BOLLINGEN SERIES XXX

PAPERS FROM THE ERANOS YEARBOOKS

Edited by Joseph Campbell

Selected and translated from the *Eranos-Jahrbücher*
edited by Olga Froebe-Kapteyn

VOLUME 4

Spiritual Disciplines

PAPERS FROM THE ERANOS YEARBOOKS

Rudolf Bernoulli • Martin Buber • M. C. Cammerloher
Theodor-Wilhelm Danzel • Friedrich Heiler • C. G. Jung
C. Kerényi • John Layard • Fritz Meier • Max Pulver
Erwin Rousselle • Heinrich Zimmer

BOLLINGEN SERIES XXX · 4

PRINCETON UNIVERSITY PRESS

Published by Princeton University Press, 41 William Street,
Princeton, New Jersey 08540

First Princeton / Bollingen Paperback printing, 1985

LCC 54-5647
ISBN 0-691-09737-2   ISBN 0-691-01863-4 (pbk.)

THIS IS THE FOURTH VOLUME
OF PAPERS SELECTED FROM THE ERANOS YEARBOOKS.
THESE VOLUMES OF SELECTIONS CONSTITUTE NUMBER XXX
IN BOLLINGEN SERIES, SPONSORED BY
BOLLINGEN FOUNDATION

These papers were originally published in German in
Eranos-Jahrbücher I (1933), II (1934), III (1935), V (1937),
X (1943), XIII (1945), and XVI (1948)

Clothbound editions of Princeton University Press books
are printed on acid-free paper, and binding materials are chosen
for strength and durability. Paperbacks, while satisfactory
for personal collections, are not usually suitable
for library rebinding.

Printed in the United States of America by Princeton
University Press, Princeton, New Jersey

Translated by

RALPH MANHEIM

except for the paper by C. G. Jung

which was translated by

R. F. C. HULL

NOTE OF ACKNOWLEDGMENT

Grateful acknowledgment is made to the following publishers for permission to quote as indicated: the Society for Promoting Christian Knowledge, London, and Macmillan, New York, for quotations from Rolt's translation of Dionysius the Areopagite; Burns, Oates and Washbourne, London, and The Newman Press, Westminster, Maryland, for passages from the E. Allison Peers translation of the complete works of St. John of the Cross; and The Clarendon Press, Oxford, for quotations from the *Hermetica*, edited by Walter Scott. Thanks are due the staff of the Warburg Institute, London, for assistance in obtaining pictures.

The advice and assistance of the following persons is gratefully acknowledged: Professor Ruth Bunzel, Dr. Chung-yuan Chang, Frau Professor Hedwig Danzel, Frau Ingrid Forner, Professor Maurice Friedman, Dr. Jolande Jacobi, Professor Karl Lehmann, Dr. Susan Miles, Professor Paul Radin, and Professor Hellmut Wilhelm.

CONTENTS

CONTENTS

viii

LIST OF PLATES

III. Ancestor image. Behind may be seen the monolith, covered by partly rotted roof

IV. Stone mausoleum. In the form of a shark, with its three fins

For C. Kerényi, "Man and Mask"

following page 154

I*a*. Masks used decoratively in a mosaic floor. Fragment of mosaic of Heraclitus
Lateran Museum, Rome. P: Anderson.

I*b*. Silenos mask in maturity rite. Fresco
Villa dei Misteri, Pompeii. P: Anderson.

II. Gorgon mask. Ornament from the archaic temple of Apollo at Veii, VI–V cents. B.C.
Museo di Villa Giulia, Rome. P: Alinari.

III*a*. Archaic mask of Acheloos. Brass
Museum, Tarquinia. P: Anderson.

III*b*. Silenos mask. From a krater
Private collection, New York. From W. Wrede, in *Athenische Mitteilungen*, LIII (1928), p. 66.

IV. Dionysiac mask from Ikaria. Attic
National Museum, Athens. From Wrede, ibid., Pl. I.

V. Dionysiac mask, formerly interpreted as Acheloos
Altes Museum, Berlin. From Wrede, ibid., Pl. II.

VI. Decorative marble mask of Silenos
Casa degli Amorini, Pompeii. P: Alinari.

VII*a*. Putto donning a Silenos mask. Antique
Capitoline Museum, Rome. P: Alinari.

VII*b*. Putto wearing a colossal mask
Villa Albani, Rome. P: Alinari.

VIII. The marriage of Dionysos and Ariadne. Roman sarcophagus, reign of Hadrian (117–138)
Lateran Museum, Rome. P: Anderson.

For Rudolf Bernoulli, "Spiritual Development as Reflected
in Alchemy and Related Disciplines"

following page 322

LIST OF TEXT FIGURES

EDITOR'S FOREWORD

Toward the task of encompassing and assimilating the world's wealth of poetic and religious visions, modes and dreams of life, and readings of the mystery of death, the Eranos lecturers first assembled in the summer of 1933, at Ascona, Switzerland. Coming together on the inspired invitation of Frau Olga Froebe-Kapteyn, seven distinguished scholars brought from the fields of their special studies the first offerings for a spiritual feast that has continued ever since, an annually celebrated festival. Three of the papers of that first meeting are included in the present volume, Heinrich Zimmer's "On the Significance of the Indian Tantric Yoga," which inaugurated the whole series, Erwin Rousselle's "Spiritual Guidance in Contemporary Taoism," and Friedrich Heiler's "Contemplation in Christian Mysticism." Two of the present offerings are from the meeting of 1934, Martin Buber's "Symbolic and Sacramental Existence in Judaism" and M. C. Cammerloher's "The Position of Art in the Psychology of Our Time"; two are from 1935, C. G. Jung's "Dream Symbols of the Individuation Process" and Rudolf Bernoulli's "Spiritual Development as Reflected in Alchemy and Related Disciplines"; and two are from 1937, Theodor-Wilhelm Danzel's "The Psychology of Ancient Mexican Symbolism" and John Layard's "The Malekulan Journey of the Dead." These represent excellently the spirit and scope of the earliest Eranos collations and yield, as well, a vivid sense of the wonder of those days, when from every field of research themes were appearing that leaped the bounds of the variously orthodox provincialisms of East and West and even of High and Primitive Culture.

The reader will recognize immediately the resonances and perhaps even share in them from within. They were not planned or intended by the participants but occurred of themselves, as one lecture followed another. And as the range of the exploration expanded in the course of the following decades of the Eranos round table, the play and counterplay of such themes increased. Three papers from the period of the middle forties, therefore, have been added to the present collection: Max Pulver's "The Experience of Light in the Gospel of St. John, in the 'Corpus hermeticum,' in Gnosticism, and in the Eastern Church," from the meeting of 1943; Fritz Meier's "The Spiritual Man in the Persian Poet 'Aṭṭār," 1945; and Carl Kerényi's "Man and Mask," 1948. These enlarge the view and complete our circumambulation of that great invisible, Man, in his quest for the gold of his own fulfillment, affording a prospect not only of his manifold yet unitary past but also, and even more impressively, of our present, actual, spiritual wealth, which, like the major part of the earth's natural resources, still lies untapped, unutilized for modern life.

The present volume is the fourth of a projected series in English, selected from the great suite of the *Eranos Jahrbücher*, which latter, as a record of all the meetings plus two festival works, now comes to an impressive twenty-eight tomes. The first volume of our English series, *Spirit and Nature* (1954), was based on the meetings of 1945 and 1946, with one addition from 1937; Volume 2, *The Mysteries* (1955), had for its base the meeting of 1944, with added papers from 1936, 1939, 1941, and 1942; Volume 3, *Man and Time* (1957), was a presentation of the meeting of 1951 with a single addition from 1949; and in the present offering we are going back in thought to the very start of this developing project of cross-cultural discussion. I wish to thank Frau Froebe for her sympathetic support and advice in the shaping of these volumes, Mr. Ralph Manheim for his translations of the frequently very difficult texts, Mr. R. F. C. Hull for his translation of Dr. C. G. Jung's lecture, the Bollingen Series editorial staff for their attention to all the work of editorial detail, and finally, Professor Mircea Eliade, one of the leading members of the present generation of Eranos contributors, for his illuminating introduction to the present volume—written from within Eranos, and therefore a testament of the bearing of these conferences not only on the work and thought of a modern scholar but also on our common task of understanding the present period of cultural catastrophe . . . and of prelude.

JOSEPH CAMPBELL

Encounters at Ascona

It is characteristic of Eranos at Ascona that the speakers do not address themselves to an audience of specialists. Yet neither do they engage in any form of "popularization"; there is no expounding the latest results gained in various departments of knowledge. The originality of Eranos lies primarily in the fact that the speakers there are able to shed both their timidities and their superiority complexes. Although they are "specialists" in some particular field of study, they are aware that they have every reason to familiarize themselves with the methods used and the results achieved in other areas of research. Nor does this spring from mere curiosity or a desire for a naïve encyclopedism. It is because Eranos at Ascona is one of the privileged places where one is made conscious of the true dimensions of culture. Sooner or later every scholar has to face this problem and learn, from his own experience, the meaning of being "culturally creative." Now, no culture is possible without a sustained effort to integrate, in one embracing perspective, the progress made in all the various fields of study. Indeed, there is no true culture if, finally, the creations that constitute it are not related to man and his destiny.

All this seems so obvious at this date that one almost hesitates to say it for fear of repeating a truism. Yet for many years certain disciplines that studied the deepest experiences of the human psyche and their cultural expressions developed side by side without their results being integrated and articulated toward a more exact and complete knowledge of man. The disciplines of the history of religions, ethnology, paleoethnology, and orientalism have seldom been regarded as *separate but interrelated* phases of a single study. It is only very recently that these disciplines have come to be thought capable of revealing human existential situations worthy of interesting not only the psychologist and sociologist but also the philosopher and theologian.

Translated from the French by Willard R. Trask.

It is perhaps the greatest contribution of Eranos to have stimulated and encouraged meetings and dialogues among representatives of the various sciences and disciplines whose field is the human mind and spirit. For it is through such encounters that a culture can renew itself, in a bold widening of its horizon. Depth psychologists, orientalists, and ethnologists interested in the history of religions are those who have most successfully achieved rapprochement and even collaboration. This is perhaps due to the fact that, in the last analysis, each of these disciplines implies encountering and confronting an unknown, strange, even "dangerous" world—dangerous because able to threaten the spiritual equilibrium of the modern West. Certainly, confronting these "strange worlds" does not always entail the same degree of danger; some of them have long been known. Thus, for example, the researches of orientalists had gradually familiarized the West with the eccentric and fabulous nature of the societies and cultures of Asia. But the ethnologist discovered obscure and mysterious spiritual worlds, universes that, even if they were not the product of a prelogical mentality (as Lévy-Bruhl believed), were none the less strangely different from the cultural landscape with which Western man had been familiar.

Obviously, it was depth psychology that revealed the greatest number of *terrae ignotae* and thus brought about the most dramatic confrontations. The discovery of the unconscious could be compared to the maritime discoveries of the Renaissance and the astronomical discoveries made possible by the invention of the telescope. For each of these discoveries revealed worlds whose very existence had been previously unsuspected. Each of them effected a sort of "breakthrough in plane," in the sense that it shattered the traditional image of the Cosmos and revealed the structures of a Universe previously unimaginable. Such "breakthroughs" have not been without consequences. The astronomical and geographical discoveries of the Renaissance radically altered the image of the universe and the concept of space; in addition, for at least three centuries, they assured the scientific, economic, and political supremacy of the West, at the same time that they opened the road that inevitably leads to a united world.

Freud's discoveries likewise represent an "opening," but this time it is an "opening" into the submerged worlds of the unconscious. Psychoanalytical technique inaugurated a new type of *descensus ad inferos*. When Jung revealed the existence of the collective unconscious, the exploration of those immemorial treasures, the myths, symbols, and images of archaic humanity, began to resemble the techniques of oceanography and speleology. Just as descents into the depths of the sea or expeditions to the bottoms of caves had revealed elementary organisms long vanished from the surface of the earth, so analyses retrieved forms of deep psychic life previously inaccessible to study. Speleology presented biologists with Tertiary and even Mesozoic organisms, primitive zoomorphic forms not susceptible to fossilization—in other words, forms that had vanished from the surface of the earth without leaving a trace. By discovering "living fossils," speleology markedly advanced our knowledge of archaic modes of life. Similarly, archaic modes of psychic life, "living fossils" buried in the darkness of the unconscious, now become accessible to study, through the techniques developed by depth psychologists.

This explains why the meetings at Ascona have been so stimulating. Specialists in various "strange," "exotic," or "unique" worlds could converse together at leisure on the efficacy of their methods, the value of their discoveries, and the meaning of their cultural adventures. Each of these specialists had devoted his life to the study of an unfamiliar world, and what he had learned during this long frequentation of the "others" obliged him to make drastic changes in the accepted clichés concerning man, religion, reason, beauty. Then too, these discoveries and confrontations formed part of the *Zeitgeist*. The rise of Eranos coincided with the political and cultural awakening of Asia and, above all, with the entrance of exotic and primitive peoples into History. Encountering these "others"— which was, as it were, the sign under which Eranos developed—had, after the second World War, become an ineluctible decree of History.

At a certain moment, the members of Eranos felt that a new humanism could well develop out of such encounters. Then, too, similar phenomena were beginning to appear elsewhere. It would be impossible in these few lines to depict an extremely complex cultural process, which, in addition, is extremely difficult to grasp since it is still *in statu nascendi*. We will only say that at Ascona each speaker felt that his scientific creation acquired a new and deeper meaning in the degree to which he undertook to present it as a contribution to the knowledge of man. It was realized, too, that the new humanism that was here coming to birth could not be a replica of the old humanism. Eranos had more than sufficiently demonstrated the need to integrate the researches of orientalists, ethnologists, and historians of religions in order to attain an integral knowledge of man.

But there was something yet further, and perhaps yet more important. The researches of depth psychologists, ethnologists, orientalists, and historians of religions had constantly brought out the human interest, the psychological "truth," and the spiritual value of countless symbols, myths, divine figures, and mystical techniques attested not only among Europeans and Asians but also among "primitives." Such human documents had previously been studied with the detachment and indifference with which nineteenth-century naturalists considered it proper to study insects. It now began to be realized that these documents express existential situations; that, consequently, they form part of the history of the human spirit. But the proper procedure for grasping the meaning of an existential situation is not the naturalist's "objectivity," but the intelligent sympathy of the hermeneut. *It was the procedure itself that had to be changed.* For even the strangest or the most aberrant form of behavior must be regarded as a human phenomenon; it cannot be understood by being taken as a zoological phenomenon or an instance of teratology.

To approach a symbol, a myth, an archaic mode of behavior as an expression of an existential situation is in itself to give it human dignity and philosophical meaning. This would have seemed the height of absurdity to a nineteenth-century scholar. For him, "savagery" or "primordial stupidity" could represent only an embryonic, and hence noncultural, phase of humanity.

If the simplest archaic myth deserved to be considered an integral part of the history of the spirit, the mystics and contemplatives of all religions could not but be given a large place. Interest in spiritual disciplines and mystical techniques—especially those of the Orient and the primitive world, hitherto little studied—has from the first been one of the characteristic aspects of Eranos. To be sure, this interest was sometimes subject to misinterpretation by uninformed outsiders, was in danger of being confused with the suspect fascination with the "occult" that is typical of modern pseudomorphoses and the countless movements of cheaply won "spirituality." But of course no subject has not been "compromised" or "compromising" at some moment in history.

For the members of Eranos, this exceptional interest in spiritual disciplines and mystical techniques arises from the fact that they are documents capable of revealing a dimension of human existence that has been almost forgotten, or completely distorted, in modern societies. All these spiritual disciplines and mystical techniques are of inestimable value because they represent conquests of the human spirit that have been neglected or denied in the course of recent Western history, but that have lost neither their greatness nor their usefulness.

The problem that now arises—and that will present itself with even more dramatic urgency to scholars of the coming generation—is this: How are means to be found to recover all that is still recoverable in the spiritual history of humanity? And this for two reasons: (1) Western man cannot continue to live on for an indefinite period in separation from an important part of himself, the part constituted by the fragments of a spiritual history of which he cannot decipher the meaning and message. (2) Sooner or later, our dialogue with the "others"—the representatives of traditional, Asiatic, and "primitive" cultures—must begin to take place not in today's empirical and utilitarian language (which can approach only realities classifiable as social, economic, political, sanitary, etc.) but in a cultural language capable of expressing human realities and spiritual values. Such a dialogue is inevitable; it is part of the ineluctible course of History. It would be tragically naïve to suppose that it can continue indefinitely on the mental level on which it is conducted today.

This new volume of Papers from the Eranos Yearbooks also has the value of familiarizing the reader with certain problems that will become painfully urgent in the more or less immediate future.

MIRCEA ELIADE

University of Chicago
November 1959

SPIRITUAL DISCIPLINES

Heinrich Zimmer

On the Significance of the Indian Tantric Yoga

I

The ritual path of the Hindu is bordered with sacraments, framed by customs, festivals, observances, as a highway is bordered by trees. In their shade he lives; they seize hold of him before he is born and they have power to find him long after his death. These observances stand side by side with the myths related in epics and countless old traditions, which guide men through life and create a bond between them by providing them with symbols and formulas for the reality of the world and of human destiny. The moral element in the myths, the example and warning, is concentrated in these observances. In their psychagogic function such observances are related to Yoga, and their specific character throws light upon the specific character of Yoga.

A young Bengali once told me of certain observances which he remembered from his childhood in the country; it was with nostalgia that he spoke of this self-contained Indian world, from which he had been uprooted by the Anglo-Indian education that had carried him into a Western and cosmopolitan civilization.

One of these observances was "the giving away of the fruit"; this is practiced by the mother who has borne a son. To bring a son into the world is the supreme duty and the supreme happiness of the Hindu woman; her husband has married her in order that his male line should be preserved, in order that through her he and his forefathers should be reborn in a son. It is solely through this supreme fruit that her life obtains meaning and justification. But however attached she may be to this veritable fruit of her life, she has not brought her son into the world in order to keep him for herself, but in order to give him to the world, once he has attained sufficient maturity.

3

Though natural and sincere, this powerful bond between mother and child, in a country where the mother's existence is built with a religious exclusiveness upon this bond and little else, holds the danger of a profound and almost insoluble crisis for mother as well as son. The threat of the crisis can poison the relation between mother and son and the son's whole life. But the natural, painful, and necessary release of the son from the mother, her giving of her fruit (*phala*) as a gift (*dāna*) to the world, is made possible by the observance (*vrata*) of the giving of the fruit (*phala-dāna-vrata*).

She who would make so great a sacrifice must begin with little things, and through them prepare for the great sacrifice. The time for the beginning of this observance is indefinite; it is somewhere around the son's fifth year, but it may be later. The observance continues for an indeterminate number of years and takes up one month each year. The house Brahman and spiritual director of the family (guru) supervises it and determines its course; it is he who decides when the mother is ready for its termination; that is, at what point, after what preliminary sacrifices, she is prepared for the actual sacrifice of her son. The woman begins with the sacrifice of little fruits of which she is very fond. She abstains from eating them, and each day brings them, with rice and all sorts of vegetables, to the house Brahman as an offering. She fasts in the morning and presents her offering to the guru when he visits the house; he partakes of it and gives her back a small portion which she reverently eats. She continues to fast until evening, and then she is again permitted to cook and to eat. On each of his visits, the guru tells the mother a mythical tale of a woman who sacrificed everything and thence derived the strength to accomplish all things; silent and attentive, holding holy grass in her folded hands, the woman listens, takes in his words and turns them over in her heart.

Each year a new and more precious fruit serves as the symbol at the center of this observance. The sacrifice advances from fruits to metals, from iron to copper, bronze, and finally to gold. These are the metals of which a woman's ornaments are fashioned. This means no doubt that the woman sacrifices her ornaments, or at least some of them, for her jewels and clothing are the only personal possessions to which she attaches importance. But objects specially made of the same metals for this purpose may be used to symbolize her ornaments.

The last, extreme stage of the sacrifice is a total fast: the woman presents fresh coconut milk to the guru and must then go thirsty all day. Brahmans,

4

relatives, and household attend this ceremony, representing the world to which the son must be given. At the end of the rite, twelve Brahmans and a few beggars belonging to the fifth caste, or "untouchables," are given ceremonial food: the highest and lowest caste, the summit and base of the social pyramid, symbolize the whole social world for which the matured boy must leave his home and sever his maternal bonds. A relative of the male line must also attend to represent the aspect of the world which is most involved in the mother's sacrifice of her son. At the end of the ceremony, the guru declares that the mother is ready to perform the act of giving her son to the world. And then, silently and inwardly, she completes the sacrifice of her life's fruit.

In this observance, myth and rite combine to effect the necessary transformation in the mother: to release her from the beloved son, whose bond with her she is keenly aware of and would like to maintain forever. The rite of symbolic giving is illuminated by the myths of exemplary figures, with which the guru accompanies each stage of the sacrifice. Their attitude is evoked from the woman's unconscious, to help mold her psyche, to redeem her and preserve her from the instinctual force of the bond, which might otherwise do violence to both mother and child. The affecting yet menacing demonism of her elemental emotion is replaced by a symbolic being in her inner life which channels the flood of emotion and takes it up and transforms it.

A mother may equally well reveal her love by clinging jealously to her son or by sending him forth with her blessing. We carry all potentialities within us. It is not by reason and conscious will that we can rouse them from their deep slumber when the need arises. But the symbolic, revealed again and again in myth, practiced forever anew in the rite, has this magical, conjuring power over our unconscious, out of which the demonism of instinct arises to overpower us. We ourselves are defenseless against it. We are not masters of our emotions, but ritual observances can create guiding images in our unconscious, capable of directing and molding our emotional life.

This is the significance of another observance, which sisters perform for their brothers. Family life is often full of friction, particularly in the large Indian household, into which grown sons often bring their wives and children to live. What are the relations between the wives and sisters of the young men? The members of the family live side by side with all their little daily worries and annoyances, each exasperated by the idiosyncrasies of the

5

other. When will they come to realize how close they are to one another: one blood, one life? Important emotional functions are neglected, they atrophy and slumber, and often awaken only when it is too late.

The observance of *bhrātri-sphota* (Bengali: *bhai-phota*), the "forehead mark of the brother," is practiced in the second night of the new moon in October. All the sisters in the family invite their brothers to a gathering and perform a sacrificial rite calculated to shield the brothers from death. Other sacrifices are performed in honor of a god, whose favor is to be gained; but no god enters into this observance; here the sister offers herself to death as a sacrifice, just as the sister of the first man did for her brother Yama. The first man, Yama (meaning "twin"), had a twin sister, Yamunā (in the Vedic myth called "Yamī"), who for his sake vanquished death. She sacrificed herself to death for him each day, and in consequence he became the deathless king in the realm of the blessed and ruler over the kingdom of the dead. This mythical event serves the sisters as a model; it is repeated in their observance. The whole observance is a question of will power and faith. Because Yamunā was able by will power to make her brother immortal, each sister must develop in herself the faith that she by her own will power can perform the same miracle for her brother.

All the sisters invite all the brothers to the apartment of one of the sisters. The sisters fast and prepare for the brothers a special meal consisting only of perfectly pure, living things. After midnight the sisters go out and gather dew from the leaves, the purest water of heaven, the life-giving milk of the upper world, which refreshes and fortifies all creatures. This observance demands a pure heart, full of solicitous love, and a pure heart is revealed by the loving care with which the pure dew is gathered each night for the brother to drink. Along with the dew, rice is given; it is pure and living, for it is freshly husked; and banana, pure and living since it has just been taken from its skin, and fresh coconut milk from the newly opened fruit.

As a symbol of fresh, renewed life, the brothers receive from their sisters clean new clothing, which after bathing they put on. Then they partake of the little meal. At the culmination of the ceremony, the sisters several times paint a mark (*sphota* or *tilaka*) between the brothers' eyebrows. For this they take lampblack, oil of sandalwood, honey, sour milk, and melted butter, which each one separately stirs with the little finger of her left hand and administers. It was with these substances, which signify life, that Yamunā marked the forehead of her brother, in order to safeguard him

6

against death. And similarly the dish of the purest ingredients, the dew of heaven and the living fruit, is an imitation of "Deathless," the potion which gives the gods their eternal life. During this ceremony the story is told of how Yamunā enabled Yama to conquer death and become immortal in this very same way. At the end of the observance, the younger sisters receive a little present—usually consisting of sweetmeats—from the older brothers, and the older sisters give presents to the younger brothers.

This observance implies more than a magic spell calculated to inure the brothers against death through the love of their sisters. The imitation of Yamunā's old magic, whose mythical success guarantees the efficacy of the observance, has another significance; it invokes the hidden but ever present potentiality of an ideal relation between brother and sister, and exalts it to an inner reality, in order that it may paralyze the counterforces of everyday life and human inadequacy, the currents of ill humor and estrangement, indifference and hostility, and replace them by their opposites. The mythical archetype is intended to awaken this potentiality, submerged perhaps by the cares of the day, from the depths of the unconscious to which it has sunk, to raise it from its atrophied stage, so that it may unfold and dominate personal life.

The man who at every step is surrounded and sustained by such customs, so that without exercise of his will his life runs always in the path which they prescribe, need not ask himself conscious questions or frame conscious decisions concerning his conduct and his goals. All this has been taken care of in the wisdom of the great religious and social community which received him and blessed him with its sacraments before he was born, and which continues to bless him most particularly when it exacts the severest symbolic sacrifices and renunciations. Carried by the stream of ritual, sacramental observances, all his life unconscious of himself—as though submerged, he drifts in the river of the unconscious. Thus he drifts, in harmony with himself and with the eternal contents of life, which enter into every individual destiny with their tasks and joys, their sacrifices and sorrows.

The wonderful thing about such observances is that their symbolism is utterly apt; as perfectly apt as our deeper dreams, and sometimes as inaccessible to reason. They strike the unconscious that governs our life with the force of the symbol, just as the unconscious speaks in marvelous symbols when it sends us dreams or gives us signs by other involuntary acts.

And such observances are created by an unconscious; they are formed by the collective, suprapersonal spirit of the religious and social community, and their purpose is to appeal to something suprapersonal in us, to the profounder unconscious. They are intended to guide it, in order that the individual may mesh with the suprapersonal element in human social life, in order that he may live in harmony with the eternal contents that constitute a suprapersonal fate and exigency transcending any individual, historical situation in which they may mask themselves, the eternal contents that are common to us and to all living nature.

This unconscious, this suprapersonal sphere of our inner life, is full of formed contents; here, as the psychology of dreams and the study of other manifestations of the unconscious reveals, the experience, the destiny of man ever since he ceased to be an animal, has been deposited in symbols or archetypes. Our deeper dreams raise this deposit up to us, and it is nothing other than what the myths of all times have preserved in their figures, situations, and symbols. Accordingly, these wise observances, calculated to guide the individual by means of the unconscious through the invisible shoals on which we may founder unawares, make use of mythical figures in order to pilot man safely through the unavoidable and critical transition periods of his life. The archetypes or variants of archetypes in myths and rites speak to the unconscious, which no rational admonition or consolation can reach; in the unconscious they encounter something that is related to them, an archetype at work in its depths, which they awaken and make into an instrument of the regent within us, a guiding image which can gain power over our individuality and adapt its behavior to that of the archetype.

Thus such archetypes, awakened from their slumber within us, become visible images and effect transformations in us; when called forth by kindred archetypes in myth and observance, they rise up within us and become our guides. Our conscious will cannot create such guides; the archetype rises from within us to perform its directing function, to transform us in its image and direct our formless vital forces, by assimilating them to its primordial form, by filling itself with them, as a mold is filled with liquid metal. And this archetype summoned from our depths preserves us; it prevents our formless forces from tearing our personality apart or driving it to madness under the pressure of the eternal contents of life, of the destiny that oppresses and threatens to crush us. This primeval archetype, with its timeless validity, enables us to live at peace with our inexorable destiny. The sacred

8

and nonsacred figures that have risen to the level of mythical symbolism
—and this is their sublime function—lead us to emulate them in our
actions and our suffering. Passing over the bridge of our devotion and concentration, they evoke within us an image of potential nobility which
moves us to emulate them in our actions and in our sufferings.

Another observance of this sort, which like the "forehead mark of the
brother," functions through a mythical archetype, is the rite of Sāvitrī,
performed by the Indian widow. The fate of the Indian widow is no doubt
among the hardest to which a human being can be subjected. Marriage
among the Hindus is a bond for eternity. Even beyond death, the woman
remains the wife of this one man, i.e., the man is for her immortal. But, betrothed to him while still half a child, she often loses him before she has ever
really possessed him. And her life ends with his. If he dies an early death,
her existence becomes a mere shadow.

An observance practiced for one month each year is intended to help the
widow to bear this lot. At its center stands the legendary figure of Sāvitrī,
a princess who married the son of an exiled king, although she knew what
was hidden from him: that his days were numbered by the god of death.
When the time came for the god of death to gather in the life of her husband,
she fasted for three days and purified herself in preparation for a meeting
with the god. She did not leave her husband's side, but followed him into
the jungle; as they were gathering wood in the flowery wilderness, where all
nature was in bloom, refreshed by the summer rains, the god of death came
and caught her husband's life spark in his noose. But she spoke to him of all
that was holy and good, pleaded with him, and did not desist until he had
granted her her husband's life, until he had promised to restore her blind
father's eyesight, his crown and kingdom, and had promised to give her sons
and happiness.

In times long past, Sāvitrī restored her husband to life after death had
already taken him, and every woman whose husband has died attempts to
do the same. That is the significance of this observance, which is performed
by the widow in the same summer month and which ends on a night of new
moon, just as Sāvitrī's story came to its miraculous end on a night of new
moon. The observance comprises three full fast days, corresponding to the
fasting of Sāvitrī before her encounter with the god. It is performed in the
widow's house before an image of the household god; the god is present as
a witness. A Brahman, the widow's guru, comes each day and tells her the

story of Sāvitrī; the woman, who has fasted until his coming, holds holy grass in her hands as she listens to him. At the end of the observance, a white silk thread is wound nine times round her upper arm, signifying and constituting an indissoluble bond between her and her now intangible husband. She wears this thread until the observance is repeated in the following year. Thus the miracle of the husband's return—though not tangibly alive in space, he lives for his wife—is accomplished within her. The archetype of the love that vanquishes death is evoked in her heart and becomes the meaning of her life and destiny. The mythical Sāvitrī—a variant of this archetype—rouses it to life from the depth of the unconscious, to overpower the personality, to assimilate the vital forces which, if left to act chaotically in pain or yearning, might destroy it or drive it to madness, and thus to transform it into the likeness of Sāvitrī.

The power to bear the inevitable is the wisdom of life. Only the unconscious, which knows everything and carries this knowledge in symbols, but which, if we know how to consult it, permits us as individuals to see only as much as we deserve, and not much more than we need in order to travel our path through the inevitable contents of life—only the unconscious is equal to every exigency. It is the ageless totality, to which nothing new can happen regardless of the situation, and which watches the movement of the ego as nature calmly watches the flowering and fading of her creatures. In most men its period of greatest awakeness is childhood, hence this is truly the inspired age: enchanted, incorruptible, and close to all things.

Accordingly, the Bengalis have an observance that is practiced by children; it teaches man the one lesson that every man needs: to bear the inevitable. It consists in the veneration of Jamburī. The older children initiate the younger. The children begin to participate in their fifth or sixth year, while the younger children stand in silent attendance. Adults are not permitted to be present; they do not even know exactly when the children perform the rite, for this observance, like all others of its type, may have no nonparticipating spectators. They are all performed for their effect on the participants—not as pageantry or as a symbolic ceremonial for the enlightenment or consecration of others. Consequently the performance of the rite must be kept secret from the adults. It seems almost like a game played by the children, who have observed the ritual life of the adults as it weaves through the entire year, and who now in their little world imitate it. This they do with their parents' sense of the mystery implicit in the rites, and with the imperturbable solemnity of children—but how profoundly meaningful is this solemnity which knows all things.

The observance runs through five years and is practiced in the winter nights of the coldest month, the month of Magha, which falls in January and February. Secretly the children rise in the early morning hours, while it is still dark, before any animal is afoot or any bird has begun to sing. Each night they mold a fresh little figure of Jamburī, scarcely the size of a hand, from earth, the same earth in which they roll and play in the daytime. Every morning when the rite is over, the figure is thrown away, just as the grownups at home each day fashion little gods of clay for the cult, which after the devotion are thrown into the water, in which they disintegrate. The little figure has neither arms nor legs; eyes and mouth are barely suggested. Around it the children form a pond, retained by a little earth dike. Here the figure sits and the children bring it water, flowers, and holy grass. Meanwhile they recite such lines as: "I bring thee water before the crow has drunk of it; I bring thee flowers before the bee has sucked them." At the same time the story of Jamburī is told. The import of the story and of the observance is as follows: Jamburī has no feet and no hands, she has no proper mouth and no proper eyes, and yet she can accomplish and realize all things—for she has a will. And that is what we must learn from her.

Each day the rites become more intense; the inner process they are intended to provoke runs through the seven stages of the Yoga exercise, which is associated with the image of a god: from the contemplation of the material image to the substitution of its inner likeness, the contemplation of which no longer requires any outward contact; then from an inner contemplation of this image in which contemplator and image exist separately to a union of the two (*samādhi*), whereby the image is fulfilled in the devotee, who fuses with it and becomes one with it.

The offering of water and flowers is only an introductory ceremony, by which the child demonstrates that he comes to Jamburī in all earnestness, as a pupil comes to his guru: full of veneration and eager to serve, prepared to receive and to fulfill the teachings of Jamburī. Then follows the instruction, ascending by the stages of Yoga. The oft-repeated narration of the myth of Jamburī constitutes the bridge by which the silent, rigid instructress, the little clod of earth, gives some part of her essence to the devoted pupil.

And today we still find ceremonies of instruction and initiation (in Japanese and Tibetan Buddhism) in which teacher and pupil perform symbolic gestures and observe set forms, while not a single word of instruction is uttered. Teacher and pupil have cleansed themselves through ascetic practices and have concentrated all their forces through exercises, in order to be able to communicate to one another something that cannot be conveyed in words. The teacher gives, the pupil receives something that is more than knowledge—a power, a magical fragment of the teacher's essence, which penetrates the pupil's whole personality and unconscious and transforms him from within.

The outcome of this ascending process is that Jamburī's little pupil assimilates what she can give him, that is, her essence. It becomes reality within him: his new reality, into which he has been transformed. Her essence has flowed into him and become his essential nature. This would hardly be possible unless it were already in him in germ, one of the innumerable potentialities of his half-formed, but always formable and form-seeking, vital force, the *shakti* in him, for, just as that infinite force, the *shakti* of the universal God, unfolds and permeates the macrocosm, his *shakti* governs the little world of his body, striving to assume manifold and forever renewed form.

We are now prepared to understand that form of Yoga which, through daily worship of the god, calls forth its inner image in the devotee. The literature of the Tantras offers innumerable instructions for this form of *pūjā*, the veneration of the divine in one of its infinitely many aspects. It teaches an inner cult full of pious devotion (*bhakti*) to the god of the heart, the *ishta-devatā*—the "god to which one sacrifices" in accordance with a ritual into which one is initiated by one's guru. As in the observance of Jamburī, a little image serves as the center of the rite of offering and worship. But, at the same time, it serves to introduce the inner contemplation which little by little sates itself with the outward, sensory manifestation, until it is able to dispense with the concrete image. Then the outward cult, which mimics the reception of a respected guest with offerings, whispered formulas, a swinging of lamps and other ceremonial, is discontinued. The cult is now transferred to the sphere of pure inner contemplation. In an inner vision, the figure of the god is recreated, with train and trappings, in its own appropriate locale (palace, landscape, resting place under a tree). This occurs by degrees; piece by piece, the entire image is inwardly evoked and enduringly held fast. The god's neck and arms, breast and flanks, are adorned with "spiritual," i.e., purely visualized ornaments, from the diadem in his hair to the bracelets round his ankles; "spiritual" flowers are presented to him, and the whole outward ceremonial is repeated in a process of progressive visualization.

But in the light of the final purpose, all this is only preparation; like the offerings and formulas of the children in their nocturnal cult of Jamburī, the intense effort of inner vision expresses the faith and devotion of the believers. The actual goal is that this inner image of the deity and he who has conceived it should emerge from their duality and interpenetrate one another, that they should fuse into One (samādhi). The believer experiences the fact that the deity is not something different from himself—it does not dwell somewhere out in the world, it has not just come to visit him; it does not sit on a throne in some heaven beyond the heavens: out of his own formless inwardness he has built up every detail, and at the end of his devotions he lets it dissolve again in his formless inwardness, in the primordial waters of the unconscious, just as the Indian god unfolds the world and then, when it is ripe for dissolution, melts it down again into himself, the universal night, the primordial flood. Out of his unconscious, the believer has wrested the apparition of the divine, after the unconscious had assimilated its form to the model of the outward cult image; now he can recollect this vision in a daily process. As at the beginning of the world Brahma rises out of the primordial waters on the lotus and begins to unfold the world in creation, and as at the end of an aeon the world dissolves again in the worldless and spaceless sea of the beginning, so the form of the god rises from the innermost depths of the initiate as hieroglyph and true form of his intangible being, which had remained unknown to him as such and can be raised to consciousness in no other way.

The number of gods whom the Hindus learn to worship in inner invocation, contemplation, and immersion is legion. In ever-changing variants of aspect, dress, and gesture, the big and little gods appear, with different weapons, emblems, and trappings, with gestures of blessing or menace, gracious and sinister, accompanied by their divine forces (shakti), or wives, who reveal the divine essence as the facets of a crystal reflect the colors of light. Beside the god with his gracious aspect and gesture of blessing and giving, there often stands his shakti, menacing and dripping with blood, for only thus is he truly complete; his nature is the whole. All these gods are visualized as the creatures of our own depths, the hieroglyphs of our being. For in all of us are all things—at least as potentiality.

Within us lies the predisposition to all things: we wish to hear and obey, to follow and let ourselves be led, to serve and renounce; but we desire also to inflate ourselves and command, to dominate and fling thunderbolts; we desire to dissolve in the community and to be solitary, needful of no other. Every horror slumbers within us and every misdeed, but also every possibility of purification. The total, ideal fulfillment of this predisposition, of the *shakti* within us, would be a swift and unceasing succession like frantic lightnings, an eternal coincidence of all these contradictory potentialities; if it burst forth from within us, if it strove to flow through us into reality, to project itself into the world, it would destroy us. The real fulfillment of such a stupendous play is the existence of God, not of the creature. Its reflection is found in the behavior of the child as long as it is little; in the child this urge can find a greater measure of fulfillment than in the adult without destroying him. In childhood the inner forces, which later are gradually inhibited and masked by social life and education and thrust back into the unconscious, are freely projected. They pour forth, naïve and unrestrained. All the malice, the smiling insensibility, the cruelty, the tenderness, all the helpless clinging and cajoling, the whimsy and anxiety and fearless observation of the world; in the sovereign subjectivity of childhood, all these inner forces cloak as though by magic the limits of objective reality in dense clouds aglow with demonism.

But who may awaken within himself all the archetypes of possible behavior that lie dormant within us? Who may realize them in the community of adults, in the ordered society in which the adult lives? No one. Therefore the peoples long ago devised games, which give play to impulse, yet restrain it by rules; these were the great festivals with their luxuriant splendor and their peculiar observances. By temporarily lifting the rigid rules of morality, by transforming boundaries and fences into roads and gates, by permitting or even ordaining what was ordinarily forbidden, they created compensations for what the community of everyday life must deny itself if it is not to be shattered into bits, and all men with it.

How much lies blocked up in every man by the social order! For the vital force (*shakti*) in each of us would overflow all measure were it to fulfill its nature, which is totality. Even the fool sometimes wants to play the king, and his anointed majesty demands on occasion to play the fool. Harun al-

14

Rashid and his Grand Vizier disguise themselves and mingle with the people, with porters, fishermen, Negro slaves; they long to taste the common, impure things which cannot approach the Commander of the Faithful on his throne. The dauphine Marie Antoinette leaves the royal seclusion of Versailles and drives out in disguise to the carnival in Paris; even the chastest soul is visited in a balmy night by the burning breath of disordered desires and images that make it freeze with horror: it feels soiled by some totally alien thing—but this thing has welled up from deep within itself. It is the inexorable *shakti* in us, whose nature it is to manifest itself to the full in every possible shape and gesture of life.

We see this when we behold those woodcuts and etchings of Hans Baldung Grien and of the Hausbuchmeister, showing the aged Aristotle: upon his naked back rides the naked courtesan Phyllis; with her whip she strikes his sunken flanks, guides him by a bridle attached to the bit in his mouth —that mouth which when young discoursed with the divine Plato, that mouth to whose words the world-conquering Alexander listened with veneration. The great sage, that noble model of *Homo sapiens*, the erect biped— here we see him creeping on all fours. Something in him impels him to renounce everything that has made him great and exemplary in his own eyes and those of the world, something he had never allowed to emerge, of which he had never become conscious—"Eros undefeated in battle," as the Theban maidens called it in Sophocles—something which had remained crippled and stunted within him and had therefore grown angry, transforming itself from visage to grimace, from pure to sordid; and then one day it had risen up and seized the mastery, and taken its cruel, demonic revenge upon him.

Or what of Nebuchadnezzar, the great king who said: "Is not this great Babylon that *I* have built for the house of the kingdom by the might of *my* power?" [1] Was there not something more in this king than power and glory and the urge to enjoy these two to the full? Almost the direct opposite was also in him, but amid the iron necessity of his fate always to be a great king, greater than all the kings around him, it could not be manifested. But while he was speaking so grandly, "there fell a voice from heaven, saying: ... The kingdom is departed from thee. And they shall drive thee from men, and thy dwelling shall be with the beasts of the field; they shall make thee to eat grass as oxen, and seven times shall pass over thee ..." And thus it befell him. "He was driven from men, and did eat grass as oxen, and his

1 Dan. 4:30 ff.

body was wet with the dew of heaven, till his hairs were grown like eagles' feathers, and his nails like birds' claws."

For seven years Nebuchadnezzar forgot his glory and lived like a beast of the fields, compelled by a voice that was stronger than his power and his glory. It is not said that he was unhappy during these years, but merely that he was insane. And because he was mad, men drove him forth to the beasts who lived like him. It does not even appear that these years harmed him, for: "At the end of the days I Nebuchadnezzar lifted up mine eyes unto heaven, and mine understanding returned unto me, . . . at the same time my reason returned unto me; and for the glory of my kingdom, mine honor and brightness returned unto me; and my counsellors and my lords sought unto me; and I was established in my kingdom, and excellent majesty was added unto me."

Transformed and refreshed, greater than ever before, the king returns from his retrogression to the animal and attains to the highest nobility. In his renunciation of all kingly and human dignities lay hidden the possibility of regaining them to a higher degree. When he became a beast, Nebuchadnezzar vanished for men; to them it was as though he had died. He was less than a shadow; no shadow of his kingliness lay upon him, his very countenance had been taken from him like his diadem. His road to the beast and back again was like the journey across the threshold of Proserpina to the realm of the shades, traveled by the ancient adepts of the mysteries of Isis, and like an initiate he returned transformed, sustained by new knowledge and a new psychic balance.

Before becoming a beast, Nebuchadnezzar had exalted the kingly *I* in his concept of himself until it became the dominant function of his self. In the destiny that made him an oriental despot of a great empire, he could only fulfill himself by clutching in his hands the power and the glory of great Babylon; it was by this gesture, continuously intensified, that he lived. And in this convulsive gesture, imposed upon him by his situation as well as his nature, lay the danger that he would lose his inner balance, that he would cease to be anything other than this I, this despotic *I*, to the detriment of all the infinite unconscious possibilities which the *shakti* carries within it. And the balance of the whole could only be restored when a totally disregarded, never experienced aspect of his nature, that had sunk into the unconscious, seized the mastery over Nebuchadnezzar as completely and as ruthlessly as the despotic idea before it. Thus he became like a beast.

16

But he recognized the force that had thrust him down and transformed him; he called it God: "And at the end of the days I Nebuchadnezzar lifted up mine eyes unto heaven, and mine understanding returned unto me, and I blessed the most High, and I praised and honored him that liveth for ever, whose dominion is an everlasting dominion, and his kingdom is from generation to generation: and all the inhabitants of the earth are reputed as nothing: and he doeth according to his will in the army of heaven, and among the inhabitants of the earth; and none can stay his hand, or say unto him, What doest thou?" The regent in us, which can thus accomplish all things in our soul, he called the "King of heaven," and concluded the story of his miraculous transformation, as it is written in the Book of Daniel, with the words: "Now I Nebuchadnezzar praise and extol and honor the King of heaven, all whose works are truth, and his ways judgment: and those that walk in pride he is able to abase."

What Nebuchadnezzar found in the heavens of the macrocosm is felt by the adept of Tantric Yoga to dwell corporeally within him in the depths of his microcosm, and like the King of Babylon he calls it "God." To it he dedicates himself in inner veneration, and evokes it in one of the innumerable forms it can assume. Thereby he aims at achieving consciousness of it, for only by taking form can a thing enter our consciousness and exist for our consciousness. He adorns the divine manifestation of the unconscious which he evokes with every charm, every excellence, and every power; he worships it appropriately and in so doing worships the omnipotent, formless, and omniform power it embodies. Thus at the same time he pours forth the charm, the nobility and greatness, and all the potentialities that constitute the demonism of his own nature; he engenders them from himself, reaches for their forms in space, clutches them and shapes them into the ornament and expression of the divine figure. Instead of projecting into the outside world all those unconscious potentialities of his vital force, which his human situation permits him to realize only in shadowy fragments, he projects them into an inner godhead. For these potentialities are infinite in their dimension and insatiable in their urge, measured by the confined situation of most human lives. He projects them all into the god-image, they become its charm and its greatness; and thus they do not destroy him in their eruption, do not turn into something evil and diabolical, as they might if they had been repressed. They are saved from the danger of remaining imprisoned in the unconscious, of aborting into evil demons; they are carried upward, substantiated and molded into the image of the inwardly visible godhead of the heart. The believer projects and discharges them into their image by his attitude of pious devotion (*bhakti*) which renounces the ego, and says to the godhead: "Thou art my true being—not I. It is not I but thou, who movest this cosmos of my personality and my world. Everything is thine."

In this attitude, the devotee renounces his conscious ego and gives himself piously to the unconscious in himself, the regent that is in us. Thus he avoids the host of dangers that lurk within us and in us alone—the legions of hell which can break out of us and whose arbitrary power is clearly manifested to us in the image of Aristotle and Nebuchadnezzar crawling on all fours.

The innumerable manifestations of the divine as gods and goddesses full of nobility and youthful charm, majestically calm or grimly menacing, and all the hosts of the demonic—all of them are outward prototypes expressing the inward abundance of the vital force, the *shakti*. They correspond to the innumerable basic gestures and elemental potentialities of the believer's unconscious, which may project themselves in this or that attitude. These potentialities are present in varying strength in the individual human type, their germ is unequally developed. We have within us the seed of all things, but all things will not germinate and sprout, many of the fruits that our garden might bear will never ripen. But that potentiality among all those that are in us in germ, which is so constituted that it can really germinate, that potentiality which is not vague but actual, constitutes our type that shows hostility or affinity to other types. Type, temperament, age, and habituation hold us spontaneously in the orbit of one or another form of the divine or the demonic; the potentialities which germinate in us disclose an affinity to one or another archetype in myth or history.

Accordingly, it is a part of the wisdom of the spiritual guide who wishes to direct the formative urge of the unconscious vital forces within us, to withhold demonic and other unsuitable archetypes from these inner forces, but to offer them in cult and observance an archetype to which they bear affinity, in order that they may attach themselves to this archetype and mold themselves to its nature. Certain Catholic women have a secret affinity for St. Anne; when her example is held up to the formative urge of the unconscious, it often evokes a corresponding inner image to mold and direct the woman in question; the devotee can learn from her as the child learns from Jamburī, and the primordial waters of the unconscious, always pregnant with form, can create a world in her image. To others St. Agnes or St. Mary Magdalen offers a similar possibility; St. Aloysius is often held out as an example to young people. St. Francis and St. Ignatius, the bridegroom of poverty and the soldier of Christ, are mutually exclusive as guiding images for self-transformation and the crystallization of the self-sated, self-emanating *shakti*; similarly Vishnu and Shiva, two different supreme aspects of the universal divine being, mutually exclude one another, and on a lower plane the elephant-headed, rice-bellied Ganesha, the god of peasant prosperity, and his brother, the agile boy war god, who seven days after his birth freed the world from a demon who had overthrown all the gods and brought tyranny and confusion into the world. Just as Sāvitrī represents the ideal of self-sacrificing conjugal love, as Yamunā embodies the highest love among brothers and sisters, and Jamburī the power to bear every fate, thus do all the archetypes of the unconscious in myth and cult embody in ideal purity a specific attitude and gesture of man. Here all that is pure and all that is demonic are embodied in symbolic figures: every horror and every mischief, but also all the angelic power of the sublime, which carries in its hands the key to the abyss and the great chain with which to bind Satan.

The Buddhas and Bodhisattvas represent luminous knowledge, as the highest potentiality of the *shakti* within us, through which, when it has wholly purified itself of beclouding passion and sodden animality, it can overcome its frantic natural urge to engender and project itself into a world of form. They represent the miracle of a conversion by which the *shakti* itself assuages the urge which impels it to project its form-seeking forces, leave them free play in a limitless Māyā, and maintain the world process. They embody the sublime compassion which strives to redeem the whole world from itself as world, as the continuously germinating product of this world-creating potency—the compassion which desires to free the world from its own chains, in which it tosses about in pleasure and pain like a dreamer in the chains of sleep, assailed by luring and terrifying images in breath-taking succession.

All the figures that live in cult and myth are corporeal ideas such as these; as variants of archetypes that lie dormant within us they can, according to our predisposition and situation, serve us as models for good and evil. But we are not free to choose: we cannot, for example, elect Indian forms for ourselves and Christian forms for the East. Here man's powers of adaptation are limited, and here lies the danger of all missionary activity; our Western unconscious contains the same archetype as the Eastern unconscious, molded in a different variant. We are little blossoms on the ancient tree of the West, and the sap of this tree presses into our unconscious; it bears and engenders symbolic variants according to its own species.

This is evinced in our remoteness from the mythical figures of the Greeks, despite all our humanistic love for the ancient world. Both Greek and German mythology know the blacksmith-magician, the wonder-working craftsman: Daedalus and Wieland. When man miraculously discovered how to smelt liquid metal from hard rock and pour it into shapes, a new age arose. A demonic force was here at work: the hardest of all things was vanquished by fire, it became like water, but when molded it retained its shape. From stone, the weapon and implement of an age, man brought forth its multiform conqueror. The miracle of this Promethean achievement descended into the human unconscious in the form of the mythical smith, the magical worker in metals, so that even today his trade carries a magical aura (e.g., in Britain, the smith of Gretna Green who forges marriages). But how different are the forms assumed by this hieroglyph of the collective unconscious in the Greek and in the German tradition. The mythical smith frees man from the prison of the stone age and similarly frees himself from his bondage to the king. He achieves the infinite scope of a new age of man; on the wings which he has fashioned, he flies heavenward. How tragic is the new freedom for the Greeks: the wings which free Icarus and Daedalus bring Icarus to an early death. Like Euphorion, the birdlike Icarus, borne by the spirit of the new age, rises too impetuously toward the sun, and meets his death in the sea. His father Daedalus pays for his Titanic gift of invention with the gravest loss; the loss of his alter ego, his son, his reborn future. In this penalty, the Greeks, filled with terror by the unlimited new possibilities, by this Titanic mastery over nature and destruction of the old stone order, found a balance with the powers which the magical inventor had offended.

With Daedalus compare his sinister brother Wieland, the dark avenger of his imprisonment and of the wounded sinews of his feet, which the king had ordered to be cut to prevent the wonder-worker from escaping him— even his successful flight was bound up with the taking of innocent life. And here the darkness is not illumined by the pathos of a flight into the sun. Wieland strikes off the heads of the king's two sons, as they bend covetously over his treasure, and, after making her drunk, violates the king's daughter, who has come to the smith with the broken gold hoop of his beloved; and this immoderate revenge, striking the king in that which was dearest to him, in his second life, his future, this revenge which makes ornaments and baubles out of the skulls, eyes, and teeth of the boys, which presents the king with a bastard, lies evil and oppressive on the demonic figure of the magical inventor. The collective unconscious of each of these two cultures fashions its own variants of the same primordial figure, each with its special coloration. And the manner in which this collective unconscious recalls the old times in song and legend, reflects the difference between the Hellenic world and the northern night.

The mythology of many cultures includes the figure of the singer and musician, possessed of magic powers. Here the magical power of music, which more than anything else directly penetrates the unconscious to madden or soothe it, has found its symbolic deposit in the collective unconscious. In India it is Krishna, the incarnate all-God Vishnu, who has descended into the world with a fraction of his infinite being, in order to free it from the tyranny of the demons disguised as human despots. As with Zeus it has been prophesied that he will usher in a new age, like Zeus he is persecuted even in his mother's womb; but miraculously protected, he grows up unknown among shepherds and herdsmen, until the time is ripe for him to set the world in order and redeem it. As a boy, meanwhile, he subdues the demons of the wilderness, who have been ordered to upset the bucolic idyll and to do away with him before he can grow up. In his young manhood, he is loveliness itself; the shepherd women and young girls worship him. In games and dances on moonlit nights he gives them a foretaste of the heavenly joy of being united with him in his paradise. He sings and dances with them and leads the harvest round; burning their hearts with the arrows of his glance, he initiates them into the mysteries of Eros—of Eros the lover of life, who makes man one with God (see Pl. I). He plays the flute—a pied piper of women's hearts, seductive in the bloom of his youth. All hearts fly out to him, all hearts adore him in painful sweetness. A pied piper—but how different from his dark brother in the legend of Hamelin town, the German variant of the magical musician.

The demonism of music—with us Germans it is embodied in a vagrant piper, one of the evil, strolling people, a dark and sinister figure from who knows where. But precisely because of his questionable origin he is in league with the powers by which the respected burghers, the well-fed, self-righteous rich behind their walls and towers, feel beset, the dark powers they are unable to exorcise. His affinity for the sinister gives him mastery over it, he rids the city of the noxious plague of rats which threaten to destroy it. These rats—what a gruesome symbol! The unclean, malignant, dangerous beast, viler than any other and yet man's house-companion, feeding on his refuse—what an uncanny and appropriate symbol for the unconscious! The strange musician liberates the city from the plague of its own guilt, from these living, swarming, biting creatures of its own foulness, from the demons of its own filth of every kind. But what avails it? Out of their own respectability and entrenched self-righteousness, the burghers bring forth this filth and must keep on heaping it up forever—that is their nature, and from their nature he cannot save them. No vagrant adventurer can clean out the Augean stable of our soul, were he Herakles himself; we ourselves must lend a hand to sweeping the filth from our psyche; and the vilest of all its filth is ingratitude. Hence the punishment of the ungrateful city, which thinks it can cheat the strolling piper, the outlawed vagrant, of his promised wages; it is deprived of its life in the future, of the hope and innocence, the promise of living eternity, which are miraculously present even in the basest of men: the piper lures the children, and they must follow him like rats. What a cruel punishment, as pitiless as it is just—an arrow inexorably hitting its mark. And what a gloomy unconscious that shoots such arrows into its own heart. How far removed it is from the people whose magical musician with his song and his harp liberates all nature from the bonds of its own inertia, its fear and rage; for when Orpheus plays, the wild chaotic rocks arise, moved by the rhythm; the harmony shapes them into walls and staircases, gates and palaces, citadels and temples (for harmony means just proportion). And all the animals forget their innate nature, their voracity and terror, and gather around the singer, whose harmonies soothe and compose all conflict, whose sacred name the Hellenes gave to the occult doctrines disclosing how man can progress towards perfection and gain eternity within himself. The demonic forces that rend each other are seized with rage and despair at their impotence. When finally they assail the magician to destroy him, they must deafen their ears with insensate howls, lest they hear his heavenly voice and his music which have power to subdue the demonic. For if they heard it, they would be compelled to renounce their nature, to become peaceful and full of inner harmony like his song.

The religious man lives by the archetypes which myth and ritual hold out to him as guiding images, always in their specific variants. And those who have ceased to belong to a religious community endowed with rite and myth are guided by the poets. Like priest and guru, the true poet—and there are not many—is the guardian of the archetypes of his culture's collective unconscious. His function is not to invent, but to rediscover and to animate. What distinguishes him from the common writer is that he serves the timeless genii and renews their image for his own time. The writer takes from the street motifs that have significance for his time and only for his time; when the times change, his writings pass into the morgue of that which has merely existed, and carry on a shadow existence in the waxworks of literary history. Writing that does not reach down to the archetypes molded by collective experience is limited by the social horizon and dies with social change, which makes it irrelevant. It cannot help but be patently or covertly ironic and untragic, for, seen from the plane of our deeper self, or our timeless and deathless unconscious, the conception that our essential destiny is determined solely by social forces is a true irony, a monstrous humbug. The religious man knows better, as does the man who knows how to consult the regent within. Hence the ironic character of *Madame Bovary* and of all the social novels of the nineteenth century, hence the merely three-dimensional character of the social and psychological novel in general. It can achieve pathos only by taking a critical attitude, by fighting for a better social reality, e.g., Zola. Balzac remains three-dimensional, that is his greatness and his limitation, and it is this very limitation that becomes evident when the giant in him tries to transcend it. His attempts to evoke the fourth dimension, the realm of spirits, angels, and demons (*Séraphita, La Recherche de l'absolu*), are failures if only because of the naïveté with which he chooses as his subject what ought to be no more than framework and style. There is no thing that possesses this dimension in such a way that one need only stretch out one's hand to grasp it; it is bound to no subject matter, but through style it can be revealed in any subject matter, as in Goethe's fairy tale *Die Neue Melusine* or in his *Novelle*.

Christ and the Buddha have entered as archetypes into the Western and Eastern unconscious; their historical lives had such power that they superimposed themselves on an already existing image in the unconscious, as variant and development. It is characteristic of their historical rank that they could enter into older, pre-existing archetypal forms, which they replaced and adapted to themselves—Christ into the ancient oriental figure of the dying, sacrificed, and resurrected god of the seasons, the Buddha into the old Indian sun god. Because in their own right they possessed such stature that only those lofty, venerable forms could cloak and preserve them down through the ages, it became their historic function to inspire the unconscious of men remote from them in time, to touch their inner image in us with their outward image, as though with a magical, life-giving finger, and to awaken it from profound sleep in order that it may guide us and transform us in emulation of itself. By fusing them with the older archetypes, the unconscious, in a solemn assumption, gathered their historical figures among the eternal symbols, and placed them amid the constellations in the night sky of men's souls.

The learned question whether Christ and the Buddha were historical figures or "only" the transference of fragments of a mythological complex to the historical plane loses its significance in this perspective; that both these allegedly historical figures could attain such mythological power argues for their historical reality. The unconscious cannot be fed on inventions and fabrications; "All his works are truth," says Nebuchadnezzar, who had experienced the workings of the unconscious so drastically in his own flesh. The form-hungry unconscious seized upon their coming as a rare opportunity to stamp a new and more distinct archetype; an infinity of forces attached to them, emanating from them, flowing into them, circling around them. Hence, they alone are living and immortal, while the men of the millenniums that have passed between them and us are nearly all forgotten, and scarcely a name re-echoes. And because the unconscious granted him so much life, Jesus is called the son of God, just as Herakles, by reason of the same force, became for the Greeks the son of Zeus, and Krishna for the Indians an incarnate fragment of the universal God.

To worship this Christ within us, and only within us, and not in any paradise above the heavenly spheres, to imbue ourselves with him by evoking his inner presence, developing his enormous potentiality into our own most personal reality—this would be a true "imitation of Christ." Thus to worship him, in reliance on grace, that is to say, in the faith that he really slumbers within us and can be resurrected in us, would be a Christian *bhakti-yoga*.

In its fully developed form as the "Great Vehicle" (Mahāyāna), Buddhism goes so far as to deny the historical reality of its founder. There has never been a Buddha, nor for that matter any monastic order or any Buddhism: so say the monks who wear the dress of the order, live in its cloisters, and within their walls keep images of the Buddha for the pious to worship. In this paradox, the monastic adept of Buddhistic Yoga is taught to free himself of all things temporal and spatial, of all things nameable and all things formed, which he may imagine to exist outside himself, and to which he might cling, if his *shakti* continued to project itself in worship on a Buddha who has existed. If there were a real Buddha who once dwelt on earth or who dwelt eternally in some heaven to which the layman aspires—then the ego would also be an ultimate reality. But the truth to which one must attain is precisely that the ego is only a purely phenomenal emanation of the unfathomable and nameless, a phantasm created solely by the impulse with which it clings to itself; this is what must be experienced and known. For the deeper unconscious, real events do not exist, there is no history, but only symbols which it distills from all happenings; it recalls no particular wave, but every form that waves can have. Buddhism speaks on the plane of the unconscious when it teaches that there has never been a Buddha. The adept of Buddhistic Yoga gives himself in worship to a pure symbol in the knowledge that the personal and historical origin of this symbol is as unimportant as his own ego, which results only from his own imperfection. But this symbol of unique perfection, the Buddha, helps him to awaken the hidden Buddhahood in himself, and this is the sole reality.

The unconscious remembers only in mythical symbols. Accordingly, it teaches a man to become Buddha, although it recognizes no historical Buddha or anything else that is historical. Of all the individuation through which it passes, of all the shifting phenomena it gathers in—fading blossom amid evergreen foliage—it preserves only what transcends the ephemeral and historical and attains to the timeless and symbolic that is appropriate to it. Hence the life of the Buddhist yogi is full of symbolic acts: he must perform sacrifices beyond measure as gestures symbolic of his nonattachment to anything whatsoever. The Buddha in process of becoming (Bodhisattva) must learn to maintain the same relation to himself and to every situation in which he becomes entwined on his path of self-sacrifice as the deep unconscious maintains to ourselves: for it does not cling to us; it is not bound to ego and world by its own gesture; he must learn to live like the unconscious: timeless and deathless, unattainable.

II

We are not simple, and the duality of "body and soul" does not express our being. The ancient conception of man was highly complex, as is shown in the following lines telling what becomes of him after death:

> Ossa tegit terra, tumulum circumvolat umbra,
> orcus tenet manes, spiritus astra petit.

> (Earth covers the bones, the shade flies round the mound,
> the soul descends to the underworld, the spirit rises to the stars.)

The conception that the soul, or life principle, is something simple arose only later and has again been discarded; the ancient Egyptians and many "primitive" peoples knew better; the ancient Chinese developed a particularly many-sided picture, rich in implications. "Man consists of the effective forces of heaven and earth," says the *Li Chi*, or Book of Rites,[2] "he consists of the union of a *kuei* and of a *shên*." *Kuei* and *shên* are the innumerable living infinitesimal particles of the infinite forces of earth and heaven, of *yin* and *yang;* "the breath is the concentrated manifestation of *shên*, and the 'corporeal soul' is the concentrated manifestation of *kuei*. The union of *kuei* and *shên* is the highest of doctrines. All living beings must die; in death they must return to the earth, this is called *kuei*. Bones and flesh rot beneath the ground, mysteriously they become the earth of the fields; but the breath rises upward and becomes heavenly radiant light *(ming)*." When a man is born, the first thing to develop is the "corporeal soul," the principle of vegetative vital force, the manifestation of *kuei/yin;* next develops man's share of the celestial *yang*, that is the "spiritual soul"; it is also identified with the breath. In contact with the outward world, the "subtlest force" is formed, its growth strengthens corporeal soul and spiritual soul, and their growth in turn strengthens the "subtlest force." And thus there develops ultimately *shên*, related to the breath and to the spiritual soul; it is the celestial and spiritual element, the growth of which is the aim of all ethical and ascetic education. He who strives for perfection, for transfiguration, endeavors to become pure *shên:* force from heaven, light of its light *(ming,* the sign for which is sun and moon side by side, the symbol of all that is

---

2 [The author's quotations of the *Li Chi* are from an unidentified German source and have been translated as they are. Cf. James Legge, tr., *The Li Kî* (SBE, 27, 28), Vol. I, pp. 38off.—ED.]

radiant)—this purification and exaltation is the Chinese road to immortality, the way to divine being.

In the interpenetration of *kuei* and *shên*, i.e., of *yin* and *yang*, man is a little cosmos, for "the whole *yin* and the whole *yang* are called Tao," i.e., the world circling in the great life rhythm of the seasons. But the corporeal soul, a fragment of the *yin* in man, never leaves the body, hence it lives with him in the grave: "It is the noblest part of the material man," and the grave in which it is to dwell is prepared with loving care and veneration. "After death, body and corporeal soul descend into the earth"—but with the inevitable decay of the body, the corporeal soul also gradually decays: "Body and corporeal soul dissolve and pass away, but spirit and breath retain the power to feel and move, and do not pass."

The ancient Chinese was aware of multiple forces within him; his conception of the celestial male principle and the earthly female principle as cosmic forces whose interplay re-forms the world forever anew provided him with the framework and the insights by which to comprehend the enduring play of forces he felt within himself. For us his definitive system can be no more than a parable and a suggestion, for our inquiry and questioning, our ostensible knowledge, are based on other conceptions, traditional and acquired. And it is too soon for us to realize that they are as questionable and as far from the eternal truth as those of the ancient Chinese. In any event, the Chinese conceptions, considered apart from their link with the cosmic dualism of Tao, embody an original magic, an inborn force: this corporeal soul, the first thing to arise in the body, bound to the body and with it passing away, this hidden soul that prevents the dead man as he lies there from being totally dead—it not only suggests old ideas, held by our ancestors before us, ideas that we bear within us as dim memories, the heritage of our body; no, it brings up to us an immediate feeling, something we have always felt when we have seen a man dying, whether we admit it or not. And that "subtlest force," essence and elixir of the corporeal and spiritual soul (*hsing*, i.e., literally, "finest, choicest rice,") a pure substance, whose posthumous name is "light of heaven," contains within itself the sublimest of the ideas that man, in the West as well as the East, has attached to the conception of the soul as the vehicle of all eternal destiny, of all high hopes.

In his profound remarks "On an apparent purposiveness in the individual destiny," Schopenhauer discusses the ancient doctrine of the daimon, who

27

is set over the conscious ego as a destiny to guide its life. He cites Menander: "A daimon stands at the side of every man; from birth it is his guide, a good guide through the mystery of his life." [3] Plato tells how this daimon and the soul meet in the realm of the dead and begin their journey through a new life together, ". . . and when all the souls have chosen their lives, they go before the Fate in the same order in which they have chosen their destinies. To each she gives the daimon he has chosen to guard his life and fulfill the destiny he has chosen; 'the daimon does not elect you, it is you who choose him for yourselves.' " [4]

This idea of a power within us that is stronger than the ego and acts as regent, even against our will, according to the necessity of a pre-elected fate, is stated in Seneca's aphorism: "The fates guide the willing, the unwilling they drag"—*ducunt volentem fata, nolentem trahunt.*[5] The astral lore of late antiquity situates this daimon, who holds the key to our fate and knows it better than the conscious will, in the stars; hence the astrologer can read our fate and character by their conjunctions. In this connection Schopenhauer remarks: "Theophrastus Paracelsus has very penetratingly formulated the same idea, when he says: 'in order that the fatum should be known, each man has a spirit that dwells outside him and establishes its seat in the upper stars.' " [6]

We are not free to appropriate the great symbols of other times and places as our own, and speak of ourselves directly through them. They are a picture writing that summons us to capture a reality that has always been present, in ourselves as in the men of the past, and to live by it in new images and concepts, if the picture writing of our own tradition has either become meaningless to us, or as metaphoric as that of other vanishing historical eras. If we cannot raise our spiritual eye and find our regent in the heavens, we can discern it in inward voices and signs, as Socrates did; and, after all, is its situation in space anything more than imagery, a metaphoric visualization? What is the deeper relation of outward to inward, of macrocosm to microcosm? The merit of the new depth psychology is that it unearths that which is timeless in us, in a form appropriate to our time, so that we can

3 Arthur Schopenhauer, *Sämtliche Werke,* ed. Arthur Hübscher (7 vols., Wiesbaden, 1949–50), Vol. V, p. 224 (citing from Menander, as quoted by Plutarch, *De tranquillitate animae,* c. 15).
4 *Republic* 620d.
5 Seneca, *Epistola* 107, 11.
6 Schopenhauer, *Werke,* ed. Hübscher, Vol. V, p. 224.

comprehend it and live by it. This psychology and the analytic method by which it operates constitute no more than a symbolic and visual means of obtaining knowledge about our being; it is a science born of our time and our predicament with which it will also pass away, but for that very reason it is to us more intelligible than any other set of symbols; precisely because it is the only form in which we can validly explain to ourselves how we live, it puts us into relation with the very same reality which speaks through the fading hieroglyphic systems of other ages. It is our way of giving name and form to the intangible reality within us, it is the special form of *māyā* through which the reality of the soul can manifest itself in our historical moment. A meaningful doctrine can never be anything other than an arrow aimed at reality, the intangible reality which transcends the sphere of the intellect and of speech. The arrow, however, can graze this sphere, and our comprehension follows. Every age has different arrows; some ages have but a single arrow.

Depth psychology has destroyed the primitive dualism of body and soul, which looked upon these two as a simple duality. Those who held to this conception viewed the soul as a unit, and also failed to realize that the body was a fragment of the soul. The dark waters of the unconscious upon which floats the little ship of consciousness—or we might better say the amniotic fluid which cradles and nourishes the embryo—is physically tangible in the diversified world of organs and cells that is our body. The Hindus feel that an immense force is present in its actions, its spontaneous yes and no which leap over the commands and prohibitions of the ego and mock its aspirations by failures, and they call this stupendous something "the gods." For according to the Indian conception, all the gods of the world dwell in our body, where they represent the same forces as they do in the macrocosm. By the ceremonial laying on of hands (*nyāsa*), accompanied by inner concentration on the essences of the gods and by the whispering of the magical syllables that embody them in the realm of sound, the adept of Tantric Yoga evokes them in himself and thus rouses himself to the consciousness that he is the epitome of the divine *māyā*, which differentiates all the forms in the microcosm and macrocosm and unfolds them as divine forces made manifest. Thus the gods are not only in the body of man, they not only are his whole body, this aggregate of manifold forces and functions, they are also in all other life; this is an aspect of the world's unity, for all its multiplicity is formed out of *one* fluid, living substance, the *shakti* of God.

29

The Indian textbook of elephant medicine, the *Hastyāyurveda* ("science concerning the long life of the elephants" [7]), describes in its discussion of the embryo the distribution of the diverse substantial forces of the gods (*devaguna*) in the body of the elephant (III, 8): "Brahma is located in the elephant's head, Indra in the neck, Vishnu in the body. In the navel (the seat of the body's heat) the fire god, in the two eyes the sun god, in the hind legs Mitra." Two aspects of the creator of the world (Dhatar and Vidhatar) are in the two sides of the belly, "in the organ of generation is the 'lord of emanations' (Prajāpati), in the entrails (the snakelike, winding intestines) are the snake gods that bear the yoke of all the worlds." For in the elephant there dwells the ageless and eternal being, fundamental and inherent in all things (*pradhā-ātman*). "In the forelegs are the mounted twin gods," corresponding to the two arms in man, of which the priest in the old ritual of the Vedas says: "with the two arms of the riding twins I grasp . . ." In the ears dwell the goddesses of the directions in space, the rulers of the spatial element, which in the form of sound is captured in the shell of the ear; the rain god Parjanya dwells in the heart of the elephants, for they are the mythical brothers of the rain clouds, their presence magically attracts the water of their original celestial home.

Thus all the gods are in our body; this means that the body is surrounded and filled with forces, forcelike individualities that are not subservient to us but can lead a self-willed life of their own. Otherwise we should not need the long and difficult training in Yoga, the extreme and tenacious exertion of the will, the respectful association with these gods in us through *pūjā* and *nyāsa*, in order to become master in the house of our body and gradually teach it those activities and processes which the aims of Yoga require. These gods live independently of us, they sicken and fail in their function, without consulting us. In fear and expectation, we are dependent on them, dependent on two gestures which in India as everywhere else in the world are the two most significant gestures of all gods: the gesture that grants wishes and bestows gifts (*varada*) and the gesture that says: "Fear not!" (*abhayada*). There is scarcely any image of an Indian god in which these gestures are not present.

All things are in us; we are, as the poet said, *"dei gorghi d'ogni abisso, degli astri d'ogni ciel"*—"we partake of the vortex of every abyss, of the stars of every heaven."

7 Cf. Zimmer, *Spiel um den Elephanten: Ein Buch von indischer Natur* (Munich, 1929).

All the gods are in us: there is in us a mighty mysterious power, greater than ourselves. We can only strive to gain its good graces by showing it daily attentions in ritual worship. Our association with it must be regular, otherwise the principle of power, multiform, dark and supple, escapes us. It escapes us, teases, surprises, torments us with undesired presences and absences, with disguises and threats. It ignores our needs, becomes alien and hostile to us, evades us like a goblin, refuses to hear our pleas. By daily, respectful association with it (and a part of this is its evocation through *nyāsa*), we can keep it near us and well disposed to us.

The correct form of association is equally important, for it is powerful, many-faced, and many-limbed. In its forest of hands it holds all things at once: every weapon of defense and revenge, every weapon with which to preserve or destroy us, every implement, ornament, and flower—symbols for all things. And it shows many faces at once, looks in every direction. When the face that is turned toward us smiles, another, that is mercifully turned away from us, bears the hideous features that turn us to stone. It acts out every gesture at once, loving care, terrifying violence, and world-removed equanimity; the manly and the womanly, the luring and the motherly, radiant heroism and the mocking laughter of annihilation, are manifested in turn, and over them all the divine repose of the other world. All the animal forms in their eloquent symbolism of the bestial and soft, the cruel and warm, the voracious and gentle, are its shifting facets.

The proper association with this divine and demonic element in us, with its manifestations as diverse as all life—for we with our body are life itself—can rest only upon a long tradition which has sifted the diverse and uncertain experience of many generations, and shaped that part of it which is forever confirmed anew into a canon. Such association with the divine is association with our totality in its essential facets, with the unconscious, the body, the world in which the gods dwell as they dwell everywhere else. For him who no longer worships them in wind and crag, in source and stars, or in any celestial or supracelestial zone, but only in the one place where he feels them directly, in his own body—for him his body can become the world, for him as for the yogi the reality of his body becomes reality pure and simple. He discovers that it contains all things and that all outward contents are mere reflections of his inward being, projections of the force which forever builds him inwardly; for him, the inner event becomes the event as such.

31

The cult of Tantric Yoga is directed toward man's own unconscious, the divine that is in us, which it conjures, awakens, and ritually worships. In the old cult of the Vedas, the gods come forth on their chariots externally though invisibly. Only the priest sees them corporeally, in an inner visualization effected by liturgical verses which describe them in their glory and carry them into the sphere of the cult. In Tantric Yoga the same occurs in the inner space of the body, in the inner field of vision, into which the figure of the deity rises from its—our—intangible depth.

All the gods are in our body; nothing else is meant by the visual schema of the Kundalinī Yoga, whose adept guides the world-unfolding, world-bearing life-serpent of the macrocosm out of its slumber in the depths, up through the whole body to its supraterrestrial opposite. On its upward path it passes through the lotus centers of the body, in which all the elements, the material from which the form-hungry vital force makes every form and every gesture, are gathered together; and in the same centers the apparitional forms of the godhead, along with the facets of their *shaktis*, are seen and worshiped.

That all the gods and demons come from within us, even though they seem to approach us from without, is an open secret of Buddhism in its developed form, the "Great Vehicle," and is also taught in the Vedānta, which serves as the philosophical basis for the Tantras. Nowhere is this more effectively expressed than in the Tibetan Book of the Dead, the *Bardo Thödol*.[8] For according to the doctrine inherent in this Buddhist ritual, every man, even if he has not suspected or wished to suspect this truth in his lifetime, learns it in the "intermediate state" (*bardo*) which follows his death and precedes the new incarnation of his aggregate of psychic forces and potentialities.

The dead man's guru or a lama who is also his friend speaks to him and advises him during this intermediate state, in which he is assailed by extraordinary terrors and visions:

> Thou seest thy relatives and connexions and speakest to them, but receivest no reply. Then, seeing them and thy family weeping, thou thinkest, "I am dead! What shall I do?" and feelest great misery, just like a fish cast out [of water] on red-hot embers. Such misery thou wilt be experiencing at present. But feeling miserable will avail thee nothing now. . . . Even though thou feelest attachment

8 W. Y. Evans-Wentz, *The Tibetan Book of the Dead* (London, 1927; 3rd. edn., 1957).

for thy relatives and connexions, it will do thee no good. So be not attached. Pray to the Compassionate Lord [Buddha]; thou shalt have naught of sorrow, or of terror, or of awe.[9]

Such words accompany the dead man on his entire journey through the intermediate realm, and by them the guru strives on each new stage of his road to save him from the peril of rebirth in upper or lower worlds. Only the man who in his lifetime has attained to the goal of Yoga and learned that all forms of world and ego are mere phantasms rising out of the formless and intangible, a *māyā* in which our being cloaks itself, can dispense with the explanations and advice in which a final effort is made to preserve him from his own demonic force, from imprisonment in himself. Before the eyes of each man who must leave the flesh, there shines the pure light of reality, an empty, formless, all-filling radiance; but only he who as a yogi in his life was illumined by it does not shrink back in terror. The man who is imprisoned in himself can neither comprehend nor bear it, and continues on the road of his aptitude for gesture and form.

The outer world pales around him, he has grown light as ether.

> . . . when thou art driven by the ever-moving wind of *karma*, thine intellect, having no object upon which to rest, will be like a feather tossed about by the wind. . . . Ceaselessly and involuntarily wilt thou be wandering about. To all those who are weeping [thou wilt say], "Here I am; weep not." But they not hearing thee, thou wilt think, "I am dead!" And again, at that time, thou wilt be feeling very miserable. Be not miserable in that way.
>
> There will be a grey twilight-like light, both by night and by day, and at all times. In that kind of Intermediate State thou wilt be either for one, two, three, four, five, six, or seven weeks, until the forty-ninth day. . . . Because of the determining influence of *karma*, a fixed period is not assured.
>
> . . . the fierce wind of *karma*, terrific and hard to endure, will drive thee [onwards], from behind, in dreadful gusts. Fear it not. That is thine own illusion. Thick awesome darkness will appear in front of thee continually, from the midst of which there will come such terror-producing utterances as "Strike! Slay!" and similar threats. Fear these not.
>
> In other cases, of persons of much evil *karma*, karmically-produced flesh-eating *rākshasas* [or demons] bearing various weapons will utter, "Strike! Slay!" and so on, making a frightful tumult. They will come upon one as if competing amongst themselves as to

9 Ibid., pp. 160f.

which [of them] should get hold of one. Apparitional illusions, too, of being pursued by various terrible beasts of prey will dawn. Snow, rain, darkness, fierce blasts [of wind], and hallucinations of being pursued by many people likewise will come; [and] sounds as of mountains crumbling down, and of angry overflowing seas . . .

When these sounds come one, being terrified by them, will flee before them in every direction, not caring whither one fleeth. But the way will be obstructed by three awful precipices—white, and black, and red. They will be terror-inspiring and deep, and one will feel as if one were about to fall down them. . . . They are not really precipices; they are Anger, Lust, and Stupidity.[10]

When the customary world which comes to man in his lifetime through his senses dissolves in the formless gray of the intermediate realm that enfolds him now that he is released from the mechanism of his corporeal senses, his inner energies take on form and spatiality, and they assail him as though from without. In his hallucination he sees his own inwardness as a sphere around him, just as a dreamer, from whom the world of the day has fallen away, sees his own tensions and impulses transmuted into alluring or nightmarish landscapes and figures which beset his dream self.

Like the dreamer, the departed is all alone; but just as one can speak to a dreamer and he weaves the words into his dream, the lama, the guide of his soul, speaks to the departed. And now all the impulses and potentialities for good and evil that were in him emerge, as figures of saints, gods, and demons; he looks upon these spirits of his heart and mind, and the dazzling light of the ones, the haunting awfulness of the others, is more than he can bear. But the voice of the guru teaches him to pray:

> May I recognize whatever appeareth as being mine own thought-forms, . . .
> [May I] fear not the bands of the Peaceful and Wrathful, Who are [mine] own thought-forms.[11]

In death, with the dissolution of consciousness, our unconscious is set free and bursts forth all-powerful. All the impulses and predispositions that governed our living world—the individual world that surrounds each one of us with its special distribution of emphasis, with all the valuations which we attach to things, all the colorations we give them in love and rejection,

10 *The Tibetan Book of the Dead*, pp. 161f.
11 Ibid., p. 204.

Flute-playing Krishna (Venu-gopāla). Wood, South Indian,
c. XVII *cent.*

Dākinī ("Fairy of All Buddhas"). Nepal or Tibet, gilded bronze

acceptance or flight—all this is projected outward, as has been the case throughout our lives. But now there is no longer a world of corporeal forms, corresponding to our own body, a neutral gray world to which this projection lends luring or menacing tonalities—there is instead the formless gray of the intermediate realm. The archetypes of the sacred, seductive, and terrifying forms which in life we projected upon others, whom we honored, desired, or hated, now strike upon no corporeal world; like mirages of our inwardness they fall upon the gray mist of the intermediate realm: and the mist stares back at us in a thousand aspects, blinding us with intolerable radiance, terrifying us with demonic rage—how shall we learn to withstand it?

But the voice of the lama is heard:

> These . . . perfectly endowed deities, issuing from within thy heart, being the product of thine own pure love, will come to shine. Know them. . . . These realms are not come from somewhere outside [thyself]. . . . They issue from within thee, and shine upon thee. The deities, too, are not come from somewhere else: they exist from eternity within the faculties of thine own intellect. Know them to be of that nature.[12]

And, when, beginning with the eighth day after death, the mild emanations of the heart are followed by the horrible emanations of the brain, spewing flame, wielding all the weapons of destruction, raising to their lips skulls full of human blood, the voice of the guru resounds:

> Be not awed. Know it to be the embodiment of thine own intellect. As it is thine own tutelary deity, be not terrified. . . . In reality [these demons are] the Bhagavān Vajra-Sattva, the Father and Mother. Believe in them. Recognizing them, liberation will be obtained at once. By so proclaiming [them], knowing them to be tutelary deities, merging [in them] in at-one-ment [samādhi], Buddhahood will be obtained.[13]

Only he who, while still living in the flesh, has striven for Buddhahood as a yogi, and penetrated the essence of these projections of his inwardness, who has recognized that it is they and they alone who lend all coloration, value, and weight to the outside world, and transform the infinite into his own finite world which lures and frightens him—only a yogi is prepared to

12 Ibid., pp. 121f.
13 Ibid., pp. 137f.

meet this all-powerful, volcanic *māyā* of his *shakti*. Consequently the *Bardo Thödol* is not only a ritual for the instruction and guidance of the dead, but also a book of Yoga for the living, a book with whose help, while still alive, he may through inner vision and outward observances come to terms with the projections of his inwardness, and learn to recognize them without fear when he encounters them in the intermediate realm. He who in his lifetime has been initiated by his guru can withstand their terrors in the hereafter and realize in himself the pure light of knowledge, which transcends all these phantasms.

The *Bardo Thödol* teaches the Buddhist yogi to venerate the demonic forces of his inwardness as his own tutelary deities; then he need have no fear of them when he encounters them in the intermediate realm; for he has always humbly revered them. We must learn while it is still time to deal with the dark aspects of our being; not in order to exert a demonic influence on the world or to amuse ourselves—that would be black magic or a court-ing of the devil; no, we must recognize them and hold them in veneration as dark and dangerous forces within us. They have power and sovereignty, because equally with our oft-praised angel-like potentialities for purity and beauty, they are forms of our form-hungry *shakti*, of the divine vital energy we embody. To him who closes his eyes to them and refuses to recognize their mighty omnipresence, they will some day demonstrate their existence in a terrible way; but with him who humbly venerates them, without attempting to unleash them for his own advantage, they will live as neigh-bors and tutelary deities. For their fierce diabolic power is only the nocturnal aspect of their nature, and it prevails only when we attempt to exclude them from our consciousness; their sinister aspect is the apt hieroglyphic of our unconscious, into whose night we have thrust them back; and what it ex-presses is our own horror and shame and refusal to recognize them. We must accept and honor the wholeness of our being, from which we cannot sub-tract one particle, any more than man can remove from his body that part of it which his modesty conceals, without becoming an utter monstrosity.

Yet to be sure, this association with the wholeness of our being, which is in danger of remaining unconscious and disordering us with its demonic force, demands a pure heart. He who seeks it while clouded by the whirling dust of passion, while sullied by animality, succumbs to the powers he has conjured up to serve his desires. That is the meaning of the fear of hell that we find in the tales of demonic sorcerers. Dr. Faustus in the

36

old legend and Dr. Cenodoxus of Paris (in the baroque drama [14]) are carried off by the devil they had summoned. He serves them until they are entirely in his power. He has known from the outset that he is the stronger; how, in the long run, can man withstand this multiform power which tempts him with blandishments and terrors? The unconscious which man awakens in order to use it for conscious ends instead of worshiping it in awe and veneration is infinitely more powerful than the conscious ego, as much more powerful as the body—the body of the unconscious—which, whenever it pleases, can submerge the waking ego in sleep.

The *Bardo Thödol* orders the adept to make his peace with the most diabolical projections of his own inwardness, if he would save himself from them and from the menace of rebirth; it orders him to undertake the journey into his own hell. The road to the perfect sphere passes, as in Dante, through it alone. Oedipus performed this terrible descent into his own depths when he inquired after the accursed, fateful child whom his father had destined to early death—the child that he himself was, without knowing it: this is his striving for wholeness and in it he succeeds; it is his typically tragic destiny. He has a foreboding that he is also someone other than the savior of Thebes, the hero and king, the husband of this woman and the father of these children. He feels in himself something else, something terrible that blots out all this, but its nature and name remain for him unfathomable; and how can he remember, since he has slain his father unbeknown to himself, and taken his mother to wife, and begotten three children on her. "The circle is closed!" is his terrible cry after he has unearthed the doom within him, the sphinx that has oppressed him and his kingdom, the dark guilt which he could not exorcise, which he could not conquer as he had conquered the other sphinx. Now he is whole again, both the one and the other: both savior and criminal carrier of doom; the light and the darkness in him flow into one mighty stream. Now he no longer needs eyes like other men—eyes which are given man in order to distinguish the one from the other, to reveal one road among several; in his wholeness, the one is the other, the savior is the victim, his greatness is his curse, his innocence his guilt. And so he casts his eyes away; and like Ajax gone mad, his tragic Sophoclean

---

14 [*Cenodoxus* (1602), drama by the German Jesuit playwright Jakob Bidermann. A "dramatic concretion of the struggle between free thought and divine faith . . . a kind of morality play of Faustian flavor."—Allardyce Nicoll, *World Drama* (London, 1949).—ED.]

37

brother, he might have welcomed his self-chosen death with the cry: "Darkness! O thou my light!"

A similar motif occurs in the story of Christ: Jesus' rejection of the Pharisees, his devotion to the socially and morally tainted, his choice of the children as an example, not because they are pure and innocent, but because they live by their wholeness, without inhibition. He commands the disciples to stop by the carcass of the dog, to endure its stench, to behold its beauty, its white teeth, amid its putrefaction, to look upon it as a part of the world's beauty, instead of rejecting it as vile. And similarly in the story of St. Julian, which Flaubert relates after the legend: the ferryman beds the leprous wanderer on his breast, and the hideous leper is the grace-giving savior. In embracing and letting himself be embraced by what is most repugnant to him, a man can achieve possession of a wholeness in which that most repugnant thing and everything else he has shunned dissolve along with everything he has ever desired. These antitheses all require one another; they strive to form a totality in which they will disappear. This immersion in the Other, in the thing which has always inspired one with horror, but which one must nevertheless accept as one's own, reminds one of the prison bath in which all the convicts plunge their crimes, and in which after them Oscar Wilde, "the king of life," immerses his body in order to complete the life which he has always felt to be the object of his art, by fusing its oppositions into a totality. As a rite symbolizing this need to become whole, we might conceive of a Mass, in which the chalice would not be filled with the blood of Christ, the Lamb of God who took upon himself the sins of the world; instead, it would contain all the sin and vice and lewdness of priest and congregation. Both priest and flock would drink from the cup, partaking of all their hidden, but now revealed, sin; a magic transformation would occur; out of the horror and filth, ineffable purity would be distilled, the potion of the gods, that cleanses from sin and confers divine life. And this divine life is the same as the hidden Buddhahood which in the *Bardo Thödol* is disclosed to the adept as he journeys through his own inner hell; it is a wholeness above all antitheses, impervious to schism and conflict. This conquest of wholeness is represented in many legends of those about to become Buddhas (Bodhisattvas), who take upon themselves all manner of hardships and terrors, because they realize that their ego, which they are striving to dissolve, is each day recrystallized just as much by attitudes of rejection and denial of repulsive things as by feelings of attraction and

38

possessiveness toward pleasant things. But the Illumined One (*buddha*) is "without fallow land, without wasteland" in himself (*a-khila*) and therefore "whole" (*a-khila* means also "entire" or "whole"). He has not established his ego like a garden and marked it off from the wholeness of his being, and of all being, safeguarding it against the menacing desert of the unconscious that lies round it unnoticed: accordingly, the desert cannot assail him with its terrors, no beast or demon can rise up out of his unconscious part to terrify and destroy him.

All the gods and powers are within us; the body expands to a cosmos, and woe to him who disregards it. This divine being in us can never—as has been said in mockery of other gods—be asleep or away on a voyage; if it seems to sleep or to be far off, that is a sign that it is angry, because we have lost our relation to it and have not been able to preserve it. In that event, we no longer enjoy its grace: it is already in process of metamorphosing itself into a dangerous devil, which, like all stupidity and despair, must behave malignantly toward us. Each of us has in himself the godly in the form he deserves; he can nurture and preserve it in daily devotion. We nurture the godhead in us with our heart's blood, as the priest in certain Aztec frescoes offers the blood of his tongue to the god. Novalis noted: "Every word is an exorcism; whatever the spirit that calls, a kindred spirit will answer." The rationalistic unbeliever, for whom all this does not exist, has no gods left in his heart; that is his fall from grace. Instead, he is tormented by the devils of his brain: "Chance" or "force of circumstances" or "ineluctable causality" or the "fault of the others," for he must seek outside himself all the demons which he does not wish to find and resolve in himself. "Where there are no gods," said Novalis, "there are ghosts." And like true ghosts, they evade any real capture by their faculty for continually assuming new and unexpected forms: he who cannot exorcise their demonism and transform it into the higher thing it cloaks and disguises lives in impotent servitude to it; he is his own malignant and stupid devil.

Tantric Yoga teaches its adepts to respect and live at peace with the world of the unconscious; by evoking the unconscious, they preserve their balance; total and repeated immersion in it is indeed the very core of Tantric Yoga. Out of the dark waters rises the godhead like a glittering wave, and with it the conscious ego fuses. Thus the adept lives on, continually relieved of his burden, because he is not split off from his inwardness, but in full communion with it. "As all flowing rivers find peace in the ocean, where they lose their name and form," says the Upanishad, "the Knowing Man, relieved of name and form, attains to the divine essence, which is higher than the highest." Similarly the yogi, by a daily smelting down of his tangible part with its form and name, and of his consciousness that confers concepts and names, returns home to his divine opposite. And thereby he derives the strength to bear up against every eventuality.

III

Numerous attempts have been made to formulate the doctrines of Indian Yoga in Western terms, and these simplifications have given rise to all kinds of interpretation, but it has never been made really clear to what mode or sphere of reality the experiences of Yoga have reference. Only the new psychology of the unconscious has penetrated the sphere in which the experiences of Yoga are at home. Additional light has been cast on the subject by the studies of a solitary thinker, still little known except to specialists in psychopathology. In 1912, Dr. Ludwig Staudenmaier, professor of experimental chemistry at the Lyceum in Freising, Bavaria, published an amazing book, *Die Magie als experimentelle Naturwissenschaft* (Magic as an Experimental Science). He was well aware of the misgivings his findings would arouse in strictly scientific circles, to which he himself belonged, and to which he addressed his book; for this reason he submitted a first draft in 1910 to the judgment of a positivist, the chemist Wilhelm Ostwald, whose "comprehensive scientific knowledge in the most important related fields" would enable him to deliver a considered opinion as to whether Staudenmaier "should venture to publish his work." By way of an answer, Ostwald accepted the paper for the *Annalen der Naturphilosophie* (Annals of Natural Philosophy), and it is to be found in the 1910 volume of that leading scientific journal. The psychiatric world, it is true, probably regards Staudenmaier's book as nothing more than an interesting autobiographic case history of a sufferer from schizophrenia.

Staudenmaier's outward career was rather colorless and uneventful; all the more noteworthy were his inner adventures. This relation between outward and inward was similar to that prevailing in the ascetic life of a yogi or a saint. In the preface to his book, he tells us that he graduated from a Bavarian Latin school in 1884, and then for four years attended a lyceum, a "special academy for philosophy and Catholic theology," attended by students of theology who for one reason or another did not wish to attend a university. Here he studied philosophy for one year and theology for three years. But after a year as a clergyman, Staudenmaier abandoned both theology and the ministry and undertook a different line of study that was to open up a new career to him. He went to Munich, where he studied "nothing but natural science, specializing first in zoology and later in chemistry." He continues: "After passing the state examinations in descriptive natural science and chemistry, as well as the examination for the doctorate in chemistry at the University of Munich, I served for a year and a half as an assistant at the scientific institute of that university; in 1896 I was appointed professor of experimental chemistry at the Royal Lyceum in Freising, where I shall soon have completed my sixteenth year."

Thus, except for a few years spent in intensive study and for his brief term as an assistant in Munich, his whole adult life was spent amid the uneventful calm of a provincial school. He was of a celibate nature, sitting patiently over his chemical experiments like the eternal student, living a quiet, frugal life, seeking no academic honors. Freising was a dead end, a backwater; here he was far removed from the vanities of the large universities, the competition for appointments, the faculty politics; and by disposition he was also alien to such interests. Eros and Kratos, love and the lust for power, the two manifestations of the *shakti* that move the social world, did not influence his conscious life.

It was what we call an accident that brought him to his study of "magic as an experimental science." A friend asked him whether he believed the manifestations of phosphorescence seen at spiritualist séances "could be explained by chemistry or other physical causes." The same friend persuaded the skeptical professor to attempt the writing experiments customary among spiritualists: one holds a pencil loosely over a sheet of paper and lets it move of its own free will until it produces some sort of script or signs. At first his inhibitions led to failures, but his friend encouraged him to go on, and finally results were obtained: the pencil described "the strangest loops and curlicues," then it began to form letters, and to answer questions which he had asked inwardly. The writing flowed more and more easily, and various spirits seemed to speak in it. Staudenmaier doubted whether they could be real spirits, for his "own thoughts were involved in the answers." "Nevertheless," he remarks, "I absolutely had the impression of having to do with a being utterly alien to me. At first I could tell in advance what was going to be written, and from this there developed in time an

41

anticipated 'inner' hearing of the message." Now the association with the inner voices no longer required paper and pencil, though for a transitional period he continued to use them to introduce and stimulate the process. "As the spiritualists say, I had become an 'auditory medium.'" Any number of voices presented themselves.

> In the end there were too many of them; they importuned me, for no good reason and quite against my will. [They were] often malicious, scheming, mocking, quarrelsome, angry, etc. For days an intolerable and repugnant squabbling went on, quite against my will. And often the statements made by these beings proved to be utterly false.
>
> [In addition to these] acoustical hallucinations, as a psychiatrist would call them, I soon had others of an optical nature. The manner of behavior of these beings unquestionably revealed a certain measure of independent intelligence, but on the other hand, their conduct was so strange, so biased, their whole attitude towards me was often so completely contingent on my own nervous state, that obviously the causes of these magical phenomena lay largely within myself. In naïve, medieval terms, I was possessed. Gradually, individual hallucinations became more and more distinct, and recurred more and more frequently; finally, the more frequent visual images entered into regular combination with corresponding auditory images, and definite personifications resulted; the figures that now appeared began to talk to me, to give me advice, to criticize my actions, etc.

Several personalities now become differentiated within Staudenmaier, each with a self-willed existence of its own. At first three were most conspicuous, and these, in keeping with their character and appearance, he named "His Highness," "The Child," and "Roundhead." It seems worth while to describe these figures as accurately as one might describe the experiences in a Yoga exercise, especially as Staudenmaier's book is not likely to be known to many. "While watching a military drill," he had occasion "to see a certain prince at close quarters and to hear him speak. Some time later I had a distinct hallucination of hearing him speak again." This hallucination developed into a feeling that this prince was near by. Other personifications of kings and nobles appeared.

> The figure assumed the disguise of the German Emperor, then of Napoleon; gradually I was invaded by a strange, exalting feeling

42

that I was the ruler and commander of a whole people; my chest expanded and broadened almost without any participation on my part, my whole posture became strikingly erect and military—a proof that this personification was gaining a powerful influence over me. . . . Out of the aggregate of the royal personifications there gradually developed the type, "His Highness." His Highness is very much addicted to military pageantry, high life, lofty manners, fine dress, good posture, gymnastics, hunting, and other sports; he favors order and elegance in my home. He tries to influence my mode of life accordingly, by means of advice, admonition, commands, threats. His Highness is opposed to children, to charming little trinkets, to jokes and merriment . . . he has a particular distaste for humorous magazines containing caricatured portraits . . . moreover, I am a little too short to suit his taste.

This ideal caricature of a provincial nobleman in 1900 arises from the total irony and incorruptibility of the unconscious toward the whole social sphere. His Highness "seeks to influence and interpret all my actions and plans in his aristocratic way, to ennoble my whole mode of life and manner of thinking."

And if he really can not be the German Emperor, or seriously suppose himself to be the German Emperor, he can at least think of him often and he wants me to do the same. When I return to reality, he wants me at least to feel like a real professor, to take pleasure in the position I have acquired, to live, eat, and drink as befits my class, and not just keep on studying and speculating like the eternal student, utterly forgetting the enjoyment of life.

A far more important role is played by the personification of "The Child": "I am a child. You are my papa. You must play with me." This personification hums children's songs . . . he is so sensitive, so wonderfully childlike and naïve; no real child could be so touching. . . . On my walks in the city, he makes me stop outside the windows of the toyshops, makes me examine the toys at length, makes me buy some of them, watch children playing, and makes me want to play about on the ground like a child; in other words, wants me to behave in a thoroughly un-aristocratic way. Occasionally, when at the insistence of "The Child" or "The Children" (sometimes there is a split into several related personifications) I visit the toy department of a department store in Munich, this personification is beside himself with joy, and often exclaims in a childlike voice: "Isn't it marvelous! This is heaven!" And he expresses the hope that I shall soon set up a playroom.

Roundhead took his name and visual aspect from a little rubber ball with the good-natured face of a "beer student" painted on it; when you pressed the ball, the student stuck his tongue out. A peddler had sold it to Staudenmaier's mother in a beer garden.

> She took it home and we sometimes played with it. Some years later this head, but now in life size, seemed to be near me, and at the same time an inner voice corresponding to the figure said to me: "I'm feeling good today. Don't be such a bore. Think of me. I like to do things too. I want to have some fun!" Then he would crack a few jokes and perform various ludicrous tricks. All of a sudden he would make his hair stand up on end, make faces, and stick out his tongue like the rubber ball, etc. This Roundhead was enthusiastic about the Munich humorous magazines, and comic papers in general; he would study the pictures at great length. He liked entertaining company, and he liked to sit for hours drinking beer, etc. . . . But soon I heard other inner voices, complaining angrily about the "boorish vulgarity" of this personification. That would soon spoil his fun, he would make a wry face, and the joking was over. Inside me, I could hear a voice saying: "That's no way to treat a fellow. I wanted to cheer you up." Later I perceived bad, I might even say very bad, qualities in Roundhead. In certain respects he seemed to be utterly dissolute, and to possess grave defects of character. Then I would forget him for quite a long time, until one day it struck me that an alien power was trying to move my tongue from one side to the other, or to make it stick out. It then turned out that Roundhead was performing exercises for the purpose of making "his" tongue larger and more agile and in every way more mobile than the tongue of the rubber ball. Although I claimed the tongue as my own, he frequently attempted from this time on to do exercises with it. . . . Meanwhile I must admit that Roundhead had once done a good thing. For one night as I lay in bed, extremely agitated and angry over other personifications, suddenly the visual hallucination of a black and white rooster appeared. There was no doubt in my mind that Roundhead had sent it. In his bill he held the olive branch of peace and immediately laid an egg. I could not help laughing and the entire situation was changed.

Here apparently Staudenmaier had unconsciously remembered one of the crude black and white woodcuts from Kortum's "Jobsiade": Hieronymus Jobs, the "dissolute student vagabond," has become a village schoolmaster. It causes much headshaking in the village when he draws on the blackboard a rooster laying an egg in his nest.

44

In reality, it was Staudenmaier's unlived life that rose up out of him in the form of these personifications; they were the natural contents, the unrealized, unconscious potentialities of a man's life, which, barred from outward expression by the life he had chosen to lead, had seized upon a belated inner reality in which they could act as they pleased. The imposing, austere gesture, the Jovian host and family head, the respected academic leader, all this had never come out in him, had never had an opportunity to express itself in his narrow, celibate existence, in this small provincial Lyceum, devoted entirely to teaching and learning and sheltered by the great hierarchy of which it formed a part, in this modest, quiet life far from the great world. Nevertheless this penchant for aristocratic splendor and the lofty manner was in him, though he had never noted it, for all things are present in all of us as potentiality.

And the predisposition to fatherhood which is in every man, which in him had had no opportunity to develop, expressed itself in "The Child." Once when he bought a tiny little doll to use as an object of fixation for certain experiments on optical hallucinations, The Child cried out in enthusiasm: "That's the beginning of the children's room. But now you'll have to take real children as models . . ." Soon it was no longer a single child, but a whole chorus of the unborn that spoke within him—"and then we'll show you who we are and what we can do." This was the voice of all the children and grandchildren that he, in accordance with the potentiality of every male, man or animal, might have had and loved, but he had never developed this potentiality, he had allowed his life to pass it by. With joyous promise, The Children cried out; an absurd little doll had sufficed to awaken them, to fill them with enthusiasm, like the chorus of the unborn in Hofmannsthal's *Frau ohne Schatten* (Woman without a Shadow):

> wäre denn je ein Fest
> wären nicht insgeheim,
> wir die Geladenen,
> wir auch die Wirte

> (for if there were ever a banquet
> would not secretly
> we be the guests
> and the hosts too).

But never had he celebrated the banquet of his life, he had never invited the guests and had never accepted their invitation.

45

He had never known the commonplace gaiety of a night out, the mild dissipation of young Jobs; the lighthearted student with his beer and his barmaids, his jokes and his foolishness and his smug complacency had never had a chance to come out in him, but had been stifled by his clerical education and his intensive study of the natural sciences. And now all this lifted up its round head from the depths of the unconscious, in which it had been left to slumber—to slumber like the unborn babes which the stork finds in the marshes.

But more surged upward than Staudenmaier's unrealized personal potentialities; hell itself and its heavenly counterpart, the pacific and menacing powers of the *Bardo Thödol* in the variants of the Christian unconscious. There was one figure which Staudenmaier recognized as God the Father, "a personification of the godly and sublime, a venerable old man with a full, powerful voice and a flowing beard; he is the natural adversary of the diabolical personifications and strives to inspire me with virtue and lofty aims." And there were two "personifications, usually wearing horns," who "play an important role: 'Goat-foot' and 'Horse-foot,' whom I must treat with great caution, since they continually threaten me with the most dangerous developments, especially when I over-exert myself." But the devil, the emanation of his own inwardness, also showed himself in other ways: "sometimes all the devils seemed to be let loose. Repeatedly, I could discern fiendish faces with the utmost clarity and sharpness. Once as I lay in bed I had the distinct feeling that someone was winding a chain around my neck. Immediately afterward I perceived a foul smell of hydrogen sulphide and an uncanny inner voice said to me: 'Now you are my prisoner. I'll never let you go. I am the devil.'"

Thus he experienced in his own flesh the demons that beset St. Anthony and other Christian ascetics, that swarm through the world of the Tantric Yoga and constitute the subject matter of lamaistic art. Nor was the temptress, the phantom of Helen—who, as Mephisto said, lurks "in every woman"—lacking:

> Among the optical hallucinations, this is the most noteworthy. Once a pretty young woman visited me for several days. She made a certain impression on me, which soon vanished, however, after she had gone. A few nights later, I was lying in bed, on my left side, conversing a little from time to time with my inner voices as they presented themselves. When I turned over on the other side,

46

I was dumfounded to see this girl's head emerging from the bed-clothes to the right of me, as though the girl were lying beside me. Her face was magically transfigured, charmingly beautiful, ethereal and translucent; it gave off a gentle glow in the near darkness, the room being lit only by a street lamp some distance away. At first I was utterly amazed as though at a miracle, but a moment later the nature of the hallucination became clear to me, particularly as a strange, raucous voice whispered mockingly from within me. I let out a violent curse and indignantly turned back on my left side, paying no attention to the phantom. Later a friendly voice said to me: "The young lady has gone." I looked, and seeing that nothing was there, I fell asleep. I am absolutely certain that I was entirely awake, and also that I had not previously been thinking of the person in question.

Staudenmaier's resolute conduct in the face of this temptation would have done honor to a good many saints; but on the other hand the dry celibate nature by which he withstood the temptation is probably just what had led him to experimental chemistry and away from the clerical career that might have made a saint of him. So much was dammed up in his unconscious that he had visions like any saint or yogi, but he lacked the outlet of passionate faith, by which his pent-up vital forces, surfeited with themselves, might have issued forth, to be transformed by worship and veneration into the crystal-clear figure of the divine. Lamaism is also acquainted with this "young lady," shimmering in her nakedness and presenting the cup of desire; but lamaism has broken the demonic power of her allure and has transformed her through ritual worship into the friendly "fairy of all Buddhas" (*sarva-Buddha-Dākinī*). She is the tutelary deity of the Saskya sect of red-capped lamas. In her diamondlike aspect with the boar's head (*Vajra-vārābī*), she is one of the *shaktis*, and also an emanation of the diamond sphere of supraterrestrial reality (Pl. II).

Staudenmaier also encountered the devil in various forms when out of doors: "To help me recover from my nervousness, my doctor, smiling at my experiments, had advised me to put magic 'on the shelf' and study as little as possible, but to take long walks and particularly to go hunting. As far as the hunting was concerned, I acceded to his advice." Why should hunting have appealed to him more than aimless wandering? Characteristically, he "hunted only beasts of prey. But in my own way, I soon put a certain passion into it and became particularly interested in hunting magpies and

47

ravens." Staudenmaier does not tell us whether he had any clear idea of the meaning of his predilection for ravens and magpies. An explanation is perhaps to be sought in the fact that these are among the forms taken by the devil in Christian legend and iconography. In Hieronymus Bosch's *Nativity* (Cologne), a great black and white magpie is sitting beside Mary and Joseph; to the right an ox thrusts his head into the picture and the ass is nuzzling in the crib; in the center appears the rustic face of a shepherd who has come to congratulate the pair: here all the actors in the great drama are united, the parents, brute nature, the rough shepherd representing the world that rejoices at the birth of the Saviour as it will also rejoice at his entry into Jerusalem, and that will crucify him in the end. God lies in the manger, and the devil is also there, for the event concerns him more than anyone else. Similarly, in the form of a black and white magpie he perches on the thatched roof of the manger in Bethlehem in Piero della Francesca's *Nativity* (London), and participates in the event just as fervidly as the angels from heaven with their paeans of praise and playing of harps. In the Louvre there is another Italian Nativity, in which the devil in the form of a magpie sits on the wall of the tumble-down manger in Bethlehem.

But, as Staudenmaier was to discover, the devil, the dark aspect of our all-powerful *shakti*, can assume any form he pleases:

> Instead of magpies, I often saw, scattered among the trees and bushes, mocking figures, shadowy but clearly outlined, big-bellied fellows with crooked spindly legs and long fat noses [who does not know them from Breughel's hell?] or great-trunked elephants staring at me. The ground sometimes seemed to swarm with lizards, frogs, and toads. Sometimes they were of fantastic size. Every bush, every branch assumed weird forms that infuriated me. On another occasion, there seemed to be the figure of a girl sitting on every tree and every bush, and clinging to every reed. On the passing clouds I saw shapes of girls, smiling seductively or mocking me, and when the wind moved the branches, girls waved at me. Anyone who knows the stories of the saints of various religions knows that they suffered from similar visions.

And anyone familiar with the *Bardo Thödol* knows that, after these emanations of the unconscious vital forces that had been dammed up to create a hell for him, there was little more that could happen to him when he entered the intermediate realm; he needed no voice to say to him: "Be not awed.

Know it to be the embodiment of thine own nature." Thus, unawed by his "illusions and hallucinations," Staudenmaier proceeded in his study of experimental magic.

Up until now, the Indians have learned more about the unconscious than any Westerners, more indeed than anyone else; therein lies their specific gift, as ours lies in the unparalleled development of a rational understanding of nature, as a basis for the rape of creation, for the triumph of the brain and its demons. However, Staudenmaier came close to the achievement of the Indians. He prodded his unconscious until it welled up in its might— but not in order to honor it as his superhuman and eternal part, but to explore it and hang contemptuous names on its children. Both his positivistic, scientific habits of thought and his critique of materialistic occultism led him to apply such terms as "hallucination" and "illusion" to something that had power over him by day and by night. He rejected as mere appearance something that was a very tangible part of his total nature and that imperiously proclaimed its reality. By bedeviling him as it did, his unconscious repaid him for not evaluating more highly the parts of his Self which had assumed personal contours side by side with his ego, for his inability to understand them as projections of his *shakti*, as aspects of his vital energy, which cast them up, just as it cast up his conscious ego.

Nevertheless, Staudenmaier discovered for himself the technique and specific reality of Yoga phenomena. It began with the hand that wrote of its own accord, without his conscious volition; he observed a strangely increased current of energy which flowed into his fingers and brought about the involuntary act. Then he noted a similar phenomenon in connection with his eyes, when he compelled them to produce hallucinations of certain images. He found that he could voluntarily increase the stream of energy behind the involuntary writing, and use it for "motor hallucinations" in space:

> When with continued practice the current of energy moving into the fingertips has become stronger and a perceptible quantity of energy moves beyond their periphery, one will attempt to hold the pencil less and less by direct contact, but rather by means of the energy issuing from the fingers, until one is able to direct it from a certain distance, and thus write with it.

He also found he was able to project energy through the eyes, and this brought him to his "optical hallucinations":

At first we have to do with a purely hallucinatory copying of a visual image; through intense and prolonged concentration on an object, one obtains a protracted optical "echo," even after the eyes have been closed for some time. With practice one can learn to obtain a very clear hallucination of the object in question, with closed eyes. The essential is to practice the unaccustomed, reverse stimulation of the visual apparatus, so that one really *sees* the image, i.e., develops it into a hallucination. . . . Once this first step has been taken, and one really sees the visual image, it will soon be a simple matter to immerse oneself entirely in the visual image and intensify it by the use of muscular energy. Gifted individuals can add to the quantities of energy available, by inducing a perceptible diminution in the action of the heart and respiratory apparatus, such as the great spiritualist mediums, Indian Yogis, etc., have often carried to the extreme.

Here Staudenmaier seems really to have arrived at the technical principle by which images are visualized in Yoga, and at the intrinsic reality of these visions. He also seems to have grasped the magical principles whereby the yogi (as is attested in innumerable tales and accounts) projects such visions and makes them appear real and corporeal to others.

When once the hallucination begins to be really visible, one can go into a darkened room and keep one's eyes open. . . . If one wishes to photograph the image, one projects it as accurately as possible on a photographic plate set in place at the same time. In order to counter certain objections at the outset, I wish to emphasize that the magician does not in the ordinary sense "see" the real optical image he has created, for unlike the real images of the outward world, it sends no radiation into his eyes; on the contrary, the radiation issues from his eyes. He perceives only the stimulation of his visual apparatus, he feels the adjustment of his eye muscles to the proper distance, so that the effect for him is the same. An outside observer, however, can perceive the image just as one perceives an image cast by a common convex lens, i.e., within the cone of rays issuing from the lens. The image (or the phantom of the spiritualists) becomes visible to all only when each of the participants in a (spiritualistic) séance projects it outward from his own standpoint but towards a single spot prescribed by the medium.

From his own experiments, Staudenmaier derived the basic principles of Hatha Yoga, the ability to transform the pneumatic energy of the organism, by muscular contraction, direction, and diversion, into hallucinations of all sorts, pre-eminently of a visual and acoustic nature, but also into the motor hallucinations of the Kundalinī Yoga:

> Magical experiments often revolve around the transmission of the specific energy of the system in question, in a direction opposite to that of its normal function. In seeing, hearing, smell, touch, etc., the specific stimulus is transmitted centripetally from the peripheral organs, the eye, ear, etc., to the higher centers in the brain and finally to consciousness. In the production of optical, acoustical, and other hallucinations, one must learn to transmit the specific energy in the reverse direction from the higher brain centers to the periphery. Often one drives the form of energy in question beyond the confines of the body, e.g., motor energy beyond the fingertips, hands, etc., whereas in the normal function of the body, energy does not leave the body in perceptible quantities. One must, in accordance with the law of the transformation of nervous energy [that is, the Prāna of Yoga, which runs through the *sushumnā*, the spinal artery], learn to conduct large quantities of energy, particularly muscular energy, from one system to another system and there to transform it. All magicians of the past made much use of this law of the transformation of nervous energy. All sorts of means, most of them painful, such as hunger, cold, lack of sleep, holding of the breath, unnatural body exercises, such as protracted kneeling, even torture, were used in order to gain nervous energy. Nevertheless, we need not pity the Indian Yogis, the Mohammedan fakirs, since in the main they probably experience more pleasure than pain, even though we may find a certain element of perversion in their methods. A scientific magic will attempt to obtain nervous energy from the place where it is present in the greatest quantities and most easily tapped, i.e., from the muscles.

Even though he differs a little from the yogis in technical details connected with the obtaining of energy and, like a good Occidental, favors the muscles, this professor of chemistry, better than any Westerner before him, understood the psychophysical alchemy of Yoga, which begins with *tapas*, the accumulation of energy by means of self-imposed physical torment, and rises to the higher forms.

To be sure, the self-willed products of his *shakti* accumulated the free transformation-hungry energy of his microcosm and transformed it after their own pattern, as it suited their demonism. The hallucinations of his conscious ego remained obedient to him; when he went walking in his garden, three figures walked straight ahead of him and kept step with him, three

Staudenmaiers exactly like himself: if he stopped, they stopped; if he raised an arm, they raised an arm; four arms rose in unison, in a single gesture; but the egos within him, the "personifications," carried on a sinister alchemy with the energy of the whole. Roundhead had taken possession of Staudenmaier's tongue, he claimed it as his own, drove additional energy into it and wanted to enlarge it. Goat-foot and Horse-foot played their diabolical tricks in his intestines; they were the demons of the digestive disturbances from which Staudenmaier suffered for many years. "Thus, in part, as the personifications themselves made it clear to me, the specific peripheral nerve ends for aristocratic and noble sentiments lie in the region of the pylorus, those for the religious and sublime in the region of the upper small intestines"—while those for the diabolical sentiments were situated further down. No wonder that the center of aristocratic sentiments was located in the gateway to the intestine: it is in the nature of the aristocrat to refuse, and persist in refusing, to assimilate and digest the whole of life indiscriminately, as it pours in upon us in its mixture of the sublime and the vulgar.

And so Staudenmaier was discovering in himself the Indian experience that "all the gods are in our body," and even the significance of their locations became clear to him. But what in the inner experience of the Tantric Yoga the series of layingon of hands (*nyāsa*) and the cosmology of the Kundalinī Yoga hallows, orders, and by ritual exercise shapes into a balanced cosmos remained for Staudenmaier frightful conflict and confusion: angry jurisdictional disputes among the demons called for clear demarcation of their realms. The miracle of the mythical act, which would have ordered the chaos of his bodily world with its conflicting forces into a cosmos, in which the various provinces would willingly co-operate, was denied to Staudenmaier. The condition which he describes is well known to Indian mythology: the welter of self-willed, unrestrained forces, which periodically overtakes the universe, the chaos which shatters the order in which each force is a divine personification working modestly in its allotted place. The mythology of the Vedas, as of Hinduism, tells again and again of the divine cosmogonic act, which restores this order and quells the arbitrary demonic power which had been giving free and unlimited rein to its force, its *māyā*, swallowing up all things and spewing them forth again, thus dislocating the body of the universe. In just such a world-ordering act, Indra cut off from the mountains the wings with which they had been flying about free like the cloud banks piled upon their summits—making the earth tremble with the confusion. But with the weight of the wingless mountains, as with heavy stones, Indra fastened down the shifting surface of the earth. With the thunderbolt he slew the great dragon that lay over the mountains—the cloud that had sucked up all the earth's water into itself and would not release it; the cloud that had gathered in the all-nourishing vital forces burst, and life-giving they streamed down the channels that Indra traced for them: again life flowed in its circuit through the body of the universe, which had been in danger of death from inanition. But Staudenmaier's microcosm brought forth no such divine savior as Indra, or as the avatars of Vishnu after him, or as the heroic Zeus who ushered in a new era. The best he could hope was to hold his own against the rapacious self-will of his demons.

Staudenmaier died on August 20, 1933, in Rome, where he had spent the last years of his life—in the hospital of the Brothers of Mercy on the Tiber Island. A friend, who had been his colleague at Freising, reports: "He had been admitted to the hospital some weeks before, totally exhausted and thin as a skeleton. Under the good care, he soon began to recover; but when he felt his strength returning, he insisted on going back home, letting no one restrain him. There he suffered several fainting fits and had to be brought back to the hospital where he died, showing symptoms of uremia. Probably he had resumed his exercises while at home. The reasons for his collapse may be sought in overexertion over a period of years, coupled with an irregular, unbalanced, and frequently insufficient diet, and in his consternation over the fall of the American dollar, since he had converted his savings into that currency. . . ." At the time of his death, Staudenmaier was still warring resolutely against the demons who threatened his microcosm with anarchy; the last postcard which he wrote to this same friend on the occasion of his own sixty-sixth birthday, two and one-half years before his death, attests this, as does his desire, during his last few weeks, to return to his "exercises," or magical experiments. February 8, 1931, he wrote from Rome to his friend in Freising:

> . . . I accept your best wishes for my sixty-sixth birthday as though I had received them, and thank you in advance. I have written to Fräulein D. that one should no longer be congratulated at such an age, but condoled with, as each birthday takes one closer to the grave. Of course I beg to be considered an exception! I have not yet answered your New Year's letter, for I kept hoping that I

53

should soon have completed my experiments and be able to write you at length, and now it will soon be my birthday on which you have always written me; therefore I make haste to send you a postcard, if nothing more. I am continuing my work with desperate energy, but it is very slow and difficult. Although all four of the recalcitrant centers have received ample blows in their personifications, partly from one another and partly from me, they fall back again and again into their old errors, so that it really takes the patience of a lamb to persevere; this month it will be just thirty years since I took up the study of spiritualism, but the rest of it began when I was fourteen, in the boys' seminary.

Up to the end Staudenmaier remained in every way true to himself; he lived in Rome like a Tibetan yogi in his mountain cell: ". . . it is pretty much *stile zingaresco* [gypsy style] here. . . . I almost moved out, as the weather has been beastly cold since yesterday and there is no heat anywhere in the house. Yesterday, even after the sun had begun to come round, there were little icicles at the southern end of the house, and the floor was covered with ice where water had dripped. . . . A German family, consisting of a woman and her two young daughters, has left after three months. She often expressed surprise that we were able to stick it out so long. They were always sick, first the one and then the other. It hasn't upset the two of us up to now, for I have made great *progress* compared to last year." The progress seems to refer to his alchemy of bodily energy, particularly the transformation of muscular energy into the body heat by which to compensate for extreme outward cold. In this feat, Staudenmaier made himself the equal of the Tibetan adepts, who live through the mountain winter in caves on the meagerest fare, without freezing. Alexandra David-Neel relates [15] how they would cause cloths immersed in icy brooks to be laid on their skin and rapidly dry them by their own body heat, which they increased through Yoga exercises. He was as much at home in this physiological form of Yoga (*tapas*, or Tibetan *tumo*), which transforms energy into heat and stores it, as in his association with gods and devils; truly, as his friend says, he was "a highly original, very much misunderstood, and yet outstanding pioneer."

We are all of us Staudenmaiers, always in danger of such a disturbance in the circulation of our microcosm, always in danger that the divine potentialities of our *shakti* may be perverted into demonic forms that will

15 *My Journey to Lhasa* (Harmondsworth, 1940), p. 129.

make a chaos of us. This danger carried Staudenmaier so far that he came to resemble the Tibetan adepts of Tantric Yoga, who move in the Lamaistic world of devils and demons as in their real world. But the situation into which he fell without his wishing, they strive to induce voluntarily, by conscious renunciation of the natural attitude in which the *shakti* is connected with the outward world and projected into it, illumining it with alluring and malignant colors. They awaken within themselves a host of personifications modeled after the saints and devils known to them from the pantheon of Lamaism. Their Yoga systematically evokes hallucinations taken from their religious painting, whose linear style lends itself perfectly to reproduction in hallucination; these hallucinations they nurture and cultivate with wholehearted devotion. They struggle to keep them alive and present; and, as with Staudenmaier, their hallucinations represent a demonic interplay between the outward and the inward. Inherent in such a struggle is the constant temptation to let oneself be swallowed up by the preponderant power of the personifications, to succumb to madness, or to join in league with the personifications and regard oneself as a demonic magician. The proper goal in this perilous journey is, however, to see through them, to realize that they are projections of one's own inwardness, and by this knowledge and the power it confers to melt down the very real diabolical elements of one's own nature, the demonism of one's *shakti*, into the serenity of Buddhahood.

It is in the nature of the *shakti* to overflow and to project itself in an abundance of forms: thus in the Indian myth, the god, at rest above the world, unfolds, out of himself and his *shakti*, the *māyā* of the world; the One, resolving in himself and embracing all antitheses, projects them again into the world. And thus, day after day, the deep unconscious spontaneously puts forth the ego, as the germ puts forth the flower in order that its seed may be fertilized and develop into fruit. He who does not put forth his impulse has the world drama, the eternal cosmogony, in himself, in his own body, as Staudenmaier had within him the anarchy of his partial personalities; and it breaks out in hallucinations. To be sure, anyone who radiates these urges without realizing that they, and all the coloration, all the weight and reality of the world, through which the world acts upon us, are something we have wrought ourselves, just as the spider spins his web which becomes his world in whose center he sits—anyone who is unaware of all this is entirely Samsāra: caught in his demonic inwardness as though it were something outside him, shining upon him, terrifying and fascinating him, he lives for his own *māyā*, and is caught in the meshes of his own *shakti*.

Because a man has vanity, other people exist as a mirror of his behavior; because he is attached to things, others are an object of his exploitation and envy; they are rivals and represent danger, because they are capable of taking the thing to which he is attached. Every relation in which they might stand to him springs from a spontaneous affective attitude in himself; only from this do others obtain their attractive or repellent coloration, only through this do they obtain the weight and existence of their own, by which they affect him; without it, they are not really present, are not really perceived, do not touch him. Out of the shadowy, thin possibility of existence, they attain to reality only through the measure of affectivity, the natural urge which shines on them and attaches to them. As Odysseus must give the shades of Hades blood to drink, before they can depart sufficiently from their shadowy nature to talk to him as the men he once knew, we diffuse blood into the shadowy, unreal world around us, in order that it may mean something to us; but it is our own heart's blood, our vital force and *shakti*, that we pour into it: and then, all at once, it is full of lures and terrors, of contours soft and sharp, of lights and shades of every color. It reflects all our innermost potentialities for action and reaction, we fill its dull mirror with our light, and what it reflects we call our world. There is no world as such; no science, as long as it is pure, ventures to say what the world is; any science that purports to do so has been colored by a *shakti*. Noteworthy as the relations which the inquiring mind regards as objective may be, they are unimpressive when measured by the *shakti's* share in shaping the network of the world in which each of us is caught. A flash from the clouds can burn us to ash, poison gases or other vapors of the demons of our brain can destroy us: the precariousness of the creature's existence is a fundamental motif in the symphony of life; but the coloration of its effect on us comes from us alone. Because every demonism possible in the world is within us, the world is the same outside us as inside. We ourselves have infinity in our depths, therein lies the irony and the glory of our existence— the threat of its hell and the promise of its heaven. The adept of Tantric Yoga lives in awe of himself because God and the world lie within him, and from his devotion to the divine he derives absolute power over himself.

Life itself stands ready to initiate every man into this knowledge: time passes, and that which once glittered with brilliant colors, an object of love and yearning, lies like cold slag, all its glitter spent. Or a man is passionately attached to certain persons and things, and when, after an interval, he sees them again, he realizes that his former ego has become alien to him. The things and the people have undergone little change, the change must have occurred within himself, even though he is continually discovering, to his own disillusionment and even embitterment, how little he can change in the direction he chooses. Life has carried him onward, along one of its universal and secret pathways. The light that he formerly diffused over so many things—as a child projects upon his toys a light that makes them glitter beneath his eye—has changed with him; now it falls in another direction and has taken on a different tone; the same things upon which it formerly shone so radiantly now lie gray and ugly. Such was the experience of Prince Gautama after he had encountered the messengers of mortality: old age, sickness, and death; then the yogi—and thereafter the message that a son had been born to him. The beautiful women of his harem who upon his return home tried to delight him with their songs and their lute-playing, and the sparkle of their limbs as they danced, and all the radiance of their emotion—these all meant nothing to him. And when, dismayed at his indifference, they were overcome by lethargic slumber and sank down in a disordered heap, they seemed to him a heap of corpses, and this heap of corpses seemed to him the face of reality. And the transformed light which he suddenly cast upon these beautiful women showed him the way to the tree of illumination.

The important thing is to find the right mode of association with ourselves, with the God of Nebuchadnezzar within us; with ourselves and with God, that is one and the same thing. The contemplation of Indian observances and the exercises of the Tantric Yoga can make us aware of the need for immersing ourselves in a similar process. Many of these exercises involve the visualization of a circular diagram (*mandala* or *yantra*). The spider in its web is to the Indian a metaphor for the divine principle which out of itself brings forth the world of substance and form. But this divine principle —Brahmā—is our own deep unconscious. We all of us sit in the web of our world, which we have wrought with the projections of our *shakti;* it is the *māyā* in which we are caught. To overcome this nature-given imprisonment, the yogi learns to develop out of himself, in inner visualization, a structure corresponding to the spider web; he himself is its center and source. He weaves it into a circular design of the world, filled with figures (*mandala*),

57

or into a linear diagram full of symbols, representing the world, or the divine forces, which unfold into macrocosm and microcosm. This structure he develops out of himself in inner vision; he holds it fast as his reality, and by degrees takes it back into himself. Thus he learns to understand the genesis and passing away of the world as a process of which he himself is the source and middle. Freely and without constraint, he can now contemplate the world, as it wells out of him in accordance with nature's processes, and holds him imprisoned: can see it as the product of the mysterious will of his inwardness, of its demonic urges and impulses. He learns to see through his *shakti*, proliferating in hourly cosmogony, and to take the play of her projections as that which the world is for God: as *māyā*, which he inwardly permeates and governs, but which does not touch him.

Erwin Rousselle

Spiritual Guidance in Contemporary Taoism [1]

Confucianism established for Chinese man his ethics and politics; but even though it preserved a complete political and social system by its universalistic, cosmic idea of the emperor's "heavenly mandate" and cemented family morality by sustaining the ancestor cult, it did not satisfy the soul's metaphysical need to fathom and know the unknowable. It has been chiefly the Taoist trend which encouraged the mighty impulse of man's genius to descend into the depths of his own being and of the cosmos, and thence—fortified by the potion of immortality—to return to the tasks of everyday life. This is the path by which man is assimilated to the Tao; by pursuing it, Taoism met the unsatisfied yearning of the Chinese spirit, and indeed of many great Confucians.

True, where the field of experience is thus broadened, the Aristotelian theorem that the truth can only be one loses its universal force; the concept of truth becomes more dynamic. There are different levels of truth, and each man has as much depth, as much truth, as his own inner experience brings within his reach. But, it is believed, when it comes to the ultimate depths of truth, all illumined spirits will agree. The Tao is indeed ineffable, but it can be apprehended by the man of genius, whereas little minds cling without understanding to the surface, they grow rigid and doctrinaire, and are full of ridicule for the true depths. "When the man of highest capacities hears Tao, he does his best to put it into practice. When the man of middling capacity hears Tao, he is in two minds about it. When the man of low

1 [Chapters 1 and 3 were published under the same title ("Seelische Führung im lebenden Taoismus") in *Chinesisch-Deutscher Almanach 1934* (Frankfurt a. M.), and chapter 2 in the journal *Sinica*, VIII (1933), 207-16, both issued by the China-Institut of the University of Frankfurt.—ED.]

capacity hears Tao, he laughs loudly at it. If he did not laugh, it would not be worth the name of Tao." [2]

Different from the empty laughter of the little man is the wholehearted laughter of the wise man, who, detached and yet in close contact with the world process, understands life and the world and accepts them. Here there is no obsession, no cramping of the spirit, and also no residue of mortal clay seeking to assuage its painful tensions in the laughter of irony; no, here there is clarity and freedom of spirit, the responsibility and kindness which lead the truly profound spirit back to the performance of the day's tasks.

The high metaphysical plane on which such a spirit dwells implies a heretical ideal: the type of the "saint, or man with a calling" (*shêng jên*), a title traditionally attributable only to the emperor, the "Son of Heaven" (*t'ien-tzu*) with his heavenly mandate, and to the greatest heroes—such as Confucius. Confucius himself taught the aristocratic ideal of the "gentleman" (*chün-tzu*), but Taoism always had for its goal the holy sage, a metaphysical ideal, and viewed the Confucian image of man as a kind of preliminary stage and an ideal for the many. And it must be admitted that many Taoists did not escape the dangers of presumption and of "cloud-walking"—of a sterile severing of all human and political ties.

However, the Taoist type reveals such outstanding traits and in the last millennium, indeed up to this day, it has—below the surface of Confucianism—played so immense, though often hidden, a part in the life of the Chinese people that the neglect of this field by Sinologists can be justified only by the difficulty of obtaining knowledge of living Taoism. This knowledge cannot be obtained from books; one must spend years in China and gain admittance into the intimate circles which guard the spiritual heritage of Taoism; one must learn through one's own inner experience. Our Western mystics used to say: *lex orandi—lex credendi;* and here we can say: *lex contemplandi—lex cognoscendi,* i.e., the crucial knowledge is the knowledge obtained by which one is transformed. Once we overcome the European— and Confucian!—prejudice according to which the whole of living Taoism is "nothing but crass superstition," we shall find that the heritage trans-

2 *Tao Tê Ching,* XLI, tr. Arthur Waley, *The Way and Its Power* (New York, 1942). [The author's original German translation: "Hören hohe Meister vom Tao, so werden sie angeregt und handeln darnach. Hören mittlere Meister vom Tao, nehmen sie's bald auf, bald lassen sie's fahren. Hören niedere Meister vom Tao, lachen sie darob gewaltig. Lachten sie nicht, wäre es noch nicht als Tao anzusehen."]

mitted in these circles is not a superstitious faith in the efficacy of objects of contemplation, but an age-old tradition of experience in guiding the human psyche to maturity.

I shall not consider the innumerable ancient societies to one or another of which most Chinese belong. Assuredly they too have great value. Their Confucianism is in a certain sense deepened by Taoist or Buddhist elements. But the little we know of them seems to warrant the conclusion that despite their careful transmission of a—highly syncretistic—doctrine of allegorical actions and symbols, they offer relatively little of anything worthy to be considered as a clear and systematic spiritual guidance. And the occasional aberration of these societies from their proper functions into surface activity and political bustle, without philosophical perspective, lends strength to the suspicion that we are here not necessarily drawing on the pure and precious source.[3]

As for the Taoist monasteries, they too have generally speaking become too rigid to offer much promise of a living Taoism, except among a few outstanding abbots. Our guides will rather be individual Taoist scholars and the modern Taoist study associations.

Systematic instruction and guided meditation in a Taoist brotherhood of this sort can give us a far profounder knowledge of living Taoism than can be obtained from the old societies, the monasteries, or even from inspired individual scholars. Meditation systematically unfolds the entire psyche, creates communication between consciousness and unconscious, raises the contents of the unconscious to the light of consciousness, and forms a new whole personality, the personality of a man integrated with everything in himself, in his fellow men and in the cosmos—all this provided that the man is the right man. For "in the wrong man even the right means work in the wrong way." [4] The whole path is in the last analysis charismatic.

The following is written on the basis of my experience in one of these study associations. Like Richard Wilhelm, and through his introduction, I was privileged to be admitted to membership in a Taoist study association, and was ultimately received in its inner circle. One important consequence

---

3 Concerning these societies, see among others J. J. M. De Groot, *Sectarianism and Religious Persecution in China* (Amsterdam, 1903); J. S. M. Ward and W. G. Stirling, *The Hung Society or the Society of Heaven and Earth* (3 vols., London, 1925–26).

4 [Cf. *The Secret of the Golden Flower*, tr. from Chinese by Richard Wilhelm with a psychological commentary by C. G. Jung, all tr. from German by C. F. Baynes (London and New York, 1931), p. 70.—ED.]

of Wilhelm's experience is his translation of the essential chapters of *The Secret of the Golden Flower*, published by him in conjunction with C. G. Jung. But Wilhelm has said next to nothing in explanation of the whole, and—as has been customary from time immemorial—he has passed over in silence certain important aspects of this path that is not without its psychological dangers.

Oriental meditations are in large part unsuited to the European. He should undertake them, if at all, only under the direction of an experienced master, like every Chinese. A bar to excessive curiosity is provided by the so-called "signs" or "impediments" which occur in meditation. By them the spiritual guide can tell whether his pupil has meditated correctly. And only after these ·signs have been experienced is the next meditation assigned. In most cases, it is impossible to pass by the signs and impediments without experienced guidance. Faithful to the Chinese practice, Richard Wilhelm has said nothing of them or their solution—he has not so much as mentioned their existence. It is my intention likewise to pass over the signs and impediments. An account of the path loses nothing by this omission. Meditation is no concern for curious persons wishing to perform psychological experiments, but only for men of integrity, still capable of devotion, veneration, and profound feeling. Even the few venerable old ceremonies and symbols, whose profound meaning also can be penetrated only through meditation, are unsuited to a public disclosure, since, as experience has shown, they are always misunderstood and misinterpreted by outsiders. A few indications here will suffice.

1. Ju Shê: Initiation

As in Eleusis, all mystery cults are transmitted through sacred actions (δρώμενα), words (λεγόμενα), and symbols (δεικνύμενα). Our first brief glimpse of the sacred actions occurs in the initiation into the inner circle of Tao Tê Hsüeh Shê, my Taoist study society in Peking.

The usages connected with this initiation are of a Confucian simplicity, quite in contrast to the elaborate ritual characterizing the old associations. The initiation consists of five parts: the preparation, the performance of the "great ritual" (*ta li*) by way of introduction, instruction as the climax, leave-taking through the "great ritual," and finally bestowal of the disciple's certificate of admission. The preparation consists in the sending of the petition requesting admittance to the narrower circle and its instruction. Approval of the petition depends on knowledge of the candidate and his gifts and the Master's meditations concerning him based on the eight characters representing the hour of his birth, and on the *Book of Changes;* it is conveyed by messenger and then the introduction is effected by performance of the "great ritual." In the great ritual the candidate bows down before the altar of the acting, that is, personal God (*yu wei shang ti*) or *deus manifestus*, in the Hall of Ritual (*li t'ang*), and repeats the same ceremony before the altar of the nonacting God, *deus absconditus*, in the Hall of Supreme Beatitude (*chi lo tien*); this is done in the usual Chinese manner nine times (three times three) on the command of the master of ceremonies. Candles are lighted, sticks of incense are burned, and the gong is struck three times. Then the candidate bows in the same way, but only four times, before the panel of the founder of the tradition in the Hall of Original Humaneness (*pên jên t'ang*), which is the chapel of the Master.

There could scarcely be anything simpler. No idols adorn the halls, but all the rooms are designed and arranged with choice taste and a sense of dignity and solemnity. On the altars stand only incense burners, two candlesticks, two vases with flowers, and the name tablet indicating the presence of the godhead. On the tablet of the manifest God—who was proclaimed especially by Confucius (but also, as it is taught, by Christ)—the inscription runs: "Seat of the great holy former teacher and supreme God of all religions"; on the panel of the hidden God—as proclaimed by Lao-tse in particular (and in the deepest sense by all the religions of the earth): "Seat of the supreme true Lord and originating master of all religions."

Thus the familiar titles of the two great masters recur in the designation of the divine. The basic fact, that we know the divine only in its manifest aspect, but that its true essence is closed to us and accessible to no speculation is here clearly expressed. Echoing the *Shu Ching* (III, 3), the personal aspect of the godhead is said to be "the God who flows down into the men who live below." Man is an image of the divine. The suprapersonal aspect of the godhead is to the personal as the spirit to the consciousness. Both aspects originate in the "Ultimatelessness" [5] (*wu chi*) of the cosmos.

5 [Professor H. Wilhelm has pointed out that *Urgrund*, "fundament," is apparently a typographical error in *EJ 1933* for *Ungrund*, "the ultimateless," which translation he advocates for *wu chi*.—Ed.]

After this introduction follows the strictly individual instruction, by the Master, in the path of salvation and the meditations that accompany it.

The Master himself is a charismatic personality and is in possession of inner experience relevant to spiritual guidance. He has rejected the methods, in many respects superficial, of the old societies and founded a scholarly study group with a view to separating the wheat from the chaff by strictly objective psychological methods and to establishing a system of spiritual guidance that will be as perfect as possible. A fusion of the Confucian and Taoist doctrine seems to him the obvious premise for Chinese man, Confucianism providing the ethical, social, and political training, while Taoism must provide the foundation and roots.

The strength in metaphysics peculiar to Taoist philosophy as opposed to Confucianism has given the Master the conviction that the mystical core of all religions is the same and constitutes what is deepest in them. The essential is therefore to experience this deepest element in oneself, but otherwise to stand firmly within that historical religion, whether it be Confucianism, Taoism, Buddhism, Christianity, or Islam, which lives in one's own unconscious and thus constitutes the most effective instrument of training.

To experience this deepest content of all religions, to find one's own depth and to become a personality which is one with itself and socially and cosmically integrated, that is the aim, and the way to it is introversion, meditation. Aim and crown of this inward life, this *vita contemplativa*, is active life, *vita activa*, which then loses all compulsiveness and constraint, and becomes effortless action.

What is "right" is laid down in the solemn rites and customs which have come down from antiquity. He who keeps to the rites, keeps to the right (he who holds to the mores, *li*, holds to the right).

> The man who desires to cultivate *tao* (the truth), must first know *tao* (the truth). If he does not know the truth, it is as though he were "a blind man tending a blind fire," as though he were "grinding a pebble to make a jewel," or "boiling sand to make it into rice"; never does he see the day of success. Today you have entered upon the path (*tao*), that is, you have entered into the gate (school) of the "great doctrine," to be "the beloved children of the great *tao* and the worthy ministers of the universe (heaven and earth)." Formerly the emperor was addressed with veneration as the "son of heaven." That was the title of a nominal son of

64

heaven, for the *Chung Yung*, or Doctrine of the Mean, says:[6] Only an emperor can enact the forms (rites), "and even if he sits on his throne yet does not possess virtue, he should not venture to enact the forms and the (sacred) music. However, if a man possesses virtue but not the throne, he should likewise not dare to enact the forms and the (sacred) music." So verily, the emperor is not (merely by virtue of his office) the "son of heaven"; but the right and true cultivator (of *tao*) is the true "son of heaven," because the cultivator (of *tao*) possesses inwardly the virtue of sanctity and outwardly the dignity [7] of the sovereign. He has the merit of essential nature and of heavenly *tao*, hence he is worthy to be addressed as the "true son of heaven." He is truly the "beloved son of the supreme God." Hence he must also have the right heart and truly cultivate (tao) . . . .: "Cultivate your own personality, then there will be order in the cosmos." [8,9]

The performance of the "great ritual" with its traditional inclinations represents an act of inner devotion to the highest godhead, "an act of faith and trust." This devotion or trusting faith (*hsing*), which will henceforth be the student's essential attitude, includes faith in the great tradition of the Master and is cultivated through meditation. Other fundamental attitudes include the regulation of life by diligence, leisure, serenity, and by daily reflection on *tao*.

He who has faith preserves his heavenly essential nature (*hsing*). Tao keeps the cosmos alive, it is in a sense its center, its polestar. The seat of psychic power and faith is the "heart." The heart is the polar star within us. The cultivation of trusting faith leads to union, the *unio mystica* of man with heavenly *tao*. The seat of vital force (*ming*) is in the middle of the body (solar plexus)—at the level of the navel. Its cultivation leads to prolonged, indeed to endless life. These two forces, "essential nature" and "vital force," are related to one another as *yin* and *yang* in the cosmos, and it is the task of man to combine them in a *communio naturarum*. He must further culti-

---

6 *Chung Yung*, 28, 4. Cf. the translation by James Legge, The Chinese Classics, Vol. I (2nd edn., rev., Oxford, 1893).

7 Pun: the words for "dignity" and "throne" are both pronounced *wei*.

8 *Book of Mencius*, VIII, B, 32. Cf. Legge tr., The Chinese Classics, Vol. II (London, 1861), p. 495.

9 From an "Address to Beginners" in the Hall of Instruction (after their reception into the inner circle). The Hall of Instruction faces the Hall of Ritual and its middle courtyard, while the Hall of Ritual faces the main courtyard and its Hall of Original Humaneness. In a parallel tract are situated the courtyards with the Hall of Return to the Origin and the Hall of Supreme Beatitude.

vate the threefold I: the physical, the psychic, and the spiritual. The body and the corporeal I is descended from one's parents, the psychic I is descended as a monad from heaven and earth, the spiritual I is ultimately identical with the divine source of all being [*Urgrund*], and must first be discovered and achieved.

The road to cultivation of one's essential nature and vital force is "cultivation of the personality" (*hsiu shên*) or—to use an Indian term—Yoga (*yü ch'ia*). This consists largely in spiritual meditation and has little to do with devices of outward discipline (such as breathing exercises). The aim is to build an eternal, imperishable personality and the means is the meditative transformation and sublimation of the lower psychic forces into higher ones. In this way isolation is overcome, a bond is established with the cosmos and society. If this aim is not achieved, the higher soul, after death, is slowly dissolved in the heavenly *yang*.

According to Chinese physiology and psychology, there are in man three currents or rivers (*san ho*): the seed (*ching*), the breath (*ch'i*), and the spirit (*shên*). These three rivers are not identical with their physical equivalents, but influence them and are at the same time their psychological manifestations. The seed has the impulse to turn outward, to work independently and creatively, and to draw the higher psychic forces into its orbit. The corporeal soul (*p'o*) controls the seed and the breath, and strives to draw the conscious soul (*hun*) into its orbit, as the *yin* and *yang*, or, as in the star myth, the Weaving Maiden draws the Cowherd. But the two are separated by the River of Heaven. And so man should not be overpowered by the Weaving Maiden, the force of *yin*, but use it as a means to elevate his higher soul. If the higher soul keeps itself free from this dependence, it rises as spirit to the heavenly regions in this or in the afterlife; otherwise it roams the world as a demon (*kuei*). To prevent this and achieve immortality in the true and personal sense, one must gather the seed by a "backward-flowing movement" and not squander it. Through this meditative process, the vital force of the breath is enhanced, the seed is transformed into breath. The breath must in turn be gathered and purified till it becomes spirit.

There are three points of departure for meditation (corresponding to the conception described above), namely the "three fields of cinnabar" (*tan t'ien*), or fields of the alchemistic elixir: the "upper" field is in the middle of the forehead, seat of the "radiance of our essential nature" (*hsing kuang*);

66

the "middle" field is in the heart, the true source of the cinnabar-red elixir and of the conscious soul (*hun*); and the "true" field is in the middle of the body (approximately from the navel to the kidneys), seat of the vital force (*ming*) and of the lower soul (*p'o*).

Meditation lifts everything that is unconsciously present into consciousness and unifies the man; and it unites the unified man with the cosmos and the social community. But meditation is an art that must be learned. Only by studying its practical operation and its results can we judge the spiritual guidance peculiar to Taoism. Reading and hearsay provide no objective basis for judgment. Over a period of centuries a vast tradition, drawing from the most varied Chinese (and Indian) sources, has developed an astonishing method. Every pupil must go through his own personal experiences under the guidance of a master; the instruction is strictly individual. He is led onward step by step, in accordance with his experiences. Each week he reports on his progress or his impediments, but the task to be accomplished in the next stage of meditation is not assigned him until the—unpredictable!—experiences of the preceding stage have been realized. And there are 108 stages in 360 lessons.

An introduction to the technique of meditation, of which I shall have more to say below, concludes the first lesson, which confers new insights in many fields. So much for the words, the *legomena* of the initiation. Then occurs the leave-taking from the Master; the great ritual is again performed, but in reverse order. The great ritual is repeated each week, on the occasion of every new lesson.

In conclusion, the pupil, again waiting in the vestibule of the Hall of Return to the Origin (*kuei yüan t'ang*), receives the pupil's certificate, which is sent by the Master. The pupil himself sends the Master three symbolic copper coins, known as the "dried meat money" [10] (*hsiu chin*).

Something still remains to be said of the δεικνύμενα, the signs or symbols. In the Hall of Ritual lies a great square carpet (Figure 1) of a yellow color (earth) with a round black field (heaven) in its center. The carpet is surrounded by a border of black, white, and red (from the outside in). These are the three colors of alchemical psychology. The black is the water of purification and signifies the putrefaction of the imperfect natural man, the

---

10 This designation refers to the saying of Confucius (*Lun Yü*, VII, 7): "Beginning with those who offer a bundle of dried meat, I have never refused anyone my instruction." Cf. Legge tr. (as in n. 6), p. 197 [*Analects*].

Fig. 1. *Design of a carpet, showing the ancient Chinese symbols of
the dignity of a priest-king, the Son of Heaven*

via purgativa; the white is the white tincture, gold; the red is the true cinnabar (sulphide of mercury), the fire of the *via unitiva.* Clouds surround both
the square of the earth and the circle of the heavens. On the black field of
the heavens are represented twelve symbols of the imperial priest-king, the
"Son of Heaven"; these are the two dragons (*lung*) which seem to be biting
each other's tails, symbol of the correct backward-flowing circulation of
creative force; the mountains (*shan*) of eternity, the pheasant (*hua ch'ung*),
or red sunbird, which has descended to the water, just as the spirit must
descend into the unconscious, the *logos* into the *eros,* in order to arise with
new strength. Above the dragons is seen the fire (*huo*) of illumination,

which radiates from the middle of the forehead. Three pairs of symbols designate the three polarities: above, the sun and the moon in white and red, denoting *yang* and *yin, logos* and *eros,* essential nature (*hsing*) and vital force (*ming*); to one side, the sacrificial goblets (*tsung i*), in which thoughts (monkey) and sensuality (tiger), radiance and power, are sacrificed, and the sacrificial ax (*fu*) representing the death of the unillumined man; to the other side, below, the leaves of a water plant (*tsao*) signifying the purity of the vegetative life and, juxtaposed to them, the rice grains (*fên mi*) of generation and nourishment. Over the whole hover three stars connected by lines; these sum up the entire conception and represent the unity of heaven, earth, and man, and of the three rivers, seed, breath, spirit.

> The seed, breath, and spirit of heaven are in Taoism called *primal.* Primal Beginning (*yüan yüan shih*), the three rivers of man are called water, fire, earth. The two (heaven and man) are one. One is two. Everything is contained in pre-existence (*hsien t'ien*) and arises out of the supreme ultimate (*t'ai chi*). Hence man can attain equality with the heavens. If a man is not concerned with pre-existence, but only with the seed, breath, and spirit, of empirical existence (*hou t'ien*), he attains—although his life can be prolonged and sickness averted—unevenly to the root of the principle. Therefore one should concentrate the three principles; thus one creates the supreme ultimate, the *t'ai chi* (in oneself). The supreme ultimate is, when concentrated, *one* principle. It is perfected man in harmony with heaven; that is the (whole) science. Perfected cosmic order, perfected essential nature—that is the main thing.[11]

Finally, in the place where one kneels on the carpet, the central symbol is to be noted. It is the age-old magic sign of sublime beauty [12] and its power (*fu*). In the usual interpretation, it is composed of two characters (*chi*) reversed and turned sideways in such a way that a cross (in Chinese, the perfect figure, ten) remains free in the middle.[13] Chi means "self." The union of the "self" with the "self" is the ultimate goal and true secret of the Taoist way.

---

11 From a little treatise by the Master: "Explanations Pronounced in the Pavilion beside the Sophora Tree."

12 The arrangement of the symbols shows a certain similarity to the *Tabula smaragdina* and even more so to the *Arbor cabbalistica,* which are both of course considerably more recent.

13 Presumably both signs were originally weapons, namely bows. Their association here with the ax seems to make this likely.

Tradition has it that these twelve signs had since the oldest times been embroidered on the emperor's gown, which he wore when performing the Great Rites.[14] In Taoism they have been interpreted in many ways. Here we shall have to content ourselves with the brief suggestions given above. The main forces of the universe and of man are represented by the same signs, for macrocosm and microcosm are originally one. But the potentiality implanted in us must become effective and real. To create harmony is the task of the "son of heaven."

We have now gained a general view of the initiation, its ritual, instruction, and symbols. In contrast to the old secret societies, the utmost liturgical simplicity prevails, and yet the smallest act is filled with tradition. And even later, when greater depths are broached, the practices become only a little more elaborate. Thus for example the pupil must make a vow to regulate his way of life, and the instruction no longer takes place in the Master's chapel, but in the adjacent sacristy and in progressively more inward rooms. Finally, at a very advanced stage, the pupil must find his way alone to the Master. He passes through a series of rooms and receives the final instructions; then, dismissed as a pupil, he regains his independence.

Symbols play a rather subordinate role, for meditation must be "image-less vision."

The inner attitude is what matters most, and its fundamental characteristic must be reverence. Accordingly, at the end of the initiation, the pupil receives a "breviary," a brief prayer book, designed to induce in him again and again this basic attitude without which no higher humanity is conceivable. It creates the sacred inner "void" without which no man can communicate with his fellow men, or become one with the heavenly tao.

> Push far enough towards the Void,
> Hold fast enough to Quietness,
> And of the ten thousand things none but can be worked on by you.
> I have beheld them whither they go back.
> See, all things howsoever they flourish
> Return to the root from which they grew.
> This return to the root is called Quietness;
> Quietness is called submission to Fate;

14 The Chou dynasty is then supposed to have removed the signs for sun, moon, and stars from the imperial dress and to have transferred them instead to the imperial banner.

What has submitted to Fate has become part of the always-so.
To know the always-so is to be illumined. . . .[15]

2. Nei Ching T'u: "The Table of the Inner Warp"

According to the current Taoist conception, man can achieve this enlightenment only if his profoundest forces are awakened and the whole man, body
and soul, undergoes a transformation. The process is physical as well as
spiritual. For the body must provide the vital force through whose sublimation the spiritual, immortal man is born. Here we enter the province
of physiology, the domain of physicians. And indeed, the technique and
conception of meditation which we are here seeking to explain are unintelligible without some knowledge of certain aspects of Chinese medicine.

Accordingly we shall briefly examine these medical conceptions regarding
the chemistry, or rather alchemy, of life (but also of the spirit). We shall
not attempt to appraise them from the standpoint of our own medical
science, but shall merely consider them in their bearing on the Taoist
technique of meditation. We have principally to do with five conceptions:
1, the three rivers; 2, the main pulses; 3, sublimation; 4, the archaic anatomy
of certain organs; and 5, the cosmic analogy.

1. THE THREE RIVERS (*san ho*) or humors which flow through man are:
the spirit (*shên*), the breath (*ch'i*), and the seed (*ching*). Somewhat freely,
one might call them: spiritual force, vital force, and the force of generation
or force of immortality.[16] All three, first the stream of the breath, then the
stream of the seed, and finally, the stream of the spirit, must be regulated
by meditation, which guides and unites the streams. Out of this guidance

15 Lao-tse, XVI, tr. Arthur Waley, p. 162.
[The author's own version:
              Erreichen der Leerheit First,
              Bewahren der Stille Stärke!
              Erhöben sich dann sämtliche Wesen zugleich,
              Ich schaue, wie sie sich wenden.
              Die Wesen in all ihrer Menge—
              Ein jegliches kehrt zu seiner Wurzel zurück.
              Rückkehr zur Wurzel heisst Stille.
              Stille heisst Wendung zum Leben (ming).
              Leben heisst Ewigkeit.
              Erkenntnis der Ewigkeit heisst Erleuchtung.]

16 In Western alchemical works in some contexts called sulphur, mercury, and salt.
With regard to the system of the "three rivers," see the table in E. Rousselle, "Die
Meditation in China," *Deutsch-chinesischer Almanach*, 1932, p. 30.

and union, wrought by meditation, arises the immortal man, the "diamond body."

2. THE MAIN PULSES. According to venerable but still surviving Chinese medical conceptions, there is within the human body an entire "network" or "warp," which is composed of "pulses" or "channels" of breath. Most of these pulses belong to what we should call the circulatory system; but Chinese physiology possesses no exact knowledge of the course of the blood vessels and none at all of the nature of the circulation. Since in slaughtered animals the veins are found full of blood while the arteries are found bloodless but full of air, the Chinese arrived at the erroneous notion that the arteries were the carriers of the breath.[17] In present-day contemplative practice, these "breath pulses of the inner warp" (*nei ching ch'i mo*) are not conceived as physically visible—hence not equivalent to arteries—but he who is illumined becomes aware of them in meditation.[18] There are two reasons for differentiating the pulses from the arterial system: first, their channels lie partly outside the body, hence in open space; and secondly, according to the prevailing Chinese view, they are not discernible in the dead body. Are we dealing with collective, inherited memories of what in times long past may have been our body structure? And if so, wherein lies their efficacy for therapy and meditation? We withhold judgment. At all events these pulses are looked upon as the actual, subtly ramified paths by which the vital force travels within the body from diverse yet communicating sources; and in the course of these invisible channels, certain vital points are differentiated and localized with anatomical precision. From these points, called "hollows" (*hsüeh*) or "hollow passages" (*hsüeh tao;* the term can also signify "tomb"), a direct beneficial influence spreads to the surrounding regions. They are of the greatest importance—as is the entire network of pulses—for the medical art of acupuncture, a therapy based on pricking with needles, which along with total failures has produced astonishing cures. In addition to the minor pulses—of which twelve are enumerated—there are two main pulses, or main channels of breath, namely the channels of yang and yin, which connect the lesser channels situated on either side of the body. The main pulse of yang rises from the

17 Cf. also Dr. Reinhard Grimm, "Die Akupunktur, ein altchinesisches Heilverfahren und seine Stellung in der Geistesgeschichte," *Tientsiner Nachrichten*, 1933.
18 Current conceptions in the Japanese offshoots of Chinese meditation are similar. Cf. Shoseki Kaneko, *Über das Wesen und den Ursprung des Menschen* (Osaka, 1932).

symphysis between the legs and ascends by way of the spinal cord to the brain, then passes through the forehead to the bridge of the nose. The main pulse of yin originates in the genital zone, rises up to the vicinity of the navel, and from there continues upward through the neck to the lips. The channel of yang is believed to be particularly developed in men, that of yin in women. The main pulse of yang is also called "guide channel" (*tu mo*) and that of yin "channel of function" (*jên mo*). Through meditative union of the two channels in a closed circuit (the powers of spirit, life, and immortality contributing as in the generation of a corporeal child) one experiences the birth of the *puer aeternus*, the eternal child, that is immortal man. This may be said to be the crucial inner experience, dubious as the physiological theories surrounding it may seem.

3. SUBLIMATION. It is an axiom of Chinese—as of Indian and Arabic— medicine, that a close connection exists between the central nervous system and the generative faculty, indeed in some of these conceptions the connection is direct: the brain fluid flows downward through the spinal cord, to fulfill its generative function. But in the process, it is thought, precious seeds of immortality are lost. Hence there is reason to oppose this downward flow by meditation, so inducing the "river of heaven to flow uphill." There then occurs an alchemical sublimation or distillation of sex, the spirit is stimulated, fortified, and refreshed by this force of immortality. In this conception, the occasional practice of asceticism does not have a negative and moral, but a positive and metaphysical significance. The marriage of *logos* and *eros*, if we may use these Western terms, creates the immortal man, rejuvenates him and gives him, among other things, long life. Even though things may not be quite as simple as the Chinese believe, but in reality are far more complex, it is of course a scientific fact that the glands of internal secretion play an essential part in lending youthful freshness to the whole man, including the spiritual man.

4. THE ARCHAIC ANATOMY OF INDIVIDUAL ORGANS. As C. G. Jung has had the kindness to inform me, Western science has known since Wernicke that there is in our mind a "mental counterpart of the internal organs," by which we know of these organs and their condition. It is curious to note that in Chinese meditation (and physiology) these psychological representations of internal organs correspond only partly to the actual state of the organs in question, while in part they reflect another condition, pertaining, strange to say, to forms of life that have long since died out on our planet. We cannot

73

but think of a collective memory—as we did in connection with the pulses. Such examples of archaic anatomy are: the third eye which, as in the deep-sea fish, both sees and illumines objects (pineal gland?); the unbroken connection between kidneys and testicles; the situation of the vital center, or "field of cinnabar," in the solar plexus; the "three burners" (*san chiao*), or water secreters, which fill the whole lower body, the "sea of breath," at the level of the stomach, navel, and bladder.[19] These are no baseless fantasies. Just as rudiments of older states are still present in our anatomy— some, to be sure, only temporarily in the embryo—here mental counterparts of our organs, but in an anterior state, emerge during meditation from the collective unconscious.

5. THE COSMIC ANALOGY. In the structure of the magic-animistic system which dominates the old Chinese cosmology, analogy plays a significant part, as it usually does in archaic forms of thought. Analogies are found of course throughout Chinese medical science as well, and since meditation in its physiological aspect draws on medical conceptions, we encounter the same system with its analogies in the symbolic images, beliefs, and terminology of the meditative technique. Man is a little cosmos. "The cosmos is not great, my body is not small," says an aphorism. And since man is a part of the cosmos, the possibility of an analogy between man and cosmos cannot be rejected a priori. His spirit is the heavenly Jade City, where Lao-tse has his throne, his spinal substance is the Milky Way, the River of Heaven, the two constellations of the Cowherd and the Weaving Maiden are at work in his heart and kidneys. In his abdomen are the plowed field of earth and also the supreme ultimate; still farther down are the yin-yang gate of the underworld, and the region of the ground water. In addition to this symbolical analogy of the big and little world, the yin-yang system, embracing the five elements and their organic correspondences, finds extensive application. And a complete system of number symbolism understood as the expression of the cosmic order also enters into this concept of man. Clearly, valuable insights are here intermingled with others that are quite

19 The arrangement of the elements is: in the center of the body, "earth"; below it and farther back, "fire"; and at the very bottom, aside from the spine, "water." This is different from Indian Yoga, where "earth" is bottommost. The main centers of the five elements are distributed as follows: wood—liver and gall; fire—heart and small intestine; earth—spleen and stomach; metal—lungs and large intestine; water—kidneys and bladder. Chinese Yoga differs appreciably from the Indian: it is an independent discipline, though it has borrowed considerably from the Indian.

74

beside the point, and the system as a whole strikes us as unscientific in the extreme. Analogy is never cogent proof. But meditation does not aspire to prove: it aims to bring the deepest levels of man into communication with his consciousness, to liberate the genius in him, and to open the gates to certain valuable experiences. In the light of this aspiration, the peculiar Chinese medical concepts that enter into the technique of meditation seem to lose much of their significance.

Having briefly discussed the principal physiological conceptions without which the terminology of Taoist meditation technique would be unintelligible, we shall describe and explain the two pictures we have here reproduced (Plates I and II).

The one is a black and white rubbing made from a stone tablet to be found in the Monastery of the White Clouds (Po-yün-kuan), near Peking; the other is a colored scroll painting unquestionably based on the Po-yün-kuan stone. In their essentials, stone and painting are identical, but there are differences in detail; the stone, for example, has in the lower left-hand corner a text telling how the work was engraved in the Monastery of the White Clouds, and in the upper right-hand corner the date; it bears the heading "Nei Ching T'u" (Representation of the Inner Warp). All this is lacking in the painting. The texts also differ slightly in phraseology (but not in meaning). In the following we shall point out occasional variants. Other differences: in the painting the inscription pertaining to the kidneys was put in its proper place, while in the stone the two lines in question have been shifted for lack of space to the region of the cervical vertebrae. And the painting, unlike the stone, also shows the halo or nimbus over the head, with the red pearl as its center, and the almond-shaped aureole around the body. Rubbings from the Po-yün-kuan tablet are so widely known in Taoist circles, and their content sheds so much light on the nature of Taoist meditation, that their publication has become a scientific necessity.

An inscription in the lower left-hand corner of the stone engraving has the following to say of its origin:

> This picture has not been published up to now, because the doctrine of the elixir is exceedingly comprehensive, great, subtle, and profound, and accordingly the common man cannot understand it or make anything of it. Consequently it (the picture) is little distributed in the world. But accidentally, in the study at

75

Kao-sung-shan, when I was borrowing some books and pictures, I
saw this picture hanging on the wall and (I must say) the drawing
is very exact and subtle, the muscles, nodes, and pulses are all very
clearly explained, and all are full of excellent meaning. I examined
it at length and found that it gave me understanding, and only
then did I realize that physical inspiration and expiration are
nothing other than the fullness and emptiness of the cosmos. Indeed, once one has truly attained to a general understanding of
this and has been illumined by it, the great doctrine of the gold
elixir is more than half understood, and truly I do not dare to keep
it (the picture) for myself alone. Hence I gave it at once to be engraved with a view to its dissemination.

[Signature:] Su-yün the Taoist [by his original name] Liu
Ch'êng-yen has reverently published it and annotated it [with the
above text]. [Seal:] Ch'êng-yen.

[Postscript:] The stone engraving is preserved in the Monastery
of the White Clouds (Po-yün-kuan) near the capital [Peking].

In the upper right-hand corner the stone bears the date "the sixth month
of the year Ping-hsü of the Kuang-hsü era" (1886). These data are of course
lacking in the scroll-painting copy. Concerning Liu Ch'êng-yen, alias Su-
yün, no further information of any interest has come to light, and this
makes his distinct reference to the "great doctrine of the gold elixir" (known
as *chin tan ta tao*, or simply as *chin tan chiao*) all the more gratifying. For
this is the most significant tradition of living Taoism, and derives chiefly
from the patriarch Lü Tung-pin (b. 798). In it a number of individual
teachings and traditions are fused into a system for the transformation of
man. Thus on our picture there are several Buddhist quotations, and of
course some kind of connection with the Nestorians is also undeniable. But
the present-day bearers of the tradition—among them the Tao Tê Hsüeh
Shê study society in Peking—reject the imputation of "syncretism," declaring that their doctrine possesses a content of its own, which is at the
same time the mystical content of all the religions of the world. And indeed
the "doctrine of the golden mercuric sulphur" (i.e., sulphide of mercury, or
cinnabar), as our Western alchemists would have translated it, embraces
the quintessence—in every sense of the word—of the entire Taoist tradition.

Let us look at our two reproductions of the rubbing and the painting.
It is evident even to the layman that they represent a lengthwise section of
a human (male) body, the head and torso. The outline of a head seems to

emerge quite distinctly, and on the right side the spinal column can be seen; the heart, too, is recognizable and under it certain allegorical representations, presumably concerning the other inner organs and their functions. But on closer examination we see that the whole is allegorical; nowhere is there any realistic representation, two main pulses meet at a point where the face should be, but there is no outline of a face. The bones are not represented as such but as cliffs, and nine peaked cliffs appear at the summit of the skull, where (in this age!) they cannot signify bones (or horny scales). Hence we have pure allegories: In the head we have Lao-tse and under him a Buddhist monk; farther down the Cowherd and the Weaving Maiden; the plowman and the two water-wheel treaders are also in evidence. Over the head hangs the pearl; in the forehead in the place of the third, "heavenly" eye, the red sun, and opposite, at the optic center in the back of the head, the moon. In the mouth we discern a pond with bridge, at the neck a pagoda, under the heart a row of trees, in the region of the kidneys a representation of the supreme ultimate, under it a pond with fiery water, a flaming caldron (tripod), etc.; in short, we find ourselves in an exceedingly strange, poetic landscape, embracing heaven and earth and the Stygian waters, a landscape representing man with his three selves, spiritual, psychic, and animal. For an understanding of living Taoism and its doctrine of eternal rejuvenation, longevity, and the creation of an immortal self in the form of a metaphysical "diamond body" (*chin-kang shen*, or Skr. *vajrakāya*)—all through meditation—we must examine all the physiological (?) starting points shown on this allegorical landscape of heaven, earth, and underworld. For just as Aeneas descended unharmed to the Acherontic waters of the underworld and returned illumined and fortified, so, it is promised, will the "friend of the tao" (*tao yu*) find in his own self the true sources of life, health, eternity, and wisdom, provided only he descend—equipped with the proper light— and know the way back again; but if he does this, he will also be able to ascend to the celestial regions. Lao-tse, one of the Three Pure Ones in the Beyond and the Cowherd and Weaving Maiden, those two figures of the star myth, are, as it were, our metaphysical, divine I (diamond body), our psychic consciousness (*hun*), and our animal I (*p'o*); the three other figures: the Buddhist monk, the plowman, and the water-wheel treaders show us in essence the path to follow in meditation. But this is not the place to consider the whole sequence of Taoist meditation in the Chin-tan tradition —that we shall do in our third section. Here we shall merely explain our picture as a map of meditation. In the description we shall in general follow the course of the Taoist path of salvation, first describing those parts which belong to the "circulation of the light," i.e., orientation and awakening; secondly, the allegories pertaining to transformation, i.e., to the death of the ordinary man; thirdly, the conception and growth of the new, immortal man; and fourthly, we shall consider those images which suggest the perfect state, wise with age, fulfilled with eternity.

1. The "circulation of the light" extends from the head to the middle of the body and back up again. We begin with the figure of the Buddhist monk at the front of the head. Looking up at Lao-tse, who sits smiling in an attitude of meditation, the monk holds both arms upraised as though supporting everything that is over him. Beside him is written: "The blue-eyed [properly jade-eyed] barbarian monk holds the heavens with his hands." The "blue-eyed barbarian monk" is an old designation for the Buddhist patriarch Bodhidharma, founder of the meditation sect, who emigrated from India to China in 520. He had vainly stared at a rock wall for nine years, before the "heavenly eye" opened within him, but his persistence in meditation brought success; like all the illumined, he himself supports the heavens (a reference to a certain legend). This Buddhist monk is not, it is true, represented with the well-known bearded features of Bodhidharma, but as a very youthful man; the accompanying inscription, however, makes his identity clear.[20]

The "friend of the tao" is admonished to show similar endurance in meditation and to use the light of his eyes (in a strictly anatomical sense, the "blue-eyed monk who bears the heavens" refers to the zygomatic arch which supports the skull). But he should not stare at the wall in vain for nine years; he should direct his glance downward at the center of life and warmth (approximately at the height of the navel), where the source and junction of the main pulses and of the twelve subsidiary pulses (solar plexus) is to be found. This immersion of the thoughts and the gaze in the vital center is known as the "plowing." In the pictures we accordingly find at the level of the navel the plowman diligently at work preparing the field, i.e., stimulating the vital center and its energy. Rather high up in the trees we find this text regarding the plowman: "The iron cow plows the earth in

---

20 All persons are represented as children or young people in order to indicate that they possess eternal youth. Only Lao-tse is represented as an aged man, in reference to the treasure of ancient, eternal truth that was disclosed to this Perfect Man.

order to grow gold coin." [21] The whole region from the navel down through the abdomen to the kidneys is associated with the element of "earth"; it is known as the elixir field (*tan t'ien*); from it are distinguished an upper elixir field in the forehead, a middle one in the region of the heart (*chung tan t'ien*), and a posterior field in the middle of the body (kidneys), which is the "true elixir field" (*chêng tan t'ien*). Persistent work on this vital region is symbolized by the plowing iron cow. From the plowed earth grows true blessing; the earth is prepared to receive the seed of higher life, for the "growing of gold coin." (This last is not in the tablet, but it is in the painting, represented in two fields sowed with coins.)

Once the vital force in the lower body, the "ocean of the breath" (*ch'i hai*), is stimulated, the method used thus far is no longer adequate, it must be reinforced by the third, "celestial," eye, the "radiance of our (innate) nature" (*hsing kuang*). To this end, this eye must be aroused to efficacy. Here the blue-eyed barbarian monk appears again, perceiving the third eye by a special technique of meditation, a particular way of staring at the wall: the ball over his left hand, represented in the painting as a glowing red sun, is this eye. This third eye now contributes its light. The elixir field is powerfully plowed, its energy is conveyed by a particular method to the kidneys. The region of the kidneys is also called the "axle of the river" (presumably signifying the spinal cord). Here the current turns sharply upward, and along with the main pulse of the yang, the control pulse (*tu mo*), it passes through two important nodes, one behind the heart, the "central gate in the back," and another in the back of the head, "the upper gate in the jade city" or "jade cushion," [22] across the top of the head, the "palace of the mud ball," to the forehead (the last section of the current's path is clearly discernible on the rubbing as a radiation, on the painting as two red lines), and here the third eye, reinforced with vital energy, glows in meditation. This is the "hall of illumination" (*ming t'ang*), as it is also called, in which the emperors of olden times met for illuminating discourse with the great men of the realm. The control pulse then descends to the bridge of the nose, where it ends, but it is conceived as carrying its energy

21 As plants are grown. The "cow" is an animal "correspondence" to the "earth."
22 Written incorrectly in the Po-yün-kuan tablet, which has *chên* = "the True" for *chên* = "cushion." The term applies of course to the green jade cushion supporting the head of the Son of Heaven, the emperor, in his tomb. Everyone who enters upon the Yoga path: "cultivation of the individuality," is a "son of heaven."

onward to the elixir field—the "circulation of the light" is complete, the "wheel of dharma has turned."

The first stage of training in meditation is ended. The vital center in the solar plexus, central seat of a more archaic, semiconscious stage, with its sure instinct and wealth of images, has been connected with the "third eye"; i.e., raised to consciousness. This "circulation of the light" is the foundation for an understanding of the three higher stages of instruction. In the painting (though not on the tablet) we find, close to the "heavenly eye," the words "Here is the origin of the best path to a good life." And both pictures contain the admonitory yet mocking verses addressed to the beginner: "If you have understood the true mystery of this mysterious mystery, then there is no mystery beside this mystery." On top, in front of the head, there are two more Buddhist quotations—in the painting joined into a single band. These quotations deal with the white hairy fuzz (*pai mao*, Skr. *ūrnā*) between the eyes of a Buddha, which like the third eye confers knowledge of the cosmos and of redemption.[23] The quotations read: "Dharmagupta [24] (Fa-tsang) says: The blue eyes make the four cosmic seas clear and distinct—and the white fuzz curls as far as the (five) sumeru [= cosmic mountains]"; and "Maitreya [25] (Tz'u-shih) says: Between the eyebrows gleams the radiant white fuzz—in all creatures it can destroy the misery of rebirth."

2. The novice who has reached the meditative experience of the third eye is indeed filled with an ecstatic sense of illumination and awakening; but at present we are still in the first stage of meditation: the old Adam must die, the immortal man remains to be conceived and born. Still deeper forces are now evoked and called to consciousness, and the path of transformation is undertaken. The Chinese believe that before entering on this path, a man should be around forty years of age.

A special breathing technique is used to facilitate the peculiar ascetic exercises which because of the danger inherent in them are taught and transmitted only by word of mouth. We cannot agree with Father L. Wieger,

23 Chinese Yoga usually makes the third eye and *ūrnā* one, i.e., does not distinguish between spirit and will, whereas Indian Yoga both equates and distinguishes *ūrnā* and *ājñā*. But occasionally in Chinese Yoga as well, a distinction is made between the third eye as "big red pearl" and *ājñā* as "little white pearl."
24 Died A.D. 619. Famed Buddhist church father and translator, came from southern India.—The number 5 is in the painting, not in the rubbing. The apparent meaning is: the world mountain of our system and the four cosmic mountains of the next worlds with their paradises.
25 The well-known teacher of Asanga, who is difficult to distinguish from the Bodhisattva.

S.J., who, in speaking of this oral tradition and the need for discretion, writes:[26] "*Il doit se cacher de jolies choses sous cette phrase anodine.*" The natural is always innocent. Yet it must be owned that an attempt to create a mutually fructifying contact between consciousness and unconscious, *logos* and *eros*, cannot be entirely free from danger. In any event, the two main pulses are joined in a circuit of interaction; the yin pulse is utilized not in ascent but in descent, and sublimation is accomplished in meditation with the help of certain rhythmic breathing exercises. Thus sexuality is not repressed, but sublimated through the use for a time of a meditative technique related to the Indian Kundalinī Yoga. Accordingly, it is noted beside the waterfall—represented in the painting as flowing upward in the spinal column: "Water of the upward flowing river of heaven (i.e., the Milky Way)." And below, at the base of the spine, the "Lower Gate at the Rump Village," it is written: "The waters of the Abysmal (*k'an*)[27] flow upstream." And between the end of the spine and the kidneys we find the "tripod of the elixir," the true crucible—anatomically perhaps a gland—and the "pond where water and fire cross and turn to vapor."

The same ascetic sublimation is once more represented by the two children treading the water wheels to pump up the ground water. The children are a boy and a girl. The seminal glands—like the kidneys—are conceived as male on one side, female on the other, embodying yin and yang. Beside them, in the painting, stands the "*hsüan p'in* wheel of yin and yang," a reference to the sixth chapter of Lao-tse, and in the rubbing, the treadmill of the mystery of yin and yang (*yin yang hsüan cha ch'ê*).[28] In the rubbing we find this text given for the sublimation: "Repeating and continuing, circulating step by step, as these wheels turn, the water flows eastward. Even in the spring that is ten thousand fathoms deep, the bottom must become visible. This sweet spring flows up to the summit of the Southern Mountains (i.e., to the top of the skull)." The text in the painting uses similar terms.

In the kidney region a "cave" is designated as a vital point; this is the "cave of the mystery of the kidneys," and the inscription pertaining to it

26 Léon Wieger, *Histoire des croyances religieuses et des opinions philosophiques en Chine* ... (Paris, 1917), p. 393.
27 The dangerous element among the eight primary trigrams of the *Book of Changes*.
28 This is the true meaning of the allegory also known as *ho ch'ê*, "river wheel or water wheel." This by way of a contribution to the understanding of Lü Tsu's "Song of the Valley Spirit," where Erkes has translated the term as "river chariot" instead of "river wheel" (*Sinica*, VIII, 4), thus losing the entire sense. The Tz'u-yüan is not adequate for the explanation of specialized Taoist terms.

reads: "In this little pan mountain and water boil." [29] In China the kidneys are looked upon as the true seat of the generative power.[30] In the kidney region we therefore find pictured the Weaving Maiden, i.e., the animal soul, and beside her these verses: "The Weaving Maiden sets in motion" (a pulse in the form of a thread can be seen running upward from the spinning wheel to the spinal cord); "the godhead of the kidneys is mysterious and impenetrable, it can itself engender children"; and "the godhead of the spleen remains forever preserved in the court of the higher soul (*hun*)."

In the dark firmament of our inner world the constellations of the macrocosm and the genii or gods of our organs appear as allegorical images. Other internal organs also help to condense the vital force: "The godhead of the lungs has the name 'gray flower' and the personal name 'empty perfection,' [31] the godhead of the liver can illuminate and can itself contain illumination, the godhead of the gall bladder can itself illuminate and achieve illumination." Of the internal organs, there remains only the heart, the seat of the conscious soul and the alleged producer of the red blood (cinnabar). In the heart is written "earth of immobility (*kên*)," corresponding to the hexagram, Mountain, Keeping Still, in the *Book of Changes*, and beside it: "The godhead of the heart is the source of cinnabar and itself preserves the spirit." The "godhead of the heart" is the divine boy stonecutter, the true alchemist, who in his play tosses gold pieces into the firmament and arranges them on threads until they form the constellation of the Northern Bushel (Big Dipper, Great Bear), whence the supreme cosmic force emanates. The heavenly boy in his Cowherd aspect is also the counterpart of the Weaving Maiden; once upon a time he stole her clothes as she was bathing but, as the supreme lord of heaven has willed it, he may unite with her but once a year, on the seventh day of the seventh month. On that day she goes to him, crossing the celestial river by a bridge formed by magpies.[32]

---

29 In the rubbing, for lack of space written farther up close to the cervical vertebrae.
30 In Chinese there is one word for kidneys and testicles.
31 Likewise the text of the painting, where a distinction is made between name (*ming*) and personal name (*tzu*).
32 In the painting the seven stars are correctly arranged, but the boy by an error holds an eighth star in his hand. Beside the boy is written "the cowherd" and "the boy stonecutter lines up the money on string." In the rubbing we see him lining up the Northern Bushel. Six stars are already in place, he holds the seventh in his hand. This is, among other things, a reference to the "seven openings" of the heart and also to a saying of Confucius, *Lun Yü* [*Analects*], II, 1. Cf. Legge tr., p. 145.

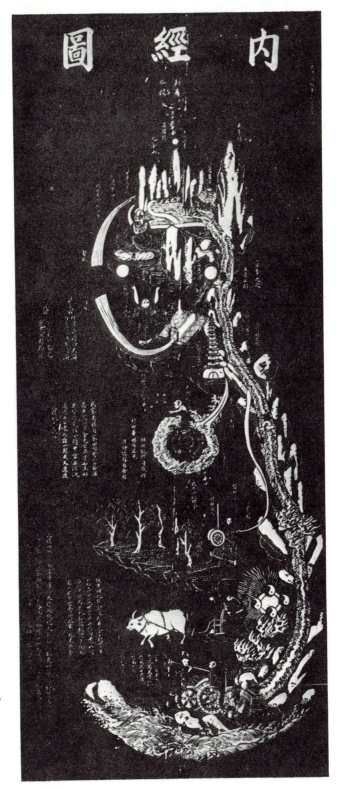

Rubbing of a
stone tablet in
the Monastery
of the White
Clouds, near
Peking

1

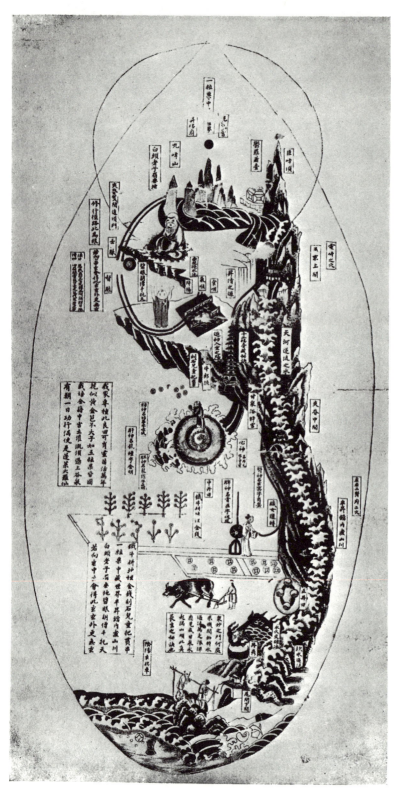

Scroll painting based on the tablet in the Monastery of the White Clouds

II

That is the night of nights. We see a suggestion of the possibility of their union pictured in the pulse which passes from the heart through the twelve-storied pagoda of the windpipe (breath!) to the occiput, where the pulse of the Weaving Maiden also ends. This is the gate to the celestial jade city. The two souls are united. But while in the painting there is a "spring of ascending truth" (*dharma*) or of purity near the "cave of the spirit field" (the spring takes its ambrosian liquid from the "moon," situated in the occiput, the optical center, which in turn has drawn moisture from the depths), in the rubbing the spring pours into the pond "where the red dragon wallows" [33]—i.e., into the breath conceived as condensed into spittle —and the pond is crossed by a "drawbridge," or "bird bridge" (*ch'iao ch'iao*),[34] recalling the bridge of the magpies.

3. In the middle of the vital center the germ of the new immortal man condenses; it matures until it is born, appearing over the crown of the head like Pallas springing from the head of Zeus, like the image of Buddha on the lotus blossom.

4. The immortal genius hovers over its human counterpart. As for the lotus blossom, the brain remains merely the "palace of the mud ball," from which the blossom rises immaculate in the light. Eternity is attained, shown by the eternal Southern Mountains of K'un-lun, or the "nine peaks." "The terrace of the deep chaotic spirit" offers a view into the ineffable from the "Supreme Summit." "The eyebrows of the white-headed Lao-tse hang down to the earth" (signs of eternal life). For thanks to the millennial tradition, the figure of Lao-tse lives in the soul of the Taoist as summation, archetype and prototype: the Taoist *becomes* Lao-tse. This is not only the Lao-tse who lived on earth, but also the transcendent "supreme ancestor," one of the figures in the Taoist trinity of the "Three Pure Ones." Resplendent the pearl rises, the "desirable treasure," the sign of the immortal over the head which has become the "house of the rising sun." The macrocosm has opened; after uniting in himself all depths and polarities, man has

---

33 In the painting two red pulses pass directly through the pond.
34 By "bridge" is meant the arching of the tongue against the hard palate (Skr. *khecarī*). This holds the controlling pulse in line, and causes the secretion of the sweet spittle, the potion of immortality. [Professor Hellmut Wilhelm, who has read this paper and given helpful advice, explains: *Khecarī* does not mean "bridge" or "hard palate," but signifies the *mudrā* (devotional posture or gesture, here of the tongue) wherein the tongue is pressed against the hard palate. Lit., *khecara* means "sky-walking," and this *mudrā* when successfully practiced is said to confer the power of "sky-walking." —ED.]

become the universe: "The whole world is contained in one grain" [35]—this stage in the Taoist view can be fully realized only by a man of sixty.

Strange as the Chinese imagery may seem to us, the *meaning* of this conception of man's path to maturity, from the circulation of the light and the death of the old Adam (in the fire of *eros*), through his transformation and rebirth from fire and water, to the eternal zones beyond the stars, is deeply related to certain aspects of our own being and recalls Western doctrines. Consider, for example, these verses by Goethe, from *Selige Sehnsucht* (Beatific Yearning):

> Sagt es niemand, nur den Weisen,
> Weil die Menge gleich verhöhnet:
> Das Lebend'ge will ich preisen,
> Das nach Flammentod sich sehnet.
>
> . . . .
>
> Und so lang Du das nicht hast,
> Dieses: Stirb und werde!
> Bist Du nur ein trüber Gast
> Auf der dunklen Erde.[35a]

3. Hsiu Shên: Individuation

The path leading through transformation, illumination, and rebirth to this mature, transcendent wisdom is designated as *hsiu shên*, "cultivation of the person," or, "of the individuality." [36] A subjectivistic interpretation must however be rejected at the outset. In meditation, as in any other system of

35 Literally, "grain of millet," here the designation of the pearl. Of those verses which repeat and sum up what has been detailed, those concerning the heart still remain to be cited:

> In my house I plow only my own field,
> In it are spiritual shoots that can live ten thousand years.
> The blossom is like yellow gold and the color changes,
> The seed is like grains of jade and the fruit is all round.
> The planting here is based solely on the earth of the middle castle,
> And the watering depends solely on the source of the supreme valley.

35a ["Tell no one but the wise, for the mob will straightway mock: the stuff of life is what I praise, that longs to die in flames.... And until you have grasped this—Die and be transformed!—you will be but a sorry guest on the somber earth."—After tr. in *The Penguin Book of German Verse*, ed. Leonard Forster (Harmondsworth, 1957), p. 227.—ED.]

36 The word *shên* really means "body." As in many other languages, it stands for the whole of the person. "My body" means "I."

self-discipline, man is concerned with himself only until an inner unity, a true individual arises, out of the union of polarities. But then this *communio naturarum* serves to integrate man with the social community and make him one with the Tao of the cosmos. It cannot be denied that many Taoists, and particularly Chuang-tzu, have manifested an extreme individualism which detaches the individual from the human community and induces an ironic attitude. In this, Confucians have justifiably sensed a symptom of anarchism. But beyond any doubt the ironic man, i.e., the clever and evil man, is inferior to the all-embracing, wise, strong, and kindly man, for the real source of irony is an unsublimated and misdirected drive towards self-assertion and recognition by others. The satirical, ironic man who in the last analysis is pessimistic because of his own imperfection, is the monkey image—and a mere torso—of the humorous, kind, strong, sage. And this latter is the true type of the Chinese "saint."

The "sage" or "saint" (*shêng*) is he "who understands with his spiritual ear and is able to teach because he stands firmly on this earth and carries out his celestial mission." He is like a radiant, warming "second sun between heaven and earth." [37]

Scarcely any man is privileged to fulfill the mission of the priest-king and guide the holy kingdom to peace; but this lofty idea works fruitfully in the depths of the soul.

Beneath the surface of history, the lofty ideal of the Taoism of the best tradition, which not only can live in harmony with Confucian statecraft but is its actual inspiration, has always been a source of national strength and renewal.

The course of training in a Taoist brotherhood is divided into stages corresponding to the path of salvation. But the path itself is nothing other than a man's inner growth to maturity, running parallel to the natural stages of his life. Its stages are: the dying of the young, world-bound man; achievement of spiritual clarity; rebirth out of the spirit; attainment of union with the primal source of all creatures and with one's fellow men; and finally, attainment of the sovereign goal: "actionless activity" or "outer passivity, inner activity" (*wu wei*). But this should not be taken to mean that one may achieve rebirth and perfection through any mere system of

---

37 Popular interpretation of the usual character, as well as of an older one for *shêng* (*jên*), the "holy" (man), a designation for the (ideal) emperor, but in Taoism also for the man with only an inner "calling."

psychotechnics. No, here the stern Christian truth applies: "For whosoever hath, to him shall be given, and he shall have more abundance; but whosoever hath not, from him shall be taken away even that he hath." Each man brings with him various gifts and aptitudes, hence the instruction varies with the pupil, and each man is instructed individually. (Though of course there are also general lectures in the Hall of Instruction (*chiang t'ang*) to which members of the outer circle are also admitted.)

The secret of this system of spiritual guidance is this: we must not repress the varied richness, the contradictions of our unconscious, but must lift them into our consciousness; the unconscious must be accepted and used for the building of a new man. This is also the way to open the gates to the genius of our hereditary, collective memory; by journeying to the Mothers, to raise the primordial dark mysteries of the soul and of life into the light of the spirit. In those of us who have the calling, there will thus arise that depth and clarity of spirit which can only be designated as "illumination" (*ming*). Depth and clarity unite, like "moon and sun." [38]

The means of experiencing the depth within oneself is contemplation or meditation. The technique of meditation is imparted in the very first lesson. The whole point of this technique is the total exclusion of every possibility of disturbance from outside, whether from the body or the mind, and the development of an attitude of waiting or listening. Its rules, which are all based on age-old experience, may be briefly summed up as follows:

1. Choose a quiet room, neither dark nor bright. In a bright room one is disturbed by outward images, in a dark room by inner images.

2. Choose a comfortable position, which the body will not be compelled to change soon, a sitting position. Crossing of the legs in the traditional tailor's posture is quite unnecessary for anyone not accustomed to it. On the contrary, it is a good idea to set the feet firmly on the ground.

3. Hold the back straight (supported by a back rest if desired) and the head high but bent backward a little, so that the tip of the nose is vertically over the navel and the "light of the eyes" can easily be directed toward the body's center (solar plexus), i.e., so that consciousness can easily be directed toward the unconscious.

38 Old interpretation of the character *ming*. It can, to be sure, also be written with "eye and moon," which well expresses the "vision of truth." The moon is a symbol of "truth."

86

4. Keep the eyes half closed. The same would be true of entirely open or entirely closed eyes as of bright or dark rooms. The eyes—their gaze converging over the tip of the nose—are directed toward the solar plexus.

5. Hold the hands together, as in the Chinese greeting—the right hand forms a fist which is held clasped by the left. This represents a *communio naturarum* of the yin and yang.

6. Before beginning to meditate, breathe from three to five times, deeply, slowly and evenly, so that the "sea of breath" (*ch'i hai*) is stimulated in the abdomen. In this way you will avoid being disturbed in the course of meditation by the need to take a deep breath. During meditation, pay no attention to breathing. The mouth must be closed, you must breathe entirely through your nose.

7. Look reverently at the picture of the Master (in the student's certificate). Thus you will be in his presence as it were, and will give yourself over to meditation with confidence.

8. Banish all thought. A total emptiness of mind is created. Meditation consists in "letting go." It is not the surface consciousness but the creative genius of the deep psyche that should speak to us.

9. This emptiness of thought is facilitated by its positive counterpart, which consists in directing consciousness toward the body's center, i.e., the unconscious.

10. You now enter upon the first of the three preparatory stages of meditation. All thoughts are bound fast in imagination to the body's center (*eros!*) like monkeys at the foot of a tree. The bond between *logos* and *eros* paralyzes the "monkey" thoughts. Consciousness by an act of the imagination is shifted to the solar plexus, i.e., the unconscious. This fixation is called *ting* (cf. in Indian Yoga: *dhārana*).

11. This produces a certain degree of relaxation, though there is still a faint striving to hold fast. This second preparatory stage of release or silence is called *ching*.

12. One now attains the third stage, in which there is no further effort or tension, the state of peaceful beatitude (*an*).[39]

Now at last the stage has been reached in which something can "happen" to you. What you now experience is the content of your meditation—but images and ideas must be expelled at once! It is impossible to guess before-

---

39 These terms go back to the beginning of the Great Learning (*Ta Hsüeh*).

hand what this content will be. Certain temporary disturbances of the meditation will occur, but these are actually an indication that you have meditated correctly.

It is recommended that you take a little exercise before meditating; otherwise your limbs may fall asleep from sitting. Meditate two or three times a day for a good half hour ("the length of a burning incense-stick") and read the "breviary" of prayer. Indeed in the beginning, it is advisable that you immerse yourself in meditation whenever you have nothing else to do. After a week's practice, you must go to the Master to report your experiences. If your experiences are the right ones, he will assign to you your next meditative task; you remain at your present one if they are not. If one day you happen to be overworked or nervous, you should not meditate; it would all 'be in vain anyway. As a means of achieving quiet it is recommended that you immerse yourself in the godhead and think of the Master.

This spiritual guidance through "His Eminence, the Master" (*shih tsun*), is supplemented by instruction of a more general, more philosophical nature, in which the master of novices, or teacher (*hsüeh chang*), elucidates the principles of spiritual guidance. There is no need to go into detail here.

We shall now go on to describe the meditative path as a whole, as it progresses parallel to the path of salvation.

1. The first thing the novice must experience is the existence in the unconscious of an opposite center, in which he immerses himself on the one hand and which on the other hand he raises up into consciousness. This stage is called the "circulation of the light" or, to borrow a Buddhist expression—the "wheel of *dharma*" (*fa lun*, Skr. *dharmacakra*), which must be "turned" (*chuan fa lun*).

His thoughts are shut off through the "binding of the monkeys" (*shuan hou tzu*); this consists in fixating the essential nature (*hsing*) and the consciousness upon their opposite, the center of vital force (*ming*) in the solar plexus. This must be accomplished without exertion or tension, for meditation, as we know, demands a state of relaxation. The union of essential nature (*hsing*) and vital force (*ming*) is the *communio naturarum* of yang and yin and may be compared to the union of the sexes. Above the heart dwells the divine primal man, the center of the spirit, who "carries the number two as a sign of his relation" to a Thou, the deity and other men (*jên*); in the vital center dwells the egocentric, individualistic, natural man (also pronounced *jên*), of whom nothing more can be said than that he "walks

88

on two legs." [40] From their union, which is fatal to the natural man, is born the new man of the spirit, the incorruptible "diamond body."

The natural man "sleeps," i.e., he is not taken up into our consciousness. But he must be awakened. To this end, consciousness is immersed in the natural man, or as it is said in the poetic language of meditation: "Sun and moon (the two eyes) shine on the earth (the body's center or solar plexus)." This earth is the "true elixir field" (*chêng tan t'ien*). This field must be "plowed" or "cultivated" by the immersion of the spirit (*chung t'ien*). The natural man is thus disturbed in his sleep, i.e., he enters into our consciousness. All the chthonic deities emerge. At this point the novice encounters two signs, and quite often also a phenomenon that he regards as a disturbance of his meditative tranquillity. I shall not discuss these signs or this disturbance at any length, but merely mention the poetic terms for them: one sign is the "awakening of the natural man" in the solar plexus; the other is the presence of "fire," also in the solar plexus. The disturbance, which accompanies the first sign, consists in a slight stirring of the watery element, which disappears of its own accord in the course of continued meditations. At this point it is a good sign, for the aim in this phase of meditation is to know—and to acknowledge all the powers of the unconscious. Once again it should be stressed that despite the poetic terminology, this soberly psychological system of training considers all visual images or visions as aberrations.

Now the next stage begins. The novice is led to perceive the third "celestial eye" (*t'ien yen*, Skr. *divya çakṣus*) in the middle of the forehead; this is the true "sun," the "radiance of our essential nature." In this he is aided by the "bodhidharma," the "blue-eyed barbarian monk," the "master of meditation," in us. By a certain form of "staring at the wall," said to have been practiced by Bodhidharma (d. 529), the novice perceives with closed eyes the third "heavenly eye," i.e., after experiencing the opposite, the vital force in the unconscious, he gains cognizance of the divine guide, the "radiance of his essential nature." From this point on, he looks at the vital center with this "heavenly eye," the essential nature irradiates its opposite pole, the life in us, as the light of heaven irradiates the earth. The consequence is a complete and violent awakening of the natural man. The vital force is condensed in the vital center, and this condensation must never again be

---

40 Usual interpretation of the two characters.

dissipated. In addition to this concentration (coagulation) and to the violent awakening, the novice encounters a third sign, the "oil" (*yu*) or potion of immortality (*kan lu,* Skr. *amṛta*). He now approaches the second section of the path. So far the path has consisted mainly of "work with the vital force" (*ming kung*), a central part of the whole technique of meditation. At this point the purifying or ennobling "work with the essential nature" (*hsing kung*) must be undertaken, if it has not begun before. For all the open-mindedness that characterizes the Chinese, the second part of the path, the "backward-flowing movement," demands a firm ethic. Once the plane beyond the opposites has been reached, no lax dalliance with good and evil can be tolerated—even though the "good" may be understood in a very profound sense rather different from that of common morality.

A new dedication is now undertaken. The novice is required to make a solemn vow to regulate his way of life according to a supreme principle, *sub specie aeternitatis*. These Confucians and Taoists made me swear to walk in the paths of Christ, understood in a very profound and ultimate sense. I confess—obviously everything that I am here describing is entirely a personal matter in any case—I confess that this unexpected demand made such a profound impression on me, though I was then already *nel mezzo del cammin di nostra vita*, with much inner experience behind me, that my readers will understand if I do not go into details about it. I should like to say only this much: what a profound understanding of the ways of the divine Logos, of the relation of historical to suprahistorical religion, of the nurturing force of the inherited religious substance, is revealed in this desire to see the Confucian firmly anchored in his Confucianism, the Buddhist in his Buddhism, the Christian in his Christianity, while at the same time the equally essential, suprahistorical, ultimate and ineffable core of the "ten thousand religions," the miraculous bridge that unites them all, is always kept in mind.

The novice is prepared for the vow through instruction in the sacristy beside the master's chapel. This was a true confidential session, an "Upanishad"! And because of its bearing on the whole path of meditation, I must add a remark in this connection: in so far as it is transmissible, the esoteric ancient wisdom was taught publicly in China up to the days of Mencius, in India up to the days of the Buddha, and in the West up to the days of Christ, but after that it was taught only in closed circles, for men were dazzled but not illumined by intellectualism. To us critical Westerners such an interpretation seems nonsense, but the fact remains that in ancient times, when the archaic way of thinking was still common to all, religion embraced the whole tribe or nation, while today spiritual guidance presupposes a restricted group, for the most part an association of two persons, student and teacher; through their unreserved confidence in one another, slowly and methodically, communication is established between consciousness and the unconscious.

The preceding course of meditation, for the completion of which some require many years, ten or more, enormously enhances the powers of the whole man (by stimulating the internal secretion?). The next stage makes great demands. According to the tradition, Buddha had "performed three thousand good deeds and won eighty distinctions" before he achieved illumination, and after that he still had to preach for forty years. To few men it is given to complete the stage of "work with his essential nature." Teaching, it may be added, is also regarded as part of the work on the essential nature.

At this point the meditative technique is changed. The pupil no longer immerses himself in the vital center; even without this fixation he retains his freedom from the play of thoughts. At most, he sends out a "thought thread" to the vital center. Preparation through the three graduated stages *"ting, ching, an"* is no longer needed; instead, he awakens in himself a mood of "joy" (*k'uai lo*). Under the guidance of the Master, the current is now carried forward from the central "seminal bladder" by way of a "thought thread"; then it is divided in two streams and carried back to the kidneys, where the streams are reunited. Thence the current is guided up the spinal cord, over the head, and down across the middle of the forehead to the chest and the vital center. The circulation of the light is complete (see Figure 2).

The "wheel of dharma is turning"! Conscious and unconscious, heaven and earth, essential nature and vital force, have been brought into fruitful interrelation by an exercise of the imagination; this relationship is an inner experience, an inalienable possession. And this is what matters in meditation quite regardless of any "objective" truth which we may or may not impute to the paths followed by the "light" in its circulation. Consciousness has been opened to the abysses of the unconscious, ready communication has been established between the two. There is no repression, no cramped tension, for the essence of Oriental wisdom is effortless mastery of the world, continence without repression, discipline without constraint, and this means: to float in freedom, to be "empty," to act "spontaneously." . . .

The chiliastic ideal of the Chinese is *ta t'ung shih chieh,* "the world of the great community," after the celebrated chapter in the Book of Rites. When this is achieved, every man will be a "gentleman" (*chün-tzu*), "inwardly a saint, outwardly a sovereign" (*nei shêng wai wang*). The true mission of the

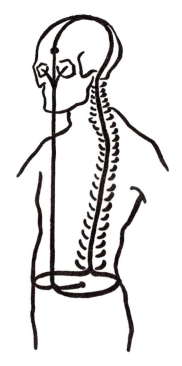

Fig. 2. *Circulation of the light*
(First part of the meditation path)

individual is to realize this type by the discipline of letting go—; and it is the mission of all, particularly the carriers of the Taoist tradition, to prepare the way for the chiliastic kingdom. Beginning and end of the myth of history become one.

In ancient times the occult doctrine was a universal possession, while now it is limited to a few. And once again it shall become a universal possession, illuminating an ennobled mankind. According to myth, virtue and holiness governed the remote past and will govern the distant future, while today man must labor for their attainment, and harvests only incomprehension and empty laughter from all the many "little masters." To dissect a myth with rationalistic critique is neither necessary nor fitting; let us not discuss the pious faith of the "heathen" world! Perhaps the rule of the *logos spermatikos* is to be seen in it also?

The phase of "work with the essential nature" (*hsing kung*) involves the following four points: 1. There must be a determined desire for individuation, for the development of a self-contained character and personality. The solemn vow marked the beginning of a new impulse, the opening of a new psychological perspective. 2. The ancient sacred texts of the Chinese must now be studied, in the light of certain Taoist commentaries, for the classics are essential aids in character training. 3. The student is to maintain a friendly, brotherly association with the "tao friends" to the end that each may inspire the others. 4. The ethical and metaphysical essence of ancient Taoist wisdom, in short, Tao itself, is to be spread wherever he goes.

At the same time the student must above all continue to receive encouragement and instruction from the Master, for that is actually the presupposition of the four points cited above. Two types of instruction are given, a "rational type" (*li hsüeh*) and a "mystical type" (*tao hsüeh*). The second cannot really be formulated in words; it is a current flowing as it were from master to pupil. This is the "school of tradition" (*ch'uan mên*) in the strict sense, that is, the wordless tradition. Its path leads from the purification (*via purgativa*) of man to his union (*via unitiva*) with the primal source [*Urgrund*] "through virtue to the light," as it is said in the West. *Chin jen ho t'ien*, "the advanced human being unites with heaven," as the Chinese say.

We now leave this "work with the essential nature" and all the various philosophical and religious studies, and return to the instruction in meditation proper. It is, as before, imparted by "an oral occult process" (*k'ou chüeh*), with which the Master favors those who "know me" (*chih chi*) or who "know the self."

In connection with the "circulation of the light," i.e., the conscious communication between conscious and unconscious, it remains to be said that there must be no division of the current, neither behind the heart, nor in the occiput, nor on the top of the head, nor beyond the middle of the forehead. In these four places are situated "gates" through which the current must pass. The pupil prevents the current from dispersing over the nose and flowing into his throat, by curling his tongue and setting the tip to his palate (*shang o*). The tongue then forms—as it is put poetically—the "bird bridge" (*ch'iao ch'iao*) or more correctly "magpie bridge," over which in the star myth the celestial fairy, the Weaving Maiden, crosses the celestial river to her husband the Cowherd.

Greatly stimulated by the circulation, the light of the "celestial eye" now becomes a glowing ball, growing slowly and sending forth its rays farther and farther. We see what we irradiate (we recognize only what is illumined by the light of consciousness!). "Between the eyes it darts forth and illumines the ten thousand worlds."

As his meditations on the circulation of the light proceed, the student—from being enclosed in the circle—is befallen by a sudden "disturbance," a sense of loneliness, forsakenness, as though the whole world were sinking and he were lost. He is filled with horror, evoked by the natural man in him, who is unwilling to renounce the world. At this point he must simply keep up his courage and persevere, for he stands face to face with the primal fundament [*Urgrund*] of the world and no longer with the appearance, so nothing can befall him. Through this confidence the horror vanishes at once, giving way to a marvelous beatitude.

Meditation should now be completely discontinued. Only if it sets in of its own accord should the pupil accept it. Here a rule applies: "*wu wang wu chu*—do not forget, but neither help along." The cessation of meditation is of the utmost importance. Meditation is after all only an instrument and a not undangerous one. Excesses lead to needless disturbances of the psychic equilibrium, whereas the desired result is a *communio naturarum* in perfect harmony.

The next "sign" is a strange "emptiness" (*hsü k'ung*, Skr. *śūnyatā*) accompanied by total tranquillity in the "heart." This is an intimation of the fundament of our own being and of the universe. "The true emptiness is not empty, the true existence is non-existence." This emptiness should not be regarded as mere nothingness, but as the ineffable, "the Wholly Other": "as though something there were and as though nothing there were." The essential thing in a vessel, as Lao-tse himself said, is not its walls, but its hollowness; and so it is with the "emptiness" of man and the universe. It is not tangible, it is the essential, it can assimilate all things in selfless kindness. This emptiness is the kernel of all things, indeed, all that goes to constitute our experience is in essence nothing other than this emptiness. "Emptiness is form, form is emptiness," as the Buddhist Diamond Sūtra puts it.

2. Our effort up to now—"the circulation of the light" and the beginning of "work with the essential nature"—corresponds to the "tao of man" (*jên tao*). Now we must go on to the second part of the path, intensified work with the essential nature and complete assimilation and sublimation of the vital forces in our essential nature. This is the stage of transformation into the "Tao of the essential nature" (*hsing tao*); and the main content of this second part of the path is the sublimation, or "backward-flowing movement," of the seeds of the vital force. They are stored up and transformed into life-giving breath. The occasional ascetic exercises necessary to this end should be performed without any constraint. For this stage the novice must have passed the middle of his life, i.e., he should be approximately forty years of age.

The Chinese have a strong feeling for the stages in the inner growth of man. It is reflected in their customs. The man of forty, usually already a grandfather, is entitled to grow a mustache; the man of sixty, who is often a great-grandfather, is permitted a full beard. The spiritual clarity of complete detachment is similarly associated with age. A man must be close to forty before he is instructed in the meditation on the backward-flowing movement; only at the approach of sixty does a man dedicate himself entirely to the "tao of heaven" (*t'ien tao*).

Here we must interpolate a psychological observation which applies both to the first part of the meditative path and to all its subsequent development. The localization of certain processes in certain parts of the body, such as the forehead, the region of the heart, the kidneys, solar plexus, etc. is a carry-over from an archaic psychology. Whether these localizations are objectively correct is a matter of indifference; what matters is the efficacy of these views and of the experience associated with them in the mind of the pupil. To arrive at fundamental and deeply moving experiences, to attain unsuspected insights, to open the way for new and meaningful shifts in our psychological components, these are the essential aims in meditation. It is of fundamental importance that man should actually experience—and not merely note intellectually—the opposite pole in himself, his unconscious and his vital force; it is of fundamental importance that he recognize as a part of himself everything, good or bad, that lies in his unconscious—symbolically called "earth, fire, water"—and make use of it all; it is of fundamental importance that all this should be raised to consciousness and that ready communication be established between conscious and unconscious; and it is of fundamental importance that the man who has passed middle life should know the terrible experience of the "death of the natural man"; only then can he progress to the perfect type of the mature, spiritually serene man; only then can he achieve a truly meaningful, organic growth to maturity, without detours and without a loss of time greatly to be regretted in view of the brevity of life. The raising of all this to consciousness does not mean an intellectualization of the profound forces within us; in reality, understanding opens the path to a new and spontaneous psychological experience.

In the above we have described the first part of the path in detail, keeping silence only with regard to the first two signs and the first disturbance. This should give the reader an adequate picture of the whole psychological method. Since the subsequent parts are intended only for those who have passed middle life and come to accept the prospect of their own slowly approaching death (a limited circle, in other words), and since moreover the second part comes to grips with highly personal matters—sexuality, for example—it will be understood that I see fit to treat the ensuing stages only in their main outlines.

In addition to seeking greater ethical and spiritual depth through "work on his nature," the student must now be instructed in certain details by experienced "tao friends." At the end of the first part, two "tao friends," known as "guardians of the law" (*hu fa*, Skr. *dharmapāla*), are accordingly assigned him. The two dharmapalas guard the student, on his right and on his left, like two archangels, like the lance-bearing "illustrious" (*to wên*) Vaisravana, the celestial king (*t'o t'a t'ien wang*), who supports the pagoda (of the sacred doctrine), and like Wei T'o (Skr. Skandha?) the youthful captain of the celestial hosts with his diamond battle-ax. Under the stanch guard of the two archangels, no great harm can befall the student as, surrounded as it were by mysterious spirits, he continues his way. In every way this institution is beneficial and necessary.

For now we approach the beatific mystery of the conception of the new man out of water and fire. Our true essential nature is the "primal spirit" in which nature and life are one, it is the great divine Tao. This primal spirit is not yet incarnated in us, but is crystallized in the "fundament [*Urgrund*], the great One," and awaits its incarnation.

In man, *logos* and *eros* (cognition and emotion), heart and kidneys are the great contradictory principles, equivalent to fire and water. The natural man allows both principles to flow out of him as thinking and begetting. But we must now gather them in, so that consciousness and the force of immortality may fructify one another. This turning back of energy, this temporary asceticism, is termed the "backward-flowing movement"; or it is described in the verse: "The river of heaven (the Milky Way) is flowing upstream." The two "water wheels" carry the "water" to higher ground. Both heart and vital force are refreshed. Man has within him the three streams of spirit, breath, and seed. The common man wastes the seed, in him the life-giving force of the breath is consumed, and with it the spirit as well. Where asceticism is practiced, the vital energy and breath are strengthened (seed transformed into breath), and finally breath is transformed into spirit.

It must be owned that sublimation is not so simple a matter as Chinese physiology here assumes. But there is no doubt that physical vitality and spiritual alertness do depend very greatly on internal secretion.

It is evident that only men of clear and stable mind may safely venture into this realm; and that is the reason for the rule that the student must have passed middle life before embarking on the second half of the path. Here it is to be noted once more that the physiological considerations we have discussed are again merely points of departure for meditation; the essential thing is the spiritual result attained through this whole impressive path. The period of one hundred days now devoted to ascetic exercises is considered a transitory phase. It is assumed that once the exercises have been performed, the body will automatically accomplish the sublimation. This is exactly as with the "circulation of the light." If the exercises have been successful, "the light" circulates without need of any further meditation. It means of course that what has once been raised to consciousness by significant and sometimes shattering experience can never again be lost.

The circulation, the wheel of dharma, must now perform a greater task. The "earth kingdom" in man was included, and the chthonic gods spoke. But now the breath and the seed must be captured. The seed is stimulated by the emission of a ray of light, but there is no release. The breathing, which in a certain sense is the vehicle of the breath-spirit, must be regulated until its rhythm harmonizes with the heartbeat. And the heart achieves tranquillity through the breathing. Sun and moon shine outward like the eyes,

97

but when the true sun and the true moon shine inward, the light, i.e., the seed of the sun and the moon, is crystallized. The conception is that in inspiration the seminal power is conveyed to the brain, in expiration it is carried back again down the front of the body. In inspiration the lower gate of energy is opened, in accordance with the tenth chapter of Lao-tse; in expiration the upper gate is closed.

In the first half of the path we have already seen that a concentration of energy occurs in the vital center which must not be lost. We pass over details, the rhythms of breathing, the washing and bathing (see Figure 3). The crystallization occurs in the eye. In the midst of the light, a new point of light appears. Suddenly the seed pearl is present.

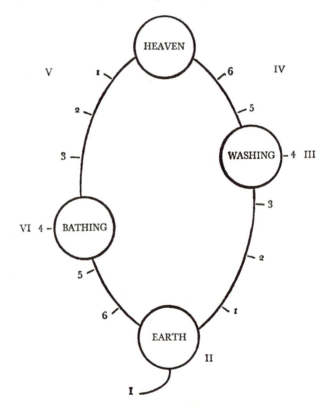

FIG. 3. *Backward-flowing movement*
(Second part of the meditation path)

The true divine primal man, *Humanus*, the vehicle of our divine essential nature, and the natural man, *Homo*, have united their seed; all polarities, including the dragons of the yang and yin pulses in man, have found their synthesis in a *communio naturarum*. The new immortal man has been conceived in the vital center.

It is self-evident that the significance of this whole conception lies in spiritual generation; the alchemical physiology is a pedagogic instrument. In this unity of the new man in us, we find our whole essence; we have risen above inner opposites.

3. The Birth of the New Man. The new man in us gains possession of us more and more. He grows in us and exacts our best energies. For ten lunar months (nine solar months) the new man, who is still a homunculus, a golden embryo (*chin t'ai*, Skr. *hiraṇyagarbha*) is nurtured within us. During this period the "gentle heating" takes place, in order to convey our force of immortality to the embryo. "At the end of a year, the ablutions and baths are warm." The divine spirit has united with our breath. Previously seed was transformed into breath, now breath is transformed into spirit. The embryo is pressing to be born. Our immortal essence assumes the imaginary form of a *puer aeternus*, rises up, bursts through the skull in the region of the third eye, and with a shout that is echoed by the heavens, is born. The reborn man sits immortal on the lotus throne over our head.

These partly alchemical, partly allegorical images convey the fact that through tremendous experiences we have found our true being in the new man, and that from this moment on we shall live by our true being.

The new man is known by the Indian term "diamond body" (*chin-kang shen*, Skr. *vajrakāya*); but we are still living in our phenomenal or "transformation" body (*hua shen*, Skr. *nirmānakāya*). Here on earth we have our task to perform, which is to fill our phenomenality with profounder meaning. According to Indian tradition, our phenomenality has five components. These five groups (*wu yün*, Skr. *pancaskandha*) are the body (*sê*, Skr. *rūpa*); the feelings or in another interpretation the sense perceptions (*shou*, Skr. *vedanā*); perception (*hsiang*, Skr. *samjñā*); the inborn potentialities or unconscious constructive forces, which lead from one existence to another (*hsing*, Skr. *saṃskāra*); and the consciousness (*shih*, Skr. *vijñāna*). Up until now the new man, the "diamond body," has dwelt lonely on his throne, above our whole being; above the world; he has been the "son of Buddha" (*Fo tzu*), the mystical Vajrasattva (*chin-kang yung*), the true "son of heaven."

99

Now each conception takes form, according to the five components of our being. We live in the midst of this process, we strive to retain our phenomenal body, but the diamond body possesses sacred "emptiness," and becomes increasingly empty. Each of the five groups again contains the full number of components; thus in each of our various manifestations, we appear as one and the same.

4. Then, on the highest plane, the activity of the "blue-eyed barbarian monk" resumes once more. All our manifestations are in the last analysis

Fig. 4. *The Chinese character* chung, *"middle"*

The vertical is symbolically related, among other things, to the world axis, to the "yellow center," that is, the axis running from the celestial eye to the middle of the body, to the ethical principle of "the middle of correct behavior," and so on, and also to the stream which flows over the forehead from above in the "circulation of the light." The oval figure through which the stream passes (originally meant to represent a target) represents the third or "heavenly eye." At the lower end of the vertical arrow, a small white space is left open. This is the seed pearl.

Fashioned in gold, and bearing a white pearl at the lower end, the character is worn by the Master on the front of his cap when he presides over a meeting in the Hall of Instruction. *Chung* further signifies the Middle Kingdom, also in the ancient sense of the crown land or personal domain of the Chinese Son of Heaven.

empty form. In recognizing this, we "stare at the wall," like Bodhidharma, and the "light of our essential nature" shines back upon the Primordial. Only then is our multiform individuality fully unified. The supreme and ultimate state experienced by the illumined, unified man is the "One without two." He becomes one with the tao of heaven. "Cultivate the tao, become the tao, be the tao." He preserves the axis of the world, which is the sacred "yellow center" (see Figure 4), and works here and now at the spot in the cosmos that has been assigned to him; "he exerts influence without willed intent," he is "empty" of all specificity, one with the world, its process and life, and with their common fundament, for he now lives out of that cosmic fundament. The state to which he has attained is well described by Liu Hua-yang in the *Hui Ming Ching:* [41]

> Without Becoming, without extinction,
> Without past, without future,
> A radiance surrounds the world of the spirit.
> We forget one another, still and pure, powerful and empty.
>
> The emptiness is illumined by the light of the heart of heaven,
> The sea is smooth and reflects on its surface the moon.
> The clouds vanish in blue space,
> The mountains glisten clear.
> Consciousness dissolves into vision,
> The disk of the moon is alone.

41 Cf. German tr. by L. C. Lo, in *Chinesische Blätter für Wissenschaft und Kunst* (Frankfurt a. M.), III (1927): 1, p. 114. [The verses are tr. by Cary F. Baynes.]

Theodor-Wilhelm Danzel

The Psychology of Ancient Mexican Symbolism

It seems to me that the symbolism of the pre-Hispanic Mexicans very much merits the interest of the cultural psychologist. Scarcely any other people not yet in possession of phonetic writing has given us such a wealth of symbolic signs and images. Yes, it is important to stress that the Mexicans had no phonetic writing: they had no accurate, literal means of registering the spoken word. Many conceptions which with us have paled to abstraction were to them still image and symbol. Much that in our culture has grown dim and conceptual remained for them concrete and visible. Other peoples, it is true, have developed rich imagery in myths and sagas, cults and tales, but I believe there is none without phonetic writing—that is to say, writing in the proper sense of the word—which has given us an equal abundance of graphic symbols. The "Pustakas" which have come down to us from the Bataks of Sumatra are indeed comparable to the Mexican books; they contain a wealth of symbols not yet fully explored by scholars, but these books are written in a phonetic system, and the images, the illustrative symbols, are subordinated to the text. A better parallel would be the "Malangans" of New Ireland, mythological representations carved in wood; though more modest in scope, these may plausibly be compared to the Mexican works. The religious art of China, India, Egypt, and Babylonia is also full of symbolic representations; but to meet their needs of expression, these peoples had not only pictorial representation but also highly developed systems of writing. The old Peruvian cultures reveal much interesting iconographical material in their Nazca ceramics; but here the symbolism is subject to ornamental and decorative limitation. Moreover, we know very little about the meaning of these representations, which we have barely begun to penetrate.

Indigenous civilizations rose to notable heights in four parts of the New

World: in Peru, where we find the civilization of the Incas, whose traditions would seem in very large degree to date back to earlier cultures; in Colombia, with the civilization of the Chibchas; and finally, in the territory of the present republic of Mexico, where we find two civilizations of leading importance: in the north that of the Aztecs, or Mexicans properly speaking, and in the south that of the Mayas, which extended over Tabasco, Chiapas, Campeche, Yucatán, Guatemala, British Honduras, and northern Honduras. These civilizations were not isolated; they were surrounded by a ring of related cultures whose traditions accord in many points. Of these I mention only the Zapotecs to the south of the Aztecs and the Totonacs in the state of Vera Cruz.

Here I shall touch only briefly on the history of these civilizations. The empire of the Aztecs with its capital city Tenochtitlan (on the site of the present capital of the republic of Mexico) was situated on the plateau of Anahuac. In the sixth century of our era, it is believed, this territory was occupied by the Toltecs, apparently a people of advanced civilization, computing the calendar and—of particular interest to us here—making use of pictorial symbols. Their empire collapsed in the tenth or eleventh century A.D., seemingly in consequence of famine and other catastrophes. The survivors—as tradition would have it—left the country and fled to Yucatán and Guatemala, where they founded the Mayan empire. The Toltec empire, which some scholars regard as entirely legendary and others take to be historical, was followed by the empire of the Chichimecs, which was in turn followed by that of the Aztecs. The actual history of the Aztecs as a great nation begins in A.D. 1376. The historical events thus briefly related involve many problems that I cannot enter into here. At any rate, the distinct quality of Aztec style and the advanced state of culture show that a development covering thousands of years must have preceded the full flowering of Aztec traditions.

It has often been asked whether indigenous American civilizations developed independently of old world cultures or whether they in some way received impulses from Asia. The fundamental importance of such questions has been very much exaggerated. The borrowing of cultural traditions is always bound up with such a variety of creative processes that it comes very close to being an independent achievement. Karl Vossler, the great Romance scholar, once said: "We do not inherit culture, and we do not borrow it; we recreate it from day to day, each of us in his own way. Nor do we learn culture; it is awakened in us." In approaching this question of cultural borrowing, we must draw a sharp distinction between habits of life and authentic traditions. (We are indebted above all to René Guenon for clarification of the concept of tradition in all its profundity.) In any event there are strong indications that the native American civilizations developed in isolation: the absence of stringed instruments, the failure to make use of iron, the absence of the wheel and cart and of the most important domestic animals of the old world.

The Aztec symbols—with which we are today concerned—have come down to us in works of sculpture and architecture, and above all in a type of book, the picture manuscript. Their writing was a symbolic script or ideography. For proper names, it is true, they did have a kind of phonetic writing, the rebus, a method similar to that employed by Europeans in ideographic heraldry. The monk in the emblem of Munich or the bear in that of Bern or Berlin is intended to symbolize the sound of the name. We occasionally find a device of this sort in the Mexican codices, but apart from this, there is only symbolic writing, ideography. The writing of the Mayas, the other great pre-Hispanic culture in the territory of the present republic of Mexico and bordering countries, is likewise ideography, although some of its signs are very much de-imagized, offering very little suggestion of the object to which they refer.

It may appear from the following what abundance of meaning enters into Mexican picture writing, and how this meaning is expressed. The moon is often symbolized by a rabbit, for the Aztecs (like the peoples of East Asia and many parts of Africa) thought they could discern the shape of this animal in the spots on the moon. The starry firmament is represented in the codices as a dark surface covered with star-eyes. I am reminded of a window in the Besserer chapel of Ulm Cathedral, dating from the year 1430, in which God the Father is represented as the creator of heaven, holding in his hand the celestial sphere, a dark surface covered with bright stars—a characterization very close to Mexican conceptions. The disk of the sun, placed behind a human figure, often serves as a kind of halo designating divinity. A half-sun, completed by a dark disk with star-eyes, signifies dusk, the dividing line between day and night. The earth is represented by a gigantic, wide-open, tooth-filled maw: the consuming earth. Sin, which sullies, is symbolized by a dog passing water; the sinner himself, the impure, is symbolized as a human form with lumps of mud clinging to his back. The mud, considered as nocturnal, is covered with star-eyes. The road that a man has traveled is indicated by a series of footprints. Death is indicated in the manner familiar to us by a skull and crossbones. And plastic representations of skulls on temple pyramids as well as skulls ground from clear crystal suggest that death is often conceived as not merely corporeal. Speech, song, and prayer are indicated by little tongues of breath before the mouth. Water, and sometimes blood, is represented by an undulating ribbon which, when it signifies water, is adorned with crowns of foam and sometimes with sea shells. Among animal symbols, we most particularly encounter the snake in many contexts. There are water snakes, rain snakes, lightning snakes. In ancient Mexico, as in many other parts of the world, the snake is associated with the penis and presumably the orgasm. The winged snake, or cloud snake, to which we shall return, may thus be presumed—if we take cloud in its extended meaning of heaven—to signify "heavenly orgasm," hence religious ecstasy. In addition to the snake we find an inexhaustible wealth of other beasts, both in sculpture and in picture writing. The old god of the dance is represented by the howling wolf, known for his musical qualities. Certain deities—and this is highly significant—are no longer represented in animal form but in animal disguise, an indication that the gods were no longer seen as purely animal. We are reminded of ancient oriental representations in which the distance between the transcendent and the animal has become even greater, and the gods are shown standing on the backs of animals.

Sacrifice plays an essential role in the old Mexican cults and takes innumerable forms. We have representations of human and animal sacrifices, and of all sorts of offerings (Pl. I). Particularly graphic is a conception underlying one of the numerous forms of sacrifice. As in the corn harvest the farmer tore the ear from the stalk, so in the human sacrifice the sun god received his harvest from the executioners who tore out the heart of the victim. The relation between victim and divinity is expressed in a representation showing a broad ribbon of blood connecting the headless neck of a sacrificial bird with the mouth of the sun god: the sun feeds on such sacrificial blood (Pl. II). It is interesting to note that conceptions of similar concreteness are encountered in the European Middle Ages. A tapestry by M. J. Doerr dating from 1603 (in the historical museum at Lucerne) shows the blessed consequences for mankind of Christ's sacrifice on the Cross. The Holy Ghost is represented by lines issuing from sacred chalices. Other lines, symbolizing a kind of magico-sacral causality, run from Christ's wounds to representations of other holy persons' good deeds and of other divine events.

In view of this symbol-creating power, it should not surprise us that the early Mexicans should have found forms and symbols for the cosmos as a whole. One of the most significant examples of this is the "Hackmack stone chest," in the Hamburg Museum für Völkerkunde, a kind of sarcophagus which presumably served to receive the remains of a warrior after his ceremonial cremation. This chest is an image and symbol of the whole cosmos. The top is identified as the heavens by the celestial snake carved in it; the bottom as the earth by a toad; the four sides are characterized by four symbols signifying north, south, east, and west as the four regions of the world.

These few examples from the inexhaustible wealth of early Mexican symbols may give some notion of the way in which the symbol was used to convey a meaning, and of the type of meaning represented.

In the present paper we shall concern ourselves primarily with the mythological symbolism of the Aztecs; and here again I should like to be selective, stressing only those myths and symbols that seem to be most interesting from a psychological point of view. The cultural relations between the Mayas and the Aztecs involve so many problems that have not yet been fully solved that I must dispense with taking them up in detail. In characterizing the Aztec and Mayan cultures, certain writers have drawn on Old World comparisons, likening the Aztecs to the Romans, the Mayas to the Greeks. By and large, the comparison is apt. The Mayas were a people split into separate communities that banded together only in times of special danger. Thus they were not remarkable for their political power. But their accomplishments in the fields of plastic art, architecture, astronomy, and arithmetic were extraordinary. The Aztecs, on the other hand, were a conqueror people who built their empire on the ruins of another nation, the Toltecs. In likening the Mayas to the Greeks and the Aztecs to the Romans, we might complete our parallel by comparing the Toltecs to the Etruscans. And the Zapotecs who, as I have said, occupied a territory between the Aztecs and the Mayas, constituted an intermediary between the two civilizations, which in many features reveal a common cultural base.

The Aztec symbols were co-ordinated above all in the calendar. This was the basic schema, the system in which the symbols were articulated. The deities were distributed through the calendar, different gods dominating different times of the year. A psychological approach may be helpful here.

Sacrificial scene

Upper left, sacrificed man; *lower left*, sacrificed dog; *lower right*, eagle and jaguar fighting, symbolizing a human sacrifice that took the form of a simulated battle between the sacrificing priest and his victim (Codex Nuttall, f. 69)

The sun god feeding on sacrificial blood

Left, the god before the disk of the sun; *upper right*, the moon with moon-spot rabbit; *below it*, a figure representing the morning star, offering a quail (headless) as sacrifice; *bottom right*, the earth gullet (Codex Borgia, f. 71)

Magical anatomy

The god of lust, his limbs and organs connected with calendaric symbols
suggesting magical associations (Codex Vaticanus 3773, f. 96)

Regions of the cosmos

On the toothed edge of the earth's maw, the hole from which the stars rise, a pyramid with steps is being built. This pyramid, symbolizing the edifice of heaven, contains a temple on the platform above with a high, pointed roof, beneath which rest the souls of ancestors and of warriors fallen in battle or sacrificed (Codex Borgia, f. 33)

a. *Pyramid of the Sun, Teotihuacan*

b. *Pyramid of Quetzalcoatl, Teotihuacan*

Quetzalcoatl

Quetzalcoatl

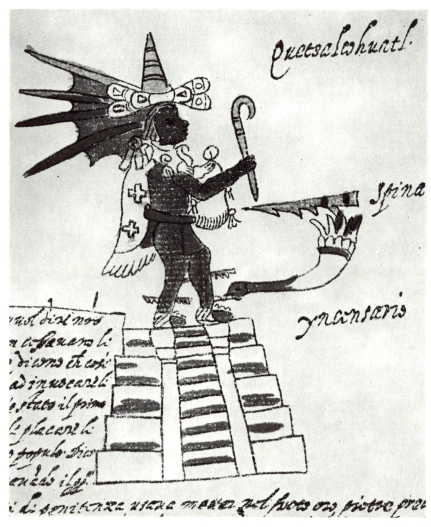

Temple pyramid with Quetzalcoatl, hero and penitent of Tollan

(Codex Vaticanus A 3738, f. 7ᵛ)

Quetzalcoatl

Life and death: the wind god and the skull-headed god of death

(Codex Vaticanus 3773, f. 75)

Xipe Totec. Stone head

The god looks out of a mask of human skin

Xipe Totec

The god is clothed in human skin, which hangs from his arms. *Right*, a snake devouring a man, presumably a symbol for the moon sinking into the sea (Codex Borbonicus, f. 14)

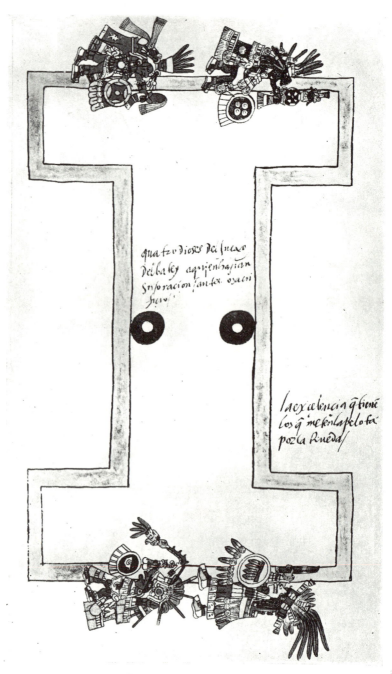

quatzo dioses dei Juego
Dei ba ley aquijenhazian
Su foracion fantes oyaciri
fierof·

laexcelencia q̃ tiene
los q̃ metenlapelota
por la ruedas

Four gods on the ball court

Middle, the two stone rings; to throw the ball through them was the main
purpose of the game (Codex Borbonicus, f. 27)

First let us consider the "magical anatomy" represented in various picture manuscripts. In one of these (Pl. III) we find the usual figure of a man. Various parts of the body are marked by calendaric symbols, indicating that these organs and limbs are controlled by demonic powers that are important also in controlling certain segments of the calendar. It is interesting to note that this notion of the control of certain organs by gods and demons occurs among other peoples—for example, the Maoris of New Zealand, the ancient Egyptians, the Chinese, and the cabalistic scholars of the European Middle Ages. The psychological approach offers us a key to the understanding of these very strange conceptions. In the course of his self-induced hallucinations and visionary states, Ludwig Staudenmaier [1] found that a very definite connection existed between certain bodily organs and the fantastic forms, the chimeras, which he saw in his hallucinations and visions; he discovered that very definite visionary forms corresponded to certain organic stimuli. In the imaginative life, there would appear to be a definite relation between specific organic sensations and certain specific phantasms. In other words, what to us appears as a relation between certain parts of the body and certain phantasmal forms appears to the mythically thinking man as a relation between parts of the body and demons.

Psychology throws a similar light on the magical calendar. I have said that in Mexico the calendar was a basic schema of religious symbolism. It was regarded as the "book of good and bad days"—that is, a guide to the periods favorable and unfavorable to human undertakings. The calendar had this same significance in Babylonia, in China, in ancient Egypt, in Indonesia, in Europe during the Middle Ages. In ancient China there was a high imperial authority that supervised the drawing up of the calendar; and from Egypt a sort of textbook in the art of choosing days has come down to us. In general, it may be said that the calendar came into being on the basis of time intervals resulting from changes in natural phenomena, especially the movements of heavenly bodies. But another element entered into it. The periodicity of human life must also have played its part. A number of recent scholars, such as Kamerer and Swoboda, have shown that human life is subject to certain rhythmic fluctuations of vitality. This periodicity, determined by man's own nature, would account for a certain sequence of favorable and unfavorable days. It may be presumed that such periods played a part in the conception of these mythological calendars, and

1 [See the paper by Zimmer in this vol., pp. 40ff.—ED.]

the rhythm of psychophysically favorable and unfavorable days disclosed by modern scientists would explain why the calendar came to be taken as a book of destiny.

In addition to the temporal schema of the calendar, in which the sacral symbols of the Aztec scholar-priests were ordered in the picture manuscripts, there are also spatial schemas. According to Aztec mythology, the cosmos is divided into zones, or levels (Pl. IV): the heavens consist of thirteen, the underworld of nine layers. The number of these regions indicates—though I cannot here discuss this in detail—arithmetical relations with the moon. In this connection it is interesting to note that in the Egyptian "Book of That Which Is in the Underworld," the world of the dead is divided into twelve parts, which as in Mexico correspond to the number of the hours of night. The stratified structure of the world—here I follow Seler's interpretations—is expressed in Mexican pictographic representations showing the cosmos as a gigantic pyramid with stairs, resting upon the fanged edge of the maw of earth. This motif takes us to the Aztec temple pyramids (Pl. V), many of which—according to Seler—were images of cosmic phenomena and processes. There was one rite in which a man destined to be sacrificed was made to ascend slowly the steps of a temple pyramid. This ascent had cosmic significance, symbolizing the slow ascent of the sun in the firmament. Here an Oriental analogy comes to mind. In the ancient Orient the steps of the temple sanctuary were similarly conceived as an image of the cosmic ascent to heaven; according to Alfred Jeremias there was in Lagash, at the time of King Gudea (c. 2600 B.C.), a pyramid with steps, known as the "temple of the seven zones," the zones referring to cosmic spheres. There is also a Polynesian conception of cosmic strata, and in many other mythologies celestial and infernal levels are distinguished. Such conceptions are in part based upon astronomical, particularly lunar, phenomena. But another element enters into them. Adolf Bastian was first to point out that the cosmic levels and strata, such as we find among the Polynesians, demand a psychological interpretation along with the cosmographical and astronomical. To state this in terms consonant with the findings of our modern cultural psychology: cosmic levels in mythology symbolize levels of consciousness. To the subconscious with its dark animal impulses corresponds the subterranean region; to consciousness sublimated and exalted to intuitive, ecstatic states correspond the celestial regions; to the waking consciousness finally corresponds the terrestrial region. We find a late echo of such conceptions in Dante's *Divine Comedy*, in which the mountain of Purgatory with its gradations corresponds to our "levels." And we may take it as one more echo when Romano Guardini writes in his little book *Von heiligen Zeichen:* "When we mount the steps [of the church], it is not only our feet that mount, but our whole being;—we mount spiritually as well." In such insights we find confirmed what may be taken as the basic trait of mythical thinking, namely that a perception which to us splits into a psychological or subjective component on the one hand and an objective component on the other, presents itself to the mythological mind, the mythologically thinking man, as a single unit. In myths and in cultic actions based on a mythological attitude both a subjective and an objective content is inherent. This is a fundamental insight of cultural psychology, an insight which at one stroke clears up a vast number of baffling questions. Cosmology is at the same time psychology, and cosmic phenomena become the correspondences of psychological life.

In his penetrating investigations Konrad Theodor Preuss has pointed to the transformation of darkness into light as a motif running through the whole of Aztec religion. In manifold cults and myths we find symbolizations of the change from dark beings into light. Light, in line with what we have elucidated above, is to be taken in a twofold sense: first in an astronomical-physical sense as an illumining force, but at the same time as an inner force, the force of inner illumination.

This brings us to one of the most venerable figures of the Aztec pantheon, Quetzalcoatl (Pls.VI–IX), who has sometimes been designated as the savior of the Aztecs. In function, Quetzalcoatl is primarily the wind god who, according to one legend, blows up storms to clear the road for the rain gods. Here we shall leave open the question of any analogy between this "wind" and our concept of the *pneuma*. Quetzalcoatl, another saga tells us, founded in olden times a realm of beatitude, plenty, and growth. There were turquoises and other jewels in abundance; prince and people lived in sanctity, atonement, and purification. In this realm the calendar and the sciences of the priests were invented; colored cotton grew in the fields; the ears of the corn and the pumpkins were the size of a man. But Prince Quetzalcoatl succumbed to temptation and sinned. He was given a beverage which he took for a potion of immortality but which merely made him drunk. By this infringement of the sacred injunction of abstinence, he forfeited his happiness and lost his kingdom. He departed from it, taking with him—

as the legend tells us—picture manuscripts, songs, and flutes. He traveled eastward toward a locality called the "place of burning," that is to say, place of sacrifice. With him went a strange host of hunchbacks and dwarfs, who died miserably on their way through the snowy mountain regions. At the edge of the celestial water (the sea), Quetzalcoatl began to weep and lament. He cast off his plumed headdress and his turquoise mask and voluntarily consumed himself with fire. His ashes scattered to dust and turned into many kinds of birds with brilliant plumage, and his heart was transformed into the morning star. From the standpoint of nature mythology, we may designate Quetzalcoatl as the moon: the waning moon which at the end of the month dies under the beams of the morning sun, for the moon like the god's heart seems to turn into the morning star, that rises just as the moon vanishes. But this does not complete the mythological characterization of Quetzalcoatl. In the pictographic books he is often represented with the instruments of mortification and of sacral blood-letting, a bone dagger and the point of a maguey leaf—the instruments that prepare the road to inner illumination through ascetic torment. All these motifs make it understandable that Quetzalcoatl should sometimes appear split into a living figure, or one destined to life, and a dead figure, or one destined to death. In the codices we often find him represented in this duality, as god of life and of death (Pl. IX). This again is expressive of his relation to the moon, which in waxing symbolizes life; in waning, death.

Frequently Quetzalcoatl becomes the god pure and simple. As Seler once said in his commentary to the Borgia Codex, even these polytheists "amid the swarming abundance of their gods, surmised a unity in their being." Seler presumes that there existed in Mexico a school of priests who worshiped Quetzalcoatl as the original creator of the world, the god of generation and the creator of man. Quite consonant with this theory is the legend that Quetzalcoatl once took a bone from the god of the underworld, crushed it, and mixed it with blood which in ritual manner he took from his penis. The mixture yielded the substance from which the first human pair were formed.

In another legend Quetzalcoatl is the son of a pair of primal gods. This pair—in the opinion of Seler—may be taken to represent heaven and earth. The primal god is heaven, which arches over the earth and fecundates it with its sunbeams and rain. The primal goddess is the earth, stretched out beneath him, which receives the seed from him. The son born of the two is the air that lies between them. I have already referred to Quetzalcoatl as the wind god. Other peoples, such as the Maoris of New Zealand and the ancient Egyptians, also have myths in which heaven and earth are separated by the air god. In Babylonia we find a similar cosmological triad in Apsu, the primal father, Tiamat, the primal mother, and Mummu, the son-emanation. As early as 1922, in the first volume of my book on Mexico, I pointed to the analogy between such doctrines and the triad *anima, corpus, spiritus* as expounded in hermetic philosophy. But to discuss this in detail would take us too far.

All these characteristic traits of Quetzalcoatl are highly interesting from the standpoint of the psychology of religion. For in him we find qualities otherwise encountered among peoples at more advanced stages of development only in the revered figures of founders of religions. It is safe to say that in the mythology of the Aztecs we discern the first intimations of a process which, if it had been allowed to continue unobstructed, might have given rise to a full-fledged redeemer religion. But the Aztec religion did not progress far toward unification. No dominant doctrine emerged, embracing all religious themes in a distinct order. This is particularly evident from the following: I have said that in some legends Quetzalcoatl was represented as the son of a pair of primal gods. But there is a saga of the creation which scarcely accords with this. In one of the Old Norse myths the world was created from the body of the giant Ymir, and we find similar conceptions in ancient Mexico. The legend has it that two gods fashioned the world from the body of the goddess Atlatentli, making trees from her hair, rivers and caverns from her mouth, mountains and valleys from her nose and shoulders. We are reminded of an Indian legend in which the gods at a great feast sacrificed the primal man Purusha. His spirit became the moon, his eye the sun, his mouth the weather god, his breath the wind, his head the heavens. According to a south Chinese saga, the first man or demiurge was P'an-ku, whose breath when he died became the wind, his voice the thunder, his left eye the sun, his right eye the moon, his hair the vegetation that covers the earth. All these sagas of the creation reveal a conception to which we find numerous analogies elsewhere. Paracelsus once said: "And it is a great thing—consider for once, that there is nothing in heaven or in earth that is not also in man." [2] And Swedenborg

---

2 [From the *Paramirum, c.* 1535; tr. Norbert Guterman in *Paracelsus: Selected Writings,* ed. Jolande Jacobi (2nd edn., New York, 1958), p. 45.—Ed.]

writes: "The whole heaven is in the human form and likeness and is therefore called the Grand Man, and . . . each member of the human being has a
relation with this Man or with heaven." [3] In the *Ascension of Isaiah* we
read: "And as above so on the earth also: for the likeness of that which is
in the firmament is here on the earth." [4] And the Buddha says: "I proclaim
to you that in this animated body no more than a fathom in height, the
world dwells." [5]

The conception ultimately underlying these cosmogonies is again a reflection of a psychological process in which cosmic events and phenomena
become symbols and images of subjective states. The mythological man
takes cognizance of the world as an image, an analogy of the self. In myths
the world is created from subjective—that is, corporeal—parts, since the
objective and cosmic actually does take form in the consciousness as an
analogy and counterpart to the subjective.

I come now to certain other sagas and symbols which in a very interesting
way express the same "heavenly-earthly parallelism," as Jeremias once
said with regard to Babylon.

In the legendary West, an Aztec saga relates, there is a hole in the earth,
from which in olden times the races of men came forth, just as a child issues
from its mother's womb. Another saga has it that in the age that was known
as the "water sun," there were giants—and we are reminded of the small
child overawed by the existence of people so much larger than himself.

A similar interpretation gives us a key to the understanding of two of
the strangest Aztec cults. There was a festival consecrated to Xipe Totec
(Pls. X, XI), a god who appears to present certain parallels to Quetzalcoatl.
In this feast a man was sacrificed to the god. The victim was flayed, and
one of the priests donned the skin. This cruel sacrifice, as Seler observed,
occurred in the spring, when the rains resumed and the earth began to take
on a greener hue. Seler correctly interpreted the flaying of the skin and its

3 [Swedenborg, *Heaven and Hell*, par. 94 (cf. Everyman's Library, p. 40).—ED.]
4 [*Ascension of Isaiah* 7:11, tr. R. H. Charles (Translations of Early Documents, Ser. I;
London, 1917, p. 46).—ED.]
5 [Cf. *Sangyutta-Nikaya*, I, 62, in *The Book of the Kindred Sayings*, tr. Mrs. C. A. F. Rhys
Davids (Pali Text Society Translation Series, 7; London, 1950), p. 86: "It is in this
fathom-long carcase, friend, with its impressions and its ideas that, I declare, lies the
world. . . ." Also Edward Conze, *Buddhism: Its Essence and Development* (Oxford,
1951), p. 97: "Within this very body, mortal as it is, and only six feet in length, I do
declare to you are the world and the origin of the world, and the ceasing of the world,
and likewise the Path that leads to the cessation thereof."—ED.]

donning by the priest as a symbolization of the earth's renewal in vegetation. This accounts for the objective side of the rite. But such sacrifices would remain unintelligible to us without some insight into the motive behind them, the appeasement or relief of tension which they confer—in other words, their subjective aspect. Frobenius once said that the rites and usages of mythological man were in a sense his means of expressing things that for us are reflected in speech, thought, consciousness. We speak of "burying a quarrel," but mythological man (as is shown in American and African examples) often enacts an actual symbolic burial. How then, in the light of these remarks, shall we account for the flaying rite to which we have just referred? To me it seems presumable that one meaning of this cruel rite comes very close to the thought expressed in the German phrase "to slough off the old Adam and put on a new skin." What with us is a mere figure of speech was acted out by the Aztecs in dire earnest in a sacrificial rite that really conveyed a sense of regeneration and renewal.

A similar symbolic significance attaches to another rite of a far gentler nature. I have in mind a ritual ball game (Pl. XII). At certain prescribed times, this game was played in a walled-in court not far from the temple. These ball courts were shaped like a double T, with stone rings affixed to the lateral walls. The purpose of the game was to throw the ball through the stone rings. In an objective sense—I follow Seler—the flight of the ball symbolized the sun, which rises heavenward from the night or earth and then is driven downward from heaven to the night or earth. And the game seems also to symbolize the passage of the moon through the heavens: when in waning the moon approaches the sun, it loses, while it wins when it takes on roundness in the western sky and becomes a full moon. In its subjective aspect, the flight of the ball through the ring offers a parallel to the sexual act. And an indication of this meaning is the cry with which the onlookers are said to have honored the successful player: "He is a great adulterer." From this we are led to assume that the strange usage was originally a kind of fertility rite.

Let us now look back over our examples of the cultic and mythical symbolism of the Aztecs. We have recognized a multiplicity of forms and meanings, a multiplicity which, as I have said, had not yet been simplified into the abstraction of a homogeneous, dominant doctrine. Seemingly contradictory and mutually exclusive conceptions existed side by side. But everywhere we have discerned the same form of imagery, characterized by a subjective-objective parallelism. As the cults have shown, this religious experience brought forth specific techniques of release and redemption. Formerly we were quite baffled by such techniques and attitudes and were far too prone to dismiss them as senseless superstition. But modern cultural psychology has begun to penetrate the meaning underlying such usages. Today we know that there are two fundamentally different but equally meaningful attitudes.

The one attitude leads to technical actions which are its specific though not exclusive manifestation. Here *homo faber* endeavors to master the world in its objective aspect.

The other attitude leads to magical actions, which again are its specific but not exclusive manifestation. Here *homo divinans* seeks mastery over the world in its subjective aspect.

The recognition, appreciation, and understanding of the two attitudes has vastly broadened our horizons. I have endeavored to show to what high degree the paths and techniques of religious salvation were already shaped in the cult and myth of a people which had not yet attained to such higher forms of abstraction as we find in later cultural stages, for example in China and India. And I hope I have succeeded in giving some insight into the religious life of an extremely remote and alien stage, which created very strange forms of redemption and appeasement, forms which precisely by their strangeness admonish us that if we would be truly world-embracing in our attitudes, we must not formulate too narrow a concept of redemption. For as Bastian once said, the ultimate goal of the study of cultures is to see the positive everywhere.[6]

6 [Among Professor Danzel's works on this theme, as cited by him: *Babylon und Altmexico; Gleiches und Gegensätzliches* (Mexico City, 1921); *Mexiko I: Grundzüge der altmexikanischen Geisteskultur; Altmexikanische Bilderhandschriften* (Hagen and Darmstadt, 1922); *Mexiko II: Kultur und Leben im alten Mexiko; Mexikanische Plastik* (Hagen and Darmstadt, 1922); *Kultur und Religion des primitiven Menschen* (Stuttgart, 1924); *Magie und Geheimwissenschaft in ihrer Bedeutung für Kultur und Kulturgeschichte* (Stuttgart, 1924); *Handbuch der präkolumbischen Kulturen in Lateinamerika* (1927; 2nd edn., Hamburg and Berlin, 1937); *Gefüge und Fundamente der Kultur vom Standpunkte der Ethnologie (Prolegomena)* (Hamburg, 1930); *Symbole, Dämonen und heilige Türme. Bildtafeln zur ethnologischen Religionskunde und Mythologie* (Hamburg, 1930).—ED.]

John Layard

The Malekulan Journey of the Dead [1]

1. Introduction

The subject of this lecture is the belief in a Journey of the Dead, prevalent among the natives of the island of Malekula, in the Melanesian archipelago of the New Hebrides, among whom I have worked.

Seldom has a statement on religion been so illuminating as Professor Jung's observation that those taking part in a ritual performance rarely seem to have conscious awareness of its full significance; for what gives a myth or rite its inner power is the fact that it is rooted in the unconscious. This serves to explain how fruitless it often is to seek to wrest from the natives a concrete interpretation of their myths. But it also imposes a grave responsibility upon those who attempt their own interpretations. Consequently, in speaking of the Journey of the Dead in Malekula I shall try as far as possible to let the facts speak for themselves, giving a minimum of psychological interpretation, and that only on the sociological level, but amplifying the material to a certain extent by means of references to related cultures, leaving for future works the discussion of some deeper problems which it suggests.

---

1 [This paper was given at the 1937 Eranos meeting in German as "Der Mythos der Totenfahrt auf Malekula." The English original having been lost during the war, the German version has been retranslated into English by Ralph Manheim and revised by the author. Dr. Layard has since published a general review of mythology from the aspect of external observation as performed in the small Malekulan island of Vao, entitled *Stone Men of Malekula* (London, 1942). He is now engaged on a more detailed psychological study of religion in the neighboring Malekulan island of Atchin, including the nature and meaning of sacrifice as it is there conceived, of which some of the beliefs cited in this article form part of the mythological background. Subsequent papers by Dr. Layard published on this subject in the *Eranos-Jahrbuch* have been "The Incest Taboo and the Virgin Archetype" (1945), "The Making of Man in Malekula" (1948), and "Identification with the Sacrificial Animal" (1956).—ED.]

It is now generally recognized that megalithic culture such as is found in Malekula is by no means an isolated phenomenon there, but forms part of a network of similar cultures diffused by means of maritime migrations which spread over a large part of the globe in late neolithic or early Bronze Age times (the Malekulans have implements of polished stone and shell) and which fused with pre-existing cultures wherever it went. Some features of it, therefore, in places like Malekula, may be taken as primitive, while others may have become degraded by being misunderstood or taken too superficially by peoples unable to grasp their deeper meaning as conceived or developed in the centers of higher culture in which they had their origin. I shall make no attempt in the present paper (except in one instance in which I discuss the labyrinth designs) to disentangle this aspect of the problem, but I should like the fact to be borne in mind while I describe the Journey of the Dead as part of the religious system of these Pacific islanders.

Megalithic Culture in Malekula; the Ritual Cycle Called the Maki

The island of Malekula is approximately sixty miles long and includes a number of cultural districts. In all these districts social affairs are guided by public opinion, the wielding of which lies chiefly in the hands of the older men of the tribe. There are chiefs only in a single tribe, the Big Nambas, who inhabit the northeastern plateau of the island. It should not be supposed that each cultural district has only one language; at least two hundred languages or separate dialects are spoken on the island.

The district in which I chiefly worked was the minor archipelago of small coral islands lying off the northeastern coast of Malekula. These islands, Vao, Atchin, Wala, Rano, and Uripiv, locally called the "Small Islands," form a cultural unit. The inhabitants call themselves "Sea Folk" in contrast to the inhabitants of the main island of Malekula itself, most of whom have no canoes. Each of the Small Islands has its own dialect. None of them is larger than a half-mile square, and the population of each ranges between four and five hundred souls. At the time of my visit, the population of Atchin was about four hundred.

Although the culture of each district, village, or small group of villages within a district differs significantly from that of the neighboring groups, one feature is common to all: the megalithic culture manifested in a great public rite, which in the different districts is called *Maki*, *Mangki*, or *Menggi*. This rite is closely related to the belief in a Journey of the Dead, of which

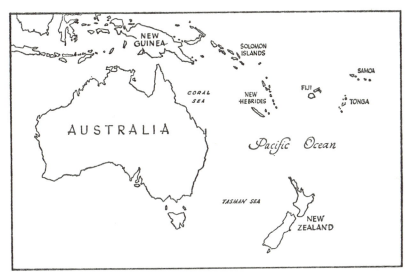

Sketch map showing the position of the New Hebrides

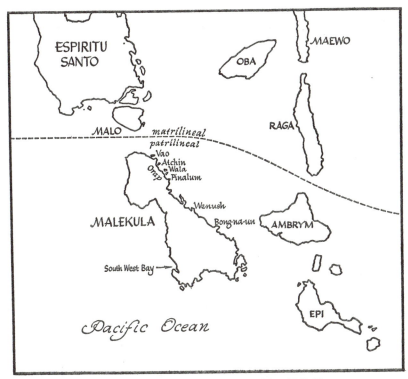

Sketch map of part of the northern New Hebrides

Illustrating the Journey of the Dead from the Small Islands (Vao, etc.), down
the coast of Malekula, and across to Ambrym, where the volcano is.

I shall here give three versions recorded by myself from the Small Islands of Vao, Atchin, and Wala, and a fourth recorded by a colleague from South West Bay on the Malekulan mainland.

In the opinion of the natives, this megalithic culture was introduced from outside. All the coastal districts have legends telling of its introduction by immigrants who arrived in canoes and then went elsewhere. In South West Bay these immigrants are said to have been white-skinned, with aquiline noses. Their chief—for the immigrants had chiefs, whereas the present inhabitants have none—is said to be buried sitting on a stone seat in a stone chamber. This chamber was covered with a mound of loose stones and earth. In Europe we should call this a tumulus or round barrow. The body of this chief is said to be incorruptible. In the fertility rite, on which the health and survival of the people are said to depend, the main observance consists of displaying images of his body and that of his wife, and in reanimating them by ritually washing them. The chief's ten grandsons are said to have been incarnated in stones, which still exist and serve as seats for the heads of the ten families of which the clan consists to sit on during their assemblies.[2]

In Atchin the corresponding ten brothers are represented to this day by ten natural coral blocks standing on the shore.

In order to place our account of the Journey of the Dead in its proper setting, I shall begin with a brief description of the megalithic ritual in the Small Islands; this ritual, as has been said, is closely related to the Journey of the Dead. If we enter that part of the village in which the dwelling huts are situated, the first stone monuments to be encountered are two stone seats or dolmens (Pl. I*a*) on either side of the entrance to each of the ten lodges or "men's houses," which are the assembly places for the male members of the ten great families into which each Atchin village is divided. From the roofs of these lodges hang the jaws of the tusked boars that were sacrificed when each lodge was consecrated. These stone seats are used by the older men of the clan, a practice found in many megalithic cultures; among the Nagas in Assam, the spirits of the dead are said to sit on similar stone seats.

These Small Island lodges are in one sense temples of the dead as well as of the living, being surrounded by the graves of departed ancestors. We

2 See A. Bernard Deacon, *Malekula: A Vanishing People in the New Hebrides* (London, 1934); and my "The Making of Man in Malekula," pp. 216, 272ff.

often hear of primitive peoples' fear of the dead. The dead are feared in Malekula only when they have been offended by omission or neglect of the proper attentions due them. They then punish the offender with sickness or death; they cause his pigs to sicken and his crops to fail. But the prevailing sentiment toward ancestors is one of veneration, gratitude, and affection, and the favorite place of assembly for the male members of the tribe is in the proximity of their graves.

Each lodge is surrounded by a stone wall, in which there is an entrance, called "shark's jaw," symbolically expressing the consecrated character of the enclosed space, which may be entered only by men.

Other stone monuments in the form of dolmens or monoliths are to be found in various parts of the village, but chiefly lining the sides of the dancing ground. The most important rite for which they are erected is the above-mentioned Maki, a ritual cycle extending over a period of from fifteen to thirty years, corresponding to a generation of men. There is no aspect of the native's life that is not intimately bound up with it. It has to do both with society and with the individual's aspiration toward a future life, which is its basic function, and one of its main features is the sacrifice of numerous tusked boars in order to propitiate and thereby circumvent the destructive power of a cannibalistic Female Devouring Ghost, whose object is to "eat" or annihilate the spirits of the dead and thus prevent them from accomplishing the long journey to the Land of the Dead.

The ritual cycle as a whole falls into two halves. In the first half of the Maki on Vao the most important sacrificial monument is a large dolmen. This dolmen represents, first, a stone tomb; secondly, the Cave said to be inhabited by the Female Devouring Ghost through which the dead man is supposed to pass on his journey to the Land of the Dead; and thirdly, the womb through which the living achieve rebirth by means of sacrifice. A wooden image is set up in front of the dolmen, representing all those ancestors who have previously performed the rite. The wooden image serves as a support for the roof erected over the dolmen. The rooftree resting on it ends in a carved representation of the mythical nighthawk, which is believed to hover and to preside over all these rites. No part of this composite erection is ever removed, and every dancing ground is littered with the rotting remains of many such shrines.

In the second part of the ritual cycle on Vao, the sacrifice is performed on a stone platform which is set up directly behind the shrines. The sacrificer mounts the platform, sacrifices a tusked boar, kindles a new fire, and assumes a new name to symbolize the fact that he has entered upon a new life. This division of the ritual cycle into two halves corresponds to a similar duality in the beliefs concerning the Journey of the Dead which the departed must undertake. In the first part of the rite the maternal uncles of the sacrificer bar his way to the dolmen, just as the Devouring Ghost, female in certain regions, bars his way into the Cave of the Dead; both the mother's brothers (in the rite) and the Female Devouring Ghost (in the belief) have to be propitiated by an offering of tusked boars. In the second part of the rite, the fire which the sacrificer lights on the stone platform parallels the belief that the ghosts of the dead of high Maki rank, after having successfully passed through the Cave of the Dead, proceed to a final Home of the Dead on an active volcano on the neighboring island of Ambrym.

In order to throw light on the significant variations in this ritual cycle in its relation to the Journey of the Dead, it is necessary at this point to refer to one fundamental aspect of native social organization, namely the kinship system. In the Small Islands this system is based on a number of what are called "open" kinship sections, not unlike those found in some parts of Australia, founded on a simultaneous recognition of matrilineal and patrilineal descent. Overt matrilineal descent dominates social organization in many parts of Melanesia, including the islands immediately to the north of Malekula. The sketch map on page 117 shows the division between the overtly matrilineal culture to the north and the overtly patrilineal culture to the south. The patrilineal organization, which according to native accounts infiltrated from the south many generations ago, is now the dominant factor in almost all parts of Malekula, though the matrilineal element also subsists side by side with it in the regulation of the kinship system.

Corresponding to the two aspects of kinship organization, matrilineal and patrilineal, that are thus intermingled in northeastern Malekula, there are two forms of Maki rite, an older and a later. The great dolmen that is erected on Vao during the first half of the rite belongs to the older, more matrilineal form.

I have mentioned the close relationship between the dolmen and female fecundity giving the hope of rebirth. With the introduction of overt patrilineal descent into the Small Islands and particularly into Atchin and Wala, the great dolmen was replaced in the first half of the rite by ten Maki shrines (Pl. II), each of which, though still containing a dolmen, consists chiefly of a monolith representing the male ancestors and having in front of it a wooden ancestor image (Pl. III). The shrine is covered by a roof, the tree of which is as usual carved in the likeness of the mythical nighthawk. The wooden image and the monolith together represent the sacrificer's male ancestors, and when he is dead they will represent him too. A study of the corresponding rites in other parts of Malekula shows that for the higher ranks in the sacrificial hierarchy the monolith itself is carved to represent a human figure—that is to say, it becomes a portrait statue. With the deterioration in material culture that set in after the early waves of megalithic immigration, the natives lost the art of working stone and transferred these images to wood. Thus the plain monolith, in conjunction with the carved wooden image, represents the male ancestor. Neither of the two is effective without the other, and the rope with which the sacrificial tusked boar is attached to the monument must be tied round them both. In time, the wooden figure rots and only the stone remains as the dwelling place of the ancestral spirit, particularly that of the last in the long line of sacrificers for whom the stone was set up.

For a better understanding both of the Maki and of the Journey of the Dead, it will be necessary to say a few more words concerning the sacrificial animals, the tusked boars (*Sus papuensis*). Although these animals are eaten after the sacrifice, they are raised primarily not for their flesh but for their tusks. The natives artificially promote the growth of these tusks by knocking out the upper canines, so that the tusks grow unobstructed, curving first upward, then back, then downward again, in such a way as to pierce first the cheek and then the jaw, finally reappearing in front to form a complete spiral.

If the boar does not die, the growth of tusks continues until a second or even a third turn of the spiral is made. The boars thus reared are here referred to as circle-tuskers, or double or triple circle-tuskers, as the case may be. The growth of a good tusker takes at least seven years. Rearing and trading in tusked boars constitutes one of the chief preoccupations of the natives. Without a tusked boar with which to propitiate the Female Devouring Ghost, no man can be reborn or attain to the Land of the Dead. Without such boars he cannot marry—for boars serve also as bride price in the acquirement of wives, and the value of this form of currency is estimated according to the length of the tusks. Without tusked boars the native would be lost, both spiritually and socially.

To sacrifice these animals the natives strike them on the head with a special wooden instrument, wonderfully carved. After the sacrifice the jaws are removed and exhibited on racks to enhance the glory of the sacrificer. On certain important ritual occasions, as many as five hundred of these valuable animals may be sacrificed on a single day.

Identification of Sacrificer with Victim

In some parts of Malekula human sacrifice occasionally takes place as well as that of tusked boars. In the village of Matanavat on the north coast, bastards are raised for this very purpose, and on reaching the age of puberty are prepared, though without their knowledge, for sacrifice.[3] On the Small Islands only enemies wounded or killed in battle are used for this purpose. The relation between human and animal sacrifice is made clear by the fact that in warfare every effort is made to keep wounded enemies alive until they can be brought home to the village, where they are sacrificed on a stone platform, just as though they were boars. But if the death of an enemy is thought to be imminent on the field of battle, a stone altar (dolmen) is hastily erected just where he lies, and the victor ritually "sacrifices" his victim on it, kindles a new fire, and takes an appropriate new name.

The identification of sacrificer with victim is a further fact of the highest importance if we wish to understand fully the idea underlying the Journey of the Dead. It is implicit in every sacrificial rite. In Malekula human and animal victims are interchangeable. But this is not all, for the sacrificer himself is in a deeper sense also the victim. The most striking proof that the sacrificer in sacrificing his tusked boar during the Maki rites is symbolically sacrificing himself is to be found in the circumstance that each successive new rank and title which the sacrificer assumes in the hierarchy of the protracted Maki ritual is one that has previously been conferred upon the boar he sacrifices, and which has thereby been already sanctified. For in the course of this ritual the ranks and titles are conferred first not on the man but on the animal, and the sacrificer, in sacrificing his boar, at one and the same time symbolically sacrifices what we may think of as part of his own animal nature and by this act also becomes himself sanctified in simultaneously acquiring the degree of sanctification previously bestowed upon the boar.

Thus the central act of the whole Maki is the *self-sacrifice* of a man who

3 Thomas H. Harrison, *Savage Civilisation* (London, 1937), pp. 38-39.

122

symbolically immolates part of himself in the form of his tusked boars, these most precious possessions which he has spent his life in raising, with which he ritually identifies himself.

The Devouring Ghost

So much for the basic sacrificial nature of the Maki rite, which represents the extravert aspect of religious life in Malekula; the introvert aspect is to be found, among other things, in the islanders' corresponding belief in the Journey of the Dead.

The chief figure in this Journey is a Devouring Ghost who bars the road to the new life. To make clear the peculiar nature of this being, I shall render literally a conversation with a native of the Small Island of Vao.[4] This conversation followed a discussion on the nature of a divine being named Taghar, who is at one and the same time (1) the creator of all men and things; (2) a man who arrives paddling a canoe and bringing the first tusked boars, yams, and coconuts; and (3) the principle of light, which as the "man in the moon" begets human children on the moon, who thence descend into and are born out of their mothers' wombs. In the course of the conversation, the notable fact came to light that this god, who has created men and foodstuffs and all other good things in the world, is not worshiped in any way; in fact, that no one gives him much thought, since he is always "good" and therefore need not be too much bothered about.

To the question "What being do you think of then?" came the answer "Of that other, of that which wishes to devour us as soon as we are dead."

"And what do you call that other?" "Le-hev-hev."

"Who is Le-hev-hev?" "Le-hev-hev means: That which draws us to It so that It may devour us."

On the island of Vao the natives do not know whether this Devouring Ghost is male or female; but it is interesting to note that in the matrilineal region to the north of Vao it is male, while in the patrilineal south, including the Small Islands of Atchin and Wala, it is female. In Vao, which lies between the two regions, we find a kinship system based almost equally on patrilineal and matrilineal descent, and here the sex of the being is unknown. For this interesting phenomenon I can find only a psychological explana-

4 Recorded by Jean Godefroy, S. M., former Marist missionary on Vao, in a series of articles entitled "Une tribu tombée de la lune," *Bulletin de l'Association Amicale des Anciens Élèves, Institution Libre de Combrée* (Angers, 1932-34). See my translation, with comments and additional material, in *Stone Men of Malekula*, pp. 218-39.

tion, namely that in those regions to the north, where consciousness is directed almost exclusively toward the female line of descent, the unconscious compensates for the overemphasis on the female aspect by experiencing the Devouring Ghost as male; while in the southern area, where consciousness is directed toward the male line of descent, the compensation of the unconscious produces a mythical female ghost. In Vao, where both lines of descent have equal weight, the unconscious does not know which to choose, and so the sex of the being remains unknown.

Another highly significant fact is that the general term used to designate old men of high rank is simply a variant of the word for the Devouring Ghost, namely *na-humbe* (*humb* = *hev*), showing that old men of high rank become *ipso facto* identified with the Devouring Ghost. This is of the utmost importance for an understanding of the native mentality. From the psychological standpoint it would suggest that the Devouring Ghost not only symbolizes each individual man's anima, but at the same time represents the reverse side of the social organization. This reverse side is, in the predominantly patrilineal Small Islands, the female element, which is heavily repressed in overt social organization and gives mythological expression to the nameless horror and self-accusation of a devouring monster dwelling in the unconscious, which has to be propitiated by sacrifice.

To return to our conversation. To the next question, "You say It wants to eat you? How? With Its teeth?" the answer was "No, not with Its teeth. It has no body. It is like a ghost, It's terrible . . . We are in great fear of It . . . It is to save ourselves from Le-hev-hev that we sacrifice our pigs, that we dance, that we perform all our rites." Thus the most important aspect both of the Maki ritual cycle and of the Journey of the Dead is the need to conciliate and propitiate this being, so that the sacrificer after his death can enter unhindered into a new life.

Just as, through the Maki ritual cycle, a man gains the possibility of a future life by sacrificing tusked boars, so also during his lifetime he must have in his possession a special boar for his relatives to sacrifice at his death, in order that his spirit may be protected against the Devouring Ghost. For this reason a man will never part with this special boar—later referred to as the "death pig"—which is his spirit's indispensable passport to the Land of the Dead.

During the ensuing mortuary rites, additional tusked boars are sacrificed, and it is said that these sacrifices are performed "to prevent the ghosts from tormenting us and haunting us, for they demand unceasingly to eat pigs." This makes it apparent that the Devouring Ghost is also a representative of all the long-dead ancestors, who are thus, in sociological terms, the real object of the natives' religious veneration and awe.

2. The Journey of the Dead

The encounter with the Devouring Ghost is, however, only one of the concepts connected with the dead man's journey to his future home. I recorded three different versions of the same mythological belief, from the Small Islands of Vao, Atchin, and Wala; and a colleague has recorded a fourth version from South West Bay.

The four versions differ considerably in details which at first glance might seem irreconcilable. But if we compare them with other characteristic cultural elements in the areas in which they are found, particularly with regard to differing forms of Maki ritual, we can perceive distinct stages of historical and psychological development.

As we have seen, the Maki in Vao falls into two parts, the chief sacrificial monument for the first part being the dolmen and for the second part the stone platform. We also know that a new form of Maki came to Atchin and Wala from the south, and that in this form of the Maki the great dolmen erected in Vao during the first part of the rite became replaced by other stone monuments, the most important of which was the monolith. In the various districts we find an exact parallel to all these facts in the development of beliefs regarding the Journey of the Dead.

The Vao Version [5]

I will speak first of the form current on Vao, the seat of the older form of Maki, lying nearest to the overtly matrilineal area of the northern New Hebrides.

We cannot here go into the highly complicated mortuary rites with which the ghost of the dead man is sped on his way; it need merely be stated that his body is buried in his paternal village, while certain objects from among his personal possessions are sent back in a canoe to his mother's village, to which, in one level of belief, his spirit also is said to return.

5 Parts of this section are taken from an article by the author entitled "The Journey of the Dead, from the Small Islands of North-eastern Malekula," in *Essays Presented to C. G. Seligman* (London, 1934).

At sunset the dead man is buried in a squatting position. His body is arranged in all the finery and insignia due to him on account of the rank he has achieved in the Maki rites. Immediately before burial, a communion feast is held in which a morsel of food is actually placed in the mouth of the dead man. This is the first of many subsequent communion rites, which do not concern us here. The body, wrapped in fine mats, is lowered into the grave; many pigs are then sacrificed, including the "death pig," which is thrown alive into the grave for the dead man to use as ransom to redeem his spirit from the Devouring Ghost, which will otherwise destroy it.

What is here called "dead man" is a literal translation of the Vao word *ta-mat* (Atchin *ta-mats*), since *ta* means "man" and *mat* (A. *mats*) means "dead." But in the native mind it has a wider connotation, which we render "ghost" but which the Malekulans think of as something that a man can possess even while he is yet alive, which we might term "spirit" or "soul" or a mixture of both. There is no clear distinction between the two, since the word indicates all that a man possesses of unseen psychic qualities, which are there recognized as resulting from sacrifice, both internal and external in the form of ritual. They are what some neighboring Melanesian islanders call *mana*, a word sufficiently familiar to us now in the West as indicating psychic power in this life, leading to survival in the next. It is such psychic quality giving the hope of immortality which the Devouring Ghost is jealous of and wishes to destroy. But the word *ta-mat* is used also for a corpse (the psyche's shell), and the natives' figurative view of this life after death is of the spirit in the form of a corpse reanimated and living on, always at the age at which it died, with the amount of *mana* that the man may have acquired while yet alive.

Beliefs as to what kind of existence the dead have when they die are as various as ours are, though there is a certain logic in what they say, namely that the body stays and rots in the grave in a man's father's village where he has lived all his life (i.e., in the cemetery surrounding the men's lodge to which he belonged and on the site of which he can be spoken to by his immediate descendants in a personal way), while of his immaterial essence one part, as we have seen, goes back to his mother's village. This is the matrilineal element which we may tentatively equate with the feminine "soul." But it is confidently believed that that part of him which has been transformed through sacrifice now seeks to join the spirits of all previously departed ancestors and merge with them in that spirit world which is the tribe's reservoir of psychic heritage that looks both backward and forward: back toward origins and, acting as the collective tribal conscience, forward toward a future life and individual immortality. This may be called "spirit," and it is this spirit part of a man which sets out on the Journey of the Dead into the other world, which is the "other world" of the living as well as of the dead, since it is they who have the premonition of it symbolized by the myth.

But since the myth is told in terms of the "dead man" himself undertaking this journey, we will not spoil the native figurative imagery by using any other term—bearing in mind, however, that in this terminology "dead" means "psychic," that which has come into being through sacrifice, which is a mystic concept for which the myth itself acts but as an outer garment.

Quite naturally the Devouring Ghost, symbolizing all that is retrograde and psychically mother-bound, is jealous of transformation which she thinks of as depriving her of her "natural" maternal rights over men's lives, and so she does her utmost to prevent it by what the natives think of as annihilating the man's spirit and thus hindering him from reaching his goal. We may ourselves think of her as being also the prime initiatress, by thus being known to challenge his psychic gains: and this thereby stimulates him to preserve them by undertaking this Journey to rejoin the ancestors who have similarly overcome her by seeing through her trickery, as she has also caused them to ward it off by repeated sacrifice throughout all their lives. But the native's conscious attitude is mainly a kind of mystic fear, which a man's own kinsmen help him finally to overcome by their last sacrifices for him during burial.

The myth has all the setting of an actual journey on foot down the familiar Malekulan coast. As the natives conceive it, the "dead man" or "ghost" first makes his way to the long, black-sand beach called Orap, situated on the Malekulan mainland between Atchin and Wala. Here he enters a cave called *Barang na Tamat*, "Cave of the Dead." As he goes in, his way is blocked by the Devouring Ghost Le-hev-hev, whose sex, as we have said, is there not known.

As the dead man's ghost tries to enter the Cave, Le-hev-hev pulls him back. But there is another mythical ghostly being, called Ta-ghar Lawo, an aspect of the benevolent creator-god Ta-ghar, who intercedes for the newcomer and says to Le-hev-hev: "Leave him alone. Let him come and join all his friends—in there" (indicating the interior of the Cave). Le-hev-

hev then releases the dead man's spirit, which at the same time presents her with the ghost of the pig sacrificed at his burial. If he had not such a pig, Le-hev-hev would devour him. The newcomer also pays a pig to Ta-ghar Lawo for having pleaded for him, and then goes inside the Cave "to join his dead friends who are gathered there."

He does not stay, however, but continues his lonely way for some forty miles down the coast until he comes at sundown to a promontory called Tsingon Bong-na-un, where he lights a great fire to attract the attention of a ghostly ferryman on Ambrym (where the volcano is); he also gathers a particular kind of seaweed and beckons with it, whereupon the ghostly ferryman pushes off from the beach on Ambrym in his ghost canoe, to fetch him over. Such ghostly craft are not canoes in anything but name, but simply any kind of flotsam floating on the water. The name of this ghost canoe was first given me as *wuwun*, which means "banana skin," but later it appeared that any other minute object floating on the water would serve the ghostly purpose as well. The ferryman now paddles over in his flotsam craft and takes the newcomer back with him to Ambrym, where he is escorted up to the big volcano called *Bot-gharambi*, "Source of Fire."

This is all that is known of the Journey of the Dead on Vao, except that the dead on the volcano dance all night and sleep all day. The variant current on Wala (to be referred to later) to the effect that the dead dance in the form of skeletons, that their bones fall apart and their heads roll to the ground at dawn, is vehemently denied on Vao.

The fiery path. There is still another account current on Vao, which reveals a certain mixture of the two episodes I have cited, according to which the fire flowing from the volcano seems to cover the whole of the dead man's path. I will now quote this version, because of the interesting light it throws on the attitude of the natives to fire.

According to this account, the boars that have been sacrificed are laid on the dead man's grave, and the "death pig" thrown into it in order to "buy the fire." To the question "What fire?" came the answer "The fire of Le-hev-hev."

"What does that mean: buying the fire of Le-hev-hev?" "That means that the dead man must pay Le-hev-hev not to devour him, but to leave him alone to follow the path of fire."

"Where is Le-hev-hev when the dead man's ghost arrives?" "It stands upright on the path of fire. It throws itself forward to devour us, but . . ."

"But what?" "But we give It the boars we have caused to be sacrificed for It. It throws Itself on them and devours them instead of devouring us."

"Does that mean that you would prefer walking in the fire to being devoured by Le-hev-hev?" "Indeed, yes."

Thus "walking in the fire"—that is to say, being inside the volcano—means beatitude, since to the native, fire means power and life, and the attainment of life after death in the volcano is the positive goal toward which every native strives. The same man had more to say of the volcano, which he called "the great fire of Le-hev-hev, the fire of chiefs [i.e., the narrator's term for those who have attained to the highest ranks in the Maki hierarchy]. It is there that Le-hev-hev sends the ghosts of 'chiefs,' the *na-humbe*."

Nor is there any fear, or even thought, of being burned in it, since to the question "Do your ancestors tell you that this fire burns them?" the emphatic answer was "No." We may compare this to the burning bush which was not consumed, in Exodus 3:2.

So much for the Journey of the Dead as it is described on Vao.

The Versions from Wala and Atchin

I have mentioned how for several generations a strong new patrilineal current had been coming in from the south, bringing new forms of Maki ritual to Atchin and Wala, thrusting the male principle of the monolith into the foreground in contrast to the dolmen, which in Vao symbolizes the womb and matrilineal kinship.

Corresponding to these new forms of ritual, new concepts have also entered into the beliefs concerning the Journey of the Dead. Above all, the Devouring Ghost has undergone a significant change. In the first place this Ghost no longer dwells in the Cave but on the rocky coast of Malekula at the spot from which the ghosts of the dead are ferried across to Ambrym. In the second place, this being is no longer a sexless "It" but is definitely female, the mother of ten mythical petromorphic brothers. She herself is likewise a Stone, a great block of natural coral standing on the rocky shore. This variant is in keeping with the late megalithic tendency, found not only in Malekula but also elsewhere, which represents the actual human dead in carved stone, but chooses natural stone blocks of superhuman dimensions to symbolize the greatness and unfathomable nature of mythological figures.

Some of the details of this later form of the belief as it is found in Wala are significant. Here the dead of high rank are wrapped in finely woven mats and buried either in the sitting or in the extended position. In either case they are, as in Vao, first dressed and decorated with the insignia of their rank in the Maki hierarchy. A bamboo stick, called *ne-row*, "measuring stick," is cut to the exact length of the dead man's body and laid beside him in the grave. Later this stick turns out to be a kind of magic wand, with the help of which the dead man divides the waters of the rivers he must cross in the course of his journey. At the same time a fowl is sacrificed, to be eaten at some later time by the four men who bury him. But here again it is the ghost of the fowl that plays the principal role, for the spirit of the dead man now takes the wand, and, slinging it over his shoulder with the ghost fowl hanging from the hinder end, makes its way on foot to the Cave of the Dead on the coast near a place called Orap, which in an Atchin version is said to lie at the foot of a high mountain.

Outside the Cave there grows a magic fruit tree known by the special name of *nu-wi men-men*. The first act of the dead man on arrival there is to gnaw at the bark of this tree. In the Atchin variant he eats the fruit of the tree. In some mysterious way the mourners at his grave at once become aware when he has done this—it occurs immediately after burial—and they feel relieved, cease weeping, and laugh, saying, "He has gone away now," meaning that he will not come back, "for he has gnawed the *nu-wi men-men* tree."

Outside the Cave there is also a stone, called *ni-wet wen-wen*, "the whistling stone." Having gnawed at the tree, the dead man shoulders the wand with the ghost fowl slung on the end of it and walks twice around the stone, softly whistling.

Then he enters the Cave. No Devouring Ghost here bars the way, nor is there any mention of meeting here with other dead. He walks right through the Cave, and coming out at the other end proceeds southward along the black-sand beach of Orap.

Halfway along the beach there is a river. When the dead man comes to it, he strikes it with his wand, and the waters part, retreating on either side to let him pass through and closing up again behind him when he has gone. He continues southward, until at the southern end of the beach he comes to a place called Wetu, "Stone," where there is a solitary upright stone called "Nose-devouring Stone." This stands alone in the sea and is a spirit.

a. *Sacrificial dolmen, Atchin*

b. *Profile of shrine, Atchin*

I

One of ten shrines in an Atchin village

The carved ancestor image is capped with a carving of a hawk, and
immediately behind it stands its monolith

Ancestor image, Atchin

Behind may be seen the monolith, covered by partly rotted roof

Stone mausoleum, Atchin

In the form of a shark, with its three fins

It is related that the ghost of a man from Vao was followed on his journey by two living Atchin women, who saw this stone rise up and hit the nose of the dead man with its finger, not in order to break it but to make it flat, which would mean to deprive him of his psychic masculinity, since noses are phallic symbols and a well-formed nose is prized as being symbolic of psychic strength. For this reason the dead man hurriedly presents the Stone with the ghost fowl he has been carrying with him. If he delayed in presenting it, his nose would be flattened. And if he had no ghost fowl to give, the Stone would devour him.

The exact route followed from here on is not known; the next fixed point is the promontory of Pinalum, where the dead man takes off the mats in which he was wrapped at burial. The people of this place frequently find the tassels of these mats lying about on the beach and say, "A dead man seems to have passed in the night." Next, he comes to a place called Wenush close to a promontory corresponding to the rocky coast of Bong-na-un in the preceding version. Here the deceased encounters the Devouring Ghost, whose name in Wala is *Le-saw-saw* (a philological variant of the Vao *Le-hev-hev*), and who dwells in a stone standing in the sea. This stone is also said to be a shark, and on it is perched a bird which in some way lures to it the passing ghost. If the dead man has no boar with which to ransom himself, he is devoured by it and drowned. In the ritual of initiation into manhood this ghost is represented by a giant mask. The mask, some twenty feet high, is carried before the assembled people, and the men shoot at it while the women weep. This takes place in the evening, evidently recalling the time of day when the dead man encounters the shark stone. The mask itself has a human face painted in geometrical design, surmounted by a tall, narrow superstructure, tapering off at the top, on which are represented in conventionalized design a shark, a bird, a crescent moon, and three pentacles.[6] The shooting of the Devouring Ghost is a symbolic act of deep psychological significance, symbolizing the overcoming of the Devouring Mother.

At Wenush, where the dead man has now arrived, there is a village of living people. Here he steals a brand from one of their fires when they are not looking, and with it lights his own beacon on the rocky coast. The ghostly ferryman on Ambrym sees the fire and paddles over in his canoe

6 [For an illustration of this, see my "The Making of Man in Malekula," *EJ 1948*, p. 254, fig. 5b.—J. L. (1959).]

to find out from what village the dead man hails. He does not ferry him over at once but first returns alone to Ambrym, to tell the former members of the dead man's village that one of their number is waiting on the other side. Then they all go over in their flotsam canoes to meet him, and in their company he finally reaches the Land of the Dead on the volcano there.

On the volcano the dead dance every night and all night long till the appearance of the morning star, when their heads fall off and their bones fall asunder until they join together again the following evening. The newly arrived ghost dances with them, but his head does not fall off till the seventh night after his arrival, when the body lying in its grave is believed to rot, and the mourners at home blacken their faces and begin the prescribed fasts.

Analysis of the Preceding Versions

a. *The Devouring Ghost.* We shall examine later some of the details of this version of the myth. I first want to stress the importance of the belief in the Devouring Ghost for everyday life. We may take as an example the story of the stone mausoleum which an Atchin native, an old friend of mine named Melteg-tò, built for himself (Pl. IV). This was some nine yards in length, built in the traditional Atchin way except for one entirely novel detail: he shaped it like a shark, with three great oval stones laid along the ridge to represent its fins. As we have seen from the description of the giant mask, the shark in the Wala version of the Journey of the Dead is one of several symbols for the Female Devouring Ghost. Melteg-tò not only erected his own mausoleum in this unusual shape, but, as is customary among old men, he performed while yet alive that part of his own mortuary rite called *metsen*, which signifies that a man is already symbolically "dead." This means that he has "made his soul" (*ra-mats*) sufficiently well through continual sacrifice to be considered worthy, from the psychic and ritual point of view, of joining the ancestral spirits while he is yet alive. Furthermore, by means of the fins affixed to his mausoleum, he made sure that after his physical death he would be one with the Devouring Ghost, in whose "body" in the form of a stone shark he intended his own body to be laid.

The shark aspect of the Devouring Ghost was an imported belief. A mausoleum with shark fins added to it had never before been built on Atchin, although the form was quite current on the Malekula mainland. But new customs are not imported with impunity; and when Melteg-tò fell sick shortly after completing this mausoleum, another old man came to him and told him he had had a dream, and that in this dream two ancestors had appeared and said that the reason for Melteg-tò's sickness was his unwarranted importation of a custom which hitherto had been unknown on Atchin. But Melteg-tò, very proud of his edifice—which moreover guaranteed his oneness with the Female Devouring Ghost—would not listen to the old dreamer. He continued, however, to be sick. Then another old man presented himself, this time from the other side of the Small Island, reporting a similar dream; but in this case the two ancestors had added that Melteg-tò would die of his sickness if he did not take his mausoleum down. Despite all this, Melteg-tò was not to be moved; nevertheless, his sickness took a turn for the worse, whereupon his son persuaded him to remove the shark fins from the tomb. He did so and recovered.

This story shows how deeply the belief in the Female Devouring Ghost stirs the imagination of the natives; and at the same time it hints at a transformation process connected with her. If I may suggest a psychological interpretation, I should say that in this late patrilineal myth, originating in male minds, the Female Devouring Ghost represents a kind of mother image. The sacrificer identifies himself with this mythological figure by taking her name; he fears and at the same time desires to be swallowed up by her. Hence it is the aim and purpose of his life to appease and win her over. To accomplish this, a man spends a large part of his life rearing and sacrificing tusked boars; and after his death, his spirit must purchase new life by offering her one last ghost pig. In Malekula the tusked boar acts as vehicle for a man's spiritual striving, and only by constant sacrifice can he hope to attain forgiveness for the "sin" of overcoming the mother image, involving the exclusion of women from the benefit which he strives to attain through his lifelong observance of the rites, and from his hope in a future life.

b. Two levels of belief. A brief analysis of this mythical Journey of the Dead shows first of all that it consists of two distinctly different parts, one of which has the appearance of being superimposed upon the other. The mere fact that in the Vao version the dead, although living on the volcano, are also present in the Cave, and that the dead man meets both Le-hev-hev and Ta-ghar Lawo there, shows plainly that formerly the Cave and not the volcano was the ultimate goal of the dead. This assumption is supported by the account recorded by Codrington from the overtly matrilineal region of northern Raga, where the Devouring Ghost—here, as to be expected, male—is located in a deep gorge in the interior of that island. In his account there is no mention of a volcano, though Raga is nearer than Vao to Ambrym. Thus it might have seemed at first reasonable to suppose that the earlier belief in an abode of the dead within the Cave had had a later myth of a Home of the Dead on the volcano superimposed on it.

On closer scrutiny, it becomes evident that these two levels of belief belong to two different psychic levels, sociologically expressed as matrilineal and patrilineal, in such a way that when the matrilineal element predominates the Home of the Dead is conceived of as being in a cave; while in those areas where patrilineal influence was on the increase the Cave came to be looked on only as the first stage in a longer journey to the volcano, which is, after all, only another more fearsome cave or crater spewing fire from the top of a high mountain. It seems that formerly, even on Atchin, only those who had attained to very high rank in the Maki ritual cycle were able to reach a Home of the Dead on the volcano, whereas the others who had not risen so high were doomed to remain within the Cave. Since the belief in a Home of the Dead in the volcano is connected with the later, monolithic, form of Maki, there can be little doubt that of the two simultaneous levels of belief, the one which places the abode of the dead within the Cave is the older or more primitive matrilineal one, and that the concept of a ghostly life on the more skyward volcano was a result of further development, which is in line with more highly developed psychic experiences and shows every sign of having been introduced later.

If we now compare the beliefs concerning the Journey of the Dead with the Maki ritual cycle, two points of similarity emerge.

1. There is an identity between, on the one hand, the Cave which the dead have to enter and, on the other hand, the dolmen in the first part of the Maki on Vao, which symbolizes the mother's womb to which in the Maki the sacrificer's access is barred by his maternal uncles, just as his path into the Cave is barred by the Devouring Ghost.

2. There is an identity of the volcano with the stone platform on which the sacrificer in the second part of the Maki ritual cycle must kindle a fire before assuming his new name, which corresponds to a second rebirth into a patrilineal world.

The connection between the stone platform and the patrilineal spirit striving ever upward is further demonstrated by the fact that the mythological tales dealing with the development of Maki ritual state that stone platforms were formerly so high that they approached the sky. In the ritual as it is performed today, the same upward striving is expressed when the sacrificer standing on the stone platform imitates the posture of a hawk in flight and sings a song about the stars.

c. Further comparisons. We know from archaeological evidence that in antiquity burial in a cave or tomb was more primitive than cremation, which came later; similarly we can observe in the Maki ritual that the sacrifice was (and is) first performed on the dolmen and later on the stone platform corresponding to the volcano.

The purpose of cremation in other places was to establish a union between the departed and the celestial world by means of the smoke. That the actual volcano on Ambrym, though real, had only a symbolical significance in the eyes of the natives is made clear by the following story. It is credibly reported that in the year 1903 a few old men of Wala and Rano took it into their heads to paddle in their canoes over to Ambrym in order to "buy the fire" of the volcano and "bring it back" with them and install it on top of the mountain nearest them, namely Mount Lalemp on the neighboring Malekulan mainland. In their opinion they were perfectly justified in speaking of "bringing it back" because, as they said, there had formerly been fire on Mount Lalemp, but the men of Ambrym had stolen it in order to magnify the power of their own volcano. To this end, the men of Wala and Rano assembled a whole fleet of seagoing canoes, laden with tusked boars with which to "buy" the fire. But after they had gone no farther than a nautical mile and a half, as far as the promontory of Pinalum, which is known as the gathering place of the ghosts of this whole region of Malekula, the ghosts objected violently, releasing winds and waves and creating such a storm that the little fleet found itself compelled to return home. And so the fire remained on Ambrym.

In the Wala variant of the belief in the Journey of the Dead, as compared with that from Vao, the Cave is relegated to the background, although this relic of former belief still survives in attenuated form. For there are in the Wala version no longer any dead living within the Cave, and the Devouring Ghost has left it too; she is now thought to dwell in a natural monolith standing on the rocky coast of Bong-na-un. This, as well as the fact that the Devouring Ghost, the shadowy adversary of the departed, is now definitely female, clearly reveals the influence of the later strongly patrilineal social form.

The number seven, referred to as the "seventh day" on which the dead man becomes fully initiated, is the resurrection number in the later, more patrilineal, form of megalithic culture on Malekula, in contrast to the number five, which was dominant in the older, more matrilineal, form. The falling off of heads is to be correlated with the later form of mortuary ritual in which the head is removed from the body and is preserved in a diminutive dolmen erected in the burial ground especially for this purpose, which is not done in the matrilineal area. The magic wand—an obvious "double" of the dead man, since it is cut to his own length—appears to represent his psychic or spiritual force, which can divide the waters of death, just as in the Old Testament the waters of the Red Sea were divided to let the people enter into their new life.

Some of these features strongly suggest comparison with more familiar facts, particularly the alleged incorruptible body of the "white-skinned" culture-hero in South West Bay lying within his tumulus.[7]

First I should like to point out that in this Journey of the Dead, conceived of as extending over a distance of more than forty miles, we find in dramatized form some of the motives implicit in the forms of many megalithic beliefs and mortuary monuments elsewhere. In the first part of the journey the Cave corresponds to the stone cist; the mountain over the Cave (in one version), to the mound of earth or tumulus covering it; the magic tree, to the tree of life so often found in close connection with it; and the water that common mortals cannot cross, to the well-known waters of the Styx, sometimes called the "waters of death."

The same motive, without mound and magic tree but with the later adumbration of cremation, occurs in the second part of the journey, in which the volcano is the ultimate goal, which also, though from a great height, opens into the earth; around the volcano lie the waters of death—here symbolized by the actual sea.

Both levels of belief allude to individuation rites (initiation into a higher state of consciousness), one superimposed upon the other. The belief found on Raga, that the dead have their home inside the Cave (corresponding with the fact that they are still overtly matrilineal), is of course found

7 [For detailed comment see my later contribution on this subject in "The Making of Man in Malekula," *EJ 1948*.—J. L. (1959).]

elsewhere, and this suggests that at least two megalithic waves reached Malekula. Professor S. H. Hooke (London University) has pointed out that if we compare these two versions with the religious forms of the ancient world, the older Malekulan version coincides closely with Egyptian matrilineal beliefs, but the later version shows similarity with the more complex and elaborate forms of Mesopotamian mythology. Professor Hooke is so convinced of these similarities that he has subjected the legends of Atchin and Wala to a thorough analysis, comparing them step by step with the epic of Gilgamesh, which deals with the hero's difficult progress in his quest for immortality.[8]

3. The Labyrinth Motive in the Journey of the Dead: Sand-tracings in South West Bay

Finally I should like to refer to a particular feature of the Journey of the Dead which does not occur in the versions so far recounted from the Small Islands off the northeast coast of Malekula but is recorded in a fourth one from South West Bay, at the opposite end of the Malekulan mainland.[9] This version belongs to a yet older belief in which the motive of the volcano is totally lacking. In all the versions so far discussed we have encountered the waters of death which the dead man must cross or pass around, but must not touch. In this fourth version the waters of life also occur. The encounter with the waters of death still takes place outside the Cave, and the ghost of the dead man overcomes this obstacle not by dividing the waters with his magic wand as in the Wala story, but simply by being wafted over them. His escape from this peril is followed by an encounter with the Female Devouring Ghost, who in this version sits at the entrance of the Cave. After he has withstood a certain test imposed upon him by her, the dead man enters the Cave and suddenly finds himself by the side of a sea channel. On the shore of this sea there grows a tree; climbing it, he dives into this water—the water of life—and swims to the other shore, where he joins the spirits of all those who have preceded him.

It is not, however, on these two waters that I propose now to concentrate,

---

8 S. H. Hooke, "Some Parallels with the Gilgamesh Story," *Folk-Lore* (London), XLV (1934), 195ff.

9 A. Bernard Deacon, "Geometrical Drawings from Malekula and Other Islands of the New Hebrides," *Journal of the Royal Anthropological Institute* (London), LXIV (1934), 129ff.

but I now wish to call your attention to the remarkable test to which the Female Devouring Ghost subjects the ghost of the dead man at the entrance to the Cave. She has drawn with her finger, in the sand, a geometric figure, and she sits beside it, waiting for the dead man to come. He sees her from a distance. He is confused at the sight of her, and loses his way. When he regains his path and approaches the Devouring Ghost, she rubs out half the design. The dead man must know how to complete it. If he succeeds,

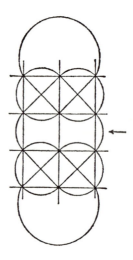

Fig. 1. "The Path" or "The Way." This is the design drawn in the sand by the Female Devouring Ghost. The figure consists of a single continuous line drawn around a framework of straight lines. As soon as the dead man approaches, the Devouring Ghost rubs out half the design, which the dead man must complete before he can pass through the middle of the sand-tracing in the direction indicated by the arrow. (South West Bay, Malekula.)

he passes through the lines of the geometric design into the Cave. If he does not succeed, he is devoured by this terrible ghost.

Figure 1 is an illustration of the design she draws, which the natives of all these islands also draw sometimes in the sand; it is called "The Path," which might be better translated "The Way." First a framework of straight lines is drawn. Around and within this framework a continuous line is traced; the finger must under no circumstances be taken off until the design is complete.

The question is, what does this drawing mean? To explain it, we must examine a number of sand-tracings which the present natives of Malekula and neighboring islands execute as a game of skill. Here I can mention only some of the most important types.[10]

Figure 2 is from the neighboring island of Oba; the framework (the thick

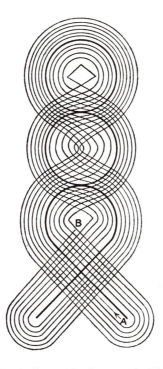

Fig. 2. The dark line indicates the framework. The continuous line begins at *A* and ends at *B*. (Oba Island.)

line in the figure) is in the form of a spiral. The rest of the drawing consists of a single continuous but not endless line, for it has both an end and a beginning. It begins at *A*, not far from the edge, and ends at *B*, almost at the center of the design.

10 Detailed interpretations are to be found in my article "Maze-Dances and the Ritual of the Labyrinth in Malekula," *Folk-Lore* (London), XLVII (1936), 123ff.

Figures 3a and 3b are from the same island. In 3a the framework is formed of a rectangle with two diagonals. The remainder of the drawing consists of a continuous line which meanders from point A to point B, constantly inter-

Fig. 3a. The framework is a rectangle, with corners connected by two diagonals. The rest of the design consists of a single continuous line beginning at A and ending at B. (Oba Island.)

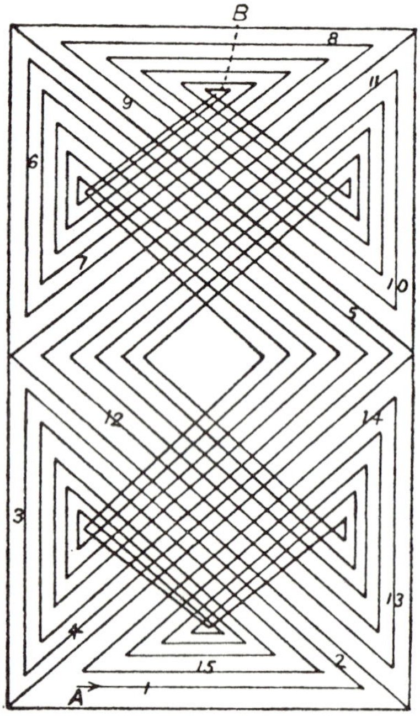

Fig. 3b. The framework is a rectangle, with sides connected by four diagonals. The single continuous line begins at A and ends at B. (Oba Island.)

secting itself during its course. Figure 3b is a more complex version of the same motive. In both cases the continuous line begins near the outer edge and ends somewhere near the middle.

The connection between these three figures and the first, called "The Way," will become clear when we examine the various stages of elaboration of the original labyrinthine motive, for all the evidence points to these designs essentially representing labyrinths in the true classical sense of the word. How is it that we thus find labyrinths in Malekula, and how do they come to be used as an essential test of the dead man's fitness to enter the Land of the Dead?

Figure 4 may give us a hint of their hidden meaning. This drawing is strikingly reminiscent of the church labyrinths of Europe, although there is no question here of European influence. In the Middle Ages such laby-

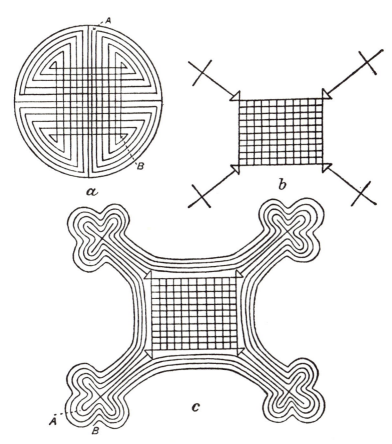

Fig. 4. The first part of the design to be drawn is *a*, of which the framework consists of a circle intersected by two lines at right angles to each other; here the continuous line begins at *A* and ends at *B*. Next, the outer contours are rubbed out and four crosses drawn at the corners, as shown in *b*. A continuous line is now begun at the tip of one cross and traced all around the figure four times from *A* to *B*, as shown in *c*. (Oba Island.)

141

rinths were used for penance; the penitent had to make his way through
them until he finally found Jerusalem, heaven, or a saint in the center. In
his work on the labyrinth, Hermann Güntert [11] demonstrates the close relationship between the structure of such labyrinths, together with the purpose
for which they were constructed, and that of the megalithic tombs of the
pre-Indo-Germanic peoples of the Mediterranean region.

What is the real meaning of these labyrinths? The best starting point for
such an inquiry is provided by the important discovery of C. N. Deedes,[12]
who, on the basis of detailed studies of Egyptian and Mesopotamian seals,
found that the labyrinths, from which the later mazes were derived, originally served to safeguard the kings' tombs against intrusion by uninitiates.
The author traces the architectural development of the tomb from simple
to complex form with labyrinthine passages.

With the removal of the mortuary temple to outside the tomb proper, the
labyrinth came in time to be transferred from tomb to temple, where "the
funerary rites of the dead king-god were performed. Here was his portrait
statue and here he was daily fed." [13] Summing up a considerable body of
evidence, the author declares:

> the Labyrinth was the centre of activities concerned with those
> greatest of mysteries, Life and Death. There men tried by every
> means known to them to overcome death and to renew life. . . .
> There the living king-god went to renew and strengthen his own
> vitality by association with the immortal lives of his dead ances-
> tors. . . . The break-up of the archaic civilisations, together with
> the diffusion and democratization of the ancient pattern of religious
> belief and ritual, resulted in degradation of ritual, confusion of
> beliefs, and loss of technical knowledge and ability to reproduce the
> old forms. . . . Labyrinth forms . . . were preserved as art-motives
> in decoration.[14]

The same observations apply also to Malekula. Here, too, the motivation
for the Journey of the Dead is to be sought not in the fact of death itself
but in the desire for the renewal of life through contact with the dead ancestors who are already leading a life beyond the grave.

The juxtaposition of tomb, labyrinth, and portrait statue of the dead,
which we find in Egyptian funerary monuments, can accordingly be brought
into a direct parallel with that Malekulan variant of the Journey of the

11 *Labyrinth; eine sprachwissenschaftliche Untersuchung* (Heidelberg, 1932).
12 "The Labyrinth," in *The Labyrinth*, ed. S. H. Hooke (London and New York, 1935),
    pp. 3–42.   13 Ibid., p. 14.   14 Ibid., p. 42.

Dead in which the female figure of the Devouring Ghost sits beside a stone with which she is identified; she sits outside the Cave, which represents the tomb, having before her a labyrinthine design, whose mazes the dead man, who is said to have lost his way, must understand if he is to pass through.

In the sand-tracings shown in Figures 2, 3, and 4 the continuous line runs parallel to itself. The most prevalent kind of design, however, is that seen in Figure 1, "The Way," a framework of straight lines at right angles to one another, with the continuous line curved in and out of it.

Figure 5a shows a second type of labyrinth design. Here the continuous

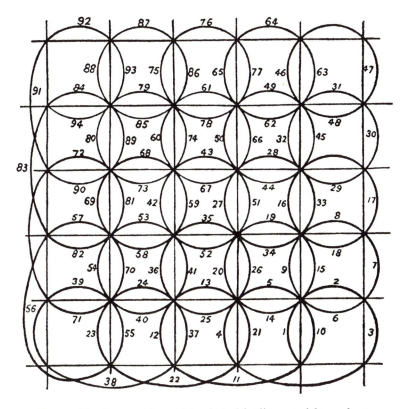

Fig. 5a. The framework consists of straight lines at right angles to one another. The remainder of the drawing is a single continuous line, beginning at one corner and ending in the opposite corner. The continuous line can be followed with the help of the numbers from 1 to 94. (Oba Island.)

line, instead of running from the outside inward toward the center, begins at one corner, passes diagonally across the frame, intersecting itself over and over again, and ends in the opposite corner. This is a first step in the evolution of the labyrinth motive whose very essence consists of a striving from outside inward toward the center; here the basic concept of a passage toward the center is replaced by the new idea of a passage through the labyrinth toward some goal beyond it. This corresponds to a similar process in Egypt, where the labyrinth at first surrounded the tomb itself, but later became a temple outside the tomb, whose complicated entrance it now constituted.

Unfortunately, most of the sand-tracings here recorded from Malekula have been redrawn for purposes of reproduction by a professional draftsman using compass and ruler—implements which, it goes without saying, are unknown in Malekula. Figure 5b is a sand-tracing similar to 5a but made by a native of Atchin and recorded by myself. Apart from the fact that this freehand design is far more beautiful than any Europeanized and conventionalized mechanical redrawing, one interesting feature of it is that the continuous line does not pass through the intersections of the framework but curves around them like a man adroitly turning a sharp corner. If it is true that these sand-tracings are derived from architectural maze or labyrinth forms, it would appear that the framework represents the basic structure of an actual labyrinth, while the continuous line symbolizes the path followed by one who enters it. While the actual knowledge that the continuous line itself represents the mazelike path through the labyrinth has evidently been lost, the natives nevertheless remember that it has something to do with a path or "way" which the dead man must find out and travel along in order to reach the Land of the Dead and of the future life; and they also realize that this path is in some way connected with the geometric figure.

Since the native has lost the knowledge of the identity between the "path" and the continuous line, and since the idea of "confusion" is here associated less with the "path" than with the Devouring Ghost, at first sight of whom the deceased is so confounded that he loses his way, the geometric sand-tracing itself has lost its original shape as depicting a true labyrinth, with the continuous line representing the actual Way. But since it is still known that this sand-tracing in some way represents a maze, the "test" sand-tracing called "The Path" or "Way," drawn by the Devouring

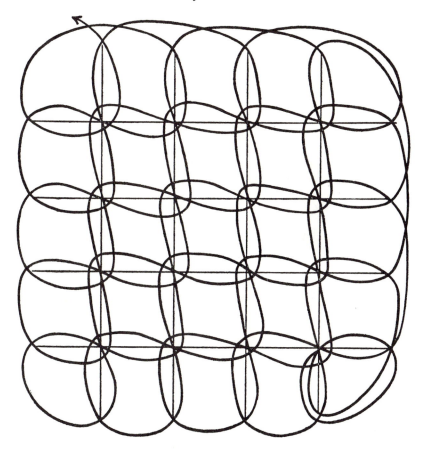

Fig. 5b. This design is very similar to Fig. 5a, except that it is drawn freehand, instead of with compass, in such a way that the continuous line runs around the corners formed by the framework, instead of intersecting them. (Atchin Island.)

Ghost, is nevertheless contrived so as to have a relatively empty space in the middle, and it is through this central cleft in a technically degraded labyrinth design that the ghost of the dead man now goes toward his future life.

The further development of these sand-tracings furnishes us with an interesting example of the fusion of two originally separate motives that is easily understandable and psychologically as well as culturally illuminating. This arises from a combination of the continuous-line motive (representing the Way that has to be trodden from one end to the other) with that of the conventionalized outline of the human figure, and the human figure thus represented is that of the Female Devouring Ghost herself.

Figure 6 represents in outline this very primitively conceived being, more

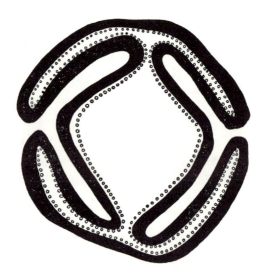

Fig. 6. This design, painted on the mask of one of the
Secret Ghost Societies, represents the Female Devouring
Ghost. (South West Bay, Malekula.)

like a fetus than an actual person. It is painted on a mask belonging to one of the Ghost Societies in South West Bay and is almost identical in shape with another design painted on a funeral coverlet representing the Female Devouring Ghost. Here the outline is not only a continuous line but also a never-ending one. There is no space in this paper to enter into the detailed development of the type of design based on this motive, in which the never-ending line is constructed on a framework not of straight lines, as in the simple labyrinth motive, but of small dots or circles, originally representing eyes and nostrils. This has been illustrated and discussed elsewhere.[15] What happened, briefly, is that the motive of the never-ending line outlining the primitive form of the Female Devouring Ghost became merged with

15 See above, n. 10.

146

that of the continuous-line labyrinth designs in such a way as to produce a totally new art form with infinite possibilities of representations of every kind of object, either real or imaginary.

Figure 1, "The Path" or "Way," is itself of such a type, combining both features, that of the continuous line representing a "way" and that of the never-ending line returning on itself, based on the primitive outline of the human figure.

Figure 7 is a much more complicated example of this type of development, in which the never-ending line is manipulated in such a way as to suggest the body and flippers of a giant tortoise.

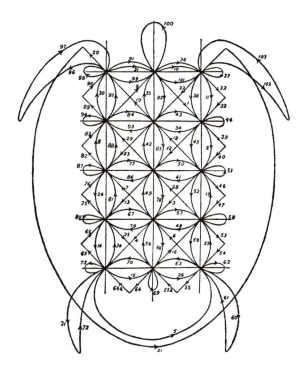

Fig. 7. "The Tortoise." Framework of straight lines at right angles to one another. A single never-ending line begins at 1 near the base of the loop representing the "head" and runs to 100, where it joins on to 1 again. An unintentional interruption occurs between 31 and 32; at this point the continuous line runs along part of the framework. (Ambrym Island.)

Figure 8, constructed in a similar way, resembles a mandala, but it is said to represent "a little black bird with a red head." Apart from a diamond-shaped center unconnected with the other parts, the whole design is formed of a single never-ending line.

These are only a few examples of the pure art forms that have developed in Malekula out of the labyrinth motive combined with that derived from the outline of the human form.

Fig. 8. A mandala-type figure to which the natives give the same name as to a little black bird with a red head. In this complex design the never-ending line begins at 1 and continues to 131, whence it returns to 1, running along the framework for a short stretch. Note the unconnected diamond-shaped motif in the center. Several mistakes have crept into the numbering; nevertheless the endless line can be followed without difficulty. (Ambrym Island.)

148

From the Near East to Malekula is a long way. However, there are connecting links that suggest the itinerary which these combined motives apparently followed. One such link is to be found in South India, where ritual and labyrinth designs almost identical with those made in Malekula are still in use.[16] This field of study has only begun to be investigated, but already it is possible to throw light on certain obscure points in classical tradition by comparison with the living beliefs of Malekula. The sibyls of classical and medieval lore may well be compared with the Malekulan Female Devouring Ghost sitting beside her Cave guarding the labyrinth. Through caves or clefts guarded by these mythical figures mighty heroes of antiquity started on their journeys to the underworld to visit the shades of their ancestors.

Virgil describes such a descent in the sixth book of the *Aeneid*, in which Aeneas goes into the underworld. Hitherto scholars have, very understandably, failed to appreciate why, in his introduction to this book, the Latin poet interrupts his otherwise consecutive tale with a till now apparently unintelligible interpolation concerning a labyrinth. Aeneas, who has finally landed at Cumae on Latin soil, approaches a cave, guarded by the sibyl, through which he wishes to descend to Hades. But here Virgil, in a passage often criticized as having apparently nothing to do with the story, breaks off his account to describe a representation of the Cretan labyrinth, depicted on the rock beside the entrance to the cave. Judging from the Malekulan material, it now appears not only that this labyrinth depicted at the entrance to the Cumaean cave is in its right symbolic place, but also that for the Roman reader the scene would have been charged with all the emotion connected with initiation rites and the journey into the land of the dead.[17] In this same book of the *Aeneid* are also described the two "waters"; outside flows the Styx nine times round, the river of death, which Aeneas can be ferried over only after he has shown the sibyl the famous golden bough or magic wand which, judging from the Malekulan evidence, is his own counterpart, his spiritual "double." Inside, he comes to Lethe, the water of forgetfulness leading to the inner life, in which, for full initiation, he must immerse himself in order to achieve new life on earth.

16 John Layard, "Labyrinth Ritual in South India: Threshold and Tattoo Designs," *Folk-Lore*, XLVIII (1937), 115ff.
17 See W. F. Jackson Knight, *Cumaean Gates; a Reference of the Sixth Aeneid to the Initiation Pattern* (Oxford, 1936).

Thus, even for an interpretation of Virgil, we may find help in a study of the religious concepts that are still alive among the natives of Malekula, while in them also many of our own inner problems are to be found dramatically expressed.[18]

18 [For further parallels from classical antiquity and from many cultures, ranging from aboriginal Australians to the high civilizations of Mesopotamia, there could be no better introduction than that to be found in Gertrude Rachel Levy's book *The Gate of Horn* (London and Chicago, 1948), especially on pp. 151 to 164 dealing with some matters mentioned in this paper in relation to other mythological beliefs and ritual practices. Her book was published after the original publication of this paper, or it would certainly have been mentioned in it.—J. L. (1959).]

C. Kerényi

Man and Mask

Ancient fables are terse. They stick to essentials; most of all they provide
an unforgettable image. "The fox once saw a tragic mask. 'Oh,' he cried
out, after turning it this way and that for some time, 'what a big face to
have no brain!'"

> Personam tragicam forte vulpes viderat:
> quam postquam huc et illuc semel atque iterum verterat,
> "O quanta species," inquit, "cerebrum non habet!"

In the classical text of this fable of Phaedrus, the words about the fox turning
the mask this way and that are dropped.[1] But supposing it should occur to
us to ask: Where did the fox find the mask? The question actually did come
to the mind of late classical writers who transmitted the tale. Greek narra-
tors presumed that the fox had crept into the house of an actor, musician,
or mask maker.[2] Romans of the same late day seem to have had other information. In their version it is the wolf who meets the tragic mask, and the
encounter takes place in the open fields: *personam tragicam lupus in agro
invenerat. . . .*[3]

Masks in woods and fields, hanging from trees, or set up on altarlike
elevations were still familiar images to the Roman of the late empire. He
found sacred landscapes dominated by masks, or open-air still lifes consisting entirely of masks, on sumptuous goblets in the Alexandrian manner,[4]

---

1 Restored by J. P. Postgate (Corpus Poetarum Latinorum), on the strength of the
Codices Periphrastarum.
2 Cf. O. Crusius' edition of Babrius (Leipzig, 1897) with critical apparatus.
3 Postgate, following the Periphrastae.
4 F. Drexel, "Alexandrinische Silbergefässe der Kaiserzeit," *Bonner Jahrbuch,* CXVIII
(1909), 176ff.; E. Pernice and F. Winter, *Der Hildesheimer Silberfund* (Berlin, 1901),
pp. 35ff., pls. XII–XVI; T. Schreiber, "Die Alexandrinische Toreutik," *Abhandlung
der Sächsische Gesellschaft der Wissenschaften,* XIV (1894), 451.

in murals,[5] reliefs,[6] and mosaic floors.[7] Into the Roman house the mask brought a suggestion of nature, a glimpse of the ancient landscape, and certain types of mask conveyed a special intimation of a mystery inherent in the landscape. Of that mystery nature was the arena, the mask the instrument. There is a mystery common to all masks: a common function for which this primal human instrument was devised. It will not be easy to state in words what this original function was. But in any event we shall be justified in assuming that one type of Greek mask, the mask of Dionysos, to which most other types of mask—tragic, comic, and satyric—are subordinated in their function of cultic playthings, was originally associated with the realm of nature or, indeed, the wilderness.

Equally primordial is the association between man and mask. Both associations are archaic, originating in a state of man which is suggested by the general concept "natural man" and which justifies us in speaking of a "primordial" implement. The original function of this implement was not at all what comes to the mind of modern man. Modern man speaks of "throwing off the mask" which he continuously wears, in order that he may at last be "himself." Or he suddenly casts off the mask: what a hideous sight. The uncivilized, inhuman enemy of man is revealed. Thus it is supposed that the mask was invented solely to conceal its wearer. The criminal actually does use a mask for this purpose. When, by a survival of archaic ritual as it were, one dons the mask at carnival, one becomes the uncivilized man one would otherwise not dare to be. Metaphoric mask and authentic mask: both have today a purely negative function, determined by our civilization. The mask cannot help being an implement of self-concealment, but this is a secondary function at most.

Another, almost inevitable function of the mask is to frighten. There is a

5 Le pitture antiche di Ercolano e contorni, Vol. IV (Naples, 1765), pp. 170ff. (of especial interest is the picture on p. 170 and the top of 171); W. Helbig, Wandgemälde der vom Vesuv verschütteten Städte Companiens (Leipzig, 1868), pp. 414ff.; H. G. Beyen, Über Stilleben aus Pompeji und Herculaneum, The Hague, 1928.
6 T. Schreiber, Die Wiener Brunnenreliefs aus Palazzo Grimani (Leipzig, 1888), pp. 87ff. and Die hellenistischen Reliefbilder (Leipzig, 1899), pls. 98–101; A. Sogliano, Notizie degli scavi di antichità, 1907, pp. 558ff.; D. Mustilli, Il Museo Mussolini (Rome, 1939), pls. 35–36.
7 The signed Asaroton of Heraklitos in the Lateran: W. Helbig, Führer durch die öffentlichen Sammlungen klassischer Alterthümer in Rom (3rd edn., Leipzig, 1912–13; 2 vols.), no. II, 1231; B. Nogara, I Mosaici antichi (Milan, 1910), pl. 5. See our Pl. Ia. Another example, in the Vatican, is from the Villa Adriana in Tivoli: Helbig, Führer, I, pp. 158ff.; Nogara, pl. 31.

particular archaic type of mask to which almost more than to any other this function is specific: the Gorgon. Myths impute to this figure a killing emanation.[8] Thus the special function of the Gorgon's mask is not merely to terrify but to kill by turning to stone. Stonelike rigidity is a quality common to all masks, even to the oldest theatrical masks, made of cloth, and in a sense to the still more primitive face painting.[9] But in the Gorgon myth this rigidity is enhanced as the efficacy of a superhuman creature, a face which has power to turn to stone even after it has been severed from the body. Mask and Gorgon cannot be separated, they are identical. The two oldest types of Greek mask—the male prototype Dionysos and the female Gorgon—have this in common. They are the masks par excellence, the masks which were first able to stand by themselves, without human bearer. At an even earlier day, to be sure, there must have been a human bearer; without him the mask as invention is inconceivable.[10] Aside from those non-Greek masks found in Mycenaean tombs or in the tombs of Trebeniŝce, which covered the faces of the dead so that the hidden face and the face represented by the mask were identical, the relation between man and some other being is inseparable from the idea of the mask. The mask conceals, the mask terrifies, but, most of all, it creates a relation between him who wears it and the being it is made to represent.

By its inherent rigidity the mask is associated first of all with the dead, whom among various archaic peoples it represented.[11] It creates a relation between the living and the dead. The one is transformed into the other; or, more accurately, the mask accomplishes a fusion between them, and this fusion is not purely external but penetrates deep into the soul of the mask-wearer. The mask—perhaps we shall thus best indicate its function—is an instrument of unifying transformation: negatively, in that it annuls the dividing lines, e.g., those between the dead and the living, causing something hidden to be manifested; positively, in that through this liberation of the hidden, forgotten, or disregarded, the wearer of the mask becomes identified with it. Anyone who is inclined to limit this primordial function of the mask to evoking spirits of the dead—which would then have to be considered

8 Cf. Pindar, *Pythian Odes* X, 47, and XII, 12; Aeschylus, *Prometheus* 798; and the quotations in K. Ziegler, "Gorgo," PW, VII, 1630ff.
9 Concerning these types of mask, see M. Bieber, "Maske," PW, XIV, 2070ff.
10 Kerényi, "Gedanken über Dionysos," *Studi e materiali di storia delle religioni*, XI (1935), 36.
11 Cf. K. Meuli, *Schweizer Masken* (Zurich, 1943).

only as daemons of fertility (and this too is an annulment of dividing lines)
—could well adduce the words of Shakespeare: "To die is to be a counterfeit;
for he is but the counterfeit of a man who hath not the life of a man." [12]
The association of the mask with the dead is indicated among the Greeks
by its use in tragedy: "the dead," i.e., the heroes of olden time, appear
in rigid masks and are restored to animation by the vital atmosphere
of the Dionysos cult. In comedy it was the reverse. By enhancing the absurd,
the rigid mask helped to suspend the base and oppressive: here there was
liberation in the deathly effect,[13] which indeed went beyond any association with the dead. The same is true of the tragic mask, which was no spirit
mask, no disguise, but an implement of the poet and actor with which to
effect a fusing transformation into the figures represented.[14]

If we have not limited ourselves to the view that the essence of every
masquerade, whether secular or religious, is to transform the masquerader
into a special being,[15] it was because we wished to take into account those
uses of the mask which involved more than a mere masquerade. In the
archaic and classical period something more than a masquerade was always
involved. And similarly in the tragic drama as we experience it today, the
function of the Greek poet and actor was not to represent some imaginary
being but to evoke one who actually existed. The words of W. F. Otto come
very close to the reality, even if they go on to lose themselves in the ineffable: "The full radiance of the dead is brought compellingly close, yet
at the same time it is lost in the infinite. The wearer of the mask is gripped
by the sublimity and dignity of those who have ceased to be. He is himself
and yet another. Madness has touched him, something of the mystery of
the raving God, of the spirit of a double being which lives in the mask and
whose latest descendant is the actor." [16] In this conception the fusion is so
overwhelming that it scarcely requires the mask.

12 *I Henry IV*, V, iii, 115 (as cited by Meuli).
13 Cf. Kerényi, *Dionysos und das Tragische in der Antigone* (Frankfurter Studien, XIII;
   1935), pp. 6ff.
14 Cf. P. Girard, *Revue des études grecques*, VII (1894), 1ff.; E. Krüger, *AM*, XXVI
   (1901), 126; the literature on the Menander relief in the Lateran in Helbig, *Führer*, II,
   24; the 78 words of Fronto (ed. S. A. Naber, Leipzig, 1867), p. 147, cited by Carl
   Robert, *Die Masken der neueren attischen Komoedie* (Hallisches Winckelmannspro-
   gramm, no. 25, Halle, 1911), p. 78, n. 1; and the remark of Cicero in *De legibus*, I, cap.
   9, par. 26, to the effect that the Greeks had no word exactly equivalent to the Latin
   voltus. The closest Greek equivalent is at the same time the word for mask.
15 M. Bieber, "Die Herkunft des tragischen Kostüms," *JAI*, XXXII (1917), 69.
16 W. F. Otto, *Dionysus* (Frankfurter Studien, IV; 1933), pp. 194f.

a. *Masks used decoratively in a mosaic floor. Roman*

b. *Silenos mask in maturity rite. Fresco, Pompeii*

Gorgon mask. Ornament from the archaic temple of Apollo at Veii
VI–V *cents.* B.C.

a. *Archaic mask of Acheloos. Brass, Etruscan*

b. *Silenos mask. From a Greek krater*

Dionysiac mask from Ikaria. Attic

Dionysiac mask, formerly interpreted as Acheloos

Decorative marble mask of Silenos. Pompeii

a. *Putto donning a Silenos mask.*
Antique Roman

b. *Putto wearing a colossal mask.*
Roman

The marriage of Dionysos and Ariadne. Roman sarcophagus, reign of Hadrian (117–138)

VIII

What we are speaking of, however, is the mask actually used by the Greeks. Its principal function is to transform and thereby to unite or, perhaps more fundamentally, to unite and thereby transform. But this must not lead us to forget its inherent secondary functions: concealment and terror. An implement which combines these three is an implement of mystery or—in other words—the implement of a secret cult. Warding off by the elaborate use of figures which inspire terror and at the same time represent higher beings is characteristic of the primitive secret cults.[17] These cults might more aptly be called archaic, although we have little evidence of such cults from the Greek archaic period; the classical mysteries of the Greeks are quite different. It has been possible to show that at least one primitive implement of secret cults aside from the mask, namely the bull-roarer, was in use in archaic Greece.[18] Certain *mysteria*, or *teletai* as the Greeks called their secret cults, preserved other traces of their archaic character up to the age of imperial Rome, and there is evidence that masks were used in connection with them.

The protective, terror-inspiring mask of the archaic secret cults was meant to be seen only by the initiate or those undergoing initiation—others might at most hear its voice—for to the profane the sight of the mask meant death. The mythologem of the Gorgon's fatal power corresponds exactly to this menace. But the Greek mysteries early abandoned the use of such terrible means of repelling the profane. From the seventh century on, the Gorgon's head became widespread as a symbol of special divine protection or apotropaism through mysterious forces.[19] The use of an apotropaic mask in an archaic cult of Demeter in Arcadia is first reported by Pausanias. In the "greater mysteries" of Demeter at Pheneos, the priest took a mask from the round vessel that lay on the sacred stone of the goddess, the *petroma*. This was the mask of Demeter Kidaria, a manifestation of the great mystery goddess. With it were associated a certain headdress and a certain dance,

17 Cf. J. E. Harrison, *Themis* (Cambridge, 1912 and 1927), pp. 18ff.; J. Gregor, *Die Masken der Erde* (Munich, 1936), pp. 12ff. and the literature therein cited, particularly L. Frobenius, *Masken und Geheimbunde Afrikas* (Halle, 1898). See the entire chapter "Der Geheimbund" in Frobenius, *Monumenta Africana* (Weimar, 1929).
18 Harrison, p. 61; R. Pettazzoni, *I Misteri* (Storia delle religioni, 7; Bologna, 1923), pp. 1ff.
19 A. Furtwängler, "Gorgones und Gorgo" Roscher's *Lexikon*, I, 1700ff., and K. Ziegler, "Gorgo," PW, VII, 1652. The earlier instances found in Homer are testimony to the greater religious freedom of the nobility and the poet himself. The usual hypothesis of "widespread belief in the evil eye" (Ziegler) or in evil spirits, which originally the Gorgon mask was supposed to frighten away, is a mere explanation *faute de mieux*.

both called *kidaris*. The priest put on this mask and struck the "earthly ones"—a mysterious epithet which Pausanias perhaps quoted from a versified legend of the cult [20]—with a stick. We do not know the mask, but we do know that the angry Demeter, Demeter Erinys, and her daughter Brimo (a name suggestive of "roaring") sometimes assumed the form of the Gorgon.[21] Here the mask of the goddess "transformed" her male priest; elsewhere this function was performed by her dress: [22] an archaism which has perhaps been preserved only in traces and which would seem to account for the beard in certain archaic Gorgon's masks [23] or the male designation of the wearer of the Gorgon's head in early Etruscan representations.[24]

The presumable line of development, which as always in such cases is concurrently a line of decadence and banalization, might easily be shown. The implement of a secret cult developed on the one hand into a protective, "apotropaic" mask of terror and as such into a theme of decorative art.[25] On the other hand, it became a mask to frighten children, and here we might mention the various "Gorgons for children" as they might be called: Akko, Alphito, Gello, Empusa, and the entwining Lamia, as well as the Roman Mania and the other manifestations of the Mater Larum, sometimes taken very much in earnest and sometimes in jest.[26] But we must limit our present inquiry to more general notions, which it is hoped will serve as working hypotheses for future studies. Hence we shall content ourselves with a single indication that the Dionysos mask shared its function of terror (in this case

---

20 VIII, 15, 3. The change from the "earthly" (ἐπιχθόνιοι) to the "subterranean" (ὑποχθόνιοι) would be justifiable only if we knew the λόγος to which Pausanias refers and if it favored this change.

21 Cf. the representation of the Gorgon as a horse in an archaic relief pithos reproduced in R. Hempe, *Frühe Griechische Sagenbilder aus Böotien* (Athens, 1936), pls. 36 and 38, and the remarks in this connection in Jung and Kerényi, *Essays on a Science of Mythology* (New York, 1949)(or *Introduction to a Science*, etc., London, 1950), pp. 175ff.; βριμάζειν also means to roar. Roaring was characteristic of the Gorgon; cf. Ziegler, PW, VII, 1636.

22 The classical example is the oath of men wearing the dress of the goddess, which is also worn by the mystagogue in the Demeter sanctuary in Syracuse: Plutarch, *Dion* 56. Pausanias tells of the oath in the Demeter sanctuary in connection with the above-cited passage concerning the mask of the goddess. A late (less certain) example: Galliena Augusta, A. Alföldi, *Zeitschrift für Numismatik*, XXXVIII (1928), 180.

23 Furtwängler in Roscher's *Lexikon*, I, 1707.

24 Cf. the bronze reliefs from Orvieto, *Archäologische Zeitung*, XXXV (1877), pl. 11, 1, and the references of G. Körte on p. 111.

25 Cf. our Pl. II.

26 Cf. E. Tabeling, *Mater Larum* (Frankfurter Studien, I; 1932), in which most of the terror-inspiring monsters known to the Greeks are cited. With regard to Alphito: O. Crusius in PW, I, 1637.

secondary) with the other masks of secret cults. Dionysos, the mask god as he had been called [27] because a mask could represent the god as a fully valid cult image, shows the closest similarity to Acheloos, the typical river and source god, half bearded man, half bull, and usually bearing horns. The Ikaria mask (from a rural cult site of Dionysos in Attica), this to us most impressive archaic epiphany of the mask god, is still $\tau\alpha\upsilon\rho\eta\delta\grave{o}\nu\ \beta\lambda\acute{e}\pi\omega\nu$; it has the gaze of a bull.[28] But it is characteristic that a second, already classical example of this type was at first taken for an "Acheloos." [29] In archaic horned male masks,[30] a purely typological distinction is scarcely possible: they reveal one prototype, one and the same male secret cult mask.

Dionysos in the form of a bull may have been welcome to the women who carried on so many of his secret cults—the women of Elis are known to have evoked him in the form of a "worthy bull." [31] However, it would seem that this same form was used to frighten away the profane. A tragedy of Aeschylus, dealing with the introduction of the cult of Dionysos in Thrace (named *Edonoi* after a Thracian tribe), described the tones which announced the advent of the god among his companions, the devotees of the secret cult. "Shrill stringed instruments resounded," the account begins; "deep as a bull the terror-inspiring imitators"—i.e., imitators of the bull's blare—"roar from some invisible place, and it is like the tone of a deeply moving drum, a subterranean thunder. . . ." Strabo, who is familiar with such matters, adds [32] that the same occurs in Phrygia, that is, in the Phrygian cult of Dionysos. Modern scholars have associated this voice with another archaic implement of secret cults, the bull-roarer.[33] The bull's voice, regardless of the instrument by which it is produced, demands a bull mask and announces the coming of a god who will appear in that mask and whom all

27 W. Wrede, *AM*, LIII (1928), 66ff., who in his otherwise fundamental paper makes use of what we have called a hypothesis *faute de mieux*.
28 Our Pl. IV after Wrede, pl. I, in the National Museum, Athens.
29 Our Pl. V after Wrede, pl. II, in the Altes Museum, Berlin, interpreted as Acheloos, because the head has dowel holes over the forehead, perhaps for horns; cf. Wrede, pp. 76ff., to the contrary.
30 Cf. our Pl. IIIa.
31 Plutarch, *Quaestiones Graecae* 36, 299 A; M. P. Nilsson, *Geschichte der griechischen Religion*, I (Handbuch der Altertumswissenschaft, V, 2; Munich, 1941), pp. 538ff.
32 Strabo X, 3, 16, to whom we owe the quotation (fr. 57, Nauck); cf. L. Séchan, *Études sur la tragédie grecque* (Paris, 1926), pp. 63ff., and S. Srebrny, in *Mélanges Franz Cumont* (Université libre de Bruxelles: Annuaire de l'Institut de philologie et d'histoire orientales et slaves, IV, 1936), pt. I, p. 423, n. I.
33 Harrison, *Themis*, and Pettazzoni, *I Misteri*.

the uninitiated should flee in terror. It is from this substratum that the Greek Dionysos raises his head, devoid of animal traits; but the animal features are retained by the benign but not unmysterious river and source god Acheloos. The Greeks had many legends concerning the father role of the river gods; in the marriage rite the river god preceded the bridegroom.[34] Ultimately, the same mask became that of Father Okeanos himself,[35] the Homeric "source of all things."

The mask of Dionysos without a wearer, hanging from a tree or—after the sylvan god had moved into the city—from a pillar [36] entwined in ivy and branches, has become a cult image. The god himself is with it and in it, unassisted by any human wearer. Even by itself it accomplishes the fusing transformation of the maenads who dance around it and celebrate beneath it: now they are transformed and fused with their god. Even a mask that is not worn creates between god and men a bond which far transcends the evocation of the godhead through a cult image. Here one may speak with Otto of a "primordial phenomenon of duality, of distance made physically present, of a shattering encounter with that which cannot be brought back, of a brotherly meeting between life and death." [37] But the word "death" must be taken in a broad sense. In the realm of Dionysos there is no real death; there are dead people who by their presence attest the irreducibility of life.[38] By virtue of the mask, a being who is only seemingly remote is placed in this world. And this can be done even with the gods: a mask can place them in this world so that they not merely appear but actually live among us, though remaining at the same time far off and never relinquishing their remoteness. This paradoxical phenomenon is still evident in the the-atrical masks used as ornaments on many ancient sarcophagi. For the ancient mask is by this duality forever bound up with the tomb.

The original connections, contexts, references, in which an ancient cult implement had had its full meaning—not an allegorical meaning as the ex-pression of a dogma, but the fundamental being that made it exactly what it was—remain inherent in it; they are never entirely lost, and are always

34 Cf. O. Weinreich, *Der Trug des Nektanebos* (Leipzig, 1911), pp. 34ff.; O. Waser, "Fluss-götter," in PW, VI, 2774ff.
35 Bieber, "Maske," PW, XIV, 2118, and A. Hartmann, "Silenos und Satyros," PW, series 2, III, 42.
36 Wrede, pp. 83ff.
37 *Dionysus*, p. 194.
38 Cf. Kerényi, *Pythagoras und Orpheus* (Albae Vigiliae, n. s. IX; Zurich, 1950), p. 37.

capable of reviving. The theatrical masks not only retained their association with the tomb; but like the olden "mask god," in whose rural or urban sphere they originated, they hark back to the wilderness. While not original to the tragic and comic masks, this association, with which our present discussion began, is fundamental to the Dionysian mask. As we know, furthermore, it was extended to the theatrical masks. Accounts of the great Dionysian festivals of the Alexandrian and Roman era tell of artificial grottoes and arbors in imitation of the primitive nature in which Dionysos had originally been worshiped. These woodland scenes were decked out with all the trappings of the Dionysian cult, among them the tragic, comic, and satyric masks.[39] These last, to be sure, might have found their way back to nature without this circuitous route through the theater.

Among all the masks which arose within the cult of Dionysos, or had become associated with it, the *satyroi*—both the satyrs and the actors who portrayed them—had from time immemorial belonged to wood and mountain; they were spirits of nature or dancers possessed by such spirits. It may be mentioned in passing that in archaic times, when the sublime Artemis still occasionally bore the face of a Gorgon,[40] such dancers, including men in female guise, participated in her cult.[41] The masked dancers express a contradiction; they are a cultic society, a θίασος, appearing openly before the public, but at the same time they constitute a kind of secret league, whose members remain hidden beneath their masks.[42] In the Greek cults this hidden element—which, as in all mysteries,[43] was from the outset a "sacred open secret"—receded more and more. In the classical era the companions of Dionysos appear totally distinct from their actualization by masked dancers, and take the form of phallic half-animals half-gods. At least one satyr's mask, however, retains the clear character of a cult implement: the mask of Father Silenos, *Sileni patris imago*, as Propertius calls it in his description of a Dionysian grotto.[44] As a bearded, male face it shows considerable resemblance to the masks of Acheloos and Dionysos, but it is

39 Athenaios IV, 148 B, and V, 198 D.
40 See the Rhodes plate in Nilsson, pl. 30, 2, and the gable of the archaic temple of Artemis in Corfu in Jung and Kerényi, *Essays*, p. 178.
41 Cf. E. Buschor, *AM*, LIII (1928), 105ff.
42 Cf. Adolf E. Jensen, *Das religiöse Weltbild einer frühen Kultur* (Studien zur Kulturkunde, IX; Stuttgart, 1948), pp. 152ff.
43 Kerényi, *Die Geburt der Helena* (Albae Vigiliae, n. s. III; Zurich, 1945), pp. 48ff.
44 II, 3, 29.

distinguished from the latter by a certain animal, or excessively physical, quality.[45]

The mask of Silenos appears in three aspects: as apotropaic mask,[46] as cult implement, and as theatrical property, though the theatrical mask is not without its cultic implication. Here we must limit our remarks to a few essential points. The motif to which we refer occurs on a Roman sarcophagus of Hadrian's age now in the Lateran Museum,[47] and is emphasized by repetitions. The sacred event represented on this sarcophagus is the marriage of Dionysos and Ariadne. In the large relief, the two of them are driving to meet one another in chariots drawn by centaurs. On the back of the centaur drawing the god stands a little Eros with a mask of Pan on his head but not covering his face, and with a shepherd's staff in his hand. A corresponding Eros sits on the centaur drawing Ariadne, he too holding a shepherd's staff. To this Eros the divine bride holds out a mask of Silenos. The masks of Pan and Silenos seem to be variations of one and the same cult implement; in the one the animal, in the other the human, aspect is more emphasized. They appear as variants in a mural in the hall of Ixion of the Casa dei Vetti in Pompeii, since first one, then the other, appears in combination with a winnowing basket, the *liknon*.[48] This utensil of mysteries, the *mystica vannus Iacchi*, was also borne about in the marriage procession; in Athens it was filled with bread,[49] otherwise, as shown in most representations, it was full of fruit and contained a phallus. The mask of Silenos often lies beside it or near it.[50] Ariadne extends it to her Eros, in expression of her evident willingness to wed the bridegroom, whose Eros wears the mask of Pan. This interpretation is confirmed by the relief on the cover of the sarcophagus. It shows the wedded pair lying together and kissing: the marriage is nearing its consummation. An Eros, bearing in his hand a mask of Silenos and a shepherd's

---

45 Cf. our Pls. III*b* and VI: the first, according to Wrede, p. 66, is from a krater now in New York and represents an early example; the second is a later type, a decorative marble mask from the Casa degli Amorini, Pompeii.

46 This purpose is particularly clear where the mask is used as an ornament on a shield. Cf. Bieber in PW, XIV, 2113.

47 Helbig, *Führer*, II, no. 1200; our Pl. VIII.

48 L. Curtius, *Die Wandmalerei Pompejis* (Leipzig, 1929), figs. 17 and 18.

49 Cf. J. E. Harrison, *Prolegomena to the Study of Greek Religion* (Cambridge, 1903), pp. 522ff., and *Journal of Hellenic Studies*, XXIII (1903), 292ff.

50 The finest of these appear on the votive tablet of the relief "Lioness with young," in Schreiber, *Die Wiener Brunnenreliefs*, last plate; a Verona relief in Schreiber, *Die hellenistischen Reliefbilder*, pl. 101; two cameos in the Bibliothèque Nationale, Paris, E. Babelon, *Catalogue des camées . . .* (Fondation E. Piot; Paris, 1897), pl. VIII, 62, 63.

staff, hastens toward the kissing pair. Vainly a satyra lying beside him seeks to draw the little Eros to herself.

The prelude to the marriage of Dionysos and Ariadne is differently represented on a Roman sarcophagus now in Baltimore.[51] The god, accompanied by maenads and satyrs in festive train, comes to Ariadne as she sleeps on Naxos. Here again there is a little Eros; behind him, the mask of Silenos; beside it, a utensil associated with the mystery. This is the *cista mystica*, a basket from which there crawls a snake and which, like the *liknon*, is often associated with this mask.[52] Here, however, Silenos himself appears, leading Eros, the divine child who shrinks back in fear of the snake and who at the wedding will handle such mysterious utensils. In this connection we might mention another group of scenes with Erotes and masks of Silenos: that of the Palazzo Mattei.[53] Here an Eros holds the snake through the mouth of the Silenos mask, which he carries on his head, and frightens another Eros with it. The relation between the contents of the *cista mystica* and *mystica vannus*, snake and phallus, and the ensuing marriage feast is obvious. The Silenos mask seems to have the same significance in these nuptial and pre-nuptial scenes, but we do not yet understand why.

A mural in the famous Villa dei Misteri in Pompeii gives us the answer. In these pictures we encounter the same parallelism. To the left of the divine pair, Dionysos and Ariadne, who dominate the sacred events, the *mystica vannus* and its contents, the still veiled phallus, serve to initiate a virgin into the marriage rites.[54] It has never been doubted that the same series of pictures also represents an initiation of boys.[55] A rite involving the Silenos mask,[56] represented to the right of Dionysos and Ariadne, apparently shows the climax of such an initiation, but the meaning of neither the scene nor the initiation is as evident to the modern observer as in the case of the *liknon* rite on the other side. Maturity rites, by which boys are received among full-fledged men, and which are prerequisite for marriage, are indeed

---

51 K. Lehmann-Hartleben and E. C. Olsen, *Dionysic Sarcophagi in Baltimore* (Baltimore, 1942), fig. 9.
52 The Dresden relief in Schreiber, *Die hellenistischen Reliefbilder*, pl. 101, and the Munich relief, pl. 100, 2.
53 S. Reinach, *Répertoire de reliefs grecs et romains*, Vol. III (Paris, 1912), p. 295, [fig.] 3.
54 Cf. M. Bieber, *JAI*, XLIII (1938), pp. 306ff., and A. Maiuri in his publication *La Villa dei Misteri* (Rome, 1931), pp. 166ff.
55 This was the basis of the interpretations of G. E. Rizzo, *Memorie di R. Accademia delle belle arti* (Naples), III (1918), 61ff., and V. Macchioro, *Zagreus*, 1920 and 1930.
56 Our Pl. I*b*.

well known to the ethnologist.[57] On the third day of the festival of Apaturia those Athenian boys who had reached puberty were entered in the list of a *phratria*, and this sacred action was known as *gamelia*, "marriage sacrifice"—this can scarcely be regarded as anything other than a form of maturity ceremony, the acceptance of the boy in the "secret league" of the men, which also registered eligible girls as possible mates.[58]

This brings us close to the interpretation of the ceremony represented in the mural that seems most compatible with careful observation of the rite. Three persons participate in a strange game: a Silenos and two boy satyrs. The leader and initiator of the game is the Silenos. This is in keeping with his invocation in the Orphic hymn as "mystery leader of the shepherds' league."[59] An inscription of one of these cultic leagues in Pergamon, a *thiasos* dedicated to Dionysos Kathegemon, mentions in addition to the chief shepherd, the ἀρχιβουκόλος, and the shepherds, the βουκόλοι, two "teachers of hymns" and three "Silenoi," one of whom was the leader of the chorus.[60] This function of the Silenos in the *thiasos* finds its expression in mythology: Silenos appears as the tutor of Dionysos or as teacher of the mythical flute player, Olympos.[61] The pastoral scene which in the Villa dei Misteri series—and assuredly throughout the initiation of the boys—precedes our scene is, presumably with this implication, dominated by the towering figure of a lyre-playing Silenos.

In the scene with which we are concerned, the Silenos, seated, holds out a deep silver cup to a boy satyr. A Dionysian implement, a mighty drum, lies between them. Two other utensils involved in the game or ceremony—both terms seem apt—are present. The first is a silver bowl. The boy peers deep into it, yet his lips do not touch the edge; he is not drinking. But what

57 Cf. the above-cited work of Jensen and his early book *Beschneidung und Reifezeremonien bei Naturvölkern* (Studien zur Kulturkunde, I; Stuttgart, 1933).

58 Analysis of texts in A. Mommsen, *Feste der Stadt Athen* (Leipzig, 1898), pp. 323ff., and V. Magnien, *Mélanges Franz Cumont* [as in n. 32 above], pp. 305ff. Concerning the *phratriai* as rudiments of primitive clans, cf. H. J. Rose, *Primitive Culture in Greece* (London, 1925), p. 167. In his elucidation of Spartan usages, H. Jeanmaire, *Couroi et Courètes* (Lille, 1939), pp. 145ff., cited the African secret societies. F. Cumont, *Les Religions orientales dans le paganisme romain* (Paris, 1929), p. 201, had done the same in connection with the secret cult of Dionysos.

59 Θιάσου νομίου τελετάρχα, Hymni Orphici 54, 4; A. Delatte, *La Catoptromancie grecque et ses dérivés* (Liège, 1932), p. 199.

60 Dittenberger, *Sylloge inscriptionum graecarum*, Vol. III (3rd edn., Leipzig, 1920), col. 1115; F. Cumont, *American Journal of Archaeology*, XXXVII (1933), 245.

61 Cf. E. Kuhnert, "Satyros," Roscher's *Lexikon*, IV, 505 and 509.

he sees within the bowl can be calculated with mathematical precision.[62] The silver bowl serves as a concave mirror, a type which is attested in a temple inventory.[63] Thus the boy does not, as he might have expected, see his own face in the mirror, but another object, which hovers outside its focus. This other object is the Silenos mask, which the other boy satyr, as the Silenos' assistant in the game, holds behind the back of the first boy at such an elevation that, instead of his own face, he sees the mask. It appears, to be sure, in reverse in the concave mirror, but the cause of the boy's amazement is so much more profound that this passes almost unnoticed. The boy thinks that he sees himself, and he recognizes himself as one of those older men, fathers and teachers, who had dominated and led him up to now and to whose number he now belongs. It is a uniting transformation, accomplished by the mask as image of the father: *Sileni patris imago*. The boy is united with the fathers and is initiated as a procreating man.

This subtle use of the mirror image is not indeed archaic. It is presumably an invention of the Hellenistic era, attested by a second Pompeiian mural.[64] The scene, disclosed by a mural in the so-called Hall of Mysteries in the Casa del Criptoportico, does not, to be sure, as Rostovtzeff still believed, represent a regular, well-planned ceremony with Silenos mask and silver bowl. What is here represented is rather the surprise at the first observation of the phenomenon, the accidental "find." This is how Rostovtzeff describes the scene: "On a couch or a natural rock lie a Silenus and a Maenad. The Silenus is highly excited. He lifts his right hand in admiration and looks attentively into a round mirror or a shallow bowl of mirrorlike appearance which a Satyr who stands behind the couch is holding in his right hand before a Satyrisk who kneels and gazes into a mirror. The mouth of the Satyrisk is wide open. The Satyr who holds the mirror or the bowl makes with his left hand a gesture which probably invites the Satyrisk to look into the mirror. The Satyrisk is evidently telling something to the great amazement of the Silenus. Behind this group there is a girl with a sacrificial dish in her left hand. She is also fixing her eyes *in admiration and terror* [italics

---

62 This was done by Macchioro, *Zagreus*, pp. 94ff. and 82ff., checked and confirmed by Delatte, pp. 190ff., and also by a more recent pictorial parallel, fig. 22. Macchioro and Delatte believed that the mask and its reflections were intended to provoke "hallucinations" of some sort.

63 Pliny, *Naturalis historia* XXXIII, 129; cited by Macchioro.

64 Cited by M. I. Rostovtzeff, *Mystic Italy* (New York, 1928), p. 66; a better reproduction in Delatte, fig. 23.

mine] on what is going on among the four members of the Dionysiac rout."
The fiction represented in this painting is presumably this: Satyrs helping
to serve Silenos at a feast discovered the optical phenomenon which was
subsequently used in the initiation of the boys—the initiation of the Satyr-
isks into the mystery that they, as male beings, are identical with Father
Silenos.

How the actual implement of uniting transformation, the mask, was
originally used in such a ceremony, is shown in turn by late Roman works
of art showing little boys, Erotes or wingless putti, handling gigantic Silenos
masks. Two statues in Rome are particularly worthy of mention. A putto
sits on a goatskin, a festive fillet round his head, and tries to draw an immense Silenos mask over his face.[65] Or a putto stands half hidden behind
the colossal mask and protrudes his hand through the mouth of the bearded
face.[66] These sculptures—presumably from tombs—become intelligible only
as elements of larger compositions. The putto who protrudes his hand
through the mask's mouth, and who, as we have said, may also hold a snake,
requires as his complement another putto, who falls on his back for fear [67]
or who stands terrified with a defensive gesture.[68] In certain sarcophagus
reliefs these motifs are combined with others which recur in the same context, particularly with two putti beginning to wrestle. A sarcophagus with
garlands in Porto di Roma shows exclusively these two juxtaposed motifs.[69]
Perhaps the most instructive composition is that of the above-mentioned
sarcophagus relief in the Palazzo Mattei. Aside from the motifs we have
described—Silenos mask, snake, and wrestlers—it contains others, among

65 In the Capitoline Museum, Rome, our Pl. VIIa: Helbig, *Führer*, I, no. 869; H. Stuart
   Jones, *The Sculptures of the Museo Capitolino* (A Catalogue of the Ancient Sculptures
   ... in the Municipal Collections of Rome, I; Oxford, 1912), text, p. 317, no. 8; falsely
   interpreted by W. Klein, *Geschichte der griechischen Kunst*, Vol. II (Leipzig, 1905),
   page 243. [Another example was found in the grotto of Sperlonga; see my *Abenteur
   mit Monumenten* (Olten, 1957), p. 44.—C. K., 1959.]
66 In the Villa Albani, Rome; our Pl. VIIb.
67 Thus on the sarcophagus in the Lateran, Room XI, no. 672: Lateran Museum cat.,
   ed. O. Benndorf and R. Schöne (1867), p. 256. A small-scale example in the Palazzo
   Doria. A similar game of two Erotes with the mask of a child—presumably the infant Herakles—adorning the inside of a colossal marble bowl in the museum of the
   Palazzo dei Conservatori, is also most likely associated with the Apaturia; cf. below,
   n. 73. Reproduced in Mustilli, *Il Museo Mussolini*, pl. LXX, 275, 276. See the two
   snakes at the edge, which may suggest the child Herakles.
68 In all three of the sarcophagi about to be mentioned: those in Porto, in the Palazzo
   Mattei, and in the Villa Albani.
69 G. Calza, *La Necropoli del Porto di Roma nell'Isola Sacra* (Rome, 1940), pp. 190ff.,
   figs. 94 and 95.

them one which, like the wrestler motif, seems to point to the Apaturia, the Athenian festival in which boys were initiated into the state of maturity.

The general nature of this inquiry permits only brief intimations of the context. The motif in question is the great mixing vessel in the background, no common krater, but rather a giant bowl from which an Eros is taking wine with a pitcher. At the opposite edge lies another Eros, the upper part of his body plunged deep into the great bowl. A second giant bowl, into which two Erotes empty a wine pitcher,[70] stands likewise in the background, behind two little wrestlers, while the first vessel constitutes the background of the mask scene. Other Dionysian utensils are also present: a great *thyrsos*, a drum, a basket full of fruit, and a vase, perhaps also filled with fruit. The author of the *Vetera Monumenta Matthaeorum* called the whole a vintage festival.[71] But there is no visible sign of the grapes which otherwise characterize these festivals.[72] The old interpretation is surely false. A libation of wine, known as *oinisteria*, occurred on the third day of the Apaturia. And descriptions of it mention a gigantic drinking vessel.[73] The boys themselves and not merely their fathers partook of the wine.[74] The festival was dedicated to various deities, among them Dionysos Melanaigis, the Dionysos with the black goatskin.[75] Use of the goat as a sacrificial beast is attested.[76] The fruits suggest the autumnal month of Pyanopsion, in which this festival occurred.

The motif of the wrestlers has its correspondence in the cultic legend of this festival. The Athenians derived the name "Apaturia" from ἀπάτη, "deception," associating the festival with a legendary duel fought at the border between Attica and Boeotia, in which Melanthos (the "black") deceived his adversary Xanthos (the "blond"). Melanthos accused the other of having brought a helper with him into the duel, and when Xanthos looked around for the supposed helper, Melanthos killed him from behind. This legend does not speak of a real helper.[77] But there was another version

---

70 After the description of F. Matz, *Antike Bildwerke in Rom*, ed. F. von Duhn, Vol. II (Leipzig, 1881), p. 208, whereas Helbig, *Führer*, II, 446, mistakes the corresponding giant vessel in the Villa Albani relief for a "great water basin."

71 Vol. II (Rome, 1778), pl. 47, 1.

72 Cf. G. Rodenwaldt, *JAI*, XLV (1930), 171ff.

73 Athenaios (XI, 494 F, after Pamphilos) mentions in his explanation of this libation (οἰνιστήρια) the great drinking vessel (μέγα ποτήριον) which is known as οἰνιστηρία, and from which the Ephebes drink in honor of Herakles. Cf. also Pollux III, 52–53, which suggests the lively movements of the boys.

74 Cf. R. Hänslik, Οἰνιστήρια, in PW.

75 Cf. the analysis of the texts by W. R. Halliday, *Classical Review*, XL (1926), 177f.

76 Pollux III, 52.   77 Halliday, loc. cit.

of it, in which a beardless boy [78] or a terrifying form in a black goatskin [79]—in both cases Dionysos—really appeared behind the deceived Xanthos. Aside from the libation and the duel, which on the basis of this cultic legend would seem at this festival to have taken the form of a wrestling match between boys, something else seems to have taken place at the Apaturia: a sacred action which consisted in a deception not only through words but through a terrifying figure—actually a beardless boy. The game with the Silenos mask, by which one boy frightens another, runs parallel to the wrestling match on the sarcophagus relief.

The game of the putti was originally a serious rite, with an older boy frightening the younger ones in order to disclose himself as the wearer of the mask and in this way to manifest the identity of the youths with the older men. The Silenos mask as implement of such an initiation, prerequisite for marriage, became a symbol suggestive of future marriage—another form of "uniting transformation." Are we justified in assuming that not only the Silenos mask but also the *cista mystica* with snake played a part in the Attic initiation of boys? On a sarcophagus relief in the Villa Albani, which closely resembles the one described in the Palazzo Mattei and combines all the motifs we have discussed,[80] an Eros opens the basket in which the snake had been concealed, while another, frightened by the sight, falls on his back. On closer inspection, a *cista mystica* opened by two putti is discernible in the Palazzo Mattei relief: the snake which protrudes through the mouth of the mask comes from the mystery basket. Whether this association of snake and Silenos mask goes back to a real ceremony remains an open question. We only know that every possible initiatory rite undergone by young people in Greece was a welcome subject to the artists of the Roman sarcophagi. Their works sometimes went back to models which were inspired by the great art and religious life of Attica.[81] Another model with the Dionysiac initiation of a boy, done in two variants in Attica itself, indicates the path by which such representations found their way to Rome.[82]

The union of mask with putto in the sarcophagi accomplishes a transformation. A transformation not of the little boy who, with or without wings, represents the timeless figure of the child, but of the mask itself. Hitherto,

78 Konon XXXIX in Jacoby, *Die Fragmente der griechischen Historiker*, Vol. I (Berlin, 1923), p. 204.   79 Suidas, see Jacoby.

80 Helbig, *Führer*, II, no. 1907; G. Zoega, *Li Bassirilievi antichi di Roma*, Vol. II (Rome, 1808), pl. 90.   81 Cf. F. Cumont, in *Syria*, X (1929), 219.

82 The one example is in the museum of the catacomb of Pretextatus; cf. M. Gütschow, in *Memorie della Pontificia Accademia Romana di Archeologia*, ser. III, IV (1938), 142ff.; the other in the Museum of Ostia: cf. Calza, *Necropoli*, pp. 210ff.

with its rigidity it suggested the dead; with the emptiness of its mouth and eyes it suggested a kind of nonbeing, which, to be sure, under the aspect of Dionysos transforms itself back into the most radiant life, while now this radiant life itself issues from the mouth of the mask with the child's hand. The game enhances the terror and at the same time annuls the deathlike rigidity. It gives the mask life and soul. On the Porto sarcophagus, a butterfly appears between the frightened putto and the face of Silenos,[83] thus uttering in pictorial language the word "psyche"—its name in Greek. The playing with the paraphernalia of the mystery retained the force of a mystery play.

In the present discussion the animal masks [84] of the Greeks—as well as other important mask types [85]—have purposely been disregarded. Our starting point was an animal's encounter with the mask of a man, but what has eminently concerned us is the meeting of man himself with the non-individual—whether divine or animal, heroic or only typical—human face. It is an overwhelming encounter, whether it takes place in the secret cult or in the theater. How—the psychologist will say—can an encounter with the archetype, in the case of the Silenos mask assuredly a father archetype, fail to be profoundly moving? The human face—otherwise the vehicle of individual features, the features of a "personality," as this unique entity is named by a shift in meaning of the Latin word for mask, *persona*—is here the form in which the universal and collective are manifested. The situation of man between an individual being and another, Protean being which assumes every shape is made visible in the mask. Hence the creative, participating ecstasy which the mask calls forth and disseminates. It is a true magic implement, which enables man at any moment to apprehend that situation and find the road into a broader, more spiritual world, without departing from the world of natural existence. If anyone were to wear a mask permanently, he would be a dead man or a monster. In antiquity it was worn only ceremonially and employed with art, as one might, for example, say of musical instruments, the instruments of a similar magic.

83 Calza, fig. 95.
84 Cf. Bieber, *JAI*, XXXII (1917). This line leads back to the Old Stone Age—cf. M. Hoernes and O. Menghin, *Urgeschichte der bildenden Kunst in Europa* (Vienna, 1925), p. 669—and would lead us from our topic Man and Mask to a discussion of Man and Beast.
85 Masks from the sanctuary of Artemis Orthia in Sparta, cf. G. Dickins in R. M. Dawkins, *The Sanctuary of Artemis Orthia* (London, 1929), p. 163; masks from Carthaginian and Punic-Sardian tombs; old Italic masks, including the Etruscan Phersu mask and the Roman *imagines*, etc.

Martin Buber

Symbolic and Sacramental Existence in Judaism [1]

Not only is human existence the area in which symbols and sacraments are manifested or the substance they assume: the tangible existence of a human person can itself be a symbol, a sacrament.

It is not in the essence of the symbol to hover timelessly over the concrete and contingent. Precisely because a symbolic act is by nature unique and unpredictable, it can occur at any time. The symbol derives its permanence from its transience. Thus when we have reached the end of our life span, we may look back and realize that all things transient are "only" a symbol; but our experience teaches us that *only* the transient can become symbol. For the representation of the unmutilated meaning, its authentic utterance, compared to which everything we call speech is mutilation, can originate only in the begotten, mortal body; all else is repetition, simplification, imitation. The mind with its timeless works is self-contained—it does not point beyond itself; only the body, enmeshed in time, can achieve transparence in its fleeting gesture. The covenant which the absolute, reaching beyond the universal—the "idea"—concludes with the concrete always selects a sign more fugitive than the rainbow of Noah's covenant: a movement, attitude, or action of the human form. And this sign endures. It can indeed lose some of its immediate force, its "credibility," but it can also gather fresh life from new—newly enacted—human existence. Every symbol is in constant danger of degenerating from a real sign sent down into life to an

---

1 [Since its original publication in *EJ 1934* the present paper has appeared (in other translations) in *Mamre* (Melbourne and New York, 1946); *Hasidism* (New York, 1948); and *The Origin and Meaning of Hasidism* (New York, 1960). The last is Vol. II of *Hasidism and the Way of Man*, a definitive edition of Professor Buber's essays on Hasidism edited and translated by Maurice Friedman. Biblical quotations are from *The Holy Scriptures according to the Masoretic Text* (Jewish Publication Society of America, Philadelphia, new edn., 1955), with occasional modifications to conform with the author's German text.—ED.]

intellectual, arbitrary construction; every sacrament may cease to be a living interaction between above and below and become a surface experience on the "religious" plane. Only through the man who gives himself can the power of the primal source be saved for renewed actuality.

*

Plato in the *Timaeus* (72 b) distinguishes between the μάντεις, whom he conceives as μανέντες—those who are ravished by the god and "prophesy" in mysterious sounds what they have received from him—and the προφῆται, the "divulgers," who translate these mysterious sounds into human speech. The passive element in the former recedes, but the basic relation remains the same when Pindar (fr. 150) says that the Muse "prophesies," while the poet "divulges": the Muse gives the poet the keynote, the poet frames it in word and verse; but the Muse does not express herself; she expresses the god by whom she, a superhuman Pythia, is possessed—her lord Apollo. And he, too, as he confesses in Aeschylus,[1a] is both μάντις and προφήτης, serving a higher god, Zeus, who has endowed him with wisdom; he does not speak his wisdom; to the Muse or Pythia he conveys no word, but only a mystery, of which he moans inarticulately and which finally the "prophetic" interpreter divulges.

To the Greek, μαντεία is not "finished" discourse. It bursts forth unshaped and to the nonprophet unintelligible; only the προφήτης can give it shape and fashion it into λόγος. The prophet translates, but from a language which to the ear of the profane is no language at all. When a man combines both functions, we must assume that for a time he is only a μάντις and then becomes a προφήτης; the personal differentiation is replaced by one of condition, a differentiation between states of mind, a transformation within the person. The duality remains.

Not so the Biblical *nabi*. It is significant that this term is not also used in a profane sense, as in Greek, where the interpreter of a philosophy or even a crier at the games can be called προφήτης, signifying one who publicly proclaims. The *nabi* exists only in the relation between God and man; he is one who "carries the word along the vertical,"[2] and this not only downward as the bringer of God's message, but also upward: Abraham "inter-

---

1a *Eumenides*, 17ff.; cf. 615ff.

2 Buber, *Königtum Gottes* (Vol. I of *Das Kommende*, Untersuchungen zur Entstehungsgeschichte des messianischen Glaubens; Berlin, 1932), p. 165. [3rd edn., enlarged, 1955; English tr. in prep.—M. B. (1959).]

cedes" for the king of the Philistines (this is the basic meaning of the Hebrew word for "pray"); it is as a messenger that Miriam sings and that Deborah proclaims her song of thanksgiving and victory. The mission of the *nabi* is to let the dialogue between God and man be accomplished in his speaking. God elects him "in the womb," in order that through him the divine cry of admonition and promise should strike the ear of man, but also that through him the cries of men's hearts should be gathered and borne on high. True, the divine purpose is not mediation but immediacy; however, the intermediary is the road to this aim—to the longed-for day when all God's people will be prophets with the spirit upon them (Numbers 11 : 29).

The Biblical concept of the *nabi* stands out most clearly in one passage (Exodus 7 : 1), where it is used metaphorically, where two men stand to one another in precisely the relationship of Elohim, the divine power, and *nabi*, His herald. "See," God says to Moses, "I have made thee as Elohim to Pharaoh: and Aaron thy brother shall be thy *nabi*." The metaphor clearly reveals the relation between the two, Elohim, the inspiring power, and *nabi*, the speaker. The full intimacy of this relation is shown by a parallel passage (4 : 16) earlier in the narrative: "And he shall be thy spokesman unto the people: and it shall come to pass that he shall be to thee a mouth, and thou shalt be to him as an Elohim." To be the *nabi* of an Elohim means then to be his "mouth." His mouth and not his mouthpiece: the *nabi* does not communicate a finished utterance that might have been heard before; he puts into words a hidden, soundless utterance, God's primal word, for man anterior to all words; just as a man's mouth puts into words the hidden, soundless speech of his inwardness. This fundamental conception attains its full force where God speaks of His relation to the *nabi* in exactly the same image and preserves the Biblical distance between God and man merely by saying: not "my mouth," but "as my mouth." In a critical hour Jeremiah has prayed God for help against his persecutors (15 : 15). In answering him, God not only rejects his prayer, in which the prophet has been unfaithful to his mission, but tells him (15 : 19ff.) that only if he returns from the all too human path on which he has strayed to the path of God, will He reinstate him and cause him to "stand before my face": "And if thou bring forth the precious out of the vile, thou shalt be as My mouth."

Here it is essential to note that God does not declare His intent to use the man's mouth as His own: it is the man's whole person that shall serve Him as a mouth.

This the Greek προφήτης is not, and this he cannot be. It is his mouth and not his person that "divulges." Likewise, the μάντις is not the mouth of the god, nor can he be. His person, entranced and possessed by the god, utters but does not divulge. As long as a man functions as a μάντις, he remains unintelligible to those who receive his message; and once he becomes his own προφήτης, he is merely the speaker of a word that is distinct from himself.

In the world of Biblical faith, it is not two men who confront God, one immediately and one mediately, but one; the man upon whom the storm of the divine spirit descended, to "clothe him" (Judges 6 : 34), is not with his mouth and tongue alone but with his whole life and being the spokesman of the secret voice, the "still, small voice," that blows through him (I Kings 19 : 12).

"Here there was no separation between Pythia and interpreting priest-poet: the Israelite prophet was both in one person" (Max Weber). This means that in the prophetic word of the Bible, unlike that of the Delphic oracle, speech *in statu nascendi* and finished speech are identical, whereas for the Greeks an ecstatic babbling must be transposed into ordered discourse. The speech that bursts forth from the Biblical prophet is already stamped into words; it is rhythmically articulated, "objective" speech. And yet it is not a discourse separable from the speaker, which he merely utters: it embraces the whole person, the whole speaking human body, alive in itself and now inspired by the *ruach*, the *pneuma*; it embraces the whole existence of this man: the whole man is mouth.

Here there is no distinction between the passivity of μαίνεσθαι, trance and ecstasy, and the action of προειπεῖν, expressive and effective discourse. The form of the speech is here not "received"; it is born in the original impulse to utter sound—and this is why all rules of metrics must fail the scholar, because the "ready-made" meter is always overwhelmed by the unique stream of prophecy. The man who has been seized by the *ruach* and compelled to speak does not stammer before he speaks; even when God has touched his mouth, the language he speaks has a rhythmic rigor, but it is flooded with the headlong surge of the moment. And to speak of a "development" from the "primitive ecstatic seer" to the "articulate prophet" is misleading: in the Bible the former never appears distinct from the latter, and though we read of a wild, frantic—but not unmusical—outpouring, we hear no inarticulate babbling or ranting; we encounter the voice of the *nabi* only as word, and his word only as discourse. And chronologically, the passive and active elements are not divided; they are one. There is a single comprehensive function, and this indivisible function demands the undivided man.

For a sound appreciation of the nature of prophetic existence, we must inquire into the purpose of prophecy.

Both the Greek oracular utterance and the utterance of the Biblical prophet are bound up with a specific situation. But the oracle responds to a situation described by an embassy in quest of advice, while the *nabi*, sent by God, addresses himself unbidden to the biographical or historical situation. The response of the oracle is the prediction of an unalterable future; the utterance of the *nabi* refers to an hour that is undecided but bears within it the potentiality of decision. In the answer of the Greek oracle the future is written on a scroll, the unrolling of which constitutes history; in Biblical prophecy nothing is fixed or foreordained, and God mysteriously holds his sheltering hands over the free play of human responses to events as they occur: his power, which is greater and more mysterious than the formal omnipotence of dogma, can spare a little power for the moment of his creature.

In Herodotus (I, 91) the Pythia proclaims that even a god cannot evade the destiny that has been decreed. The paradigmatic book of Jonah relates that God sent a prophet to announce the doom of the sinful city of Nineveh, and this was no conditional, avertible doom: "Yet forty days, and Nineveh shall be overthrown," cries the prophet (3 : 4). But Nineveh turned back from its ways, and God too "turned and repented." This reciprocity of repentance was the secret import of Jonah's message; it was unknown even to himself, and that was why he shrank back from it. And the Jewish tradition offered a sound interpretation of Biblical faith when it asserted that the prophets prophesied "only on behalf of penitents." [3] Speaking to the people in a given situation, the *nabi* assumes a real power of decision inherent in them. His words are not, like those of the Pythia, merely called forth by a situation: they are entirely contingent on that situation. Only this contingency can penetrate the mysterious depths of existence in creation. And just because the words of the prophets refer to the historic hour and are in keeping with it, they retain their force for all generations and peoples.

Prophecy is grounded in the reality of history as it is enacted. In contra-

3 Babylonian Talmud, *Berakoth*, tr. Maurice Simon (London, 1948), 34 b.

distinction to all mantic historiosophy, to all knowledge of the future, whether of dialectical or of gnostic origin, we have here an insight into the true character of decision, determined by so many factors and yet so determining in its simplicity.

But the spoken word alone cannot be adequate to this character of the moment, so pregnant with decision. To be adequate to it, to cope with its limitless reality, the word must be complemented by the symbolic attitude and action which alone can enable the word to express and evoke the free choice that lives in the historic moment. It is not the word as such that acts on reality, but only that word which is an integral part of a whole human existence, which springs from it and epitomizes it.

The Biblical sign can encompass proof or confirmation; but in essence it is neither one nor the other. This may be illustrated by one example among many. When Moses expresses his misgivings: "Who am I, that I should go unto Pharaoh, and that I should bring forth the children of Israel out of Egypt?"—God replies (Exodus 3 : 12): "Certainly I will be with thee; and this shall be the token unto thee, that I have sent thee: when thou hast brought forth the people out of Egypt, ye shall serve God upon this mountain." This "token," or sign, is not to be taken as an authentication. In the Bible, "sign" has a different meaning. Biblical man and with him the Biblical God demands that the spirit manifest itself more fully, more "really" than in the spoken word, that it materialize itself. Stated in Biblical terms, man asks a sign of God—that is, asks substantiation of His message; while God "proves" a man—that is, brings out what is in him, makes him manifest himself; so did God in His relentless mercy prove Abraham (Genesis 22) by giving him the utmost opportunity to embody his inner devotion. And God wants man to desire the embodiment of His spirit; he who asks a sign from Him is confirmed in his belief; he who refuses a sign offered by God to man attests not faith but lack of faith (Isaiah 7 : 11–13). The mission conferred on Moses by the voice from the burning bush is embodied in a sign when the people led out of servitude in Egypt come to the burning mountain [4] and serve the God who has borne them "on eagles' wings" and brought them unto himself (Exodus 19 : 4).

This sign cannot be rendered in words or replaced by words; there is no book of signs in which one can look up its meaning; but the spoken word is

---

4 In the original Hebrew there is an untranslatable pun: *seneh* = both "bush" and "Sinai."

fully incarnated in the sign. Precisely through being spoken the spoken word is itself a part of that corporeity: it is part of a living attitude and action.

Only the transient can become a symbol. Both sign and symbol are irreducible, a statement cannot be distilled from them; both state what cannot be stated otherwise—body and image cannot be paraphrased, the body like the image is needed to render all the depth of the word; and the bodily sign is no proof, any more than the imaged symbol is a comparison.

The prophecy of the *nabi* is not an oracle but the exact opposite. It aims at an event which may or may not take place, according to the either-or implicit in the moment. Such an aimed-at event can be adequately expressed only by a symbolic act. Only a symbolic event or action can do justice to the plenitude and freedom inherent in the moment of decision.

It is from this standpoint that we must understand all the symbolic actions of the Biblical prophets, whether, like Jeremiah's shattering of the pitcher in the presence of the elders or Ezekiel's fitting together of the two blocks of wood, they are acts of a moment, or whether they thrust deep into a life, as when Hosea marries a harlot and to the children of this marriage gives names of doom. This last, cruel example makes it plain that the symbolic act is not a practical metaphor but a literal acting out in his own flesh. The marriage is meant to represent in the human world the marriage between God and the whore Israel. "Go," says the voice in its first proclamation to the *nabi* (1 : 2), "take unto thee a wife of harlotry and children of harlotry; for the land doth commit great harlotry, departing from the Lord." This "for" states brutally that God exacts the physical life of his just-elected prophet as a sign, as a physical image of His experience with Israel. Here we have a sacred action in terrible earnest, it is a vital *dromenon*. The narrative of the marriage and the directly identifying word of God are gruesomely intertwined. The naming of the children of whoredom—that is, the legitimate children of Hosea and the whore—is recounted. One daughter is named "That hath not obtained compassion" ("for I will no more have compassion upon the house of Israel, that I should in any wise pardon them"); one son is named "Not My people" ("for ye are not My people, and I will not be yours"). And now suddenly (2 : 2) the voice of God in these children speaks to the children of Israel: "Plead with your mother, plead; for she is not My wife, neither am I her husband; and let her put away her harlotries from her face, and her adulteries from between her breasts." Here it is sharply brought home to us into what depths of reality the "sign" penetrates.

The *nabi* does not merely act by signs; his whole life is a sign. In the last analysis it is not what he does that is the sign; in the act of doing it, he himself is the sign.

But the symbolic existence of the prophet becomes most intense and also clearest in Isaiah (8 : 11–22). It is a time of the greatest confusion in which the future catastrophe of the people is foreshadowed; truth and falsehood are so mingled that the soul can scarcely distinguish between them, can scarcely recognize which is the right; God himself is misunderstood and misused "for a gin and for a snare to the inhabitants of Jerusalem." Even in this situation, to be sure, there is a consolation pointing beyond the coming catastrophe (Isaiah 9 : 1–6). But to utter it now would be to expose it to misunderstanding and abuse. And so Isaiah's word of the hour is "Bind up the testimony, seal the instruction among My disciples" (8 : 16). As one binds up and seals a book, so does the prophet bind up the testimony which he has handed on to his disciples: they themselves now represent the sealed book, which shall be broken open only when, in the midst of the catastrophe, the call "for instruction and for testimony" (v. 20) goes out to the people who in vain have been consulting the oracles, the "wizards that chirp and that mutter" (19). In the approaching "distress and darkness" (22) the prophet, in the midst of the people that have "no light" (20), will wait for the day when God, who now "hideth His face from the house of Jacob" (17), will take pity on his repentant "remnant"—he and his disciples and his own children, to one of whom, plainly at God's bidding, he has given the prophetic name "Remnant repent ye." And thus does he speak of this waiting: "Behold, I and the children whom the Lord hath given me shall be for signs and for wonders in Israel from the Lord of hosts, who dwelleth in mount Zion" (8 : 18). These men, the nucleus of the holy remnant, exist as signs; they live their lives as signs. This whole man as sign is the mouth of God. What needs to be said at such a moment is said through his symbolic existence.

This is something rather different from what is often spoken of as symbol. But no symbol, no timeless elevation, can ever achieve and recapture reality otherwise than by such incarnation in a living and dying human existence.

2. SACRAMENTAL EXISTENCE IN THE WORLD OF HASIDISM [5]

Symbol is the manifestation, the radiation of meaning in incarnate form. In it the bond between the absolute and the concrete is manifested. But the sacrament is the binding of meaning to body, the tying, the enactment of the bond. It is in the sacrament that the absolute is bound up with the concrete.

The manifestation of the symbol is a movement in one direction, from above to below; it descends and is incarnated. But the binding has two directions: the upper attaches itself to the lower and the lower attaches itself to the upper; the upper binds the lower and the lower binds the upper; they bind one another—meaning and body bind one another. Where the bond is manifested, it is like the reflection of one invisible; where the bond is enacted, it is like a hand within a hand. Hand in hand, the bond is concluded and renewed.

To connect the divine and the human though without fusing them, to form them into a living Beyond, compounded of transcendence and immanence—that is the chief though not the only function of the sacrament. Even when it is only two human beings who sacramentally consecrate themselves to each other—in marriage, in brotherhood—that other bond, the bond between the absolute and the concrete, is secretly enacted; for the source of consecration is not any power in the human beings; it is the power of the eternal wings that hover over them. Every absolute relation into which men enter with one another derives its force from the presence of the absolute.

The sacrament has rightly been called "the most dynamic of all ritual forms." [6] And the important thing about this dynamism is that it loses its authenticity if it ceases to encompass an elementary and living experience of the *other*, of otherness as an effective force. The sacramental rite is not merely something that man "performs" or "experiences"; it seizes him and exacts his whole being, and he requires his whole being to fulfill it. This is what constitutes its three-dimensional character, the reality of its dimension of depth. The sacral convention of the church or other institution flattens the event into a gesture, while mystical enthusiasm contracts it

---

5 In preparing the present version of this part for publication, even more than in the preparation of the first part, above, I have incorporated material suggested by questions from the audience.

6 Robert R. Marett, *Sacraments of Simple Folk* (Oxford, 1933), p. 9.

to an inwardness so inward as to be no more than an ardent, glowing point.

Every sacrament requires a natural activity drawn from the natural course of life—and consecrates that activity. It requires also a substantial or material otherness with which a sacred contact is established. In this contact the secret force of the *other* becomes effective.

"Primitive" man is a naïve pansacramentalist. For him everything is full of sacramental substance; everything, every thing and every function, can appear in a sacramental light. He knows no selection of objects and activities, only one of methods and favorable moments. The "substance" is everywhere; one needs only the power to capture it. For this there are rules and rhythms; but these one can acquire only by daring, and even he who has the knowledge and power must continually renew the dangerous grip and challenge of the contact.

The crisis of primitive man occurs when he discovers the essentially unholy, asacramental—the things which resist his methods and have no "hour"; and this province becomes constantly larger. This critical phase, in which the world threatens to become neutralized, to evade the sacred contact, can be found among certain tribes which we are accustomed to regard as primitive, though sometimes only in marginal individuals. The Ba-ilas of Northern Rhodesia, for example, characterize this phase when they say of their god: "Leza has grown old" or "Leza is no longer what he ought to be." [7]

What we call religion in the more restricted sense has perhaps always come into being in such crises. All historical religion is a *selection* of sacramental substances and actions. Through the separation of sacred elements from all those now abandoned as profane, the sacrament is saved. The consecrated bond is concentrated in certain objects and functions.

But now the sacrament enters into a realm of new and more difficult problems. For a concrete religion can preserve its living significance only if it exacts not only faith, but the whole person of the faithful. But such is the power of the sacrament, based on the separation of the sacred from the profane, that it easily beguiles the believer into feeling secure in a mere "objective" performance of ritual, a mere *opus operatum* without personal devotion. And so he evades the grip and challenge of his own wholeness.

7 Edwin W. Smith and Andrew M. Dale, *The Ila-speaking Peoples of Northern Rhodesia* (London, 1920), Vol. II, pp. 200ff.

But when the vital substance of the faithful ceases to flow into it, the sacrament loses depth, three-dimensional reality, substantiality. As, for example, when in the sacramental sacrifice of Biblical Israel the central intention of self-sacrifice (where the believer is actually "represented" by an animal) is lost in the security of an objective, ritual atonement.[8] Or when the Biblical anointment of kings, which confers a living responsibility on him who is entrusted with God's eternal stewardship,[9] degenerates in Western coronation rites to a pompous confirmation of arbitrary power.

Where the inner crisis of sacramentalism has placed the original content, the original force, of a religion in question, an attempt at reformation has sometimes been successful. Such an attempt strives also to save the consecration of the bond: by reviving an attitude of seriousness toward the presence of man. (The controversy between Luther and Zwingli regarding the divine presence in the Last Supper was secretly concerned with the human presence as well; Luther sensed, as Zwingli did not, that a merely symbolic presence could not capture the whole man and summon his full presence.)

But the reformer does not tamper with the principle of selection as applied to sacramental substances and actions; only sectarians occasionally assail it, though they never transcend or replace it. It would seem as though the man who had experienced the discovery of the essentially profane could never regain a sacred relation to the whole cosmos; as though reduction of the life of faith to a single sphere were indispensable and central to all religion, the only possible bulwark against the pantheism which threatens concrete religion with dissolution. "He alone existing," says the poet of the South Seas of his god Taaroa or Tangaroa, "he transforms himself into a world. The axis on which it turns is Taaroa, the blocks which sustain it Taaroa; Taaroa is the primal grain of sand." [10] Concrete religion must see to it that the image of the Lord, the eternal religious confrontation, does not dissolve into primal dust.

But there is one great religious movement, essentially of a reform character, which has devised a new pansacramentalism. This was not a retreat into the time before the critical discovery of which we have been speaking—the road to such a return is barred, and anyone seeking to travel it can arrive only at madness or mere literature—but a progression to a new, com-

8 Cf. Buber, *Königtum Gottes*, pp. 99ff.

9 Buber, *Der Gesalbte* [unpublished Vol. II of *Das Kommende*; see n. 2, supra].

10 Jacques A. Moerenhout, *Voyages aux îles du Grand Océan* (Paris, 1837), Vol. I, pp. 419-20.

prehensive vision. This movement knew that the sacramental substance cannot be found or grasped in the totality of things and functions, but that it can be awakened and released in every object and every action—not by any method that can be acquired, but by the fulfilling presence of the whole, wholly devoted man, by sacramental existence.

This great movement, Hasidism, came into being two centuries ago (according to the legend, its founder was "revealed" about 1735) in an obscure corner of Eastern Europe and there—degenerated, but still capable of regeneration—it has remained. But this movement must go down in religious history as an incomparable attempt to rescue the life of man from the ruin of everydayness.

For Hasidic pansacramentalism the sacred in things is not, as it was for primitive pansacramentalism, a power over which man can gain mastery; it is embedded in them, it inheres in them like sparks, waiting to be released and fulfilled by the devoted man. The man of sacramental existence is no magician; he not only ventures to approach the sacrament, but really and absolutely dedicates himself; he exerts no power but performs a service, *the* service. He dedicates himself in service; and this means always, on every occasion. What is important (in the sacramental sense)? The answer: "Whatever a man happens to concern himself with." And the momentary, when it is taken seriously in its momentary, unique contingency, proves to be that which cannot be anticipated or prepared for. The man of sacramental existence is aided by no acquired rules and rhythms, by no traditional methods, no special knowledge or aptitude; he must continually withstand the unforeseen and unforeseeable moment; he must continually, in the on-flowing moment, offer release, fulfillment to a thing or creature encountered. And he can effect no selection, no division, since it is not for him to decide what will come his way and what will not; and there is no such thing as the profane, there is only the not-yet-sanctified, the not-yet-redeemed-into-sanctity, which it is his mission to sanctify.

Hasidism is commonly interpreted as a rebellion of "feeling" against a religious rationalism which exaggerated and rigidified the doctrine of divine transcendence, and a ritualism which made religious practice independent and barren. But the actual force at work in this rebellion is not covered by the term feeling; it is the resurgence of an authentic vision of unity and a passionate longing for wholeness. It is not merely a repressed emotional life demanding its rights, but a magnified vision of God and a stronger desire

179

for realization. The sharp boundary drawn between God and world in doctrine, and between sacred and profane in life, no longer satisfies this twofold growth, because both boundaries are static, rigid, timeless, because they allow no room for unique, concrete events. The magnified image of God demands a more dynamic, fluid boundary between God and world, for it implies knowledge of a force striving to pour itself out and at the same time limiting itself, a resistant but also pliable substance. And the increased desire for realization demands a more dynamic, fluid boundary between sacred and profane, because it cannot leave the redemption, which will, it is promised, assimilate the two realms generically to the Messianic Age; it must actively give to the moment whatever may be its rightful due.

And yet, from a historical point of view, we must recognize that all the elements of this "new" world were alive, struggling for dominance, and making headway in the "rabbinical" world against which the struggle was directed. In order to understand this, we must realize (though this is far too seldom done) that there had always been a strong tendency toward sacramental life in Judaism. Contrary opinions notwithstanding, it can be shown that there is scarcely any Christian sacrament without its sacramental or semisacramental Jewish prototype. And moreover, throughout Jewish history, even in the Talmudic period, there have been masters of an unmistakably sacramental form of existence, men whose whole life and attitude represented and enacted the consecration of the bond. The historical series of such men is well-nigh unbroken. The "Zaddik" of the early Hasidic period, the classical Zaddik,[11] is only a particularly clear, theoretically circumscribed form of the one archetype, originating in the Biblical world and foreshadowing a future world.

But a study of the relation between Hasidism and the cabala [12] reveals a still more significant aspect of Hasidic pansacramentalism. Hasidism did not, like rabbinical Judaism, oppose the cabala; it took over the concepts, often the style, and to some extent the doctrine of cabalism; and the cabalistic works of Hasidic authors remain within the late cabalistic tradition. Theurgic practice of a cabalistic character makes several appearances in the history of Hasidism, sometimes in strangely anachronistic form. Yet, fundamentally, Hasidism rejected the basic principles of the cabala;

---

11 Concerning the Zaddik, cf. my *Die chassidischen Bücher* (Hellerau, 1928), pp. 352–70.
12 The authoritative and comprehensive work on the cabala is G. Scholem's article by this name in the *Encyclopaedia Judaica*, IX (1932), 630–731.

where it concerns itself with its true object, life within the bond, it speaks from an entirely different source and in essential points reveals a nowhere uttered, perhaps never conscious, and yet evident opposition to the cabalistic doctrine and attitude; and even more important: leading figures of Hasidism, and above all the many *zaddikim* as described in Hasidic legend—whose equal for scope, variety, vitality, and wild popular charm I do not know— are very far removed from cabalistic existence; these men are open to the world, they have an attitude of piety toward this world, they are in love with the world.

A difference that may at first seem superficial but is nevertheless significant: the cabala is esoteric. What it says conceals something that is unsaid. The ultimate meaning is disclosed only to the initiate. Even from the point of view of access to the reality of God, a dividing line runs through mankind. This is a conception intolerable to Hasidism: as regards access to the kingdom, there may no longer be division; here stands the brotherhood of all God's children, the secret is manifested to all or to none, to all or none is the heart of eternity open. What is reserved to a knowing segment of mankind, what is withheld from the simple, cannot be the living truth. Lovingly, the Hasidic legend praises the simple man. He has oneness of soul; where there is oneness of soul, there will God's oneness dwell. The sacramental bond signifies a life of oneness with oneness.

In its origin, but also in its central nature which continually emerges, the cabala is a gnosis, but unlike every other form of gnosis, it is antidualistic.[13]

The source of all gnosis—forgive me a simplification which I believe to be necessary in the present context—is the primal question, intensified to the point of despair in the world: How can the corrosive essence of existence in the world, the insoluble contradiction in every life and historical context, be reconciled with God's being? The question did not become thus acute until after the Old Testament period; all true gnosis originated in a cultural sphere touched by the Old Testament, and almost every branch of it was a more or less explicit rebellion against the Old Testament. The Biblical experience of unity—One essential power, One superior counterpart to man —meets the experience of contradiction, rising as it does from painful

---

13 I believe that the doctrine of Plotinus will also be seen to be fundamentally antidualistic when the significant work of Hans Jonas, *Gnosis und spätantiker Geist* (Vol. I, 1934) becomes available in its completed form; but then we shall have to regard it as gnosis transformed into philosophy and not, like the cabala, as gnosis pure and simple. [The work was completed by a second vol. in 1954.—ED.]

depths, with insistence on the mysteriousness of the mystery: the meaning of that which is manifested as contradiction or irrationality surpasses the limits of knowledge (Job), but can be surmised in the living mystery of suffering (Deutero-Isaiah); and here occurs the most powerful manifestation of sacramental existence: suffering itself becomes sacrament (Isaiah 53). But the apocalyptic Jewish writings can no longer meet the question; the Apocalypse of Ezra (Fourth Book of Ezra), for example, has lost the pious acceptance of the mystery and reveals merely a mechanical subjection, which amounts to renunciation of the world and a drying up of sacramental life. Here gnosis intervenes, taking stones from the crumbled giant edifices of the ancient oriental religions and fitting them into the strangest new structure. It interprets the conflicts of the world as conflicts of the godhead: either the good God is confronted by an evil, or merely inferior, negative principle; or else the good God engenders frail or seducible powers which fall into the sphere of evil and become a world soul caught in contradiction, until they are permitted to rise up again. The Other, the Opposing principle, the contrary power or contrary world, is always more or less explicitly posited, though sometimes it is spoken of merely as "spaces of shadow and emptiness." To take away from this Other its independence, to draw it into the dynamic of the divine oneness—that is the striving of the cabala.

Using an amalgam of gnostic and Neoplatonic schemata, the cabala takes a Talmudic doctrine and expands it prodigiously. This is the doctrine (developed in opposition to apocalyptic resignation) of the divine attributes of sternness and mercifulness, and of their dialectical interrelations: the drama of the world process appears as a drama enacted within God. This dual dialectic, which must be construed as real and yet not as dualistic, is multiplied by the cabala in the interrelations of the Sephiroth,[14] the divine primal numbers or primal radiances, of the powers and orders which it, the cabala, evokes from the eternally hidden inwardness of God, which is called "the endless," by a "limitation" and a "sifting"; these powers and orders remain in God and yet they are the foundation of the world. Their hierarchy reaches down into all the levels of the cosmos, even to the lowest, corporeal "husk" world; the dynamism of their veilings and unveilings, effusions and obstructions, bindings and unbindings creates the dialectic of cosmic and terrestrial being. Like such precosmic catastrophes as the "death of the primal kings" or the "breaking of the vessels"—catastrophes with cosmic repercussions—

14 [See the paper by Bernoulli, below, pp. 325ff.—ED.]

so likewise every obstruction and disturbance in the world, down to the daemonic powers which assail the human soul, are the consequence of bindings, shifts of weight, overflowings in the realm of the aeons. And yet it is precisely in this world that something can be done toward resolving the conflict: it is the sacramental act of man—who in his prayers and actions aims at the elementary mysteries of God's names and their interrelations and works toward the unification of the divine forces—that the second, the perfecting, unity of being is prepared. The cabalistic reconciliation of the experience of unity with the experience of contradiction, like the Biblical reconciliation of the two, is ultimately sacramental.

Never explicit but nevertheless very real, there is in Hasidism a twofold opposition to the cabala.

First, Hasidism rejects the schematization of the mystery. Like any other system of gnosis the cabala purports to penetrate the contradiction of existence and to rise above it, while the essential attitude of Hasidism is to endure the contradiction in piety and thus redeem the contradiction itself. The cabala draws a map of original mysteries, and on this map the sources of the contradiction also have their place; Hasidism may imitate the cabala (this is often the case, though even here its cabalism is purely peripheral); it may retain a cabalistic picture of the upper world, precisely because it knows no other with which to replace it—but in its own province it is agnostic; it is concerned not with objective, formulable knowledge, susceptible of schematization, but with a vital knowledge, with a Biblical "knowing" which consists in a reciprocal relation with God. To be sure, "the classical cabalists deny over and over again that the movement into the finite world, of the goodness inherent in God, described in those cabalistic doctrines which combine theology and cosmogony in such a way as to make them indistinguishable, is an objective process, i.e., a process manifested by God." [15] But this is merely a parenthetical, metaphysical-epistemological principle without application; it never enters into the system itself, and the whole cabalistic edifice rests upon a certainty which almost never pauses, almost never trembles, almost never sinks to its knees. But it is precisely through pausing, through openness to emotion, through a profound awareness of the frailty of all positive knowledge, of the incongruity of all possessed truth, through "holy uncertainty," that Hasidic piety truly lives. This is the reason for the Hasidic love of the "fool." What is the essential?

15 Scholem (n. 12, above), p. 670.

You may "climb about in the upper worlds"—suddenly the storm strikes and everything is blown away; in the infinite, inarticulate darkness you will stand before your own presence. And it is only the hand of the insecure man, stretched forward without defense, that is not paralyzed by the thunderbolt. We have been sent down into a world of contradiction; to glide off into spheres where the contradiction seems transparent is to evade our mission. It is contrary to the faith and humor of our existence (Hasidism is distinguished by both faith and humor) to suppose that there is a level of being to which we need only lift ourselves in order to fathom the contradiction. Contradiction is given me to endure along with my life and also to fulfill; this endurance and fulfillment of the contradiction is the only meaning accessible to me.

Hasidism also rejects the cabalistic magicalization of the mystery. Magic is not identical with belief in the transcendental efficacy of man's acts— that is, in the influence of human being and human life beyond the sphere of logical causality; no, within faith, magic is the belief that there are certain transmissible and transmitted, inward and outward, actions and attitudes through which a definite effect can be obtained. Thus where magic (which can exist both inside and outside of sacramentalism) is connected with gnosis, it is simply its reverse side: its definition of the instruments—here the instruments for combating the contradiction of existence—goes hand in hand with the gnostic claim to penetrate the contradiction. In the cabala these traditional magical methods can be applied in connection with very diverse activities; these are the *kavanot*, the intentions which, gathering from the rich store of name and letter mysticism, aspire through manipulations of letters and names to influence the essences themselves. And again: as Hasidic doctrine retains the cabalistic schemata in a peripheral sense but centrally disregards them, so in practice it retains all those manipulations that can be learned, and indeed all sorts of cabalistic-magical trappings, such as magical formulas and amulets, but its true nature is often realized in actual, and not seldom in programmatic, opposition to these elements. In opposition to the intelligible *kavanot*—you must meditate thus and so remember this and that—there rises the single *kavanah*, encompassing all life, of the man dedicated to God and His work of redemption. As Hasidism strives to transcend the split between the sacred and the profane, it also opposes the isolation of fixed manipulatory procedures out of all the abundance of living action. Not by accompanying any action with a preconceived mystical method, but by performing this action with his whole being turned toward God, does man practice a true *kavana*. That which can be known in advance is not suited to release the central content of the act; for it is not in any arbitrary, self-willed way, but solely as a countermovement to that which meets us, that the sacramental act may be performed; but that which meets us cannot be known in advance; God and the moment cannot be known in advance, and the moment is God's cloak; hence we can always prepare ourselves for the act, but we cannot prepare the act. Always the substance of the act is given, or rather offered us: by what befalls us, by what crosses our path, by everything that crosses our path. The consecration of the bond is the consecration of contingency. All things—all secular things in their secularity—want to be sanctified, consecrated. They desire not to be desecularized, but within their secularity to be consecrated in the *kavana* of redemption—all things desire to become sacrament. Creatures and things seek us out. Whatever crosses our path needs us for that path. Ye shall pray "with the plank and with the bench"; [16] they want to come to us, all things want to come to us, all things want to reach God through us. What are the upper worlds, if such there be? Our task is "to make the hidden life of God shine in this lower world, the world of matter."

The word *yihud*, unity or unification, which Hasidism took over from the cabala as a designation of the sacramental act, has a threefold sense. Originally, it means the unity of God, which embraces and sustains all the multiplicity and multiformity of being. Next, it means the human profession of this unity, wherein man apprehends all the powers in nature, history, life, as emanations and rays of the one power, and by his word restrains the striving for independence of any among them, transforming it into worship and humility. And finally it means the unifying act of man. For the cabala this means: participation in the marriages of the Sephiroth. For Hasidism this means: to draw all impulses and passions of the person into a unity moved toward God, a unity utterly open to the world, which sanctifies all things and even their resistance to unity. It means to offer this unity of immanent sacramental existence to God for the work of his redeeming unification—that is to say, the "union of the transcendent God with his immanent glory."

16 Buber, *Die chassidischen Bücher*, p. 470.

Friedrich Heiler

Contemplation in Christian Mysticism

1. The History of Christian Contemplation

The hallmark of present-day Western culture is an unlimited dynamism. The intense organizational activity, the rationalization and mechanization, characteristic of this culture have also seized hold of the Christian Churches of the West. Protestantism seems particularly in danger of succumbing to this *Zeitgeist*, to conceptions that are here today and gone tomorrow.

In contrast to this restless activity of the Western Churches, the great religions of the East maintain a majestic tranquillity. They are all contemplative religions, the Taoism of China, Vedāntic Brāhmanism, Buddhism in both its Hīnayāna and Mahāyāna forms, and even Islam, with its unchanging daily prayer, not to mention the mysticism of the Ṣūfīs.

This contemplative repose makes the Eastern religions, particularly those of India, a revelation to the cultivated Westerner. In them he believes that he can find peace and certainty for his heart, which breathless activity has deprived of all calm. And yet objective comparison shows that none of the lofty values or reliable methods that the Oriental religions offer the West is totally lacking in Christianity. All forms of contemplative piety can be found in the two-thousand-year-long history of the Christian religion. Christianity, too, is a contemplative religion, even though its modern Protestant representatives have greatly neglected and even negated this aspect of it.

Contemplation is the ancient word used by Western theologians for what the Greek theologians designated *mystērion* and *mystikē theologia*—the now current word "mysticism," an abbreviation of "mystical theology," has only quite recently gained full acceptance in the West. The clearest definition of contemplation was perhaps presented by St. Thomas Aquinas, the prince of Scholastics, when he said: "Contemplatio est simplex intuitus divinae veritatis a principio supernaturali procedens" ("Contemplation is the simple intuition of divine truth, proceeding from a supernatural principle").[1] Contemplation is spiritual vision, a total vision, directed toward the divine reality in its transcendental totality, a vision that is not voluntarily induced by human activity but that arises without our volition, that—speaking in religious terms—is inspired, infused, bestowed as a divine *charisma*.

A proper understanding of Christian contemplation, both in its corporative-ecclesiastical and in its individual forms, can be gained only if we keep in mind a general picture of the origin and development of contemplative piety in Christianity. The root of Christian contemplation is threefold:

(1) Jewish prophetism and the Jerusalem Temple cult;

(2) the Hellenistic-syncretistic mysteries;

(3) Platonic and Neoplatonic mysticism.

The Jewish religion from which Christianity sprang was prophetic and active in character, but from the beginning it contained a strong mystical, contemplative element. Even in the tales of Genesis, this element finds plastic expression. In his dream, Jacob beholds "a ladder set up on the earth, and the top of it reached to heaven: and behold the angels of God ascending and descending on it" (Gen. 28 : 12)—a vision that was to become a favorite image with the Christian mystics. At the ford of Jabbok, Jacob meets the God Yahweh face to face, and wrestles with Him until he receives His blessing; and he names the place of this spiritual wrestling bout Peniel; i.e., face of God—"for I have seen God face to face, and my life is preserved" (Gen. 32 : 22 ff.). The amazing intimacy of the Prophets with their God, Yahweh, was accomplished through their visions of the Eternal in sensible forms. Moses sees Yahweh as fire in the bush that is burned but not consumed; from the midst of it, he hears the voice of Yahweh—"and Moses hid his face; for he was afraid to look upon God" (Exod. 3 : 2 ff.). From this moment on, Moses stands in the closest relation to the God who has called him; he encounters Him again and again on the mountaintop (Exod. 19 : 18). "With him will I speak mouth to mouth, even apparently" (Num. 12 : 8). To be sure, this is a limited vision. Moses' yearning "to behold the glory of Yahweh"—i.e., to know God in His eternal essence—could not be satisfied, for such a vision must destroy a man: "Thou canst not see my face: for

1 *Summa theologica*, II–II, q. 180, a. 3 and 4 (summarized).

there shall no man see me, and live." But the Lord grants Moses a partial vision—"thou shalt see my back parts"—and gives him a glimpse of His radiant light through the veil of the cloud (Exod. 19 : 9 ff.; 33 : 7 ff.). When this covert vision was conferred upon him, Moses "bowed his head toward the earth, and worshipped" (Exod. 34 : 5 ff.). This contemplation has a miraculous transfiguring power; it lays hold of the whole man, body and soul. Whenever Moses returned from speaking with God on the mountain or in the tabernacle, the people saw that "the skin of his face shone"; and because his countenance revealed the radiance of the Eternal Himself, "they were afraid to come nigh him" (Exod. 34 : 29 ff.).

And others among the Hebrew Prophets beheld similar indirect visions of God. Elijah on Mount Horeb sees the Lord "pass by," but not in the usual forms assumed by the volcanic mountain god, not in the wind, not in the earthquake, and not in the fire, but in "the still small voice." And "when Elijah heard it . . . he wrapped his face in his mantle"—for even thus cloaked, the divine glory blinds the human eye (I Kings 19). The most grandiose contemplative experience of the Hebrews was vouchsafed to Isaiah, Israel's greatest Prophet after Moses, at the time of his calling. He sees Yahweh on a "throne, high and lifted up, and his train filled the temple. Above it stood the seraphims. . . . And one cried unto another, and said, Holy, holy, holy, is the Lord." And so overwhelming is this vision that it terrifies the sinful man, and brings only a lamentation from his lips: "Woe is me! for I am undone . . . for mine eyes have seen the King, the Lord of hosts" (Isa. 6). Upon the great priest-Prophet Ezekiel a similar vision is bestowed within the Temple—he sees the throne of Yahweh "above the head of the cherubims," "and the house was filled with the cloud, and the court was full of the brightness of the Lord's glory" (Ezek. 10).

The experience of contemplation, however, was not limited to the great Jewish Prophets; it spread to the people and became their common heritage in the cult of the tabernacle and the Temple. The stories of the cloud that concealed the glory of Yahweh, which covered the tabernacle and glowed like fire at night (Exod. 40 : 34; Num. 9 : 15), reflect the contemplative experience as a vision of light by the congregation in its Temple cult. The yearning for this joyful contemplation is stirringly expressed in the Temple Psalms. The Psalmist prays again and again for the veiled vision of God that had been bestowed upon the Prophets: "As the hart panteth after the water brooks, so panteth my soul after thee, O God. . . . When shall I come and appear before God?" (Ps. 42 [Vulg. 41]). The longing of the Psalmist for the tabernacles and courts of the Lord (Ps. 84 [83]), for the Temple and the "beauty of the Lord" (Ps. 27 [26]), the infinite love of the pious Jews for their Temple as the place of Yahweh's presence, have their source in the experience of liturgical contemplation, which allows the worshiper to see the eternal light in earthly reflections: "in thy light shall we see light" (Ps. 36 : 9 [35 : 10]); "Make thy face to shine upon thy servant" (Ps. 31 : 16 [30 : 17]).

The Temple in Jerusalem had stood at the center of Jewish contemplation; its destruction brought about a complete transformation in Jewish piety. Nevertheless, the contemplative mysticism of the Prophets and of the Temple cult remained alive in the individual mysticism of the Jews, in the subtle, gnostic cabala, and in the simple piety of the Hasidim. Contemplative mysticism is no peculiarity of "Aryan" religions; it is universal. The Jewish vision is an essential link in the general history of mysticism. It finds its highest fulfillment in Christian contemplation.

Jesus completes the series of the contemplative men of God under the old covenant: Moses, Elijah, Isaiah, Ezekiel. Like all pious Jews, he dwelt from childhood on in the Temple, the abode of Him whom he knew to be his Father. Like Elijah, he repeatedly fled into the solitude of the mountains and the desert, in order to spend the nights in contemplative prayer and in converse with his Father. The most wonderful contemplative experience befell him while he was with three of his Apostles on Mount Tabor (Mark 9): "He was transfigured before them. And his raiment became shining, exceeding white as snow; so as no fuller on earth can white them," "and there was a cloud that overshadowed them"—the same cloud in which Moses and his people had beheld the glory of Yahweh—and a voice from heaven confirmed him as God's Son. In this wondrous vision Jesus and his Apostles were not alone, but in communion with the greatest contemplative Prophets of the Old Testament, Moses and Elijah; contemplation is for Jesus not only the most fervent communion with God, but at the same time a *communio sanctorum*, a communion with the departed holy men who are dwelling with God. Jesus enjoined upon his disciples not to speak of this most sacred contemplative experience until his resurrection. But the contemplative ideal as such constituted a part of his public preaching. "Consider the lilies of the field . . ." he says, "they toil not, neither do they spin: And yet . . . even Solomon in all his glory was not arrayed like one of these" (Matt. 6 : 28). Thus he places the contemplative life above all the restlessness of worldly endeavor. And in the same spirit he praises the tranquil Mary, who, unlike her busy sister Martha, "hath chosen that good part" (Luke 10 : 42). Yet man cannot achieve the serene vision and knowledge of God by his own strength; it is a free gift of God's grace; it is hidden "from the wise and prudent" and revealed "unto babes" (Matt. 11 : 25).

Not only was Jesus an example and a teacher of mystical contemplation; he himself became an object of such contemplation. In the piety of St. Paul, the mysticism of God became the mysticism of Christ. St. Paul inextricably interwove contemplation with the Christ of the Gospel history, with Christ incarnate, crucified, and risen again. The life of a Christian was for him essentially a *vita contemplativa*—"your life is hid with Christ in God" (Col. 3 : 3). The life of the Christian is in the world beyond—"our conversation is in heaven" (Phil. 3 : 20); it is a constant seeking of "those things which are above, where Christ sitteth on the right hand of God" (Col. 3 : 1 ff.), an ἐν Χριστῷ εἶναι ("being in Christ") (Rom. 8 : 1; II Cor. 5 : 17). This mystical unity with Christ is nourished by the sacrament of the bread and wine, the communion of the body and blood of Christ (I Cor. 10 : 16). Although this mysticism reveals ecstatic peaks, in which the soul is "caught up to the third heaven" (II Cor. 12 : 2), it nevertheless bears an ethical character; all mystical gnosis—i.e., all contemplative immersion in the divine mysteries—is nothing without active brotherly love. And as long as man dwells in this temporal world, he can only "know in part," he sees "through a glass, darkly." Perfect contemplation, the seeing of God "face to face," is reserved for the glory of the eternal kingdom of God (I Cor. 13 : 9 ff.).

Mystical contemplation takes on still another form in the writings of St. John. The Fourth Gospel is the contemplative or, as the Fathers said, the pneumatic Gospel. The image of the eagle that Christian symbolism attaches to the fourth Evangelist indicates his contemplative clarity. St. Augustine writes: "Aquila ipse est Joannes, sublimium praedicator et lucis internae atque aeternae fixis oculis contemplator" ("A veritable eagle is John, who narrates things sublime, and contemplates the internal and eternal light with steadfast gaze").[2] In the Fourth Gospel, Jesus initiates his disciples into the mysteries of contemplation: "Hereafter ye shall see heaven

---

2 *Tractatus in Joannem*, XXXVI, 5; quoted in Cuthbert Butler, *Western Mysticism* (London, 1922), p. 86n.

open, and the angels of God ascending and descending upon the Son of man" (John 1 : 51). Indeed, the speeches of Jesus, with their constant ἐγώ εἰμι ("I am"), compel mystical vision: "I am the light of the world," "I am the resurrection and the life," "I am the bread of life," "the good shepherd," "the way," "the truth," "the life," "the true vine," etc. The human face of Jesus gives the beholder a glance into the depths of the Eternal Father. "Lord, shew us the Father, and it sufficeth us," says Philip. And Jesus answers: "He that hath seen me hath seen the Father" (John 14 : 8). And as in Jesus' lifetime the incarnate God was visible to the eyes of the disciples, those who believe in him continually see, touch, taste him in the sacramental bread and wine, his "flesh" and his "blood" (John 6 : 54 ff.). The divine and eternal glory is manifested visibly and tangibly in the face of the incarnate Son of God—"No man hath seen God at any time; the only begotten Son, which is in the bosom of the Father, he hath declared him" (John 1 : 18). "We beheld his glory"—in these words of his prologue the Evangelist sums up the import of his contemplation; at the end of the Gospel, the incredulous Thomas, converted to belief, cries out: "My Lord and my God." This is the creed of the corporeally present Son of God. And when in his First Epistle John writes: "We shall see him as he is" (I John 3 : 2)— he is pointing to the fulfillment of contemplation in the glory of the afterlife.

Contemplation is an essential element in early Christianity. Much as it inevitably varies in Jesus, St. Paul, and St. John, nevertheless, when compared to the contemplation of the Oriental religions, or of the contemporaneous Hellenistic cults, it reveals four distinguishing features. (1) It is bound up with the Gospel; the road to the vision of God is through Christ incarnate and crucified. (2) It is closely associated with the sacraments, particularly that of the Lord's Supper. (3) The touchstone of its authenticity is ethical activity, whose essence is active brotherly love: "For he that loveth not his brother whom he hath seen, how can he love God whom he hath not seen?" (I John 4 : 20). "Vidisti fratrem, vidisti Dominum tuum" ("If thou hast seen thy brother, thou hast seen thy Lord").[3] (4) It is incomplete in the present age, and achieves its fulfillment only in the kingdom of God to come.

In the ensuing nineteen hundred years this early Christian contemplation, grown on Jewish soil, gained ever-increasing richness and scope. In this process of growth the contact of Christian-Biblical religion with the Hellenistic mysteries and with Platonic and Neoplatonic mysticism played an

3 An extracanonical saying of Jesus (cf. Matt. 25 : 35 ff.).

191

essential part. It was indeed the fusion of these two currents, of Biblical Christianity and Hellenism, that created the incomparable wealth of Christian contemplative piety. It began in the age of the New Testament and continued in the following centuries. The profoundest contemplative experience of the ancient world entered into Christianity, where it was purified and completed. In its ability to assimilate such "heathen" elements, Christianity demonstrated its all-embracing catholicity.

The mysteries led their devotees from κάθαρσις (purification) to ἐπόπτεια (vision), and finally to ἕνωσις (union). A sacred drama, δρώμενον, or the showing of a cultic object (δεικνύμενον), enabled the initiate to see the godhead in sensible images and signs. It was in the Egyptian mystery cult that the contemplative element was most highly developed. Porphyry tells us that the Egyptian priests spent their whole lives in meditation and contemplation of things divine (τῇ τῶν θείων θεωρίᾳ καὶ θεάσει). Cumont, the great student of Hellenistic-Roman syncretism, rightly says that "Egypt is the country from which contemplative piety came to Europe." [4] In the Roman Isis cult, the images of the godhead were set up in special sacramental chapels from early morning to late at night for the worship of the faithful. Apuleius tells of the *inexplicabilis voluptas* that came over him at the sight of the unveiled divine image.[5] Another devotee, when he saw the divine image, burst into the cry of thanks: "Thou hast deified us by the vision of thyself" (ἀπεθέωσας τῇ σεαυτοῦ θέᾳ).

Under the direct or indirect influence of these mysteries, the Christian cult, and particularly its central act, the celebration of the Lord's Supper, acquired an even stronger mystical and contemplative cast than had been given it by its Jewish origins. Christianity became the great school of contemplation, not only for the individual mystic recipient of grace, but for the simple folk as well. The incarnation, crucifixion, and resurrection of Christ were the sacred δρώμενον, accomplished in the rite of the Eucharist; the flesh and blood of Christ actualized in the form of bread and wine were the δεικνύμενον.

An even greater stimulus to Christian contemplation than the ancient esoteric mysteries was the individualistic mysticism of Platonism and Neoplatonism, which was itself influenced by the mystery cults. In the grandiose visions of Plato (d. 347 B.C.), the divine Eros leads the soul upward from the

4 Franz Cumont, *Les Religions orientales dans le paganisme romain* (Paris, 1929), p. 89.
5 *Metamorphoses*, XI, 24.

192

contemplation of earthly beauty to that of absolute reality, of true being (ἡ τοῦ ὄντος θέα), of eternal truth, goodness, and beauty. With stirring eloquence, Plato described this vision culminating in ἐνθουσιασμός and in ἔκστασις.

He will "perceive a nature of wondrous beauty—a nature which in the first place is everlasting, not growing and decaying, or waxing and waning; secondly, not fair in one point of view and foul in another, or at one time or in one relation or at one place fair, at another time or in another relation or at another place foul, as if fair to some and foul to others." He will see "the divine beauty . . . pure and clear and unalloyed, not clogged with the pollutions of mortality and all the colors and vanities of human life." "Beholding beauty with the eye of the mind, he will be enabled to bring forth, not images of beauty, but realities." [6]

This Platonic vision was theoretically and practically elaborated by the greatest religious thinker of late antiquity, Plotinus (d. c. A.D. 270). Prerequisite for the vision of God is the soul's kinship and similarity to God— "Never did eye see the sun unless it had first become sunlike." [7] But first the soul must detach itself from the unclean and the transitory; it must cast off all veils, just as he who enters the holy of holies, or the mystic who enters the imageless ἄδυτον, must leave behind all images. In ecstasy the vision of the absolute becomes a vision of the self—the ecstatic beholds himself as one grown simple, "a self wrought to splendour, brimmed with the Intellectual light, become that very light, pure, buoyant, unburdened, raised to Godhood or, better, knowing its Godhood." [8] Because in this vision soul and God coincide, it is different from sensory and intellectual vision; it is a going out, a becoming simple, a giving of oneself (ἔκστασις, ἅπλωσις, ἐπίδοσις); "beholder was one with beheld," what was before a seen object has now become the seeing itself. "He is merged with the Supreme, sunken into it, one with it: centre coincides with centre." [9] "There were not two; beholder was one with beheld; it was not a vision compassed but a unity apprehended" (οὐχ ἑωραμένον, ἀλλ᾽ ἡνωμένον). [10] This vision culminating in ἕνωσις is the highest joy and bliss—for nothing would the soul exchange this vision, even if it were offered the whole of heaven. Such vision, to be

6 *Symposium*, 210f., in B. Jowett, tr., *The Dialogues of Plato* (New York, 1937), I, 334–35.
7 Plotinus, *Enneads*, I, 6, 9; tr. Stephen MacKenna, rev. B. S. Page (London and New York, 1956), p. 64.
8 Ibid., VI, 9, 9; tr. MacKenna, p. 623.
9 Ibid., VI, 9, 10; tr. MacKenna, p. 624.   10 Ibid., VI, 9, 11; tr. MacKenna, p. 624.

sure, cannot be voluntarily induced, it cannot be forced by any psycho-technics, but can only be humbly awaited. Just as the wanderer waits for the rising of the sun, so the pious man waits for the ecstatic vision of God; the vision comes he knows not whence; it is ultimately an effect of that which is seen; only by the light can one see the light ($αὐτῷ αὐτὸ θεάσασθαι$). Here Plotinus utters the same great insight as the Psalmist: "In thy light shall we see light" (Ps. 36 : 9 [35 : 10]). In this temporal, corporeal world the vision is still incomplete, for it remains limited to a few blissful hours of ecstasy; but it points beyond, to an uninterrupted eternal contemplation.

Plato and Plotinus became the great teachers of the Christian mystics; their rich and profound contemplative experience entered into the treasure house of Christian mysticism. Though St. Augustine does not name them, it is they whom he has in mind when he speaks of "magnae quaedam et in-comparabiles animae" ("certain great and incomparable souls") who in his opinion had beheld reality and testified concerning it.[11] The contempla-tion of Christians at the summit of their inner life re-echoes the contempla-tion of the Hebrew Prophets; that of Jesus, St. Paul, and St. John, and of Plato and his successors. This fusion of Biblical-prophetic piety and of Pla-tonic-Neoplatonic mysticism is the most grandiose synthesis of diverse religious forms known to the history of religion, greater even than the memorable synthesis of old Islamic religion and Gnostic-Neoplatonic-Indian mysticism that occurred in Ṣūfism.

The first decisive step toward this synthesis was taken by a Jew. Philo of Alexandria (d. c. A.D. 50),[12] the author of a treatise *On the Contemplative Life*, saw the powerful mystical and contemplative elements in Jewish prophetism with an eye sharpened by the study of Plato. For him the patriarch Jacob became the prototype of the contemplative soul; he explained his name "Israel" as "seer of God" ($ὁ θεὸν ὁρῶν$). Moses seemed to him the "seer of the invisible world and of God" ($ὁ τῆς ἀειδοῦς φύσεως θεατὴς καὶ θεόπτης$). Much as Philo Platonized the religion of the Law and the Prophets, he never lost sight of the Biblical belief in the transcendence of God. To his mind mystical vision was not full comprehension; for God re-mained essentially invisible ($ἀθέατος$); even Moses, the greatest of the Old Testament seers, saw God only veiled in the dark cloud ($θεῖος γνόφος$).

11 *De quantitate animae*, 76; quoted in Butler, p. 60 & *n*.
12 [Dates revised according to *The Oxford Dictionary of the Christian Church* (London, 1957).—ED.]

Walking in the footsteps of Philo, the great Alexandrian catechists, Clement (d. *c.* A.D. 215) and Origen (d. *c.* A.D. 254), accomplished the synthesis of Biblical Christianity and Platonism. Clement introduced the ἐποπτικὴ θεωρία of the Platonic mystics into Christian theology. Origen was the first to offer a theological discussion of contemplative prayer. The highest degree of prayer was for him the worshiping vision, the "gnosis" of the divine glory that deifies the soul. The entire activity of the Christian mystic should consist in prayer; his whole life should be one continuous prayer. The duality of the contemplative and active life (θεωρητικὸς καὶ πρακτικὸς βίος) is symbolized by Origen in the figures of Martha and Mary, and this dual symbol was to gain general acceptance in Christian mysticism.

The external conditions for a contemplative life were created by the Christian monasticism that came into being in the fourth century. Its ideal was the "angelic life" (βίος ἀγγελικός); the monk should be an "angel on earth" (ἐπίγειος ἄγγελος)— i.e., he should live in constant remembrance of God (μνήμη θεοῦ), in incessant worship of the divine Majesty. All outward forms of prayer, though recited a hundred times, serve only as preparation for the spiritual prayer (προσευχὴ πνευματική, νοερά) of vision, which has its culmination in the contemplation of the hypostatic light (ἔλλαμψις τοῦ ὑποστατικοῦ φωτός). Macarius, Mark the Hermit, Nilus of Sinai, John Climacus, and later Simeon the New Theologian (d. 1022) are the monastic mystics who, themselves at home in spiritual contemplation, became the preceptors of the Eastern Church in mystical meditation and contemplation.

The practical contemplation of these monks was deepened by a continual return to Platonic and Neoplatonic philosophy and mysticism. All the Eastern Church Fathers were Platonists; among them it was first and foremost Gregory of Nyssa (d. *c.* 395) who, under the direct influence of Philo and the Neoplatonic philosophers, developed a comprehensive theory of the mystical contemplation of God.

But Neoplatonism influenced the Christian mysticism of the East and West still more through the mysterious figure who called himself Dionysius the Areopagite, after the man mentioned in the Book of Acts, and who for centuries enjoyed a kind of apostolic authority (fl. *c.* 500). Even though many modern Protestants may regard him as a dangerous smuggler who surreptitiously introduced a heathen mysticism into Christian theology and piety, careful inquiry reveals that, like Philo, he combined the transcendence of the Biblical faith with the immanence of the mystical experience. In rich, metaphoric terms he expressed the sublimity, intangibility, and ineffability of God. For him God is the "inaccessible light" ($\dot{\alpha}\pi\rho\dot{o}\sigma\iota\tau o\nu\ \phi\tilde{\omega}s$) that can be seen only in a "nonseeing" that transcends all sensory perception and intellection ($\delta\iota'\ \dot{\alpha}\beta\lambda\epsilon\psi\dot{\iota}as\ \dot{\iota}\delta\epsilon\tilde{\iota}\nu\ a\dot{v}\tau\tilde{\omega}\ \tau\tilde{\omega}\ \mu\dot{\eta}\ \dot{\iota}\delta\epsilon\tilde{\iota}\nu$). In this nonseeing, imageless vision lies for him the secret of the $\mu\nu\sigma\tau\iota\kappa\dot{\eta}\ \theta\epsilon\omega\rho\dot{\iota}a$, of mystical contemplation. Yet at the same time the Areopagite created a bridge leading from this imageless mysticism of infinity to the imaged mystery of the cult. The importance of the cultic, sacramental symbol for the highest spiritual contemplation has not often been so deeply comprehended as by this unknown mystical theologian. The writings of the Areopagite gained a profound influence over the inner life of the Eastern Church, in both its Orthodox and Monophysite branches, both in the cultic meditation of the masses and in the individual contemplation of the monks and saints. His influence extended beyond the borders of the Christian Churches, even to the Islamic mysticism of the Ṣūfīs.

The Areopagite also wielded great influence on the Western Church. Both the Scholastics, headed by Thomas Aquinas, and the mystics, particularly Meister Eckhart, the greatest of them all, looked up to him with veneration. Yet the great Neoplatonist could not have enjoyed so wide an influence in the West if a still greater Neoplatonist, St. Augustine (d. 430), had not paved the way for him. It was from St. Augustine that the Western world had learned the very meaning of mystical contemplation. In a wealth of metaphoric terms he had described the nature of intellectual contemplation, which was for him the highest level attained by the soul. Its purest and most powerful form is the ecstatic *raptus*, the sudden *"ictus trepidantis aspectus"*; its psychological effect is infinite bliss, purity, and certainty; its metaphysical effect is a likeness to God, a deification (*conformari Deo, deificari*). But Augustine did more than glorify contemplation in the Neoplatonic sense; he also fused the contemplative and ecstatic experience of the Neoplatonic philosophers with the simple Biblical prayer. And it is precisely the mixture of Neoplatonic sublimity with Christian-Biblical grace and prayer that gives Augustinian mysticism its unprecedented scope and vitality. This fusion of Neoplatonic vision with the Christian-Biblical prayer of praise, thanks, and supplication has found its most magnificent expression in the *Confessions*, which is also the first document in which a Christian mystic records his own psychological experience. In Augustine's famous conversation with Monica, his mother, before her death (IX, 10), a masterfully described ecstatic experience is permeated with simple Christian faith in creation and the life after death.

St. Augustine has been the preceptor of innumerable Christian thinkers and mystics; through the centuries his rich and abundant writings have remained a school of the contemplative life. And in Benedictine monasticism Western Christianity has known another, living school of contemplation. Contemplation is the profoundest content of the prayer of the "canonical hours" that St. Benedict (d. *c.* 550) looked upon as the *opus Dei* par excellence, over which "nothing has precedence." The contemplation of the prayer of the hours is continued in the *silentium* of the monks and completed in the *pura oratio*, the unspoken contemplative prayer of the individual. St. Benedict combined the contemplation of St. Augustine with the early monks' exercises in meditation and contemplation, and added Roman balance and restraint. In the religious life of the Benedictine monks contemplative fervor is strongly checked and tempered. Pope Gregory the Great (d. 604), a son of the Benedictine order, further developed this moderate mysticism, which contrasts sharply with the visionary exuberance of the Eastern Church. This serene, lucid mysticism is distinguished for its lack of emphasis on extraordinary phenomena such as ecstasies, visions, and auditions. Here "mystical contemplation is no boiling over, no flash of lightning, but a tranquil, flowing line of loving sojourn with godly thoughts and delights"; here there is an "instinctive distaste for everything flaming, ecstatic, ardent" (Butler). This classical Benedictine mysticism preserved a unique balance between the *vita contemplativa* and the *vita activa;* the motto "Ora et labora" originated with the Benedictines.

In Bernard of Clairvaux (d. 1153), the great Cistercian abbot, we find a transition from the tranquil, predominantly intellectual meditation of the Benedictines to a more visual, emotional, and ecstatic mysticism, nurtured by meditation on the life, Passion, and death of Jesus. In the era of the Crusades, the human figure of Jesus as he dwelt on earth assumed, as was only natural, a central position in Christian meditation. "To know Jesus, Jesus crucified, that is the kernel of my philosophy," says the credo of St. Bernard.[13] But for him, just as for Origen, visual meditation on Jesus is a preliminary stage, leading up to the imageless contemplation of the Logos.

No less important than this incursion of the affective element into the

13 *Sermons on the Canticles,* XLIII, 4; cf. Butler, p. 173.

sphere of meditation and contemplation is the reflection on the contemplative experience itself, which began with St. Bernard and ultimately led to the development of what might be called a psychology and theology of contemplation. Richard of St.-Victor (d. 1173), author of a treatise *De gratia contemplationis,* was the first author to analyze and classify contemplative experiences with psychological subtlety and to develop a systematic curriculum of meditation and contemplation. Strongly influenced by the Areopagite, he carried a renewed Neoplatonic current into Christian mysticism; he has rightly been called one of the main channels through which "the antique mystical tradition . . . was . . . transmitted to the mediaeval world." [14] Thomas Aquinas (d. 1274), the prince of Scholastics, also devoted a special discussion (*Summa,* II, 2, 180) to the *vita contemplativa* as contrasted with the *vita activa,* and in his harmonizing way created a synthesis between the intellectual aspect of contemplation (*contemplatio veritatis*) and the affective aspect (*amor et delectatio*). Such a synthesis is also characteristic of the poetic *summa theologica* of the Middle Ages, Dante's *Divine Comedy,* which reveals a clearly contemplative character in the *Paradiso;* the poet's visionary eye, schooled by St. Augustine, St. Thomas, and St. Bonaventure, was turned toward the "intellectual light full of love" (*luce intellettuale piena d'amore*). In the last years of the Middle Ages, Denis the Carthusian (d. 1471), the *doctor ecstaticus* who walked in the footsteps of Richard, St. Thomas, and St. Bonaventure, continued the theological systematization of contemplation; perhaps his chief contribution to mystical theology was the distinction between "acquired, active" contemplation and "infused, passive" contemplation.

The theological systematization and dogmatization of contemplation begun by St. Bernard and Richard of St.-Victor found a powerful counterweight in the naïve piety of the great medieval saints. The most original of all these was Francis of Assisi (d. 1226), who was entirely uninfluenced by mystical literature. His mystical life was one simple, fervent prayer, nourished by the contemplation of nature, of Calvary, of the Lord's Supper. For him all nature became a transparency of the Creator's beauty and love; the poor, humble, and suffering Jesus became an image of God's self-sacrificing love—his contemplation of Christ's wounds, his at-one-ness with Christ's love and agony, even gained plastic power over his flesh, and burst forth visibly in the stigmata; and finally, the sacrament of the Eucharist

14 Evelyn Underhill, *Mysticism* (12th edn., London, 1930), pp. 458–59.

198

became for him a pledge of the eternal, loving presence of his Saviour. Through St. Francis the love of nature, the mysticism of the Passion and the sacraments, became a constant source of contemplation for the members of the Franciscan order of both sexes, including the lay tertiaries. It was above all in the Capuchin order, which revived the early Franciscan ideal, that contemplative prayer—in permanent conjunction with the activity of preaching—found a home.

In these years contemplation flowered not only in the Romance countries, but in the Germanic North as well. Rich mystical experience coupled with a fine gift of expression was given to four women, the Benedictine Hildegard of Bingen (d. 1179) and Gertrude of Helftä (d. c. 1302), the Beguine Mechthild of Magdeburg (d. c. 1280), the greatest mystical writer of the German Middle Ages, and the English seer and poet Juliana of Norwich (d. after 1413), surnamed *Theodidacta, Profunda, Ecstatica*. In the three great German Dominican mystics, the contemplative life assumed three different aspects: Meister Eckhart (d. 1327) impresses us with his profound metaphysical vision, Henry Suso (d. 1366) with his emotional devotion and enthusiasm, Johannes Tauler (d. 1361) with his ethical gravity. All three qualities are combined in the Fleming Jan van Ruysbroeck (d. 1381), whom some regard as the greatest of medieval mystics. Like Eckhart, he stands on the shoulders of the Areopagite; and not without reason he has been called "another Dionysius," though he is "clear where the Areopagite is obscure." [15] Beside this Netherlands mystic stands the English mystic, Richard Rolle of Hampole (d. 1349), who departed from the mystical theories of Richard of St.-Victor, Bernard of Clairvaux, and Bonaventure, and turned back to the immediacy of the contemplative life.

None of these theorists and practitioners of contemplation, however, attained anything approaching the influence of the author of the little book *The Imitation of Christ*, which after the Bible is the most widely read book in Christian literature. The *Imitatio Christi*, attributed no doubt rightly to Thomas a Kempis (d. 1471), offers neither a dogma nor a psychology nor a psychotechnic of contemplation; it makes sparing use of the terms meditation and contemplation, and nevertheless it is not only the most popular but also the best work on these subjects. This book embodies spiritual guidance in the truest and innermost sense of the term, and for this very reason is the best of textbooks on contemplation. The whole wealth

15 Underhill, p. 465, quoting Denis the Carthusian.

of the medieval mysticism of God, of Jesus, the Passion and the sacraments, is here summed up in a succinct, balanced, and well-tempered form.

In the latter half of the Middle Ages the contemplation that the medieval mystics practiced and the mystical theologians described was widely disseminated in three ways: (1) the cultus of the Eucharist (the elevation of the Host during the Mass and the veneration of the exposed Sacrament), which taught the people to see and worship the Saviour made present in the sensible sign; (2) the lay folk's prayer book, in which the meditation and contemplation of the great mystics were set forth in simple forms accessible to the unlearned; (3) the religious of the various orders (Benedictines, Carthusians, Dominicans, Franciscans, Brothers of the Common Life), whose cloisters—homes and schools of contemplation—gave the simple folk a shining example of the contemplative life.

In post-Tridentine Catholic mysticism there was a further systematizing and psychologizing of contemplation. Ignatius Loyola (d. 1556) created in his book of *Spiritual Exercises*, the material for which he took from the medieval literature of meditation (especially from Ludolf of Saxony), an easily handled technique of meditation and contemplation; at the same time, he made meditation and contemplation into a sure instrument for the ascetic training of the will. For centuries his method of exercises dominated the higher clergy of the Roman Catholic Church, and it was not until quite recently that its exclusive role was contested by Benedictine and Franciscan contemplation.

Whereas Loyola consciously placed mystical contemplation at the service of practical Church affairs, the two great reformers of the contemplative Carmelite order, St. John of the Cross (d. 1591) and St. Teresa of Ávila (d. 1582), brought about a new flowering of the classical Catholic ideal of contemplation. They revealed true mastery in developing the psychological analysis of the mystical experience and its stages; Teresa possessed a particular gift for psychological self-observation. Yet despite their virtuosity in observation, description, and classification, the contemplative life loses none of its original freshness and power in the work of these two Spanish mystics. Whereas in St. Teresa we find a strong leaning toward extraordinary visions and ecstatic experiences, St. John of the Cross, despite all his poetic fervor, is distinguished by an ethical temperance and a restraint that seem almost puritanical.

The contemplative art of the Spanish mystics was continued (1) in the refined, yet somewhat secular and sentimental popular mysticism of Francis of Sales (d. 1622), whose writings were widely read; (2) in the quietist mysticism of Miguel de Molinos (d. 1697) and Mme. de la Mothe Guyon (d. 1717), which represents a one-sided reaction from the emotional and imaginative mysticism of the Middle Ages and replaces the enthusiastic Eros with cool indifference (in its extreme manifestations quietism was condemned by the Church, whereas in its healthy forms, that, for example, of the Carmelite Brother Lawrence, it remained unmolested); (3) in an elaborate systematization of mystical experience, a "scholastic of mysticism," characteristic of numerous theological and didactic authors of the last three centuries: Suárez (d. 1617), Alphonsus Liguori (d. 1787), Scaramelli (d. 1752), Poulain, Saudreau, and Maumigny.

In general, the post-Tridentine development has been one of increasing one-sidedness and narrowness; there has been a partial degeneration from the purer creative mysticism of the ancient and medieval Church. However, the great liturgical movement in the Church today may be regarded as a conscious return to the classical communal mysticism of the past; and the preoccupation of modern religious thinkers with medieval mysticism cannot fail to focus general attention on the purer prototypes of Catholic individual mysticism. Moreover, there are still serene contemplative souls in whom the rich tradition of classical Catholic mysticism lives on. An example is the woman who in our own time founded a free, primitive-Franciscan sisterhood, which now occupies a venerable Franciscan cloister near Assisi.[15a]

In Protestantism, even more than in post-Tridentine Catholicism, the contemplative life seems weakened, and sometimes even totally buried. The exaggerated dynamism of the concept of God that recognizes only a "Deus semper actuosus et numquam otiosus," a God always active and never idle, and the related hostility to the static Platonic conception of God, have given rise to a highly anticontemplative attitude. Nevertheless, the contemplative attitude is not entirely lacking, but has merely been submerged. It cannot die as long as the Old and New Testaments continue to be generally accepted.

Even Luther (d. 1546) passed through the school of contemplative mysticism. His preceptors were St. Augustine, Bernard of Clairvaux, Tauler, and the Frankfurt canon who wrote the *Theologia Germanica*, which Luther

15a [Sister Maria Valeria Pignetti (b. 1876), founder of the "Larks" at Campello sul Clitunno, in the 1930's, still active.—ED.]

edited and of which he said that after the Bible no book had meant so much to him. With this grounding in contemplative mysticism, however, he combined a number of anticontemplative traits: a mortal hostility to the monastic ideal, a lack of understanding for Francis of Assisi and Thomas Aquinas, a bitter animosity toward the Areopagite, who seemed to him "plus Platonisans quam christianisans." Since Luther's time the anticontemplative attitude of his Church has been further intensified and vulgarized by rationalism, Ritschlianism, and recently by Barthianism; to Karl Barth contemplation is nothing but "a sea of mischief." Despite Luther's deviation from classical contemplation, we must nevertheless give him credit for his own brand of mysticism and contemplation. The joyful, confident faith attained through the simple prayers in which he carried on his dialogue with God is in its way contemplative, for it enables the worshiper to "see into the fatherly heart of God" through the mirror of the incarnate Christ. For Luther all contemplation is indissolubly bound up with faith in the story of redemption; unlike the ecstatic mystics, he does not allow the possibility that the soul may leave this faith behind in its mystical ascent to God.

Yet not only in the fervid Luther, but in the harsher and harder Geneva reformer Calvin (d. 1564) as well, we encounter a contemplative element. Despite the even more pronounced dynamism of his conception of God, despite his greater emphasis on belief in the kingdom of God, beside which all individual religious experience pales to nothingness, Calvin most particularly insists that the faithful sink down in reverence before the majesty of the Eternal God, to whom all glory is due—*soli Deo gloria*. In Calvin's prayers, as in the old Calvinist hymns, there survives something of the grandiose contemplation of the early Church.

> Venez, chrétiens,
> et contemplons
> la gloire du roi des rois,
> du monarque des cieux.

> (Come, ye Christians,
> let us contemplate
> the glory of the king of kings,
> of the monarch of the heavens.)

The mystical element in Luther and Calvin accounts for the steady stream of early Christian and medieval contemplative mysticism that has flowed into the religious life of their Churches. From the late sixteenth century on, the Lutheran prayer book took over numerous motifs and formulas from the late medieval missals. The Lutheran hymnal of the seventeenth century was fed on this mystical literature of prayer. And among the Lutherans were several outstanding contemplative mystics: Johann Arndt (d. 1621), who remained within the limits of Lutheran orthodoxy; Jakob Boehme (d. 1624), whose religious and metaphysical views ran counter to this orthodoxy; and Count von Zinzendorf (d. 1760), who revived St. Bernard's mysticism of Jesus and the Passion in a form transcending denominational barriers. Side by side with these Lutheran mystics stand significant Calvinists, Pierre Poiret (d. 1719), who introduced the religious writings of the French and Spanish mystics into the Protestant world, and above all Gerhard Tersteegen (d. 1769), a mystic of extraordinary tenderness and delicacy, who was highly considered by Lutherans as well as Calvinists, and gave to the German Protestant hymnal its finest contemplative songs. Even amid the poverty and barrenness of the evangelical Church service with its emphasis on the sermon, these songs create a warm glow of contemplative intimacy with God.

> Mache mich einfältig,
> innig, abgeschieden,
> sanft und still in deinem Frieden;
> mach mich reinen Herzens,
> dass ich deine Klarheit
> schauen mag in Geist und Wahrheit.

> (Make me simplehearted,
> fervent and withdrawn,
> gentle and quiet in thy peace;
> make me pure of heart,
> that I may see thy clarity
> in spirit and in truth.)

Of all the reformed Churches it is the Anglican that has left most scope for mystical contemplation. William Law (d. 1761) and William Blake (d. 1827) were two heralds of mystical piety. And the fathers of the Oxford movement of renewal, Newman (d. 1890) and Pusey (d. 1882), restored mystical contemplation to an Anglican world disrupted by rationalism. In the most recent period, Platonic mysticism found a spirited advocate in Dean Inge, one of the most significant of Anglican theologians, while Evelyn

Underhill showed herself both a sound interpreter of classical Christian mysticism and a practical teacher of contemplation.

The modern German *Gemeinschaftsbewegung*,[16] inspired largely by the British Free Churches, has also done much to foster contemplative mysticism. The evangelists Vetter and Binde have introduced mystical prayer into these circles.

Beside all these more or less ecclesiastical mystics stand the great lonely mystics of modern Christianity, above all Sebastian Franck (d. *c.* 1542), whose mysticism dispenses with evangelical mediation, and George Fox, the founder of the Quakers (d. 1691), who, detaching himself from all church organization and sacramental cults, combined the mysticism of the "inner light" with inspired prophecy, and procured for this purely individualistic piety a wide dissemination.

*

Even a brief and dry survey of the history of Christian mysticism shows what a wealth of contemplation the experience of the Christian mystics embraces. In this experience, which itself covers two millennia, a thousand years of Hebrew prophetism and five hundred years of Orphism and Platonism still live. And there is an intrinsic bond between this infinitely rich world of contemplative piety and the mysticism of the great religions of the East. Despite all the differences between historical, eschatological Christianity and the ahistorical, acosmic religions of India, there is an ultimate unity. All contemplative souls have beheld an infinite light of the spirit, even though they may describe it in entirely different images and words. It is, to speak with the prologue to the Gospel of St. John, "the . . . Light, which lighteth every man that cometh into the world" (John 1 : 9). But despite this ultimate inner unity, Christian mysticism overshadows non-Christian mysticism by its scope, its richness and diversity. There is no truly religious mode of meditation, nor any contemplative and ecstatic experience known to non-Christian piety, that cannot be found exemplified many times over in the history of Christian mysticism. Accordingly, though non-Christian forms of meditation and contemplation can give valuable stimulus and suggestion to Christian mysticism, they cannot contribute anything entirely new. If the cultivated world of today feels so strongly attracted by Oriental mysticism, it is largely because the authentic tradi-

16 [A movement arising in the 1880's, marked by pietism, evangelism, missionary activity, etc.—ED.]

tion of Christian mysticism has remained unknown. Once again we may say with Goethe:

> Willst du immer weiter schweifen?
> Sieh, das Gute liegt so nah.

> (Wilt thou roam forever farther,
> When the good is close at hand?)

2. Contemplation in the Mysticism of the Christian Community

In non-Christian mysticism the soul often appears as a monad—Plotinus, the prince of non-Christian mysticism, concludes his wonderful *Enneads* with the words: φυγὴ μόνου πρὸς μόνον ("the flight of the alone to the alone"). And St. Augustine, greatest of the Western Church Fathers, said that he desired to know only "God and the soul," and nothing else in the world. Indeed, that ultimate aloneness of the soul with God, of which Plotinus speaks in his grandiose phrase, was known to Christian and non-Christian mysticism alike. Yet it is characteristic that the same Augustine who put forward the motto *"Deus et anima"* should have been the great herald of ecclesiastical faith, proclaiming the glory of the *corpus Christi mysticum* and preaching world-wide Catholicism (*"communicare orbi terrarum"*). Mystical unity with Christ comprehends unity with all the members of Christ's body in the here and in the hereafter. The individual does not remain isolated in his communion with God, but is intimately bound up with all his brethren, living and dead, just as when Jesus was transfigured on Mount Tabor there were with him the three chosen disciples, representing the earthly community, and Moses and Elijah, representing the heavenly church. The community is no obstacle, but, on the contrary, an aid to contemplative communion with God; sustained by all the faithful, the believer rises more easily to the vision of God. The contemplation of the community in the cult is the tranquil source out of which the individual contemplation of Christian mysticism rises. All the great Christian mystics are rooted in the sacramental and liturgical life of the Church, even when they are not aware of it. Even when they break loose from the bonds of the cult, they remain under the influence of its sacraments. All mystics, even among extreme spiritualists like the Quakers, reveal the imprint of the cult in their language.

But the sacramental cult is not only a source of contemplative life for the great mystics; it is also the main school of contemplation for the mass of those who partake in it. In Christianity, contemplation is not the prerogative of the elite, not a technique that can be learned only by a few recipients of special grace; no, every believer, even the poorest and simplest, can participate in the great vision conferred by the Church. Gregory the Great says significantly: "It is not the case that the grace of contemplation is given to the highest and not given to the lowest; but often the highest, and often the most lowly, and very often those who have renounced, and sometimes also those who are married, receive it. If therefore there is no state of life of the faithful, from which the grace of contemplation can be excluded, anyone who keeps his heart within him may also be illumined by the light of contemplation; so that no one can glory in this grace as if it were singular." [16a] The cult of the Church is "a mysticism for all," a path to which all are called. Without conscious design, the entire cult is adapted to contemplation: the holy place, the holy object, the holy season, but above all the holy of holies, the mystery of the Eucharist, leads upward to the vision of God.

The church building in itself is a material symbol of the invisible, of the Eternal, encouraging the contemplation of God, and this is true equally of the Byzantine circular and basilican styles and of the Western Romanesque and Gothic. (Only secularized Renaissance, baroque, and rococo architecture can provide no contemplative impulse.) The cruciform plan of the Romanesque or Gothic church strongly suggests the mystery of the death of Christ. The ἄδυτον, or sanctuary, which is separated from the nave either by the chancel rail as in the West or by the iconostasis as in the East, appears to the congregation as a symbol of the higher, celestial world. The raised altar with the cross, in Romanesque art delimited and overshadowed by the baldacchino or ciborium (κιβώριον), in Gothic art striving heavenward with its superstructure, in Byzantine churches visible only through the royal doors in the iconostasis, attracts the gaze of all the faithful. It is the place where the Eucharistic memorial of Christ's suffering is solemnized, and as such it actualizes Golgotha, the point at which time and eternity meet, the point of communion between fallen mankind and the holy God, and the point at which God's condescending, forgiving love enters the world of man. In the modern Western Church, the altar supports the taber-

16a *Homily on Ezechiel*, II, 5, 19; quoted in Butler, p. 238.

nacle, where Christ lives and is present beneath the sacramental veil of bread.

In the Eastern Church another object of contemplation is provided by the icons, the sacred images of Christ, the mother of God, and the saints, which are attached primarily to the iconostasis, but also to the walls and the pulpits. With their strangely immobile, hieratic solemnity, they are a symbol of the eternally serene reality of God; their linear incorporeity suggests the pure world of spirit, their golden background reflects the glory of the beyond. These icons, which are nothing if not sacral, capture the eye and draw it away from the sensory world; imbedded in the community of Christ and his elect, the spirit is led to contemplate the celestial world. And icons, often crude and artless, also serve as aids to meditation and contemplation in the private dwellings of the faithful, who from contemplation of the earthly copy are raised, in accordance with Plato's doctrine of ideas, to the vision of the celestial prototype; every honor shown the image—prostration, inclination, the kiss—is directed toward the transcendent prototype. In the Western Church, to be sure, statues and pictures are not so directly bound up with the cult as in the Eastern Church, but here too they are a living actualization of Christ and his saints and thus a constant stimulus to meditation and contemplation. Often in the lives of the great mystics special visionary experiences have been associated with the contemplation of such pictures and statues, as, for example, when St. Francis of Assisi, kneeling in prayer before the crucifix in San Damiano, heard the voice of the crucified Saviour himself.

In addition to pictures and images there are numerous symbols to stimulate meditation and contemplation, above all the symbol of light. The burning candles and lamps are symbolic of the eternal light shining in the darkness of the world, of God's everlasting love, and also of the pious soul burning with love of God and of his brethren. In the Easter Vigil liturgy, a candle is lighted while the officiant exclaims: "Lumen Christi—Deo gratias"; this is the symbol of Christ rearisen in the light of transfiguration. In the Eastern Church, the τρικήριον (three joined candles), held by the bishop when he blesses his flock, serves as a symbol of the holy Trinity, and the δικήριον (two joined candles) as a symbol of the divine and human natures of Christ. The incense is a symbol of the prayers of the faithful rising up to God and of the fragrance that should issue from the inward and outward life of the Christian; it also symbolizes the love of God and of one's brother: "Accendat in nobis Dominus ignem sui amoris et flammam aeternae caritatis" ("May the Lord kindle in us the fire of His love and the flame of eternal charity") are the words of the priest in the Roman High Mass at the incensing of the altar. These and other liturgical symbols (water, oil, salt), the holy vessels (chalice, monstrance), the vestments and insignia, are transparencies of the eternal divine reality and its workings in body and soul and nature, whereas all the liturgical gestures and movements serve as expressions for the soul's devotion to the invisible reality of the divine. *"Per sensibilia ad invisibilia"*; man as a physical and spiritual duality cannot attain directly to pure spiritual contemplation of God, but requires a sensible sign and image as stimulus, springboard, and vehicle. By virtue of the *analogia entis* (analogy of being) between creature and divine Creator, all sensible things are a copy, a shadow, a footprint of the invisible eternal God, and can accordingly guide man to the ultimate, absolute reality. Very aptly the Areopagite speaks of the "emanations and copies of the divine writing, the visible images of the ineffable, supernatural wonders" (τῶν θείων χαρακτήρων ἔκγονα καὶ ἀποτυπώματα καὶ εἰκόνες ἐμφανεῖς τῶν ἀπορρήτων καὶ ὑπερφυῶν θαυμάτων). Especially in times of spiritual weariness, barrenness, and dejection, when the body presents obstacles, man requires such outward aids to meditation and contemplation. When mental concentration alone cannot give sufficient strength, then often an inconspicuous symbol helps to uplift the searching, anguished soul, as though on wings, to the highest contemplative and ecstatic experiences. To be sure, it is always essential, as Dionysius says, that the beholder penetrate the outward sheath "to the core of the holy symbols" (εἴσω τῶν ἱερῶν συμβόλων διαβαίνειν) and thus come to behold the "naked and pure divine mysteries in their essence" (αὐτὰ ἐφ᾽ ἑαυτῶν γυμνὰ καὶ καθαρὰ γενόμενα). Before "true lovers" of holiness the veils fall; by "simplicity of the spirit" they penetrate to the "simple and sublime truth of the spirit."

Side by side with the spatial, earthly, and corporeal symbols stand the holy hours as stimuli to and object of meditation. In the Church's prayers for the "hours," the natural course of the day becomes a plan of meditation. The daily hymns of the Latin Breviary make the sun's passage into a symbol of the most fervent relations between the soul and God. By night, at Matins, the congregation waits with yearning for the coming light; in early morning, at Lauds, it sings the praise of the dawning light; at Prime (6 A.M.), it humbly worships the rising spiritual sun, Jesus Christ; at Tierce (9 A.M.), it contemplates the growing light; at Sext (noon), its climax; at None (3 P.M.), the waning light; at Vespers, the dawning of the eternal light as the earthly light departs.

The days of the week likewise encourage meditation. Thursday reminds the communicant of the institution of the Lord's Supper, the great bond that unites all the members of Christ, and of Christ's agony on the Mount of Olives; Friday recalls his Passion and death; Sunday his resurrection and the spiritual resurrection of the Christian in the sacrament of baptism.

But the greatest plan of meditation is the Church's year, in which the diverse acts of the drama of salvation are shown, each in its season: Advent recalls the expectation of the Messiah; Christmas, the incarnation of the Son of God; the days of Holy Week, his suffering and death; Easter, the resurrection; Pentecost, the coming of the Holy Ghost. And when the story of salvation is ended, the Church contemplates the inner triune life of God on the festival of the Trinity. The cycle of the festivals of Christ is framed in the twofold wreath of the festivals of Mary and of the saints. Each single mystery of Christ, each single recollection of a witness to the life of God on earth, becomes for the congregation that contemplates it a medium of the ultimate and deepest divine secret of all, of eternal love. As in the prism the rays of the one sun are broken up into different colors, so in the Church's year is the plenitude of the eternal divine sun broken up. The gaze of him who regards the separate rays will be carried upward toward the one sun from which they emanate. The Church's calendar offers constantly changing objects for meditation, and this is a particular aid to contemplation. Those who live with the liturgy of the Church's year require no special plan of meditation; they possess inexhaustible material on which to meditate. The hymns on any particular day constitute a running meditation, and the same is true of the prayers and festivals of the Church's year. At Advent the congregation, immersed in the darkness of night, beholds the gleam of the re-deeming light on the distant horizon; at Christmas and Epiphany "the people that walk in darkness behold a great light," and hear the waking cry: "Be enlightened, thy light has come!" At Easter it bursts into the cry of rejoicing: *"Gaudeat et tellus tantis irradiata fulgoribus; et aeterni Regis splendore illustrata, totius orbis se sentiat amisisse caliginem. Laetetur et mater Ecclesia tanti luminis adornata fulgoribus."* ("Let the earth rejoice, being bathed in such effulgence, and illumined by the radiance of the eternal King; let it feel that it has cast off all darkness. Let Mother Church also rejoice,

209

adorned in such flashing light." [17]) At Pentecost, it beholds the tongues of flame over the heads of the Apostles and begs to be kindled with the fire of divine love—"tui amoris ignem accende."

Like the holy place, the holy ritual object, the holy season, so also does the holy word become a stimulus to contemplation: not only the visible sign, but also the audible sound is charged with sacred power. First of all, the liturgical recitative, the soft murmur, so dissimilar to the common speech of every day, induces meditation; the same effect is produced by the strange-sounding Byzantine melodies of the Eastern Church and the Gregorian chant of the Western. This sacral song has an eschatological character; it does not issue from the earth, but seems to emanate from a transcendent world. What a mighty force of meditation and contemplation lies in the "Sursum corda" of the Preface at High Mass, the Magnificat of Vespers, the Lamentations of the days before Easter, the "Ecce lignum crucis" at the unveiling of the Cross on Good Friday, the Exultet of the Easter Vigil liturgy! These sacral songs capture men's thoughts and concentrate them wholly on the mystery of salvation. It is characteristic of both the Eastern Orthodox and the Roman Catholic church service that the active part originally played by the congregation has been curtailed in favor of the priest and choir, and this gives the faithful the quiet and leisure needed for inward contemplation and silent prayer. For the same reason the anthroposophical *Christengemeinschaft* ("Community of Christians") has designedly excluded from its services all activity on the part of the congregation; only priests and altar boys act and speak.

Not only the form but also the content of the liturgical prayer bears an unmistakably contemplative character and inspires contemplation of the divine mysteries. The liturgical prayer is a school of concentration. From the formal point of view the contemplative character of the liturgical prayer is more pronounced in the Eastern than in the Roman Church, where—in distinction from other old Western liturgies—the *oratio* has a concentrated, succinct, juridical form. But even in the Roman liturgy supplication, praise, and thanks lead to contemplation of the heavenly mysteries. Even the emotional moderation and restraint—only rarely, as in the Easter-night Exultet, is an unrestrained cry of joy allowed to break through—facilitates contem-

---

17 Exultet of the Easter Vigil Service in the Roman Missal. Numerous translations are available; e.g., *The Missal in Latin and English*, ed. J. O'Connell and H. P. R. Finberg (London, 1949).

plation; the muffled fire, the restrained passion, of the liturgical prayer leaves room for a long, serene meditation on the divine majesty and love. And, moreover, the transition from the intimate Thou to the respectful He, from the direct to the oblique, creates a distance favorable to contemplation; the classical example of this is the Trisagion (Thrice-holy), taken from the Hebrew Temple cult, and the Psalms, with their constant alternation between Thou and He. Many of the prayers of the Eastern Church circle incessantly around the infinite God, who transcends all human power of comprehension; the communicant at prayer does not think of himself, of his distress and desires, but immerses himself in a sea of divine being and divine action; "O Lord our God, whose might surpasses understanding, whose glory cannot be measured, whose mercy is infinite and love of men unspeakable," runs the "prayer of the first antiphon" in the Liturgy of St. John Chrysostom. No less distinct is the contemplative character of the priest's prayer in the same liturgy:

> Holy God, who dost rest among the saints, who art praised by the seraphim with the cry of Thrice-holy, who art glorified by the cherubim and adored by all the powers of heaven; thou who didst bring all things from nothing into being, who didst make man to thine own image and likeness, who didst adorn him with all the gifts of thy grace, who dost give wisdom and understanding to them that ask; thou who dost not scorn the sinner, but hast ordained repentance for his salvation, who has granted to us, thy lowly and unworthy servants, to stand at this moment before the majesty of thy holy altar, and to offer thee due worship and honor; do thou, O Lord, receive from the mouth of us sinners the hymn of the Thrice-holy . . . for thou our God art holy, and we give glory to thee, Father, Son, and Holy Ghost.[18]

Though this particular kind of contemplative prayer may be rare in the liturgy of the Roman Church, contemplative prayer itself plays a large part. Every Psalm concludes with the doxology: "Glory be to the Father and to the Son and to the Holy Ghost, as it was in the beginning, is now, and ever shall be, world without end." Thus the communicant rises again and again to the contemplation of the mystery of the Trinity. The belief in the triune God does not imply the threefold nature of God's external works, but of the eternal inner movement of the Godhead. The Gloria Patri, of frequent occur-

18 *The Divine Liturgy of Our Father Among the Saints, John Chrysostom,* tr. Adrian Fortescue (London, 1908), pp. 64–65, 72–73.

rence in both the Eastern and the Western liturgies, moves the congregation forever anew to the contemplation of that ocean of light, wisdom, love, beauty, and beatitude which constitutes God's innermost, eternal, and unchanging essence.

Similarly, the tenor of the daily prayers at the hours shows that the Western Church unceasingly summons its children to contemplation. Matins summon to midnight meditation in accordance with the cry: "Mine eyes prevent the night watches, that I might meditate in thy word" (Ps. 119 [118] : 148). In the Invitatory Psalm at Matins, "Venite adoremus" (95 [94]), the gaze of the worshipers is raised to the infinite greatness of God: "The Lord is a great God, and a great King above all gods." The peculiar character of those Jewish Psalms which have been adopted for the Church's prayers at the hours lies in the constant interplay of supplication, thanks, and praise with pure meditation and contemplation. Over and over again the wondering, worshiping soul stands in silence before the glory and the beauty of God, His compassion and His love; in Him is its joy and its strength: "Whom have I in heaven but thee? and there is none upon earth that I desire beside thee" (Ps. 73 [72] : 25). The Psalms of Matins are three times interrupted by meditative readings from Scripture and from the Fathers, and each reading is followed by a meditative dialogue. The climax of Matins is the glorious Te Deum, with its adoring threefold "Holy." In Lauds the meditation continues, with Psalms and other Old Testament songs, to culminate in the Benedictus, the hymn of Zacharias, joyfully contemplating the morning light: "The dayspring from on high hath visited us, to give light to them that sit in darkness and in the shadow of death, to guide our feet into the way of peace" (Luke 1 : 78 f.). The Little Hours (Prime, Tierce, Sext, and None) reveal an active character—Psalm 119 [118] of the monastic hours is a preparation for work and struggle in the world, but this preparation takes place through meditation on the greatness and glory of the divine ethical law: "Thy word is a lamp unto my feet, and a light unto my path" (Ps. 119 [118] : 105). When the work and the struggle of the day are over, the soul turns back to contemplation at Vespers: "The works of the Lord are great, sought out of all them that have pleasure therein" (Ps. 111 [110] : 2). In the gathering darkness, the soul sees a spiritual light flare up; "but darkness shall not be dark to thee, and night shall be light as the day: the darkness thereof, and the light thereof are alike to thee" (Ps. 138 : 12 [Vulg.]). Vespers reach their climax in the joyful meditative hymn of the Mother of God, the Magnificat: "My soul doth magnify the Lord, and my spirit hath rejoiced in God my Saviour" (Luke 1 : 46 f.). The meditative prayer ends with the serene contemplation of Compline, in which the weary soul sinks happy and confident into the fatherly arms of God: "He shall cover thee with his feathers, and under his wings shalt thou trust" (Ps. 91 [90] : 4); "Into thine hand I commit my spirit" (Ps. 31 : 5 [30 : 6]). In the contemplative hymn of the aged Simeon, the Nunc Dimittis, the soul looks back upon the wonderful vision of God it has enjoyed in the contemplation and prayer of the day: "For mine eyes have seen thy salvation" (Luke 2 : 30).

Yet all the daily prayers, all the ritual gestures and objects, places and times, words and songs, are only frames around the center of the cult that is truly the great center of contemplation: the sacrament of the Eucharist. In it the most holy and most immediate vision of the eternal Christ and his Cross is opened up to the congregation through humble earthly signs. In the Eucharist, Christ becomes truly present in the elements of bread and wine. Through the invocation of the creative spirit of God and the repetition of Christ's own words, bread and wine are hallowed and transfigured into the vehicles of Christ's body and blood. The simplest, most everyday things, food and drink, become the sign and pledge of the presence of the Most High: "[We] do not bow to flesh and blood, but to thee, the dread God," [19] runs one of the prayers in the Liturgy of St. John Chrysostom. Whether the sacramental elements are presented to the faithful in veiled form, as in the Eastern liturgy, or uncovered, as at the Elevation of the Host in the Roman Mass, the Eucharist remains the highest object of all cultic contemplation. All the love, devotion, self-sacrifice of the flock is concentrated on the sacramental Christ.

But the Eucharist is even more than the actualization of Christ; it is the visible representation of the drama of salvation: Christ's incarnation, atoning death, and resurrection. The story is not told in a protracted mystery play, but is concentrated in the brief and simple action of the breaking of the bread and the lifting of the cup, that humble metaphoric action in which Jesus symbolized the breaking of his body and the pouring out of his blood for the salvation of mankind. In the solemnization of the Eucharist, the congregation beholds again and again the great event on the Cross at Golgotha; "Christ is mystically slaughtered," according to the formula of the

19 *The Divine Liturgy of . . . John Chrysostom,* tr. Fortescue, p. 112.

Eastern Church; or, as Western theology puts it: "The bloody sacrifice of the Cross is bloodlessly represented on the altar." What happened once in history as a revelation of eternal, divine love and spirit of self-sacrifice is made continually present, symbolized in the liturgical-sacramental act.

In the Christian liturgies of both East and West, this simple act has been elevated to the level of a great contemplative drama which, like the ancient mystery cults, reveals the threefold mystical path of salvation: purification, illumination, and union.

The Greek Liturgy of St. John Chrysostom may serve us as an example of the Eastern liturgies. An act of preparation, the προσκομιδή, serves to purify the officiating priest and the sacrificial elements. The priest solemnly prostrates himself before the holy icons; amid symbolic prayers, the theme of which is detachment from the world and the invocation of divine sanctity and justice, he dons the holy vestments, washes his hands as a sign of inner purification, "slaughters the lamb"—i.e., divides and arranges the morsels of sacrificial bread—incenses, veils, and presents the gifts and with them body and soul, and incenses the altar and the tabernacle as a symbol of the transfiguring "cloud" that will veil the sacred place like a Mount Tabor.

This act of purification is followed by the different parts of the ἐπόπτεια, the holy vision. At the Little Entrance in the Liturgy of the Catechumens, the priest carries the gospel book from the sanctuary into the nave. Christ, preceptor of the world, proclaims the gospel. At the Great Entrance in the Liturgy of the Faithful, the priest carries in the sacrificial gifts—Christ, redeemer of the world, makes his entrance. The Cherubic Hymn, one of the most wonderful contemplative texts in the liturgy, serves as an inner preparation for this appearance of the Lord before His congregation: "We who mystically represent the cherubim, who sing to the life-giving Trinity the thrice holy hymn, let us now put aside all earthly care; that we may receive the King of all things, who comes escorted by unseen armies of angels." [20]

The kiss of peace, which unites all the disciples of Christ in his forbearing love, is followed by the Eucharistic prayer, introduced by the contemplative summons: "Lift up your hearts" (which goes back to the earliest days of the Christian church service), and culminating in contemplation of the infinite God: "Thou art the ineffable God beyond understanding, unseen, incomprehensible, eternally the same, thou and thine only-begotten Son and thy Holy Spirit. Thou didst bring us from nothing into being, and didst raise

20 *The Divine Liturgy*, tr. Fortescue, p. 121.

us up when we had fallen." [21] The prayer concludes with the "Holy, holy, holy," the great contemplative prayer of the Hebrew Temple cult, to which is appended a contemplation of God's holiness: "Holy art thou and all-holy, thou, thine only-begotten Son and thy Holy Ghost. Holy art thou and all-holy, and wonderful is thy glory." [22]

Now, behind a drawn curtain, the act of consecration is accomplished with the recitation of the words of institution and of the ἐπίκλησις (calling down of the Holy Spirit upon the elements); the sacrosanct event remains veiled—for, in this temporal world, only through veils can God be seen. The awe-inspiring greatness and holiness of this act of consecration is incomparably expressed in the Syrian-Jacobite liturgy: "The gates of heaven open and the Holy Ghost descends upon these holy mysteries and permeates them. We stand in a terrible, awe-inspiring place, along with the cherubim and the seraphim; we have become brothers and fellow servants of the angels, and with them we perform the service of the fire and the Spirit."

In the presence of Christ actualized in the sacrament, the congregation conveys all its pleas to God's throne in the great prayer of intercession ending with the Our Father. In the solemn elevation, the priest shows the veiled gifts to the faithful with the contemplative cry: "Holy things to the holy," which the congregation answers with the words: "One is holy, one is the Lord," etc. In this cry, the infinite distance between sinful man and holy God is brought home to the congregation; then the gulf between human misery and divine glory is closed in the *unio mystica*. In communion, the soul is made one with the eternal Son of God, is permeated by his light, transformed, renewed, hallowed, deified. Blissfully the congregation sings after communion: "We have seen the true light, we have received the heavenly Spirit, we have found the true faith." [23]

Like the Eastern liturgies, the Roman Mass reveals in its structure the schema of the mystical path of salvation: *via purgativa, illuminativa, unitiva.*

The priest's preparatory prayers serve to purify the heart and make it ready for the mystery. As he washes his hands, he prays to be "cleansed of all taint, to the end that I may serve thee in body or soul"; as he puts on the amice, he prays God to "place upon my head the helmet of salvation to ward off the assaults of the devil"; as he puts on the alb, he prays that God may "make me white and cleanse my heart, in order that, washed white in the blood of the Lamb, I may enjoy bliss eternal"; as he draws the girdle round

21 Ibid.   22 Ibid.   23 Ibid.

his waist, he prays that God may "gird me with the girdle of purity and quench all sensual desire in my loins, that I may be confirmed in the virtue of continence and chastity"; as he dons the stole, he prays to be "clad in the vesture of immortality, which I have lost by the sin of our first parent"; and as he puts on the chasuble, he says: "O Lord, who hast said: my yoke is sweet and my burden light, grant that I may so bear it as to obtain thy grace."

The priest's act of purification is continued in a common act of purification for both priest and people, the prayer on the steps of the altar. In the Psalm Judica (Ps. 43 [42]), the oppressed soul struggles with the hostile powers of the world, who have followed him even into the temple, but, illumined by the divine light, he wrests himself from their grasp and confidently climbs upward to the "holy hill" and to God's "tabernacles." In the Confiteor, priest and people avow to each other their guilt, and plead in turn for divine release, that they may enter the holy of holies with a pure heart. The repeated supplicatory cry of the Kyrie eleison completes the preparatory purification of the congregation.

The second stage in the path of salvation, illumination, begins with the hymn Gloria in Excelsis. All earthly misery is forgotten. In worshiping contemplation, the congregation glorifies the divine majesty: *"Laudamus te, benedicimus te, adoramus te, glorificamus te, gratias agimus tibi propter magnam gloriam tuam"* ("We praise thee, we bless thee, we worship thee, we glorify thee, we thank thee for thy great glory"); these simple, succinct words of praise are a compendium of the purest contemplation. Everything earthly and unholy falls away; the holy God in His unapproachable greatness stands before the worshiping congregation: *"Tu solus sanctus, tu solus Dominus, tu solus altissimus."*

After attaining by a steep ascent to the first summit of contemplation, the congregation descends again into the valley, thence again, but this time more gradually, to climb an even higher peak. The sequence of the remaining parts of the Mass distinctly reveals the schema of contemplation of the medieval mystics: *lectio, meditatio, oratio, contemplatio.* The reading of the Epistle and the Gospel, separated by the meditative Gradual Psalm, is followed by the contemplation of the Creation and Redemption in the Nicene Creed. In a series of prayers, the priest implores acceptance of the votive offerings of bread and wine, and offers himself and the congregation as a sacrifice. Then, in accordance with the injunction of the "Sursum corda," supplication yields to contemplation of the divine glory and love in the Eucharistic prayer, the so-called Preface; at the center of this prayer stands the particular mystery of the feast being celebrated. The contemplative character of this great prayer of thanks is most strikingly apparent in the words of the Christmas Preface: "*Quia per incarnati Verbi mysterium nova mentis nostrae oculis lux tuae claritatis infulsit, ut dum visibiliter Deum cognoscimus, per hunc in invisibilium amorem rapiamur*" ("For by the mystery of the Word made flesh, a new ray of thy glory has appeared to the eyes of our mind, that while we behold God visibly, we may be carried by Him to the love of things invisible"). As in the Eastern Church, this contemplative prayer κατ᾽ ἐξοχήν ends in the angelic hymn: "Sanctus, sanctus, sanctus."

The central point of the whole liturgy of the Mass, the act of consecration, which is accomplished in complete silence, places the mysteries of Christ's incarnation and death on the Cross before the eyes of the faithful. For both the medieval and the modern Roman Catholic Church the Elevation of the Host and the chalice is the most important moment of the Mass. Through the veil of the earthly elements, the congregation beholds the hidden Son of God, falls down before him, and worships him in silence. No less a saint than Francis of Assisi has described this sacramental contemplation in eloquent words:

> As He appeared in true flesh to his holy apostles, so now He shows himself to us under the form of bread. And as they with the eyes of their body saw only his flesh, but contemplating him with their spiritual eyes, believed him to be their Lord and their God— so we who see only bread and wine with our bodily eyes, believe most firmly that it is his most holy body, and true and living blood. . . . Man should be seized with fear, the earth should tremble, and the heavens rejoice exceedingly, when Christ, the Son of the living God, descends upon the Altar in the hands of the priest. O admirable greatness! O stupendous condescension! O humble sublimity! " [24]

Before the earthly altar upon which the consecrated offerings rest, the praying congregation, guided by the angel, rises up in spirit to the heavenly altar, where the eternal Christ sacrifices himself unceasingly to the heavenly Father, and achieves a vision of the saints made perfect, in communion with whom it is devoutly united with Christ. All thoughts concentrate upon him

24 St. Francis, *Works*, tr. by a Religious of the Order (London, 1890), pp. 28, 95.

as the head of the body, the center of the drama of Creation and Salvation. This basic Christocentric attitude of the liturgy is wonderfully expressed in the contemplative formula uttered by the priest as he holds the Host over the chalice: "*. . . per quem haec omnia . . . bona creas, sanctificas, vivificas, benedicis, et praestas nobis, per ipsum et cum ipso et in ipso est tibi Deo Patri omnipotenti in unitate Spiritus Sancti omnis honor et gloria*" ("[that Christ] by whom thou dost always create, hallow, quicken, bless, and bestow upon us all these good things, through him and with him and in him, is to thee, God the Father Almighty, in the unity of the Holy Ghost, all honor and glory"). After the Our Father, the congregation in the thrice-repeated invocation: "*Agnus Dei, qui tollis peccata mundi,*" turns to the divine sacrificial Lamb which, mystically slaughtered, rests upon the altar. At the summons to receive Communion, "Behold the Lamb of God, who taketh away the sins of the world," the priest, now turned toward the congregation, raises the Host for the third time so that all may look once again upon the eternal God in the earthly symbol.

The holy vision ends in the *unio mystica,* by which vision and beholder become entirely one. The distance between sinful man and holy God is great—that is why the communicant utters the humble words of the heathen centurion: "I am not worthy that thou shouldst enter under my roof"; but divine grace bridges the gulf and condescends to miserable man—"But speak but the word, and my soul shall be healed." The union of the soul with Christ, accomplished in the taking of the consecrated bread, extends beyond this temporal realm to the transcendent realm of perfection; hence the formula: "May the body of our Lord Jesus Christ preserve thy soul unto eternal life." Indeed, the power of this celestial food extends also to the body, in which it implants the seed of immortality. In the Communion, body and soul are "transformed into a new creature."

The prayer of thanksgiving after Communion (Postcommunion) guides the soul from the heights of divine contemplation and union with God back to active life, in which the fruit of this heavenly food will show its efficacy, and then from life in this world it leads back to the realm of perfection, to that eternal heavenly banquet, of which the Lord's Supper, as solemnized here on earth, gives only a foretaste. Thus the Roman Church prays at the festival of Corpus Christi: "*Fac nos, quaesumus, Domine, divinitatis tuae sempiterna fruitione repleri, quam pretiosi corporis et sanguinis tui temporalis perceptio praefigurat*" ("Grant us, we beseech thee, O Lord, to be filled with

218

the everlasting fruition of thy divinity, which is prefigured by the temporal reception of thy precious body and blood").

After the blessing, the liturgy of the Mass concludes with the recitation of the prologue to the Gospel of St. John, one of the most contemplative texts in the New Testament. With the Evangelist, the congregation contemplates the essence of the eternal God, who eternally creates the Logos, who through its medium created the world in time, who through it reveals himself to all mankind, who became flesh— i.e., descended, in space and time, into a finite human person, Jesus of Nazareth. In the ceremony of the Eucharist this very incarnation has once again been made manifest to the congregation, in the descent of the Logos-Christ upon the bread and wine. Thus the Mass ends with the Evangelist's magnificent cry of rejoicing as he contemplates the mystery of the incarnation, and at this both priest and congregation genuflect: *"Et Verbum caro factum est, et habitavit in nobis, et vidimus gloriam eius, gloriam quasi Unigeniti a Patre, plenum gratiae et veritatis"* ("And the Word was made flesh, and dwelt among us, and we beheld his glory, the glory as of the only begotten of the Father, full of grace and truth"). The fundamental experience of the Hebrew congregation in the tabernacle and the Temple is also the fundamental experience of the Mass: it is the contemplation of the divine glory (*kabod*, δόξα, *gloria*).

So powerful is this contemplative experience of the eternal glory of God in the sensible sign that the Western Church of the second millennium created an opportunity for the flock to contemplate the sacramental Christ even outside of the Eucharistic liturgy proper: in the exposition of the sacramental bread, visibly in the monstrance, or unseen in the ciborium (pyx). At the sight of the humble white wafer, contemplation of the invisible God is kindled forever anew; in the infinitely small the beholder sees the infinitely great: the everyday object becomes a pledge of the enduring divine glory and love. In the epoch of the Counter Reformation, contemplative orders of nuns arose who devoted themselves especially to "perpetual adoration"; the sisters relieved one another in perpetual prayer before the exposed Sacrament. From these convents the custom of "perpetual adoration" passed into the lay world. On each day of the year a different parish maintains the watch of honor before the monstrance, and every night a different cloister takes over, so that the adoration of the Eucharistic Christ is uninterrupted. In big cities "Chapels of Perpetual Adoration" have recently been established, where the *Sanctissimum* is permanently exposed for the benefit of pious fugitives from the tumult of the big city, who pause for a while to worship in contemplative calm.

But not only the monstrance, even the closed tabernacle that holds the consecrated bread, constitutes a powerful point of attraction for mystical souls in the Roman Church. The tabernacle, before which the perpetual light burns, serves as a pledge of the presence of Christ and as an outward point of concentration for meditation and contemplation. Before Christ present in the tabernacle, the heart hungering for consolation pours forth its distress, the soul avid for God is inspired to worship, praise, and give thanks. According to the great Roman Catholic lay theologian, Friedrich von Hügel, the contemplative worship of the exposed Eucharist has "created saints, great saints."

True, these outward forms of reverence should not be overesteemed, but they are valuable because they give millions of simple souls an opportunity for contemplation. What the great Christian mystics have experienced in their solitary prayer is imparted, through these cultic symbols and forms, to the many who are "poor in spirit." *"Alles Vergängliche ist nur ein Gleichnis"* ("All things transitory are merely a parable") [25]—the outward objects of the cult are merely transparencies through which the contemplative soul beholds the glory and the beauty of the other world. Perhaps none of the great mystics has described this vision of the hidden God under the sacramental, sensible veil so movingly as has Thomas Aquinas in his *Rhythmus eucharisticus:*

> Adoro te devote, latens Deitas,
> quae sub his figuris vere latitas;
> tibi se cor meum totum subicit,
> quia te contemplans totum deficit. . . .
>
> Jesu, quem velatum nunc aspicio,
> oro, fiat illud, quod tam sitio,
> ut te revelata cernens facie
> visu sim beatus tuae gloriae.
>
> (Humbly I adore thee, hidden Deity,
> Which beneath these figures art concealed from me;
> Wholly in submission thee my spirit hails,
> For in contemplating thee it wholly fails. . . .

25 Goethe, *Faust*, II, Act 5.

Jesu, whom thus veiled I must see below,
When shall that be given which I long for so,
That at last beholding thy uncovered face,
Thou wouldst satisfy me with thy fullest grace? [26])

The suppliant soul sees through the temporality of the sensible sign to the infinite, thus anticipating the eternal vision of God. Removed from the world and its misery, it rests immersed in the light and radiance of beauty and love everlasting.

In Protestantism this sacramental cult has virtually vanished, and mystical contemplation with it. But in one of the Reformed Churches, the Anglican, it has been revived through the Anglo-Catholic movement founded some hundred years ago. The Anglo-Catholics have restored the daily celebration of the Eucharist, frequent Communion, and the monstrance. What this Eucharistic cult means to the masses is shown by the attractive churches with their tabernacles and perpetual lights, which form oases of stillness and beauty in the slums of London. Through the Eucharistic cult, a ray of divine light falls into this world of dark misery. Through its sacramentalism the Catholic Church is able to educate the simple, dull, and uneducated masses in mystical contemplation, and raise them up to the heights of meditative prayer. It invites all men, great and small, the rich and the poor in spirit, to drink from the sacramental springs of mystical contemplation. To all it proclaims the words of the Psalm that accompanies Communion in the Eastern liturgies: "O taste and see that the Lord is sweet" (Ps. 33 : 9 [Vulg.]).

3. Contemplation Among the Great Individual Mystics

Christianity is a contemplative religion in the full sense of the word. The Scriptures of the Old and New Testaments and the sacramental cult are the great schools and practice grounds of contemplation. Every Christian who penetrates to the core of Scripture or lives in the liturgy of the Church is led to contemplation, however imperfect in form. But above this mysticism of the congregation there rises an individual mysticism, more or less strongly influenced by Neoplatonic ideas. This individual mysticism goes beyond the mysticism of the congregation in three ways: (1) it achieves consciousness

26 See *Missale Romanum*, Gratiarum Actio post Missam; tr. John Mason Neale, *Collected Hymns, Sequences, and Carols* (London, 1914), p. 63.

of the contemplative experience through theological and psychological reflection; (2) it systematically cultivates contemplation and often makes use of a highly developed technique of meditation; (3) it develops an extraordinary intensity of contemplative life, often attaining to astonishing ecstatic and visionary experiences. Even so, it never entirely detaches itself from the mysticism of the congregation, from which it gathers nourishment and which it nourishes in turn; and for this reason it must always be considered an intrinsic part of the Christian faith and cult.

Contemplation is a stage in the great mystical path of salvation; it is a part of the "illumination" (*via illuminativa*), in its ascent to the final stage, "union" (*via unitiva*). It must be preceded by the hard, self-sacrificing road of "purification," the *via purgativa*. "Contemplative sweetness not without full great labour is gotten, and with joy untold it is possessed. . . . And yet from the beginning to this day never might man be ravished in contemplation of Love Everlasting, but if he before parfitely all the world's vanity had forsaken." [27] But this process of purification should not be conceived in terms of time; the *via purgativa* is as long as life itself; as the inner life progresses, the soul merely becomes more deeply rooted in the higher experiences of mystical contemplation and union. The contemplation of the eternal, transcendent God is possible only if the soul continually renews its detachment from transient things and men, only if the passions and desires are constantly held in check, only if all sinful will is killed, only if the soul frees itself unceasingly from the finite ego. In a "creative death," the individual ego must make way for a higher, God-filled self. To sacrifice the individual ego means to overcome: (1) attachment to outward possessions; (2) sexual passion; (3) the individual will. This process of self-sacrifice is most radically accomplished through individual poverty, celibacy, and total subordination to an ecclesiastical superior; hence in the realization of the three *consilia evangelica:* poverty, chastity, and obedience, which constitute the foundation of the Christian monastic life. However, the "evangelical counsels" are not an indispensable premise for the achievement of mystical perfection; they are, as Thomas Aquinas classically formulates it, only the best *instrumenta perfectionis*. A number of the greatest Christian mystics did not belong to the monastic orders; Ruysbroeck was a secular priest, Rolle a hermit, Tersteegen an artisan; St. Catherine of Genoa, Jakob

---

27 Richard Rolle, *The Mending of Life*, XII; quoted in Underhill, p. 336.

Boehme, and Mme Guyon were married. But though the higher mystical life does not require the cloister, it cannot dispense with discipline in detachment from the world, from men, and from the self. The most important "technical" instrument of this discipline is asceticism—i.e., practice and training in detachment from neutral (i.e., morally permissible) objects. It consists above all in fasting, in the renunciation of pleasures and comforts, and in silence. To these is added confession—i.e., the laying bare of one's inner life to a spiritual guide, submission to his control, and obedience to his instructions. Many great Christian mystics had confessors who were not on a plane with them, who sometimes dealt harshly with them, and nevertheless they willingly submitted, in order to break their individual will. These outward acts of purification are accompanied by the inner purification of the soul through self-abasement before God, in the contrition of the heart, motivated by love of God.

The *via purgativa* of asceticism leads to the *via illuminativa* of meditation and contemplation. The first act of illumination is introversion, inner concentration. Introversion means not only detachment from the confusing turmoil of the sensory world, but also immersion in the divine ground of the soul. Since the soul is made "in God's image and likeness," it reflects the glory and love of the Eternal Creator, once it is cleansed of impurity and sin. For this reason the great contemplative mystics continually counsel introversion, as, for example, St. Augustine: *"Redi in temetipsum, in interiore homine habitat veritas"* ("Return within yourself. In the inward man dwells truth").[28] In his innermost heart the mystic, who has closed the outward gates of his senses ($\mu\upsilon\epsilon\tilde{\iota}\nu$, the root of "mystic," means to close), experiences the presence of the infinite God. The purpose of narrowing down the spiritual horizon to the innermost soul is accordingly to expand it infinitely; "sese angustat ut dilatetur" ("it narrows itself, that it may be enlarged"), as Gregory the Great aptly said of the soul concentrated upon its inwardness.[29] Having died to the outward world, it is reborn in the divine inner world; accordingly, Bernard of Clairvaux speaks characteristically of the *"vitalis vigilque sopor,"* a "sleep alive and watchful," which "enlightens the inward senses."[30]

This inner concentration does not consist merely in a heightening of

28 *De vera religione*, XXXIX, 72.
29 *Homily on Ezechiel*, II, 2, 12; quoted in Butler, p. 93.
30 *Sermons on the Canticles*, LII, 2, 3; in Butler, p. 154.

attention, in freeing the soul from its outward bonds, that it may turn toward God; in meditation, the inner void is, on the contrary, filled again with concrete content, resulting from a relative and regulated extraversion, from the silent contemplation of nature, but most of all from the reading or recitation of a passage in Scripture or a verse of prayer, from the contemplation of a ritual object or sacred image, or from preoccupation with a religious fantasy. For the most part the contemplation of nature plays an unsystematic part in the meditation of the Christian mystics. The Christian hermits and monks usually constructed their cells and cloisters amid a magnificent landscape, and this in itself reveals an intimate relation to nature. The importance of nature for meditation and contemplation is manifest both in the famous saying of St. Bernard to the effect that he had learned more about God from forests than from books and in St. Francis' *Canticle to the Sun*. But a systematic use of natural objects for purposes of meditation is rarely found in Christian mysticism.

An important source of contemplation for the Christian mystics has been the reading of Holy Scripture. Because, as the Apostle said, its authors were "moved by the Holy Ghost" (II Peter 1 : 21), the contemplation of a passage in Scripture, "in spirit"—i.e., in devotion to the God who is present in a man's innermost soul—can disclose its spiritual kernel. The contemplative soul first reads a passage in the Old or New Testament "cursorily." He then stops at a sentence that speaks directly to him and ponders its meaning, not the "historical" meaning, which it possessed originally for the author or the contemporary reader, but the present meaning that opens up to the contemplative soul in its concrete situation. But because it is one and the same God who spoke to the godly men of the Old and New Testaments and who speaks to meditative souls in the present time, the historical meaning and the present meaning of a passage in Scripture are ultimately one, both being aspects of its transcendent "pneumatic" meaning.

Side by side with the reading of Scripture stands the recitation of liturgical texts as a wellspring of contemplation. The Our Father, the Hail Mary, the Apostles' Creed, such classical hymns as "Vexilla regis prodeunt," "Veni Sancte Spiritus," sung at Pentecost, the sacramental "Adoro te devote," the antiphons of Mary, the mysteries of the rosary, but also more individual prayers such as the "Soul of Christ, sanctify me" of St. Ignatius —these and other prayers are uttered a sentence or half a sentence at a time, and their meaning is pondered.

Meditation is also cultivated through ritual objects and pictures of the saints: the altar, the tabernacle, the exposed *Sanctissimum* (see above, p. 219), the crucifix, the Stations of the Cross, pictures of the Blessed Virgin and the saints. All these objects and pictures are outward aids and stimuli to the contemplation of God's presence, His mercy, His condescension and sacrificial death; while the pictures of the saints encourage contemplation of heroic *caritas* and love of God.

But meditation need not be based upon any sensible object; it can also originate in certain imaginings. Aided by concrete memories or fancies, the contemplative soul considers the transience of earthly existence, the suddenness and the terrors of death, the ugliness of sin; or he may evoke in his imagination the various acts in the drama of salvation, the life, Passion, death, and resurrection of Christ, or the life and death of the Virgin and the saints; finally, he may seek to actualize the divine attributes of omniscience, wisdom, beauty, justice, and love, concrete examples from nature, from history, and from his own life.

Psychologically speaking, all meditation is characterized by the voluntary activity of the mind, which can be either intellectual and discursive or more imaginative and intuitive; the meditative soul seeks to analyze or examine the substance of his meditation from every angle, and thus to exhaust its inner meaning.

In Christian mysticism, meditation on God's being and His works passes into prayer, which is a direct turning to God in personal dialogue, in a living Thou-and-I relationship. In prayer the results of meditation are summed up and uttered in the form of supplication, praise, or thanks to God. Prayer comprehends all the stages of the mystical path of salvation: purification, illumination, and union. The suppliant prays for forgiveness, rebirth, and sanctification, for the strength needed for dedication and devotion to God, for the love of God, for the unclouded vision of God; he prays to be made like unto God, to be deified. All these different pleas are mere circumlocutions for the central plea of the mystic: the prayer for God Himself. With incomparable insight, St. Augustine stated the mystical object of prayer: *"Nolite aliquid quaerere a Deo nisi Deum"* ("Ask nothing of God but God").[30a] One of the Greek hymns of Simeon the New Theologian [31] may serve as an example of this mystical life of prayer:

30a Sermo 331 (*De Diversis* 100), par. 5; in Migne, *PL*, XXXVIII, 1461.
31 *Divinorum amorum liber*, 19 (Migne, *PG*, CXX, 548).

First of all, O King of all things, shine forth within me, dwell in me and illumine my base soul; show me openly the face of Thy Godhead, and manifest Thyself altogether to me invisibly, O my God. . . . Give Thyself to me now, that I may take my fill, that I may kiss and embrace Thine ineffable glory, the light of Thy countenance, and be filled, and tell all others of it, and after death come all glorified to Thee. May I stand before Thee made light by Thy light, and freed from the care of all these evils, be delivered also from fear and changed no more.

All these prayers disclose one essential feature of Christian mysticism: ascetic and meditative techniques can facilitate and pave the way for contemplation and union, but cannot induce them; they are given by grace alone. "The grace of contemplation," says Bernard of Clairvaux, "is granted only in response to longing and importunate desire." [32] Indeed, not only are contemplation of God and union with God free gifts of divine grace; so also are the desire and the longing for them that find their expression in prayer. It is not man who seeks God, but God who seeks man, and this call and appeal of God finds its echo in man's longing to see God and be united with him. The prayer of the Christian mystics is an *oratio infusa*, infused, imparted, inspired from above.

The effect of contemplation and of the prayer that sums up and expresses its results is an inner peace, ease, and suppleness, a *passivity* that releases the creative forces of the subconscious or, in religious terms, opens up a way to the full efficacy of divine grace. Tauler says aptly: "The best and most exalted thing that you can do in this life is to be silent and let God work and speak; when all your energies are withdrawn from your own works and thoughts, then will this (divine) word be spoken." Only in this condition of passive openness and readiness is true contemplation possible.

Contemplation enters into the life of the mystic as a new and wonderful experience. This experience has often been described by Christian mystics, but few accounts of it reveal such depth and subtlety as a passage in the *Enneads* of Plotinus. If we quote this passage *in toto*, it is because Platonic-Neoplatonic mysticism became the strongest element in Christian contemplation, and because even St. Augustine, one of the greatest of Christian mystics, recognized the inspired nature of Neoplatonic contemplation when

---

32 *Sermons on the Canticles*, XXXII, 3; quoted in Butler, p. 145.

he referred to Plotinus and others as "magni homines et paene divini" ("great men and almost divine").[33]

> Beholding this Being . . . resting, rapt, in the vision and posses-
> sion of so lofty a loveliness, growing to Its likeness, what Beauty
> can the Soul yet lack? For This, the Beauty supreme, the absolute,
> and the primal, fashions Its lovers to Beauty and makes them also
> worthy of love. . . . And one that shall know this vision—with
> what passion of love shall he not be seized, with what pang of
> desire, what longing to be molten into one with This, what wonder-
> ing delight! . . . He will be flooded with awe and gladness, stricken
> by a salutary terror; he loves with a veritable love, with sharp
> desire; all other loves than this he must despise, and disdain all
> that once seemed fair.
> This, indeed, is the mood even of those who, having witnessed
> the manifestation of Gods or Supernals, can never again feel the
> old delight in the comeliness of material forms: what then are we
> to think of one that contemplates Absolute Beauty in Its essential
> integrity, no accumulation of flesh and matter, no dweller on earth
> or in the heavens—so perfect Its purity—far above all such things
> in that they are non-essential, composite, not primal but descend-
> ing from This? [34]

Contemplation is directed toward the ultimate, the highest, the absolute, toward God in His totality and infinity, in "His unutterable plenitude." In contemplation the spirit gazes into an abyss, an ocean, a dazzling sun. All concrete conceptions and imaginings, all *corporales similitudines*, are left far behind; vanished are all the religious and cultic symbols; even the humanity of the Son of God, the child in the manger, the sufferer on the Cross, are left behind. ". . . Though we have known Christ after the flesh, yet now henceforth we know him no more" (II Cor. 5 : 16). Jesus the man is forgotten; only the eternal God-Logos stands before the contemplating soul, only the "immutable light" in its nakedness and purity, in its "color-less beauty"—"*bellezza contemplando, la qual non ha colore*" ("contemplating beauty that has no color").[35] This total detachment from all sensual and spiritual concreteness does not, however, exclude the contemplation of all creation within God. St. John of the Cross speaks eloquently of this universal

---

33 *De ordine*, II, 28; in Butler, p. 60.
34 Plotinus, *Enneads*, I, 6, 7; tr. MacKenna, p. 62. [The first two sentences have been transposed from end to head of quotation.—ED.]
35 Jacopone da Todi, *Laude*, XCI; cited from Underhill, p. 374.

vision, which is bound up with the vision of God: "The soul is able to see, in that tranquil wisdom, how of all the creatures—not the higher creatures alone, but also the lower, according to that which each of them has received in itself from God—each one raises its voice in testimony to that which God is. . . . Thus all these voices make one voice of music, extolling the greatness of God and His marvellous knowledge and wisdom." [36]

As all sensory concreteness is excluded from the contemplation of the Highest, so also are all willful activity, all logical deductions and ethical value judgments. The contemplator does nothing and strives to do nothing; as Plotinus puts it in his fine metaphor, he resembles the wanderer watching the sunrise. Not with the light of his own eyes, but only with the divine light, can man behold the eternally Divine. "Here there is nothing but an eternal seeing and staring at that Light, by that Light, and in that Light." [37] "And to it none can attain through knowledge or subtlety, neither through any exercise whatsoever. Only he with whom it pleases God to be united in His Spirit, and whom it pleases to enlighten by Himself, can see God, and no one else." [38]

This passive, grace-induced character of contemplation is what chiefly distinguishes it from meditation, with its activity and participation of the self. Richard of St.-Victor has aptly formulated the psychological differences: "Meditation with great mental industry plods along the steep and laborious road keeping the end in view. Contemplation on a free wing circles around with great nimbleness wherever the impulse takes it. . . . Meditation investigates, contemplation wonders. . . . Meditation [arises] from the reason, contemplation from the intelligence." [39]

For the Christian mystic contemplation signifies profoundest bliss, inner sweetness (*interior dulcedo*), a holy drunkenness (*sancta inebriatio*), as St. Augustine puts it. Richard Rolle describes the beatitude of the contemplative soul: "To me it seems that contemplation is joyful song of God's love taken in mind, with sweetness of angels' praise. This is jubilation, that is the end of perfect prayer and high devotion in this life. This is that mirth

36 *Spiritual Canticle*, XIV–XV, 27; in *The Complete Works of St. John of the Cross*, tr. and ed. E. Allison Peers (3 vols., London, 1934–35), II, 273.

37 Jan van Ruysbroeck, *Adornment of the Spiritual Marriage*, tr. C. A. Wynschenck Dom (London and New York, 1916), p. 171. (Cf. Underhill, p. 345.)

38 Ibid., p. 167. (Cf. Underhill, pp. 333–34.)

39 Richard of St.-Victor, *De gratia contemplationis seu Benjamin major*, I, 3, in *Selected Writings on Contemplation*, tr. Clare Kirchberger (London, 1957), p. 136.

in mind, had ghostily by the lover everlastingly, with great voice outbreaking. . . . Nothing merrier than grace of contemplation!" [40]

In the words of Richard Rolle, this contemplative bliss is a "great voice outbreaking"; it finds spontaneous expression in brief outcries within the prayer; the soul stammers as it strives to utter the glory and the greatness of the contemplated God. Two prayers of the greatest Western mystics, St. Augustine and St. Francis, give us an example of this enraptured prayer:

"*Summe, optime, potentissime, misericordissime et iustissime, pulcherrime et fortissime*" ("O Thou, the greatest and the best, mightiest, almighty, most merciful and most just, most beautiful and most strong").[41]

"Thou art holy, O Lord God; thou art the God of gods, who alone workest wonders, thou art strong, thou art great, thou art most high, thou art omnipotent. Thou art the eternal Father, king of heaven and earth. Thou art the triune God. Thou art good, all good, the greatest good, O Lord God, true and only God. Thou art love and charity, thou art wisdom, thou art humility, thou art patience, thou art beauty . . . thou art happiness . . . temperance, thou art all riches." [42]

With the advance of contemplation, the power of expression vanishes. In the presence of the ineffable God, prayer is silence. The contemplation becomes wordless, silent, *oratio pura, oratio mentalis*, inward prayer; the contemplative mystics use any number of terms to distinguish this type of prayer from the usual spoken dialogue with God. "For all words and all that may be learnt and understood in a creaturely way are foreign to, and far below, the truth which I mean." [43]

But it is not speech alone that becomes inadequate and slips away from the contemplative soul; his inner thoughts leave him as well—"all divine names, all modes and all ideas that are formed in the mirror of divine truth, have fallen into the nameless realm where there is neither mode nor reason" (Tauler). Angela of Foligno gives an intimation of the unfathomable and unthinkable nature of the object of contemplation: "I beheld a fullness and a clearness, and felt them within me so abundantly that I cannot describe it, or give any likeness thereof. I cannot say I saw anything corporeal. It

40 *The Mending of Life*, XII; in Underhill, pp. 336, 342.
41 St. Augustine, *Confessions*, I, 4; tr. F. J. Sheed (London and New York, 1944), p. 2.
42 St. Francis, *Works*, p. 163.
43 Ruysbroeck, *Adornment of the Spiritual Marriage*, p. 168. (Cf. Underhill, p. 334.)

was as though it were in heaven: a beauty so great that I can say nought concerning it, save that it was supreme Beauty and sovereign Good." [44]

In its highest and richest form contemplation is a relatively rare and brief experience. Bernard of Clairvaux laments: *"Heu rara hora et parva mora!"* ("Alas, how rare the hour and how brief its duration!") [45] And St. Augustine indicates the suddenness and brevity of the experience in a number of striking terms: the contemplation of the infinite beauty occurs *"perstrictim et raptim, quasi per transitum"* ("briefly and quickly, as in passing"),[46] *"in ictu trepidantis aspectus"* ("in the flash of a trembling glance"),[47] *"rapida cogitatione attingimus"* ("in swift thought we touched [the Eternal Wisdom] ").[48]

But even this beatific contemplation of the infinite God is not the ultimate and highest mystical experience; vision leads finally to the perfect union of the contemplating soul with the seen or rather the seeing God. In contemplation there is still a strong consciousness of the distance between the soul and God. Man in his paltriness and sinfulness feels himself unworthy to stand before God's face, and believes himself unable to bear the sight of the eternal divine purity.

> Tainted and sullied in body and soul, how shall I stand before Thee? How shall I behold Thee, wretched as I am, how shall I stand before Thy face? Must I not flee from Thy glory and the flashing light of thine Holy Spirit? [49]

But this sense of the essential difference between soul and God struggles with the opposite sentiment of consubstantiality. St. Augustine expressed this tension in incomparable words: *"Inhorresco, in quantum dissimilis ei sum; inardesco, in quantum similis ei sum"* ("I draw back in terror in so far as I am different from Him; I am on fire with longing in the degree of my likeness to Him").[50] In the contemplation of the divine beauty the mystic discovers the copy of this beauty in his own soul; he recognizes that he is not surrendering himself to an alien being that is only outside and above him, but to a consubstantial being, present in his innermost soul. And from

44 Blessed Angela of Foligno, in Underhill, p. 342.
45 *Sermons on the Canticles*, XXIII, 15.
46 *Enarrationes in Psalmos*, XLI, 10 (Migne, *PL*, XXXVI, 471); in Butler, p. 67 & *n.*
47 *Confessions*, VII, 17; in Butler, p. 66*n.*
48 Ibid., IX, 10; in Butler, p. 66*n.*
49 Simeon, *Divinorum amorum*, 17 (Migne, *PG*, CXX, 534).
50 *Confessions*, XI, 9; tr. Sheed, p. 214.

this twofold contemplation of the transcendent and immanent God arises the *unio mystica*, the essential union. In one of his prayers, St. John of the Cross gives us an intimation of how this union arises from the contemplation of God and self:

> ... That I may be so transformed in Thy beauty that, being alike in beauty, we may both see ourselves in Thy beauty ... so that, when one of us looks at the other, each may see in the other his beauty ... and thus I shall see Thee in Thy beauty and Thou wilt see me in Thy beauty; and I shall see myself in Thee in Thy beauty, and Thou wilt see Thyself in me in Thy beauty; and thus I may be like to Thee in Thy beauty and Thou mayest be like to me in Thy beauty, and my beauty may be Thine, and Thine mine; and thus I shall be Thou in it, and Thou wilt be I in this same beauty of Thine, and thus we shall each see the other in Thy beauty.[51]

"Tu totus meus et ego totus tuus" ("Thou art all mine, I am all thine")— in this brief prayer formula of Thomas a Kempis [52] the union of the soul with its God is expressed. Mechthild of Magdeburg describes the same experience in the powerful verses:

> I am in thee and thou in me,
> We could not be closer,
> For we two are fused into one,
> Poured into one mould,
> Thus, unwearied, we remain forever.[53]

In this perfect union, the soul is entirely illumined and transfigured by the primal divine light; it takes on the form of light. Union means transformation of the soul into its divine prototype, deification in the true sense of the word. The fervent communion of God and soul has become a total immersion. As John of the Cross eloquently sings:

> Amado con amada,
> Amada en el Amado transformada!
>
> (Lover and lov'd, as one,
> Lover transform'd in lov'd . . . ! [54])

51 *Spiritual Canticle*, xxxvi, 5; tr. Peers, II, 380–81 and n. 1.
52 *De imitatione Christi*, ii, 5.
53 *The Revelations*, iii, 5; tr. Lucy Menzies (London, 1953).
54 "Songs of the Soul," etc., tr. Peers, II, 441.

For the Christian mystic this union and deification does not mean a suspension of man's created nature. Even in the perfect *unio mystica* man remains man—i.e., God's creature. No more than the sponge loses its essence in water, the iron in fire, the air in the sunlight, although they are entirely permeated and filled by the other element, does the soul lose its own being in God. Unlike other mysticisms, Christian mysticism knows no pantheism, and where pantheism has appeared, the official Church has pronounced an immediate and clear-cut no. For the Christian mystic the words of the Psalm are still in force: "The Lord he is God: it is he that hath made us, and not we ourselves" (Ps. 100 [99] : 3).

When this experience of union reaches its summit in ecstasy, not only is sensory perception excluded as it is in contemplation, but all psychic function is suspended as well: "So wondrously remembering, we do not remember, and not remembering we still remember; seeing we do not discern, beholding we do not perceive, and our effort does not penetrate." [55] Consciousness of space and time is suspended, the soul is dissolved in the infinite, its life is a *nunc aeternum*, an eternal today. Even the consciousness of Thou-and-I, still present in contemplation, is now extinguished. Physically, the state of ecstasy is characterized by total anesthesia, often outwardly manifested by catalepsy or even apparent death. For this very reason, the duration of ecstasy is greater than that of pure contemplation; the ecstatic soul can remain for hours in this state of total absorption. When he returns from ecstasy to his normal waking state, all concrete memory has vanished, he knows only that he has experienced the infinite and that in some unutterable way he has become one with it. Christian mystics find a Biblical example of this ecstatic experience in St. Paul, who was "caught up to the third heaven" (II Cor. 12 : 2).

For the Christian mystic, pure contemplation and ecstatic union on earth are an anticipation of eternal contemplation of God and union with Him in the hereafter, but for this very reason they are not the ultimate, the absolute, the perfect. "It doth not yet appear what we shall be: but we know that, when he shall appear, we shall be like him; for we shall see him as he is" (I John 3 : 2). Christian mysticism, like all Christian religion, is eschatological; hence even in its highest and purest experience, it points beyond, to ultimate fulfillment in the eternal kingdom of God. Accordingly, the

55 Richard of St.-Victor, *De gratia contemplationis*, in Kirchberger, p. 179. (Cf. Underhill, p. 370.)

Christian mystics never weary of stressing the imperfection and limitation of all contemplation and union this side of the grave. All mystical contemplation of God is a "night vision," "a seeing in the darkness," "through a dense cloud of unknowing," "a vision through nonvision," "a cognition through noncognition." Darkness as well as light plays a prominent part in the imagery of the Christian mystics. Dionysius the Areopagite combined the two in his subtle paradox, "light darkness." Or, as St. Paul said, we can only hope in this world to "see through a glass, darkly" (I Cor. 13 : 12). "God lifts the veil a little" for the pious man in his earthly pilgrimage; He lets a few rays of light from His venerable countenance shine down upon man's soul, but it is only in the perfection of the life after death that man will "see Him face to face." "God now appears as He wishes, not as He is. No wise man, no saint, no prophet, is able to see Him as He is, nor has been able in this mortal body." [56] Indeed, even in the perfection of the afterlife, the created nature of the soul places a limit upon the possibility of seeing God "face to face"; the perfect soul's knowledge of God consists precisely in "knowing God as unknowable."

The ascent of the mystical soul from meditation to the heights of contemplation and ecstasy is a highly differentiated process, which can be described only by a more or less crude and artificial schematization. The mystics themselves have often attempted to classify the separate stages of this process and have arrived at a great variety of subdivisions. Of the innumerable attempts to classify contemplation and mystical prayer, St. Teresa's ladder of prayer [57] is not only the most famous, but also unquestionably the most psychologically penetrating and graphic. She distinguishes four stages: the prayer of recollection, of quiet, of union, and of ecstasy. The prayer of recollection is the meditative prayer, in which the soul actively moves into the presence of God. Teresa likens the activity of the soul at this stage to the "great labor" of a man drawing water from a well. In the prayer of quiet, the soul rests in profound contentment in God; He grants it an unutterably sweet and peaceful joy, which fills all its faculties with deepest contentment and the purest sense of beatitude. The soul enjoys the supreme good. Teresa likens the diminished activity in this stage to the turning of a wheel, by which the bucket is placed beneath the waterspout. She calls

56 St. Bernard, *Sermons on the Canticles*, XXXI, 2; in Butler, p. 175.
57 St. Teresa of Jesus, *Life*, XIff.; in *The Complete Works*, tr. E. Allison Peers (3 vols., London, 1946), II, 88, 96, 105.

the prayer of union the "sleep of the soul's faculties." The soul enjoys nameless delight. It sinks into a celestial inebriation, a celestial folly; it floats in the purest and highest bliss. It would wish to pour itself forth in praise of the divine love; it yearns only for God; it belongs no longer to itself, but only to Him. Teresa likens the slight activity at this stage to the diversion of water into a brook or river. Finally, in the prayer of ecstasy, all inner activity has vanished. All feeling ceases, and the suppliant sinks into a swoon; the "soul is immersed in blissful enjoyment, without understanding what it enjoys." In this beatitude, it knows a foretaste of eternal glory. The total passivity of this delight is likened by Teresa to flooding by heavy rain—without human participation, the Lord waters the garden.

In its higher stages, contemplation is accompanied by extraordinary manifestations, which, however, do not belong to its essential realm of experience. Not infrequently, especially in women mystics, there are visions and auditions, lights, colors, shapes, lending sensory expression to purely spiritual experience. The living union with Christ crucified is manifested with immense plastic power in the stigmata. Total ecstatic detachment from the sensory world is accompanied not infrequently by levitation: gravity is overcome, and the body is raised from the ground. Finally, the mystical soul achieves through constant contemplation an extraordinary faculty for the "discernment of spirits," a clairvoyance in the psychological and ethical judgment of other persons, extending as far as cardiognosis, the perception of the heart's innermost thoughts. All these parapsychological phenomena are, however, mere marginal manifestations of contemplation; their presence is no criterion for the elevation and purity of the contemplation; their total absence does not in any way diminish the value of the mystical experience.

The contemplative life no doubt involves grave dangers. Mystical and ecstatic experience often borders closely on the psychopathological. Above all, there is the danger of confounding objective, transcendent reality with subjective experience that is merely a projection of human emotions and desires. But the great Christian mystics did not succumb to these dangers. They were not fantasts and crackpots; indeed, their sobriety never ceases to amaze us. They possessed a number of unerring criteria for the metaphysical authenticity of their contemplative and ecstatic experience.

(1) The first hallmark of a mystic's religious authenticity is his distrust of all extraordinary experiences, especially of all ecstasies and visions. The

desert monks already recognized this rule: one's first thought in the presence of a miraculous experience must be that it is a delusion sent by the Devil. St. John of the Cross declares that as soon as signs of an approaching ecstasy are manifested, one should turn one's attention to other things. Ignatius Loyola wrote: "Visions . . . must never be desired or demanded; in accordance with the counsels of the saints and the doctors of spiritual life, one must, to the limit of one's powers, shun them and look upon them with suspicion." St. Philip Neri advised his students to reject all visions; this resistance, he said, was the surest means of distinguishing true visions from false ones.

(2) With his distrust of all extraordinary experiences, the true mystic combines a punctilious silence concerning all his mystical experiences. "Blessed is the servant, who keeps the secrets of his Lord in his heart," says St. Francis of Assisi.[58] And, accordingly, he concealed the miraculous stigmata that he bore on his body. Many mystics have spoken or written of their experiences only at the command of their confessors.

(3) Another characteristic of the true mystic is that he sets less store by unusual and exalted experiences than by simple, everyday piety and active love of God. The Apostle Paul regarded his miraculous visions, ecstasies, and miracles as trifling compared to the true worship, which consists in charity and the love of God (I Cor. 13). "How much more in God's sight," says St. John of the Cross, "is one work or act of the will performed in charity than are all the visions and communications that they may receive from Heaven. . . . Many souls who have known nothing of such things have made incomparably greater progress than others who have received many of them." [59] Pope Benedict XIV stresses that "many perfect men have been canonized, without the least mention having been made, in this process, of infused contemplation." [60]

(4) A no less trustworthy sign of the authenticity of mystical love of God is perseverance in perfect devotion and trust in God despite total absence of contemplative experience. The intensification of inner emotion in such experiences is inevitably followed by a psychic lethargy in which the wellsprings of beatitude dry up. Ecstatic plenitude is followed by a terrifying

---

58 *Works*, p. 103.
59 *Ascent of Mount Carmel*, II, 22, 19; tr. Peers, I, 184.
60 *Opera omnia*, III, 26, 8; cited in Albert Farges, *Mystical Phenomena*, tr. S. P. Jacques (London, 1926), p. 225.

condition of inner emptiness, for which the mystics have a number of striking terms: "Dark night of the soul," "barrenness," "despair," "mystical purgatory," "temporal hell." The radiance of the vision of God permeates the sinful and insignificant soul of man so strongly that it painfully recognizes its remoteness from God. St. John of the Cross describes this process with sure psychological insight:

> Because the light and wisdom of this contemplation is most bright and pure, and the soul which it assails is dark and impure, it follows that the soul suffers great pain when it receives it in itself, just as, when the eyes are dimmed by humours, and become impure and weak, they suffer pain through the assault of the bright light. And when the soul is indeed assailed by this Divine light, its pain, which results from its impurity, is immense; because, when this pure light assails the soul, in order to expel its impurity, the soul feels itself to be so impure and miserable that it believes God to be against it, and thinks that it has set itself up against God. This causes it so much grief and pain (because it now believes that God has cast it away). . . . When this purgative contemplation is most severe, the soul feels very keenly the shadow of death and the lamentations of death and the pains of hell, which consist in its feeling itself to be without God, and chastised and cast out, and unworthy of Him; and it feels that He is wroth with it. All this is felt by the soul in this condition—yea, and more, for it believes that it is so with it for ever.[61]

Most mystics have passed through these terrible depths of Godforsakenness, like their divine Master, who cried out in despair on the Cross: "My God, my God, why hast thou forsaken me?" But precisely in this state of desolation, it becomes manifest whether the soul in its contemplative experience has been seized by the reality of the eternal God or has merely grown drunk on delusive feelings and images of its own ego, whether its piety is rooted in a transcendent reality or is only the reflection of a sublimated egoism. St. Mary Magdalen dei Pazzi writes: "A soul that has tasted the goodness of the Lord must veritably be a bride of the Cross if it would continue to serve God just as faithfully in aridity as it did amid consolations."

(5) The last and royal criterion for the authenticity of the *vita contemplativa* is its effect on the *vita activa*. Just as Jesus descended from the mountaintop, where he had spent his nights in prayer, into the cities, to proclaim the

61 *Dark Night of the Soul*, II, 5, 5; II, 6, 2; tr. Peers, I, 407, 410.

word of God and to heal the sick, so does the mystic descend from the Mount Tabor of contemplation into the plains of daily life, to serve his brethren, to serve indeed all creatures in "all-embracing love," "to enrich all things in true generosity from his divine abundance" (Ruysbroeck). By this active love he transmits the love of God he has experienced through contemplation, and thus becomes a "messenger of divine love" (Gertrude of Helftä), "an intermediary between God and all men" (Ruysbroeck). All the great contemplative souls (St. Augustine, St. Benedict, Gregory the Great, St. Bernard, Meister Eckhart, St. John of the Cross, St. Hildegard of Bingen, St. Catherine of Siena and St. Catherine of Genoa, St. Teresa of Ávila) were also great in their active lives, consuming themselves in the service of the Church. "They . . . in quiet imbibe by contemplation," says Gregory the Great, "what in employment they may pour back to their neighbours by word of mouth. For by contemplation they rise into the love of God, but by preaching they return back to the service of their neighbour." [62]

> Holy men are sent and go forth as lightnings, when they come forth from the retirement of contemplation to the public life of employment. They are sent and they go, when from the secrecy of inward meditation, they spread forth into the wide space of active life. But after the outward works which they perform, they always return to the bosom of contemplation, there to revive the flame of their zeal, and to glow as it were from the touch of heavenly brightness. For they would freeze too speedily amid their outward works, good though they be, did they not return with anxious earnestness to the fire of contemplation. [63]

The life of the Christian mystic is carried on in constant interchange between contemplation and deed. As in human breathing inspiration and expiration, as in the working of the human heart systole and diastole, are forever alternating, so likewise in man's relation to God do unworldly contemplation and the worldly service of sacrifice and love succeed one another. In the transcendent life the arduous sacrifice ceases, making way for the eternal, undisturbed vision of God. During their days on earth, all the longing of the mystics is toward this perfect vision of God. And this yearning for the ultimate and the most high has found wonderful expression in innumerable works, in prayers, hymns, and homilies. But perhaps it has been

62 Gregory the Great, *Morals on the Book of Job,* VI, 56; in Butler, p. 222.
63 Ibid., XXX, 8; in Butler, p. 224.

most marvelously expressed by Plotinus, the prince of non-Christian mystics, who was to become the preceptor of Christian contemplation:

> And for This, the sternest and the uttermost combat is set before the Souls; all our labour is for This, lest we be left without part in this noblest vision, which to attain is to be blessed in the blissful sight, which to fail of is to fail utterly.
>
> For not he that has failed of the joy that is in colour or in visible forms, not he that has failed of power or of honours or of kingdom has failed, but only he that has failed of only This, for Whose winning he should renounce kingdoms and command over earth and ocean and sky, if only, spurning the world of sense from beneath his feet, and straining to This, he may see.[64]

64 *Enneads*, 1, 6, 7; tr. MacKenna, p. 62.

Max Pulver

The Experience of Light in the Gospel of St. John,
in the "Corpus hermeticum," in Gnosticism,
and in the Eastern Church

1. Light in the Gospel of St. John

"In him [the Logos] was life; and the life was the light of men. And the light shineth in darkness; and the darkness comprehended it not."

The word καταλαμβάνω, here translated "comprehended," can also mean "find," "know," "hold down," and "oppress."

These words, ambivalent in a twofold sense, constitute verses 4 and 5 of the Fourth Gospel: ἐν αὐτῷ ζωὴ ἦν, καὶ ἡ ζωὴ ἦν τὸ φῶς τῶν ἀνθρώ-πων· καὶ τὸ φῶς ἐν τῇ σκοτίᾳ φαίνει, καὶ ἡ σκοτία αὐτὸ οὐ κατέλαβεν.

This prologue deals with the Logos, the Word, which was with God, πρὸς τὸν Θεόν, and which was God. "The same was in the beginning with God."

This passage speaks of the unrevealed God, hidden and immanent before His self-unfolding in the Trinity or in the creation of the world.

However, the still unmanifested godhead already contained a differentiated structure, a beginning of articulated life. And this life is said to be the light of men. But were there men in this time preceding time?

Or did it later become the light of men? Thus God, even while He remained a *deus absconditus*, was not alone; in Him and with Him were the Word, life, and light. And all had relevance to man.

But in addition to God and His inner forms or creations—Word, life, and light—and in addition to His relation to men (who perhaps were created only later), something else was present, a fourth entity, if we call God the first, Logos the second, and man the third: this was darkness, or, more correctly translated, the shadow. ἡ σκοτία means darkness, night, blindness, impotence, concealment. All these meanings are among its overtones.

The shadow is the opposite of light, the adversary of light, not its mere absence, not the mere lack of light; it resists the light and hence has a certain autonomy. It is said not to have *ap*prehended or *com*prehended the light. If we translate *ap*prehend, the shadow was at least an independent power or force; if we translate *com*prehend, it is an independent person, the adversary of God's person.

Thus the opening lines of the Fourth Gospel speak of four entities, of the still unuttered godhead, of the darkness as its counterpart, of the first Thou, the Logos that is with the godhead, and of man for whom light is life.

After verse 5 the prologue breaks off and the text shifts to the story of John the Baptist.

Out of this obscure series or sequence, let us remember one thing: life was the light of men. For man life was, or perhaps still is, the same as light; and light was the same as life. But what kind of human life can be called light? Here Colossians 1 : 12 comes to mind: "Giving thanks unto [God] the Father, which hath made us meet to be partakers of the inheritance of the saints in light: who hath delivered us from the power of darkness . . ." (μετὰ χαρᾶς εὐχαριστοῦντες τῷ [Θεῷ] πατρὶ τῷ ἱκανώσαντι ἡμᾶς εἰς τὴν μερίδα τοῦ κλήρου τῶν ἁγίων ἐν τῷ φωτί· ὃς ἐρρύσατο ἡμᾶς ἐκ τῆς ἐξουσίας τοῦ σκότους κ.τ.λ.). But we do not require these words of St. Paul in order to fathom our strange prologue, although the Epistle to the Colossians was written in the year 60, hence considerably earlier than the Gospel of St. John (written between 100 and 110). When we read these opening words of the Gospel, another world emerges behind the Christian world of the Evangelist. And the same is true when the motif of light is further developed and it is said of John the Baptist (1 : 8–9): "He was not that Light, but was sent to bear witness of that Light. That was the true Light, which lighteth every man that cometh into the world. He was in the world, and the world was made by him, and the world knew him not. He came unto his own [things], and his own [οἱ ἴδιοι = initiates] received him not," they failed either to apprehend or to comprehend him. "But as many as received him, to them gave he power to become the sons of God, even to them that believe on his name." Thus this light must be apprehended or comprehended—i.e., received—if man is to be redeemed, if he is to become the son of God; God wants to be known by his own, as

240

is taught in the initiation of Hermes: ὃς γνωσθῆναι βούλεται καὶ γινώσκεται τοῖς ἰδίοις.[1]

The introductory sentences of the Gospel of St. John are Hermetic formulas, and, as we shall see, they are also descended from Gnosticism. We have chosen them as an introduction to this type of experience because they are as well known as they are obscure. What is here expressed is light, not as a metaphor, not as a mere image, even the purest possible image, for the imageless God, not as a symbolical or even metaphorical expression for the ineffable. These words refer to light in its psychic function, as the inner process of illumination and as the psychic content of illumination; they refer to light as a path, in the sense that the Tao is a path. This light gives insight, inner sight; it is illumination and wisdom in the Gnostic sense. This illumination, in which the illumined one himself illumines, this φωτίζειν, is a process and no static image. The act of gnosis is an illumination; its fulfillment is a psychic light.

The gnostic illumines because he is himself illumined. An invocation of gnosis reads: "O Holy Knowledge, by thee am I illumined, and through thee do I sing praise to the incorporeal Light . . . I rejoice in joy of mind." (γνῶσις ἁγία, φωτισθεὶς ἀπὸ σοῦ, διὰ σοῦ τὸ νοητὸν φῶς ὑμνῶν, χαίρω ἐν χαρᾷ νοῦ.)[2] And St. Paul declares similarly in II Cor. 4 : 6: "For God, who commanded the light to shine out of darkness, hath shined into our hearts, to give the light of the knowledge of the glory of God in the face of Jesus Christ." (ὅτι ὁ Θεὸς ὁ εἰπών· ἐκ σκότους φῶς λάμψαι, ὃς ἔλαμψεν ἐν ταῖς καρδίαις ἡμῶν πρὸς φωτισμὸν τῆς γνώσεως τῆς δόξης τοῦ Θεοῦ ἐν προσώπῳ Ἰησοῦ Χριστοῦ.) Christ is the Thou to God's I.

This illumination is no poetic image. It is, rather, a technical term for the experience gained in a technical exercise. φωτίζειν means not only to illumine but also to turn into light, as in the mystery prayer: "May all that is within us save [or bring to life] our life, make the light shine, awaken pneuma and God." (τὸ πᾶν τὸ ἐν ἡμῖν, σῷζε ζωή, φώτιζε φῶς, πνεῦμα-(τιζε) θεέ).[3] The Iranians also believed that the divine part of our psyche was—light.

---

1 *Corpus hermeticum*, I, 31; ed. A. D. Nock and tr. A.-J. Festugière (4 vols., Paris, 1945–54), I, 18.
2 Ibid., XIII, 18 (from the *hymnodia krypte*); Nock-Festugière, II, 208; tr. Walter Scott, *Hermetica* (4 vols., Oxford, 1924–36), I, 250–51.
3 Ibid., XIII, 19; Nock-Festugière, II, 208; tr. Scott, I, 252–53.

In all religious experience the saint is inwardly luminous. Light shines forth from him, illumining his cloak over his heart. Luminous letters or symbols appear upon him; at moments he becomes transparent. The Parsis, Manichaeans, and Mandaeans know of luminous garments and the luminous wreath, *hvarena*, the halo.

Among the Mandaeans baptism is performed in the river of light, the Jordan. From this Mandaean baptism possibly is descended the baptism of John, which is in turn connected with that of the Christians.[4] Thus the φωτισμός is a rite of initiation. Apuleius equates φωτίζεσθαι and τελεῖσθαι, to be illumined and to be initiated. But very early in Christianity, an allegorical interpretation was introduced: Justin[5] calls the baptismal bath illumination, because those who bathe are illumined in spirit.

Φωτισμός is primarily the inward experience of a world-removed brightness and clarity; it is illumination and transfiguration. And it is this experience that we wish here to follow, not merely the image of light that ultimately pales to a mere phrase. We wish to follow the experience of the soul's illumination.

According to the Persian and later the Manichaean tradition, "the pious man had a second immaterial self (Persian *grev* = *soma* or nature, Aramaic *qnuma*, which is used to translate the Greek *autos*), and this was the reflection of his luminous soul and at the same time the divine emissary who would one day guide this luminous soul to heaven."[6]

Later the luminous self, which becomes identified with the luminous soul, is often called Jesus. In the so-called Liturgy of Mithras, a work that is assuredly pre-Manichaean, the luminous self is seen as a body placed in the luminous world by the primal god, and consisting of four or five luminous elements. "This luminous self in its bodily form is a divine being to whom the initiate must pray if he wishes to rise to the world of light." This σῶμα = τέλειον dwells with the primal god, while in the material world the primal man Gayōmart represents gnosis or knowledge of God. Thus illumination here means to return to oneself, to find the way back to one's divine nature, to the luminous body within us that is composed of the elements of light.

The spiritual body is distinguished from the body of the flesh. This is a fundamental distinction that forms the basis of many different religious

---

4 Richard Reitzenstein, *Die hellenistischen Mysterienreligionen* (Leipzig, 1927), p. 264.
5 Justin, *Apology*, I, 61; in Migne, *PG*, VI, 422.
6 Reitzenstein, p. 279, n. 1.

disciplines. While the body of the flesh is strictly limited in space, the spiritual body (the somatic consciousness) can extend far beyond the limits of the body or contract into a particular region of the body; layers of varying sensibility will then form around the adept, outside the skin.

These things were already known to the Babylonian magi. Perhaps, as de Rochas has suggested, Paracelsus' *mumia* should also be considered in this light.[7] In any event, this notion of the luminous self forms a basis for the understanding of certain so-called parapsychological phenomena; in the following it will interest us primarily as a religious experience. Here a brief intimation of the Iranian views on the connection between light and self must suffice, but there are large religious areas that might serve to illustrate our point.

Thus the prologue to the Gospel of St. John makes use of an existing religious idea when it speaks of the light that enlightens all men who come into this world. Yet there is no indication that the writer had in mind the luminous self of the Iranian tradition, even though he does employ the dualism of darkness and light. Probably the author of this Gospel would not, like the Zoroastrians, impute an individual luminous self even to a saint. Yet it would be an error to distinguish too sharply between the rather popular mystical notion of the prologue and the Persian conception. The Manichaean fragments recently found in Turfan designate Jesus as the luminous self of the individual soul, but also of all souls. In this conception the nature of the soul is defined, it has a definite content, it is substantial, but not material, not even in a subtle sense as Reitzenstein still supposed; and the godhead is also substantial, it is light and life, $\phi\tilde{\omega}s$ $\kappa\alpha\grave{\iota}$ $\zeta\omega\acute{\eta}$.

God has an essence, and to have an essence is to have content, structure, and substance. In Christianity the pneuma is understood in the same way; it lives in the individual and in the $\grave{\epsilon}\kappa\kappa\lambda\eta\sigma\acute{\iota}\alpha$, and Paul's $\sigma\tilde{\omega}\mu\alpha$ $\pi\nu\epsilon\upsilon\mu\alpha\tau\iota\kappa\acute{o}\nu$ is a spiritual body, hence substantial.

Light and life, then, are attributes of the soul. The soul is by nature luminous and living.

2. Light in the "Corpus hermeticum"

We have suggested the significance of these conceptions in nascent Christianity. Now we shall examine the role and the scope of the experience of

---

7 Albert de Rochas, *I'Extériorisation de la sensibilité* (Paris, 1895), p. 73.

light in that strange *Corpus hermeticum* whose conceptions stand between the late Stoics and the Gospel of St. John, and many of whose fundamental insights, like those of Paul and the Fourth Gospel, may be classified as Gnostic.

If the soul is called luminous and living, it is not in our sense of these terms and not for our reasons. Like Plato in the *Phaedo*, the *Corpus hermeticum* regards life on earth as a misfortune, as, for example, in IX, 4, where earth is called the abode of evil, and as frequently in the *Logia* of Stobaeus.[8] Such statements belong to the catechism of the *Corpus hermeticum;* to be luminous and living means not to live in the earthly sphere. On earth the soul is in exile, in εἰργμός, in prison, in narrowness and captivity. For it is of divine and celestial origin. The body is the tomb and dungeon of the soul, sometimes its garment, but then in guise of punishment. But beside the mortal body there is the immortal, spiritual body, which is indissoluble. For man is twofold—διπλοῦς . . . θνητὸς μὲν διὰ τὸ σῶμα, ἀθάνατος δὲ διὰ τὸν οὐσιώδη ἄνθρωπον. "And that is why man, unlike all other living creatures upon earth, is twofold. He is mortal by reason of his body; he is immortal by reason of the Man of eternal substance." [9]

This essential man is the human soul, or, expressed in Iranian terms, the luminous self in man. Life, ζωή, is defined as the union of spirit and soul; death is not the destruction of the two, but the dissolution of their union. ζωὴ δέ ἐστιν ἕνωσις νοῦ καὶ ψυχῆς· θάνατος δὲ οὐκ ἀπώλεια τῶν συναχθέντων, διάλυσις δὲ τῆς ἐνώσεως.[10]

Thus what is truly alive in man is the union of soul and spirit. But man, the third god, ὁ τρίτος θεός, as the *Corpus hermeticum* calls him,[11] is not only living but also luminous. And he has this inner luminous body from the first (and second) god, from the primal god, and from the cosmos, which is the second body of God.

The primal god is formless. Sometimes, however, he is called the Nous, from which the second Nous issued. But often the second god is called Nous or Logos, sometimes the world-creating Nous (νοῦς δημιουργός). This Nous is also in man, but it must cast off its fiery form in order that man may bear it. It is called the god of fire, θεὸς τοῦ πυρός, and reminds us of

8 Ed. C. Wachsmuth (Berlin, 1884), I, 274ff.; see Nock-Festugière, III, 54ff.

9 *Corpus hermeticum*, I, 15; Nock-Festugière, I, 11; tr. Scott, I, 123.

10 Ibid., XI, 14; Nock-Festugière, I, 153.

11 E.g., Stobaeus, ed. Wachsmuth, I, 275, 3; Nock-Festugière, III, 54: πρῶτον ὁ θεός, δεύτερον ὁ κόσμος, τρίτον ὁ ἄνθρωπος.

244

the fiery god, πύρινος θεός, in the related Gnostic systems—e.g., of the Naassenes, Peratae, and Docetae. According to *Poimandres*, the first treatise of the *Corpus hermeticum*, the supreme Nous engenders the celestial anthropos. "But Mind the Father of all, He who is Life and Light, gave birth to Man, a being like to Himself. And He took delight in Man, as being His own offspring." [12] Here the substance of the supreme God is defined as light and life. If man is like him, then man's spiritual substance must also be light and life. This enables us to understand the vision with which the cosmogony of the *Poimandres* is introduced: "And I beheld a boundless view, all was changed into light, a mild and joyous light; and I marvelled when I saw it. And in a little while, there had come to be in one part a downward-tending darkness, terrible and grim . . ." καὶ ὁρῶ θέαν ἀόριστον, φῶς δὲ πάντα γεγενημένα, εὐδιόν τε καὶ ἰλαρόν, καὶ ἠράσθην ἰδών· καὶ μετ' ὀλίγον σκότος κατωφερὲς ἦν, ἐν μέρει γεγενημένον, φοβερόν τε καὶ στυγνόν, σκολιῶς ἐσπειραμένον.)[13] This reminds us of the cosmogonic fantasies of the Nicolaitans and Sethians. The light comes first, but after a brief time the darkness descends, and this is the beginning of cosmic dualism.

In the eleventh treatise we find still another vision of light, a vision of the πλήρωμα φωτός. The Nous declares: "Look upon things through me, and contemplate the Kosmos as it lies before your eyes, that body which no harm can touch, the most ancient of all things, yet ever in its prime and ever new. See too the seven subject worlds, marshalled in everlasting order, and filling up the measure of everlasting time as they run their diverse courses. And all things are filled with light, but nowhere is there . . . fire; for by the friendship of contraries, and the blending of things unlike, the fire of heaven has been charged with light, which is shed on all below by the working of the Sun." [14]

In the beginning, in the origin, there was light, ὁ Νοῦς, ὁ θεός, and it is

---

12 *Corpus hermeticum*, I, 12: ὁ δὲ πάντων πατὴρ ὁ Νοῦς, ὢν ζωὴ καὶ φῶς, ἀπεκύησεν Ἄνθρωπον αὐτῷ ἴσον, οὗ ἠράσθη ὡς ἰδίου τόκου (Nock-Festugière, I, 10; tr. Scott, I, 121).

13 Ibid., I, 4; Nock-Festugière, I, 7; tr. Scott, I, 115.

14 θέασαι δὲ δι' ἐμοῦ τὸν κόσμον ὑποκείμενον τῇ σῇ ὄψει, τό τε κάλλος αὐτοῦ ἀκριβῶς κατανόησον, σῶμα μὲν ἀκήρατον, καὶ οὗ παλαιότερον οὐδὲν ἔσται, διὰ παντὸς δὲ ἀκμαῖον καὶ νέον καὶ μᾶλλον ἀκμαιότερον. ἴδε καὶ τοὺς ὑποκειμένους ἑπτὰ κόσμους κεκοσμημένους τάξει αἰωνίῳ καὶ δρόμῳ διαφόρῳ τὸν αἰῶνα ἀναπληροῦντας, φωτὸς δὲ πάντα πλήρη, πῦρ δὲ οὐδαμοῦ· ἡ γὰρ φιλία καὶ ἡ σύγκρασις τῶν ἐναντίων καὶ τῶν ἀνομοίων φῶς γέγονε, καταλαμπόμενον ὑπὸ τῆς τοῦ θεοῦ ἐνεργείας κ. τ. λ. (*Corpus hermeticum*, XI, 6; Nock-Festugière, I, 149–50; tr. Scott, I, 211–13).

not known whence the darkness came. The light is certainty, it is the first thing; the light is the oldest and the youngest. Often the formula recurs: "I am that light, the Nous [the creative mind], thy God." (τὸ φῶς ἐκεῖνο ἐγώ εἰμι Νοῦς, ὁ σὸς θεός). As Eduard Norden has shown, "I am"— ἐγώ εἰμι—is the Greek adaptation of an old Oriental formula.[15]

The visionary, the prophet, sees in spirit the prototype of the world, the ἀρχέτυπον εἶδος, the light, τὸ φῶς, an inner light that confers illumination. In order to find his way back to his luminous body, man must experi· ence this inner light through exercises and a process of initiation. Man, the microcosm, is essentially luminous body, while the world, the macrocosm, is essentially the body of God. Man's central striving is to return to his essence, to find his way back to his luminous body or self, and this homeward road, as Novalis calls it, is the road of gnosis, leading man to know God and to be known by that God, of whom our luminous self remains a part. This is made clear by the prayer to Hermes that ends the *Poimandres* or by the invocation in the *hymnodia krypte* of the thirteenth treatise of the *Corpus hermeticum:* "Let all that is in us save life, make light, O light, turn to spirit, O God." Or otherwise translated: "All our inwardness save, O life, illuminate, O light, spiritualize, O God." [16]

At the end of the *Poimandres* the prophet prays for the nine-times sacred gift mentioned in the preceding chapter: ". . . put power into me, that so, having obtained this boon, I may enlighten those of my race who are in ignorance, my brothers and thy sons. . . . Wherefore I believe and bear witness that I enter into Life and Light. Blessed art thou, Father; thy Man seeks to share thy holiness, even as Thou hast given him all authority." [17] This enthusiasm enables the prophet to penetrate to the essence of God, which is here equated always with light and life. The prophet is a model for the others, who remain in the ignorance of genesis, of the creature, of birth, the species, the human race—for *genos* can mean all these.

Fortified with God's power and filled with His grace, a man bursts out of his material body and passes into the life of light. This is "His man," the

15 *Agnostos Theos* (Leipzig, 1923), p. 190.
16 *Corpus hermeticum*, XIII, 19; Nock-Festugière, II, 207ff.
17 καὶ ἐνδυνάμωσόν με, καὶ [πλήρωσόν με] τῆς χάριτος ταύτης, [ἵνα] φωτίσω τοὺς ἐν ἀγνοίᾳ τοῦ γένους, ἐμοῦ [μὲν] ἀδελφούς, υἱοὺς δὲ σοῦ. διὸ πιστεύω καὶ μαρτυρῶ· εἰς ζωὴν καὶ φῶς χωρῶ. εὐλογητὸς εἶ, πάτερ. ὁ σὸς ἄνθρωπος συναγιάζειν σοι βούλεται, καθὼς παρέδωκας αὐτῷ τὴν πᾶσαν ἐξουσίαν. (*Corpus hermeticum*, I, 32; Nock-Festugière, I, 19; tr. Scott, I, 131–33.)

man of God, the initiate, the chosen one—ὁ ἐλλόγιμος—in his perfection, which is his return to his profoundest self. This man is a prophet when he becomes an instrument that sees and expresses the divine revelation. The possession of ἐξουσία is "characteristic of the prophet, who combines supernatural powers with the immediate intuition of the godhead." [18] Secret knowledge of the godhead confers supernatural power. He is a gnostic when he takes the step beyond and becomes a "stander" (ἐστώς) like the supreme God Himself.

How does the initiate return to the Nous, to the mind or spirit which is God, to the mind, the father of the universe,[19] whose essence is life and light, and who has engendered man in His likeness? For empirical man has fallen under the order and domination of the planet gods, hence under the power of fate, *heimarmene;* he has become a slave of the spirits of the spheres, of the starry influences, of the rulers of the stars—ἐναρμόνιος δοῦλος. "He is immortal, and has all things in his power; yet he suffers the lot of a mortal, being subject to Destiny. He is exalted above the structure of the heavens, yet he is born a slave of Destiny. He is bisexual, as his Father is bisexual, and sleepless, as his Father is sleepless; yet he is mastered by carnal desires and by oblivion." [20]

How does man redeem himself "from the body of this death"? How does his soul ascend to God? First the initiate must come to know that he himself is made of life and light like his God and father. Then he can pass over into life. "Let the man who has mind in him recognize himself" (ὁ ἔννους ἄνθρωπος ἀναγνωρισάτω ἑαυτόν).[21]

Then the ascent of his soul can begin—ἡ ἄνοδος, the road upward. It is a difficult road (ἄνοδος = *invius*). Here, as in other parts of our text of *Poimandres,* two different versions are intermingled; chapter 24 reads: "At the dissolution of your material body, you first yield up the body itself to be changed, and the visible form you bore is no longer seen." [22] The ethos, the individual character, is given over to a daimon, probably the personal guardian spirit. In this pantheism the individual is cast off, for it is regarded as evil.

At the next stage, the sensory functions of the body return to their

18 Reitzenstein, *Poimandres* (Leipzig, 1904), p. 48, n. 3.
19 *Corpus hermeticum,* I, 12; Nock-Festugière, I, 10.
20 Ibid., I, 15; Nock-Festugière, I, 11–12; tr. Scott, I, 123.
21 Ibid., I, 21; Nock-Festugière, I, 14; tr. Scott, I, 127.
22 Ibid., I, 24; Nock-Festugière, I, 15; tr. Scott, I, 127–28.

sources; they leave the soul and unite with the energies—i.e., either with the spiritual activities conceived by the cosmos as great man or with the energies of the elements. And the two lower parts of the soul, the *thymos* and the *epithymia*, emotion and desire or impulse, return to mindless nature. Only the Nous (mind) remains, and probably the spiritual or immortal body, the νοητὸν or ἀθάνατον σῶμα.

The thirteenth treatise of the *Corpus hermeticum* treats of these matters; chapter 3 runs: "By God's mercy there has come to be in me a form which is not fashioned out of matter, and I have passed forth out of myself, and entered into an immortal body" (ἐξ ἐλέου θεοῦ, καὶ ἐμαυτὸν ἐξελήλυθα εἰς ἀθάνατον σῶμα). "I am not now the man I was; I have been born again in Mind" (καὶ εἰμι νῦν οὐχ ὁ πρίν, ἀλλ' ἐγεννήθην ἐν νῷ).[23]

In chapter 14 of the same treatise, that body which consists of the forces, the δυνάμεις, is described and distinguished from the body of physical perception. This body is called the body of essential genesis—τῆς οὐσιωδοῦς γενέσεως.[24] The whole thirteenth treatise must be regarded as a continuation of the first, the *Poimandres*.

Now only spirit and immortal body have remained behind, and as he continues to rise, the redeemed man enters the first planetary sphere, that of the moon, where he loses the energy to increase or diminish.

But here the text leaps from one version to the other. For we would now expect an account of the attributes discarded in each of the other spheres, that of the sun, etc., but instead we suddenly find a listing of the vices that the soul casts off in its ascent from the second to the seventh sphere, vices which, as Reitzenstein remarked, it could no longer have had, because the personal attributes had been cast off with the ethos and because *thymos* and *epithymia*, emotion and desire, had also been discarded. Servius wrote of these vices in his commentary on *Aeneid*, VI, 714. In *Poimandres*, the vice cast off at the second stage signifies malice, guile, and contentiousness, and that of the third stage the delusions of concupiscence (τὴν ἐπιθυμητικὴν ἀπάτην) = Venus. At the fourth it is domineering pride (τὴν ἀρχοντικὴν ὑπερηφανίαν) = Jupiter; at the fifth it is irreverent boldness and audacity (τὸ θράσος τὸ ἀνόσιον), *iracundia*, the rage of Saturn and Mars. At the sixth it is seduction by wealth (τὰς ἀφορμὰς τὰς κακὰς τοῦ πλούτου) = Mercury; at the seventh, the lurking lie. It is the lie that is last discarded,

---

23 Ibid., XIII, 3; Nock-Festugière, II, 201; tr. Scott, I, 241.
24 Ibid., XIII, 14; Nock-Festugière, II, 206.

it extends upward to the highest planetary sphere, it is the main enemy of the self. This evaluation of veracity and its opposite seems definitely Persian and indicates that this hierarchy of vices is not purely Greek in origin.

It is also noteworthy that no vice is cast off at the sphere of the sun, and that though the moon nominally occupies second rank in the hierarchy, what is cast off in this sphere is the faculty of growth and not a vice. In the second period of Parsiism, in the Sassanid era, five of the planets, as here, were evil spirits and creatures of Ahriman.[25] And the same conception is to be found in the *Pistis Sophia*,[26] where the planets Kronos, Ares, Hermes, Bubastis-Aphrodite, and Zeus are the five evildoers.

After casting off these astral influences acquired in its descent, the soul returns to the realm of eightness, the Ogdoad. The self enters its heavenly home, the realm of divine abundance. The ellipse of descent and reascent is closed. This is the Hermetic experience of light.

3. The Light in Gnosticism

As we have seen from the *Poimandres*, the universe opens to the initiate's prayer, and this because man is of divine nature. Inwardly he is made of the same substance as his godhead; a celestial body, $\sigma\tilde{\omega}\mu\alpha$ $\tau\acute{\epsilon}\lambda\epsilon\iota\nu o\nu$; the substantial, but not material, element in God as in man is called nous and psyche, the spiritual faculty of perception, or spirit and soul. These two elements compose the essence of both God and man. In other words, it consists of light and life, of $\phi\tilde{\omega}s$ and $\zeta\omega\acute{\eta}$. This is the self of both God and man. Porphyry[27] speaks of the $\sigma\acute{\upsilon}\mu\phi\upsilon\sigma\iota s$ $\tau\tilde{\omega}$ $\theta\epsilon\omega\rho o\tilde{\upsilon}\nu\tau\iota$ $\kappa\alpha\grave{\iota}$ $\theta\epsilon\omega\rho o\upsilon\mu\acute{\epsilon}\nu\omega$ (the congruence of seer and vision), and of their $\epsilon\grave{\iota}s$ $\tau\grave{o}\nu$ $\check{o}\nu\tau\omega s$ $\alpha\grave{\upsilon}\tau\grave{o}\nu$ $\sigma\acute{\upsilon}\mu\phi\upsilon\sigma\iota s$, growth into true selfhood.

This luminous vision of him who is seer and vision in one is pure intuition. This $\tau\acute{\epsilon}\lambda os$, this goal, this culmination in perfection, has been achieved by the Gnostic. As we have seen, he has taken the step beyond and there—in the realm of the spirit—he has become a "stander." He is *ennus*, standing in the divine spirit, anchored in the celestial Nous, in the Vohū Manah of the Persians.

Porphyry gave to this vision through which man merges with the divine

---

25 Wilhelm Spiegelberg, "Ein aegyptisches Verzeichnis der Planeten und Tierkreisbilder," *Orientalistische Literatur-Zeitung*, V (Berlin, 1902), 6–9.

26 *Pistis Sophia*, v, chs. 136, 139; tr. G. R. S. Mead (London, 1955), pp. 298, 303ff.

27 *De abstinentia*, I, 29.

self the characteristic name ἀναδρομή, ascent or betterment. In his own native Syriac, he found the word *qnuma*, which fluctuates in its meaning, sometimes signifying αὐτός, sometimes nature, φύσις, sometimes essence, ὑπόστασις, sometimes person, sometimes the body, which in the most remote period passed as the authentic essence. *Qnuma* thus epitomizes the various meanings implicit in Porphyry's ἀναδρομή.

Oldenberg has demonstrated a similar range of meaning for the word *ātman*. Etymologically, it is probably associated with breath; but though it is a substantive, rather than a pronoun like the Greek αὐτός, it designates the self, a man's own person, in distinction from relatives, possessions, and the outside world. Within the person, it designates the body as a whole in distinction from its individual organs or limbs. It further signifies the inward, the essential, that which animates and governs, the invisible force at work in the senses and the mind, and at a later date the conscious self that is active in us as in the cosmos.[28]

This self is conceived almost impersonally, as a celestial body, and precisely because it is impersonal it is looked upon as divine. The *Poimandres* also says: ". . . man [the original man] became from life and light [i.e., from the attributes of God] soul and spirit, from life soul, from light spirit" (ὁ δὲ Ἄνθρωπος ἐκ ζωῆς καὶ φωτὸς ἐγένετο εἰς ψυχὴν καὶ νοῦν, ἐκ μὲν ζωῆς ψυχήν, ἐκ δὲ φωτὸς νοῦν.)[29]

This theory of the prototype, the divine original man, whose copy is man, is common to various Gnostic schools. But gnosis as a way, as practice, as an exercise, and as a permanent condition achieved through exercises is essentially the experience of light—of the inner light, of a light that is above its opposite—darkness or shadow—of an inner illumination and radiance created by God. For Clement of Alexandria and other Gnostics who thought in Biblical images, this inner light was made on the seventh day of creation:

> The seventh day, therefore, is proclaimed a rest—abstraction from ills—preparing for the Primal Day, our true rest; which, in truth, is the first creation of light, in which all things are viewed and possessed. From this day the first wisdom and knowledge illuminate us. For the light of truth—a light true, casting no shadow, is the

28 Hermann Oldenberg, *Vorwissenschaftliche Wissenschaft, die Weltanschauung der Brahmana-Texte* (Göttingen, 1919), p. 86, and *Die Lehre der Upanishaden* (Göttingen, 1915), pp. 52ff.

29 *Corpus hermeticum*, I, 17; Nock-Festugière, I, 12.

Spirit of God indivisibly divided to all, who are sanctified by faith, holding the place of a luminary, in order to confer the knowledge of real existences. By following Him, therefore, through our whole life, we become impassible; and this is to rest.

(ἡ ἑβδόμη τοίνυν ἡμέρα ἀνάπαυσις κηρύσσεται, ἀποχῇ κακῶν ἑτοιμάζουσα τὴν ἀρχέγονον ἡμέραν τὴν τῷ ὄντι ἀνά-παυσιν ἡμῶν, ἣ δὴ πρώτη τῷ ὄντι φωτὸς γένεσις, ἐν ᾧ τὰ πάντα συνθεωρεῖται καὶ πάντα κληρονομεῖται. ἐκ ταύτης τῆς ἡμέρας ἡ πρώτη σοφία καὶ γνῶσις ἡμῖν ἐλλάμπεται· τὸ γὰρ φῶς τῆς ἀληθείας φῶς ἀληθές, ἄσκιον, ἀμερῶς μεριζόμενον πνεῦμα κυρίου εἰς τοὺς διὰ πίστεως ἡγιασμένους, λαμπτῆρος ἐπέχον τάξιν εἰς τὴν τῶν ὄντων ἐπίγνωσιν. ἀκολουθοῦντες οὖν αὐτῷ δι' ὅλου τοῦ βίου ἀπαθεῖς καθιστάμεθα, τὸ δ' ἔστιν ἀναπαύσασθαι.)[30]

The Gnostic, then, is he who has found peace; he stands in his selfhood, which is also the selfhood of God; he has become a "stander"—*hestos*. He has become true light, truth; the truth, for us a fact, a correct meaning, or a valid statement, is for the Gnostic—and not only the Christian Gnostic— no condition of fact, concept, statement, or meaning, but a person. The Saviour is truth, his person is the truth. Not only is what he says true; he himself is the truth. The truth is here "made flesh and dwelleth among us."

The Gnostic pairs of cosmic and psychic powers, the *syzygiai* (from συζάω, to live together, or συζεύγνυμι, to yoke or harness together), are just such hypostases. Perhaps the most celebrated are the Ophitic pairs: Pater-Phronesis, Nous-Sophia, Logos-Dynamis. In Valentinus we find: Pater-Aletheia and the pre-existent Tetras: Bythos-Sige, Pater-Aletheia. From this last *syzygia* is descended the pneumatic, male-female Tetras: Anthropos-Ecclesia, Logos-Zoe. From the union of Anthropos and Ecclesia springs Dodekas; among the six male components of these pairs is Theletos (the Desired), who is the light. Life, Zoe, as well as Light, occur later, Zoe paired with the Logos.

We shall not pursue these hypostases any further; we merely wished to show that they embody mythical, sexual fantasies that merely have the appearance of abstract concepts. This is the atmosphere of Babylonia and Syria, not of Greece. Valentinus, for example, with his Light = Theletos

---

30 *Stromateis*, VI, 16, § 138, 1–4; tr. in *Clement of Alexandria*, tr. Rev. William Wilson (2 vols., Edinburgh, 1867–69; ANCL IV and XII), II, 386.

and Life has nothing in common with the conceptions discussed above, of life and light as an expression of the human and divine self.

When the Fourth Gospel and the *Corpus hermeticum* and Clement of Alexandria speak of light, they do not, like Valentinus, mean a mere subsidiary force or a particle in the pleroma, but a crucial and concrete inner experience. It is not a fantasy or an adventure, but an experience, the essential experience of the true essence.

Guardini points out that to the Christian mind "[by saying that] truth and goodness are a Person, Himself, Christ, it is not suggested that any personal element would intrude and blur the impartial validity of truth and goodness." [31] What he means is that the living thought and love of Christ is truth, in almost the same sense as in the above-mentioned texts light and life are the essence and content of the human and divine self. The truth here is a person, because the self, in contrast to certain Indian conceptions, is regarded as a person. Precisely herein lies an important difference between the Indian and the Western-Greek mind. In the *Corpus hermeticum* the Nous, the Spirit, also fluctuates between a personal and a cosmic-pantheistic meaning; sometimes it seems to be a person, sometimes it appears as impersonal law and world-creating power.

But let us pursue the road to experience of the inner light. Clement tells us that this light is essential—that is, real in the Platonic sense and not a mere sensory phenomenon. It is without shadow, but above the opposition of light and dark. It was first, prior to this dualism. It conveys adequate insight; it is comprehensive vision viewed as an act, and, as result of this act, pure intuition. Through this light all things are received as a heritage—i.e., given in their appropriate form, as pure object and pure content. When we accomplish this experience of light, when we repeat it as μιμηταὶ τοῦ θεοῦ, imitators of God, we remain unharmed, we preserve ourselves in the world of pure knowledge. This pattern appears over and over again in the bright mesh of Clement's *Carpets* [*Stromateis*]; and the skillful weaver modulates it more and more richly: this light is immutable and formless, it is a glittering pillar; "The pillar indicates that God cannot be portrayed. The pillar of light, too, in addition to its pointing out that God cannot be represented, shows also the stability and the permanent duration of the Deity, and His unchangeable and inexpressible light." (σημαίνει δὲ ὁ στῦλος

---

31 Romano Guardini, *The Last Things*, tr. Charlotte E. Forsyth and Grace B. Branham (London, 1954), p. 97.

τὸ ἀνεικόνιστον τοῦ θεοῦ, ὁ δὲ πεφωτισμένος στῦλος πρὸς τῷ τὸ
ἀνεικόνιστον σημαίνειν δηλοῖ τὸ ἑστὸς καὶ μόνιμον τοῦ θεοῦ καὶ τὸ
ἄτρεπτον αὐτοῦ φῶς καὶ ἀσχημάτιστον.) [32]

To him who has become gnostic, to the friend of God, the φίλος τοῦ
θεοῦ,[33] the contemplation of this light gives the eternal bliss that never
satiates:

> For what rational cause remains any more to the man who has
> gained "the light inaccessible," for reverting to the good things of
> the world? Although not yet true as to time and place, yet by that
> gnostic love through which the inheritance and perfect restitution
> follow, the giver of the reward makes good by deeds what the
> Gnostic, by gnostic choice, had grasped by anticipation through
> love. For by going away to the Lord, for the love he bears Him,
> though his tabernacle be visible on earth, he does not withdraw
> himself from life.

> (τίς γὰρ ὑπολείπεται ἔτι τούτῳ εὔλογος αἰτία ἐπὶ τὰ
> κοσμικὰ παλινδρομεῖν ἀγαθὰ τῷ τὸ "ἀπρόσιτον" ἀπειληφότι
> "φῶς", κἂν μηδέπω κατὰ τὸν χρόνον καὶ τὸν τόπον, ἀλλ'
> ἐκείνῃ γε τῇ γνωστικῇ ἀγάπῃ, δι' ἣν καὶ ἡ κληρονομία καὶ ἡ
> παντελὴς ἔπεται ἀποκατάστασις, βεβαιοῦντος δι' ἔργων τοῦ
> μισθαποδότου, ὃ διὰ τοῦ ἑλέσθαι γνωστικῶς διὰ τῆς ἀγάπης
> φθάσας προείληφεν ὁ γνωστικός; ἢ γὰρ οὐχί, ἀποδημῶν πρὸς
> τὸν κύριον δι' ἀγάπην τὴν πρὸς αὐτόν, κἂν τὸ σκῆνος αὐτοῦ
> ἐπὶ γῆς θεωρῆται κ.τ.λ.) [34]

The same passage in the *Stromateis* rejects suicide as a means of has-
tening one's entrance into the kingdom of heaven. This admonition was
not superfluous, as is evident to anyone who knows the African character, who has followed the schism of the Donatists and the acts of the
Circumcellions.[35] What interests us most in this passage from Clement
is the positive statement that even in his physical lifetime the Gnostic
can inherit fully, can be fully reinstated in the kingdom, by receiving and
conceiving the "inaccessible" light within him. In those who have con-

32 *Stromateis*, I, 24, § 163, 4; tr. Wilson, I, 458.
33 Ibid., VI, 9, § 76, 3.
34 Ibid., VI, 9, § 75, 2; tr. Wilson, II, 346–47.
35 Edward Gibbon, *The Decline and Fall of the Roman Empire*, ed. J. B. Bury (7 vols.,
   London, 1897–1900), II, 387ff.; Optatus of Milevis, *Against the Donatists*, III, 4; tr.
   O. R. Vassall-Phillips (London, 1917), p. 146; see also the anti-Gnostic Augustine.

ceived the light, the sacrament of the bridal chamber, the ἱερὸς γάμος, is enacted.

As we have seen from the *Acts of St. John*,[36] the Gnostics attached a different significance to the eucharist than did even the early Church. The same is true of the sacrament of baptism, as the Mandaeans and Elkesaites bear witness.[37] In all Gnosticism there is an element of archaic nature religion, something material and untransfigured that has been preserved in the primal depths of man's being and that bursts forth from time to time, sometimes after an interval of centuries. For the Gnostics baptism was a lustratory bath, but it was also a magic rite invoking the name or the symbol of the supreme God; it is not only a purging of sin, but also an exorcism of demons.

Pistis Sophia says, for example, that the various baptisms destroy with their fire all the sins that the *antimimon pneuma* had affixed to man externally as it were, like an illness.[38]

A few words concerning this *antimimon pneuma*, because it is the antithesis of our experience of light. *Pistis Sophia* sets forth the doctrine, which is archaic throughout.[39] It distinguishes five parts in man: the divine force, soul, body, fate, and *antimimon pneuma*, which is a contrary imitation of the divine Pneuma. The *antimimon pneuma* is the origin and cause of all the evils besetting the human soul.[40] In Isidore, son of Basilides, the same component is called προσφυὴς ψυχή, the appended soul; in Basilides himself, it is designated as the προσαρτήματα, the attachments or appendages. These are the attributes and garments that the human soul dons in its passage through the planetary spheres. According to *Pistis Sophia*, the new souls are taken from the leaven of the purified light and shaped by the five great archons (the old planet gods without the sun and moon) of the *heimarmene*. The latter knead the substance of the souls and divide the leaven, each contributing his component. The *antimimon pneuma* is the outer shell of the soul,[41] its cloak in its journey through the planetary world—it is the

36 M. Pulver, "Jesus' Round Dance and Crucifixion According to the Acts of St. John," in *The Mysteries* (PEY, 2), pp. 169ff.
37 Epiphanius, *Haereses*, XXX, 17; ed. Karl Holl (Leipzig, 1915; GCS XXV: vol. I of Epiphanius' works), 355–56; and Hippolytus, *Elenchos*, IX, 15; ed. Paul Wendland (Leipzig, 1916; GCS XXVI: vol. III of Hippolytus' works), 253.
38 *Pistis Sophia*, III, ch. 115; tr. Mead, pp. 247ff.
39 Ibid., III, ch. 111; IV, 131–33; tr. Mead, pp. 235ff., 278ff.
40 Wilhelm Bousset, *Hauptprobleme der Gnosis* (Göttingen, 1907), p. 366.
41 *Pistis Sophia*, III, ch. 111; tr. Mead, pp. 236ff.

evil contribution of the planetary spirits. This notion is carried over into Manichaeism, and Augustine devoted a whole treatise to combating it.[42]

In Gnostic baptism man is cleansed of his sinful nature; the sacrament is a seal protecting him from the power of demons. The malice of the archons, the rulers, the planet gods, is scrubbed away.

The sacrament of the bridal chamber, of the mystical marriage if you will, seems to be peculiar to Gnosticism. It is in this sacrament that the mystes "conceives" the "inaccessible" light. There are indications, however, that the mystai of Mithras also learned to raise themselves up in ecstasy to the highest heaven while still in this bodily life.[43]

The so-called Liturgy of Mithras shows us such an ecstatic ascension to heaven, and Bousset has demonstrated that this art of rising to heaven while still in the flesh was known to the rabbis of the first Christian century.[44] And St. Paul wrote: [45] "I knew a man in Christ above fourteen years ago (whether in the body, I cannot tell; or whether out of the body, I cannot tell: God knoweth); such an one caught up [ἁρπαγέντα, from ἁρπάζω] to the third heaven." The Gnostic sources also have accounts of these ecstatic ascensions. Hippolytus [46] quotes from the Gnostic *Book of Baruch* a passage relating how the mystes after being caught up to heaven drinks the living water, and in the *Clementine Recognitions* (II, 61) we read Simon Magus' instructions to Peter regarding the ascension: ". . . *et nunc sensum tuum extende in coelum, et iterum super coelum . . .*" [47]

In the Gnostic mysteries we find indications of how this ascension was effected. Particularly among the Valentinians it was a spiritual marriage. It concerns us here because of its relation to the gnosis of light. In his account of the Cainites, Irenaeus tells us that their main concern was to destroy the works of Hystera, the womb.

> I have also made a collection of their writings, in which they advocate the abolition of the doings of Hystera. Moreover, they call

42 *Opus imperfectum contra Julianum*, I, 172 (Migne, *PL*, XLV, 1051ff.); *De duabus animabus contra Manichaeos* (Migne, *PL*, XLII, 93ff.). (Bousset, Exkurs IV, p. 368.)
43 See Origen, *Contra Celsum*, VI, 22 (tr. Henry Chadwick [Cambridge, 1953], p. 334), for an account of the soul's passage through the seven gates, and Porphyry, *De antro nympharum*, 6.
44 *Hauptprobleme*, p. 314, and "Die Himmelsreise der Seele," *Archiv für Religionswissenschaft*, IV (Tübingen, 1901), 229ff.
45 II Cor. 12:2.
46 *Elenchos*, V, 27, 2; ed. Wendland, III, 132–33.
47 "And now stretch forth thy understanding unto heaven, yea, above the heaven." Migne, *PG*, I, 1277.

this Hystera the creator of heaven and earth. They also hold, like Carpocrates, that men cannot be saved until they have gone through all kinds of experience. An angel, they maintain, attends them in every one of their sinful and abominable actions, and urges them to venture on audacity and incur pollution. Whatever may be the nature of the action, they declare that they do it in the name of the angel, saying, "O thou angel, I use thy work; O thou power, I accomplish thy operation." [48]

This veiled reference may seem strange at first, but the Church Father looked upon the sacred marriage of the Gnostics as a sinful and shameful act. It seems odd that an angel should be present encouraging the impurity that lies in the sinful act, and that the mystes should cry out: O thou angel, I do thy work, I accomplish thine act!

This angel is man's celestial double, his luminous body or luminous self, which we have described above. What takes place in the seclusion of the νυμφών, the bridal chamber, Irenaeus passes over in silent indignation— *cum tacent, clamant*. The mystes must do the angel's work and accomplish his act. In so doing, he imitates his cult god. In the Valentinian schools, the savior and redeemer, Soter, celebrates his marriage with Sophia. The savior is the νυμφίος and Sophia the νύμφη, and similarly the initiate, the pneumatic man, is the bride of his angel; at the end of the world's history, when the supreme Sophia is forever united with Soter, the betrothed initiates and their angels (their celestial doubles and guardian angels) will enter forever into the pleroma, into celestial abundance. The *nymphon*, the bridal chamber, is the celestial pleroma itself. And the sacrament of the bridal chamber offers a foretaste of this bliss. Referring to the followers of Marcus of the school of Valentinus, Irenaeus writes: "For some of them prepare a nuptial couch, and perform a sort of mystic rite (pronouncing certain expressions) with those who are being initiated, and affirm that it is a spiritual marriage which is celebrated by them, after the likeness of the conjugations above." (οἱ μὲν γὰρ αὐτῶν νυμφῶνα κατασκευάζουσι καὶ μυσταγωγίαν ἐπιτελοῦσι μετ' ἐπιρρήσεών τινων τοῖς τελειουμένοις, καὶ πνευματικὸν γάμον φάσκουσιν εἶναι τὸ ὑπ' αὐτῶν γινόμενον κατὰ τὴν ὁμοιότητα τῶν ἄνω συζυγιῶν.) [49]

Thus it appears that the Marcosian Gnostics preserved the age-old custom

48 Irenaeus, *Against Heresies*, I, 31; tr. in *Writings of Irenaeus*, tr. Alexander Roberts and James Donaldson (2 vols., Edinburgh, 1868–69; ANCL V and IX), I, 113.
49 Ibid., I, 21, 3; tr. Roberts and Donaldson, I, 82.

of the real, and not merely symbolic, marriage of the devotee with his God; and in this marriage the feminine role fell to the mystes. The human soul is the bride, and we are reminded of the fantasies of certain paranoiacs, such as Schreber, who believed God had castrated him to make him a woman for God. Bousset writes of this sacred marriage: "In the bridal chamber the mystagogue leads his soul to its bridegroom, the angel . . . the aim and purpose of the action is clearly the marriage of the devotee with a celestial spirit." [50]

Irenaeus has preserved what appears to be a fragment of the liturgy of this marriage rite strewn in among his accounts of the insidious magic arts with which Marcus deceived women. "May that Charis who is before all things, and who transcends all knowledge and speech, fill thine inner man, and multiply in thee her own knowledge, by sowing the grain of mustard seed in thee as in good soil. . . ." (ἡ πρὸ τῶν ὅλων ἡ ἀνεννόητος καὶ ἄρρητος χάρις πληρῶσαί σοι τὸν ἔσω ἄνθρωπον καὶ πληθῦναι ἐν σοὶ τὴν γνῶσιν αὐτῆς ἐγκατασπείρουσα τὸν κόκκον τοῦ σινάπεως εἰς τὴν ἀγαθὴν γῆν.) [51] "I am eager to make thee a partaker of my Charis, since the Father of all doth continually behold thy angel before His face."

Here the angel is called τὸ μέγεθος, greatness, as later among the Manichaeans. This angel is man's celestial double, his guardian angel.

The passage continues: "Now the place of thy angel is among us: it behoves us to become one. Receive first from me and by me [the gift of] Charis. Adorn thyself as a bride who is expecting her bridegroom, that thou mayest be what I am, and I what thou art. Establish the germ of light in thy nuptial chamber . . ." [52] This "seed of the light" shows light gnosis regressed to the level of an archaic nature cult, whose initiates enter into a sexual union with their god. Hippolytus [53] describes a similar mystery among the Naassenes or Ophites; here the initiates cast off their clothes and become as bridegrooms to the virginal spirit. And in the first chapter of his treatise against the Valentinians, Tertullian [54] suggests a similar rite when he speaks of the Eleusinian pandering (*Eleusinia lenocinia*) practiced by the Valentinians

50 *Hauptprobleme*, p. 316.
51 *Against Heresies*, I, 13, 2ff.; tr. Roberts and Donaldson, I, 52.
52 Ibid., I, 13, 3; tr. Roberts and Donaldson, I, 52–53. καθίδρυσον ἐν τῷ νυμφῶνι τὸ σπέρμα τοῦ φωτός.
53 *Elenchos*, v, 8, 44; ed. Wendland, III, 97.
54 Migne, *PL*, II, 543.

when they enact something and say: "*altum est,*" it is sublime, or profound, or hidden and mysterious.

Here light gnosis goes back to the earliest nature religions. But Gnosticism as a historical phenomenon is not only a revival of the archaic; it discloses also the most subtle spiritual differentiations. Here we shall consider it only in so far as it represents tangible inner experience or inner knowledge of salvation. Therefore, we shall not pursue the fantasies and theologico-mystical speculations of the Gnostics, and we leave the question open as to whether they involve mere imagination or hallucination, or whether they contain an element of real inner experience.

We shall not speak of the garment or garments of light that run from the religious writings of the Persians through the Slavonic *Book of Enoch,* in which Enoch by being anointed obtains the celestial body of light, through the *Ascensio Isaiae,* to the *Pistis Sophia,* in which after the resurrection of Jesus his celestial garment of light is sent down to him. This garment of light is his celestial likeness, his double.

Nor shall we speak of the Manichaean earth of light, nor of the corresponding treasure of light that lies directly underneath the world of the supreme light with its aeons. Nor, finally, shall we speak of the virgin or virgins of light, the παρθένος τοῦ φωτός of the Coptic Gnostic books. This virgin is a double of Barbelo, who judges the souls in the middle region. She sends the souls back down into existence and sets a seal upon them that decides their destiny. The sacraments in the second *Book of Ieu* [55] have to do with the function of the virgin of light—e.g., the three baptisms, the baptism of water, the baptism of fire, the baptism of the Holy Ghost.

The virgin of light is deserving of a special monograph. In any event, she cannot be regarded as an object of inner experience in the same sense as the "life and light" we have discussed above. She is an imaginary object, a vision transmitted by Gnostic tradition, not a simple intuition of an immediate inward reality.

As a sample of extreme subtlety in spiritual differentiation, we shall quote at random from an anonymous Coptic book emanating from the same milieu as the *Books of Ieu.* I have it before me in the English translation of the Rev. F. Lamplugh. [56] This text is evidently a Coptic translation of a

55 Chs. 45–47, in Carl Schmidt, ed., *Koptisch-gnostische Schriften* (Leipzig, 1905; GCS XIII), I, 308–12.

56 *The Gnosis of the Light, a Translation of the Untitled Apocalypse Contained in the Codex Brucianus* (London, 1918), pp. 60–61.

Greek original, presumably written at the time of Basilides and Valentinus.

> O Alone-begotten of Light, I praise thee.
> O Light unengendered, I praise thee.
> O Light self-begotten, I praise thee.
> O Forefather of Light, more excellent than every Forefather . . .
> O Light Invisible, who art before all those beyond vision, I praise
> thee.
> O Thought of Light, surpassing all thought . . .
> O God of Light above all Gods . . .
> O Gnosis of Light passing all knowledge . . .
> O Unknowable One of Light, who art beyond all that is unknown,
> I praise thee.

And the doxology goes on ad infinitum with its predicates of the unknown God. Here are a few more samples:

> O Thou who hast begotten [Thyself] in the absence of all generation,
> Whom none has engendered, I praise thee.
> O True Self-born of Light, who art before all those self-born, I
> praise thee.
> O Silence of all things, Silence of Light, I praise thee.
> O Saviour of all things, Saviour of Light, I praise thee.

The names of the ineffable are heaped up interminably. We have quoted enough to suggest the mood we shall encounter in Eastern Christianity as we continue our pursuit of the experience of light.

4. The Experience of Light in the Christian East

Clement of Alexandria repeatedly struck the motif in his *Stromateis*, when he spoke of the immutable and formless light, of its shadowlessness and indivisibility, when he spoke of the vision of the illuminated pillar. He described the infinite, never-satiating bliss of the Gnostic, the friend of God, in the contemplation of this light. Clement called this light "inaccessible," the ἀπρόσιτον φῶς. And yet it is evidently accessible to the gnostic, who perseveres in his earthly existence for its sake. Clement here describes a practice that he did not invent but found already in existence, a practice older than Christianity. In some respects it reminds us of the κάτοχοι, the prisoners of the god in the Serapeion at Memphis and elsewhere. Though we shall not go so far as to call this voluntary imprisonment the source of

259

Christian monasticism, the intention of the "prisoners" was clearly to make themselves incorporeal, to achieve, at least for a time, a state of perfection. These prisoners were bound in ecstatic rapture by their god—κατέχεσθαι ἐκ θεοῦ;[57] they were possessed by a god, and were therefore said to "bear god"—θεοφορεῖσθαι—and to be enraptured—κορυβαντιᾶν.

In describing the experience of light, Clement could invoke both a Christian and a non-Christian practice, yet he had as yet no name for the experience. Pseudo-Dionysius the Areopagite, who was probably identical with the Monophysite patriarch Severus of Antioch, gave a detailed account of the phenomenon later called "the light of Mount Tabor" in his treatise *On the Divine Names* (περὶ θείων ὀνομάτων). We are in Syria at the end of the fifth and the beginning of the sixth century; we have before us an Oriental writing in Greek, educated in the Platonist and Neoplatonist school of Proclus, but versed also in the Bible and the Church Fathers. This man wrote:

> But at present we employ (so far as in us lies), appropriate symbols for things divine; and then from these we press on upwards according to our powers to behold in simple unity the Truth perceived by spiritual contemplations, and leaving behind us all human notions of godlike things, we still the activities of our minds, and reach (so far as this may be) into the Super-Essential Ray, wherein all kinds of knowledge so have their pre-existent limits (in a transcendently inexpressible manner), that we cannot conceive nor utter It, nor in any wise contemplate the same, seeing that It surpasseth all things, and wholly exceeds our knowledge, and super-essentially contains beforehand (all conjoined within Itself) the bounds of all natural sciences and forces (while yet Its force is not circumscribed by any), and so possesses, beyond the celestial Intelligences, Its firmly fixed abode.[58]

Here, as the Pseudo-Areopagite says, we encounter the superessential light—εἰς τὴν ὑπερούσιαν ἀκτῖνα . . . ἐπιβάλλομεν. This light is no doubt the godhead itself. A few lines before, we read: "But hereafter, when we are [in]corruptible and immortal and attain the blessed lot of being like unto Christ, then (as the Scripture saith, I Thess. iv, 16) we shall be for ever with the Lord, fulfilled with His visible Theophany in holy contemplations, the which shall shine about us with radiant beams of glory (even as

57 Reitzenstein, p. 200.
58 *On the Divine Names*, I, 4; in C. E. Rolt, *Dionysius the Areopagite on the Divine Names and the Mystical Theology* (London, 1920), pp. 58–59.

once of old it shone around the Disciples at the Divine Transfiguration)." [59]
This is a reference to the transfiguration of Christ on the high mountain
(Matt. 17 : 1, Mark 9 : 2) or the sacred mountain (Luke 9 : 28), the ἅγιον
ὄρος or the ὑψηλὸν ὄρος. And this mountain, which is not named in the
Gospels, merely being called "high" or "sacred," is Mount Tabor. These
early passages prepare the way for the "theory"—first in the sense of vision,
later of doctrine—of the spiritual light, of that "originating beam" and of
that "overflowing radiance," ἀκτὶς πηγαία καὶ ὑπερβλύζουσα φωτοχυ-
σία.[60]

This superabundant stream of light shines on all the spirits over the world,
around the world, and in the world; it rejuvenates all their spiritual powers.
The presence of this sacred light has the power to unite and perfect all
whom it illumines. It has the power to unite "their different perceptions,
or rather fancies, into one true, pure and coherent knowledge," etc.[61] Indeed, the Pseudo-Areopagite's whole work is a single hymn to this light.

These passages refer to a supersensory organ of illumination, to the hidden light that shines down from Mount Tabor, Θαβώρ, תָּבוֹר, at the southern border of the Galilean highlands. This is the mountain mentioned in the
Book of Judges (4 : 6 ff.) and in Psalm 89 [88], which speaks of the Messiah
and his reign. Verse 12 of the Psalm runs: "The north and the south thou
hast created them: Tabor and Hermon shall rejoice in thy name." And
this same Mount Tabor appears in a fragment that has come down to us
from the Gospel According to the Hebrews. Here the Saviour says: "Even
now did my mother the Holy Spirit take me by one of mine hairs, and carried me away unto the great mountain Thabor." [62] See also Origen [63] and
St. Jerome.[63a]

In about the year 1000, Simeon, called the New Theologian, gave this
conception of Mount Tabor its basic and most beautiful expression. In his
hymns, some forty of which are available in the Latin translation of Pon-
tanus,[64] he carries on the tradition of practical mysticism that is discernible
in Eastern Christianity from the late fourth century on. The title of these

59 Ibid.; tr. Rolt, p. 58.
60 Ibid., IV, 6; tr. Rolt, p. 94.
61 Ibid., tr. Rolt, p. 95.
62 M. R. James, *The Apocryphal New Testament* (Oxford, 1924), p. 2.
63 *Commentary on John 2:12; Homily on Jeremiah 15:4.*
63a Mentioned in divers passages.
64 Migne, *PG*, CXX, 507ff.

hymns is scarcely translatable; they are called ἔρωτες τῶν θείων ὕμνων— "loves of the divine hymns." "Hymn" means approximately "truth," and the word *eros*, "love," as in Pseudo-Dionysius,[65] is used interchangeably with *agape*.

Erotic love and worshiping love permeate one another in the language of the ecstatic writers. Even God's own love is not excepted from this state of *ekstasis*, says Pseudo-Dionysius.[66] "And we must dare to affirm (for 'tis the truth) that the Creator of the Universe Himself, in His Beautiful and Good Yearning towards the Universe, is through the excessive yearning of His Goodness, transported outside of Himself in His providential activities towards all things that have being, and is touched by the sweet spell of Goodness, Love and Yearning, and so is drawn from His transcendent throne above all things, to dwell within the heart of all things, through a super-essential and ecstatic power whereby He yet stays within Himself." [67] A strange echo of the Gnostic Anthropos!

Simeon, prior of the cloister of Mamas, was deposed, not for his dangerous doctrine of the Trinity, but (and this is what concerns us here) because, after the death of his πατὴρ πνευματικός, his spiritual father and guru, he worshiped him as a saint. Here for the first time we encounter the spiritual father as master and initiator—an institution that has endured down through the Hesychasts to the *startsi* movement in Russia.

This spiritual father of Simeon, a Studite monk also named Simeon, set the crucial imprint on the New Theologian's religious life. Ecstasy became, as with Pseudo-Dionysius, "the natural form of union with the godhead." In particularly exalted moments a sensory vision of the godhead is obtained. To him who has been favored with grace there appears a wonderful supernatural light, an emanation of the glory (δόξα) of God. In the eighth century, St. John Damascene had written of the Messalians, "that when they pray, the Saviour sometimes appears to them in a beam of light" (ὅτι τοῖς εὐχομένοις δύναται φανεροῦσθαι ὁ σωτὴρ ἐν φωτί).[68]

His father confessor, the Studite, taught Simeon to see the light of Tabor. From him, as Holl has said, he learned to regard attainment to the light as the aim and epitome of religious striving. Simeon considered the surprising apparition of that light, with which he was frequently favored, as a revelation of God given him by God's grace, through which he entered into

65 *Divine Names*, IV, 11–13; tr. Rolt, pp. 102ff.
66 Ibid., IV, 13; tr. Rolt, p. 106.
67 Ibid.

68 Migne, *PG*, XCIV, 732.

a personal relation with Christ. Christ spoke to him out of a luminous cloud, new strength poured into him, the light entered into him and filled him with joy and divine radiance.[69] This light was a revelation conferred by grace, not a distinction. Every man must be capable of beholding it, just as every man is under obligation to live in the light.

Man must so order his life that the light of Mount Tabor can shine upon him. Only what the individual himself experiences has true religious value for Simeon. Here truth is again a person, Christ in person, corporeal in his luminous transfiguration—life and light. Spiritual insensibility, $\dot{\alpha}\nu\alpha\iota\sigma\theta\eta\sigma\dot{\iota}\alpha$, is the mortal sin. It is by grace and not by works that we gain this vision of light and with it our beatitude and freedom in God.

Later there developed a systematic course of training for the attainment of the light of Mount Tabor. It began with baptism, the bath of rebirth, and included penance and ascetic and sacramental acts under the direction of a "spiritual father." This method was introduced on Mount Athos in the thirteenth century by the monk Gregory of Sinai. Or it may have been introduced at an earlier date. This was the birth of the Hesychast movement.[70]

For the Hesychasts, silence resounded; they "heard" serenity. They might have written the words from *Poimandres:* "Thou whom no words can tell, no tongue can speak, whom silence only can declare" ($\dot{\alpha}\nu\epsilon\kappa\lambda\dot{\alpha}\lambda\eta\tau\epsilon$, $\ddot{\alpha}\rho\rho\eta\tau\epsilon$, $\sigma\iota\omega\pi\ddot{\eta}$ $\phi\omega\nuο\dot{\upsilon}\mu\epsilon\nu\epsilon$).[71] And they might also have uttered the words of Pseudo-Iamblichus on the nature of God: "For he is served through silence alone" ($\ddot{o}$ $\delta\dot{\eta}$ $\delta\dot{\iota}\alpha$ $\sigma\iota\gamma\ddot{\eta}s$ $\mu\dot{o}\nu\eta s$ $\theta\epsilon\rho\alpha\pi\epsilon\dot{\upsilon}\epsilon\tau\alpha\iota$).[72]

$\Sigma\iota\gamma\dot{\eta}$, silence, becomes prayer; $\dot{\eta}\sigma\upsilon\chi\dot{\eta}$, peace, becomes the essence of God. Again Christ issues forth from God—$\dot{\alpha}\pi\dot{o}$ $\sigma\iota\gamma\ddot{\eta}s$ $\pi\rho\sigma\epsilon\lambda\theta\dot{\omega}\nu$, "come forth from silence," as Ignatius says.[73] "It is better to be silent and be real, than to talk and to be unreal" ($\ddot{\alpha}\mu\epsilon\iota\nu\dot{o}\nu$ $\dot{\epsilon}\sigma\tau\iota\nu$ $\sigma\iota\omega\pi\ddot{\alpha}\nu$ $\kappa\alpha\dot{\iota}$ $\epsilon\ddot{\iota}\nu\alpha\iota$, $\ddot{\eta}$ $\lambda\alpha\lambdaο\ddot{\upsilon}\nu\tau\alpha$ $\mu\dot{\eta}$ $\epsilon\ddot{\iota}\nu\alpha\iota$).[74]

The Hesychasts were the heirs to the mysteries of the Near East. In-

69 Karl Holl, in *Realencyklopädie für protestantische Theologie und Kirche*, ed. Albert Hauck, XIX (Leipzig, 1907), 218.

70 See Joannes Cantacuzenus, *Historiae*, II, chs. 39, 40; IV, chs. 3, 23–25 (Migne, *PG*, CLIII, 661ff., and CLIV, 29, 179ff.); and Nicephorus Gregoras, *Byzantinae Historiae*, XI, ch. 10; XV, chs. 3, 7ff. (Migne, *PG*, CXLVIII, 759ff., 991ff., 1007ff.).

71 *Corpus hermeticum*, I, 31; Nock-Festugière, I, 19; tr. Scott, I, 131.

72 *De mysteriis*, VIII, 3; ed. G. Parthey (Berlin, 1857), p. 263.

73 *Letter to the Magnesians*, VIII, 2; cf. Kirsopp Lake, tr., *The Apostolic Fathers* (2 vols., London and New York, 1912; LCL), I, 204.

74 *Ignatius, Letter to the Ephesians*, XV, 1; tr. Lake, I, 189.

evitably, this revival of ancient experience by Simeon and by Gregory of Sinai aroused controversy in the Church. The doctrine of luminous vision found an adversary in the Calabrian monk Barlaam, a champion in Palamas. Theologians argued that if the light of Mount Tabor were transcendent and divine, it must be equated with God, and that to speak of perceiving God with the senses was blasphemy. We need not consider this controversy, which agitated clergy and laity alike, and even had its political repercussions. It was a battle of Aristotelian concepts and not concerned with the true experience of the light, which alone interests us here.

Those who saw the light of Mount Tabor called it an energy of God, an emanation of the Trinity, supernatural and visible at once, eternal and uncreated—ἄκτιστον. It had the property of transfiguring everything it permeated and raising it into the realm of the uncreated. So said its adversary Nicephorus Gregoras.[75] The predicate "uncreated" was meant to designate a middle term of divinity, which makes possible a contact between the absolute and the finite. The absolute can "inform" things earthly with its essence. A related view had long been current on Mount Sinai, as attested by the κλῖμαξ τοῦ παραδείσου (Ladder of Paradise) of John Klimax (Climacus), a Sinaitic monk, who died early in the seventh century. A century earlier, Pseudo-Dionysius and, later, his commentator Maximus the Confessor, who professed the strictest orthodoxy, had held similar opinions. Nevertheless, Simeon was a pioneer, both in his perception of the light and in his insight into the inner workings of this experience. Nicholas Cabasilas, Metropolitan of Thessalonica, who died in 1371, also defended the Hesychasts in his treatise λόγοι περὶ τῆς ἐν Χριστῷ ζωῆς (Discourses concerning the Life in Christ).

The Hesychasts saw in the light of Mount Tabor an energy of God, but not His essence, which was regarded as unattainable. But their adversaries stressed God's αὐτοενέργεια, His auto-energeia, which precluded any division between His essence (οὐσία) and His energy (ἐνέργεια).

The Greek Fathers already had held that divine transcendence was inaccessible to man's spiritual as well as his corporeal eye. But in order to make possible a contact with God, it was necessary to conceive of God's efficacy as accessible to man; otherwise, there could be no living bond between Creator and creature. Ultimately, the Greek Church adopted the view of the Hesychasts, but without comprehending it clearly, for the

75 Byzantinae Historiae, XI, ch. 10 (Migne, PG, CXLVIII, 759ff.).

Hesychasts posited the existence of deities (θεότητες) emanating from God or the Trinity. But the view of the Hesychasts was and still is in keeping with the fundamental line of Eastern orthodoxy. Holl writes: "The struggle for Hesychasm is the struggle for the authentic Greek view that the spirit of God, today as in the apostolic age, is still creative and active in the Church." [76] Hesychasm was also the bulwark of the Eastern Church against Western scholasticism. Rome subsequently approved Barlaam's polemic against Palamas.

The Eastern Church still sustains the doctrine of the vision of the divine light, which in recent centuries has received its greatest impetus on Mount Athos. In 1801, Nicodemus, a monk of Mount Athos, wrote his Ἐγχειρίδιον συμβουλευτικόν (Handbook of Advice). Others working in the same direction were Eugenios Bulgaris, author of a Θεολογικόν, who directed the academy on Mount Athos from 1753 to 1758; Leontopoulos, and Athanasios, who in 1806 published an Epitome. Finally, in 1854, Archimandrite Sophronios of the Mount Athos cloister of St. Paul wrote his Νοερὰ σύνοψις τῆς νοερᾶς προσευχῆς (Inner Epitome of Inner Prayer). Mount Athos has preserved this tradition. Under the Palaeologi, under the influence of the Serbs, and later under Turkish rule, the Hagiorite monks championed and developed this inner prayer. But their doctrine of the light of Mount Tabor had triumphed as early as the time of the Hesychast controversy of 1341–51.

Independently of the outside world, they formed their ἰδιορρυθμία, which made the individual monk independent of the cloister and its *hegoumenos*. This idiorrhythmia, self-regulation, was life according to a new order. Presumably it is not unrelated to the individual experience of the light of Mount Tabor, for in 1394, soon after the controversy, reference was made to idiorrhythmia in the so-called Third Typicon.

Idiorrhythmia revived the ancient form of monastic life, the *skiti* or monastic villages, inhabited by anchorites. The *skiti*, derived from the sketes in Upper Egypt, are settlements dependent on cloisters. Today half of the Hagiorites still live idiorrhythmically.

But let us return to the light of Mount Tabor. It has survived outside of the Greek Church, among the Russians who have come to play an increasing role on Mount Athos. From the Russian cloister of St. Panteleimon on Mount Athos a new Hesychast movement, the Imyaslaviya, has gone forth, nourished on the tradition of Mount Tabor and reaching down to our own

76 *Enthusiasmus und Bussgewalt beim griechischen Mönchtum* (Leipzig, 1898), p. 221.

day. The Hesychasts had developed a strict training in the discipline of prayer, with the following degrees: oral prayer, prayer of the chest, intelligible prayer, prayer of the heart. God's name was first uttered by the mouth. But then, as the training advanced, the initiate prayed in his larynx, his chest, finally in his heart. Having learned to pray in his heart, he enters into an intelligible ecstasy, so that his whole person participates in the prayer with every heartbeat and every breath. Like Yoga, Hesychasm has also its breathing regulations. It practices a union of the person first with the breath and then with the heartbeat.

Once the training has advanced sufficiently, the divine name appears inwardly with an all-embracing flame and force. A saying of John Chrysostom is taken literally: "Preserve the name of God in your heart, that the heart may absorb God and God the heart and the two become one." This is a Hesychast exercise. In 1913 (I owe the following to René Fülöp-Miller),[77] Hilarion, a Russian monk from the cloister of St. Panteleimon, wrote a treatise entitled *In the Caucasus Mountains*. A dialogue between master and pupil, between an old and a young monk, it teaches that the name of God must be worshiped as such, the name being magically identical with the person. The so-called prayer to Jesus is spoken in the manner described above. If one prays correctly, the light of Mount Tabor, the light that shone at the transfiguration of Christ, is kindled. The words of the prayer are uttered by the initiate with closed eyes, standing or sitting, with or without genuflections, several hundred times. The prayer consists of the words spoken by the publican when he saw the Pharisee praying beside him in the temple (Luke 18 : 13): "God be merciful to me a sinner" (ὁ θεός, ἱλάσθητί μοι τῷ ἁμαρτωλῷ). The words are uttered in Church Slavonic:

Bozhe, milostif budi mnye grieshniku.

For Hilarion this sentence has a magical efficacy. The name of God must be repeated until it is transformed into the reality of God. Hilarion's treatise found adversaries, but it also met with powerful friends throughout Russia, such as Anton Bulatovich and Florensky, and it is related to Fyodorov's doctrine of the true collectivity. The movement operates secretly in Russia today,[78] and high state officials are said to belong to it.

Bozhe, milostif budi mnye grieshniku.

77 *The Mind and Face of Bolshevism*, tr. F. S. Flint and D. F. Tait (London and New York, 1927), pp. 258ff.   78 [I.e., in 1943.—Ed.]

Fritz Meier

The Spiritual Man in the Persian Poet 'Aṭṭār [1]

I

The Persian historian Ibn al-Kalbī (d. 204 or 206/819 or 821) [1a] tells in his book on ancient Arabic idols [2] how the descendants of Cain carved five images of five upright men of their number who had died in one and the same month, and how the third generation worshiped these idols as gods. Although God sent the prophet Idrīs-Enoch [3] and later Noah to put an end to this idol worship, erring mankind did not desist from its ways and the consequence was the Flood in which all were drowned.

Anyone who wishes, on the basis of this report, to speculate on the origin of idolatry may choose between two conceptions. His first thought will be that idolatry came into being when a memorial was endowed with the prestige of the divinity; such an interpretation not only accords with the text, but is also supported by the general Islamic view of the origin of idol worship. [4] But if we consider that the veneration here accorded the images of the Cainites could not have been simply nonexistent before this time, but must have been directed toward some other being, and perhaps, as the wording of the passage indicates—since for the Moslem, polytheism was identical with idolatry—toward the rightful deity, we might just as well say that this passage ascribes the origin of idolatry to the sluggishness of the human spirit, which in all times has made it hard for man to lift his

---

1 [The author has omitted a section of the paper originally printed as the conclusion (*EJ 1945*, pp. 333–53), having subsequently come to consider it irrelevant to his argument.—Ed.]

1a [Double dates indicate, first, the year in the Mohammedan calendar (A.H.), which reckons from A.D. 622, the year of the hegira, and, second, the year in the Christian calendar. Single dates are A.D.—Ed.]

2 Julius Wellhausen, *Reste arabischen Heidentums* (2nd edn., Berlin, 1897), pp. 14f.; *Le Livre des Idoles*, ed. Ahmed Zeki Pasha (2nd edn., Cairo, 1924), pp. 51–53.

3 The first prophet; Ibn Hishām, *As-sīra an-nabawiyya* (Cairo, 1936), I, 3, 2–3.

4 C. Snouck Hurgronje, "Kusejr 'Amra und das Bilderverbot," *ZDMG*, LXI (1907), 188, 1–11.

gaze above material things. According to this view, idolatry would have arisen through a concretistic misunderstanding, by which man falsely identified the supreme being with a thing, and from this it would follow that the mission of the Prophet was to call men away from this concretistic misunderstanding.

But despite the outward separation between man and godhead actually effected by the founder of Islam, Mohammed, certain of his followers were impelled to seek contact with God from within. To their mind the intellect, for which God was absolutely inaccessible, was not the only means of achieving knowledge of Him; they found within themselves other forces, which promised to establish a new bond between themselves and the godhead and to give them a certainty of their supersensory existence, similar to the certainty concerning material things conferred by sight.

If we consider that the sphere of pure ideas offers no help in this direction but is often a wall that, once man has turned inward, deters him by reminiscences of the outward, material world from the experience of an immaterial reality, we shall understand that man himself had to change in order to become aware of God from within. A detailed account of Islamic mysticism would have to define the superiority of born mystics over those who had to undergo this change. For us it will suffice to say that this altered state enabled the mystics to know not only that God was exalted above all things, but also that they themselves could not be considered in the same category as any concrete thing. For only if man himself had being outside of any sensory existence could he arrive at experience that was not transmitted to him by his corporeity.

To what degree the phenomenon of prophecy gave rise to the development of Islamic mysticism has yet to be investigated. But the relation between mystical experience and the legend of Mohammed's ascent to heaven, as related in the commentaries on Sura 17 of the Koran, has always been felt by mystics, and may be the reason why Mohammed's ascent is particularly glorified by the Persian poets of mystical inspiration in the introductions to their works. In comparison to the Prophet who, in the general acceptance, had "seen God," the common man was only half a man, for in his lifetime he had no access to the hereafter. We know, to be sure, that even before Islam, one Khālid ibn Sinān believed that he would be able in his tomb to overcome the death that separated him from the hereafter; but since his relatives, for fear of being accused of desecrating the grave, were unwilling to disinter him as he had ordered,[5] it was not given him to become the explorer of the hereafter for the Arabs as Er the Pamphylian [6] had been for the Greeks and Ardā Wīrāf for the Mazdaists.[7]

Be that as it may, it is certain that the Islamic mystics, the Ṣūfīs, believed they could attain to a kind of higher existence above what man in general takes to be the totality of his experience. And in view of the interpretations that the mystics give to their experiences, it can be taken as characteristic of them that in their higher states they regarded themselves as exalted above space and time. They might say, for example, that they had transcended the planetary world, and this brings us again to the image of Mohammed's ascent. Mawlānā Jalāl ud-dīn-i Rūmī (d.672/1273) says: "The friends of God [an Islamic term for mystics, taken from the Koran but already current in classical antiquity [8]] have, in addition to these (known) heavens, seen other heavens; for they no longer esteem these (known) heavens which seem to them too paltry. They have transcended them and left them behind. And how can it surprise us that one of us men should be enabled to pass beyond Saturn?" [9] These words clearly show that the Ṣūfī was sometimes

5 Masʿūdī (d. 345–46/956–57), *Murūj adh-dhahab* (*Les Prairies d'or*, ed. and tr. Barbier de Meynard and Pavet de Courteille [Paris, 1861–77], I, 131f.; IV, 21f.); Ibn ʿArabī (d. 638/1240), *Fuṣūṣ al-ḥikam*, including the commentary of Bālī Effendi (d. 960/1553) (Constantinople, 1309/1891), pp. 418f. — The story assuredly belongs to the reports on burials as initiation ceremonies known to us from the Hellenistic period; Albrecht Dieterich, *Eine Mithrasliturgie* (2nd edn., Berlin and Leipzig, 1910), p. 167.
6 Plato, *Republic*, 614 b ff. Dieterich, *Nekyia* (Leipzig, 1893), pp. 114f. Cf. also Aridaios, whose three-day death is even more reminiscent of Khālid b. Sinān; *Nekyia*, pp. 145f.
7 W. Geiger and E. Kuhn, eds., *Grundriss der iranischen Philologie* (Strassburg, 1896–1904), II, 108. Modern Persian translation by Rashīd-i Yāsimī, "*Ardā-Wīrāf-Nāma*," *Mihr* III (Teheran, 1314/1896), 9ff. For date and parallels, see Dieterich, *Mithrasliturgie*, p. 189, and Tor Andrae, "Die Person Muhammeds in Lehre und Glauben seiner Gemeinde," *AEO*, XVI (1918), 43.
8 Cf. Max Pulver, "The Experience of Light," in this volume, pp. 253, 259.
9 *Fīhi mā fīh* (Aʿzamgarh, 1928), 224, 4–6. Cf. ʿAṭṭār (6th/12th century), *Haylājnāma* (lith., Teheran, 1353/1934), 180, 12:
    If thou comest to our religion,
    Thou wilt pass beyond the seventh heaven [text?].
And this, it may be presumed, is not a mere poetic image as in ʿAṭṭār's *Ilāhīnāma*, 328, 8; 371, 1. Awḥadī-i Marāgha'ī (d. 738/1337), *Jām-i Jam* (Teheran, 1307/1889), 61, 12:
    For if this knot is untied to thee,
    Thy dwelling will be the head of Saturn.
Khwājūy-i Kirmānī (d. 753/1352), *Rawḍat ul-anwār* (Teheran, 1306/1888), 38, 6 from foot:
    Why dost thou rest on this edifice of four arches [= the four elements]?
    Arise! Plant thy tent above these nine tents of heaven.

able to create a consciousness that raised him above everything he could verify by sensory perception and to a certain extent enabled him to cast off his body.

Schooled in similar views of the ancient Gnostics, the Ṣūfīs felt the separation thus accomplished between body and soul, corporeity and spirit, to be quite in keeping with their origin. The body had been taken from the "earth," the substance of the sensory world, but the spirit did not originate in this world.[10] But since the mystic, when he attained to states in which his spirit left space and time behind it, never experienced himself as that part which remained below with the body, but always as the spirit which soared heavenward, it is clear that it was not the outward aspect, but the spiritual essence itself that he took to be the true man. The Ṣūfīs therefore found Adam's descent from paradise and his first contact with the earth on the isle of Ceylon [11] (where his footprint is still exhibited on Adam's Peak [12]) significantly repeated in every human life. Najm ud-dīn-i Dāya (d. 654/1256) describes the journey of the individual human soul (*rūḥ*) from the vicinity of God to earthly birth as a journey through several thousand worlds, which more and more obscure its origin until, entirely separated from its home, it wakes up in this world:

> Thus we spent the night in defiance of the envious, enjoying
> A colloquy fragrant as musk mingled with wine.
> But when the morning shone, it parted us.
> Ah, what bliss that is clouded by no vicissitude!

And though the newborn child, Dāya continues, still retains an echo of his intimacy with God prior to birth, and this loss is the reason for his constant wailing, he forgets the supersensory as he imbibes his mother's milk and accustoms himself to the appearances of the sensory world. On the basis of a paraetymology of the Arabic word for "man," Dāya illustrates the two poles between which man, according to this conception, moves: whereas the singular *insān*, man, indicates that before his birth man was

---

10 See also 'Aṭṭār, *Ilāhīnāma*, 171, 16; *Dīwān* (Teheran, 1319/1901), 401, 9835; and Asadī, *Garshāspnāma* (Teheran, 1317/1899), § 8, 1.

11 Max Grünbaum, *Neue Beiträge zur semitischen Sagenkunde* (Leiden, 1893), p. 65.

12 Fritz Sarasin, *Reisen und Forschungen in Ceylon* (Basel, 1939), p. 65. The very oldest Arab geographers speak of this footprint of Adam (the Buddhists regard it as Buddha's footprint); Ibn Khurrādhbih, *al-Masālik wa'l mamālik* (written 232–72/846–86), ed. T. J de Goeje (Leiden, 1889), 64, 10–11; Ibn al Faqīh al-Hamadhānī, *Kitāb al-buldān* (written about 290/903), ed. de Goeje (Leiden, 1885), 10, 4–5.

the intimate, *anīs*, of God, the plural *nās*, men, makes it apparent that with birth he becomes one forgetful, *nāsī*, of his true origin.[13] The only means of safeguarding man from total dissolution in this-worldliness is the seed of faith, which in some men has survived as a relic of their original intimacy with God.[14]

Thus the Ṣūfī's ascent beyond Saturn becomes a return to his home. The question of the relation of this return to death would take us too far. But let us briefly enquire: what is the relation between this spiritual experience of the Ṣūfīs and the utterances in which they even claim to be God Himself? Two statements to this effect, that of Ḥallāj (executed 309/922): "I am God,"[15] and the other by Bāyazīd (d. 261/875): "Praise be to me, praise be to me, how great is my glory,"[16] in which he transferred a doxology of God to himself, the first person, have become actual articles of Ṣūfism. If in the Ṣūfī view—it will be asked—the true man is so very different from his corporeity, how then can he be identical with God? Is there not between a spiritual man and God at least as great a difference as between body and soul?

Even the Ṣūfīs were aware of the blasphemy inherent in such utterances, and in discussions with theologians they were often obliged to disparage them as theopathic babblings (*shaṭḥ*). Here, however, we can only ask what meaning this strange equation, "I am God," holds in our present context. To arrive at an answer, we must bear in mind an illuminating remark of ʿAdī ibn Musāfir (d. 557/1162) in which he says: "Know that for me there are times when nothing holds me and nothing sustains me, but it is I who hold and sustain all things."[17] This of course can apply only to times when the subject of human knowledge has "passed beyond Saturn." If we assume that a man can develop a spirituality that embraces everything present and thinkable, there still remains one thing it cannot comprehend: the subject of this knowledge. In so far as the subject of knowledge always remains the

---

13 The Druses know of a "forgetting ('corporeal') Adam," *Adam an-nāsī (al-Jirmānī)*; Silvestre de Sacy, *Exposé de la religion des Druzes* (Paris, 1838) I, 21–23; II, 115. Cf. the Nusayris in Edward E. Salisbury, "Sulaiman on the Nusairian Religion," *JAOS*, VIII (1866), 284, 11. With regard to the scientific etymology of *insān*, pl. *nās*, most recently Ludwig Koehler in the *Theologische Zeitschrift*, I (Basel, 1945), 77 (originally "the frail one," from the Accadian *enshu*, "weak").

14 *Mirṣād ul-ʿibād min al-mabdaʾ ilaʾ l-ma-ʿād* (Teheran, 1312–52/1894–1933), pp. 57–62.

15 Louis Massignon, *La Passion d'al-Ḥallāj* (Paris, 1914–21), index, s.v. *anaʾl Ḥaqq*.

16 Massignon, *Essai sur les origines du lexique technique de la mystique musulmane* (Paris, 1922), p. 249.

17 Rudolf Frank, "Scheich Adi, der grosse Heilige der Jezidi's," *Türkische Bibliothek*, XIV (Berlin, 1911), 81.

more comprehensive entity, which is not known, there must be a stage, since it comprehends everything else, at which the indefinable character of the godhead coincides with the indefinable character of the subject—i.e., at which God appears at the back of human knowledge, as its subject, whereby the equation "I am God" is fulfilled.

Thus those Ṣūfīs who admit the possibility of this identification must tend to construe Mohammed's traditional "seeing" of God, not as actual "seeing" but as the prototype of such a union of man with God.[18] But no one will imagine that such an identification of God and man constitutes a relapse into the idolatry that Ibn al-Kalbī ascribed to the Cainites, although at first glance both conceptions of God, that of the Cainites and that of the Ṣūfīs, seem to amount to the same thing. But far from worshiping a person's historical aspect, or even his image as God, as according to Ibn al-Kalbī the Cainite heathen did, the Ṣūfīs identify with God a self that is the opposite of a material thing, and just as far removed from all tangibility as the godhead in apophatic monotheism. Thus the two utterances of Ḥallāj and Bāyazīd, and there are many others like them, do not draw God back into the realm of sensory perception, but aim at showing that in the last analysis man too can be defined only apophatically.

With this we have arrived at the other Gnostic conception that man in his highest state of perfection becomes God, the idea of the Perfect Man.[19] The age of the two utterances of Ḥallāj and Bāyazīd shows that this idea lived in Islam and that Mohammedans strove to realize it even where it was not, or not yet,[20] known under this name.

18 See, for example, 'Aṭṭār, Ilāhīnāma, 17, 11:
  Aḥmad [Mohammed] was no more. God was there.
  The seeing was the fusion of the two.
 And in the same author's Muṣībatnāma (lith., Teheran, 1354/1935), 23, 3:
  The m in Aḥmad [Mohammed] was utterly effaced,
  So that only Aḥad [the one] remained and Aḥmad left the place.

19 In his Überlieferung (Tradition) (Leipzig, 1936), esp. pp. 437ff., Leopold Ziegler has discussed the place of this idea in the history of human thought. For detailed treatment, the reader is referred to him and to Hans Heinrich Schaeder, "Die islamische Lehre vom vollkommenen Menschen, ihre Herkunft und ihre dichterische Gestaltung" (The Islamic Doctrine of the Perfect Man, Its Origin and Poetic Treatment), ZDMG, LXXIX (1925), 192ff. Valentine Zhukovski, "The Idea of Man and Knowledge in the Conception of the Persian Mystics" (tr. from the Russian by L. Bogdanov), Bulletin of the School of Oriental Studies, London Institution, VI, 1 (London, 1930), 151ff., also casts light on this theme.

20 Cf. Fritz Meier, Vom Wesen der islamischen Mystik (Basel, 1943), p. 41, n. 43.

The two Gnostic, Ṣūfic conceptions outlined above have, to be sure, this in common with nonmystical Islam and other exoteric religions: they see the goal of man not in this world but in eternity; but they differ in that they believe that man can and should realize this goal in his lifetime. Thereby life obtains special meaning, the meaning of the moment in which man must gather all his forces to transcend it. Hence it would be a misunderstanding to find the meaning and purpose of life in the fulfillment of desires that do not transcend the antinomy of happiness and unhappiness. On the contrary, such desires must be regarded merely as a challenge to rise above them and attain to a state of being that no longer knows any such desires.

II

This is the problem that the Persian poet Farīd ud-dīn-i 'Aṭṭār [21] took up in the twelfth century. He dealt with it in his early works, but in his *Ilāhī-nāma*, the *Book of the Divine*—i.e., the book of 'Aṭṭār's divine inspirations— it became the core and central theme of his thinking. This work, available to us in the edition of Hellmut Ritter,[22] must be counted, both for its form

---

21 The most recent work on 'Aṭṭār is H. Ritter, "Philologika X," *Der Islam*, XXV (Strasbourg, 1938), 134–73. He still places the year of 'Aṭṭār's death in the late sixth century/twelfth century. But as Louis Massignon tells me, Ibn al-Fuwaṭī (d. 723/1323) speaks of a meeting between 'Aṭṭār and Naṣīr ad-dīn aṭ-Ṭūsī (597–672/1201–74), which would support the tradition that he did not die until 627/1230 or 632/1236. This report is not to be found in the printed text of Ibn al-Fuwaṭī's *Ḥawādith al-Jāmiʻa waʼt-tajārib an-nāfiʻa fiʼl-miʼa as-sābiʻa* (Baghdad, 1932) (containing the Annals from 626–700/1228–1300).

22 *Ilahi-Name. Die Gespräche des Königs mit seinen sechs Söhnen. Eine mystische Dichtung von Faridaddin Attar* (Leipzig and Istanbul, 1940; BI XII). Above all I wish to call attention to the apt conjectures on 99, 8; 109, 11; and especially 142, 14. Here I cannot go into particular questions that the editor raises in his critical apparatus, but I should at least like to remark that *nishāna-i* (136, 10ff.) reveals the same metrical irregularity as *jigargūsha-i* (263, 14, and 275, 15) and should therefore presumably be retained. Similar irregularities occur in Firdawsī's *Shāhnāma:* the *nabīra* (-i) in the construct state (see passages in Fritz Wolff, *Glossar zu Firdosis Schahname* [Berlin, 1935], 803a, and in Mawlānā, *Mathnawī*, ed. R. A. Nicholson [London, 1925–33; Gibb Memorial Series, n.s. IV]; e.g., bk. 3, vv. 1217, 1269, 1347; see Nicholson's introd., I, 8). A related irregularity occurs in Firdawsī, *Shāhnāma*, ed. J. A. Vullers (Leiden, 1878–84), I, 154, v. 461 var.; I, 158, v. 527; I, 160, v. 569: *tangī (-i) dil, pākī (-i) dil*, etc. Furthermore, my pupil Gertrud Spiess rightly judges that in 217, 13, the traditional rendering must be restored (*mardumān* instead of *zumrudān*). In 250, 2–5; 287, 9; and 366, 15, *basand* is perhaps preferable to *pasand*. It also seems questionable to me whether the completely wrong order of the Arabic numbers above 10 originated with 'Aṭṭār, since in others of his books the order is correct. — Here I should like also to describe a manuscript of 'Aṭṭār's belonging to Dr. Rudolf Tschudi of Basel. Its text of the *Ilāhīnāma* is closely related to that of Ritter's MS I: 347 pp.; 23 ll.; 25½ × 19; 16½ × 13; on pp. 100b–96b, with margin the text measures 21½ × 16. Arranged in four columns, ex-

and content, among the masterpieces of world literature. By way of elucidating the title, 'Aṭṭār states (366, 5ff.) that he has "opened the door to the divine treasure" and that his work "originated in the divine emanation" (*fayḍ-i ilāhi* [23]), and this he clarifies by two turns of phrase to the effect that he has fed on the supersensory and that he has enjoyed divine instruction. Though in another passage (391, 6) he refers to the treasure disclosed by him as the "treasure of expression," this should not be construed as a mere reference to the success of his poetic endeavor. By these words, 'Aṭṭār wishes rather to explain that the wisdom he imparts is a special gift of grace, which he is privileged to receive from God and pass on to men.[24] Even if we did not know that 'Aṭṭār was a Ṣūfī, these pious and yet so ambitious words would make us aware of his certainty concerning man's higher destiny, in comparison to which all the treasures of this world are mere willo'-the-wisps.

The story itself may be briefly summed up as follows:

A king has six sons. One day he gathers them round him and bids them disclose their heart's desire in order that he may grant it. The first wishes to marry the daughter of the king of the fairies, for he has heard of her dazzling beauty. He promises that if he can possess her, he will ask nothing more to the day of his death; for who would strive after any perfection beyond the possession of such beauty? The king, however, instead of fulfilling his wish, reproaches him for sensual desire, in the toils of which a man can lose his whole being. Thereupon—I shall pass over the stories

---

tremely clear calligraphy, small *nastaʻlīq* on yellowish paper. Gold margins, red, blue, and more rarely golden headings. Dark leather binding embossed in gold (two gazelles) mended. Scribe: Muḥammad b. Aḥmad al-Ḥallāj, in Samarkand. Contents: 1. *Ushturnāma*, 1b–99a; writing completed on Sunday the fifth of Dhu'l-qaʻda, 821/December 4, 1418. 2. *Ilāhīnāma*, 100b–178a. 3. *Wuṣlatnāma*, 178b–196b. 4. *Manṭiq uṭ-ṭayr*, 198b–258b. 5. *Muṣībatnāma*, 259b–347a; completed on the last Wednesday in Muḥarram, 828/December 22, 1424. In the margin: 6. *Asrārnāma*, 100b–170a. 7. *Bulbulnāma*, 170b–197b.

23 Concerning *fayḍ*, see *EI*, Suppl. s.v. *faiḍ*; A. M. Goichon, *Introduction à Avicenne* (Paris, 1933), p. 27; Andrae, pp. 306ff.

24 As Ignaz Goldziher showed, in his *Abhandlungen zur arabischen Philologie*, vol. I (Leiden, 1896), it would be a mistake to suppose that 'Aṭṭār wished to distinguish his work from the ancient Arabic poetry that was inspired by a djinn or the Shayṭān. The questions raised by J. Rypka with regard to the title of the book, in his review of Ritter's ed. (in *Orientalistische Literaturzeitung*, XLVI [Berlin, 1943], pp. 468–74), have no relevance. However, it should be mentioned that 'Aṭṭār claimed also to have received his quatrains (Ritter, p. 154) and the *Ushturnāma* (MS. Tschudi, 10b, 7) from the supersensory world, so that the choice of the title *Ilāhīnāma* would have been justified for those also.

with which the king illustrates each of his objections [25]—the son replies
that without sexual desire the world and its order would cease, and neither
he nor his father would exist. But the father explains that nevertheless
sexual desire is not the ultimate purpose of existence, as he seems to believe,
but that one must strive beyond it for the eternal intimacy (*jāwidhānī
khalwat*), for love (*ʿishq*) and adoration (*maḥabbat*),[26] which culminates in
the dissolution of one's own soul in the beloved. Even the child, for whose
sake, as the son argues, a woman is desirable, could be a disadvantage if
he were born to one so preoccupied with him as to forget knowledge.

> If thou hast the religion of Abraham,
> Let the sacrifice of his son be a lesson to thee. [59, 19]

Then the king's son asks why he is so powerfully drawn toward this girl
whom he has never seen; and the king tells him a story that not only answers
his question and thus concludes the enlightenment of this first son, but also
establishes the central theme of the entire work. The story deals with a
young man who falls in love with the princess of China and then hears of
a powerful Indian wise man with whom the emperor of China and his
daughter are acquainted. Pretending to be deaf and dumb, the youth takes
employment with the inaccessible wise man and in the course of ten years'
service secretly acquires all his wisdom. At this time the Indian crown
prince falls gravely sick, and in treating him the young man excels the old
sage and publicly corrects him. The overwhelmed sage dies of grief and the
young man is appointed Sarpātak [27] in place of his master. Then, in a mysterious chest that his predecessor never opened for him, the youth finds the
"description of the beloved." After that he cannot rest; he draws a circle,
sits down in it, and recites spells until, at the end of forty days, the loved

---

25 An ancient type of Ṣūfic sermon and colloquy used by ʿAṭṭār in the *Asrārnāma, Manṭiq
uṭ-ṭayr*, etc.
26 In 48, 10 (as well as 232, 9; 299, 6; 347, 16), we should read *sar* (Vullers, *Lexicon
Persico-Latinum Etymologicum* (Bonn, 1855–67), s.v., No. 7) instead of *sir(r)*: "A
tête-à-tête is never desirable for the sake of sexual lust. He who is not so guided is
in error." (See also Vullers, II, 248b, s.v. *sar-i chīzē dāshtan*.)
27 Here taken as a title. Sarbātak al-Hindī was an Indian prince, who, like Ratan, was
said to have been a lifelong companion of the Prophet (d. allegedly 333/944–45);
Goldziher, *Mohammedanische Studien*, II (Halle, 1890), 172, where reference is made
to Ibn Ḥajar al-ʿAsqalānī, *Al-iṣāba fī tamyīz aṣ-ṣaḥāba* (Calcutta, 1856–73), 2, 354ff.
In his *Abhandlungen*, II (Leiden, 1899), lxxv, n. 3, Goldziher also refers to de Jong's
introd. to Ibn al-Qaysarānī, *Ansāb* (Leiden, 1865), p. xvii, and Dhahabī's *Mīzān
al-iʿtidāl*, 1, 81, s.v. Isḥāq b. Ibrāhīm aṭ-Ṭūsī.

one appears.[28] But when he sees her, he realizes that she is in his own heart.

> At this he was astonished and spake:
> Why didst thou choose to dwell in my soul, O thou who art fair as the moon?
> And she who was fair as the moon, who illumined the heart, replied:
> From the first day on I have been with thee.
> I am thy soul, and thou art in search of thyself.
> Why dost thou not make thine intellect seeing?
> If thou seest [correctly], thou thyself wilt be the whole world,
> Thou wilt be the friend without and [the mistress] within.
> [76, 11–14] [29]

At first the Sarpātak cannot understand that his soul should appear to him as beauty, since he has always conceived it as a snake, dog, or pig.[30] But the soul explains to him that it is ugly only so long as it is not purified and translated from the state of "commanding evil" to the state of the "pacified soul."

Then the king in the frame narrative admonishes his son:

> Thus what thou seekest, my son,
> Is all within thyself, and thou art merely sluggish in seeking it.
> But if thou art virile in the performance of God's work,
> Thou wilt be all, thou wilt be the companion [31] [of God].
> Without thyself thou wilt be lost unawares,
> For thou hast taken this path in search of thyself.
> Thou art thine own beloved. Return to thyself!
> Go not forth! Return from the desert to thine home!
> Love of country [32] is pure faith,
> Because the beloved is within [33] the pure spirit. [77, 4–8]

This admonition is calculated to direct the son's endeavors inward. The true beloved is not a being of flesh and blood, but a new kind of life that

---

28 Parallels from life may be found in Edward G. Browne, *A Year Amongst the Persians* (London, 1893), p. 148 (quoted in *ZDMG*, LXX [1916], 272), and Henri Massé, *Croyances et coutumes persanes* (Paris, 1938), II, 363. For the period of forty days, see also the invocation scene in 'Aṭṭār's *Khusrawnāma*, in Ritter, pp. 165ff.

29 I.e., the friend this side of the partition (*parda*) and the mistress beyond it; thus according to 222, 20 (329, 16).

30 For the instinctive soul as cow and wolf, cf. *Asrārnāma* (MS. Tschudi), 159a, margin; as dog, ibid., 159b, margin.

31 *Hamkhāna*, as in 84, 8 (cf. 190, 4).

32 Arabic quotation. The saying is attributed to Mohammed; see Henry Corbin, *Sohrawardt d'Alep* (Paris, 1939; Publications de la Société des Études Iraniennes XVI), p. 37: "L'amour de la patrie véritable procède de la foi."

33 *Andarūn-i* prepositive as *darūn-i*, 166, 13.

since his birth has been waiting to be lived by him, a being that he is not to possess but to become through an inner metamorphosis. The road to this being leads not into a new outward environment but to the state of "pacified soul," which receives from God the summons to return to him (76, 19; Sura 88, 28), whereby man, as 'Aṭṭār says, becomes God's companion. The fairy princess is thus a mere phantom goal and, if not recognized as such, a concretistic misunderstanding of the true great beloved, the *anima principalis*. Our subsequent discussion will show how deep 'Aṭṭār has taken us into the meaning of his poem with this story.

The second son (fifth to eighth dialogue) desires to learn magic, in order to be able to make his way according to his whim and fancy throughout the world, to fly through the air like a bird, to climb mountains, to swim through the oceans, to enjoy all beauties—in short, to have access to everything. The king replies that he is possessed by the devil and seeks only his own pleasure, which makes him a candidate for hell. The son points out, however, that the present epoch is one of the (instinctive) soul, in which no one acts out of other than selfish motives, so that if he, the son, should do penance in the end, the harm could not be so great. But his father admonishes him not to squander his life to no purpose, and invokes the fate of the masters of all magic, the fallen angels, Hārūt and Mārūt, who were hung upside down in a well shaft in Babylon, their mouths only a hand's breadth from the water, powerless to help themselves with all their magic.[34] His father advises him to renounce himself entirely and describes this state by numerous examples. This the son cannot resolve to do, because he considers such self-renunciation a condition too lofty for him ever to attain to. The father replies that man must nevertheless set himself a goal that is just before God, since everything else must lead to ruin. The son demands enlightenment concerning the secret of magic that seems to him so attractive, whereupon the father, on the basis of a few stories, expounds the doctrine that man should welcome even the curse of God as a sign of the attention He bestows upon him (cf. 138, 13).[35] As an example of this attitude, he cites

---

34 Victor Chauvin, *Bibliographie orientale*, VIII (Liége, 1904), 131. Edward W. Lane, *Arabian Society in the Middle Ages* (London, 1883), pp. 82ff. Abū Bakr 'Atīq-i Sūrābādī (fifth century/eleventh century), *Tafsīr*, in Mahdī-i Bayānī, *Numūna-i sukhan-i fārsī*, vol. I, pt. 1 (Teheran, 1317/1899), 119-20. 'Aṭṭār, *Bulbulnāma* (lith. Teheran, 1312/1894), 15ff.

35 Cf. 'Izz ad-dīn b. Ghānim al-Maqdisī (d. 678?/1279?), *Al-ḥadīth an-nafīs fī taflīs Iblīs*, in Ritter, "Philologika IX," *Der Islam*, XXV (1938), 46. According to the tradition, the most celebrated follower of these maxims was the mystic Shiblī (d. 334/945), who

the devil, who, when God commanded all the angels to fall down before Adam, preferred to take upon himself God's curse rather than do obeisance to anyone other than God. This excessive love of God and self-abnegation is the true, permissible magic that he should learn from the devil. And then the devil in his heart (127–29; 138, 20), nourished on false desires, would be overcome.

The third son (ninth to twelfth dialogue) wishes for the goblet of Jam, in which everything one seeks is visible, so that through its possession all the secrets of the world will be revealed to him.[36] How much would he, an ignorant man, then know! The king believes that this desire conceals a striving for glory, and expresses the opinion that he will succumb to everlasting pride if the wish is fulfilled. Moreover, it would profit him nothing in death. But just as the second son, in defense of his desire to learn magic, argued that all men sought their pleasure in some way, the third states that no man (at least none who is superior to the beasts) is free from the love of glory. The king advises him to seek greatness not through glory but rather through obedience to God, but the son defends his desire for glory by saying that it can be pursued with moderation. To which the king replies that even the slightest measure of glory is harmful; for if even a glance at one's own obedience is a pitfall, how much worse must be the striving for glory. The son now asks what the true goblet of Jam is, and the father tells a few stories to show that it can be obtained only through the self-renunciation and self-dissolution of man:

But know then, if thou willest the goblet,
Thou must die to thyself during thy lifetime! [197, 15]

Thereupon (197, 17) he defines it as intellect ('aql; understanding, reason), which is the "kernel" around which the senses form a "husk." [37] Although

---

in the hour of death is said to have granted Satan the curse of God; 'Aṭṭār, *Manṭiq uṭ-ṭayr*, ed. Garcin de Tassy (Paris, 1857), vv. 3254–68 (tr. by the ed., *Le Langage des oiseaux* [Paris, 1863], p. 181); Maḥmūd b. 'Uthmān, *Firdaws ul-murshidiyya* (written 728/1327–28), ed. Fritz Meier (Leipzig and Istanbul, 1943; BI XIV), Persian text, 267, 21–23.

36 Source material on the goblet of Jam in Arthur Christensen, "Le Premier Homme et le premier roi dans l'histoire légendaire des Iraniens: IIᵉ Partie, Jim," *AEO*, XIV, 2 (1934), 119, 128ff. According to the passages here listed, our present passage is one of the oldest in which the goblet is mentioned.

37   Each little grain of dust in both worlds,
    Everything is visible in the goblet of thine intellect.
    Thousands of arts, mysteries, and descriptions,

'Aṭṭār's attitude toward religious tradition and the position he ascribes to the intellect (198, 1b) are fully in keeping with Ṣūfism and also presuppose a certain self-renunciation, one might at first regard the dithyrambic manner in which the self-destruction of man has just been demanded as out of place or exaggerated; for the development of the intellect has nothing to do with mysticism. But here it must be pointed out that the intellect is also the receptacle of knowledge of the other world, which to be sure can be known already through the reading of the holy scriptures, yet reveals itself in a new aspect to the consciousness broadened by mysticism. Therefore the intellect, in which, according to 'Aṭṭār, not merely one but "both worlds" are reflected (197, 18), becomes enriched as man multiplies his experience and advances into the realm of perfection and self-renunciation. Only when the ultimate has been experienced does it become the true goblet of Jam, revealing all.[38]

The father's lesson to the fourth son is similar (thirteenth to fourteenth dialogue). This son wishes for the water of life, which the king interprets as a longing for eternal life. He accuses his son of harboring selfish hopes, when he would do better to make proper use of the short life with which he has been entrusted, and to be thankful to God. The son then asks his father to describe the true water of life, and the father replies that it is knowledge and "disclosure of mysteries" (198, 16; 218, 14–15; 219, 4).

The fifth son (fifteenth to eighteenth dialogue) desires Solomon's seal ring, with the help of which he hopes to conjure fairies and demons into his power, to understand the language of birds and ants, and thus become an especially powerful king.[39] As might be expected, the king dissuades him from this wish, points to the transitoriness of kingship, and informs him that the true kingdom is not of this world, but that it is the other world

---

Thousands of commandments, prohibitions, decisions, and ordinances,
Rest on thine intellect; it suffices.
What goblet could ever give thee greater clarity? [197, 18 – 198, 2]

The meaning "enough" for *tamām* is attested by many other passages (50, 17; 52, 1; 58, 4; 134, 16; 136, 13; 196, 12; 329, 17, etc.). "To have enough of" is expressed by *dil-i man migiradh az* (120, 17; 166, 14; 179, 14/16; 194, 17; 282, 8) or by *dil-i man ser āmadh az* (225, 10).

38 Also in 'Aṭṭār's *Manṭiq* (v. 3456), knowledge is a mystical station, which, as here, follows love. Cf. Christensen, p. 136: "Chez les ṣūfīs la coupe de Jim devient le symbole du savoir mystique."

39 Lane, *Arabian Society*, p. 40.

(245, 14). The son argues that all men strive for such power and that he would be willing to give his life for it; but from these words the king concludes that his son has not yet heard of the otherworldly kingdom, for if he had, this earthly realm would have lost its value in his eyes. To this the son counters that the great men whom his father has represented as examples of the good life all seek their livelihood among kings, that he can think of no one who is not dependent on the court. But the father asks why he wishes to take upon himself the responsibility for all mankind, when he is incapable of responsibility for himself:

> Since it is hard to die as a poor man,
> How, in the end, wilt thou die as a king? [269, 17]

And again the father reminds his son that the kingship he desires is ephemeral. The son then asks him the secret of the true ring of Solomon, and the father shows him, through the story of Baluqyā and 'Affān,[40] that the kingdom of Solomon, the eternal kingdom, is self-sufficiency (qanā'at) or is gained and retained through self-sufficiency (286, 10–12; 287, 3–4/7).

The sixth and last son (nineteenth to twenty-second dialogue) desires to learn alchemy in order to make people happy and rich. In this wish the king sees merely a fruit of desire, and once again he points out the worthlessness of all that is worldly. The son argues that poverty often creates unbelief, whereas, conversely, money sets both religion and worldly considerations right. The father replies that religion and worldly considerations have never been compatible. But all the examples with which the father illustrates this remark apparently cause the son to forget its content; for when he speaks again, he repeats that what he loves is a combination of religion and worldliness, and in this the art of gold making will serve him. The father replies that he who cannot contribute happiness and sorrow in equal quantity can be regarded as a lover only in a metaphorical sense. True love demands tears, fire, and blood. The son then asks the father for enlightenment as to the true alchemy, and, through a story about Plato, the father tells him that true alchemy is by no means the making of gold, but the distillation of one's own soul substance into an elixir (353, 16).[41]

40 Concerning this story and its sources, see Josef Horovitz, "Buluqja," ZDMG, LV (1901), 519–25.
41 Presumably this is also the elixir that Ibn 'Arabī claimed to have known; Ibn Shākir al-Kutubī, Fawāt al-Wafayāt (Cairo, 1299/1881), 2, 241, 2 from foot.

If the elixir that illumines the world
Is unknown to thee, learn it then from Plato!
Why dost thou labor to distill an elixir from eggshells and even
from hair
For the making of gold and silver?
Transform thy body into heart and grieve thy heart,
For this is the way in which true men make their elixir. [355,
10–12]

The king, and with him ʿAṭṭār, who thus returns to the Gnostic sphere of the story of the Sarpātak, defines the elixir itself as the "light of God." Since this passage clearly reveals the basic philosophy of the whole work, and at last states in conceptual terms the idea of the eternal man, the Ṣūfī prototype of man, I shall translate from this passage at length, in order to confirm my previous statements and also to throw light on the new concept "light of God":

He who has been dissolved in the [true] gold forever,[42]
Who knows no more of himself, he has been instructed.
But the elixir remains forever
What the travelers of the path call light of God. [43]
If it shines for a time [44] upon an infidel,
He will, in consequence of the light, comprehend the whole world.
When that light fell upon Pharaoh's sorcerers,
They who had been so remote from God became near to Him.[45]
If it shines for a time upon an old woman,
It makes her the man of the whole world, like Rābiʿa.[46]
And if it elects a spadesman to shine upon,
It makes him as glorious as Kharaqānī.[47]

42 *Maḥw-i zar* and *maḥw-i Allāh*, ʿAṭṭār, *Haylājnāma* (lith. Teheran, 1353/1934), 85, 3 from foot (see below, n. 51).
43 *Nūr Allah:* the second syllable of Allah is short (as in 302, 6; 367, 14).
44 The *zamānē* that occurs here and several times in the following means both "for a time" and "once." Because of 362, 3, where *yak dharra*, "a little," takes the place of *zamānē*, I translate according to the former alternative.
45 After Moses' miracle of the serpents, Pharaoh's magicians believed in the God of Moses and Aaron; Sura 20, 42–76, and commentaries; Muḥāsibī (d. 243/857), *Faṣl min Kitāb al-ʿAẓama* (MS. Jarulla, Istanbul), 1101, 27b; Ṭabarī, *Annales*, ed. de Goeje and others (Leiden, 1879–1901), I, 471, 5 – 478, 14. (ʿAṭṭār, *Manṭiq*, vv. 2570–74.)
46 Woman mystic, d. 185/801. See Margaret Smith, *Rābiʿa the Mystic* (Cambridge, 1928). Rābiʿa is often cited by ʿAṭṭār as the model of a "man" (*Manṭiq*, vv. 558ff., 1776, 3081ff.).
47 Mystic, d. 425/1033. He "sowed and set trees"; ʿAṭṭār, *Tadhkirat ul-awliyā'*, ed. R. A. Nicholson (London, 1907), 2, 201, 15. I use the familiar form Kharaqānī instead of Kharqānī. Since ʿAṭṭār often changes two short syllables for metrical reasons into one

And if, for a time, it goes to Maʿrūf,[48]
   He, the Christian, is invested with the true religion.
And if it appears before Fuḍayl,[49]
   From a highwayman he changes to a revealer of secrets.
And if it enters the spirit of Ibn-i Adham,[50]
   His heart becomes the prince of both worlds [the here and hereafter].
And if it falls upon the body, that dust turns heart.[51]

---

syllable long by position, his Kharqānī (see *Der Islam*, XXIV (1937), 38, n. 1) cannot be accepted as proof of the correct pronunciation. Examples of such elimination of vowels for metric reasons from the *Ilāhīnāma:* 29, 20: *kalmat* (instead of *kalimat*); 51, 12: *ʿAlwī* (instead of *ʿAlawī*); 87, 11: *jawlāngah* (instead of *jawalāngah*); 97, 17: *naknadh* (instead of *nakunadh*); 116, 17: *Hamdān* (instead of *Hamadhān*); 176, 17ff.; 212, 11: *Ḥabshī* (instead of *Ḥabashī*); 197, 2: *binadham* (instead of *binadiham*); 221, 10: *ṣadqa* (instead of *ṣadaqa*); 225, 16: *naknam* (instead of *nakunam*); 238, 8: *maṭlab* (instead of *maṭalab*); 240, 6: *bifrūkhtan* (instead of *bifurūkhtan*); 241, 13: *bukhshadh* (instead of *bikushadh*), etc.; 361, 18: *sahra* (instead of *sahara*); 376, 11: *ʿArfāt* (instead of *ʿArafāt*). Similar instances may be found in all the works of ʿAṭṭār. For Firdawsī, see Theodor Nöldeke, *Das iranische Nationalepos* (2nd edn., Berlin and Leipzig, 1920), pp. 95ff.

48 Mystic, d. 200/815–16. Originally a Christian; Qushayrī, *Risāla* (Cairo, 1346/1927), 9, 25ff.

49 Mystic, d. 187/803. A highwayman before his conversion. Qushayrī, 9, 11.

50 Ibrāhīm b. Adham, mystic, d. 161–66/777–83. He was Prince of Balkh; Hujwīrī, *Kashf ul-maḥjūb*, tr. Nicholson (2nd edn., London, 1936), p. 103. With regard to our passage, cf. ʿAṭṭār, *Tadhkirat ul-awliyāʾ*, I, 85, 18, where Ibn-i Adham is praised as the "Prince of this world and of religion." An article is also devoted to all these mystics in *EI*, s.vv.

51 Cf. 355, 12 (here translated, above, p. 281); 364, 13ff. Also ʿAṭṭār, *Muṣībatnāma*, 55, 11:
   He [the man who meditates] wanders, until he exchanges the body for the spirit,
   Letting his body attain to the spirit while still alive.
Asrārnāma (MS. Tschudi), 113a, margin, 14 from foot ff.:
   Then they wandered from the body to the heart,
   And from the heart on to the spirit, and then to the court [of God]. [Corr. *ba-dargāh* instead of *zi-dargāh*.]
Similarly, in the *Haylājnāma*, 279, 3 from foot:
   Here from the heart wander on to the spirit
   [And then] cast both, heart and spirit, into sheer nonbeing!
Such passages refer primarily to the change in man's position toward what he considers himself: from self-identification with his corporeal manifestation, he progresses to self-identification with God. But they refer at the same time to the increase in the faculty of sight until it passes beyond the sensuous and corporeal, or passes through it, to the spirit at work behind it. For in the *Asrārnāma*, 115a, margin, 8 from foot – 115b, 28, the poet writes:
   Whenever the self ceases to exist in thee,
   The duality of spirit and body remains no longer.
   When spirit and body are quickly illumined,
   The body quickly becomes spirit and the spirit body.
   Thy body with its darkness is like the back of a mirror,

And if it falls upon the heart, the heart becomes pure spirit [*jān*].
And when the spirit finds within it that light,
  It finds both worlds to be far from [true] being.
And if the spirit is absolutely extinguished by that light,[52]
  It bursts forth with "Praise be to me" and "I am God." [53]
And if in uprightness it enters the court of paradise,
  These are the words in which the supreme majesty [God] ad-
  dresses it:

But the spirit is the bright side of the mirror.
If the back of the spirit be cleansed,
  The two become one. . . . [115b]

Thine whole body is even today spirituality [*ma'nē*];
  For the body will remain here [corr. instead of "there"], since it is of this
  world.
But when the body dissolves the chain of the spirit,
  Then thy whole body appears there as spirit.
It will be the same body of thee, but luminous,
  And if thou art recalcitrant, a dull, cloudy body.
The hidden spirituality will then be fully manifest;
  This doubtless is the meaning of the words of the Koran, "when the secrets
  are slit" [Sura 86, 9].
Since now for Mohammed spirit was body and body spirit,
  He ascended to heaven with one as well as the other.
When thou sayest: I know that the body is dust;
  How can the body that consists of dust be pure spirit?
I answer thee: Look into the tomb!
  Thou thyself art blind. Who hath said: Blind man, see!
For thine eye the tomb is earth and grains of dust.
  But for the eye of another it is a green field. . . .
He who knows what appears as dust to be a green field,
  How should he not see the body as a pure spirit?
But as long as thou art confined in time and space,
  Thou canst never see thy body in its spirituality.

Cf. also *Haylājnāma*, 331. — A special study ought to be undertaken of 'Aṭṭār's "doctrine of transubstantiation."
  In this connection the Persian *jān* in 'Aṭṭār = Arabic *rūḥ*: *Muṣībatnāma*, 423–45
(39th to 40th *maqāla*); *Haylājnāma*, 314. — *Jān* = *rūḥ* (Sura 15, 29, etc.): *Manṭiq*,
v. 3230. By way of distinguishing *jān* from *nafs* (instinctive soul), *Ilāhīnāma*, 77, 2;
Manṭiq, vv. 2878, 3147: "The seat of the Supreme [God] is the kernel of thy spirit
[*jān*]. The husk of thy spirit is thy recalcitrant [instinctive] soul [*nafs*]." (Garcin de
Tassy's tr. is erroneous.) Similarly, in the fable of the fox (*jān*) and wolf (*nafs*) in the
Asrārnāma (MS. Tschudi), 159a–b. — But of course one can also translate "soul," if
one grants such a rendering of Arabic *rūḥ*.
52 Cf. Arabic *faniyat arwāhunā* in 'Adī b. Musāfir; Frank, p. 232; 'Aṭṭār, *Haylājnāma*,
85, 3 from foot:
    Until heart and spirit have been *extinguished* in God,
    How shall they perceive the "Speak, He is God" with their own eyes?
53 The two classical theopathic utterances; see p. 271, above.

"This letter is transmitted from the one king
    To the eternal king!"
Since one has [here] put on Thy [God's] very own dress,
    The letter is from a sacrosanct being to a sacrosanct being.
Since thou art sacrosanct, thou canst become eternal,
    Thy whole body can become heart, thy whole heart spirit.
Since He has given thee fair form and quality,
    Come, that He may give thee this knowledge as well! [361,
    15 – 362, 13]

Although, in this rather unclear passage, the previous definition of the elixir as something that a man distills from his own substance (353, 16) is forgotten, and replaced by the "light of God" that "shines upon man" and requires of us only that we clear the way for it, nevertheless there is no doubt that the distillation of the better man and the dawning of God's light must be considered as simultaneous and as inextricably connected as sunrise and daybreak. The elixir is both: the light of God and the eternal king. It is the place where man changes his temporal life for life everlasting, the condition in which he realizes the eternal and incommensurable, and for this very reason a goal equally exalted above the concrete that is within and the concrete that is without. Whereas all things of the world, money, women, raiment, and so on, are "goals for the sake of something else" (*maṭlūb li-ghayrih*), money for the sake of bread, woman for the sake of children, clothing for the sake of warmth, God alone is the "goal for his own sake" (*maṭlūb li-dhātih*), to which everything else is subordinate, and He is represented to the sixth son and hence to the reader as the true elixir.

Here it may be thought that I have gone too far in citing these words of Mawlānā,[54] since in 'Aṭṭār the eternal man is clearly distinguished from the one God and the two borrowed Arabic phrases, "Praise be to me" and "I am God," might be used with a certain poetic freedom. But a closer examination of the text shows unmistakably that these utterances have retained and must retain their full meaning. For not merely are man and God both represented as kings, hence equals,[55] but both are "sacrosanct" (*quddūs*),[56] and man's power to become eternal is based upon this sacrosanctity. Thus we find in the quality of the sacrosanct the common denominator between

54 *Fīhi mā fīh*, 109, 14 – 110, 1.
55 Cf. also the passage in *Manṭiq*, vv. 1659–63.
56 This attribute is given to God also in 'Aṭṭār's *Manṭiq*, v. 96, and in the first quatrain of his *Mushtārnāma*.

God and mystic, which permitted 'Aṭṭār to regard the elixir sought by the mystic now as a substantiality to be distilled from man, now as a light emanating from God. If we compare this light of God with the New Testament illumination through the Holy Spirit (as in Heb. 6 : 4), there can be no doubt that the light of God in our passage must mean something very close to what the Holy Spirit represents in Christianity [57]—and here it may be mentioned purely in passing that 'Aṭṭār also attributes the quality of sacrosanctity to the Islamic Holy Spirit, the angel Gabriel.[58] Thus 'Aṭṭār, in an act of autonomous thought, appears to have effected, partially at least, that division of God which Christianity formulated in the dogma of the Trinity, the divinity of whose second Person no one now will be likely to contest. Here, to be sure, we have not to do with the Christ of the Church, but it is clear that our mystic has in mind the Son of God, and this can be denied only if, aside from considerations of a general nature that must lead us beyond the letter, we disregard the passage in the *Corpus hermeticum* in which the mystic who has arrived at his goal is called God and son (παῖς) of the One (God),[59] the place in the Mithras Liturgy in which the mystic

---

57 "Light of God" occurs in the Koran as a poetic term for guidance in the faith (Sura 4, 174; 5, 15; 5, 44; 5, 46; 6, 91; 6, 122; 9, 32 [*nūr Allāh*]; 24, 35; 24, 40; 39, 22; 42, 52; 57, 28; 61, 8 [*nūr Allāh*]), and 'Aṭṭār also interprets it in this sense. But in the Christian view, this guidance is a work of the Holy Ghost, as countless Pentecost hymns show. In the Koran the spirit of God is once (Sura 42, 52) designated as light. In 'Irāqī (d. 688/1289), '*Ushshāqnāma* (*The Song of Lovers*), ed. and tr. A. J. Arberry (Oxford, 1939), v. 32, God is "the light of heaven and earth" (Sura 24, 35), but the Holy Ghost is "the ray" of this light. — Concerning the Islamic doctrines of light, see T. de Boer in *EI*, s.v. Nūr.

58 *Ilāhīnāma*, 310, 7; *Muṣībatnāma*, 65, 2. It may be remarked in passing that the ground for the Islamic identification of the Holy Ghost with Gabriel was laid by a tradition current in Arabia that the angel who announced the birth of Jesus to Mary was also Jesus' father. Whereas in the Gospel of St. Luke (1 : 26ff.), Gabriel merely announces that the Holy Ghost shall come upon her, Umayya b. Abi's-Ṣalt, a contemporary of Mohammed, relates in his *Dīwān*, ed. and tr. Friedrich Schulthess (Leipzig, 1911), Poem No. 38, that after the annunciation the same angel (not mentioned by name) enters into a union with Mary. The Montanists, who were widespread in Arabia, also looked upon a (heavenly) archon as the father of Jesus; Franz Joseph Dölger, *Antike und Christentum*, I (Münster, 1929), 112–16. The Koran passage (Sura 19, 16–22) presumably contains a deposit of this view; cf. Wilhelm Rudolph, *Die Abhängigkeit des Qorans von Judentum und Christentum* (Stuttgart, 1922), p. 77. The problem has been touched upon by Eduard Norden, *Die Geburt des Kindes* (Leipzig and Berlin, 1931), p. 87.

59 Bk. XIII, § 14, in W. Scott, *Hermetica* (Oxford, 1924), I, 239–55. Richard Reitzenstein, *Die hellenistischen Mysterienreligionen* (2nd edn., Leipzig and Berlin, 1920), pp. 34ff. The appellative significance of "son of God" is also presupposed by the heretic Ebion (cf. the passage in Adolf Hilgenfeld, *Die Ketzergeschichte des Urchristentums* [Leipzig, 1884], p. 429, n. 737) and by Celsus in his polemical work (see Gillis P. Wetter, "Der

calls himself "the son," [60] and Philo, for whom the hierophant becomes the son of God.[61] Christian mystics such as Eckhart and Tauler, who had no Koran to forbid a belief in God's engendering and being born (Sura 112, 2–3), fully conscious of the extended, or we might say real, meaning of the term, designated themselves sons of God.[62] But the best indication that 'Aṭṭār really means this "son" is provided in the apostolic passage (Rom. 8 : 14) which not only reveals that for the early Christians men in general can become the sons of God (though adopted sons; Christ is the *Monogenes*), but also that this becoming, just as in 'Aṭṭār, is made dependent on the power of the spirit: "For," this passage reads, "as many as are led by the

---

Sohn Gottes," *Forschungen zur Religion und Literatur der Alten und Neuen Testaments,* n.s. IX [Göttingen, 1916], 4ff.; cf. Reitzenstein, p. 168). According to Wetter (pp. 7, 146), παῖς Θεοῦ and υἱὸς Θεοῦ are "not distinguished in meaning." The "sons of God" (*bagpūhr*) of the Manichaeans, on the other hand, are individually specified. See A. V. Williams Jackson, "Studies in Manichaeism," *JAOS,* XLIII (1923), 19; Ernst Wald-schmidt and Wolfgang Lentz, "Die Stellung Jesu im Manichäismus," *Abhandlungen der Preussischen Akademie der Wissenschaften* (Berlin, 1926), Phil.-hist. Kl. IV, 48, 60 (*yazdan pūhr*).

60 Dieterich, *Mithrasliturgie,* 6, 2. Reitzenstein, pp. 33, 131ff.

61 Joseph Pascher, 'Η Βασιλικὴ ὁδός. *Der Königsweg zur Wiedergeburt und Vergottung bei Philon von Alexandreia* (Studien zur Geschichte und Kultur des Altertums, XVII, 3–4 [Paderborn, 1931]), pp. 26–36.

62 Dieterich, p. 140: " 'The Father bears His son without ceasing,' says Eckhart (ed. Pfeiffer, p. 205), 'and I say more: he does not bear me alone as his son, but more: he bears me as himself, and himself as me, and me as his essence and his nature.' The image positively turns a somersault in the headlong rush to represent the complete union with God. Tauler says (in C. Schmidt, p. 127): 'And as the Son is born from the Father, so this man is born in the Son of the Father and with the Son flows back into the Father and becomes one with Him.' Another such passage occurs in *Das Buch der geistlichen Armut* (quoted from A. Ritschl, *Zeitschrift für Kirchengeschichte,* IV, 358), a work originating in related German mystical circles: 'When the soul comes to the point where the eternal word is born in it, it is a son of God, not a natural son like the Word in the godhead, but rather a son by grace, and it says: Father, transfigure thy Son with thy clarity.' " To these passages we may add a quotation from the *Cherubinischer Wandersmann* of Angelus Silesius:

I also am God's son. I sit beside His knee.
His Spirit, Flesh, and Blood are known to Him in me.

My Christian, dost thou ask where God hath set His throne?
Is it in thee, where He gives birth to thee, His son?

Man, be thou born of God! for standeth by His throne
His own begotten Son—and other standeth none.

When God for the first time unto His Son gave birth,
His choice was me and thee for childbed upon earth.

O dignity most great! God springeth from His Throne
And setteth me thereon in His beloved Son.

Spirit of God, they are the sons of God" (υἱοὶ Θεοῦ).[63] In this appellative sense, then, the term "son of God" can be applied to the mystic, in order to indicate also in our, Christian, language the unity and at the same time the diversity of the "one" and "eternal king." [64]

Thus 'Aṭṭār's image of man accords with the ancient esoteric conception according to which man contains a divine self, into which he must work and live himself in order to be redeemed. Among other religions, we come perhaps closest to this conception in Manichaeism, where it is likewise possible for man (I quote Schaeder), "by concentrating his spiritual forces and by contemplating the divine nature of his innermost self, to find the homeward path, redemption." [65] The Manichaeans even go so far as expressly to identify Jesus Christ (whom they also recognize as the Son of God) with the "light-self," the "living," the "perfect," "uppermost self" (grēv) of man.[66] It is not our intention to discuss in any detail the difference between 'Aṭṭār's eternal man and the original man found in the systems of Mazdaism, the cabala, and the Clementines [67]—it might, for example, be exemplified in the relation between the thinking of the Ṣūfīs and the Shiites—but 'Aṭṭār himself (in a later work) reminds us of this original man: by way of explaining his own "I am God," he has God justify His demand that the angels worship Adam by saying that Adam is no one other than He (God) Himself. God says this to the devil, who, as we have already noted,[68] was, according

---

63 Here we may also mention Christ's words from the Oxyrhynchus fragment: "The [kingdom of] heaven is within you, and [whoever] shall know [himself] shall find it . . . know yourselves, and [ye shall be aware that ye are sons] of the Father" (Bernard P. Grenfell and Arthur S. Hunt, *New Sayings of Jesus and Fragment of a Lost Gospel from Oxyrhynchus* [Oxford, 1904], p. 15).

64 "The transference of the father-concept to God, sharply rejected in the Koran, occurs repeatedly in the [Mohammedan] interpretation of dreams: 'If someone dreams that he is fleeing from God while God pursues him, this means, if the dreamer [still] has his father [alive], that he will be unchildlike and recalcitrant towards him.' 'If someone dreams that God is angry with him, this points to the anger of his parents.' 'He who sees God in a dream in the form of a [*sic*] father, who is friendly to him and blesses him, will suffer harm in his body, for the sake of which God will increase his reward' " (P. Schwarz, "Traum und Traumdeutung nach 'Abdalganī an-Nābulusī," *ZDMG*, LXVI [1913], 489, n. 1). Additional and related material in Louis Massignon, "Le Hadīth al-Ruqya musulman," *Revue de l'histoire des religions*, CXXIII (Paris, 1941), 58–60.

65 Schaeder, "Die islamische Lehre," p. 207.

66 Waldschmidt-Lentz, pp. 65, 72–77, 94, 115ff.

67 Louis Ginzberg in *The Jewish Encyclopedia* (New York and London, 1901–06), I, s.v. Adam Kadmon; Israel Friedländer, "The Heterodoxies of the Shiites," *JAOS*, XXIX (1908), 104.

68 On the Christian origin of this story from the *Vita Adae et Evae*, see J. Windrow Sweetman, *Islam and Christian Theology* (London and Redhill, 1945), I, 9–10.

to the Koran, the only one of the angels who declined to fall down before Adam (Sura 15, 26–35). 'Aṭṭār's words are:

> God—be He exalted—spake: O thou accursed one,
>> Who hast turned off from God's path,
>> Who hast not rightly seen Adam and his spiritual reality [ma'nē],[69]
>> His pure spirit is a mercy to the nations! [Sura 21, 107]
> He is I, and I am he, thou heedless one,
>> Blind and deaf to the spiritual reality.
> Hadst thou eyes for Us,
>> Thou wouldst see our Adam like Us!
> But since thou dost not see man truly,
>> We have named thee "accursed devil." [70]

III

This adequately characterizes 'Aṭṭār's image of man, but I must still confute certain objections that might arise through a closer reading of the *Ilāhīnāma*. 'Aṭṭār admonishes (see p. 278) man to die to himself (197, 15). This in itself might incline us to wonder if the conception of an eternal man can be basic in his work, and what might occasion even greater doubt is the recurrent idea that it is man who must be renounced. In such passages, man is hardly an image of permanence; he is the source of all evil. Man should not come to himself but seek precisely to escape from himself, for with his egoism *he* is the origin of his error in pursuing outward goals and stubborn delusions.

> When thou thinkest of thine error,
>> May it be granted that thou thinkest of Him [God],
> But as long as thou art confronted with the obstacle of selfness,
>> Thy thinking of Him is only thinking of thyself. [123, 3–4]

---

69 Since *ma'nā* in 'Aṭṭār rhymes more or less with *dunyā* (*Manṭiq*, v. 2053; *Asrārnāma*, 148a, margin, etc.), the writing of the word as *ma'nē* might be regarded as false or at least questionable. For though today it is usually pronounced as *ma'nī, dunyā* remains the current pronunciation. But in the *Asrārnāma* (148b, margin, 3–4), *dunyā* rhymes with *nē*, "not," and must therefore be read as *dunyē*. In rhyme with *dunyē* (written with *yā'*) we can of course also read *ma'nē*; cf. also *ta'ālē* (*Ilāhīnāma*, 114, 9; 163, 11; 291, 17; 301, 17; 302, 8). On the other hand, *ma'nā* (written with alif) also rhymes to some extent with *istighnā* (*Manṭiq*, v. 3558), which justifies the pronunciation *ma'nā*. Thus we have both possibilities, in 'Aṭṭār as today. In 'Aṭṭār's *Dīwān*, 173, 4232–41, we should probably read *-ē* throughout.

70 *Bīsarnāma* (lith. Teheran, 1352/1933), 10 ult. – 11, 4. Cf. Dāya, *Mirṣād*, 183, 4 from foot – 184, 1.

Wishest thou to go forward at every step,
  Then, for good or evil, renounce thyself.
If thou dost not renounce thyself and the world,
  Thou wilt do so when death comes, even if thou dost not expressly
    state as much.
Since sleeping and eating do not endure eternally,
  What wilt thou do when death comes? [143, 19 – 144, 2]

Whether I am near or far,
  As long as I am I, I am forsaken. [181, 2]

Move away from thyself,
  That this thing may lodge well in thy mind;
For as long as thou comest everlastingly to thyself,
  The beloved will slip away from thee. [193, 1–2]

As long as thou hast thine own existence before thee,
  Thou shalt be eternally haunted.
When thy heart has had enough of the foulness of polytheism,
  It will take up lodging in the selfless. [194, 16–17]

But as long as thou art thou, imprisoned in thyself,
  Thou wilt remain wounded at heart.
Thou must through love become without thyself,
  Free from thyself and blind to thine own commission and omis-
    sion;
For as long as thou watchest thine own doings,
  Thou wilt bear the [Christian] *zonarion*, although thou wearest
    the patchwork coat [of the Ṣūfīs]. [221, 5–7]

Even if thou performest complete ablutions a hundred times a day,
  As long as thou art with thyself, thou wilt still be ritually un-
    clean. [222, 6]

Every moment thou must die a hundred times,
  If thou wouldst travel through this valley. [236, 7]

I need one who has suffered,
  Who has in one day a hundred times practiced mourning over
    himself,
Who through God has come alive and died unto himself,
  Who is not numbered among the survivors, but has anticipated
    death. [240, 1–2]

Thou must depart from thyself,
One cannot be both loving and sound of body. [298, 3]

Thy misfortune is not *before* thee,
Thy soul creates all evil out of itself.
And what happens to thee through thy soul,
Thou hast performed with thine own hand. That is clear. [143, 10–11]

Seekest thou understanding of thyself,
Die to thyself! Regard thyself no longer!
If the puppets [pupils] of thine eyes be small,
It is because they died to themselves before thou didst so; [71]
Therefore they never saw their own face even in the slightest,
Because, ever since they were, they chose their own death.
They can never see themselves,[72]
Because the dead can never see themselves.
Wouldst thou live in death,
Thou must recognize life's delusion as death.[73]

Wouldst thou find the eternal image,
It can be found only in absence of image.
Wouldst thou become like us, take heart! Become like us [i.e., the goblet of Jam]! [74]
Renounce thyself! Become unself!
Thy village requires a fortress of unselfness,
Else it will suffer blows from all sides. [185, 13 – 186, 1]

---

71 Khwājūy-i Kirmānī, *Rawḍat*, 32, 8:
   Become the pupil of thine eye and see thyself not!
   Open thine eyes well and see not what is evil!

72 In 'Aṭṭār *az 'iz(z)* with negative verb seems to intensify the negation (189, 4; 205, 13; 206, 16; 314, 9); and the same is probably true of *az 'izzē* (*Manṭiq*, v. 1910). Similarly, *zi bun* in Firdawsī. Other instances of *'izz* in the *Ilāhīnāma* (12, 10; 13, 5; 135, 3; 239, 13; 241, 9; 264, 7; 315, 9; 329, 3).

73 I cannot judge Paul Tedesco's attempt ("*a* = Stämme und *aya* = Stämme im Iranischen," *Zeitschrift für Indologie und Iranistik*, II [Leipzig, 1923], 306–08) to construe such forms as *dānī* as imperatives of the causative form in = *aya* > *-e*, upon which the present is historically based; but it should be remarked that such forms are preceded by the negation *na*, not *ma*; *Ilāhīnāma*, 64, 15; 208, 12; *Manṭiq* (in the Indian lith.), 33, 8 from foot (= v. 703): "How many seas, how many lands are on the way! Do not believe [*tu na pindārī*] that it is a short way," etc. An exception is the *ma-bādhī* (= *ma-bāsh*) in Firdawsī; but *bādhī* itself is assuredly a secondary formation. *Bādhī* (= *bāsh*) occurs in 'Aṭṭār.

74 The dividing line in 185, 12, should be deleted. The dividing line in 186, 8, belongs to 186, 7.

Of him who has drowned, there is no trace,
    And those who sit on the shore have no report of him.
Thou too art caught utterly in the whirlpool,
    Knowest thou not, thou art immersed in sleep;
For in relation to Us, thou art a block of ice in the sun
    Or a handful of clay on the water.
Forasmuch as thou liest shipless upon the sea,
    The sea tells thee what thou art. [186, 8–11]

The misfortune that hath fallen on my shoulders,
    I know that it came from myself. [370, 17]

I lay entire in the blood of my spirit [jān],
    For since I was, I have been my own grief. [371, 17]

I brought great ruin upon myself.
    Mi Deus, serva me ex memetipso, mi Deus! [75]
If thou freest me, free me from myself;
    For whatever thou willest is in thy power.
Hold me not back with myself, but make me free of myself!
    I am sated with myself, prepared to renounce this self. [383,
        10–12] [76]

75 [The author of the lecture uses Latin where Arabic occurs in the original Persian text.
    — Tʀ.]
76 From the abundance of parallel texts I cite only the following: *Asrārnāma* (MS.
Tschudi), 143a, margin, 1–4:
    Our permanence is our misfortune;
        For our joy lies in our ceasing to be.
    Whether we have joy or sorrow, it all comes from ourselves;
        For all that comes to us comes always from ourselves alone.
143a, 9–12:
    Doubtless our [own] being [hastī] is our worthlessness [pastī];
        For we have our nonbeing from our being.
    If our being were our unbeing,
        It would be safe from so much nonbeing.
143a, 27–32:
    All thy salvation is thy nonbeing.
    In nonbeing lies thy peace.
    What greater joy dost thou know and what pleasure
        Than to cease to be and become free from thyself?
    Once thou wert not. Cease again from thy being!
        For if thou ceasest from thyself, thou wilt be safe.
146b, 1–6:
    As long as thou comest not out of thy skin,
        Thou wilt achieve no safety at the court of the Friend [= God].
    As long as the end of a hair remains of thee,
        Be certain, safety is not possible.

Such passages, declaring man to be worthless, deserving of destruction, vastly overshadow those in which man is esteemed as the highest treasure:

> Gaze not scornfully at thyself!
>> Recognize that both words [here and hereafter] are nothing other than body and spirit [*jān*]!
> Thou thyself art everything! Why art thou so afraid of hell's fire?
>> Thine own heart is God's throne, thine own bosom his footstool.
> [148, 15–16]

> If thou learnest the secret [*sirr*] that lies in the depths of thy pure spirit,
>> It is to be feared thou wilt die.
> Who knows what this miraculous secret is,
>> Or what is the cause of so wondrous a secret?
> If so much grief has come to thee, it has not been to tell thee
>> That thou art nothing, nothing,
> But all this has happened
>> To make thee aware of thyself.
> Since thou wert [God's] beloved, He
>> Hid thee from thine own eyes and from the people.
> He set up thousands of screens, the causes,
>> And behind them all He set up His bed.
> But now thou canst lie down to sleep with the beloved
>> In the bed behind the screens without a third. What bliss!

> Here the criterion of safety is assuredly this.
> This is the ascension night. *Relinque te ipsum.*

156a, 11–12:

> We ourselves are the bane of the days of our life,
> We ourselves are the screen before ourselves.

156b, 15 from foot:

> Thou thyself art the misfortune, thou thyself. Get thee away!

Cf. Mawlānā, *Fīhi*, 236, 5 from foot ff.: "As long as thou forgettest not thyself, thou art not conscious of Us [= God]."

Awḥadī: *Jām-i Jam*, 171 ult.:

> As long as thou art aware of thine own existence,
> Thou inclinest toward idolatry of thyself.

Further, Pīr Jamāl (d. 879/1474–75), in R. A. Nicholson, "Pīr Jamāl" (in *A Volume of Oriental Studies Presented to Edward G. Browne* [Cambridge, 1922]), 370, 15–20:

> The wall before thee art thou thyself. Get thee away at once!
> This means: ceasing to be is the permanence of the dervish.
> If dervishhood depended on the wool [of the garment] and the felt [of the hat],
> Goats and sheep would be the leaders of the Ṣūfīs.

Since the beloved is quite invisible,
   It [the secret] is best said to be the *place* of the beloved;
For to disclose the beloved is never seemly,
   He must above all [77] be kept hidden. [152, 3–11]

If for a time thou bringest thine head down to thyself,
   Thou wilt find a token of the thing thou hast been speaking of
   [the elixir]. [359, 15]

But a closer examination of the injunction, or the decision to die, will reveal the paradox involved in it. In the passages we have cited, man does not die, but only "dies to himself"—that is, he breaks off a certain relation to himself. Where man himself is enjoined to die (236, 7), it is "a hundred times a day," and "in order to travel through this valley unharmed"; that is to say, he is actually expected to survive. Moreover, man "lives without himself." [78] The self that is to die is identical with the ego of which, ʿAṭṭār declares in another passage, man should divest himself, but it is something other than the subject that is called away from it.

Since self-renunciation in a purely philosophical sense is impossible, it becomes necessary to divide man into a mortal and an immortal being. Since a subject can never act upon itself, but only upon an object, which, being an object, must be different from the subject, even if it is expressed by means of a reflexive pronoun, the self that is to die or be renounced can never be the same as the self that undertakes the act of destruction or renunciation, but must rather be regarded as a state of the latter, which it can either assume or relinquish. The self (or whatever else one wishes to call it) thus reveals itself to be a homonym for two basically different things, for a pseudo subject, which should properly be called a condition, and a subject, which permits man a survival transcending that condition.

This distinction in itself suffices to confute those who believe that the above-mentioned passages vitiate the conception of the "eternal king," or Eternal Man. Since this supposed contradiction might be sought not only in the *Ilāhīnāma*, but also in others of ʿAṭṭār's books, it may be worth our while to examine a few relevant passages with this in mind. In doing so, let us disregard the general content of the passages in question, in order to concentrate upon our particular problem.

---

77 Here again, presumably, *az ʿiz(z)* is only an intensification of the "must."
78 *Muṣībatnāma*, 440, 2 from foot.

At first man finds himself entirely in that state which he should transcend.

> Why dost thou inquire after the story of Alexander's wall? [79]
> Thou art thyself thy wall. Pass beyond thyself!
> Thine own existence lies before thee like a wall,
>   And thou art imprisoned in that wall as in thyself.
> Thou thyself art Gog and Magog in thy wall;
>   For thy necklace is a wall as it was to Og.[80]
> If thou takest from thyself this great curtain,
>   As Og, son of 'Unuq,[81] the necklace,
> If thou freest thy neck,
>   Thou wilt be free of all thy woe.
> If not, thou wilt see hundreds of thousands of curtains,
>   And in each curtain thy dead spirit [*jān*]. [200, 11–16]

> God hath made thee for Himself,
>   Hath purchased thine [instinctive] soul and possessions.
> But thou hast given thyself up to thine own existence,
>   And hast grown greater in self-conceit than Satan. [291, 6–7]

But man can renounce the mode of life to which he inclines and wrest himself away from his ego through a movement from within.

> With stubbornness thou art stubborn and drunk.
> Emerge from thyself, be of God, and thou art free! [316, 6]

> How canst thou attain to God, as long as thou art with thyself?
> But when thou art without thyself, thou wilt find the way.
> [364, 5]

Man is admonished to return to himself only when he is able to accept sorrow with joy, or transform it into joy.

> Become so that in the hour of thy death
> Thy body will already have been abandoned and thy spirit [*jān*]
> gone forth without thee!

79 Which Alexander built in order to keep the nations Gog and Magog out of the civilized world.

80 When the giant Og wished to shatter the camp of the Israelites with an immense cliff that he had broken off the mountain, the hoopoe and other birds made a hole in the rock and it fell round his neck like a necklace; thereupon Moses brought him down with one blow (*EI*, s.v. 'Ūdj; Grünbaum, *Neue Beiträge*, pp. 180–82).

81 'Unuq (properly, "neck") was the mother of Og; Ibshīhī, *Al-mustaṭraf* (Cairo, 1935), 2, 128, 2 from foot (tr. G. Rat, *Al-Mostatraf* [Paris, 1899–1902], II, 316). 'Aṭṭār of course uses the word by way of allusion to the story of Og and the necklace of rocks.

If thou hast a death before the hour of thy death,
Needest thou fear eternal death?
A light in the desert is thy spirit [jān],
Hidden by the niche of thy flesh.
If the niche falls, the desert
Will become eternally radiant like the sun.
Innumerable are the wonders in thine heart.
If thou becomest aware of it, there is much to be done.
At every moment advance anew in religion!
Die to thyself and return again and again to thyself!
For each time thou art without thyself and in thy self,
Thou puttest a whole world of evil behind thee,
So that, on the road of the mystery, thou exchangest [82]
Every evil thing for a whole world of beauty.
Everything that He [God] giveth thee, let it rejoice thy heart,
And if He giveth it not, nevertheless remain happy and free!
Do not give back what cometh thence,
And if it displease thee, utter no word! [208, 3–12]

Thus man can become his own counterpart and attain to a perspective in which his misfortune appears to him a blessing. This division of man into a twofold being is apparent when the king summons the son to renounce himself, but in the same breath admonishes him to new fullness.

Thou must pass entirely beyond,
Increasing always in thyself. [170, 5]

And there are further indications in 'Aṭṭār that the fullness of the new life that man gains through his victory over his self is far greater than the renunciation of so many of the usual props of existence would lead us to suppose.

Since thou knowest that inexorably thou wilt die,
Why is thy death not the object of thy care? [83]
Thou art in sap no longer than the leaves. Arise!
Tremble, turn yellow, and decay! [84]
If thou fallest in this manner, [85]
Glory will open to thee.

82 On this passage, cf. 172, 17; 173, 12.
83 Barg, "care"; bī-barg, "without care" (97, 14); bā-barg, "object of care" (245, 2).
84 The same image—that one should fall like the leaves—occurs in the story of the parrot in Asrārnāma, 131b.
85 Scarcely "to fall at this door," which at most could be understood as a reference to the poor beggar who falls down at the door of a house and waits for someone to come out.

If thou fallest thus faded,
  Thou wilt arise and become a sun. [170, 6–9]

There was one who asked Shiblī: [86] Who
  Guided thee first to the court [of God]?
I saw, he said, a dog at the edge of the water,
  Which was thirsty beyond endurance.
When he saw his own face gleaming in the water,
  He thought he had another dog before his eyes.[87]
For fear of the other dog, he drank not,
  But leaped hastily from the water's brink.
But for thirst his heart could no longer rest,
  And his waiting exceeded all measure,
He cast himself suddenly into the water,
  Whereupon that other dog vanished.
Once he had departed from his own eyes—
  He himself was that screen—the other vanished.[88]
When this lesson was ended,[89]
  It became clear to me that I was the screen before myself.
I turned away from myself. In this I succeeded.
  And thus a dog was my first guide on the path [of mysticism].
Thou too, remove thyself from thine eyes!
  Thou art the screen before thyself. Remove thyself!

---

86 Mystic, d. 334/945.
87 It seems to me that the most suitable meaning for the difficult *mu'ayyan* is the one to be found in 84, 7:

  He spoke and death became visible [*mu'ayyan*] in him.
  Pitifully his pure spirit struggled from his body.

Similarly, 307, 13:

  In consequence of the many amber-scented candles
  Every single hair was *visible* that night.

Here we evidently have a confusion of *mu'āyan* and *mu'ayyan*, of frequent occurrence. Another meaning of the word that does not occur in the dictionary is given by Mawlānā, *Fīhi*, 176, 5 from foot ff. The import of this passage is that God is too close to us to be seen, just as the intellect at work in an action is not visible, but only the action itself. This is then compared with the warmth of a bath, in which the action of the fire is discernible but not the fire itself. "But if we now go out and view the fire directly [*ātash mu'ayyan bīnad*], we know that we have become warm through the fire." Thus when we leave this world, we see directly the essence of reason (*mu'ayyan dhāt-i 'aql-rā bīnī*) and know that all the intelligence we had was nothing other than an emanation of reason (*tābish-i 'aql būda ast mu'ayyan*). Here *mu'ayyan* seems to stand for *bi-'aynihī*.
88 Or: "He himself was that screen that now was lifted." It is necessary to make a separation between *ān* and *ḥijāb*: "He himself was that [other dog]—so the screen vanished."
89 *Bar-khāst = az miyān bar-khāst*. Yet the translation "appeared" would also be possible. In place of "lesson," *Manṭiq*, v. 3767, offers the possibility of "review," "demonstration."

If one little hair of selfness remains,
A heavy fetter is laid upon thy feet.
Better were it for thee, O frail man,
To have been carried straight from cradle to coffin.
Moses received from God his exalted rank,
Because he found his way straight from cradle to coffin [the ark
of bulrushes in the Nile].
If thou needest [God's] presence forever,
Return no more to thyself! Let this wine [God's presence] suffice
thee! [90]

Return not to thyself! Without thyself, come away from thyself!
For all selflessness is "light above light." [91] [195, 16 – 196, 13]

To the mystic who has died to himself, a new world of light is opened.
He himself celebrates his resurrection as light.[92] These last verses, it is true,
refer only in a general way to the closer relation into which man enters with
God, but in view of the promised light, there can be no doubt that even
here the meaning is that man becomes God. This is clearly stated in the
following verses:

The silver-breasted Ayāz [93] lay in deep sleep,
Resting for a time his heart and eyes.
Then to his pillow stepped Maḥmūd, warrior of the faith,
His heart was still governed by glory.
From his deep slumber he did not wake him,
But pressed a thousand kisses on both his cheeks.
And when the king was done with kissing,
He rubbed his feet until dawn.[94]

90 *Tamām*, as in 106, 11; I have already referred to this *tamām*, above, p. 278, n. 37. Another meaning for *tamma* occurs in *Ilāhīnāma*, 66, 1: *mātam* < *mā tamma* = "what
was left over" (Benjamin as the eleventh brother remained alone at a table), a form
that ʿAṭṭār uses also in *mā-taqaddam, mā-ḥaḍar, mā-jarā*, etc. A contrary development
was undergone by *sāʾir*, which from the meaning "the remaining" (*bāqī*) assumed the
meaning of "all" (*jamīʿ*); often in *The Thousand and One Nights*, but condemned by
Ḥarīrī (d. 516/1122), *Durrat al-ghawwāṣ*, ed. H. Thorbecke (Leipzig, 1871), text p. 3,
l. 3 from foot.
91 Sura 24, 35.
92 Cf. *Asrārnāma*, 132a, 13–14:
But if whilst thou art awake, thou emergest from thyself,
Thou wilt in sleeping be *light* in thy selflessness.
There are numerous examples and parallels of this doctrine of light in the Orient before
ʿAṭṭār.
93 Beloved of King Maḥmūd of Ghazna (ruled 389–421/999–1030).
94 This often-mentioned labor of love (*maghmazī kardan*) is found represented in Indian

When at last Ayāz awoke from his deep sleep,
  In shame he darted up like a fire before the king.
When the king saw him, he spake: O thou, may thy beauty increase,
  Now that thou hast returned, I shall depart.[95]
When thou wert without thyself,
  Thou wert exalted above all description that I could give of thee.
While I beheld thee, O charming one,
  Thou wert not here, I was in thy place.
But now that thou hast returned to thyself, the beloved is lost.
  Now that thy will is with thee, that which was willed is gone.
Be not, O friend, then thou wilt be beloved;
  For while thou art thyself, thou art thwarted by thyself.
Transcend thyself; for without thyself thou art all We.
  Since thou art happier without thyself, why art thou with thyself?
When thou art not, then thou art in reality.
  When thou aimest at nothing, then thou art estimable.
As long as thou art with thyself, no one speaks of thee.
  But as soon as thou art without thyself, all seek after thee.
  [193, 4 – 194, 2]

If thou art accepted, count it not as booty!
If thou art rejected, never take flight! [96]
For only if never for a moment well-being beguiles thee
  Will persecutions fail to grieve thee.
Beyond all these varicolored colors,[97]
  Thou wilt emerge in a very different color.
If this color falls upon thy rags,
  Both worlds will become like amber with thy fragrance.
If thou attainest to this color, unique one,
  Thou wilt need nothing more forever.
Since all things will then grow out of *thee*,
  How shouldst thou know desire?

---

miniatures; Ernst Kühnel, *Miniaturmalerei im islamischen Orient* (Berlin, 1923), pl. 104; Heinrich Glück and Ernst Diez, *Die Kunst des Islams* (Berlin, 1925), pl. 39.

95 Preterit as in 311, 2: "I too went away."

96 Here *ghanīmat shumurdan* does not yet have the weakened meaning of "seize the opportunity" (*istighnām al-furṣa*), but still evokes the full military image, as indicated by the contrary *hazīmat shudan*, "to be put to flight"; a similar opposition of *ghanīmat* and *hazīmat* in *Manṭiq*, v. 3123.

97 The reference is to the patchwork coat worn by the Ṣūfīs. The varied colors refer also to the varied inclinations and disinclinations felt by man for the vicissitudes of fate. In *Asrārnāma*, 156a, the many colors of which man must divest himself signify the human passions and weaknesses: greed, pride, arrogance, lust, coquetry, lies, avarice, anger, indifference.

Since thou wilt then be forever thou, without pretense,
    Thou wilt have all things forever.
Since thou wilt then be forever extinguished in the godly,
    Men will ask after thee, but thou wilt ask no longer. [360, 4–11]

We might be inclined to interpret the last verse, in which man, after transcending himself, is extinguished in the godly, as a denial of man's eternity. Granted—one might argue—that man does not necessarily cease to be when he casts off the individual life that circles round the idea of self; nevertheless, the wording of the last verse seems to indicate that the surviving subject that is summoned away from the self must someday meet its end. Can this self cease to be? Since bliss would be no bliss if it were not experienced, the subject of the experience must continue to exist if it is to find bliss in dissolution in God. God and eternity would have no relevance for man if his individuality ceased before they could enter into his existence. Thus we must interpret man's dissolution in God, not as a cessation of man's existence, but as a metamorphosis that occurs simultaneously with the renunciation of the self and as a necessary consequence of this act—that is, as a transference of man into a state in which he is no longer a second beside God, but is himself this supreme being.[98] This is confirmed in the second

98 *Asrārnāma*, 134a, 15–16:
    Thou wilt become a stayer if thou becomest a vanisher.
    Thou becomest all, if thou remainest without thyself.
  143a, 16:
    In ceasing to be lies permanence.
Manṭiq, v. 3730:
    I know not if Thou art I or I am Thou.
    I am extinguished in Thee, and lost in duality.
Of the numerous examples of this paradox from other poets, cf. Khwājūy-i Kirmānī, *Rawḍat*, 38, 6:
    Sink into cessation of being and strive for permanence!
    Leave thyself and strive toward God!
  45, 11:
    Take thy hand from the cup and be drunk!
    Be extinguished by nonbeing and so achieve being!
  58, 4:
    The nonbeing of those who have lost themselves is being.
    The being of those whose heart is awake is drunkenness.
  79, 5 from foot:
    Leave the worship of wine and be drunk!
    Leave being and gain being!

FR I T Z M E I E R

half of the verse, for if man were by this time completely extinguished, he could not be sought after. It is confirmed also by the parallel passage (193, 14): "Without thyself thou art all We," and a number of other variations on the "I am God" theme, all of which exclude the possibility of a cessation of man. That man must dissolve himself in God as the earth-clod in water (as in 186, 13-18) must not be taken as an indication of man's finite nature; it indicates merely that the subject has changed his predicate. Thus 'Aṭṭār says:

> If then thou hast freedom from thyself,
> Then thy selflessness is Godness.[99]
> When one has vanished, that is cessation of being.
> When there has been cessation of being, behold, from it springs survival.[100]

And in a later work, he writes:

> When thou hast died to thyself, thou wilt endure forever,
> Thou wilt endure in the eternal essence.
> If thou diest to thyself, thou becomest eternal,
> Through the light of God's essence thou wilt become a sun.[101]

> Die to thyself, in order that thou mayst live;
> For when thou art dead, thou wilt be the spirit of the spirit [God].[102]

> If then beyond a doubt I remain no longer, I shall be He [God].[103]

> Thy survival is thy last extinguishing.
> Thou wilt become God. That is the ultimate.
> Thou wilt be extinguished at the end of things.
> Thou wilt be God at the end of things.
> When this aspect vanishes entirely,
> Thou wilt attain to full, eternal life.[104]

> Extinguish me, that I may be Thou! [105]

99 Manṭiq (MS. Tschudi), 249a, 11 (var. lith. Lucknow, 197, 3). This line is missing in Garcin de Tassy's edn. (before v. 3942), which has a considerable gap in this place.
100 Manṭiq, v. 3942.
101 Haylājnāma, 185, 4 from foot ff. Cf. ibid., 162ff.; 234, 6 from foot ff.
102 Ibid., 259, 6 from foot. Jān-i jān = God; Ilāhīnāma, 6, 1; 7, 3 (transformed to Mohammed, 12, 14). See 'Azīz-i Nasafī, in my Vom Wesen, p. 44, n. 51 ("soul of the soul"). The term is already Hellenistic; Dieterich, Mithrasliturgie, Text 2, 11-12 (πνεῦμα πνεύματος).
103 Haylājnāma, 60, 5 from foot.
104 Ibid., 239, 9-12.
105 Ibid., 305, 11; 328, 6: "Thy Thouness is here beyond doubt He." The fact that in

According to this conception, one might almost be tempted to define God as the reflexive predicate of the absolute subject; for the mystic becomes God only when he has moved so far away from himself that only pure existence remains to him. But this line of thought would lead us away from ʿAṭṭār to a discussion of the philosophical content of his mysticism; and perhaps I have already gone too far in this direction by seeking to confirm ʿAṭṭār's belief in the eternity of man. However, it strikes me that this knowledge is essential to the reader who in other passages will find the movement of the mystic from self to God represented as a movement of man to himself. We have already encountered this conception in the story of the Sarpātak (p. 276), where it is said that the mystic seeks only himself (76, 13; 77, 6). But it occurs in other passages, as for example: "Thou wilt be thine own essence, but in the way that thou knowest." [106] In this conception, God is a secret mode of man's being, and the mystic, in order to attain to Him, moves from a peripheral mode of being, in which he is imprisoned in the temporal, back into himself; from a concretistic misunderstanding of himself to a truer self. The supreme mode of being is present in his innermost depths; he can enter into it through a movement to himself. "Since thou art sacrosanct, thou canst become eternal" [107] (362, 12). Hence it can be said that what the mystic seeks is not lost and never can be lost.

> And so one spake to a sifter of dust [gold-seeker]: [108]
>> There is one thing that astonishes me;
> That thou, poor man,[109] shouldst seek after that which is unlost.
> That which is not lost thou wilt never find.
> But, said the sifter of dust, there is another thing yet more astonishing:
>> It is when I am powerless to find something that has not been lost

---

Manichaeism the pious man also "becomes a god" after death is related in content to our passage, but there is surely no literary connection; Ibn an-Nadīm, Al-fihrist, ed. G. Flügel (Leipzig, 1871–72), 1, 335, 17; A. V. Williams Jackson, "The Doctrine of the Bolos in Manichaean Eschatology," *JAOS*, LVIII (1938), 232. Also in the Pythagorean-Orphic view the mystes becomes a god after death; Dieterich, *Nekyia*, 85/88. Similarly in Philo; cf. Pascher, p. 251.

106 *Haylājnāma*, 332, 4.
107 Cf. *Asrārnāma*, 130b, 16 from foot:
> At the time of the death struggle thou wert guilty of an oversight:
>> Thou lettest a bird [the bird of the soul] that thou hadst not caught go free.
108 As in *Manṭiq*, v. 3301; Awḥadī, *Jām-i Jam*, 62 ult.
109 *ʿAjiz*, as in 121, 17.

That I am most deeply grieved. That is far more
Astonishing than what thou saidst before.—
One can neither find it nor lose it.
Neither silence nor elucidation is the right way.[110]
By this it is meant: thou shouldst not be at all,
Thou shouldst be neither this nor that, but both.[111] [374, 2–7]

Whether we conceive the mystical path as a dissolution of man in God,
"a merging of I-ness into He-ness," [112] or as the apparent opposite, a search
for oneself, in either case that self which represents nothing other than the
soul's *status quo* must be abandoned; only then is eternal being manifested.
The incompatibility of the two modes of life is illustrated by the story of
Maḥmūd and Ayāz (p. 297). The mystical life is a process of becoming,
whose end product must necessarily be different from its beginning and
cannot exist simultaneously with it. Man must first bring forth this hidden
mode of being out of himself before he can say: "I am God." Only by re-
nouncing his self (the subject of self-love and the will to self-preservation)
and transforming himself (231, 6–15) can he break through encirclement by
the outward world (304 ff.) and overthrow his selfish aims (370, 7) like
idols.[113] It is a moving passage in which 'Aṭṭār represents his own poetic
gift as an idol that he has not yet overthrown (369, 10; 370, 12 ff.).[114] Through
the example of Abraham, who, tempted by Gabriel, first sacrifices all his
sheep in order to hear him utter God's ineffable name, then in obedience to
God consents to sacrifice his son, and finally, when Nimrod threatens him

110 *Rāh*, "the right way," "the right," is already known from Firdawsī and is frequent
in 'Aṭṭār: *Ilāhīnāma*, 36, 12; 137, 5; 163, 13; 237, 2; *Manṭiq*, vv. 130, 660 ("Further
[*bēsh*] to be without a king is not right"), 1692 (*rāh dīdan*, "to regard as right");
Muṣībatnāma, 182, 4, etc. To be distinguished from *ba . . . rāh nēst* = Arab. *lā sabīla
ilā!*
111 *Muṣībatnāma*, 435, 4:
    What thou hast lost, if thou hast lost it,
      Is in thyself; thou thyself art standing before it.
112 *Muṣībatnāma*, 59, 4 from foot.
113 'Aṭṭār repeatedly attacks this type of idolatry, elsewhere as well. *Haylājnāma*, 68,
    2 from foot:
    All on the journey of their own being are idolaters,
      They are in reality idolaters who worship themselves.
114 The idea that toward the end of his life 'Aṭṭār ceased to write poetry and merely re-
    corded his mystical experiences and inspirations in quatrains, as Dawlatshāh asserted
    in his *Tadhkirat ush-shu'arā'* (written 892/1487 [lith. Lahore, 1924], 123, 5 from foot),
    is probably derived from these passages in the *Ilāhīnāma* and the foreword to the
    Mukhtārnāma, and in this form is probably not in keeping with the facts.

302

with death by fire, rejects Gabriel's help because God alone must decide his fate (309, 17 – 312, 4), he shows all the stages of egoism that must be transcended if man wishes to find the way from the transitory to perfection (381, 7–8).[115] For, says ʿAṭṭār,[116] "the perfection of the knowing lies in non-being." "Be absolutely not!" he cries out, "this is perfection, this is the finished work." [117]

The *Manṭiq uṭ-ṭayr* (Language of Birds),[118] from which this last quotation is taken, sums up and confirms our view of man's relation to God in ʿAṭṭār; again we find that God is man's opposite only as long as man fails to destroy himself; once he extinguishes his self, the two become one. This work tells how the birds of the earth, yearning for a king, decide to fly, under the leadership of the hoopoe, to the legendary giant bird, Sīmurgh, and to make him their king. But only thirty birds withstand the hardships of the journey, which leads them to total self-annihilation. The thirty birds (*sī murgh*) who are successful in this self-annihilation then discover that in their present state they themselves are the Sīmurgh for which they have been seeking.[119]

> He [man] is not and yet he is. How can that be?
> It lies beyond the conception of reason.[120]

The *Ilāhīnāma*, at any rate, speaks of the transfiguration experienced by the mystic after his self-annihilation. The mystic's death and resurrection are compared to the waning of the moon in the lunar eclipse (*ijtimāʿ* = *conjunctio* [*solis et lunae*]) and its rebirth in the new moon:

> The moon spake: Out of love for the sun
> I shall make the world eternally full of light.
> To which one answered: If that is thy true intent,

115 In the strength of the same attitude Abraham, in *Manṭiq* (vv. 3443–55), is unwilling to give his soul to the angel of death. He expressly states that he paid no heed to Gabriel, who wished to help him.
116 *Asrārnāma*, 113b, 29. Cf. also *Ilāhīnāma*, 71, 16–21.
117 *Manṭiq*, v. 114. Cf. *Ilāhīnāma*, 85, 4–5:
> Everything that thou seest before thee and behind thee,
> Thou must go beyond it and beyond thyself.
> For only when the picture before thee is put aside
> Will the absolute painter grant thee his presence.
118 Written 573/1177–78 (Ritter, "Philologika X," p. 135).
119 Ritter, p. 47, and in his "Das Proömium des Matnawi-i Maulawi," *ZDMG*, XCIII (1939), 175.
120 *Manṭiq*, v. 3936.

Thou must hasten day and night
To reach her, and when thou hast reached her,
Thou must dissolve thyself unseen in her,
Thou must burn under her rays,
And thine own existence must dwindle before her sublime
    existence.
If then thou emergest under her rays,
All men [121] will be purchasers of thy beauty.
All will point at thee with their fingers,
And open their eyes to behold thee. [194, 4–9] [122]

---

121 *Khalqē* (as in 364, 11; 65, 19; 78, 2; 96, 16; 111, 6; 128, 17; 131, 5, etc.) means strictly "the whole of mankind," then "many people" and "everybody," corresponding to the *jihānē*, "a whole world," "many," "everybody," etc., so common in Firdawsī, 'Aṭṭār, and others. Fritz Wolff's statement in *Glossar*, 282b, must therefore be corrected and made more precise. Like *jihānē* and the synonymous '*alamē* (*Ilāhīnāma*, 92, 9/15, etc.), *khalqē* can stand alone or may be followed by a noun indicating what is to be measured, as in Nāṣir-i Khusraw, *Safarnāma* (Berlin, 1341/1922), 125, 6 from foot: *khalqē mardum*. *Jihānē khalq* also occurs (*Ilāhīnāma*, 49, 16; 50, 5; 78, 1; 167, 7; 183, 13; 201, 11; 266, 11; 292, 1); likewise *khalq-i jihānē* (71, 20; 141, 5; 313, 10; '*alamē*, 68, 10). To make the indication of measurement clearer, *pur* can also be added (*Ilāhīnāma*, 154, 6; 343, 4; *Manṭiq*, v. 2654; *Asrārnāma*, 157a, 19 from foot; 168a, 22 from foot): *jihānē pur;* once also *jihān pur*, "the world full" (*Ilāhīnāma*, 245, 3). For the same meaning, also '*alamē pur* (*Ilāhīnāma*, 136, 13; *Manṭiq*, vv. 2455, 4065, 4124, etc.). Also *ṣad jihān*, "a hundred worlds," as an indication of quantity, occurs (*Ilāhīnāma*, 54, 17; 168, 9; *Manṭiq*, v. 3895). Firdawsī, *Shāhnāma*, 7, 1692: *yak jihān!*

122 'Aṭṭār might have taken this metaphor from his contemporary Suhrawardī Maqtūl (d. 587/1191), who used it in his *Kalimāt adh-dhawqiyya;* see Ritter, "Philologika IX," *Der Islam*, XXIV (1937), 279, No. 21. But not only is the time relation between 'Aṭṭār and Suhrawardī unclear; moreover, the circumstances are different. According to what Henry Corbin tells us in *Sohrawardî d'Alep* (p. 37), it is not the dark moon but the full moon that represents the state of union in his metaphor.

Rudolf Bernoulli

Spiritual Development as Reflected in Alchemy and Related Disciplines

1. The Basic Elements of Alchemy

A PARABLE

A number of important alchemical manuscripts are preserved in the Vienna Staatsbibliothek. Among them I once found one entitled "The Garden Where the Task Is Found." The content of this manuscript was not accessible to me. I saw the lovely strokes of the Arabic writing but could not decipher them. Yet "The Garden" seemed strangely familiar. Was this not the "garden of inner speculation," as the cabala calls it? Was it not that same garden where I had been wandering about for years, in search of "the" task, and of ways in which to perform it, that garden to which Arab scholars long ago gave the name "Al Chimiya"?

And now I shall attempt to describe that garden as I found it. Unfortunately, I cannot speak as a scientist. I feel rather like a Cook's guide who is expected to conduct a five-day tour of "all Paris." In an hour's lecture I am hoping to give you a general view of this garden, and more: I am hoping that you will form an opinion of it.

And now let us pass through the garden gate.

If you have expected to find a neat, well-kept garden full of flowers, you will be greatly disappointed. What confusion, what disorder, what a hopeless tangle! Weeds everywhere, the paths scarcely discernible beneath the rank verdure! It is almost impossible to distinguish the plan according to which the garden was laid out. And if we ask ourselves what our task in this garden should be, one of us may say that useful work might be done with the pruning shears; another may suggest that we remove the many rotting and withered plants and roots. The European purist or patriot would like to remove all those plants imported from the East and South, which they regard as alien to the garden and unable to withstand the European climate. And still another would like to pick up a rake, uncover the paths, and thus establish the outline of the garden.

To me it seems that, justified as these proposals may be, they do not strike at the core of the matter. Let us sit quietly for a while in our garden clearing, covered with dandelion, lady's-smock, and all our familiar spring flowers and herbs. And let us listen to what the common wild flowers, the scraggly bushes, have to tell us. Perhaps they will tell us of the task that is to be found in this garden. We need only hearken; soon they will begin to speak, softly disclosing their secrets.

First comes the secret of the seed from which they all spring, the seed which might be likened to the grain of mustard in the parable. From this parched grain, which seems so utterly dead, a full life miraculously develops. Alchemy devotes much attention to the secret of the seed: The earth in which we plant it contributes its solid nutrients, the water with which we sprinkle it bestows its virtue, even from the air the seed draws subtle nourishment, while from the sun it takes fiery energy. Thus all the elements combine to confer their blessings on it. Here we have the wonder of *germinatio*, that plays so prominent a role in all alchemy.

The seedling develops, and we look with astonishment upon the *formatio* of its organs, its growth according to very definite laws that are innate in every plant.

And then comes the moment when the buds burgeon, when the blossoms burst open, the plant has reached its prime, the hour of its sacred nuptials. The blossoms are fertilized by grains of pollen borne on the wind: this is the *coniunctio* of which alchemy speaks. But now we encounter an apparent inconsistency. These flowers, which have just opened, these flowers whose creation seemed to be the whole purpose of the plant, now begin to wither and fade. The whole process would seem to have been in vain. This fading of the flowers, this seeming failure of the whole process, is also known to alchemy, which calls it the *nigredo*, the blackening. Everything appears to be lost. The lovely petals have shrunken, they are withered, dry, brown. But under the blossom the fruit grows and matures, turning from green to yellow to red. This reddening is also known to alchemy; it is the *rubedo*, the yearned-for stage leading up to the "great work" which alchemy projects. At last the fruit is ripe. The process seems to be ended, but this is not quite so. The plant is torn up, parched seeds and all. Where a moment past we beheld hopeful burgeoning and ripening, we now see a withered brown wilderness. But the seed is gathered and sown again in new earth. This is the *proiectio* of alchemy.

And now the garden reveals one of its greatest mysteries: this seed, which is sown again, will begin the cycle anew. Here we have the phenomenon of *rotatio*, the cycle, another typically alchemical concept. This cycle is the seal and true image of alchemy. There is one figure that is never absent from the old alchemical manuscripts of Egypt, scantily illustrated as they are, and that is the Uroboros, the serpent with a head like a dragon and a scaly body, biting its tail.[1] This whole metamorphosis, this growth and passing, this eternal cycle, is the first great lesson we find in our garden.

ALCHEMY IN THE HISTORY OF IDEAS

Now you may say that alchemy as we know it is not a garden, but a vast collection of books. Yet the garden in a literal botanical sense can give us a good idea of the state of alchemy. We need merely replace the flowers and plants and leaves of our garden with the numerous alchemical books and manuscripts, and we shall be a long step closer to our task. I have already told you that the garden is in great disorder and clogged with dry leaves. Alchemy is not a self-contained system, laid down once and for all, but the outcome of a long development. Side by side with familiar native plants we find remnants of foreign shrubs, early imported from the East and the South. We find withered bamboo thickets, and in the dry fish pool traces of the sacred lotus of India, which once covered the whole surface of the water; we find remains of papyrus stalks from ancient Egypt; indeed, the whole world's flora is represented. These plants are no longer green, to be sure, they no longer put forth blossoms. But should we for this reason say that they are not a part of the garden? Is it not rather our task to inquire how this garden came to be what it is, how it was originally planned, and how it may have looked in the days of its flourishing?

And this leads us to a second task: to indicate, in its outlines at least, the origin of the alchemical idea. All alchemical writings insist: We build on what went before, we do not state our own opinion, we aspire to be nothing more than a commentary on much earlier works which came into being at

---

1 E.g., the Komarios ms. Cf. Edmund O. von Lippmann, *Entstehung und Ausbreitung der Alchemie* (2 vols., Berlin, 1919–31), I, p. 51. For details on the Uroboros, p. 81.

a time when the name and the narrower concept of alchemy were still un-known.

The historians of alchemy keep telling us that there was no such thing as alchemy until the third century A.D. But the alchemists themselves dis-agree. They assure us that alchemy was divinely inspired. Some say that its founder was the Hellenistic Hermes Trismegistos, a divine figure, com-pounded of Thoth, the old Egyptian god of science, and the Greek Hermes, with his diverse manifestations: guide of souls (Hermes Psychopompos), master of discourse, crafty messenger of the gods, carrier of the highest knowledge.[2] Still others attribute the invention of alchemy to Tubal-cain or Moses, not to mention vague imputations of divine origin. But instead of considering these undemonstrable claims, let us seek to establish the link between alchemy and earlier trends of thought.

The question of when alchemy began and the precursor stage ended can be answered in any number of ways. But it is certain, at least, that alchemy can be traced back in an unbroken line to men's earliest ideas and theories on nature and the cosmos. Let us start with those proponents of alchemical ideas who are unanimously claimed for the craft. There is Stephen of Alex-andria, who delivered nine lectures on the "working of gold" before Em-peror Heraclius (610–641); and, in Phoenicia, Heliodorus, who dedicated his didactic poem on the "mystical art" to Theodosius II (410–450); and Olym-piodorus, a contemporary of Heliodorus, who wrote a letter "On the sacred art" to Petasius, King of Armenia. They all state definitely that they did nothing and intended to do nothing but interpret the teachings of Plato and Aristotle. Hence we simply obscure the truth if we draw a sharp line and say: These men are alchemists, Plato and Aristotle have nothing to do with alchemy. We must acknowledge that alchemy grew out of the theories of Plato and Aristotle, that it is built upon them and is inconceivable with-out them. This does not answer the question of when alchemy began. But, essentially, the question is meaningless. The important thing is to form a general view of its development.

Alchemy took form amid the peculiar intellectual atmosphere of dying antiquity. It was a time of overturned values; the old was being submerged by new elements which, on closer examination, turn out to be even older.

2 Concerning the so-called Hermetic philosophy, see Josef Kroll, *Die Lehren des Hermes Trismegistos* (in Clemens Baeumker, ed., Beiträge zur Geschichte der Philosophie des Mittelalters, XII: 2–4; Münster, 1914), and G. R. S. Mead, *Thrice-Greatest Hermes* (3 vols., London, 1949).

We should not forget that in all spiritual development one thing grows out of another, even if there is a certain contradiction between the two. Alchemy draws its nourishment from Greek culture and from its late echoes, Neoplatonism and Gnosis. But this same Greek culture is unthinkable without the spiritual life of the Near East and Egypt. It abounds in reminders of these earlier cultures. It is often said that the greatest fecundations of the mind came from the East. Persia, Iran, is one of the greatest riddles; what and how much may have flowed from this source can only be determined indirectly, for what has come down to us, particularly of Iranian literature, is so fragmentary that it can offer no direct answer to the most important questions.[3]

And then came a fateful development. Alchemy died out in the West, or rather was exterminated along with Gnosis, which in a sense constituted a parallel movement. Both laid claim to universality; they did not halt before the limits and claims of the religions, but drew everything into their sphere. But while Gnosis itself was almost entirely exterminated by the Church, alchemy preserved certain profoundly Gnostic elements. We may go further and say that alchemy constitutes in some degree a continuation of the mystery religions, which like Gnosis were combated by the rising Christian Church and as far as possible exterminated. Alchemy was saved by the Arabs, who took over the tradition from the Greeks. First of all we have the outstanding figure of the scientist Al Jabir, who lived at the end of the eighth century and is known to us by the name of Geber.[4] The question of the authorship of the works attributed to this supposed prince of Arabic alchemy is extremely difficult, for as I have already told you, the alchemists tended to put their ideas into the mouths of their greatest authorities. Writings bearing the names of famous alchemists often turn out to have been written by later imitators, who have thus created extraordinary confusion.[5] Moreover, just as the early alchemy was based on older speculations and conceptions which were ultimately rooted in the Near East, Arabic alchemy drew nourishment from sources far beyond the confines of

---

3 If, as has been claimed, Ostanes, one of the most frequently cited older authors, is identical with the Ostanes, brother-in-law of the King Xerxes mentioned by Herodotus, this would be an indication of vast Persian influence.

4 Cf. Ernst Darmstädter, *Die Alchemie des Geber* (Berlin, 1922).

5 Some critics, such as Moritz Steinschneider, even go so far as to regard Geber himself as an invention, or to distinguish between Geber and Jabir, as Lippmann attempts to do.

the Greco-Arabic culture. The Arab empire extended to India, far into Africa, to Spain and Portugal, and from everywhere the Arabs took the stones for their cultural edifice. In his *Kosmos*, Alexander von Humboldt tells us that the Arabs translated whole Indian codices. And the Iranians in the empire brought with them many Indian conceptions. Particularly in the field of alchemy, the Arabs were vastly indebted to India, Egypt, and Persia, along with Greece.[6]

Medieval alchemy presents a difficult problem in that here again many documents claim to be older than they really are. Some of the most important medieval texts are for good reason rejected by modern authors as late forgeries and interpolations. Some writers have attempted to represent Paracelsus as an alchemist of the golden age. But I believe that Paracelsus most particularly must be looked upon as a departure from the old alchemy. Paracelsus stood at the turning point; with him alchemy ceased to be an all-embracing world system and moved toward what today would be called a more scientific conception—more scientific perhaps and for that very reason narrower. Paracelsus stresses the chemical and physiological aspects of alchemy at the expense of its broad philosophical implications. But the seventeenth century reacted violently against this conception and once more attempted to restore alchemy to its original form.

I have given this brief historical sketch in order to show that alchemy cannot be cut away from the great skein of the history of ideas. If we do not understand its development, its place in the general texture of human thought, we cannot hope to understand its essence and meaning. And here I return to my introductory metaphor: this tangled garden can be appreciated only if we ascertain how it must have looked long ago, if we recreate before our mind's eye that lotus pond which today is no more than a foul sludge, if we see the alien plants as they were in the days of their flowering, and think away the weeds that have clogged the garden in more recent times.

THE IDEA OF CORRESPONDENCES

And now I shall take up a few of the central ideas of alchemy, by way of showing the very "archaic" character of this discipline and the antiquity

6 Albert Stange, *Die Zeitalter der Chemie* (Leipzig, 1908), p. 38. This conception is beautifully described in Ostanes' "The Vision of the Seven Gates." [Cf. A. E. Waite, *The Secret Tradition in Alchemy* (London, 1926), pp. 97–98, where it is described.—Ed.]

of the ideas it has preserved and developed. The most important conception of all, one which I regard as the very beginning and foundation of alchemy, is the idea of correspondences. This idea is taken so completely for granted by the alchemists that nowhere in the literature is it considered at any length. What do we mean by correspondences? I should like to offer a very simple illustration from modern daily life: if you strike a match in the dark, you feel the resistance of the surfaces, you feel the friction, you feel the heat that is generated by the rubbing, you hear the scratching of the wood, smell the burning sulphur, and at the same time see a light flare up. Now what in reality is the striking of the match? Is it only the light, only the smell, only the scratching, or only the heat? We cannot separate these things. The striking of the match is precisely the manifestation of an event in different sensory fields. The conception of a primal event manifested in many different fields is one of the fundamental ideas of alchemy, an idea without which there could be no alchemy. But the idea goes much farther than our example, although our example illustrates an essential point: there is no way of proving that a given acoustical impression must correspond to a given optical impression. These are things that cannot be treated logically. And no more are the great correspondences asserted by alchemy accessible to logical analysis. We cannot for example prove the basic correspondence *world = man = God*, which signifies that one fundamental fact is manifested in these three forms.[7]

And now let us briefly inquire how this fundamental conception is formulated in alchemical literature. We read for example (in connection with a chemical prescription): "Use it for the knowledge of God, nature, and yourself." This quotation clearly shows that alchemy is not a discipline with one clear application, but one which may and should be applied to the most diverse fields.

Another quotation: "The science and knowledge of all things consists in

---

The first of these is Egyptian, the second Persian, the third Indian. The inscriptions of the others prove illegible.

7 Nevertheless the works of Hermann Kopp (*Die Alchemie in älterer und neuerer Zeit*, 2 vols., Heidelberg, 1886) and Lippmann (see n. 1 above), basic for the study of alchemical literature, treat the subject exclusively from the chemical standpoint. To be sure, as early a writer as Karl Christoph Schneider (*Geschichte der Alchemie*, Halle, 1832) suspected its profounder significance, which however was first taken up systematically by Herbert Silberer in his *Problems of Mysticism and Its Symbolism*, tr. Smith Ely Jelliffe (New York, 1917), whereas F. Strunz once more stressed the purely scientific aspect.

learning of the true harmony and consonance of nature with the macrocosm and microcosm of the world and man, since all things originate in one and all things in turn flow and return to one." Here again the widespread application of theoretical alchemy is made clear. Tracing back the idea of correspondences, we find it most fully embodied in Babylonia, where it was worked out in great detail: The earth is the mirror of heaven, and conversely. One is unthinkable without the other. The lights of the heavens correspond to things on the earth.[8] This kind of thinking, so fundamental for alchemy, has today become alien to us. When we attempt it, we are thwarted by modern logic, which rejects it because it defies understanding. But the heavenly bodies are not mere optical phenomena. Plato still spoke of their singing, and indeed the ancients in general regarded them as animated, as exerting "influences." Now this animation of the heavenly bodies runs through the whole of alchemy. This is primitive thinking if you will, for we no longer believe that stone, metal, dead wood are animated. But for alchemy the stone has life, the metal has a soul.[9] And, moreover, these correspondences· pervade every field. From the stars to the parts of our body, thence to the impulses of the mind and soul, the gods, the daemons which govern the planets and of whom the planets themselves are only the bodily cloak are related in essence to our spirit, they are bound up with our spirit and soul by ties of interaction. Nothing occurs below that does not have its correspondence above, and conversely; and this correspondence extends to every sphere of the universe. It is formulated most sharply in the doctrine of the seven planets, which correspond to the seven basic metals and to the seven principal bodily organs of man.

The Chinese also developed this idea of correspondence, whether independently of the Babylonians I do not know. We find it in exactly the same form, with exactly the same implications; exactly the same thought is expressed in two languages. It matters little whether the ideas of the Chinese spread to Babylonia or vice versa, or whether the two civilizations developed the idea independently of one another. The essential here is that alchemy thinks in correspondences, and unless we remember this, we shall not be able to interpret its formulations and principles. But if we consider that the bubbling of the retort corresponds to a psychic, a physiological, and an

8 Cf. Franz Johannes Boll's comprehensive work *Sternglaube und Sterndeutung* (Leipzig, 1926).

9 This even applies to the modern alchemy of François Jollivet Castelot, *La Révolution chimique* (Paris, 1925).

astral process, that it in some way expresses a phase of the divine cosmic drama, that this specific process is reflected in every conceivable field, yet is at the same time a consequence of all these factors, then we shall recognize in alchemy a truly comprehensive analysis, an attempt to find the general in the particular. If we forget this, we are in the position of looking upon alchemy as no more than rudimentary chemistry. It *is* rudimentary chemistry, but also much more. It is a doctrine of correspondences in all fields.

True, with our present habits of thought we cannot accept such a doctrine. It is not subject to proof and hence cannot be regarded as science. But for present purposes we must accept this theory in full if we wish to gain even an approximate understanding of alchemy.

What then, given these correspondences, is alchemy? Paracelsus has given us an answer: alchemy is the voluntary action of man in harmony with the involuntary action of nature. What nature does outside him, without any help from him, man can reproduce experimentally in his inner self and in his laboratory. We often read the saying, "in accordance with nature"; it is repeatedly stressed that alchemy aspires only to produce the natural by artificial means. Thus in a certain restricted sense, it is a precursor of our modern natural science. Everything that happens in the outside world is imitated in the laboratory of the modern scientist. Today we can reproduce the flow of a river in a model, we can produce synthetic jewels and artificial lightning. Man can already perform a good many of the feats of nature. That is one side of alchemy. But alchemy also implies correspondence in all other fields; it is at this point that the modern scientist begins to smile and that alchemy begins to be psychologically interesting. For if the center of the entire world process is transferred to man, his intentions take on a new significance, since they can affect the destinies of the cosmos. Man can lift the world from its hinges, at first to be sure only the world in himself, but does not this correspond to the world outside?

Thus alchemy becomes a universal potentiality. Its aims extend to every sphere of being, ultimately transcending the possibilities given in nature. Its final goal is a transcendent perfection. Upon what foundation does it base such aspirations? By what road does it mean to attain them?

THE IDEA OF ORIGINAL UNITY

If we wish to reproduce the cosmos afresh, the first question that arises is that of the prime material. The alchemists take it for granted that there was a prime matter, an original unity, and in this they agreed with the old Greek natural philosophers. The beginning is the *prima materia*, matter in its primal state. This suggests the primal unity of Xenophanes, his theory of creation. What first appeared? What should we therefore first seek and first realize? The foundation of all things is water, taught Thales of Miletus. It flows into the depths; the ground water is the foundation of the world. In symbols of the psyche we find similar conceptions. The Egyptians also conceived the idea of water as the foundation: Osiris is the water, and all things flow from him.

But Anaximander contributed an important new element; from the primal substance he developed a pair of opposites. This is a basic alchemical conception, which we encounter also in China: out of the original unity grew two opposite poles, and contradiction is now manifest everywhere. According to Anaximander, the opposition between hot and cold on the one hand and dry and moist on the other gives rise to the four elements; Plato enlarged on the four elements and made them the foundation of all nature.

Thus we see how, very early in history, this concept of primal being was differentiated and split into separate elements, from which all other things in the cosmos arise.

But meanwhile the question of primal substance, so vital to alchemy, was answered in still other ways. Especially significant was the answer of Heraclitus. He interpreted the cosmos as a thing in a state of becoming. But what is the core of this becoming? It is fire, the fire which plays so immense a role in alchemy, since alchemy, in its chemical aspect, makes use of fire in all its operations. The alchemists are forever burning or heating something, torturing matter with fire. But did Heraclitus really mean just physical fire? No, the Greek natural philosophers were not quite so naïve. As we might expect in an alchemist, the old idea of correspondences is present: it is evident that this fire is more than the fire which the peasant kindles in the fields or which glows in the chemist's furnace. It is also the fire that is in the grape, in the wine, in speech, in the heart, in feeling, everywhere and in every aspect of life, as our language still bears witness. It is fire that gives warmth. Wherever there is warmth, there is fire. Fire in the Heraclitean sense is something quite different from the isolated phenomenon of flame. The alchemists call it "our fire," with the accent on "our." They also call it "the philosophical fire." Alchemy then is nothing other than philosophy, and most alchemists have indeed termed themselves philosophers. In this respect they follow the philosophy of Heraclitus. They are justified in looking on themselves as philosophers, for alchemy is not mere chemistry, it is an all-embracing conception of the world. Paracelsus too speaks of this fire,[10] "by which not only is lesser metal transformed into a better, but by which also all illnesses may be cured and even the mortal body of man can be preserved in long, sound, strong, and perfect life." Thus we see that the "philosophical fire," one of the main ideas of alchemy, goes directly back to Heraclitus.

The idea of primal being is encountered again and again, inside and outside of alchemy. Sometimes it is interpreted as spirit, sometimes as matter. Spinoza sees it as substance, the original substance. And it is strange to note that here a definitely alchemical language enters into philosophy.

THE IDEA OF UNITY AS THE SUM
OF THE THREE PRIMAL FACTORS

This original substance, as we have said, bears within it the germ of differentiation; it is in a sense the seed from which the whole world grows. In the cosmology of the mystical sect of the Naassenes, a system which stands exceedingly close to alchemy, we find a male-female primal being, an original principle which embraces opposing forces to such a degree that under certain circumstances separation becomes an evident possibility. This primal being consists of three principles: spirit, soul, and body, and is comparable to the three-headed giant Geryon.[11] But this idea of a fundamental primal being in threefold differentiation does not first appear with the Gnostics; it is clearly defined at a much earlier time.

The most precise formulation occurs in the Indian Sankhya philosophy, with its doctrine of the three *gunas*. Paul Deussen explains it as follows: [12] "Everything in nature, everything psychic and everything physical . . . is the product of three factors, which are for that reason called *gunas* (*guna* = factor, and its derivative, *gunayati* = multiply). Their names are *sattva* = goodness, *rajas* = passion, *tamas* = darkness. Whereas all developed things are the product of these factors, their sum constitutes that which is undeveloped (the original unity). This is the equilibrium of the three *gunas*,

---

10 Paracelsus, *Metamorphosis* [ed. Adam von Bodenstein] (Basel, 1572).
11 Hippolytus, *Elenchos*, V, 6 (ed. Wendland, p. 78). On the Naassenes. Quoted from E. Wilhelm Möller, *Geschichte der Kosmologie in der griechischen Kirche bis auf Origenes* (Halle, 1860), p. 190.
12 *Allgemeine Geschichte der Philosophie* (2 vols., Leipzig, 1906), I, sec. 3, pp. 47f.

which when thrown out of balance produce things by enchainment with one another."

These three names designate definite attitudes of the soul and of matter, none of which however is manifested in isolation but always in a mixture with the other factors: clarity of conscious being and thinking: *sattva;* blind lust, unrestrained and heedless sensuality: *rajas;* heaviness, without light or motion, obedience only to the laws of gravity and inertia: *tamas.*

This is the clearest and purest formulation of the triad, far clearer than in the sometimes unintelligible Paracelsus, or in Amos Comenius and the later alchemists.

And this in general is what repeatedly takes us back to India: certain ideas which in Europe have been formulated obscurely or unclearly seem in India to have been transmitted in a clear, intelligible language. Perhaps this is because India has suffered fewer collapses of culture than has the unfortunate West, where everything has been of so much briefer duration. In the Indian philosophical systems we find precise and clear conceptions which today, after thousands of years, still have the same immediacy as when they were new.

THE IDEA OF POLARITY AS THE BASIS
OF ALCHEMICAL DYNAMICS

Polarity plays a great part in alchemy. A picture of Roger Bacon, the famous English alchemist (1214–94), shows him with a "Treatise on Alchemy" open before him. On the open pages the signs of the sun and moon are visible; these are the symbols of polarity.[13] The symbol of the sun, a circle with a clearly accentuated center, is in its basic form descended from the Babylonians, for whom it symbolized not only the sun, but also gold and in general everything that possesses a maximum of perfection. In the Hellenistic period this seal of the sun was identified with *theta*, the first letter of *theos* = God.[14]

$$\odot \quad = \quad \ominus$$

Thus this symbol of the sun became a symbol of the godhead itself.

The symbol of the sun is at rest and fastened at the center; the moon, the continuously changing element, is symbolized by the sickle. It is the

13 Reproduced in Stange, *Zeitalter*, p. 50.
14 Franz Strunz, *Astrologie, Alchemie, Mystik* (Munich, 1928), p. 261.

sun's opposite, but it is also dependent on the other element; its light is borrowed. According to the law of correspondences this idea of opposition, as represented by the symbols of sun and moon, must be applied to all fields: it signifies the upper and lower, the difference in the sexes, father and mother, sun and moon; and it signifies light and dark, good and bad, warm and cold, in short every conceivable polarity.

The same idea is expressed by the Chinese in the basic polarity of Yin and Yang. Empedocles gave it an analogous formulation in the conflict between attraction and repulsion, from which all motion arises.

THE UNION OF OPPOSITES, THE GOAL OF ALCHEMY

But there is a still deeper polarity, that of beginning and end. As we know, beginning and end are often designated by A and Ω, the first and last letters of the Greek alphabet. Christ called himself the A and Ω. Alchemy raises the claim to universality. It uses the Latin and Hebrew alphabets in addition to the Greek. Alchemy is based on all these cultures. It draws all of them into its system. Thus in seeking a symbol for the concept of beginning and end, of first beginning and final conclusion, it uses a word which embraces beginning and end in all languages. A is the first letter of all alphabets, while Z is the last letter of the Latin alphabet, Ω of the Greek, and ת of the Hebrew. A combination of the first and last letters of the three alphabets has given rise to a strange word: "*Azoth.*" [15] In French this term has been retained to this day as a chemical term (*azote* = nitrogen). In alchemy, *azoth* means: beginning and end in all fields, summed up in one. There is a strange and important alchemical saying: "If thou hast fire and the *azoth*, thou hast all things." Or in other words: beginning and end and the means of becoming; if we clearly recognize, carry out, embody this in ourselves, then everything is solved, then to a certain degree we are at the goal. For, as we have said, alchemy strives toward a goal outside the world: not only to create the world within man, but to resolve the polarity between man and woman, above and below, bright and dark, in a new birth which follows from the union of opposites, a *hieros gamos*, a sacred marriage. Opposition is one of the great symbols of alchemy, and the union of opposites is its great mystery, its ultimate goal. In one version alchemy speaks of it as the

---

15 Cf. Basilius Valentinus in his *Azoth* (Latin edn., Frankfurt, 1613), p. 65. According to Darmstädter, *Alchemie des Geber*, p. 166, the word is derived from Arabic "*al-zawuk*," meaning nothing other than "quicksilver."

homunculus, the new man or spiritual rebirth, which is here viewed as the great desideratum. We cannot seek to identify ourselves with only one of the two poles; both poles must be transcended, transformed into new being and thus reconciled. Both are united in the new, and yet the new exceeds both of them. By way of clarifying this mystery, the alchemists adduce the image of the child "Re-bis" who issues from the union of King Sun and Queen Moon, and combines the essences of the two.

In another connection, the darkness appears purified into light, but the light cannot be manifested without the darkness, which must be present in it. Here the alchemists speak of the watery fire in which the two opposites, seemingly incompatible, are united. Modern man asks in amazement: How can this be? Something must be wrong? Such a thing is simply impossible, for it does not occur in nature. Does alchemy aspire to transcend nature?

There are then two kinds of alchemy: the one strives to know the cosmos as a whole and to recreate it; it is in a sense the precursor of modern natural science. It aspires to create gold as the supreme perfection in every sphere, the *summum bonum*. The other alchemy strives higher; it strives for the great wonder, the wonder of all wonders, the magic crystal, the philosophers' stone. This is not a substance susceptible of chemical analysis. It does not represent a spiritual or psychological state that can be reduced to a clear formula. It is something more than perfection, something through which perfection can be achieved. It is the universal instrument of magic. By it we can attain to the ultimate. By it we can completely possess the world. By it we can make ourselves free from the world, by soaring above it. This is alchemy in the mystical sense, alchemy as it was eminently conceived by the Rosicrucians of the seventeenth century, but also (if we read the sources correctly, between the lines as it were) in repeated instances in the Byzantine and Arabic period.[16]

THE PATH OF METAMORPHOSIS, ALCHEMISTIC TRANSMUTATION

And now comes the great and important chapter: How is this achieved? Where is the road that leads to the goal? It is the road of transmutation,

---

16 Cf. Kraus, quoted in Lippmann, *Alchemie*, II, p. 75: According to Geber, the task of alchemy is to "produce the elixir, in which all ingredients stand to one another in a fully harmonious relation, so that it becomes a third cosmos, side by side with the macrocosm and the microcosm, and a symbol of religious truth. Thus it can bear the religious name of 'imām,' for the human manifestation of the godhead in the 'imām' establishes the realm of God on earth."

transformation. I shall put it briefly. On the wall of the portal of the cathedral of Trogir in Dalmatia there is a small, delicately executed relief showing the alchemist seated in front of his furnace. He has set his retort on the fire. With his left hand he holds up a goblet. An angel comes to him through the air and pours the water of life into the goblet. The meaning is: on this road man cannot succeed by his own strength, but perhaps he will succeed if in some way the guide and leader within him is awakened, who will lead him to his goal. Down through the centuries this transmutation, this metamorphosis of the imperfect into the perfect and perhaps even the supraperfect, has been the task and goal of mystical alchemy. But much as we read about it, however much we seek to apprehend its essence, it will always remain a mystery. I myself have recently experienced the difficulty of communicating anything essential with regard to this process of transmutation. We strive to express ourselves clearly, but it is well nigh impossible. For the pursuit of this path involves experiences we must gain for ourselves. Speaking of these experiences, as the alchemical texts show, clarifies nothing. We gather the meaning of the texts only after we have gained for ourselves the experience of which they treat. The alchemists knew that little can be said by words alone. And that is why they had recourse to symbolic pictures, by which they strove to suggest the path to be followed.

SUMMARY

I have attempted to give an account of the three aspects of alchemy: (1) Alchemy as theory, as a great, comprehensive vision of the world, as idea of the cosmos as a whole, as analysis of man, as emanation and creation of God, as an epitome of all analytical knowledge, built on universal correspondences. (2) Alchemy as practice, as an attempt to examine these things and deal with them experimentally, not only in the realm of matter, but above all in the province of the soul, which is the true scene of becoming, the only one that is really accessible to our knowledge, since all else can be known only indirectly through psychic experience. Mere alchemy is broadened into a universal creative discipline, embracing all things from the standpoint of the soul. (3) Alchemy as a transcendental endeavor whose supreme aim is to achieve liberation from the world, after knowledge and experience of this world have been gained. The first two aspects of alchemy are consequently prerequisite to the third. Only after mastering them are we prepared for the return to the beginning.

Alchemy shows us the way from the primal beginning to the ultimate turning point of our own self, and when this is attained, back again to the beginning. This goal is reached only when a man succeeds in creating the hard and radiant philosophers' stone within himself, and this is made possible only by the intervention of the "inner master." The alchemists of the Christian era often likened this ultimate goal, this philosophers' stone, to Christ. No words or images are adequate for the communication of this alchemy, these miraculous things, and the few who have known of them have found but one means of expression: silence.

2. The System of Alchemy in Its Pictorial Representation

INTRODUCTORY

If what I have so far said is true, it will be borne out by the illustrations we sometimes find in alchemical treatises.

We should then expect the most diverse systems, emanating from similar fundamental ideas, to present parallels to alchemical notions in the narrower sense. This would bear out my assertion that if we are to fathom the true meaning of alchemy, we must view it not as an isolated phenomenon but in conjunction with related disciplines. And moreover, the principles set forth in alchemical treatises would have to apply not only to chemistry, but also to the realms of physiology, psychology, and philosophy.

The structure of those pictures which represent alchemy as a general system of thought would, in the light of what has been said, have to be more or less as follows: uppermost, we should find a figuration of the idea of primal unity, which embraces three factors and accordingly can be manifested in three realms of being.

This primal unity unfolds by engendering its opposite, thus creating polarity, duality in the most fundamental sense; this duality is represented by contrasting colors such as black and white, or by corresponding symbols.

By their tension these two original polar forces create a field of energy, characterized by the most varied interactions. The dynamics of these interactions permit three possible approaches to alchemy.

The first of these consists in observing and studying the process of genesis and development with a view to theoretical understanding. The second approach, the actual practice of alchemy, goes farther and seeks to prove the above theories by experiment. In the Paracelsan sense, it seeks to produce natural phenomena by artificial means. It aims not only to dissect but, in every sense, to build. The third approach is based on the two others. But its aims are far higher. Its problem, its goal, is not growth but a transcending, a movement away from growth; ultimately, it is redemption from the process of growing and passing away.

The interaction of forces in nature and in man, whether it implies passive experience or active participation, tends necessarily toward a goal. Alchemy does not define this goal in any one sense, and this is quite understandable in view of the diverse attitudes it embraces: it aspires not only to attain the highest perfection in the chemical, physiological, or psychological sense, but also to solve the mystery which consists in the idea of an arcanum above perfection, the philosophers' stone which engenders all perfection at all times.

And here we have the striving toward an ultimate unity which must comprehend the polar antitheses, or in a sense an involution of the process of universal unfolding or evolution which we have described; but this involution must be more than a mere reversal.[17]

A CHINESE DIAGRAM

Our first illustration (Fig. 1, p. 322), taken from the modern Chinese encyclopedia *Yu Tsei*, shows us an ancient Chinese conception of cosmic interrelations. As Erwin Rousselle informs me, it was presumably drawn in the eighth century, under Taoist influence. It would be hard to conceive of a more apposite and precise illustration of the basic theory which I have represented as the specific alchemical principle.

At the top we see the circle of primal unity, which in the next phase, represented under it, has been transformed into a polarity.[18] As in the Greek conception, the pairs of opposites give rise to the so-called elements, first as prototypes, prerequisites to the manifestation of matter. Here to be sure we have five instead of four, and in their definition they deviate somewhat from the Greek elements. But their interaction is quite analogous to that of the Greek elements, and somewhat resembles the conception known

17 In the *Thesaurus chymicus* (Frankfurt, 1675), this is briefly formulated as follows: *"Ex quatuor fiunt duo, ex duobus rursus fit unum quod dicitur mundi centrum"*: From the four (elements) arises the two (polarity), which in turn is fused into the one, the center of the world (the philosophers' stone, as we shall subsequently see).
18 Cf. Richard Wilhelm's [German] tr. of the *Tao Tê Ching: Das Buch des Alten vom Sinn und Leben* (Jena, 1911), pp. 89f.

The primal unity

Wu Chi
The undivided

The union of polar opposites

T'ai chi
The union of Yang and Yin

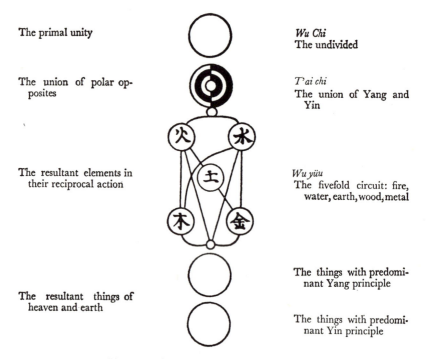

The resultant elements in their reciprocal action

Wu yün
The fivefold circuit: fire, water, earth, wood, metal

The things with predominant Yang principle

The resultant things of heaven and earth

The things with predominant Yin principle

Fig. 1. Ancient Chinese diagram of cosmic interrelations

in modern physics as the mutation of aggregate states. The Chinese call it *wu yün*, the fivefold cycle or fivefold breath of the Tao. The five elements are: earth (in the middle), wood and fire (to the left), metal and water (to the right). These elements, according to a doctrine conceived two thousand years ago by Liu An (Liu Ngan),[19] overcome, injure, or destroy one another, or else engender one another. Wood draws its nourishment from the earth, thus transforming earth into an organic cellular tissue, but it is vanquished by fire, that is, it engenders fire. Earth obstructs water by absorbing it, but on the other hand produces metal. Water destroys fire, but at the same time it produces vegetable growth, hence wood. Fire vanquishes metal by melting it, but also produces earth by burning wood to ash. Metal destroys wood, as for example when man splits wood with an ax; in its molten state it is

19 J. J. M. De Groot, *Universismus* (Berlin, 1918), pp. 120 and 370.

322

ost hec
uidi. & ecce
omia element̄a
& om̄s crea
turę̄. duro
motu ŋ eŭ
sa sunt. ignis
aer. & aqua erŭ
peruntı. & tram moueri fece
runt. fulgura & tonterua con
crepuerunt. montes. & siluę ce
ciderunt. ita ut om̄e q̄d mor
tale erat uitam exalaret. Et
om̄ia element̄a purgata sunt. ita
ut q̄cq̄d uicis sordidum fuerat.
tali m̄ euanesceret q̄d amplius
n̄ appareret. Et audiui uocem ma
xumo clamore p tot̄ū orbē trarum
uociterant̄ē & dicent̄ē. O uos filii ho
minū qui intra iacetis. surgite om̄s.
Et ecce om̄ia ossa hominū in q̄cūq;
loco trarum erant. uelut̄ i uno mo
mento ŋ gregata. & sua carne obtec
ta sunt. & om̄s homines integris
mbris & corporib; suis insexu suo sur
rexerunt. boni in claritate fulgentes.
& mali in nigredine apparentes. ita
ut & opus cuiq; in ipso apte uide
ret. Et quidam ex eis i fide signati
erant. quidam aut̄ non. ita ut

The New Heaven and the New Earth. From the "Scivias" of Hildegard of Bingen

After Van Eyck (?): "The Fountain of Living Water"

II

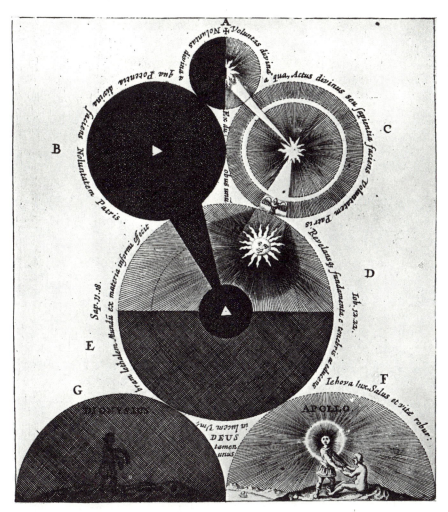

From Fludd's "Utriusque Cosmi ... Historia"

Etching by Merian, from the "Musaeum hermeticum"

regarded as a component of the aggregate water, which it thus helps to engender. All this may be a rather primitive conception, but in my opinion it is far from being "nonsense" as the Sinologist De Groot calls it.

To the Chinese mind this cycle applies not only to the transmutation and interaction of the five elements considered as aggregates. It applies also to the change of the seasons, to climatic conditions, physical organs (liver, heart, spleen, lungs, and kidneys); to the functions of the soul (anger, joy, thought, care, and fear), and to the planets, which in turn are associated with specific traits of character. Thus we have cyclic transmutation and re-formation all along the line.[20]

This dynamic is bound to the passage of time; thus in a sense it stands behind concrete things; it engenders them, and all actuality results from its action. In the Chinese conception the action of the fivefold cycle calls forth the things of heaven, in which the bright, masculine polarity predominates, and also the things of earth in which the dark heaviness of the female opposite is preponderant.

Thus interpreted, our diagram represents the process of the world's genesis. But this is only one reading, the reading from top to bottom. The figure can also be read from bottom to top: then it means that the balance of forces can be achieved through the interaction of celestial and earthly things, through prudent and purposive labor in the fivefold cycle. Once this fivefold balance is attained, it is not far to the ultimate solution, the attainment of unity.

But these two readings do not exhaust the meaning of our diagram. I have often pointed out that the chemical aspect of alchemy represents only its most external layer. In many cases the *prima materia*, the beginning of alchemical endeavor, is not the theoretical postulate of a primary or basic substance, which is put into a retort with a view to obtaining noble or perfect substances. It can also be the whole man, the natural man, as destiny has made him grow, without effort of his own. In a sense this growth is also alchemy. It is natural development. And under present conditions it can by no means be taken for granted that such natural development will proceed without difficulty. A good part of our psychiatric effort aims at restoring this natural development to its proper channels after it has been blocked or perverted in various ways. This is the alchemy of the natural process,

20 Additional correspondences in Wilhelm, op. cit., p. 94, no. 12; De Groot, *Universismus*, p. 120; Strunz, *Alchemie*, p. 74.

which has nothing whatever to do with redemption, the birth of the new man in man, the so-called homunculus, or with the magic of the philosophers' stone.

A METAPHORIC DIGRESSION

In general we should not attempt to explain other men's images in terms of our own. But occasionally when this procedure gives clarity and sudden illumination, it seems permissible. There is an image which repeatedly comes to my mind. Since its first appearance, it has never left me and has become more and more distinct.

It is the image of a well, beside which an empty bucket is waiting. It goes without saying that a thirsty man will lower the bucket, letting the chain slip slowly through his hands. But it is quite possible that the chain will become entangled, that it will jump off the roller, or that the bucket will strike some obstacle before reaching the bottom of the well. Then all possible caution will be needed to disengage the bucket and guide it to its goal, the water at the bottom of the well. If the chain is too short, all hope will be in vain. But even if it is long enough, the thirsty man must exert constant care lest it slip from his hands and fall to the bottom of the well.

If this happens, the bucket will fill with water and so seem to have attained its purpose. But if the thirsty man has lost his hold on the chain, he can no longer pull it up; it lies at the bottom of the well, and that seems to be the culmination of all his effort. It is essentially the same whether we lower the bucket because we are thirsty or merely to amuse ourselves. And since there is always a connection between the man at the brink of the well and the bucket, the man may be deluded into identifying himself with the bucket. And then he may be overcome by the same feeling as the students in Auerbach's Cellar, when they loudly roared:

> Ours is the cannibalistic bliss
> Of several hundred sows.

Meanwhile the bucket fills not only with water but, sinking deeper and deeper, with muck and slime as well, and becomes so heavy that it cannot possibly be raised.

But if the thirsty man remembers that the great work of alchemy does not consist merely in helping nature, not only in letting the force of gravity draw the bucket down to the water,[21] but actually begins only when the bucket has been let down so far that the water flows over its edge, he will summon up strength for the great final effort; he will draw it upward and will not rest until he holds it in his hands, prepared to slake his thirst.

There is a particular technique of water drawing which offers a considerable guarantee of success. We yoke an animal stronger and more persevering than man and let it move round in a circle, winding up the chain or rope. Is the relation between the words *yoke* and *Yoga* a mere accident? Does the practice of Indian Yoga not consist in harnessing all the forces at our disposal in order to quench the thirst within us which impels us to flee from the cycle of becoming and passing away? [22]

Another possibility is that if the man is too thirsty, he will not let the bucket down far enough and in his haste will draw it up empty. His failure will be all the more significant in that his good will and theoretical insight must be acknowledged. I believe that the image is clear enough. Even though it is not an alchemical image, it throws light on the fundamental situation of alchemy.

The elements of my metaphor are to be found in a number of alchemical texts. The letting down of the bucket characterizes that group of alchemist authors whose maxim it is to "follow nature." The drawing up, on the other hand, applies to those who speak of the former with unconcealed contempt as "scullery cooks" who think of nothing but "mere gold making." This "drawing up" exacts tremendous exertions; these alchemists must subject themselves to all manner of hardship and torment, to which not a few who have attempted this path have succumbed. Quite in contrast to the natural inclination to take everything in life and seek to make of it what is best and most beautiful, these authors recommend a road which runs counter to the natural trend, in total disregard of everything that can make our life beautiful and pleasant. Everything must be sacrificed to their purpose, even the

21 In certain alchemical works, this dwelling in the depths in bondage to nature is considered as the initial situation.

22 *Yoga* (Sanskrit) means literally "yoking," and sometimes by implication "the yoking of the cosmic forces." It also implies—and this strikes me as more important—the self-discipline which yokes the whole personality for the achievement of *moksha*, redemption, *"für sich sein"* (being for oneself) as Jakob W. Hauer translates it, in *Der Yoga als Heilweg* (Stuttgart, 1932), p. 76.

Nor is this expression alien to Western thought. The Apostle Peter (Acts 15:10) speaks of the "yoke [of the law] . . . which neither our fathers nor we were able to bear"; and in contrast, Christ says (Matt. 11:29–30): "Take my yoke upon you . . . for my yoke is easy."

achievements gained on the downward path. Otherwise success is not possible. In order to transcend the world, one must have experienced it, assimilated it, and utterly seen through it.

For this attitude the Indian language has the uncommonly apt term "eating of the world" (*bhoga*). It signifies an eating divorced from real enjoyment, as when one consumes food without relishing its taste. All alchemists of this school agree that this seeming detour is indispensable, that there can be no greater error than an attempt to shorten the road. And all likewise point out that so violent a reversal requires a maturity that can be attained only after a considerable time.

Again and again it is stated that the road back can be begun only by those who are called. The alchemical texts which are often cloaked in chemical formulas express this by saying that a certain chemical reaction must occur before the preliminary work can be regarded as complete and the creation of the philosophers' stone or the great elixir can be begun. Those who attempt to force such a development are condemned to failure; in the psychological sphere, blocks and neuroses arise which show clearly that the right moment has not been awaited.

Like every effort aimed exclusively at redemption, this one also culminates in injunctions that resemble the ethical postulates of our churches. Indeed, it is not easy to see why we should turn our backs on all those tasks which have been clearly and unmistakably imposed on us by nature. But how shall we transcend nature if we cede to all its drives? True, as long as we feel content in the realm of nature, the time has not come to embark on this path. Only when we are sated with the world (a term which clearly implies the "eating of the world") has the time come to think of transcending it. And once the call has gone forth and been accepted, we enter into the stream of which it is said that, contrary to everything in nature, it strives upward.

It has seemed important to me to formulate all these things as incisively as possible. I would rather be accused of occasional lapses into theology than have to reproach myself with failure to distinguish clearly enough between things which, similar as they may appear from without, are entirely different in fundamental trend.

A CABALISTIC DIAGRAM

The second example (Fig. 2) is a part of the title page to Knorr von Rosenroth's basic Latin work on the cabala, *Kabbala denudata* (Sulzbach and

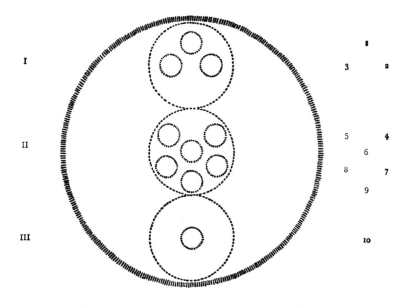

Fig. 2. The three worlds containing the Sephiroth,
or ten cosmic forces

Frankfurt, 1677). The ten divine forces, or Sephiroth,[22a] are disclosed in a glittering circle of light. These Sephiroth are essential to the cabalistic conception of the world. In the *Sepher Yetsirah*, one of the most important source works of the cabala, the world is represented as a manifestation of the Creator, who brought it forth by means of the ten numbers and twenty-two sounds or letters. This numerology recalls Pythagorean conceptions. But in the cabala the numbers are far more individualized; each one has its distinct outlines and characteristics.

In our diagram the first three Sephiroth, represented by the figures one to three, form an upper group. This is the world of the idea. Its first and uppermost Sephirah is the primary emanation from the Unfathomable, Ineffable, Indescribable. It is situated in the center, above the second and third. It represents the primal unity in its first, undifferentiated form, while the second and third Sephiroth, by their very position, express polar duality, side by side with unity. These three emanations are generally con-

22a [See the paper by Buber, above, pp. 182ff.—ED.]

ceived as static. They are not yet formed or localized; they are motionless, beyond space and time.

All this changes in the next realm downward, the world of formation, the arena of natural forces, which contains the next six Sephiroth. This world corresponds to the middle part of our Chinese diagram. Here we encounter the mighty *dynamis* and *mixis*, motion and mixture, the glittering conflict between the elements in all its potentialities: two pull to the left, two pull to the right, in the middle, in perfect equilibrium, gleams the sixth Sephirah, which is designated as "glory" or "beauty," and which in its astronomical correspondence is characterized as the sun. Below, in the realm of form, with a distinct tendency to downward action, is the ninth Sephirah, named "foundations," which is also a kind of seal, imprinting its relief on the world immediately below it. This Sephirah stands in close connection with the very lowest, the tenth, the only Sephirah in the third world, the world of consolidation and ultimate concretization. Here again we have a parallel to the Chinese diagram: the ninth Sephirah represents the sum of all things which still belong to the celestial world, while the tenth Sephirah in the lower realm represents the corresponding things in their final materialization—the ultimate products of Creation in their polar tensions.

But this cabalistic figure is no mere image of the genesis, of the gradual descent and concretization, of divine forces out of the realm of eternal transcendence which nevertheless continues, intact and undiminished, in its eternal isolation, to hover over all things. This is made evident by the commentaries that now proceed to a different interpretation of the Tree of the Sephiroth, as the complete figure is called.[23] Here the emphasis is not on the gradual re-ascent, although this too is occasionally mentioned, but on the grouping of the three axes, each of which represents a path with its own special characteristics.

Philo of Alexandria speaks of these paths, which he calls the path of Abraham, who through knowledge attains to the goal, the path of Jacob, who advances by means of continuous exercise, and the path of Isaac, which is the path of strength. These three paths are co-ordinated with the three vertical axes or "pillars," as they are more frequently called. But Philo speaks also of a fourth path, the path of Joseph, which he calls the path of

---

23 In the *Sepher Yetsirah* we read: "His word is in them [the ten Sephiroth] when they return." Knut Stenring, tr., *The Book of Formation or Sepher Yetzirah* (London, 1923), ch. I, p. 21.

politics. Here he comes close to Plato, who also finds the concrete expression of philosophical knowledge in the theory of the state.[24] We shall make no mistake if we equate this political path with the final realization in our cabalistic schema, that is, with the tenth Sephirah, which is limited to the concreteness of the manifest world, but which, though seemingly static, attains to the goal through action in this world.

OTHER RELATED EXAMPLES

Closely related to this cabalistic diagram are various pictorial representations originating in the world of Gnostic thought. One of these is found among the illustrations to the Visions of Hildegard of Bingen (Pl. I). It has little to do with the text of the Vision it is supposed to illustrate, but reveals its descent from prototypes related to our cabalistic diagrams. It also consists of three vertically arranged circles, in the uppermost God the Father, holding out a disk bearing Christ, the Lamb of God, while the dove of the Holy Ghost hovers over His head. At His right stands Mary, characterized as Ecclesia (who is mentioned by the Gnostics as one of the first of the divine emanations); at His left John the Baptist, the great herald and precursor.[25]

In the middle circle we find the saints and the perfect. This provides a certain note of incongruity. Presumably the older model on which this work is based had here the angels, representing creative forces. We shall come back to this. In the lowest circle, we see the finished Creation, the cosmos manifested in the four elements.

And here we may cite still another diagram, described in the polemic of Celsus against Origen. Unfortunately the description is none too precise, but it is clear in any event that there were again three realms represented by vertically arranged circles. Uppermost was a circle containing a smaller circle, the larger designated as Father, the smaller as Son, hence exactly the same pattern as in the illustration to the Vision of Hildegard of Bingen. The middle circle contains the names of creative genii, while the lowest circle embraces the elements of the materialized cosmos.

Centuries later we find similar patterns in Christian religious art. A particularly illuminating example is Jan van Eyck's *Fountain of Living Water*,[25a]

24 This idea was also expressed by Lao-tse. Cf. Erwin Rousselle, "Lau Dsi's Gang durch Seele, Geschichte und Welt," *EJ 1935*.
25 Certain Gnostic conceptions go so far as to make him the "initiator of Christ."
25a ["Generally held to be an old copy of a lost original—by a follower of Jan van Eyck?" —Ludwig Baldass, *Jan van Eyck* (London, 1952), p. 288. The work is also called *The Well of Life*. Errors in our author's description have been corrected.—ED.]

in the Prado (Pl. II). Uppermost the Trinity: on a vertical axis God the Father, the Dove, and the Lamb, and on a horizontal axis, God the Father in the middle, at his right the Madonna, at his left John the Baptist. The last two are related to the polarities by their characterization as man and woman, while the personification of God the Father stands above duality. In the middle ground we see six angels playing on musical instruments, embodying a kind of middle realm, a world of creative forces whose harmony (suggesting the harmony of the spheres in Plato) calls forth the world. In the bottommost section are the representatives of mankind, the virtuous who accept the Gospel and so inherit the kingdom of heaven, and the evil who close their hearts to the Message, cling to the earth, and so harvest doom.

I am well aware that some of these diagrams and pictures are related only through analogies in structure. But the mere existence of this analogy amid the utmost superficial diversity indicates a general trend at work among men dwelling in the most varied cultural climates.

THE 'TABULA SMARAGDINA' ENGRAVING

Our third example (Fig. 3) occupies a place of honor in alchemical lore. It is said to have been engraved upon the emerald medallion of Hermes Trismegistos, while the other side of the plaque bore what since the sixth century has been repeatedly quoted as the basic text of the alchemical process.[26] It is true that text and picture do not exactly correspond, but this is frequent throughout alchemical literature. Here the reason for the discrepancy may be that the engraving is possibly of far later origin than the text, although the conception is no doubt much older than any of its realizations that have come down to us, the oldest of which belong to the fifteenth century. One must study a vast number of texts in order to establish connections between specific passages and pictorial elements. But on the basis of such study, we can reconstruct a very plausible commentary to the engraving on the legendary emerald medallion, or *Tabula smaragdina*.

Two hands point from right and left toward the center. In a later version (in Becher's *Physica subterranea*, 1699) the hands bear the inscriptions "Ratio" and "Experientia," as the sources of the knowledge disclosed in the middle. The symbols in the center, as the downward flow of the essences of sun and moon indicates, can first, like our other diagrams, be read from top to bottom. Sun and moon point to the already manifest polar tension.

26 Cf. Julius Ferdinand Ruska, *Tabula Smaragdina* (Heidelberg, 1926).

Fig. 3. Engraving from the *Tabula smaragdina* (emerald
medallion) of Hermes Trismegistos
From the *Aureum vellus* (Hamburg, 1708).

The operation of this tension, i.e., the mixture of the polar elements in the
goblet at the center, gives rise to the further differentiations of matter and
of the idea of creation, which are shown to the right and left of the goblet.
These correspond to the Tetrasomia, the fourfold body of the base elements,
which already occurs in Demokritos, the Hellenistic alchemist. These too
show polar tension: At the left the sign of the fiery, violently agitated Mars,
whose correspondences are fire and iron. Across from it, the sign of Venus,
the amiable, conciliatory goddess, whose correspondences are water and
copper. In the lower rank, at the left, the dark, heavy, malignant Saturn, to
whom correspond earth and lead, and opposite him his counterpart, the
joyful ruler Jupiter, who is manifested in all things "jovial," as in the air
that caresses us, and in tin, which is easily melted and willingly assumes any
form. In the middle, equidistant from all these extremes, stands the sign

331

of Mercury, the mediator. In him the tendency to bridge all contradictions is dominant; he transforms himself from one to the other, embodying now one pole and now the other, in marked ambivalence. In his chemical correspondence he is therefore the Quinta Essentia, the hypothetical basic substance; this fifth aggregate state constitutes a refinement of the other four, a kind of subtle ether, which can be transformed by condensation into the fiery, gaseous, liquid, and finally the solid state. All five of the planetary signs taken together represent the mixture and interaction of the basic forces of nature, which draw their primal energy from the polar opposition which in our image is represented by the sun and moon.

The ring and the chain serve to link the threefold possibility of action, the workings of the three spheres characterized in alchemy as spirit, soul, body, or as being, in the absolute, divine sense, or in the sense of human existence, or in that of cosmic existence. In the alchemical writings these are often designated as "philosophical sulphur," "philosophical mercury," and "philosophical salt," referring, specifically in the physical field, to the states of the flaming and combustible, of the fusible and mobile, of the rigid and immutable. Here again a familiar parallel imposes itself. Our Chinese diagram mentioned three forms of the solid state: wood the combustible, metal the fusible, earth the immutable. And the same triad is expressed in more universal, philosophical terms in the Indian doctrine of the three *gunas*, manifested as the flaming lust of *rajas*, the flowing goodness of *sattva*, and the heavy darkness of *tamas*.

There are indeed variations in the alchemical nomenclature. Sometimes salt figures as the product of the two other polar forces, and sometimes the philosophical mercury is represented as the connecting link and middle. Indeed, when we consult the Indian version, it becomes clear to us that the three factors are equivalent, and that each in a certain sense is built on the existence of the other two.

In the *Tabula smaragdina* engraving, salt is on the left, represented as a red and white eagle, while sulphur is on the right, a green lion on a yellow background, and mercury is in the middle as a pointed star.

From the mixture of the elements in their threefold aspect arise all things that are manifested in heaven and on earth. In the figure this is stated as follows: to the right a circle with clods represents the earth (in other versions we find a map), while to the left the heavens are indicated by two crossing circular bands signifying the equator and the ecliptic.

So far our picture generally corresponds to the Chinese diagram and the cabalistic figure. But now we come to a new element: In the very midst of this escutcheon we find the symbol of dominion, the imperial orb. This dominion, which is in every way unlimited, because it embraces absolute freedom, falls to him who carries the great task of alchemy to completion by realizing the philosophers' stone. It is to be expected that this central concept of alchemy can be discussed only with the utmost caution, negatively circumscribed rather than positively defined.[27] In the field of chemistry it is a red magic powder, or else a crystal, by which base or, as it is called in alchemy, sick or imperfect metal can be transformed into the perfection of gold, or by which the quantitative miracle of multiplying existing gold can be performed. In the field of ideas, one might speak of the philosophers' stone as the harmony transcending all contradictions, as absolute freedom, as release from time, space, and causality, with the intimation that the ultimate freedom can be achieved only through this philosophers' stone.[28] It might also be defined as the point where the manifest directly confronts the transcendent and where only one last crucial step is needed to make all incommensurable things one. If we consider the definition of the "self" in its all-embracing absoluteness and transcendence, as it occurs for example in the Indian Vedānta, we may be justified in saying that the philosophers' stone induces the phenomenon whose essence it is that all barriers fall and that man liberates his "self" from the trammels of the personality. This liberated "self," which has lost all connection with the person or individual, might well be designated as "God," as for example in Angelus Silesius: "Thou must be Mary and bear God from within thee." And the gradual attainment of this state would find its correspondence in the great work of alchemy, which culminates precisely in the creation of the philosophers' stone.

A comparison of the text of the *Tabula smaragdina* with the engraving makes it clear that here too the relation between ascent and descent plays its part. But it would carry us too far afield to explore this difficult and obscure problem even in its broad outlines, not to mention its lesser im-

---

27 Thus the Arabic manuscript attributed to Ostanes uses 84 names with which to give some intimation of the nature of the stone, while Lippmann in his *Alchemie* disposes of the stone by simply calling it "superstition."

28 According to Zosimos, the divine work is performed by the arts of the *poieitai*, the makers, or workers, by means of the metal-creating stone, while Geber designates the stone as the "ferment of ferments," by which the ultimate metamorphosis is induced.

plications. The great difficulty in the study of alchemy is that we can judge the content of the texts only after we have experienced the things of which they speak. And since I must admit that my empirical foundation suffices barely for an understanding of fundamentals, I am compelled to leave the inquiry into details to those who possess the requisite experience. I only fear that they will not disclose their knowledge. And even if they were to speak, their words would be unintelligible to those who had not attained the same level of experience.

A SEVENTEENTH-CENTURY COSMOGRAM

In general structure, the preceding illustrations disclose an analogy which is not necessarily based on a common tradition. Our next picture (Pl. III), on the other hand, is obviously an interpretation and amplification of the third. It is an illustration from the *Utriusque Cosmi . . . Historia* by the English alchemist Robert Fludd (Oppenheim, 1617). In it we discern a strong theological influence and a certain psychological perception as well. Cabalistic influence, it goes without saying, plays a major role.

The three circles at the top adhere almost exactly to the cabalistic pattern: At the summit a circle which encompasses the antitheses; here, as the text tells us, the divine creative will is combined with the will-not-to-create. But the opposites strive apart and send their emanations downward, engendering the world of light on the right and the world of darkness on the left. The polar tension is developed to a maximum. But the world of darkness contains a germ of light, which in our figure is suggested by a little white triangle. This corresponds quite closely to the cabalistic realm of ideas.

The large circle below these two represents the unfolding of the world forces out of the polarity of the upper world, and corresponds to the middle realm of the six Sephiroth in the cabalistic figure, the world of formation. Light and shade join to form the manifest world; the sun appears as an emissary of light; but the symbol of the dove, situated between it and the world of light, shows that this is no purely physical but also a spiritual sun, for the dove is the symbol of the spirit of light.

It becomes evident that Fludd has more in mind than the development of matter when we consider the results of the world process as represented in his diagram. It culminates not merely in the things of heaven and earth, as in the Chinese diagram or in the *Tabula smaragdina* engraving. Here there is a reference to the realm of the soul. Like Jan van Eyck's *Fountain of Living Water*, Fludd's picture deals also with the realm of the soul. But while the Van Eyck painting divides souls into good and evil, the blessed and the damned, here, in a conception that strikes us as modern, the "realm of Apollo" is juxtaposed to the "realm of Dionysus." These are represented by two semicircles which, taken together, correspond to the bottommost realm of the ninth Sephirah in the cabalistic figure, the world of final concretization.

After what has been said, it will not be difficult to read this picture from bottom to top, as a synthetic alchemy wherein the interaction of the Apollonian and Dionysian natures results in the ultimate unity which transcends contradictions.

OTHER EXAMPLES

We might still mention a number of figures and diagrams specifically representing the process of metamorphosis that takes place between the antitheses: Above and Below, which in its descending movement implies condensation, realization, concretization, while in ascending it implies sublimation, transfiguration, or spiritualization.

In the figures thus far shown, this metamorphosis is represented as a complex of forces striving in different directions. But the *Tabula smaragdina* points to a special meaning by associating the symbols of the planets with the elements. These symbols suggest a gradation corresponding to the spheres of the planets.

Gradation, ascent, and descent: these are customary symbols of the metamorphosis. But here it must be taken into account that the seven main organs in man are correlated with the seven planets,[29] while the planet symbols may also refer to the seven principal metals, which in turn call forth definite effects in man. Upon these correspondences, the mystic J. G. Gichtel (1638–1710) built up a whole system which is not purely physiological but encompasses also psychological development. The planet symbols are not localized in particular organs of the human body, but designate certain points or foci, to which organs do not necessarily correspond. In the course of development the mind passes through these points, and consciously apprehends them; the ascent through the planetary spheres to the ultimate

29 In the calendars of the fifteenth-century Books of Hours, we almost invariably find a human figure upon which these astrological correspondences are noted.

heights of heaven leaves its traces in the human body, which are discernible only in the relative situations of the points (indicated by the planetary symbols). Gichtel insists that this unique and variable planetary system within man is based on his own experience.[30] This makes it all the more noteworthy that Gichtel's account coincides in certain respects with the Tantric system; here too we have seven centers in the body, which are looked upon not as physiological organs, but as foci of psychological experience. Furthermore, in both systems the seven degrees of experience are characterized by the names of the planets.

AN AMPLIFICATION OF THE 'TABULA SMARAGDINA' ENGRAVING

Our last picture (Pl. IV) is a dramatic representation of the ideas we have been discussing. It is taken from a collection of alchemical treatises published at Frankfurt in 1678 under the title *Musaeum hermeticum*.[31] It bears no accompanying text other than the inscription of the *Tabula smaragdina*, and this clearly identifies it as an amplification and elucidation of the diagram which served as our third figure. It is a carefully executed etching by Matthäus Merian of Basel, approximately 12 × 10 inches in size. In two places it clearly reveals its models: the five birds at the lower part of the middle circle are copied from a seventeenth-century edition of the *Twelve Keys* of Basilius Valentinus, while the nude woman at the lower right is an exact copy of an etching by Theodore de Bry in Fludd's *Utriusque Cosmi . . . Historia*, representing Dame Nature, her right hand fastened to the divine will and her left hand continuing to work upon the manifest world. These two borrowings suffice to show that Merian did not invent his whole composition, but pieced it together from various notes and models.

Merian's figure goes far beyond the conceptions we have thus far discussed. It does not stop at the limits of the ineffable. In its upper third it even attempts to represent a specifically Christian heaven, which to be sure exerts a downward influence: The Trinity is represented by three symbols—the Supreme Name, the Lamb, and the Dove, each transfigured by a nimbus; within the radiant semicircle of heaven is a semicircle of angels, which carry on the downward action, calling forth the celestial firmament characterized by the twelve signs of the zodiac; further, the annual circuit, and

---

30 Cited in *Eyne Kurze Eröffnung . . . Der dreyen Prinzipien . . . im Menschen*, published by J. G. Graber, 1736.
31 See *The Hermetic Museum*, tr. Arthur Edward Waite (2 vols., London, 1953), II, fig. iv, preceding p. 311.

within it the three fundamental qualities of the world in the order: mercury, sulphur, salt. The next concentric circle contains the four elements, and the innermost discloses the two polarities, characterized as an upright triangle and as a triangle standing on its tip; beneath these is the union of opposites, indicated by the combination of the two triangles into a star of David. At the center, within an upright equilateral triangle, we find the symbol of the philosophers' stone; this symbol, in which all the planetary symbols are united in one, resembles the sign of mercury, but has a point in the center.

The whole celestial world culminates in this central symbol, which encompasses all its forces. But the symbol is also the zenith of the lower world, radiating downward the creative forces that are concentrated in it from above. Again the elements unfold, the primal factors, the annual circuit, the world of the seven planets. Then follows the ring of the five beasts, which may be interpreted as concretized elements, but also as the phases of the alchemical process. In the middle is the omniform basilisk, which represents both the metamorphoses of alchemy and the quality of the Quinta Essentia, the ether, out of which the other four aggregate states are condensed: the fiery, represented by the phoenix, which also indicates the red glow of the stone; the gaseous by the pelican, which also connotes the yellow glow; the liquid by the swan, which stands for the white glow; and the solid by the raven, which embodies blackness, the low point in the process of development. This world of active factors is delimited at the bottom by the starry firmament and a dense semicircle of clouds.

So far, the figure shows the divine origin of the cosmos, which is formed through the harmony and hostility of active forces. But the downward manifestation of these forces has not yet been shown. The philosophers' stone is characterized by its central position in the picture, at the dividing line between the upper and the middle world.

And now, at the bottom, the multiform world is represented by personifications, seals, and symbols of its components. In direct contact with the world of forces and chained to these forces, we find the figures of man and woman; in their hands they bear the sun and moon, which identify them as personifications of polarity in the world. The sun and moon also differentiate between the diurnal and nocturnal aspect of the world; beside the sun is the lion, which we have encountered as the symbol of the philosophical sulphur, of fire and flame. Below and beside the lion is the phoenix,

337

disclosing beneath its wings the fiery and gaseous states of things. In the corresponding position, beside the moon, appears Actaeon changed into a deer, and at his feet an eagle shelters the symbols of liquid and solid matter.

Thus the two conflicting aspects of the world are dramatically indicated. In the middle rises a hill covered with trees. Seven larger trees disclose the signs of the seven planets or principal metals, twelve smaller trees below them bear the symbols of the most important metalloids. Among them, strange to say, the symbol of mercury, or quicksilver, appears for the second time. Here we have a significant reference:

A garden with twelve trees plays an important part in the Book of Baruch by the Gnostic Justin.[32] It is the garden of Eden; its twelve trees represent twelve angels, who execute the will of their Father in heaven, while twelve other angels corresponding to them do the opposite in every respect. (According to the Gnosis of Justin, there is, in addition to the first, increate principle of the world, conceived as male and inactive, a second, creative male principle which is opposed in every respect by a third, female principle. The twice-twelve angels are dominated by these opposing principles.) The third of the twelve trees, representing the paternal angel Baruch, plays a special role. This is the tree of life, to which in the picture corresponds the tree of mercury, of the "living silver" (as the ultimate material realization). The adversary of the angel Baruch is the maternal angel Nahas, the serpent seducer in paradise.

Thus the symbol of mercury appears in the ring of the twelve trees of paradise (front right); in the back row of seven trees representing the seven principal metals or planets (second from the left); and in the outermost of the three circles in the center of our figure, where it indicates one of the three fundamental states of being. Finally, it appears in the center, transformed by the point in its center into the symbol of the philosophers' stone. In diverse aspects, the mercurial element passes through all the degrees of becoming, thus connoting the descent of a supreme principle. Thereby, Hermes Trismegistos is characterized as the supreme genius and guardian of alchemy; and in every sphere his manifestations and influences are as mysterious as the essence of the strange liquid metal, quicksilver. But the sign also implies the possibility of ascent, the recovery of man's lost freedom. In the chemical aspect of alchemy this is expressed by the crucial role of quicksilver in the preparation of the philosophers' stone.

32 Cf. Hippolytus, *Elenchos*, V, 21ff. (ed. Wendland, p. 123ff.).

In this garden of paradise stands an old man whose starry gown identifies him as a magus. He signifies the union of opposites, symbolized by his black and white dress. Depending on the direction in which the figure is read, he appears as the son of the human pair to the left and right of him, or as their begetter. The old man stands on a lion with two bodies, which originated when two lions devoured one another, thus becoming one without losing their separate essences.[33] The one lion is characterized by the fire that flares up behind him, the other by a fountain of water. From the union of water and fire arises the "watery fire" as the alchemists called it, the fiery *aqua vitae* which flows from the mouth of the lion. It is from this *aqua vitae* that the philosophers' stone will be distilled. This is the meaning of our picture, and it is also formulated in a number of alchemical texts.

That this symbolism is not accidental but has taken shape according to psychological laws becomes evident when we consider that the three persons represented at the bottom of our figure—the nocturnal woman, the glittering man, and the sovereign sage who bridges contradictions—recur in the dreams of modern men.[34]

This is not the place to take up these interrelations in detail. I shall content myself with remarking that here too the law of correspondences prevails, and not as a vague hypothesis, but in actual fact. In this case, to be sure, it does not say "As above, so below" but "As without, so within," and conversely. Thus, in the last analysis, the whole process of growth and passing away tends toward the development of consciousness, and thence toward release, liberation, and redemption of the individual.

SUMMARY

All the pictures we have cited express, in diverse terms, descent and return, genesis and dissolution of the world, outward action and striving for the innermost inwardness. They aim at suggesting the foundation and essence of alchemy. It seems to me that in this they succeed better than all the copious, sometimes mutually contradictory writings, which often lose themselves in inextricable details. Precisely because the pictures deal in ambiguous signs and symbols, rather than in clear concepts, the contemplation

33 The battle of the lions is represented and explained in Michael Maier, *Atalanta fugiens* (Oppenheim, 1618), and also in the famous symbolic representation of Nicolas Flamel, here in the form of two dragons devouring one another.

34 Cf. C. G. Jung, "Archetypes of the Collective Unconscious," in *The Archetypes and the Collective Unconscious* (CWJ, 9, 1; 1959).

of them shows us the diversity of the alchemical principle of development and transmutation, now cosmological and all-embracing, now shrunken to metallurgical conceptions, now dealing in terms of physiology, now suggestive of psychology, and, finally, giving an intimation of the metaphysical in all its manifold relations. Is it any wonder that, with all its many faces, alchemy should have been misunderstood, abused, reviled as madness and despised as fraud? And yet those few who have understood its language have seen in it a valuable attempt to interpret the ultimate reality.

C. G. Jung

Dream Symbols of the Individuation Process [1]

... facilis descensus Averno;
noctes atque dies patet atri ianua Ditis;
sed revocare gradum superasque evadere ad auras,
hoc opus, hic labor est. ...
Virgil, *Aeneid*, VI, 126-29

1. Introduction

I. THE MATERIAL

The symbols of the process of individuation that appear in dreams are images of an archetypal nature which depict the centralizing process or the production of a new center of personality. A general idea of this process may be got from my essay, "The Relations between the Ego and the Unconscious." [2] For certain reasons mentioned there I call this center the "self," which should be understood as the totality of the psyche. The self is not only the center but the whole circumference, embracing both conscious and unconscious; it is the center of this totality, just as the ego is the center of consciousness.

The symbols now under consideration are not concerned with the manifold stages and transformations of the individuation process, but with the images that refer directly and exclusively to the new center as it comes into consciousness. These images belong to a definite category which I call mandala symbolism. In *The Secret of the Golden Flower,* published in collaboration with Richard Wilhelm,[3] I have described this symbolism in detail. In

---

1 [Originally published in *EJ 1935* (1936), which version was translated as "Dream Symbols of the Process of Individuation" by Stanley Dell in *The Integration of Personality*, a volume of papers by Professor Jung (New York, 1939; London, 1940). The original was revised and expanded as Part II of *Psychologie und Alchemie* (Zurich, 1944), which was translated by R. F. C. Hull as *Psychology and Alchemy* (CWJ, 12; 1953). The present version is Mr. Hull's, revised to correspond reasonably to the *EJ 1935* version.—ED.]

2 [In *Two Essays on Analytical Psychology* (CWJ, 7; 1953).—ED.]

3 [First pub. as *Das Geheimnis der goldenen Blüte* (Munich, 1929), with a European commentary by Jung; tr. Cary F. Baynes (London and New York, 1931). A revised

341

the present study I should like to put before you an individual series of such symbols in chronological order. The material consists of over a thousand dreams and visual impressions coming from a young man of excellent scientific education.[4] For the purposes of this study I have worked on the first four hundred or so dreams and visions, which extended over a period of nearly ten months. In order to avoid all personal influence I asked one of my pupils, a woman doctor, who was then a beginner, to undertake the observation of the process. This went on for five months. Except for a short interview at the very beginning, before the commencement of the observation, I did not see the dreamer at all during the first eight months. Thus it happened that 355 of the dreams (or visions) were experienced away from any personal contact with myself. Only the last forty-five occurred under my observation. No interpretations worth mentioning were then attempted because the dreamer, owing to his excellent scientific training and ability, did not require any additional assistance. Hence conditions were really ideal for unprejudiced observation and recording.

First of all, then, I shall present extracts from the twenty-two initial dreams in order to show how the mandala symbolism makes a very early appearance and is embedded in the rest of the dream material. Later on I shall pick out in chronological order the dreams that refer specifically to the mandala.[5]

With few exceptions all the dreams have been abbreviated, either by extracting the part that carries the main thought or by condensing the whole text to essentials. This simplifying operation has not only curtailed their length but has also removed personal allusions and complications, as was necessary for reasons of discretion. Despite this somewhat doubtful interference I have, to the best of my knowledge and scrupulosity, avoided any arbitrary distortion of meaning. The same considerations had also to apply to my own interpretation, so that certain passages in the dreams may

---

version of the tr. of Jung's commentary appeared in *Psyche and Symbol*, a selection of Jung's writings, ed. V. de Laszlo (Anchor Books; New York, 1958). See also "Concerning Mandala Symbolism" (orig. 1950), in *The Archetypes and the Collective Unconscious* (CWJ, 9, i; 1959), pp. 355ff., with 54 illustrs.—ED.]

4 I must emphasize that this education was not historical, philological, archaeological, or ethnological. Any references to material derived from these fields came unconsciously to the dreamer.

5 "Mandala" (Sanskrit) means "circle," also "magic circle." Its symbolism includes— to mention only the most important forms—all concentrically arranged figures, round or square patterns with a center, and radial or spherical arrangements.

342

appear to have been overlooked. Had I not made this sacrifice and kept the material absolutely complete, I should not have been in a position to publish this series, which in my opinion could hardly be surpassed in intelligence, clarity, and consistency. It therefore gives me great pleasure to express my sincere gratitude here and now to the "author" for the service he has rendered to science.

II. THE METHOD

In my writings and lectures I have always insisted that we must give up all preconceived opinions when it comes to the analysis and interpretation of the objective psyche,[6] or in other words the "unconscious." We do not yet possess a general theory of dreams that would enable us to use a deductive method with impunity, any more than we possess a general theory of consciousness from which we can draw deductive conclusions. The manifestations of the subjective psyche, or the conscious mind, can be predicted to only the smallest degree, and there is no theoretical argument to prove beyond doubt that any causal connection necessarily exists between them. On the contrary, we have to reckon with a high percentage of arbitrariness and "chance" in the complex actions and reactions of the conscious mind. Similarly there is no empirical, still less a theoretical reason to assume that the same does not apply to the manifestations of the unconscious. The latter are just as manifold, unpredictable, and arbitrary as the former and must therefore be subjected to as many different ways of approach. In the case of conscious utterances we are in the fortunate position of being directly addressed and presented with a content whose purpose we can recognize; but with "unconscious" manifestations there is no directed or adapted language in our sense of the word—there is merely a psychic phenomenon that would appear to have only the loosest connections with conscious contents. If the expressions of the conscious mind are incomprehensible we can always ask what they mean. But the objective psyche is something alien even to the conscious mind through which it expresses itself. We are therefore obliged to adopt the method we would use in deciphering a fragmentary text or one containing unknown words: we examine the context. The meaning of the unknown word may become evident when we compare

6 For this conception see my "Basic Postulates of Analytical Psychology," *The Structure and Dynamics of the Psyche* (CWJ, 8; 1960), pars. 623f.; and Toni Wolff, "Einführung in die Grundlagen der komplexen Psychologie," in *Die kulturelle Bedeutung der komplexen Psychologie* (Berlin, 1935) pp. 34ff.

a series of passages in which it occurs. The psychological context of dream contents consists in the web of associations in which the dream is naturally embedded. Theoretically we can never know anything in advance about this web, but in practice it is sometimes possible, granted long enough experience. Even so, careful analysis will never rely too much on technical rules; the danger of deception and suggestion is too great. In the analysis of isolated dreams above all, this kind of knowing in advance and making assumptions on the grounds of practical expectation or general probability is positively wrong. It should therefore be an absolute rule to assume that every dream and every part of a dream is unknown at the outset, and to attempt an interpretation only after carefully taking up the context. We can then apply the meaning we have thus discovered to the text of the dream itself and see whether this yields a working solution, or rather, whether a satisfying meaning emerges. But in no circumstances may we anticipate that this meaning will fit in with any of our subjective expectations; for quite possibly, indeed very frequently, the dream is saying something surprisingly different from what we would expect. As a matter of fact, if the meaning we find in the dream happens to coincide with our expectations, that is a reason for suspicion; for as a rule the standpoint of the unconscious is complementary or compensatory [7] to consciousness and thus unexpectedly "different." I would not deny the possibility of *parallel* dreams, i.e., dreams whose meaning coincides with or supports the conscious attitude, but in my experience at least, these are rather rare.

Now, the method I adopt in the present study seems to run directly counter to this basic principle of dream interpretation. It looks as if the dreams were being interpreted without the least regard for the context. And in fact I have not taken up the context at all, seeing that the dreams in this series were not dreamed (as mentioned above) under my observation. I proceed rather as if I had had the dreams myself and were therefore in a position to supply the context.

This procedure, if applied to the *isolated* dreams of someone unknown to me personally, would indeed be a gross technical blunder. But here we are not dealing with isolated dreams; they form a coherent series in the course of which the meaning gradually unfolds more or less of its own accord. *The series is the context which the dreamer himself supplies.* It is as if not one

---

7 I intentionally omit an analysis of the words "complementary" and "compensatory," as it would lead us too far afield.

text but many lay before us, throwing light from all sides on the unknown terms, so that a reading of all the texts is sufficient to elucidate the difficult passages in each individual one. Moreover, in the third chapter we are concerned with a definite archetype that has long been known to us from other sources, and this considerably facilitates the interpretation. Of course the interpretation of each individual passage is bound to be largely conjecture, but the series as a whole gives us all the clues we need to correct any possible errors in the preceding passages.

It goes without saying that while the dreamer was under the observation of my pupil he knew nothing of these interpretations and was therefore quite unprejudiced by anybody else's opinion. Moreover I hold the view, based on wide experience, that the possibility and danger of prejudice are exaggerated. Experience shows that the objective psyche is autonomous in the highest degree. Were it not so, it could not carry out its most characteristic function: the compensation of the conscious mind. The conscious mind allows itself to be trained like a parrot, but the unconscious does not— which is why St. Augustine thanked God for not making him responsible for his dreams. The unconscious is a psychic fact; any efforts to drill it are only apparently successful, and moreover harmful to consciousness. It is and remains beyond the reach of subjective arbitrary control: in a realm where nature and her secrets can be neither improved upon nor perverted, where we can listen but may not meddle.

2. The Initial Dreams

1. *The dreamer is at a social gathering. On leaving, he puts on a stranger's hat instead of his own.*

The hat, as a covering for the head, has the general sense of something that epitomizes the head. Just as in summing up we bring ideas "under one head" (*unter einen Hut*), so the hat, as a sort of leading idea, covers the whole personality and imparts its own significance to it. Coronation endows the ruler with the divine nature of the sun, the doctor's hood bestows the dignity of a scholar, and a stranger's hat imparts a strange nature. Meyrink uses this theme in his novel *The Golem*,[1] where the hero puts on the hat of Athanasius Pernath and, as a result, becomes involved in a strange experience. It is clear enough in *The Golem* that the thing that entangles the

1 Leipzig, 1915; tr. M. Pemberton (London, 1928).

345

hero in fantastic adventures is the unconscious. Let us stress at once the significance of the *Golem* parallel and assume that the hat in the dream is the hat of an Athanasius, an immortal, a being beyond time, the universal and everlasting man as distinct from the ephemeral and "accidental" mortal man. Circumscribing the head, the hat is round like the sun disk of a crown and therefore contains the first allusion to the mandala. We shall find the attribute of eternal duration confirmed in the ninth mandala dream (sec. 3), while the mandala character of the hat comes out in the thirty-fifth mandala dream. As a general result of the change in hats we may expect a development similar to that in *The Golem:* an emergence of the unconscious. The unconscious with its figures is already standing like a shadow behind the dreamer and pushing its way into consciousness.

2. *The dreamer is going on a railway journey, and by standing in front of the window he blocks the view for his fellow passengers. He must get out of their way.*

The process is beginning to move, and the dreamer discovers that he is keeping the light from those who stand *behind* him, namely the unconscious components of his personality. We have no eyes behind us; consequently "behind" is the region of the unseen, the unconscious. If the dreamer will only stop blocking the window (consciousness), the unconscious content will become conscious.

3 (Hypnagogic visual impression). *By the seashore. The sea breaks into the land, flooding everything. Then the dreamer is sitting on a lonely island.*

The sea is the symbol of the collective unconscious, because unfathomed depths lie concealed beneath its reflecting surface. Those who stand behind, the shadowy and demonic συνοπαθοί, "companions," have burst into the *terra firma* of consciousness like a flood. Such invasions have something uncanny about them because they are irrational and incomprehensible to the person concerned. They bring about a momentous alteration of his personality, since they immediately constitute a painful personal secret which alienates and isolates him from his surroundings. It is something that we "cannot tell anybody." We are afraid of being accused of mental abnormality—not without reason, for much the same thing happens to lunatics. Even so, it is a far cry from the intuitive perception of such an invasion to being inundated by it pathologically, though the layman does not realize

346

this. Isolation by a secret results as a rule in an *animation* of the psychic atmosphere, as a substitute for loss of contact with other people. It causes an activation of the unconscious, and this produces something similar to the illusions and hallucinations that beset lonely wanderers in the desert, seafarers, and saints. The mechanism of these phenomena can best be explained in terms of energy. Our normal relations to objects in the world at large are maintained by a certain expenditure of energy. If the relation to the object is cut off there is a "retention" of energy, which then creates an equivalent substitute-formation. For instance, just as persecution mania comes from a relationship poisoned by mistrust, so, as a substitute for the normal animation of the environment, an illusory reality rises up in which weird ghostly shadows flit about in place of people. That is why primitive man has always believed that lonely and desolate places are haunted by "devils" and suchlike apparitions.

4. *The dreamer is surrounded by a throng of vague female forms. A voice within him says, "First I must get away from Father."*

Here the psychic atmosphere has been animated by what the Middle Ages called succubi. We are reminded of the visions of St. Anthony in Egypt, so eruditely described by Flaubert.[2] The element of hallucination shows itself in the fact that the thought is spoken aloud. The words "first I must get away" call for a concluding sentence which would begin with "in order to." Presumably it would run "in order to follow the unconscious, i.e., the alluring female forms." The father, the embodiment of the traditional spirit as expressed in religion or a general philosophy of life, is standing in his way. He imprisons the dreamer in the world of the conscious mind and its values. The traditional masculine world with its intellectualism and rationalism is felt to be an impediment, from which we must conclude that the unconscious, now approaching him, stands in direct opposition to the tendencies of the conscious mind and that the dreamer, despite this opposition, is already favorably disposed toward the unconscious. For this reason the latter should not be subordinated to the rationalistic judgments of the conscious mind; it ought rather to be an experience *sui generis*. Naturally it is not easy for the intellect to accept this, because it involves at least a partial, if not a total, *sacrificium intellectus*. Furthermore, the problem thus raised is very difficult for modern man to grasp; to begin

2 *The First Temptation of St. Anthony*, tr. René Francis (London, 1924).

with, he can only understand the unconscious as an inessential and unreal appendage of the conscious mind, and not as a special sphere of experience with laws of its own. In the course of the later dreams this conflict will appear again and again, until finally the right formula is found for the correlation of conscious and unconscious, and the personality is assigned its correct position between the two. Moreover, such a conflict cannot be solved by understanding, but only by experience. Every stage of the experience must be lived through. There is no feat of interpretation or any other trick by which to circumvent this difficulty, for the union of conscious and unconscious can only be achieved step by step.

The resistance of the conscious mind to the unconscious and the depreciation of the latter were historical necessities in the development of the human psyche, for otherwise the conscious mind would never have been able to differentiate itself at all. But modern man's consciousness has strayed rather too far from the fact of the unconscious. We have even forgotten that the psyche is by no means of our design, but is for the most part autonomous and unconscious. Consequently the approach of the unconscious induces a panic fear in civilized people, not least on account of the menacing analogy with insanity. The intellect has no objection to "analyzing" the unconscious as a passive object; on the contrary such an activity would coincide with our rational expectations. But to let the unconscious go its own way and to experience it as a reality exceeds the courage and capacity of the average European. He prefers simply not to understand this problem. For the spiritually weak-kneed this is the better course, since the thing is not without its dangers.

The experience of the unconscious is a personal secret communicable only to very few, and that with difficulty; hence the isolating effect we noted above. But isolation brings about a compensatory animation of the psychic atmosphere which strikes us as uncanny. The figures that appear in the dream are feminine, thus pointing to the feminine nature of the unconscious. They are fairies or fascinating sirens and lamias, who infatuate the lonely wanderer and lead him astray. Likewise seductive maidens appear at the beginning of the *nekyia* [3] of Poliphilo.[4]

3 *Nekyia*, Νεκυία, from νέκυς (corpse), the title of the eleventh book of the Odyssey, is the sacrifice to the dead for conjuring up the departed from Hades. *Nekyia* is therefore an apt designation for the "journey to Hades," the descent into the land of the dead, and was used by Albrecht Dieterich in this sense in his commentary (entitled

5 (Visual impression). *A snake describes a circle round the dreamer, who stands rooted to the ground like a tree.*

The drawing of a spellbinding circle is an ancient magical device used by everyone who has a special or secret purpose in mind. He thereby protects himself from the "perils of the soul" that threaten him from without and that attack anyone who is isolated by a secret. The same procedure has also been used since olden times to set a place apart as holy and inviolable; in founding a city, for instance, they first drew the *sulcus primigenius* or original furrow.[5] The fact that the dreamer stands rooted to the center is a compensation of his almost insuperable desire to run away from the unconscious. He experienced an agreeable feeling of relief after this vision—and rightly, since he has succeeded in establishing a protected *temenos*,[6] a taboo area where he will be able to meet the unconscious. His isolation, so uncanny before, is now exalted into an aim, endowed with meaning and purpose, and thus robbed of its terrors.

6 (Visual impression, directly following upon 5). *The veiled figure of a woman seated on a stair.*

The motif of the unknown woman—whose technical name is the "anima"[7] —appears here for the first time. Like the throng of vague female forms in dream 4, she is a personification of the animated psychic atmosphere. From now on the figure of the unknown woman reappears in a great many of the dreams. Personification always indicates an autonomous activity of the unconscious. If some personal figure appears we may be sure that the unconscious is beginning to grow active. The activity of such figures very often has an anticipatory character: something that the dreamer himself

---

Nekyia, Leipzig, 1913) on the Codex of Akhmim, which contains an apocalyptic fragment of the Gospel of Peter. Typical instances are the *Divine Comedy*, the classical *Walpurgisnacht* in *Faust*, the apocryphal accounts of Christ's descent into hell, etc.

4 The *Hypnerotomachia Poliphili*, the work of a Dominican, Francesco Colonna (1433–1527), dates from about 1467 and was printed in 1499 or thereabout. Cf. French tr., François Béroalde de Verville, *I e Tableau des riches inventions couvertes du voile des feintes amoureuses, qui sont representées dans le Songe de Poliphile* (Paris, 1600). [Cf. also *The Dream of Poliphilo*, related and interpreted by Linda Fierz-David, tr. Mary Hottinger (New York [BS XXV], 1950).—ED.]

5 Eduard Fritz Knuchel, *Die Umwandlung in Kult, Magie und Rechtsgebrauch* (Basel, 1919).

6 A piece of land, often a grove, set apart and dedicated to a god.

7 For the concept of "anima," see "The Relations between the Ego and the Unconscious," pp. 186ff.

will do later is now being done in advance. In this case the allusion is to a stair, thus indicating an ascent or a descent.

Since the process running through dreams of this kind has an historical analogy in the rites of initiation, it may not be superfluous to draw attention to the important part which the Stairway of the Seven Planets played in these rites, as we know from Apuleius, among others. The initiations of late classical syncretism, already saturated with alchemy (cf. the visions of Zosimos [8]), were particularly concerned with the theme of ascent, i.e., sublimation. The ascent was often represented by a ladder; hence the burial gift in Egypt of a small ladder for the *ka* of the dead.[9] The idea of an ascent through the seven spheres of the planets symbolizes the return of the soul to the sun god from whom it originated, as we know for instance from Firmicus Maternus.[10] Thus the Mystery of Isis described by Apuleius [11] culminated in what early medieval alchemy, going back to Alexandrian culture as transmitted by Arab tradition,[12] called the *solificatio*, where the initiand was crowned as Helios.

7 (Visual impression). *The veiled woman uncovers her face. It shines like the sun.*

The *solificatio* is consummated on the person of the anima. The process would seem to correspond to the *illuminatio* or enlightenment. This "mystical" idea contrasts strongly with the rational attitude of the conscious mind, which recognizes only intellectual enlightenment as the highest form of understanding and insight. Naturally this attitude never reckons with the fact that scientific knowledge satisfies only the little tip of personality that is contemporaneous with ourselves, not the collective psyche [13] that reaches back into the gray mists of antiquity and always requires a special rite if it is to be united with present-day consciousness. It is clear, therefore, that

8 Zosimos lived *c.* A.D. 300. Cf. Richard Reitzenstein, *Poimandres; Studien zur griechisch-ägyptischen und frühchristlichen Literatur* (Leipzig, 1904), pp. 9ff.; Marcellin Berthelot, *Collection des anciens alchimistes grecs* (Paris, 1887–88).

9 The surmise of the ladder motif is confirmed in dreams 12 and 13.

10 "*Animo descensus per orbem solis tribitur*" (The spirit is believed [by pagans] to descend through the disk of the sun).

11 *The Golden Ass.*

12 Cf. Julius Ferdinand Ruska, *Turba Philosophorum; Ein Beitrag zur Geschichte der Alchemie* (Quellen und Studien zur Geschichte der Naturwissenschaften und der Medizin, 1; Berlin, 1931).

13 Cf. the definition of "collective unconscious" in my *Psychological Types* (London and New York, 1923).

a "lighting up" of the unconscious is being prepared, which has far more the character of an *illuminatio* than of rational "elucidation." The *solificatio* is infinitely far removed from the conscious mind and seems to it almost chimerical.

8 (Visual impression). *A rainbow is to be used as a bridge. But one must go under it and not over it. Whoever goes over it will fall and be killed.*

Only the gods can walk rainbow bridges in safety; mere mortals fall and meet their death, for the rainbow is only a lovely semblance that spans the sky, and not a highway for human beings with bodies. These must pass "under it." But water flows under bridges too, following its own gradient and seeking the lowest place. This hint will be confirmed later.

9. *A green land where many sheep are pastured. It is the "land of sheep."*

This curious fragment, inscrutable at first glance, may derive from childhood impressions and particularly from those of a religious nature, which would not be far to seek in this connection—e.g., "He maketh me to lie down in green pastures," or the early Christian allegories of sheep and shepherd. The next vision points in the same direction.

10 (Visual impression). *The unknown woman stands in the land of sheep and points the way.*

The anima, having already anticipated the *solificatio*, now appears as the psychopomp, the one who shows the way. The way begins in the children's land, i.e., at a time when rational present-day consciousness was not yet separated from the historical psyche, the collective unconscious. The separation is indeed inevitable, but it leads to such an alienation from that dim psyche of the dawn of mankind that a loss of instinct ensues. The result is instinctual atrophy and hence disorientation in everyday human situations. But it also follows from the separation that the "children's land" will remain definitely infantile and become a perpetual source of childish inclinations and impulses. These intrusions are naturally most unwelcome to the conscious mind, and it consistently represses them for that reason. But the very consistency of the repression only serves to bring about a still greater alienation from the fountainhead, thus increasing the lack of instinct until it becomes lack of soul. As a result, the conscious mind is either completely swamped by childishness or else constantly obliged to defend itself in vain against the inundation, by means of a cynical affectation of old age or embittered resignation. We must therefore realize that despite its undeniable successes the rational attitude of present-day consciousness is, in many human respects, childishly unadapted and hostile to life. Life has grown desiccated and cramped, crying out for the rediscovery of the fountainhead. But the fountainhead can be discovered only if the conscious mind will suffer itself to be led back to the "children's land," there to receive guidance from the unconscious as before. To remain a child too long is childish, but it is just as childish to move away and then assume that childhood no longer exists because we do not see it. But if we return to the "children's land" we succumb to the fear of becoming childish, because we do not realize that everything psychic in origin has a double face. One face looks forward, the other back. It is ambivalent and therefore symbolic, like all living reality.

We stand on a peak of consciousness, believing in a childish way that the path leads upward to yet higher peaks beyond. That is the chimerical rainbow bridge. In order to reach the next peak we must first go down into the land where the paths begin to divide.

11. *A voice says, "But you are still a child."*

This dream forces the dreamer to admit that even a highly differentiated consciousness has not by any means finished with childish things, and that a return to the world of childhood is necessary.

12. *A dangerous walk with Father and Mother, up and down many ladders.*

A childish consciousness is always tied to father and mother, and is never by itself. Return to childhood is always the return to father and mother, to the whole burden of the psychic non-ego as represented by the parents, with its long and momentous history. Regression spells disintegration into our historical and hereditary determinants, and it is only with the greatest effort that we can free ourselves from their embrace. Our psychic prehistory is in truth the spirit of gravity, which needs steps and ladders because, unlike the disembodied airy intellect, it cannot fly at will. Disintegration into the jumble of historical determinants is like losing one's way, where even what is right seems an alarming mistake.

It is of course impossible to free oneself from one's childhood without devoting a great deal of work to it, as Freud's researches have long since

DREAM SYMBOLS OF THE INDIVIDUATION PROCESS

shown. Nor can it be achieved through intellectual knowledge only; what is alone effective is a remembering that is also a re-experiencing. The swift passage of the years and the overwhelming inrush of the newly discovered world leave a mass of the material behind that has never been dealt with. We do not shake this off; we merely detach ourselves from it. So that when, in later years, we return to the memories of childhood we find bits of our personality still alive, which cling round us and suffuse us with the feeling of earlier times. Being still in their childhood state, these fragments are very powerful in their effect. They can lose their infantile aspect and be corrected only when they are reunited with adult consciousness. This "personal unconscious" must always be dealt with first, that is, made conscious, otherwise the gateway to the collective unconscious cannot be opened. The journey with father and mother up and down many ladders represents a making conscious of infantile contents that have not yet been integrated.

13. *The father calls out anxiously, "That is the seventh!"*
During the walk over many ladders some event has evidently taken place which is spoken of as "the seventh." In the language of initiation, "seven" stands for the highest stage and would therefore be the coveted goal of all desire. But to the conventional mind the *solificatio* is an outlandish, mystical idea bordering on madness. We assume that it was only in the dark ages of misty superstition that people thought in such a nonsensical fashion, but that the lucid and hygienic mentality of our own enlightened days has long since outgrown such nebulous notions, so much so, indeed, that this particular kind of "illumination" is only to be found nowadays in a lunatic asylum. No wonder the father is scared and anxious, like a hen that has hatched out ducklings and is driven to despair by the aquatic proclivities of its young. If this interpretation—that the "seventh" represents the highest stage of illumination—is correct, it would mean in principle that the process of integrating the personal unconscious was actually at an end. Thereafter the collective unconscious would begin to open up, which would suffice to explain the anxiety the father felt as the representative of the traditional spirit.

Nevertheless the return to the dim twilight of the unconscious does not mean that we should entirely abandon the precious acquisition of our forefathers, namely the intellectual differentiation of consciousness. It is rather a question of the *man* taking the place of the *intellect*.

14. *The dreamer is in America looking for an employee with a pointed beard. They say that everybody has such an employee.*

America is the land of practical, straightforward thinking, uncontaminated by our European sophistication. The intellect would there be kept, very sensibly, as an employee. This naturally sounds like *lèse-majesté* and might therefore be a serious matter. So it is consoling to know that everyone (as is always the case in America) does the same. The "man with a pointed beard" is our time-honored Mephisto whom Faust "employed" and who was not permitted to triumph over him in the end, despite the fact that Faust had dared to descend into the dark chaos of the historical psyche and to steep himself in the ever-changing, seamy side of life that rose up out of that bubbling caldron. The degradation of the intellect and, at the same time, the separation from the "father," are thus complete.

15. *The dreamer's mother is pouring water from one basin into another.* (The dreamer only remembered in connection with vision 28 of the next series that this basin belonged to his sister.) *This action is performed with great solemnity: it is of the highest significance for the outside world. Then the dreamer is rejected by his father.*

Once more we meet with the theme of "exchange" (cf. dream 1): one thing is put in the place of another. The "father" has been dealt with; now begins the action of the "mother." Just as the father represents collective consciousness, the traditional spirit, so the mother stands for the collective unconscious, the source of the water of life.[14] (Cf. the maternal significance of πηγή,[15] the *fons signatus*,[16] as an attribute of the Virgin Mary, etc.) The unconscious has altered the location of the life forces, thus indicating a change of attitude. The dreamer's subsequent recollection enables us to see who is now the source of life: it is the "sister." The mother is superior to the son, but the sister is his equal. Thus the degradation of the intellect frees the dreamer from the domination of the unconscious and hence from his infantile attitude. Although the sister is a remnant of the past, we know definitely from later dreams that she was the bearer of the anima image. We may therefore assume that the transferring of the water of life to the sister really means that the mother has been replaced by the anima.[17]

14 For water as origin, cf. Egyptian cosmogony, among others.
15 Albrecht Wirth, *Aus orientalischen Chroniken* (Frankfurt a. M., 1894), p. 199.
16 Cf. Canticles (Song of Sol.) 4: 12.
17 This is really a normal life process, but it usually takes place quite unconsciously. The

The anima now becomes a life-giving factor, a psychic reality which conflicts strongly with the world of the father. Which of us could assert, without endangering his sanity, that he had accepted the guidance of the unconscious in the conduct of his life, assuming that anyone exists who could imagine what that would mean? Anyone who could imagine it at all would certainly have no difficulty in understanding what a monstrous affront such a *volte face* would offer to the traditional spirit, especially to the spirit that has put on the earthly garment of the Church. It was this subtle change of psychic standpoint that caused the old alchemists to resort to deliberate mystification, and that sponsored all kinds of heresies. Hence it is only logical for the father to reject the dreamer—it amounts to nothing less than excommunication. (Note that the dreamer is a Roman Catholic.) By acknowledging the reality of the psyche and making it a co-determining ethical factor in our lives, we offend against the spirit of convention which for centuries has regulated psychic life from outside by means of institutions as well as by reason. Not that unreasoning instinct rebels of itself against firmly established order; by the strict logic of its own inner laws it is itself of the firmest structure imaginable and, in addition, the creative foundation of all binding order. But just because this foundation is creative, all order which proceeds from it—even in its most "divine" form—is a phase, a stepping stone.

Despite appearances to the contrary, the establishment of order and the dissolution of what has been established are at bottom beyond human control. The secret is that only that which can destroy itself is truly alive. It is well that these things are difficult to understand and thus enjoy a wholesome concealment, for weak heads are only too easily addled by them and thrown into confusion. From all these dangers dogma—whether ecclesiastical, philosophical, or scientific—offers effective protection, and, looked at from a social point of view, excommunication is a necessary and useful consequence. But no evil is so great that it does not have something good in it. As a counterbalance to the security offered by dogma, the excommunicate enjoys an inner freedom of spirit, a *donum spiritus sancti*.

The water that the mother, the unconscious, pours into the basin belong-

---

anima is an archetype that is always present. (Cf. *Psychological Types*, defs. 48, 49; and "The Relations between the Ego and the Unconscious," in CWJ, 7.) The mother is the first carrier of the anima image, which gives her a fascinating quality in the eyes of the son. It is then transferred, via the sister and similar figures, to the beloved.

ing to the anima is an excellent symbol for the living power of the psyche. The old alchemists never tired of devising new and expressive synonyms for this water. They called it *aqua nostra, mercurius vivus, argentum vivum, vinum ardens, aqua vitae, succus lunariae,* and so on, by which they meant a living being not devoid of substance, as opposed to the rigid immateriality of mind in the abstract. The expression *succus lunariae* (sap of the moon-plant) points clearly enough to the nocturnal origin of the water, and *aqua nostra,* like *mercurius vivus,* to its earthliness. *Acetum fontis* is a powerful corrosive water that dissolves all created things and at the same time leads to the most durable of all products, the mysterious *lapis.*

These analogies may seem very farfetched. But let me refer the reader to dreams 13 and 14 in the next section, where this symbolism is taken up again.[18] The importance of the action "for the outside world," noted by the dreamer himself, points to the collective significance of the dream, and the fact that the decision thus constellated has a tremendous influence on the dreamer points in the same direction.

The saying that *"extra ecclesiam nulla salus"*—outside the Church there is no salvation—rests on the knowledge that an institution is a safe, practicable highway with a visible or definable goal, and that no paths and no goals can be found outside it. We must not underestimate the devastating

18 These references to alchemy may strike the reader as odd, but, as dreams 13 and 14 in Sec. 3 will show, they are unavoidable because this obscure field yields such very important parallels to the processes in the unconscious. Herbert Silberer has already pointed out these connections in his *Problems of Mysticism and Its Symbolism* (tr. S. E. Jelliffe, New York, 1917). Naturally the symbolism of alchemy is only one aspect of it; another aspect is undoubtedly chemistry (together constituting the τὰ φυσικά and τὰ μυστικά of pseudo-Democritus). The alchemist's ignorance of the nature of chemical substances led him to project psychic material into the unintelligible chemical processes, with the result that, although chemical research was greatly stimulated, it also provided him with an occasion for transforming chemical procedures into speculative philosophical symbols. Thence arose the two principal branches of alchemy, which continued to intermingle for several centuries and only separated when the philosophical school became hopelessly degenerate in the 18th century. The parallels quoted here come for the most part from the Latin literature of the 12th to 14th centuries. One of the most interesting of these texts is the *Rosarium philosophorum,* by an anonymous author. It is a fairly long treatise, making use of much older sources which date back to the 12th century and, through Arabic transmission, back to antiquity. The author is very definitely a "philosopher": he is well aware that in alchemy it was not a question of ordinary gold making, but of a philosophical mystery. To the best of my knowledge the *Rosarium* was first printed in a collection of Latin treatises, together with the 2nd (?) edition of the *Turba philosophorum,* under the title *Artis auriferae.* I have used the 2nd (?) edition of 1593 (Basel), not mentioned in J. F. Ruska's edition of the *Turba.* As I was able to ascertain, the *Rosarium* is missing in the 1st edition of 1572.

356

effect of getting lost in the chaos, even if we know that it is the *sine qua non* for any regeneration of the spirit and the personality.

16. *An ace of clubs lies before the dreamer. A seven appears beside it.*

The ace, as "1," is the lowest card but the highest in value. The ace of clubs, being in the form of a cross, points to the Christian symbol.[19] Hence in Swiss-German the club is often called *Chrüüz* (cross). At the same time the three leaves contain an allusion to the threefold nature of the one God. Lowest and highest are beginning and end, alpha and omega.

The seven appears after the ace of clubs and not before. Presumably the idea is: first the Christian conception of God, and then the seven (stages). The seven stages symbolize the transformation which begins with the symbolism of Cross and Trinity, and, judging by the earlier archaic allusions in dreams 7 and 13, culminates in the *solificatio*. But this solution is not hinted at here. Now, we know from the Middle Ages that there was another movement apart from the regression to the Helios of the ancients vainly attempted by Julian the Apostate, and that was the transition to the rose as expressed in the formula *"per crucem ad rosam"* (through the cross to the rose), which was condensed in the late Middle Ages to the "Rosie Crosse" of the Rosicrucians. Here the essence of the sun descends from the heavenly Sol into the flower—earth's answer to the sun's countenance. (The solar quality has survived in the symbol of the "golden flower" of Chinese alchemy.[20]) The well-known "blue flower" of the Romantics might well be the last nostalgic perfume of the "rose"; it looks back in true Romantic fashion to the medievalism of ruined cloisters, yet at the same time modestly proclaims something new in earthly loveliness. But even the golden brilliance of the sun had to submit to a descent, and it found its analogy in the glitter of earthly gold—although, as *aurum nostrum*, this was far removed from the gross materiality of the metal, at least for subtler minds.[21] For these the gold undoubtedly had a symbolic nature and was therefore distinguished by such attributes as *vitreum* or *philosophicum*. It was probably owing to its all too obvious analogy with the sun that gold was denied the highest philosophical honor, which fell instead to the *lapis philosophorum*. For the transformer is above the transformed, and transformation is one of the

---

19 Cf. dream 23 of second series. ·
20 Also in the "golden flower" of medieval alchemy.
21 As the *Rosarium* says: *"Aurum nostrum non est aurum vulgi."*

magical properties of the marvelous stone. The *Rosarium* says: "For our stone, namely the living western quicksilver which has placed itself above the gold and vanquished it, is that which kills and quickens." [22] As to the "philosophical" significance of the *lapis*, the following passage from a treatise ascribed to Hermes is particularly enlightening: "Understand, ye sons of the wise, what this exceeding precious stone crieth . . . 'And my light conquers every light, and my virtues are more excellent than all virtues. . . . I beget the light, but the darkness also is of my nature. . . .' " [23]

17. *The dreamer goes for a long walk and finds a blue flower on the way.*

To go for a walk is to wander along paths that lead nowhere in particular; it is both a search and a succession of changes. The dreamer finds a blue flower blossoming aimlessly by the wayside, a chance child of nature, evoking friendly memories of a more romantic and lyrical age, of the youthful season when it came to bud, when the scientific view of the world had not yet broken away from the world of actual experience—or rather when this break was only just beginning and the eye looked back to what was already the past. The flower is in fact like a friendly sign, a numinous emanation from the unconscious, showing the dreamer, who as a modern man has been robbed of the certainty of his way and of the promise of salvation, the historical place where he can meet friends and brothers of like mind, where he can find the seed that wants to sprout in him too. But the dreamer knows nothing as yet of the old solar gold which connects the innocent flower with the obnoxious black art of alchemy and with the blasphemous pagan idea of the *solificatio*.

18. *A man offers him some golden coins in his outstretched hand. The dreamer indignantly throws them to the ground and immediately afterward deeply regrets his action. A variety performance then takes place in an enclosed space.*

The blue flower has already begun to drag its history after it. The "gold" offers itself and is indignantly refused. Such a misinterpretation of the *aurum philosophicum* is easy to understand. But hardly has it happened when there comes a pang of remorse that the precious secret has been rejected and a wrong answer thus given to the riddle of the Sphinx. The same thing hap-

22 "*Quia lapis noster scilicet argentum vivum occidentale, quod praetulit se auro et vicit illud, est illud quod occidit et vivere facit.*"—*Rosarium*, p. 223.
23 "*Intelligite, filii sapientum, quod hic lapis preciosissimus clamat . . . et lumen meum omne lumen superat ac mea bona omnibus bonis sunt sublimiora . . . Ego gigno lumen, tenebrae autem naturae meae sunt. . . .*"—*Rosarium*, p. 239.

pened to the hero in Meyrink's *Golem*, when the ghost offered him a handful of grain which he spurned. The gross materiality of the yellow metal with its odious fiscal flavor, and the mean look of the grain, make both rejections comprehensible enough—but that is precisely why it is so hard to find the *lapis:* it is *exilis*, uncomely, "it is found thrown out into the street," [24] it is the commonest thing to be picked up anywhere—"*in planitie, in montibus et aquis.*" It has this "ordinary" aspect in common with Spitteler's jewel in *Prometheus and Epimetheus* which, for the same reason, was also not recognized by the worldly wise. But "the stone which the builders rejected, the same is become the head of the corner," and the intuition of this possibility arouses the liveliest regret in the dreamer.

It is all part of the banality of its outward aspect that the gold is minted, i.e., shaped into coins, stamped, and valued. Psychologically speaking, this is just what Nietzsche refuses to do in his *Zarathustra:* to give names to the virtues. By being shaped and named psychic life is broken down into coined and valued units. But this is possible only because it is intrinsically a great variety of things, an accumulation of unintegrated hereditary factors. Natural man is not a "self"—he is the mass and the particle in the mass, collective to such a degree that he is not even sure of his own ego. That is why since time immemorial he has needed the transformation mysteries to turn him into something, and to rescue him from the animal collective psyche, which is nothing but a hodgepodge.

But if we reject this unseemly assortment of man "as he is," it is impossible for him to attain integration, to become a self. And that amounts to spiritual death. Life that just happens in and for itself is not real life; it is only real when it is known. Only a unified personality can experience life, not that personality which is split up into partial aspects, that bundle of odds and ends which also calls itself "man." The dangerous plurality already hinted at in dream 4 is compensated in vision 5, where the snake describes a magic circle and thus marks off the taboo area, the *temenos*. In much the same way and in a similar situation the *temenos* reappears here, drawing the "many" together for a united variety performance—a gathering that has the appearance of an entertainment, though it will shortly lose its entertaining character: the "play of goats" will develop into a "tragedy." According to all the analogies, the satyr play was a mystery performance, from which we may assume that its purpose, as everywhere, was to re-establish man's con-

24 In the *Tractatus aureus* we even read: "*in stercore eiectus . . . vilis et vilissimus.*"

nection with his natural ancestry and thus with the source of life, much as the obscene stories, αἰσχρυλογία, told by Athenian ladies at the mysteries of Eleusis, were thought to promote the earth's fertility.[25] (Cf. also Herodotus' account of the exhibitionistic performances connected with the Isis festivities at Bubastis.)

The reference to the compensatory significance of the *temenos*, however, is still wrapped in obscurity for the dreamer. As might be imagined, he is much more concerned with the danger of spiritual death, which is conjured up by his rejection of the historical context.

19 (Visual impression). *A death's-head. The dreamer wants to kick it away, but cannot. The skull gradually changes into a red ball, then into a woman's head which emits light.*

The skull soliloquies of Faust and of Hamlet are reminders of the appalling senselessness of human life when "sicklied o'er with the pale cast of thought." It was traditional opinions and judgments that caused the dreamer to dash aside the doubtful and uninviting-looking offerings. But when he tries to ward off the sinister vision of the death's-head it is transformed into a red ball, which we may take as an allusion to the rising sun, since it at once changes into the shining head of a woman, reminding us directly of vision 7. Evidently an enantiodromia, a play of opposites,[26] has occurred: after being rejected the unconscious insists on itself all the more strongly. First it produces the classical symbol for the unity and divinity of the self, the sun; then it changes into the theme of the unknown woman who personifies the unconscious. Naturally this theme includes not merely the archetype of the anima but also the dreamer's relationship to a real woman, who is both a human personality and a vessel for the psyche. ("Basin of the sister" in dream 15.)

In Neoplatonic philosophy the soul has definite affinities with the sphere. The soul substance is laid round the concentric spheres of the four elements above the fiery heaven.[27]

20 (Visual impression). *A globe. The unknown woman is standing on it and worshiping the sun.*

25 Paul François Foucart, *Les Mystères d'Eleusis* (Paris, 1914).
26 See definition in my *Psychological Types*.
27 Cf. H. L. Fleischer, *Hermes Trismegistus an die menschliche Seele* (Leipzig, 1870), p. 6; also the spherical form of Plato's original human being and the σφαῖρος of Empedocles.

This impression is an extension of vision 7. The rejection in dream 18 evidently amounted to the destruction of the whole development up to that point. Consequently the initial symbols reappear now, but in amplified form. Such enantiodromias are characteristic of dream sequences in general. Unless the conscious mind intervened, the unconscious would go on sending out wave after wave without result, like the treasure that is said to take nine years, nine months, and nine nights to come to the surface and, if not found on the last night, sinks down to start all over again from the beginning.

The globe probably comes from the idea of the red ball. But, whereas this is the sun, the globe is rather an image of the earth, upon which the anima stands worshiping the sun. Anima and sun are thus distinct, which points to the fact that the sun represents a different principle from that of the anima. The latter is a personification of the unconscious, while the sun is a symbol of the source of life and the ultimate wholeness of man (as indicated in the *solificatio*). Now, the sun is an antique symbol that is still very close to us. We know also that the early Christians had some difficulty in distinguishing the ἥλιος ἀνατολῆς (the rising sun) from Christ.[28] The dreamer's anima still seems to be a sun worshiper, that is to say, she belongs to the ancient world, and for the following reason: the conscious mind with its rationalistic attitude has taken little or no interest in her and therefore made it impossible for the anima to become modernized (or better, Christianized). It almost seems as if the differentiation of the intellect that began in the Christian Middle Ages, as a result of scholastic training, had driven the anima to regress to the ancient world. The Renaissance gives us evidence enough for this, the clearest of all being the *Hypnerotomachia*, where Poliphilo meets his anima, the lady Polia, at the court of Queen Venus, quite untouched by Christianity and graced with all the "virtues" of antiquity. (The book was rightly regarded as a mystery text in the sixteenth century.) With this anima, then, we plunge straight into the ancient world. So that I would not think anyone mistaken who interpreted the above-mentioned enantiodromia *ex effectu* as an attempt to escape this regrettable and unseemly regression to antiquity. Certain vital doctrines of alchemical philosophy go back textually to late Greco-Roman syncretism, as Ruska, for instance, has sufficiently established in the case of the *Turba*. Hence

---

28 Cf. St. Augustine's argument that God is not this sun but he who made the sun, and the evidence of Eusebius, who actually witnessed "Christian" sun worship.

any allusion to alchemy wafts one back to the ancient world and makes one suspect regression to pagan levels.

It may not be superfluous to point out here, with due emphasis, that consciously the dreamer had no inkling of all this. But in his unconscious he is immersed in this sea of historical associations, so that he behaves in his dreams as if he were fully cognizant of these curious ramifications in the history of the human mind. As an unconscious personality, he is an exponent of the unconscious development of symbols, just like the medieval alchemist or the classical Neoplatonist. Hence one could say—*cum grano salis*—that history could be constructed just as easily from one's own unconscious as from the actual texts.

21 (Visual impression). *The dreamer is surrounded by nymphs. A voice says, "We were always there, only you did not notice us."*

Here the regression goes back even further, to an image that is unmistakably classical. At the same time the situation of dream 4 is taken up again and also the situation of dream 18, where the rejection led to the preventive enantiodromia in vision 19. But here the image is amplified by the hallucinatory recognition that the drama has always existed although unnoticed until now. The realization of this fact joins the unconscious psyche to consciousness as a coexistent entity. The phenomenon of the "voice" in dreams always has for the dreamer the final and indisputable character of the αὐτὸς ἔφα, i.e., the voice expresses some truth or condition that is beyond all doubt. The fact that a sense of the remote past has been established, that contact has been made with the deeper layers of the psyche, is accepted by the unconscious personality of the dreamer and communicates itself to his conscious mind as a feeling of comparative security. The introitus can therefore proceed a step further.

22 (Visual impression). *In a primeval forest. An elephant looms up threateningly. Then a large ape-man, bear, or cave man threatens to attack the dreamer with a club. Suddenly the "man with the pointed beard" appears and stares at the aggressor, so that he is spellbound. But the dreamer is terrified. The voice says, "Everything must be ruled by the light."*

The multiplicity of nymphs has broken down into still more primitive components; that is to say, the animation of the psychic atmosphere has very considerably increased, and from this we must conclude that the dreamer's isolation from his contemporaries has increased in proportion.

This intensified isolation can be traced back to vision 21, where the union with the unconscious was realized and accepted as a fact. From the point of view of the conscious mind this is highly irrational; it constitutes a secret which must be anxiously guarded, since the justification for its existence could not possibly be explained to any so-called reasonable person. Anyone who tried to do so would be branded as a lunatic. The discharge of energy into the environment is therefore considerably impeded, the result being a surplus of energy on the side of the unconscious: hence the abnormal increase in the autonomy of the unconscious figures, culminating in aggression and real terror. The earlier entertaining variety performance is beginning to become uncomfortable. We find it easy enough to accept the classical figures of nymphs, thanks to their aesthetic embellishments; but we have no idea that behind these gracious figures there lurks the Dionysian mystery of antiquity, the satyr play with its tragic implications: the bloody dismemberment of the god who has become an animal. It needed a Nietzsche to expose in all its feebleness Europe's schoolboy attitude to the ancient world. But what did Dionysus mean to Nietzsche? What he says about it must be taken seriously; what it did to him still more so. There can be no doubt that he knew, in the preliminary stages of his fatal illness, that the dismal fate of Zagreus was reserved for him. Dionysus is the abyss of impassioned dissolution, where all human distinctions are merged in the animal divinity of the primordial psyche—a blissful and terrible experience. Humanity, huddling behind the walls of its culture, believes it has escaped this experience, until it succeeds in letting loose another orgy of bloodshed. All well-meaning people are amazed when this happens and blame high finance, the armaments industry, the Jews, or the Freemasons.

At the last moment, friend "Pointed Beard" appears on the scene as an obliging *deus ex machina* and exorcizes the destruction threatened by the formidable ape-man. Who knows how much Faust's imperturbable curiosity, as he gazed on the spooks and bogeys of the classical *Walpurgisnacht*, owed to the helpful presence of Mephisto and his matter-of-fact point of view? Would that more people could remember the scientific or philosophical reflections of the much-abused intellect at the right moment! Those who abuse it lay themselves open to the suspicion of never having experienced anything that might have taught them its value and shown them why mankind has forged this weapon with such unprecedented effort. One has to be singularly out of touch with life not to notice such things. The intellect may

363

be the devil, but the devil is the "strange son of chaos" who can most readily be trusted to deal effectively with his mother. The Dionysian experience will give this devil plenty to do should he be looking for work, since the resultant settlement with the unconscious far outweighs the labors of Hercules. In my opinion it presents a whole world of problems which the intellect could not settle even in a hundred years—the very reason why it so often goes off for a holiday to recuperate on lighter tasks. And this is also the reason why the intellect makes such frequent use of magical apotropaic words like "occult" and "mystic," in the hope that even intelligent people will think that these mutterings really mean something.

The voice finally declares, "Everything must be ruled by the light," which presumably means the light of the discerning, conscious mind, a genuine *illuminatio* honestly acquired. The dark depths of the unconscious are no longer to be denied by ignorance and sophistry—at best a poor disguise for common fear—nor are they to be explained away with pseudoscientific rationalizations. On the contrary it must now be admitted that things exist in the psyche about which we know little or nothing at all, and that these possess at least the same degree of reality as the things of the physical world which ultimately we do not understand either, but which nevertheless affect our bodies in the most obstinate way. No line of research which asserted that its subject was unreal or a "nothing but" has ever made any contribution to knowledge.

With the active intervention of the intellect a new phase of the unconscious process begins: the conscious mind must now come to terms with the figures of the unknown woman ("anima"), the unknown man ("the shadow"), the wise old man ("mana personality"),[29] and the symbols of the self. The last-named are dealt with in the following section.

3. The Symbolism of the Mandala

As I have already said, I have put together, out of a continuous sequence of some four hundred dreams and visions, all those that I regard as mandala dreams. The term "mandala" was chosen because this word denotes the ritual or magic circle used in Lamaism and also in Tantric Yoga as a *yantra* or aid to contemplation. The Eastern mandalas used in ceremonial are

29 For these concepts see my "The Relations between the Ego and the Unconscious," in *Two Essays* (CWJ, 7).

figures fixed by tradition; they may be drawn or painted or, in certain special ceremonies, even represented plastically.[1]

It seems to be beyond question that these Eastern symbols originated in dreams and visions, and were not invented by some Mahāyāna church father. On the contrary, they are among the oldest religious symbols of humanity and may even have existed in paleolithic times (cf. the Rhodesian rock-paintings). Moreover they are distributed all over the world, a point I need not insist on here. In this section I merely wish to show from the material at hand how mandalas come into existence.

The mandalas used in ceremonial are of great significance because their centers usually contain one of the highest religious figures: either Shiva himself—often in the embrace of Shakti—or Buddha, Amitabha, Avalokiteshvara, or one of the great Mahāyāna teachers, or simply the *dorje*, symbol of all the divine forces together, whether creative or destructive in nature. The text of the *Golden Flower*, a product of Taoist syncretism, specifies in addition certain "alchemical" properties of this center reminiscent of the *lapis* and the *elixir vitae*, so that it is in effect a $\varphi\acute{a}\rho\mu\alpha\kappa\sigma\nu\ \dot{a}\theta\alpha\nu\alpha\sigma\acute{\iota}\alpha\varsigma$ or $\tau\tilde{\eta}\varsigma\ \zeta\omega\tilde{\eta}\varsigma$.[2]

It is not without importance for us to appreciate the high value set upon the mandala, for it accords very well with the paramount significance of individual mandala symbols which are characterized by the same qualities of a—so to speak—"metaphysical" nature.[3] Unless everything deceives us, they signify nothing less than a psychic center of the personality not to be identified with the ego. I have observed these processes and images for twenty years on the basis of very extensive material drawn from my own experience. For fourteen years I neither wrote nor lectured about them, so as not to prejudice my observations. But when, in 1929, Richard Wilhelm laid the text of the *Golden Flower* before me, I decided to publish at least a foretaste of the results of my observations. One cannot be too cautious in these matters, for what with the imitative urge and a positively morbid avidity to possess themselves of outlandish feathers and deck themselves

1 Cf. Richard Wilhelm and C. G. Jung, *The Secret of the Golden Flower* (London and New York, 1931), and Heinrich Zimmer, *Myths and Symbols in Indian Art and Civilization* (New York [BS VI], 1946).
2 Cf. Richard Reitzenstein, *Die hellenistischen Mysterienreligionen* (Leipzig, 1910).
3 The quotation marks indicate that I am not "postulating" anything by the term "metaphysical"; I am only using it figuratively, in the psychological sense, to characterize the peculiar statements made by dreams.

out in this exotic plumage, far too many people are misled into snatching at such "magical" ideas and applying them externally, like an ointment. People will do anything, no matter how absurd, in order to avoid facing their own psyches. They will practice Indian Yoga and all its exercises, observe a strict regimen of diet, learn theosophy by heart, or mechanically repeat mystic texts from the literature of the whole world—all because they cannot get on with themselves and have not the slightest faith that anything useful could ever come out of the psyche. Thus the psyche has gradually been turned into a Nazareth from which nothing good can come. Therefore let us fetch it from the four corners of the earth—the more farfetched and bizarre it is the better! I have no wish to disturb such people at their pet pursuits, but when anybody who expects to be taken seriously is deluded enough to think that I use Yoga methods and Yoga doctrines or that I get my patients, whenever possible, to draw mandalas for the purpose of bringing them to the "right point"—then I really must protest and tax these people with having read my writings with the most horrible inattention. The doctrine that all evil thoughts come from the heart and that the human soul is a sink of iniquity must lie deep in the marrow of their bones. Were it so, then God had made a sorry job of creation, and it were high time for us us to go over to Marcion the Gnostic and depose the incompetent demiurge. Ethically, of course, it is infinitely more convenient to leave God the sole responsibility for such a Home for Idiot Children—as they conceive the world to be—where no one is capable of putting a spoon into his own mouth. But it is worth man's while to take pains with himself, and he has something in his soul that can grow. It is rewarding to watch patiently the silent happenings in the soul, and the most and the best happens when it is not regulated from outside and from above. I readily admit that I have such a great respect for what happens in the human soul that I would be afraid of disturbing and distorting the silent operation of nature by clumsy interference. That was why I even refrained from observing this particular case myself and entrusted the task to a beginner who was not handicapped by my knowledge—anything rather than disturb the process. The results which I now lay before you are the unadulterated, conscientious, and exact self-observations of a man of unerring intellect, who had nothing suggested to him from outside and who would in any case not have been open to suggestion. Anyone at all familiar with psychic material will have no difficulty in recognizing the authentic character of the results.

For the sake of completeness I begin the series with the mandala symbols which occur in the initial dreams and visions already discussed:

1. The snake that described a circle round the dreamer (5).
2. The blue flower (17).
3. The man with the gold coins in his hand, and the enclosed space for a variety performance (18).
4. The red ball (19).
5. The globe (20).

The next mandala symbol occurs in the first dream of the new series:

6. *An unknown woman is pursuing the dreamer. He keeps running round in a circle.*

The snake in the first mandala dream was anticipatory, as is often the case when a figure personifying a certain aspect of the unconscious does or experiences something that the subject himself will experience later. The snake anticipates a circular movement in which the subject is going to be involved; i.e., something is taking place in the unconscious which is perceived as a circular movement, and this occurrence now presses into consciousness so forcefully that the subject is gripped by it. The unknown woman or anima representing the unconscious continues to harass the dreamer until he starts running round in circles. This clearly indicates a potential center which is not identical with the ego and round which the ego revolves.

7. *The anima accuses the dreamer of paying too little attention to her. There is a clock that says five minutes to the hour.*

The situation is much the same: the unconscious pesters him like an exacting woman. The situation also explains the clock, for a clock's hands go round in a circle. Five minutes to the hour implies a state of tension for anybody who lives by the clock: when the five minutes are up he must do something or other. He might even be pressed for time. (The symbol of circular movement is always connected with a feeling of tension, as we shall see later.)

8. *On board ship. The dreamer is busied with a new method of taking his bearings. Sometimes he is too far away and sometimes too near: the right spot is in the middle. There is a chart on which is drawn a circle with its center.*

367

Obviously the task set here is to find the center, the right spot, and this is the center of a circle. While the dreamer was writing down this dream he remembered that he had dreamed shortly before of shooting at a target: sometimes he shot too high, sometimes too low. The right aim lay in the middle. Both dreams struck him as highly significant. (Cf. my remarks on the significance of the Eastern mandala.) The target is a circle with a center. Bearings at sea are taken by the apparent rotation of the stars round the earth.

9. *A pendulum clock that goes forever without the weights running down.*

This is a species of clock whose hands move unceasingly, and, since there is obviously no loss due to friction, it is a *perpetuum mobile*, an everlasting movement in a circle. Here we meet with a "metaphysical" attribute. As I have already said, I use this word in a psychological sense, hence figuratively. I mean by this that eternity is a quality predicated by the unconscious, and not a hypostasis. The statement made by the dream will obviously offend the dreamer's scientific judgment, but this is just what gives the mandala its peculiar significance. Highly significant things are often rejected because they seem to contradict reason and thus set it too arduous a test. The movement without friction shows that the clock is cosmic, even transcendental; at any rate, it raises the question of a quality which leaves us in some doubt whether the psychic phenomenon expressing itself in the mandala is under the laws of space and time. And this points to something so entirely different from the empirical ego that the gap between them is difficult to bridge.

10. *The dreamer is in the Peterhofstatt in Zurich with the doctor, the man with the pointed beard, and the "doll woman." The last is an unknown woman who neither speaks nor is spoken to. Question: To which of the three does the woman belong?*

The tower of St. Peter's in Zurich has a clock with a strikingly large face. The Peterhofstatt is an enclosed space, a *temenos* in the truest sense of the word, a precinct of the church. The four of them find themselves in this enclosure. The circular dial of the clock is divided into four quarters, like the horizon. In the dream the dreamer represents his own ego, the man with the pointed beard the "employed" intellect (Mephisto), and the "doll woman" the anima. Since the doll is a childish object it is an excellent image for the non-ego nature of the anima, who is further characterized as an object by "not being spoken to." This negative element (also present in dreams 6 and 7 above) indicates an inadequate relationship between the conscious mind and the unconscious, as also does the question of whom the unknown woman belongs to. The "doctor," too, belongs to the non-ego; he probably contains a faint allusion to myself. The man with the pointed beard, on the other hand, belongs to the ego. This whole situation is reminiscent of the relations in the schema of functions. If we picture the psychological functions [4] as arranged in a circle, then the most differentiated

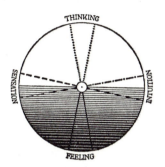

Schema of the four functions of consciousness

In this case, thinking is the superior ("differentiated") function and occupies the center of the light half of the circle. Feeling, the inferior function, occupies the dark half. The two auxiliary functions are partly in light, partly in dark.

function is usually the carrier of the ego and, equally regularly, has an auxiliary function attached to it. The "inferior" function, on the other hand, is unconscious and for that reason is projected into a non-ego. It too has an auxiliary function. Hence it would not be impossible for the four persons in the dream to represent the four functions as components of the total personality (i.e., if we include the unconscious). But this totality is ego plus non-ego. Therefore the center of the circle which expresses such a totality would correspond not to the ego but to the self as the sum of the total personality. (The center with a circle is a very well-known allegory of the nature of God.) In the philosophy of the Upanishads the Self is in one aspect the *personal* ātman, but at the same time it has cosmic and metaphysical quality as the *suprapersonal* Ātman.[5]

We meet with similar ideas in Gnosticism: I would mention the idea of the Anthropos, the Pleroma, the Monad, and the spark of light (Spinther) in a treatise of the Codex Brucianus:

4 Cf. *Psychological Types,* index, s.v. "functions."
5 Paul Deussen, *Allgemeine Geschichte der Philosophie* (Leipzig, 1906), I.

This same is he [Monogenes] who dwelleth in the Monad, which is in the Setheus, and which came from the place of which none can say where it is. . . . From Him it is the Monad came, in the manner of a ship, laden with all good things, and in the manner of a field, filled or planted with every kind of tree, and in the manner of a city, filled with all races of mankind. . . . This is the fashion of the Monad, all these being in it: there are twelve Monads as a crown upon its head. . . . And to its veil which surroundeth it in the manner of a defence [πύργος = tower] there are twelve gates. . . . This same is the Mother-City [μητρόπολις] of the Only-begotten [μονογενής].[6]

By way of explanation I should add that "Setheus" is a name for God, meaning "creator." The Monogenes is the Son of God. The comparison of the Monad with a field and a city corresponds to the idea of the *temenos*. Also, the Monad is crowned (cf. the hat which appears in dream 1 of the first series and dream 35 of this series). As "metropolis" the Monad is feminine, like the *padma* or lotus, the basic form of the Lamaistic mandala (the Golden Flower in China and the Rose or Golden Flower in the West). The Son of God, God made manifest, dwells in the flower; Buddha, Shiva, etc., in the lotus; Christ in the rose, in the womb of Mary; the seeding-place of the diamond body in the golden flower. In the Book of Revelation, we find the Lamb in the center of the Heavenly Jerusalem. And in our Coptic text we are told that Setheus dwells in the innermost and holiest recesses of the Pleroma, a city with four gates (equivalent to the Hindu City of Brahma on the world-mountain Meru). In each gate there is a Monad.[7] (Cf. the Vajramandala, where the great *dorje* is to be found in the center surrounded by the twelve smaller *dorjes*, like the one Monad with the "twelve Monads as a crown upon its head." Moreover there is a *dorje* in each of the four gates.) The limbs of the Anthropos born of the Autogenes (= Monogenes) correspond to the four gates of the city. The Monad is a spark of light (Spinther) and an image of the Father, identical with the Monogenes. An invocation runs: "Thou art the House and the Dweller in the House."[8] The Monogenes stands on a *tetrapeza*,[9] a table or platform

6 Charlotte A. Baynes, *A Coptic Gnostic Treatise Contained in the Codex Brucianus— Bruce MS. 96. Bodleian Library, Oxford* (Cambridge, 1933), p. 89.
7 Ibid., p. 58.
8 Ibid., p. 94.
9 Ibid., p. 70.

with four pillars corresponding to the quaternion of the four evangelists.[10]

The idea of the *lapis* has several points of contact with all this. The *lapis* says in Hermes: "Therefore nothing better or more worthy of veneration can come to pass in the world than the union of myself and my son."[11] The Monogenes is also called the "dark light."[12] The *Rosarium* quotes a saying of Hermes: *"Ego gigno lumen, tenebrae autem naturae meae sunt"* (I [the *lapis*] beget the light, but the darkness also is of my nature).[13]

The following passage from the *Tractatus aureus* provides an interesting parallel to the Monogenes who dwells in the bosom of the Mother-City and is identical with the crowned and veiled Monad:[14]

> The King, the Ruler, saith: "I am crowned, and I am adorned with the diadem; I am clothed with the royal garment, and I bring joy to the heart; for, being chained to the arms and breast of my mother, and to her substance, I cause my substance to keep together; and I compose the invisible from the visible, making the occult matter to appear. And everything which the philosophers have hidden will be generated from us."

It is not said in the text that the "King" refers to the *lapis*, but the qualities ascribed to him are those of the *lapis*. What is more, the *lapis* is the "Master," as is evident from the following passage in the *Rosarium:*[15] *"Et sic Philosophus non est Magister lapidis, sed potius minister"* (And thus the philosopher is not the master of the stone but rather its minister). Similarly the final production of the *lapis* in the form of the crowned hermaphrodite

---

10 Cf. Irenaeus, III, xi, and Clement of Alexandria, *Stromata*, V, vi.—Similar to the tetramorph, the steed of the Church.

11 *Rosarium*, p. 240. The Hermes quotations come from the fourth chapter of the *Tractatus aureus*.

12 Baynes, p. 87.

13 *Rosarium*, p. 239. The passages from Hermes as quoted by the anonymous author of the *Rosarium* contain deliberate alterations that have far more significance than mere faulty readings. They are authentic recastings, to which he lends higher authority by attributing them to Hermes. I have compared the three printed editions of the *Tractatus aureus*, 1566, 1610, and 1702, as well as the English translation by Mrs. Atwood (1850), and found that they all agree. The *Rosarium* quotation runs as follows in the *Tractatus aureus: "Iam Venus ait: Ego genero lumen, nec tenebrae meae naturae sunt . . . me igitur et fratri meo coniunctis nihil melius ac venerabilius"* (Venus says: I generate light, and darkness is not of my nature . . . there is therefore nothing better or more venerable than the conjunction of myself with my brother).

14 Mary Anne Atwood (1850): *A Suggestive Inquiry into the Hermetic Mystery* (Belfast, 1920), ch. IV.

15 P. 356.

is called the *aenigma regis*.[16] A German verse refers to the *aenigma* as follows:

> Here now is born the emperor of all honor
> Than whom there cannot be born any higher,
> Neither by art nor by the work of nature
> Out of the womb of any living creature.
> Philosophers speak of him as their son
> And everything they do by him is done.

The last two lines might easily be a direct reference to the above quotation from Hermes.

It looks as if the idea had dawned on the alchemists that the Son who, according to classical (and Christian) tradition, dwells eternally in the Father and reveals himself as God's gift to mankind, was something that man could produce out of his own nature—with God's help, of course (*Deo concedente*). The heresy of this idea is reason enough for mystification.

The feminine nature of the inferior function derives from its contamination with the unconscious. Because of its feminine characteristics the unconscious is personified by the anima (that is to say, in men; in women it is masculine).[17]

If we assume that this dream and its predecessors really mean something that justly arouses a feeling of significance in the dreamer, and if we further assume that this significance is more or less in keeping with the views put forward in the commentary, then we would have reached a high point of introspection and intuition whose boldness leaves nothing to be desired. But even the everlasting pendulum clock is an indigestible morsel for a consciousness unprepared for it, and likely to hamper any too lofty flight of thought.

11. *The dreamer, the doctor, a pilot, and the unknown woman are traveling by airplane. A croquet ball suddenly smashes the mirror, an indispensable instrument of navigation, and the airplane crashes to the ground. Here again there is the same doubt: to whom does the unknown woman belong?*

Doctor, pilot, and unknown woman are characterized as belonging to the non-ego by the fact that all three of them are strangers. Therefore the dreamer has retained possession only of the differentiated function, which

16 Ibid., p. 159.
17 Cf. my "The Relations between the Ego and the Unconscious."

carries the ego; that is, the unconscious has gained ground considerably. The croquet ball is part of a game where the ball is driven under a hoop. Vision 8 of the first series said that people should not go over the rainbow (fly?), but must go *under* it. Those who go over it fall to the ground. It looks as though the flight had been too lofty after all. Croquet is played on the ground and not in the air. We should not rise above the earth with the aid of "spiritual" intuitions and run away from hard reality, as so often happens with people who have brilliant intuitions. We can never reach the level of our intuitions and therefore should not identify ourselves with them. Only the gods can pass over the rainbow bridge; mortal men must stick to the earth and are subject to its laws. In the light of the possibilities revealed by intuition, man's earthliness is certainly a lamentable imperfection; but this very imperfection is part of his innate being, of his reality. He is compounded not only of his best intuitions, his highest ideals and aspirations, but also of the odious conditions of his existence, such as heredity and the indelible sequence of memories which shouts after him: "You did it, and that's what you are!" Man may have lost his ancient saurian's tail, but in its stead he has a chain hanging on to his psyche which binds him to the earth—an anything-but-Homeric chain[17a] of conditions which weigh so heavy that it is better to remain bound to them, even at the risk of becoming neither a hero nor a saint. (History gives us some justification for not attaching any absolute value to these collective norms.) That we are bound to the earth does not mean that we cannot grow; on the contrary it is the *sine qua non* of growth. No noble, well-grown tree ever disowned its dark roots, for it grows not only upward but downward as well. The question of where we are going is of course extremely important; but equally important, it seems to me, is the question of *who* is going where. The "who" always implies a "whence." It takes a certain greatness to gain lasting possession of the heights, but anybody can overreach himself. The difficulty lies in striking the dead center (cf. dream 8). For this an awareness of the two sides of man's personality is essential, of their respective aims and origins. These two aspects must never be separated through arrogance or cowardice.

The "mirror" as an "indispensable instrument of navigation" doubtless

---

17a The Homeric chain in alchemy is the series of great wise men, beginning with Hermes Trismegistus, which links earth with heaven. At the same time it is the chain of substances and different chemical states that appear in the course of the alchemical process.

refs to the intellect, which is able to think and is constantly persuading us to identify ourselves with its insights ("reflections"). The mirror is one of Schopenhauer's favorite similes for the intellect. The term "instrument of navigation" is an apt expression for it, since it is indeed man's indispensable guide on pathless seas. But when the ground slips from under his feet and he begins to speculate in the void, seduced by the soaring flights of intuition, the situation becomes dangerous.

12. *The dreamer finds himself with his father, mother, and sister in a very dangerous situation on the platform of a trolley car.*

The fall thus takes him right back into childhood, a time when we are still a long way from wholeness. Wholeness is represented by the family, and its components are still projected upon the members of the family and personified by them. But this state is dangerous for the adult because regressive: it denotes a splitting of personality which primitive man experiences as the perilous "loss of soul." In the breakup the personal components that have been integrated with such pains are once more sucked into the outside world. The individual loses his guilt and exchanges it for infantile innocence; once more he can blame the wicked father for this and the unloving mother for that, and all the time he is caught in this inescapable causal nexus like a fly in a spider's web, without noticing that he has lost his moral freedom. But no matter how much parents and grandparents may have sinned against the child, the man who is really adult will accept these sins as his own condition which has to be reckoned with. Only a fool is interested in other people's guilt, since he cannot alter it. The wise man learns only from his own guilt. He will ask himself: Who am I that all this should happen to me? To find the answer to this fateful question he will look into his own heart.

13. *In the sea there lies a treasure. To reach it, he has to dive through a narrow opening. This is dangerous, but down below he will find a companion. The dreamer takes the plunge into the dark and discovers a beautiful garden in the depths, symmetrically laid out, with a fountain in the center.*

The "treasure hard to attain" lies hidden in the ocean of the unconscious, and only the brave can reach it. I conjecture that the treasure is also the "companion," one who goes through life at our side—in all probability a close analogy to the lonely ego who finds a mate in the self, for at first the self is the strange non-ego. This is the theme of the magical traveling companion, of whom I will give three famous examples: the disciples on the road to Emmaus, Krishna and Arjuna in the Bhagavad-Gita, Moses and El-Khidr in Sura 18 of the Koran. I conjecture further that the treasure in the sea, the companion, and the garden with the fountain are all one and the same thing: the self. For the garden is another *temenos*, and the fountain is the source of "living water" mentioned in John 7 : 38, which the Moses of the Koran also sought and found, and beside it El-Khidr,[18] "one of Our servants whom We had endowed with Our grace and wisdom" (Sura 18). And the legend has it that the ground round about El-Khidr blossomed with spring flowers, although it was desert. In Islam, the plan of the *temenos* with the fountain developed, under the influence of early Christian architecture, into the court of the mosque with the ritual washhouse in the center (e.g., Ahmed ibn-Tulun in Cairo). We see much the same thing in our Western cloisters with the fountain in the garden. This is also the "rose garden of the philosophers," which we know from the treatises on alchemy and from many beautiful engravings. "The Dweller in the House" (cf. commentary to dream 10) is the "companion." The center and the circle, here represented by fountain and garden, are analogues of the *lapis*, which is among other things a living being. In Hermes the *lapis* says: *"Protege me, protegam te. Largire mihi ius meum, ut te adiuvem"* (Protect me and I will protect you. Give me my due that I may help you).[19] Here the *lapis* is nothing less than a good friend and helper who helps those that help him, and this points to a compensatory relationship. (I would call to mind what was said in the commentary to dream 10, particularly the Monogenes-lapis-self parallel.)

The crash to earth thus leads into the depths of the sea, into the unconscious, and the dreamer reaches the shelter of the *temenos* as a protection against the splintering of personality caused by his regression to childhood. The situation is rather like that of dream 4 and vision 5 in the first series, where the magic circle warded off the lure of the unconscious and its plurality of female forms. (The dangers of temptation approach Poliphilo in much the same way at the beginning of his *nekyia*.)

18 Karl Vollers, "Chidher," *Archiv für Religionswissenschaft* (Leipzig), XII (1909), p. 235.
19 According to Mrs. Atwood, this quotation from the *Tractatus aureus* is correct. The 1610 edition has: *"Largiri vis mihi meum ut adiuvem te"* (You want to give me freely what is mine, that I may help you).

The source of life is, like El-Khidr, a good companion, though it is not without its dangers, as Moses of old found to his cost, according to the Koran. It is the symbol of the life force that eternally renews itself, and of the clock that never runs down. An uncanonical saying of our Lord goes: "Whoever is near unto me is near unto the fire." Just as this esoteric Christ is a source of fire—probably not without reference to the πῦρ ἀεὶ ζῶον of Heraclitus—so the alchemical philosophers conceive their *aqua nostra* to be *ignis* (fire).[20] The source means not only the flow of life but its warmth, indeed its heat, the secret of passion, whose synonyms are always fiery. The all-dissolving *aqua nostra* is an essential ingredient in the production of the *lapis*. But the source is underground and therefore the way leads underneath: only down below can we find the fiery source of life. These depths constitute the natural history of man, his causal link with the world of instinct. Unless this link be rediscovered no *lapis* and no self can come into being.

14. *The dreamer goes into a chemist's shop with his father. Valuable things can be got there quite cheap, above all a special water. His father tells him about the country the water comes from. Afterward he crosses the Rubicon by train.*

The traditional apothecary's shop, with its carboys and gallipots, its waters, its *lapis divinus* and *infernalis* and its magisteries, is the last visible remnant of the kitchen paraphernalia of those alchemists who saw in the *donum spiritus sancti*—the precious gift—nothing beyond the chimera of gold making. The "special water" is literally the *aqua nostra non vulgi*.[21] It is easy to understand why it is his father who leads the dreamer to the source of life, since he is the natural source of the latter's life. We could say that the father represents the country or soil from which that life sprang. The water of life is easily had: everybody possesses it, though without knowing its value. "*Spernitur a stultis*"—it is despised by the stupid, because

20 Cf. the treatise of Komarios, in which Cleopatra explains the meaning of the water. M. Berthelot, *Collection des anciens alchimistes grecs* (Paris, 1887–88), III, 281ff.

21 *Aqua nostra* is also called *aqua permanens*, corresponding to the ὕδωρ θεῖον of the Greeks: "*aqua permanens, ex qua quidem aqua lapis noster pretiosissimus generatur,*" we read in the *Turba philosophorum* (1572), p. 14. "*Lapis enim est haec ipsa permanens aqua et dum aqua est, lapis non est*" (For the stone is this selfsame permanent water; and while it is water it is not the stone).—Ibid., p. 16. The commonness of the "water" is very often emphasized, as for instance in the *Turba*, p. 30: "*Quod quaerimus publice minimo pretio venditur, et si nosceretur, ne tantillum venderent mercatores*" (What we are seeking is sold publicly for a very small price, and if it were recognized, the merchants would not sell it for so little).

376

they assume that every good thing is always outside and somewhere else, and that the source in their own souls is a "nothing but." Like the *lapis*, it is "*pretio quoque vilis*," of little price, and therefore, like the jewel in Spitteler's *Prometheus*, it is rejected by everyone from the high priest and the academicians down to the very peasants, and "*in viam eiectus*," flung out into the street, where Ahasuerus picks it up and puts it into his pocket. The treasure has sunk down again into the unconscious.

But the dreamer has noticed something and with vigorous determination crosses the Rubicon. He has realized that the flux and fire of life are not to be underrated and are absolutely necessary for the achievement of wholeness.

15. *Four people are going down a river: the dreamer, his father, a certain friend, and the unknown woman.*

In so far as the "friend" is a definite person well known to the dreamer, he belongs, like the father, to the conscious world of the ego. Hence something very important has happened: in dream 11 the unconscious was three to one, but now the situation is reversed and it is the dreamer who is three to one (the latter being the unknown woman). The unconscious has been depotentiated. The reason for this is that by "taking the plunge" the dreamer connected the upper and the nether regions—that is to say, he has decided not to live only as a bodiless abstract being but to accept the body and the world of instinct, the reality of the problems put by love and life, and to act accordingly.[22] This was the Rubicon that was crossed. Individuation, becoming a self, is not only a spiritual problem, it is the problem of all life.

16. *Many people are present. They are all walking to the left around a square. The dreamer is not in the center but to one side. They say that a gibbon is to be reconstructed.*

Here the square appears for the first time. Presumably it arises from the circle with the help of the four people. (This will be confirmed later.) Like the *lapis*, the *tinctura rubea*, and the *aurum philosophicum*, the squaring of the circle was a problem that greatly exercised medieval minds. The Eastern

22 The alchemists give only obscure hints on this point, e.g., the quotation from Aristotle in the *Rosarium*, p. 318: "*Fili, accipere debes de pinguiori carne*" (Son, you must take from the fatter flesh). And in the *Tractatus aureus*, Ch. IV, we read: "Man is generated from the principle of Nature, whose inward substance is fleshy, and not from anything else. Meditate on this letter and reject superfluities."

and more particularly the Lamaistic mandala usually contains a square ground plan of the stupa. We can see from mandalas constructed in solid form that this was really the plan of a *building*. In these the figure of the square gives the idea of a house or temple, or of an inner walled-in space[23] (cf. below). According to ritual, stupas must always be circumambulated to the right, because a leftward movement is evil. The left, the "sinister" side, is the unconscious side. Therefore a leftward movement is equivalent to a movement in the direction of the unconscious, whereas a movement to the right is "correct" and aims at consciousness. Because in the East these unconscious contents have gradually, through long practice, come to assume definite forms that express the unconscious, they have to be accepted as such and retained by the conscious mind. Yoga, so far as we know it as an established practice, proceeds in much the same way even in its most modern forms.[24] It impresses fixed *a priori* forms on consciousness. Its most important Western parallel is the *Exercitia spiritualia* of Ignatius Loyola, which likewise impress fixed concepts about salvation on the conscious psyche. This procedure is "right" so long as the symbol is still a valid expression of the unconscious situation. The psychological rightness of both Eastern and Western Yoga ceases only when the unconscious process—which anticipates future modifications of consciousness—has developed so far that it produces shades of meaning which are no longer adequately expressed by, or are at variance with, the traditional symbol. Then and only then can one say that the symbol has lost its "rightness." The whole process signifies a gradual shift in man's unconscious view of the world over the centuries and has nothing whatever to do with intellectual criticisms of this view. Religious symbols are phenomena of life, plain facts and not intellectual opinions. The fact that water reaches its greatest density at 4° centigrade is an actuality beyond all criticism. If the Church clung for so long to the idea that the sun rotates round the earth, and then abandoned this contention in the nineteenth century, she can always appeal to the psychological truth that for millions of people the sun did revolve round the earth and that it was only in the nineteenth century that any major portion of mankind became sufficiently sure of the intellectual function to grasp the proofs of the earth's planetary nature. Unfortunately there is no "truth" unless there are people to understand it.

23 Cf. "city" and "castle" in commentary to dream 10.
24 E.g., among the followers of Ramakrishna.

Presumably the leftward circumambulation of the square indicates that the squaring of the circle is a stage on the way to the unconscious, that it is a *yantra*, a point of transition leading to a goal lying as yet unformulated beyond it. It is one of those paths to the center of the non-ego which were also trodden by the medieval investigators when producing the *lapis*. The "Philosophus" (one of the Latin sources of the *Rosarium*) says: [25] "Out of man and woman make a round circle and extract the quadrangle from this and from the quadrangle the triangle. Make a round circle and you will have the philosophers' stone."

The modern intellect naturally regards all this as poppycock. But this estimate fails to get rid of the fact that such concatenations of ideas do exist and that they even played an important part for many centuries. It is up to psychology to *understand* these things, leaving the layman to rant about poppycock and obscurantism. Many of my critics who call themselves "scientific" behave exactly like the bishop who excommunicated the cock-chafers for their unseemly proliferation.

Just as the stupas preserve relics of the Buddha in their innermost sanctuary, so in the interior of the Lamaistic quadrangle, and again in the Chinese earth-square, there is a Holy of Holies with its magical agent, the cosmic source of energy, be it the god Shiva, Buddha, a bodhisattva, or a great

---

25 In the scholia to the *Tractatus aureus* (*Hermetis Trismegisti Tractatus vere aureus, de lapidis philosophici secreto*, Leipzig, 1610, cum scholiis Dominici Gnosii), p. 43, it is said: "*Quadrangulum secretum sapientum.*" There is a circle surrounded by rays of light in the center of the square. The scholium gives the following explanation: "*Divide lapidem tuum in quatuor elementa . . . et coniunge in unum et totum habebis magisterium*" (Reduce your stone to the four elements . . . and unite them into one and you will have the whole magistery)—a quotation from pseudo-Aristotle. The circle in the middle is called "*mediator, pacem faciens inter inimicos sive elementa imo hic solus efficit quadraturam circuli*" (the mediator, making peace between enemies, or [the four] elements; nay rather he alone effects the squaring of the circle).—Ibid., p. 44. The circumambulation has its parallel in the "*circulatio spirituum sive distillatio circularis, hoc est exterius intro, interius foras: item inferius et superius, simul in uno circulo conveniant, neque amplius cognoscas, quid vel exterius, vel interius, inferius vel superius fuerit: sed omnia sint unum in uno circulo sive vase. Hoc enim vas est Pelecanus verus Philosophicus, nec alius est in toto mundo quaerendus.*" (. . . circulation of spirits or circular distillation, that is, the outside to the inside, the inside to the outside, likewise the lower and the upper; and when they meet together in one circle, you could no longer recognize what was outside or inside, or lower or upper; but all would be one thing in one circle or vessel. For this vessel is the true philosophical Pelican, and no other is to be sought for in all the universe.) This process is elucidated by the accompanying drawing. The quartering is the *exterius:* four rivers flowing in and out of the inner "ocean."—Ibid., pp. 262f.

379

teacher. In China it is Ch'ien—heaven—with the four cosmic forces radiating from it. And equally in the western mandalas of medieval Christendom the deity is enthroned at the center, often in the form of the triumphant Redeemer together with the four symbolical figures of the evangelists.[26] The symbol in our dream presents the most violent contrast to these highly metaphysical ideas, for it is a gibbon, unquestionably an ape, that is to be reconstructed in the center. Here we again meet the ape who first turned up in vision 22 of the first series. In that dream he caused a panic, but he also brought about the helpful intervention of the intellect. Now he is to be "reconstructed," and this can only mean that the anthropoid—man as an archaic fact—is to be put together again. Clearly the left-hand path does not lead upward to the kingdom of the gods and eternal ideas, but down into natural history, into the bestial instinctive foundations of human existence. We are therefore dealing, to put it in classical language, with a Dionysian mystery.

The square corresponds to the *temenos*, where a drama is taking place—in this case a play of apes instead of satyrs. The inside of the "golden flower" is a "seeding-place" where the "diamond body" is produced. The synonymous term "land of the ancestors" [27] may actually be a hint that this product is the result of integrating the ancestral stages.

The ancestral spirits play an important part in primitive rites of renewal. The aborigines of central Australia even identify themselves with their mythical ancestors of the *alcheringa* period, a sort of Homeric age. Similarly the Pueblo Indians of Taos, in preparation for their ritual dances, identify themselves with the sun, whose sons they are. This atavistic identification with human and animal ancestors can be interpreted psychologically as an integration of the unconscious, a veritable bath of renewal in the life-source where one is once again a fish, unconscious as in sleep, intoxication, and death. Hence the sleep of incubation, the Dionysian orgy, and the ritual death in initiation. Naturally the proceedings always take place in some hallowed spot. We can easily translate these ideas into the concretism of Freudian theory: the *temenos* would then be the womb of the mother and the rite a regression to incest. But these are the neurotic misunderstandings of people who have remained partly infantile and who do not realize that such things have been practiced since time immemorial by adults whose

26 Cf. τετράπεζα in commentary to dream 10, also the quaternion and tetramorph.
27 Wilhelm and Jung, *The Secret of the Golden Flower*, p. 24.

activities cannot possibly be explained as a mere regression to infantilism. Otherwise the highest and most important achievements of mankind would ultimately be nothing but the perverted wishes of children, and the word "childish" would have lost its *raison d'être*.

The symbolism of the rites of renewal, if taken seriously, points far beyond the merely archaic and infantile to man's innate psychic disposition, which is the result and deposit of all ancestral life right down to the animal level— hence the ancestor and animal symbolism. The rites are attempts to abolish the separation between the conscious mind and the unconscious, the real source of life, and to bring about a reunion of the individual with the native soil of his inherited, instinctive disposition. Had these rites of renewal not yielded definite results they would not only have died out in prehistoric times, but would never have arisen in the first place. The case before us proves that even if the conscious mind is miles away from the ancient conceptions of the rites of renewal, the unconscious still strives to bring them closer in dreams. It is true that without the qualities of autonomy and autarky there would be no consciousness at all, yet these qualities also spell the danger of isolation and atrophy since, by splitting off the unconscious, they bring about an unbearable alienation of instinct. Loss of instinct is the source of endless error and confusion.

The following dream is given unabridged, in its original text:

17. *All the houses have something theatrical about them, with stage scenery and decorations. The name of Bernard Shaw is mentioned. The play is supposed to take place in the distant future. There is a notice in English and German on one of the sets:*

THIS IS THE UNIVERSAL CATHOLIC CHURCH.
IT IS THE CHURCH OF THE LORD.
ALL THOSE WHO FEEL THAT THEY ARE THE INSTRUMENTS OF THE LORD
MAY ENTER.

Under this is printed in smaller letters: "The Church was founded by Jesus and Paul"—like a firm advertising its long standing.

I say to my friend, "Come on, let's have a look at this." He replies, "I do not see why a lot of people have to get together when they're feeling religious." I answer, "As a Protestant you will never understand." A woman nods emphatic approval. Then I see a sort of proclamation on the wall of the church. It runs:

SOLDIERS!

When you feel you are under the power of the Lord, do not address him directly. The Lord cannot be reached by words. We also strongly advise you not to indulge in any discussions among yourselves concerning the attributes of the Lord. It is futile, for everything valuable and important is ineffable.

(Signed) Pope . . . (Name illegible)

Now we go in. The interior resembles a mosque, more particularly the Hagia Sophia: no seats—wonderful effect of space; no images, only framed texts decorating the walls (like the Koran texts in the Hagia Sophia). One of the texts reads "Do not flatter your benefactor." The woman who had agreed with me before bursts into tears and cries, "Then there's nothing left!" I reply, "I find it quite right!" but she vanishes. At first I stand with a pillar in front of me and can see nothing. Then I change my position and see a crowd of people. I do not belong to them and stand alone. But they are quite distinct, so that I can see their faces. They all say in unison, "We confess that we are under the power of the Lord. The Kingdom of Heaven is within us." They repeat this three times with great solemnity. Then the organ starts to play and they sing a Bach fugue with chorale. But the original text is omitted; sometimes there is only a sort of coloratura singing, then the words are repeated: "Everything else is paper" (meaning that it does not make a living impression on me). When the chorale has faded away the gemütlich part of the ceremony begins; it is almost like a students' party. The people are all cheerful and equable. We move about, converse, and greet one another, and wine (from an episcopal seminary) is served with other refreshments. The health of the Church is drunk and, as if to express everybody's pleasure at the increase in membership, a loudspeaker blares a ragtime melody with the refrain, "Charles is also with us now." A priest explains to me: "These somewhat trivial amusements are officially approved and permitted. We must adapt a little to American methods. With a large crowd such as we have here this is inevitable. But we differ in principle from the American churches by our decidedly anti-ascetic tendency." Thereupon I awake with a feeling of great relief.

Unfortunately I must refrain from commenting on this dream as a whole and confine myself to our theme. The *temenos* has become a sacred building (in accordance with the hint given earlier). The proceedings are thus characterized as "religious." The grotesque-humorous side of the Dionysian mystery comes out in the so-called *gemütlich* part of the ceremony, where wine is served and a toast drunk to the health of the Church. An inscription on the floor of an Orphic-Dionysian shrine puts it very aptly: μόνον μὴ ὕδωρ (Only no water!).[28] The Dionysian relics in the Church, such as the fish and wine symbolism, the Damascus chalice, the seal-cylinder with the crucifix and the inscription ΟΡΦΕΟC ΒΑΚΧΙΚΟC,[29] and much else besides, can only be mentioned in passing.

The "anti-ascetic" tendency clearly marks the point of difference from the Christian Church, here defined as "American" (cf. commentary to dream 14 of the first series). America is the ideal home of the reasonable ideas of the practical intellect, which would like to put the world to rights by means of a "brain trust." This view is in keeping with the modern formula "intellect = spirit," but it completely forgets the fact that "spirit" was never a human "activity," much less a "function." The movement to the left is thus confirmed as a withdrawal from the modern world of ideas and a regression to pre-Christian Dionysus worship, where "asceticism" in the Christian sense was unknown. At the same time the movement does not lead right out of the sacred spot but remains within it; in other words, it does not lose its sacramental character. It does not simply fall into chaos and anarchy, it relates the Church directly to the Dionysian shrine just as the historical process did, though in the reverse direction. We could say that this regressive development faithfully retreads the path of history in order to reach the pre-Christian level. Hence it is not a relapse but a kind of systematic descent *ad inferos*, a psychological *nekyia*.

I encountered something very similar in the dream of a clergyman who had a rather problematical attitude to his faith: *Coming into his church at night, he finds that the whole wall of the choir has collapsed. The altar and ruins are overgrown with vines hanging full of grapes, and the moon is shining in through the gap.*

28 Orphic mosaic from Tramithia (Robert Eisler, *Orpheus—The Fisher* [London, 1921], pp. 271f.). We can take this inscription as a joke without offending against the spirit of the ancient mysteries. Cf. the frescoes in the Villa dei Misteri in Pompeii (Amedeo Maiuri, *La Villa dei Misteri* [Rome, 1931], 2 vols.), where drunkenness and ecstasy are not only closely related but actually one and the same thing. But, since initiations have been connected with healing since their earliest days, the advice may possibly be a warning against water drinking, for it is well known that the drinking water in southern regions is the mother of dysentery and typhoid fever.

29 Eisler, p. 271.

Again, a man who was much occupied with religious problems had the following dream: *An immense Gothic cathedral, almost completely dark. High Mass is being celebrated. Suddenly the whole wall of the aisle collapses. Blinding sunlight bursts into the interior together with a large herd of bulls and cows.* This setting is evidently more Mithraic.

Interestingly enough, the church in our dream is a syncretistic building, for the Hagia Sophia is a very ancient Christian church which, however, served as a mosque until quite recently. It therefore fits in very well with the purpose of the dream: to attempt a combination of Christian and Dionysian religious ideas. Evidently this is to come about without the one excluding the other, without any values being destroyed. This is extremely important, since the reconstruction of the "gibbon" is to take place in the sacred precincts. Such a sacrilege might easily lead to the dangerous supposition that the leftward movement is a *diabolica fraus* and the gibbon the devil—for the devil is in fact regarded as the "ape of God." The leftward movement would then be a perversion of divine truth for the purpose of setting up "His Black Majesty" in place of God. But the unconscious has no such blasphemous intentions; it is only trying to restore the lost Dionysus who is somehow lacking in modern man (*pace* Nietzsche!) to the world of religion. At the end of vision 22, where the ape first appears, it was said that "everything must be ruled by the light," and everything, we might add, includes the Lord of Darkness with his horns and cloven hoof—a mere Dionysian corybant who has rather unexpectedly risen to the rank of Prince.

18. *A square space with complicated ceremonies going on in it, the purpose of which is to transform animals into men. Two snakes, moving in opposite directions, have to be got rid of at once. Some animals are there, e.g., foxes and dogs. The people walk round the square and must let themselves be bitten in the calf by these animals at each of the four corners. If they run away all is lost. Now the higher animals come on the scene—bulls and ibexes. Four snakes glide into the four corners. Then the congregation files out. Two sacrificial priests carry in a huge reptile and with this they touch the forehead of a shapeless animal lump or life mass. Out of it there instantly rises a human head, transfigured. A voice proclaims: "These are attempts at being."*

One might almost say that the dream goes on with the "explanation" of what is happening in the square space. Animals are to be changed into men; a "shapeless life mass" is to be turned into a transfigured (illuminated) human head by magic contact with a reptile. The animal lump or life mass stands for the mass of the inborn unconscious, which is to be united with consciousness. This is brought about by the ceremonial use of a reptile, presumably a snake. The idea of transformation and renewal by means of a serpent is a well-substantiated archetype. It is the healing serpent, representing the god. It is reported of the mysteries of Sabazius: *"Coluber aureus in sinum demittitur consecratis et eximitur rursus ab inferioribus partibus atque imis"* (A golden snake is let down into the lap of the initiated and taken away again from the lower parts).[30] Among the Ophites, Christ was the serpent. Probably the most significant development of serpent symbolism as regards renewal of personality is to be found in Kundalini Yoga.[31] The shepherd's experience with the snake in Nietzsche's *Zarathustra* would accordingly be a fatal omen (and not the only one of its kind—cf. the prophecy at the death of the rope dancer).

But if the life mass is to be transformed a *circumambulatio* is necessary, i.e., exclusive concentration on the center, the place of creative change. During this process one is "bitten" by animals; in other words, we have to expose ourselves to the animal impulses of the unconscious without identifying ourselves with them and without "running away"; for flight from the unconscious would defeat the purpose of the whole proceeding. We must hold our ground, which means here that the process initiated by the dreamer's self-observation must be experienced in all its ramifications and then articulated with consciousness to the best of his understanding. This often entails an almost unbearable tension because of the utter incommensurability between conscious life and the unconscious process, which can only be experienced in the innermost soul and cannot touch the visible surface of life at any point. The principle of conscious life is: *Nihil est in intellectu, quod non prius fuerit in sensu.* But the principle of the unconscious is the autonomy of the psyche, reflecting in the play of its images not the world but *itself,* even though it utilizes the illustrative possibilities offered by the sensible world in order to make its images clear. The sensory datum, however, does not act as a *causa efficiens;* rather, it is *autonomously* chosen and exploited by the psyche, with the result that the rationality of the cosmos

---

30 Arnobius, *Adversus gentes.* For similar practices during the Middle Ages, cf. Joseph Hammer-Purgstall, *Mémoire sur deux coffrets gnostiques du moyen âge* (Paris, 1835).
31 Arthur Avalon, ed., *The Serpent Power* (London, 1919), and Sir John George Woodroffe, *Shakti and Shâkta* (Madras and London, 1920). (Avalon is pseud. of Woodroffe.)

is constantly being violated in the most distressing manner. But the sensible world has an equally devastating effect on the deeper psychic processes when it breaks into them as *causa efficiens*. If reason is not to be outraged on the one hand and the creative play of images not violently suppressed on the other, a circumspect and farsighted synthetic procedure is required in order to accomplish the paradoxical union of irreconcilables. Hence the alchemical parallels in our dreams.

Hardly have conscious and unconscious touched when they fly asunder on account of their antagonistic character. Hence, right at the beginning of the dream, the snakes that are making off in opposite directions have to be removed; i.e., the conflict between conscious and unconscious is at once resolutely stopped and the conscious mind is forced to stand the tension by means of the *circumambulatio*. The magic circle thus traced will also prevent the unconscious from breaking out again, for such an irruption would be equivalent to psychosis. "*Nonnulli perierunt in opere nostro*": "Not a few have perished in our work," we can say with the author of the *Rosarium*. The dream shows that the difficult operation of thinking in paradoxes—a feat possible only to the superior intellect—has succeeded. The snakes no longer run away but settle themselves in the four corners, and the process of transformation or integration sets to work. The "transfiguration" and illumination, the conscious recognition of the center, have been attained, or at least anticipated, in the dream. This potential achievement—if it can be maintained, i.e., if the conscious mind does not lose its connection with the center again [32]—means a renewal of personality. Since it is a subjective state whose reality cannot be vouched for by any external criterion, any further attempt to describe and explain it is doomed to failure, for only those who have had this experience are in a position to understand and attest its reality. "Happiness," for example, is such a remarkable reality that there is nobody who does not long for it, and yet there is not a single objective criterion which would prove beyond all doubt that this condition necessarily exists. As so often with the most important things, we have to make do with a subjective judgment.

The arrangement of the snakes in the four corners is indicative of an order in the unconscious. It is as if we were confronted with a pre-existent

---

32 Cf. the commentary to dream 10 (*Tractatus aureus*, Ch. IV): "Being chained to the arms and breast of my mother, and to her substance, I cause my substance to hold together."

ground plan, a kind of Pythagorean *tetraktys*. I have very frequently observed the number four in this connection. It probably explains the universal incidence and magical significance of the cross or of the circle divided into four. In the present case the point seems to be to capture and regulate the animal instincts so as to exorcise the danger of falling into unconsciousness. This may well be the empirical basis of the cross that vanquishes the powers of darkness.

In this dream the unconscious has managed to stage a powerful advance by thrusting its contents dangerously near to the conscious sphere. The dreamer appears to be deeply entangled in the mysterious synthetic ceremony and will unfailingly carry a lasting memory of the dream into his conscious life. Experience shows that this results in a serious conflict for the conscious mind, because it is not always either willing or able to put forth the extraordinary intellectual and moral effort needed to take a paradox seriously. Nothing is so jealous as a truth.

As a glance at the history of the medieval mind will show, our whole modern mentality has been molded by Christianity. (This has nothing to do with whether we believe the truths of Christianity or not.) Consequently the reconstruction of the ape in the sacred precincts as proposed by the dream comes as such a shock that the majority of people will welcome the rational Darwinian core of the dream as a safeguard against mystic exaltation. Only a very few will feel the collision of the two worlds and realize what it is all about. Yet the dream says plainly enough that in the place where, according to tradition, the deity dwells, the ape is to appear. This substitution is almost as bad as a Black Mass.

In Eastern symbolism the square—signifying the earth in China, the *padma* or lotus in India—has the character of the *yoni:* femininity. A man's unconscious is likewise feminine and is personified by the anima.[33] The anima also stands for the "inferior" function [34] and for that reason frequently has a shady character; in fact, she sometimes stands for evil itself. She is as

33 The idea of the anima as I define it is by no means a novelty but an archetype which we meet in the most diverse places. It was also known in alchemy, as the following scholium of Gnosius proves (p. 417): "*Quemadmodum in sole ambulantis corpus continuo sequitur umbra . . . sic hermaphroditus noster Adamicus, quamvis in forma masculi appareat semper tamen in corpore occultatam Evam sive foeminam suam secum circumfert*" (As the shadow continually follows the body of one who walks in the sun, so our hermaphroditic Adam, though he appears in the form of a male, nevertheless always carries about with him Eve, or his wife, hidden in his body).
34 Cf. *Psychological Types*, def. "inferior function."

a rule the *fourth* person (cf. dreams 10, 11, 15). She is the dark and dreaded maternal womb, which is of an essentially ambivalent nature. The Christian deity is one in three persons. The fourth person in the heavenly drama is undoubtedly the devil In the more harmless psychological version he is merely the inferior function. On a moral valuation he is man's sin; therefore a function belonging to him and hence masculine. The female element in the deity is kept very dark, the interpretation of the Holy Ghost as Sophia being considered heretical. Hence the Christian metaphysical drama, the "Prologue in Heaven," has only masculine actors, a point it shares with many of the ancient mysteries. But the female element must obviously be somewhere—so it is presumably to be found in the dark. At any rate that is where the ancient Chinese philosophers located it: in the *Yin*.[35] Although man and woman unite they nevertheless represent irreconcilable opposites which, when activated, degenerate into deadly hostility. This primordial pair of opposites symbolizes every conceivable pair of opposites that may occur: hot and cold, light and dark, north and south, dry and damp, good and bad, conscious and unconscious. In the psychology of the functions there are two conscious and therefore masculine functions, the differentiated function and its auxiliary, which are represented in dreams by, say, father and son, whereas the unconscious functions appear as mother and daughter. Since the conflict between the two auxiliary functions is not nearly so great as that between the differentiated and the inferior function, it is possible for the third function—that is, the unconscious auxiliary one—to be raised to consciousness and thus made masculine. It will, however, bring with it traces of its contamination with the inferior function, thus acting as a kind of link with the darkness of the unconscious. It was in keeping with this psychological fact that the Holy Ghost was heretically interpreted as Sophia, for he was the mediator of birth in the flesh, who enabled the deity to shine forth in the darkness of the world. No doubt it was this association that caused the Holy Ghost to be suspected of femininity, for Mary was the dark earth of the field—*"illa terra virgo nondum pluviis irrigata"* (the virgin soil not yet watered by the rains), as Tertullian called her.

The fourth function is contaminated with the unconscious and, on being made conscious, drags the whole of the unconscious with it. We must then come to terms with the unconscious and try to bring about a synthesis of

---

35 Cf. *Tractatus aureus*, p. 12: "*Verum masculus est coelum foeminae et foemina terra masculi*" (The male is the heaven of the female, and the female is the earth of the male).

opposites.[36] At first a violent conflict breaks out, such as any reasonable man would experience when it became evident that he had to swallow a lot of absurd superstitions. Everything in him would rise up in revolt and he would defend himself desperately against what looked to him like murderous nonsense. This situation explains the following dreams.

19. *Ferocious war between two peoples.*

This dream depicts the conflict. The conscious mind is defending its position and trying to repress the unconscious. The first result of this is the expulsion of the fourth function, but, since it is contaminated with the third, there is a danger of the latter's disappearing as well. Things would then return to the state that preceded the present one, when only two functions were conscious and the other two unconscious.

20. *There are two boys in a cave. A third falls in as if through a pipe.*

The cave represents the darkness and seclusion of the unconscious; the two boys correspond to the two unconscious functions. Theoretically the third must be the auxiliary function, which would indicate that consciousness has withdrawn completely into the differentiated function. The odds now stand 1:3, greatly in favor of the unconscious. We may therefore expect a new advance on its part and a return to its former position. The "boys" are an allusion to the dwarf motif, of which more later.

21. *A large transparent sphere containing many little spheres. A green plant is growing out of the top.*

The sphere is a whole that embraces all its contents; life which has been brought to a standstill by useless struggle becomes possible again. In Kundalini Yoga the "green womb" is a name for Ishvara (Shiva) emerging from his latent condition.

22. *The dreamer is in an American hotel. He goes up in the elevator to about the third or fourth floor. He has to wait there with a lot of other people. A friend*

---

36 Alchemy regarded this synthesis as one of its chief tasks. The *Turba philosophorum* (1572 edn., p. 26) says: "*Coniungite ergo masculinum servi rubei filium suae odoriferae uxori et iuncti artem gignunt*" (Join therefore the male son of the red slave with his sweet-scented wife, and joined together they will produce the Art). This synthesis of opposites was often represented as a brother-and-sister incest, which version undoubtedly goes back to the "Visio Arislei," *Artis auriferae* (Basel, 1593), Treatise V, where the cohabitation of Thabritius and Beya, the children of the "King of the Sea," is described.

(an actual person) is also there and says that the dreamer should not have kept the dark unknown woman waiting so long below, since he had put her in his (the dreamer's) charge. The friend now gives him an unsealed note for the dark woman, on which is written: "Salvation does not come from refusing to take part or from running away. Nor does it come from just drifting. Salvation comes from complete surrender, with one's eyes always turned to the center." On the margin of the note there is a drawing: a wheel or wreath with eight spokes. Then an elevator boy appears and says that the dreamer's room is on the eighth floor. He goes on up in the elevator, this time to the seventh or eighth floor. An unknown red-haired man, standing there, greets him in a friendly way. Then the scene changes. There is said to be a revolution in Switzerland: the military party is making propaganda for "completely throttling the left." The objection that the left is weak enough anyway is met by the answer that this is just why it ought to be throttled completely. Soldiers in old-fashioned uniforms now appear, who all resemble the red-haired man. They load their guns with ramrods, stand in a circle, and prepare to shoot at the center. But in the end they do not shoot and seem to march away. The dreamer wakes up in terror.

The tendency to re-establish a state of wholeness—already indicated in the foregoing dream—once more comes up against a consciousness with a totally different orientation. It is therefore appropriate that the dream should have an American background. The elevator is going up, as is right and proper when something is coming "up" from the "sub-" conscious. What is coming up is the unconscious content, namely the mandala characterized by the number four. Therefore the elevator should rise to the fourth floor; but, as the fourth function is taboo, it only rises to "about the third or fourth." This happens not to the dreamer alone but to many others as well, who must all wait like him until the fourth function can be accepted. A good friend then calls his attention to the fact that he should not have kept the dark woman, i.e., the anima who stands for the taboo function, waiting "below," i.e., in the unconscious. It was just for this reason that he had to wait upstairs with the others. It is in fact not merely an individual but a collective problem, for the animation of the unconscious which has become so noticeable in recent times has, as Schiller foresaw, raised questions which the nineteenth century never even dreamed of. Nietzsche in his *Zarathustra* decided to reject the "snake" and the "ugliest man," thus exposing himself to an heroic paroxysm of consciousness which led, logically enough, to the collapse foretold in the same book.

The advice given in the note is as profound as it is to the point, so that there is really nothing to add. After it has been more or less accepted by the dreamer the ascent can be resumed. We must take it that the problem of the fourth function was accepted, at least broadly, for the dreamer now reaches the seventh or eighth floor, which means that the fourth function is no longer represented by a quarter but by an eighth, and is apparently reduced by half.

Curiously enough, this hesitation before the last step to wholeness seems also to play a part in *Faust*, Part II, where, in the Cabiri scene, "resplendent mermaids" come from over the water.[36a]

NEREIDS AND TRITONS:	Bear we, on the waters riding, That which brings you all glad tiding. In Chelone's giant shield Gleams a form severe revealed: These are gods that we are bringing; Hail them, you high anthems singing.
SIRENS:	Mean these forms and slight, Vast in hidden might, Time-honored are these gods Of shipwreck and of floods.
NEREIDS ETC.:	Great Cabiri do we bear, That our feast be friendly fair: Where their sacred powers preside Neptune's rage is pacified.

A "severe form" is brought by "mermaids," feminine figures who represent as it were the sea and the waves of the unconscious. The word "severe" reminds us of "severe" architectural or geometrical forms which illustrate a definite idea without any romantic (feeling-toned) trimmings. It "gleams" from the shell of a tortoise, which, primitive and cold-blooded like the snake, symbolizes the instinctual side of the unconscious. The "form" is somehow identical with the unseen, creative dwarf gods, hooded and cloaked manikins who are kept hidden in the dark *cista*, but who also appear on the seashore as little figures about a foot high, where, as kinsmen of the unconscious, they protect navigation, i.e., the venture into darkness and uncertainty. In the

36a [Based on the tr. by Philip Wayne (Penguin Classics), though slight modifications have been necessary to accommodate his version to Jung's text.—R.F.C.H.]

form of the Dactyls they are also the gods of invention, small and apparently insignificant like the impulses of the unconscious but endowed with the same mighty power. (*El gabir* is "the great, the mighty one.")

NEREIDS ETC.:   Three have followed where we led,
But the fourth refused the call;
He the rightful seer, he said,
His to think for one and all.

SIRENS: A god may count it sport
To set a god at naught.
Honor the grace they bring,
And fear their threatening.

It is characteristic of Goethe's feeling-toned nature that the fourth should be the thinker. If the supreme principle is "feeling is all," then thinking has to play an unfavorable role and be submerged. *Faust*, Part I, portrays this development. Since Goethe acted as his own model, thinking became the fourth (taboo) function. Because of its contamination with the unconscious it takes on the grotesque form of the Cabiri, for the Cabiri, as dwarfs, are chthonic gods and misshapen accordingly. ("I call them pot-bellied freaks of common clay.") They thus stand in grotesque contrast to the heavenly gods and poke fun at them (cf. the "ape of God").

NEREIDS ETC.:   Seven there should really be.

SIRENS: Where, then, stay the other three?

NEREIDS ETC.:   That we know not. You had best
On Olympus make your quest.
There an eighth may yet be sought
Though none other gave him thought.
Well inclined to us in grace,
Not all perfect yet their race.
Beings there beyond compare,
Yearning, unexplainable,
Press with hunger's pang to share
In the unattainable.

We learn that there are "really" seven or eight of them; but again there is some difficulty with the eighth as before there was with the fourth.[37]

37 The 3 and 4 seem to have been something of a headache to the alchemists too, as we can see from the following passage: "*Est enim lapis trinus et unus, quatuor habens naturas scl. quatuor elementa et tres colores scl. nigrum, album et rubeum*" (For the stone is triune and one, having four natures, or four elements, and three colors, i.e., black,

Similarly, in contradiction to the previous emphasis placed on their lowly origin in the dark, it now appears that the Cabiri are actually to be found on Olympus; for they are eternally striving from the depths to the heights and are therefore always to be found both below *and* above. The "severe form" is obviously an unconscious content that struggles toward the light. It seeks, and itself is, what I have elsewhere called "the treasure hard to attain." [38] This hypothesis is immediately confirmed:

SIRENS: Fame is dimmed of ancient time,
            Honor droops in men of old;
            Though they have the Fleece of Gold,
            Ye have the Cabiri.

The "Golden Fleece" is the coveted goal of the argosy, the perilous quest that is one of the numerous synonyms for attaining the unattainable. Thales makes this wise remark about it:

            This is the faith in which they trust:
            The coin grows rare because of rust.

The unconscious is always the fly in the ointment, the skeleton in the cupboard of perfection, the painful lie given to all idealistic pronouncements, the earthiness that clings to our human nature and sadly clouds the crystal clarity we long for. In the alchemical view rust, like verdigris, is the metal's sickness. But at the same time this leprosy is the *vera prima materia*, the basis for the preparation of the philosophical gold. Of this the *Rosarium* says:

> Our gold is not the common gold. But thou hast inquired concerning the greenness [*viriditas*, presumably verdigris], deeming the bronze to be a leprous body on account of the greenness it hath upon it. Therefore I say unto thee that whatever is perfect in the bronze is that greenness only, because that greenness is straightway changed by our magistery into our most true gold.[39]

The paradoxical remark of Thales that the rust alone gives the coin its

---

white and red). Commentariolus in the *Tabula smaragdina* of Hortulanus (*Septem Tractatus Hermet. Trism. aurei*, 1566), p. 47. Concerning the 3 colors, see dream 59, commentary on the "World Clock."

38 See my *Symbols of Transformation* (CWJ 5, 1956), index, s.v.

39 P. 220. *Viriditas* is occasionally called *azoth*, which is one of the numerous synonyms for the stone.

true value is a kind of alchemical quip, which at bottom only says that there
is no light without shadow and no psychic wholeness without imperfection.
To round itself out, life calls not for perfection but for completeness; and
for this the "thorn in the flesh" is needed, the suffering of defects without
which there is no progress and no ascent.

Returning now to our dream, we find at the critical point—the seventh
or eighth floor—the red-haired man, a synonym for the "man with the
pointed beard" and hence for the shrewd Mephisto, who magically changes
the scene because he is concerned with something that Faust himself never
saw: the "severe form" symbolizing the supreme treasure, the immortal
self.[40] He changes himself into the soldiers, representatives of uniformity,
of collective opinion, which is naturally dead against tolerating anything
"unsuitable." For collective opinion the numbers three and seven are, on
the highest authority, sacred; but four and eight are the very devil, something inferior—"common clay"—which in the stern judgment of the pundits
has no right to exist. The "left" is to be "completely throttled," meaning the
unconscious and all the "sinister" things that come from it. An antiquated
view, no doubt, and one that uses antiquated methods; but even muzzle-
loaders can hit the mark. For reasons unknown, i.e., not stated in the dream,
the destructive attack on the "center"—to which, according to the note,
"one's eyes must always be turned"—peters out. In the drawing on the margin of the note this center is portrayed as a wheel with eight spokes.

23. *In the square space. The dreamer is sitting opposite the unknown woman
whose portrait he is supposed to be drawing. What he draws, however, is not a
face but three-leaved clovers or distorted crosses in four different colors: red,
yellow, green, and blue.*

In connection with this dream the dreamer spontaneously drew a circle
with quarters tinted in the above colors. It was a wheel with eight spokes.
In the middle there was a four-petaled blue flower. A great many drawings
now follow at short intervals, all dealing with the curious structure of the
"center" and arising from the dreamer's need to discover a configuration that
adequately expresses the nature of this center. The drawings are based partly
on visual impressions, partly on intuitive perceptions, and partly on
dreams.

40 *Faust,* Part II. The angels bear Faust's "immortal part" to heaven, after cheating the
devil of it.

394

All this goes to show that the idea of the "center" which the unconscious has been repeatedly thrusting upon the conscious mind is beginning to gain foothold there and to exercise a peculiar fascination. The next drawing is again of the blue flower, but this time subdivided into eight; then follow pictures of four mountains round a lake in a crater, also of a red ring lying on the ground with a withered tree standing in it, round which a green snake creeps up with a leftward movement.

The layman may be rather puzzled by the serious attention devoted to this problem. But a little knowledge of Yoga and of the medieval philosophy of the *lapis* would help him to understand. As we have already said, the squaring of the circle was one of the methods for producing the *lapis;* another was the use of *imaginatio,* as the following text unmistakably proves:

> And see to it that thy door be well and firmly closed, so that he who is within cannot escape, and—God willing—thou wilt reach the goal. Nature carries out her operations gradually; and indeed I would have thee do the same: let thy imagination be guided wholly by nature. And observe according to nature, through whom the substances regenerate themselves in the bowels of the earth. And imagine this with true and not fantastic imagination.[41]

The *vas bene clausum* (well-sealed vessel) is a precautionary rule in alchemy very frequently mentioned, and is the equivalent of the magic circle. In both cases the idea is to protect what is within from the intrusion and admixture of what is without, as well as to prevent it from escaping.[42] The *imaginatio* is to be understood here as the real and literal power to create images *(Einbildungskraft)*—the classical usage of the word in contrast to *phantasia,* which means a mere "conceit" or chance idea in the sense of an insubstantial thought. In the *Satyricon* the word is used even more strongly, to denote something ridiculous: *"phantasia non homo."* [43] *Imaginatio* is the active evocation of (inner) images *secundum naturam,* an authentic feat of thought or ideation, which does not spin aimless and groundless fantasies "into the blue"—does not, that is to say, just play with its objects, but tries to grasp the inner facts and portray them in images true to their nature.

41 *Rosarium,* p. 214. Quotation from a source called "Speculum."
42 Ibid., p. 213: *"Nec intrat in eum [lapidem], quod non sit ortum ex eo, quoniam si aliquid extranei sibi apponatur, statim corrumpitur"* (Nothing enters into it [the stone] that did not come from it; since, if anything extraneous were to be added to it, it would at once be spoilt).
43 Petronius Arbiter, *Satyricon.*

This activity is an *opus*, a work. And we cannot call the manner in which the dreamer handles the objects of his inner experience anything but true work, considering how conscientiously, accurately, and carefully he records and elaborates the content now pushing its way into consciousness. The resemblance to the *opus* is obvious enough to anyone familiar with alchemy. Moreover the analogy is borne out by the dreams themselves, as dream 24 will show.

The present dream, from which the drawings above-mentioned originated, shows no signs of the "left" having been in any way "throttled." On the contrary, the dreamer finds himself once more in the *temenos* facing the unknown woman who personifies the fourth or "inferior" function.[44] His drawing has been anticipated by the dream, and what the dream gives in personified form the dreamer reproduces as an abstract ideogram. This might well be a hint that the meaning of the personification is a symbol for something that could easily be represented in quite another form. This "other form" refers back to the ace of clubs in dream 16 of the first series, where we emphasized its analogy with the irregular cross. The analogy is confirmed here. I tried to formulate the situation at that time as follows: the Christian Trinity, but modified, colored, or overshadowed by the four (colors). The colors now appear as a concretization of the *tetraktys*. The *Rosarium* cites a similar statement from the *Tractatus aureus:* "*Vultur* [45] . . . clamat voce magna, inquiens: Ego sum albus niger et rubeus citrinus*" [46] (The vulture . . . exclaims in a loud voice: I am the white black and the red yellow). On the other hand it is stressed that the *lapis* unites *omnes colores* in itself. We can thus take it that the quaternity represented by the colors is a kind of preliminary stage. This is confirmed by the *Rosarium* (pp.

---

44 Prescription for preparation of the *lapis*, quoted from pseudo-Hermes, *Rosarium*, p. 317: "*Fili, extrahe a radio suam umbram: accipe ergo quartam partem sui, hoc est, unam partem de fermento et tres partes de corpore imperfecto,*" etc. (Son, extract from the ray its shadow: then take a fourth part of it, i.e., one part of the ferment and three parts of the imperfect body, etc.). For *umbra*, see p. 233: "*Fundamentum artis est sol et eius umbra*" (The basis of the art is the sun and its shadow). The foregoing quotation only gives the sense of the *Tractatus aureus* and is not a literal quotation.

45 Cf. dream 58. The alchemical vulture, eagle, and crow are all essentially synonymous.

46 This quotation from Hermes is likewise an arbitrary reading. The passage runs literally: "*Ego sum albus nigri et rubeus albi et citrinus rubei et certe veridicus sum*" (I am the white of the black, and the red of the white, and the yellow of the red, and I speak very truth). In this way three meanings are expressed by four colors, in contrast to the formula of Hortulanus which attributes four natures and three colors to the *lapis*. See note 37.

207-8): *"Lapis noster est ex quatuor elementis"* (Our stone is from the four elements). The same applies to the *aurum philosophicum: "In auro sunt quatuor elementa in aequali proportione aptata"* (In the gold the four elements are contained in equal proportions)—*Rosarium* (p. 208). The fact is that the four colors in the dream also represent the transition from threeness to fourness and thus to the squared circle, which, according to the alchemists, comes nearest to the *lapis* on account of its roundness or perfect simplicity. For this reason a recipe for the preparation of the *lapis*, attributed to Raymundus, says:

> Recipe de simplicissimo et de rotundo corpore, et noli recipere de triangulo vel quadrangulo sed de rotundo: quia rotundum est propinquius simplicitati quam triangulus. Notandum est ergo, quod corpus simplex nullum habens angulum, quia ipsum est primum et posterius in planetis, sicut Sol in stellis.

> (Take of the body that is most simple and round, and do not take the triangle or quadrangle but the round, for the round is nearer to simplicity than the triangle. Hence it is to be noted that a simple body has no corners, for it is the first and last among the planets, like the sun among the stars.) [47]

24. *Two people are talking about crystals, particularly about a diamond.*

Here one can hardly avoid thinking of the *lapis*. In fact this dream discloses the historical background and indicates that we really are dealing with the coveted *lapis*, the "treasure hard to attain." The dreamer's *opus* amounts to an unconscious recapitulation of the efforts of Hermetic philosophy. (More about the diamond in dreams 37, 39, 50 below.)

25. *It is a question of constructing a central point and making the figure symmetrical by reflection at this point.*

The word "constructing" points to the synthetic character of the *opus* and also to the laborious building process that taxes the dreamer's energy. The "symmetry" is an answer to the conflict in dream 22 ("completely throttling the left"). Each side must perfectly balance the other as its mirror-image, and this image is to fall at the "central point," which evidently possesses the property of reflection—it is a *vitrum*,[48] a crystal or

47 *Rosarium*, p. 317.
48 A quotation from Ademarus (*Rosarium*, p. 353): *"[Lapis] nihilominus non funditur, nec ingreditur, nec permiscetur, sed vitrificatur"* (But [the stone] can neither be melted nor penetrated nor mixed but is made as hard as glass).

sheet of water. This power of reflection seems to be another allusion to the underlying idea of the *lapis*, the *aurum philosophicum*, the elixir, the *aqua nostra*, etc.

Just as the "right" denotes the world of consciousness and its principles, so by "reflection" the picture of the world is to be turned round to the left, thus producing a corresponding world in reverse. We could equally well say: through reflection the right appears as the reverse of the left. Therefore the left seems to have as much validity as the right; in other words, the unconscious and its—for the most part unintelligible—order become the symmetrical counterpart of the conscious mind and its contents, although it is still not clear which of them is reflected and which reflecting. To carry our reasoning a step further, we could regard the center as the point of intersection of two worlds that correspond but are inverted by reflection.[49]

The idea of creating a symmetry would thus indicate some kind of climax in the task of accepting the unconscious and incorporating it in a general picture of the world. The unconscious here displays a "cosmic" character.

26. *It is night, with stars in the sky. A voice says, "Now it will begin." The dreamer asks, "What will begin?" Whereupon the voice answers, "The circulation can begin." Then a shooting star falls in a curious leftward curve. The scene changes, and the dreamer is in a rather squalid place of entertainment. The proprietor, who appears to be an unscrupulous crook, is there with some bedraggled-looking girls. A quarrel starts about left and right. The dreamer then leaves and drives round the perimeter of a square in a taxi. Then he is in the bar again. The proprietor says, "What they said about left and right did not satisfy my feelings. Is there really such a thing as a left and a right side of human society?" The dreamer answers, "The existence of the left does not contradict that of the right. They both exist in everyone. The left is the mirror-image of the right. Whenever I feel it like that, as a mirror-image, I am at one with myself. There is no right and left side to human society, but there are symmetrical and lopsided people. The lopsided are those who can fulfill only one side of themselves, either left or right. They are still in the childhood state." The proprietor says meditatively, "Now that's much better," and goes about his business.*

I have given this dream in full because it is an excellent illustration of how

49 There are very interesting parapsychological parallels to this, but I cannot discuss them here.

the ideas hinted at in the last dream have been taken up by the dreamer. The idea of symmetrical proportion has been stripped of its cosmic character and translated into psychological terms, expressed in social symbols. "Right" and "left" are used almost like political slogans.

The beginning of the dream, however, is still under the cosmic aspect. The dreamer noted that the curious curve of the shooting star corresponded exactly to the line he drew when sketching the picture of the eightfold flower (cf. commentary to dream 23). The curve formed the edge of the petals. Thus the shooting star traces the outline, so to speak, of a flower that spreads over the whole starry heaven. What is now beginning is the circulation of the light. This cosmic flower corresponds roughly to the rose in Dante's *Paradiso*.

The "cosmic" nature of an experience—as an aspect of some inner occurrence that can only be understood psychologically—is offensive and at once provokes a reaction "from below." Evidently the cosmic aspect was too high and is compensated "downward," so that the symmetry is no longer that of two world pictures but merely of human society, in fact of the dreamer himself. When the proprietor remarks that the latter's psychological understanding is "much better," he is making an estimate whose conclusion should run: "but still not good enough."

The quarrel about right and left that starts in the bar is the conflict which breaks out in the dreamer himself when he is called upon to recognize the symmetry. He cannot do this because the other side looks so suspicious that he would rather not investigate it too closely. That is the reason for the magical *circumambulatio* (driving round the square): he has to stay inside and learn to face his image in the mirror without running away. He does this as best he can, though not quite as the other side would wish. Hence the somewhat chill recognition of his merits.

27 (Visual impression). *A circle with a green tree in the middle. In the circle a fierce battle is raging between savages. They do not see the tree.*

Evidently the conflict between right and left has not yet ended. It continues because the savages are still in the "childhood state" and therefore, being "lopsided," only know either the left or the right but not a third that stands above the conflict.

28 (Visual impression). *A circle: within it, steps lead up to a basin with a fountain inside.*

When a condition is unsatisfactory because some essential aspect of the unconscious content is lacking, the unconscious process reverts to earlier symbols, as is the case here. The symbolism goes back to dream 13, where we met the mandala-garden of the philosophers with its fountain of *aqua nostra*. Circle and basin emphasize the mandala, the rose of medieval symbolism. The "rose garden of the philosophers" is one of alchemy's favorite symbols.[50]

29 (Visual impression). *A bunch of roses, then the sign* ⚮ *, but it should be* ✳

A rose bouquet is like a fountain fanning out. The meaning of the first sign—possibly a tree—is not clear, whereas the correction represents the eightfold flower. Evidently a mistake is being corrected which somehow impaired the wholeness of the rose. The aim of the reconstruction is to bring the mandala—the correct valuation and interpretation of the "center"— once more into the field of consciousness.

30. *The dreamer is sitting at a round table with the dark unknown woman.*

Whenever a process has reached a culmination as regards either its clarity or the wealth of inferences that can be drawn from it, a regression is likely to ensue. From the dreams that come in between the ones we have quoted here it is evident that the dreamer is finding the insistent demands of wholeness somewhat disagreeable; for their realization will have far-reaching practical consequences whose personal nature, however, lies outside the scope of our study.

The round table again points to the circle of wholeness, and the anima comes in as representative of the fourth function, especially in her "dark" form, which always makes itself felt when something is becoming concrete, i.e., when it has to be translated, or threatens to translate itself, into reality. "Dark" means chthonic, concrete and earthy. This is also the source of the fear that causes the regression.

31. *The dreamer is sitting with a certain man of unpleasant aspect at a round table. On it there stands a glass filled with a gelatinous mass.*

50 Cf. the Heavenly Rose in Dante's *Paradiso*, and Luigi Valli, "Die Geheimsprache Dantes und der Fedeli d'Amore," *Europäische Revue* (Berlin), VI: 1 (Jan.–June, 1930), 92–112.

This dream is an advance on the last in that the dreamer has accepted the "dark" as his own darkness, to the extent of producing a real "shadow" belonging to him personally.[51] The anima is thus relieved of the moral inferiority projected upon her and can take up the creative and living function that is properly her own.[52] This is probably represented by the glass with its peculiar contents which we, like the dreamer, may compare with the undifferentiated "life mass" in dream 18. It was then a question of the gradual transformation of primitive animality into something human. So we may expect something of the sort here, for it seems as if the spiral of inner development had come round to the same point again, though somewhat higher up.

The glass corresponds to the *unum vas* of alchemy and its contents to the living, semi-organic mixture from which the body of the *lapis*, endowed with spirit and life, will emerge—or possibly that strange Faustian figure who bursts into flame three times: the Boy Charioteer, the Homunculus who is dashed against the throne of Galatea, and Euphorion (symbolizing a dissolution of the "center" into its unconscious elements). We know that the *lapis* is not just a "stone" since it is expressly stated to be composed "*de re animali, vegetabili et minerali*," and to consist of body, soul, and spirit (*Rosarium*, p. 237); moreover, it grows from flesh and blood (p.238). For which reason Philosophus says: "The wind hath carried it in his belly. And therefore it

---

51 Although the theme of this study does not permit a full discussion of the psychology of dreams, I must make a few explanatory remarks at this point. Sitting together at one table means relationship, being connected or "put together." The round table indicates that the figures have been brought together for the purpose of wholeness. If the anima figure (the personified unconscious) is separated from ego consciousness and therefore unconscious, it means that there is an isolating layer of personal unconscious embedded between the ego and the anima. The existence of a personal unconscious proves that contents of a personal nature which could really be made conscious are being kept unconscious for no good reason. There is then an inadequate or even nonexistent consciousness of the shadow. The shadow corresponds to a negative ego personality and includes all those qualities we find painful or regrettable. Here shadow and anima, being unconscious, are contaminated with each other, a state that is represented in dreams by "marriage" or the like. But if the existence of the anima (or the shadow) is accepted and understood, a separation of these figures ensues, as has happened in the case of our dreamer. The shadow is thus recognized as belonging, and the anima as not belonging, to the ego.
52 Cf. what I have said about the function of the anima in my lecture "The Archetypes of the Collective Unconscious" (CWJ, 9, I, 1959). In Hermes' treatise "To the Human Soul," she is called "the highest interpreter and nearest custodian (of the eternal)," which aptly characterizes her function as mediator between conscious and unconscious.

is plain that wind is air, air is life, and life is soul. The stone is that thing midway between perfect and imperfect bodies, and that which nature herself begins is brought to perfection through the art" (p. 236). The stone "is named the stone of invisibility" (*lapis invisibilitatis*) (p. 231).

The dream certainly deals with the question of bringing the "center" to life, or—as we might say—to birth.

32. The dreamer receives a letter from an unknown woman. She writes that she has pains in the uterus. A drawing is attached to the letter, looking roughly like this:

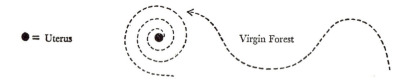

In the virgin forest there are swarms of monkeys. Then a panorama of white glaciers opens out.

The uterus is the center, the life-giving vessel. (The Grail: by Wolfram von Eschenbach called the *"lapsit exilis,"* but he may have meant *"lapis exilis."* [53]) *"Unus est lapis, una medicina, unum vas,"* says the *Rosarium*, p. 206. As the Grail is the life-giving vessel itself, so the stone is the *elixir vitae*.[54] The drawing shows a spiral with the vessel as its center. The serpentine line leading to the vessel is analogous to the healing serpent of Aesculapius (*medicina*), and also to the Tantric symbol of *Shiva bindu*, the creative, latent god without extension in space who, in the form of a point or *lingam*, is encircled three and a half times by the Kundalini serpent.[55] With the virgin forest we meet the ape motif again, which appeared before in vision 22 of the first series and in dreams 16 and 18 of this. In

53 The conjecture *"lapsus est ex illis"* is hardly tenable, nor is *"lapis ex coelis."* Wolfram could neither write nor understand Latin.
54 The center of the mandala is sometimes referred to in alchemical literature as the *vas*. It corresponds to the calyx of the Indian lotus, seat and birthplace of the gods. This is called the *padma*, a term that denotes femininity and corresponds to the *yoni*. In alchemy the *vas* is often taken as the uterus where the "child" is gestated. In the Litany of Loreto, Mary is spoken of three times as the *vas* (*"vas spirituale," "honorabile,"* and *"insigne devotionis"*), and in medieval poetry she is called the "flower of the sea" which shelters the Christ (cf. dream 36).
55 See Avalon, *The Serpent Power*.

vision 22 it led to the announcement that "everything must be ruled by light" and, in dream 18, to the "transfigured" head. Similarly the present dream ends with a panorama of white "glaciers," reminding the dreamer of an earlier dream (not included here) in which he beheld the Milky Way and was having a conversation about immortality. Thus the glacier symbol is a bridge leading back again to the cosmic aspect that caused the regression. But, as is nearly always the case, the earlier content does not return in its first simple guise—it brings a new complication with it, which, though it might have been expected logically, is no less repugnant to intellectual consciousness than the cosmic aspect was. The complication is the memory of the conversation about immortality. This theme was already hinted at in dream 9, with its pendulum clock, a *perpetuum mobile.* Immortality is a clock that never runs down, a mandala that revolves eternally like the heavens. Thus the cosmic aspect returns with interest and compound interest. This might easily prove too much for the dreamer, for the "scientific" stomach has very limited powers of digestion.

The unconscious does indeed put forth a bewildering profusion of designations for that obscure thing we call the mandala or "self." It almost seems as if we were ready to go on dreaming in the unconscious the age-old dream of alchemy, and to continue to pile new synonyms on top of the old, only to know as much or as little about it in the end as the ancients themselves. I will not enlarge upon what the *lapis* meant to our forefathers, and what the mandala still means to the Lamaist and Tantrist, Aztec and Pueblo Indian, the "golden pill" [56] to the Taoist, and the "golden seed" to the Hindu. We know the texts that give us a vivid idea of all this. But what does it mean when the unconscious stubbornly persists in presenting such abstruse symbolisms to a cultured European? The only point of view I can apply here is the psychological. (There may be others with which I am not familiar.) From this point of view, as it seems to me, everything that can be grouped together under the general concept "mandala" expresses the essence of a certain kind of attitude. The known attitudes of the conscious mind have definable aims and purposes. But a man's attitude toward the self is the only one that has no definable aim and no visible purpose. It is easy enough to say "self," but exactly what have we said? That remains shrouded in "metaphysical" darkness. I may define the "self" as the totality of the conscious and unconscious psyche, but this totality transcends our

56 Synonymous with the "golden flower."

vision; it is a veritable *lapis invisibilitatis*. In so far as anything unconscious exists it is not describable; its existence is a mere postulate and nothing whatever can be predicated as to its possible contents. The totality can be experienced only in its parts and then only in so far as these are contents of consciousness; but *qua* totality it necessarily transcends consciousness. Consequently the "self" is a pure borderline concept similar to Kant's *Ding an sich*. True, it is an idea that grows steadily clearer with experience—as our dreams show—without, however, losing anything of its transcendence. Since we cannot possibly know the limitations of something unknown to us, it follows that we are not in a position to set any limits to the self. It would be wildly arbitrary and therefore unscientific to restrict the self to the limits of the individual psyche, quite apart from the fundamental fact that we have not the least knowledge of these limits, seeing that they also lie in the unconscious. We may be able to indicate the limits of consciousness, but the unconscious is simply the unknown psyche and for that very reason illimitable because indeterminable. Such being the case, we should not be in the least surprised if the empirical manifestations of unconscious contents bear all the marks of something illimitable, something not determined by space and time. This quality is numinous and therefore alarming, above all to a cautious mind that knows the value of precisely delimited concepts. One is glad not to be a philosopher or theologian, lest one should then be obliged to meet such "numina" professionally. It is all the worse when it becomes increasingly clear that numina are psychic *entia* that force themselves upon consciousness, since night after night our dreams practice philosophy on their own account. What is more, when we attempt to give these numina the slip and angrily reject the alchemical gold which the unconscious offers, things do in fact go badly with us, we may even develop symptoms in defiance of all reason, and the moment we face up to the stumbling block and make it—if only hypothetically—the cornerstone, the symptoms vanish and we feel "unaccountably" well. In this dilemma we can at least comfort ourselves with the reflection that the unconscious is a necessary evil which must be reckoned with, and that it would therefore be wiser to accompany it on some of its strange symbolic wanderings, even though their meaning be exceedingly questionable. It might perhaps be conducive to good health to relearn Nietzsche's "lesson of earlier humanity."

The only objection I could make to such intellectual expedients is that very often they do not stand the test of events. We can observe in these and similar cases how, over the years, the entelechy of the self becomes so insistent that consciousness has to rise to still greater feats if it is to keep pace with the unconscious.

All that can be ascertained at present about the symbolism of the mandala is that it portrays an autonomous psychic fact, characterized by a phenomenology which is always repeating itself and is everywhere the same. It seems to be a sort of nucleus about whose innermost structure and ultimate meaning we know nothing. We can also regard it as the actual—i.e., effective—image of a conscious attitude which can state neither its aim nor its purpose and, because of this inability, projects its activity entirely upon the virtual center of the mandala. The compelling force necessary for this projection always lies in some situation where the individual no longer knows how to help himself in any other way. That the mandala is a mere psychological reflex is, however, contradicted firstly by the autonomous nature of this symbol, which sometimes manifests itself with overwhelming spontaneity in dreams and visions, and secondly by the autonomous nature of the unconscious as such, which is not only the original form of the psyche but also the condition we pass through in early childhood and to which we return every night. There is no evidence for the assertion that the activity of the psyche is merely reactive or reflex. This is at best a biological working hypothesis of limited validity. When raised to a universal truth it is nothing but a materialistic myth, for it overlooks the creative capacity of the psyche, which—whether we like it or not—exists, and in face of which all so-called "causes" become mere occasions.

33. *A battle among savages, in which bestial cruelties are perpetrated.*

As was to be foreseen, the new complication ("immortality") has started a furious conflict.

34. *A conversation with a friend. The dreamer says, "I must carry on with the figure of the bleeding Christ before me and persevere in the work of self-redemption."*

This, like the previous dream, points to an extraordinary, subtle kind of suffering caused by the breaking through of an alien spiritual world which we find very hard to accept—hence the analogy with the tragedy of Christ: "My kingdom is not of this world." But it also shows that the dreamer is now continuing his task in deadly earnest.

405

35. *An actor smashes his hat against the wall, where it looks like this figure.*

As certain material not included here shows, the "actor" refers to a definite fact in the dreamer's personal life. Up to now he had maintained a certain fiction about himself which prevented him from taking himself seriously. This fiction has become incompatible with the serious attitude he has now attained. He must give up the actor, for it was the actor in him who rejected the self. The hat refers to the first dream of all, where he puts on a *stranger's* hat. The actor throws the hat against the wall, and the hat proves to be a mandala. So the "strange" hat was the self, which at that time—while he was still playing a fictitious role—seemed like a stranger to him.

36. *The dreamer drives in a taxi to the Rathausplatz, but it is called the "Marienhof."*

I mention this dream only in passing because it shows the feminine nature of the *temenos*, just as the *rosa mystica* is one of the attributes of the Virgin in the Litany of Loreto (as also the *vas;* cf. dream 32).

37. *There are curves outlined in light around a dark center. Then the dreamer is wandering about in a dark cave, where a battle is going on between good and evil. But there is also a prince who knows everything. He gives the dreamer a ring set with a diamond and places it on the fourth finger of his left hand.*

The circulation of light that started in dream 26 reappears more clearly. Light always refers to consciousness, which at present runs only along the periphery. The center is still dark. It is the dark cave, and to enter it is obviously to set the conflict going again. At the same time it is like the prince who stands aloof, who knows everything and is the possessor of the precious stone. The gift means nothing less than the dreamer's vow to the self—for as a rule the wedding ring is worn on the fourth finger of the left hand. True, the left is the unconscious, from which it is to be inferred that the situation is still largely shrouded in unconsciousness. The prince seems to be the representative of the *aenigma regis;* cf. commentary to dream 10.

38. *A circular table with four chairs round it. Table and chairs are empty.*

This dream confirms the above conjecture. The mandala is not yet "in use."

406

39 (Visual impression). *The dreamer is falling into the abyss. At the bottom there is a bear whose eyes gleam alternately in four colors: red, yellow, green, and blue. Actually it has four eyes that change into four lights. The bear disappears and the dreamer goes through a long dark tunnel. Light is shimmering at the far end. A treasure is there, and on top of it the ring with the diamond. It is said that this ring will lead him on a long journey to the east.*

This waking dream shows that the dreamer is still preoccupied with the dark center. The bear stands for the chthonic element that might seize him. But then it becomes clear that the animal is only leading up to the four colors (cf. dream 23), which in their turn lead to the *lapis*, i.e., the diamond whose prism contains all the hues of the rainbow. The way to the east probably points to the unconscious as an antipode. According to the legend, the Grail stone comes from the east and must return there again. In alchemy the bear corresponds to the *nigredo* of the *prima materia*.

40. *Under the guidance of the unknown woman the dreamer has to discover the Pole at the risk of his life.*
The Pole is the point round which everything turns.

41. *Yellow balls rolling round to the left in a circle.*
Rotation about a center, recalling dream 21.

42. *An old master points to a spot on the ground illuminated in red.*
The *philosophus* shows him the "center." The redness may mean the dawn (alchemical *rubedo*).

43. *A yellow light like the sun looms through the fog, but it is murky. Eight rays go out from the center. This is the point of penetration: the light ought to pierce through, but has not quite succeeded.*
The dreamer himself remarked that the point of penetration is the same as the Pole in dream 40. So it is, as we surmised, a question of the sun appearing, which now turns yellow. But the light is still murky, which probably means insufficient understanding.

44. *The dreamer is in a square enclosure where he must keep still. It is a prison for Lilliputians (or children?). A wicked woman is in charge of them. The children start moving and begin to circulate round the periphery. The dreamer*

would like to run away but may not do so. One of the children turns into an animal and bites him in the calf.

The lack of clarity demands further efforts of concentration; hence the dreamer finds himself still in the childhood state, "lopsided" (cf. dream 26), and imprisoned in the *temenos* in the charge of a wicked mother-anima. The animal appears as in dream 18 and he is bitten, i.e., he must expose himself and pay the price. The *circumambulatio* means, as always, concentration on the center. He finds this state of tension almost unendurable. But he wakes up with an intense and pleasant feeling of having solved something, "as if he held the diamond in his hand." The children point to the dwarf motif, which may express Cabiric elements, i.e., unconscious formative powers (see dreams 56ff., below).

45. *A parade ground with troops. They are no longer equipping themselves for war but form an eight-rayed star rotating to the left.*

The essential point here is that the conflict seems to be overcome. The star is not in the sky and not a diamond, but a configuration on the earth formed by human beings.

46. *The dreamer is imprisoned in the square enclosure. Lions and a wicked sorceress appear.*

He cannot get out of the chthonic prison because he is not yet ready to do something that he should. (This is an important personal matter, a duty even, and the cause of much misgiving.)

47. *The wise old man shows the dreamer a place on the ground marked in a peculiar way.*

This is probably the place on earth where the dreamer belongs if he is to realize the self.

48. *An acquaintance wins a prize for digging up a potter's wheel.*

The potter's wheel rotates on the ground (cf. dream 45) and produces earthenware ("earthly") vessels which may figuratively be called "human bodies."

49. *A starry figure rotating. At the cardinal points of the circle there are pictures representing the seasons.*

Just as the place was defined before, so now the time. Place and time are the most general and necessary elements in any definition. The determination of time and place was stressed right at the beginning (cf. dreams 7, 8, 9).

50. *An unknown man gives the dreamer a precious stone. But he is attacked by a gang of apaches. He runs away (nightmare) and is able to escape. The unknown woman tells him afterward that it will not always be so: sometime he will have to stand his ground and not run away.*

When a definite time is added to a definite place one is rapidly approaching reality. That is the reason for the gift of the jewel, but also for the fear of decision, which robs the dreamer of the power to make up his mind.

51. *There is a feeling of great tension. Many people are circulating round a large central oblong with four smaller oblongs on its sides. The circulation in the large oblong goes to the left and in the smaller oblongs to the right. In the middle there is the eight-rayed star. A bowl is placed in the center of each of the smaller oblongs, containing red, yellow, green,* 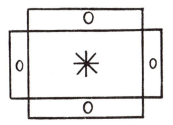 *and colorless water. The water rotates to the left. The disquieting question arises: Is there enough water?*

The colors point once more to the preliminary stage. The "disquieting" question is whether there is enough water of life—*aqua nostra*, energy, libido —to reach the central star (i.e., the "core" or "kernel"; cf. next dream). The circulation in the central oblong is still going to the left, i.e., consciousness is moving toward the unconscious. The center is therefore not yet sufficiently illuminated. The rightward circulation in the smaller oblongs, which represent the quaternity, seems to suggest that the four functions are becoming conscious. The four are generally characterized by the four colors of the rainbow. The striking fact here is that the blue is missing, and also that the square ground plan has suddenly been abandoned. The horizontal has extended itself at the cost of the vertical. So we are dealing with a "disturbed" mandala. We might add by way of criticism that the antithetical arrangement of the functions has not yet become sufficiently conscious for their characteristic polarity to be recognized.[57] The predominance of

57 Cf. the psychological functions in *Psychological Types*.

the horizontal over the vertical indicates that the ego consciousness is uppermost, thus entailing a loss of height and depth.

52. *A rectangular dance hall. Everybody is going round the periphery to the
left. Suddenly the order is heard: "To the kernels!" But the dreamer has first
to go into the adjoining room to crack some nuts. Then the people climb down
rope ladders to the water.*

The time has come to press on to the "kernel" or core of the matter, but
the dreamer still has a few more "hard nuts" to crack in the little rectangle
(the "adjoining room"), i.e., in one of the four functions. Meanwhile the
process goes on and descends to the "water." The vertical is thus lengthened,
and from the incorrect oblong we again get the square which expresses the
complete symmetry of conscious and unconscious with all its psychological
implications.

53. *The dreamer finds himself in an empty square room which is rotating. A
voice cries, "Don't let him out. He won't pay the tax!"*

This refers to the dreamer's inadequate self-realization in the personal
matter already mentioned, which in this case was one of the essential conditions of individuation and therefore unavoidable. As was to be expected,
after the preparatory emphasis on the vertical in the preceding dream, the
square is now re-established. The cause of the disturbance was an under-
estimation of the demands of the unconscious (the vertical), which led to a
flattening of the personality (recumbent oblong).

After this dream the dreamer worked out six mandalas in which he tried
to determine the right length of the vertical, the form of "circulation," and
the distribution of color.[58] At the end of this work came the following dream:

54. *I come to a strange, solemn house—the "House of the Gathering." Many
candles are burning in the background, arranged in a peculiar pattern with four
points running upward. Outside, at the door of the house, an old man is posted.
People are going in. They say nothing and stand motionless in order to collect
themselves inwardly. The man at the door says of the visitors to the house, "When
they come out again they are cleansed." I go into the house myself and find I*

58 Drawings of this kind can be found in the so-called *Muti libri* of later alchemy. Cf.
particularly the MS. in the Bibliothèque de l'Arsenal, Paris, No. 974, 8552.

can concentrate perfectly. Then a voice says: "What you are doing is dangerous. Religion is not a tax to be paid so that you can rid yourself of the woman's image, for this image cannot be got rid of. Woe unto them who use religion as a substitute for another side of the soul's life; they are in error and will be accursed. Religion is no substitute; it is to be added to the other activities of the soul as the ultimate completion. Out of the fullness of life shall you bring forth your religion; only then shall you be blessed!" While the last sentence is being spoken in ringing tones I hear distant music, simple chords on an organ. Something about it reminds me of Wagner's Fire Music. As I leave the house I see a burning mountain and I feel: "The fire that is not put out is a holy fire" (Shaw, *St. Joan*).

The dreamer notes that this dream was a "powerful experience." Indeed it has a numinous quality and we shall therefore not be far wrong if we assume that it represents a new climax of insight and understanding. The "voice" has as a rule an absolutely authoritative character and generally comes at decisive moments.

The house probably corresponds to the square, which is a "gathering place." The four shining points in the background again indicate the quaternity. The remark about cleansing refers to the transformative function of the taboo area. The production of wholeness, which is prevented by the "tax evasion," naturally requires the "image of the woman," since as anima she represents the fourth, "inferior" function, feminine because contaminated with the unconscious. In what sense the "tax" is to be paid depends on the nature of the inferior function and its auxiliary, and also on the attitude type.[59] The payment can be either concrete or symbolic, but the conscious mind is not qualified to decide which form is valid.

The dream's view that religion may not be a substitute for "another side of the soul's life" will certainly strike many people as a radical innovation. According to it, religion is equated with wholeness; it even appears as the expression of a self integrated in the "fullness of life."

The faint echo of the Fire Music—the Loki motif—is not out of key, for what does "fullness of life" mean? What does "wholeness" mean? I feel that there is every reason here for some anxiety, since man as a whole being casts a shadow. The fourth was not separated from the three and banished to the kingdom of everlasting fire for nothing. Does not an uncanonical saying of our Lord's declare: "Whoso is near unto me is near unto the

59 See *Psychological Types*, def. 8.

fire?" [60] Such dire ambiguities are not meant for grown-up children—which is why Heraclitus of old was named "the dark," because he spoke too plainly and called life itself an "ever-living fire." And that is why there are un-canonical sayings for those that have ears to hear.

55. *A silver bowl with four cracked nuts at the cardinal points.*

This dream shows that some of the problems in dream 52 have been settled, though the settlement is not complete. The dreamer pictured the goal that has now been attained as a circle divided into four, with the quadrants painted in the four colors. The circulation is to the left. Though this satisfies the demands of symmetry, the polarity of the functions is still unrecognized despite the last, very illuminating dream. From this we must conclude that the "realization" is meeting with strong inner resistances, partly of a philosophical and partly of an ethical nature, the historical justification for which cannot easily be set aside.

56. *Four children are carrying a large dark ring. They move in a circle. The dark unknown woman appears and says she will come again, for it is the festival of the solstice.*

In this dream the elements of dream 44 come together again: the children and the dark woman, who was a wicked witch before. The "solstice" indi-cates the turning point. Children, dwarf gods, bring the ring (cf. the Cabiri and the "severe form").

57 (Visual impression). *The dark ring, with an egg in the middle.*

58 (Visual impression). *A black eagle comes out of the egg and seizes in its beak the ring, now turned to gold. Then the dreamer is on a ship and the bird flies ahead.*

The eagle signifies height. (Previously the stress was on depth: people descending to the water.) It seizes the whole mandala and, with it, con-trol of the dreamer, who, carried along on a ship, sails after the bird. Birds are thoughts and the flight of thought. Generally it is fantasies and

---

60 "*Ait autem ipse salvator: Qui iuxta me est, iuxta ignem est, qui longe est a me, longe est a regno*" (The Savior himself says: He who is near me, is near to the fire; he who is far from me, is far from the kingdom).—Origen, *Homiliae in Jeremiam*, XX, quoted by Erwin Preuschen, *Antilegomena* (Giessen, 1901).

intuitive ideas that are represented thus (the winged Mercurius, Morpheus, genii, angels). The ship is the vehicle that bears the dreamer over the sea and the depths of the unconscious. As a man-made thing it stands for a system or method (or a way: cf. Hīnayāna and Mahāyāna = the Lesser Vehicle and Greater Vehicle, the two forms of Buddhism). The flight of thought goes ahead and methodical elaboration follows after. Man cannot walk the rainbow bridge like a god but must go underneath, with whatever reflective afterthoughts he may have. The eagle—synonymous with phoenix, vulture, raven—is a well-known alchemical symbol. Even the *lapis*, the *rebis* (compounded of two parts and therefore frequently hermaphroditic as an amalgam of Sol and Luna), is often represented with wings, denoting intuition or spiritual (winged) potentiality. In the last resort all these symbols depict the transconscious fact we call the self. This visual impression is rather like a snapshot of an evolving process as it leads on to the next stage.

4. The Vision of the World Clock

59. THE "GREAT VISION." *There is a vertical and a horizontal circle, having a common center. This is the world clock. It is supported by the black bird.*

The vertical circle is a blue disk with a white border divided into $4 \times 8 = 32$ *partitions. A pointer rotates upon it.*

The horizontal circle consists of four colors. On it stand four little men with pendulums, and round about it is laid the ring that was once dark and is now golden (formerly carried by the children).

The "clock" has three rhythms or pulses:

1. *The small pulse:*   *the pointer on the blue vertical disk advances by* $\frac{1}{32}$.
2. *The middle pulse:*   *one complete rotation of the pointer. At the same time the horizontal circle advances by* $\frac{1}{32}$.
3. *The great pulse:*   *32 middle pulses are equal to one rotation of the golden ring.*

This remarkable vision made a deep and lasting impression on the dreamer, an impression of "the most sublime harmony," as he himself puts it. The world clock may well be the "severe form" which is identical with the Cabiri, the four children or four little men with the pendulums. It is a three-dimensional mandala—a mandala in bodily form signifying realization. (Unfortunately medical discretion prevents my giving the biographical details. It must suffice to say that this realization did actually take place.)

Just why the vision of this curious figure should produce an impression of "the most sublime harmony" is, in one sense, very difficult to understand; but it becomes comprehensible enough as soon as we consider the comparative historical material. It is difficult to feel our way into the matter because the meaning of the image is exceedingly obscure. If the meaning is impenetrable and the form and color take no account of our aesthetic requirements, then neither our understanding nor our sense of beauty is satisfied, and we are at a loss to see why it should give rise to the impression of "the most sublime harmony." We can only venture the hypothesis that disparate and incongruous elements have combined here in the most fortunate way, at the same time producing an image which realizes the "intentions" of the unconscious in the highest degree. We must therefore assume that the image is a singularly happy expression for an otherwise unknowable psychic fact which has so far been able to manifest only apparently disconnected aspects of itself.

The impression is extremely abstract. One of the underlying ideas seems to be the intersection of two heterogeneous systems by the sharing of a common center. Hence if we start as before from the assumption that the center and its periphery represent the totality of the psyche and consequently the self, then the figure tells us that two heterogeneous systems intersect in the self, standing to one another in a functional relationship that is governed by law and regulated by "three rhythms." The self is by definition the center and the circumference of the conscious and unconscious systems. But the regulation of their functions by three rhythms is something that I cannot substantiate. I do not know what the three rhythms allude to. But I do not doubt for a moment that the allusion is amply justified. Since the figure has a cosmic aspect—world clock—we must suppose it to be a small scale model, or perhaps even a source, of space-time, or at any rate an embodiment of it and therefore, mathematically speaking, four-dimensional in nature although visible only in a three-dimensional projection. I do not wish to labor this argument, for the interpretation of the figure would considerably overtax my present understanding.

As to the comparative-historical interpretation, we are in a rather more favorable position, at least as regards the general aspects. We have at our disposal, firstly, the whole mandala symbolism of three continents, and secondly, the specific time symbolism of the mandala as this developed under the influence of astrology, particularly in the West. The horoscope is itself a mandala (a clock) with a dark center, and a leftward *circumambulatio* with "houses" and planetary phases. The mandalas of ecclesiastical art, particularly those on the floor before the high altar or beneath the transept, make frequent use of the zodiacal beasts or the yearly seasons. A related idea is the identity of Christ with the Church calendar, whereof he is the fixed pole and the life. The θεὸς Χριστος as υἱòς τοῦ ἀνρθώπου is a projection of the individual self into a symbolic figure, an obvious anticipation of the idea of the self. Hence the Gnostic (Ophitic) adulteration of Christ with the Agathodaemon serpent, and with the Horus symbolism that can still be seen in medieval paintings: Christ enthroned in the mandala with the four emblems of the Evangelists, the three animals and the angel, corresponding to Horus the Father with his four sons, or Osiris with the four sons of Horus.[1] For Horus was also a ἥλιος ἀνατολῆς (rising sun),[2] and Christ was still worshiped as such by the early Christians.

We find a remarkable parallel in the writings of Guillaume de Digulleville, prior of the Cistercian monastery at Châlis, a Norman poet who, independently of Dante, composed three "pélerinages" between 1330 and 1355: *de la vie humaine, de l'âme,* and *de Jésus Christ.*[3] The last canto of the *Pèlerinage de l'âme* contains a vision of Paradise, which consists of seven large spheres each containing seven smaller spheres.[4] All the spheres rotate, and this movement is called a *siècle (saeculum)*. The heavenly *siècles* are the prototypes of the earthly centuries. The angel who guides the poet explains: *"Quand la sainte Eglise dans ses oraisons ajoute: in saecula saeculorum, il ne s'agit point du temps de là-bas, mais de l'éternité."* At the same time the *siècles* are spherical spaces in which the blessed dwell. *Siècles* and *cieux* are identical. In the highest heaven of pure gold the King sits on a round throne

---

1 Bas relief from Philae, Sir E. A. Wallis Budge, *Osiris and the Egyptian Resurrection* (London, 1911), I, 3. In the Hunefer Papyrus the sons of Horus stand in the lotus: Budge, *The Book of the Dead* (London, 1938), Pl. 5. Sometimes there are three with animal heads and one with a human head, as in the Papyrus of Kerash. In a 7th-cent. manuscript (Gellone) the evangelists actually wear their animal heads.

2 So called by Melito of Sardis. From the *Analecta sacra*, quoted in Franz Cumont, *Textes et monuments figurés relatifs aux mystères de Mithra* (Brussels, 1894-99), I, 355.

3 Joseph Delacotte, *Guillaume de Digulleville . . . Trois romans-poèmes du XIVe siècle* (Paris, 1932).

4 An idea which corresponds to dream 21 of the large sphere containing many little spheres.

which shines more brightly than the sun. A *couronne* of precious stones surrounds him. Beside him, on a circular throne that is made of brown crystal, sits the Queen, who intercedes for the sinners. (Mary as God's wife.)

"Raising his eyes to the golden heaven, the pilgrim perceived a marvelous circle which appeared to be three feet across. It came out of the golden heaven at one point and re-entered it at another, and it made the whole tour of the golden heaven." This circle is sapphire-colored. It is a small circle, three feet in diameter, and evidently it moves round in a great circle like a rolling disk. The great circle intersects the golden circle of heaven.

While Guillaume is absorbed in this sight, three spirits suddenly appear clad in purple, with golden crowns and girdles, and enter the golden heaven. This moment, so the angel tells him, is *une fête*, like a church festival on earth:

> Ce cercle que tu vois est le calendrier
> Qui en faisant son tour entier,
> Montre des Saints les journées
> Quand elles doivent être fêtées.
> Chacun en fait le cercle un tour,
> Chacune étoile y est pour jour,
> Chacun soleil pour l'espace
> De jours trente ou zodiaque.
>
> (This circle is the calendar
> Which spinning round the course entire
> Shows the feast day of each saint
> And when it should be celebrate.
> Each saint goes once round all the way,
> Each star you see stands for a day,
> And every sun denotes a spell
> Of thirty days zodiacal.)

The three figures are saints whose feast day is even now being celebrated. The small circle that enters the golden heaven is three feet in width, and three figures likewise make their sudden entry. These signify the moment of time in eternity, as does the circle of the calendar. But why this should be exactly three feet in diameter and why there are three figures remains a mystery. We naturally think of the three rhythms in our vision which are started off by the pointer moving over the blue disk, and which enter the system just as inexplicably as the calendar-circle enters the golden heaven.

The guide continues to instruct Guillaume on the significance of the signs of the zodiac with particular reference to sacred history, and ends with the remark that the feast of the twelve fishermen will be celebrated in the sign of Pisces, when the twelve will appear before the Trinity. Then it suddenly occurs to Guillaume that he has never really understood the nature of the Trinity, and he begs the angel for an explanation. The angel answers, "Now, there are three principal colors, namely green, red, and gold. These three colors are seen united in divers works of watered silk and in the feathers of many birds, such as the peacock. The almighty King who puts three colors in one, cannot he also make one substance to be three?" Gold, the royal color, is attributed to God the Father; red to God the Son, because he shed his blood; and to the Holy Ghost green, *"la couleur qui verdoye et qui reconforte."* Thereupon the angel warns Guillaume not to ask any more questions, and disappears. The poet wakes up to find himself safely in his bed, and so ends the *Pèlerinage de l'âme.*

There is, however, one thing more to be asked: "Three there are—but where is the fourth?" Why is blue missing? This color was also missing in the "disturbed" mandala of our dreamer. Curiously enough, the *calendrier* that intersects the golden circle is blue, and so is the vertical disk in the three-dimensional mandala. We would conjecture that blue, standing for the vertical, means height and depth (the blue sky above, the blue sea below), and that any shrinkage of the vertical reduces the square to an oblong, thus producing something like an inflation of consciousness.[5] Hence the vertical would correspond to the unconscious. But the unconscious in a man has feminine characteristics, and blue is the traditional color of the Virgin's celestial cloak. Guillaume was so absorbed in the Trinity and threefold aspect of the *roy* that he quite forgot the *reyne.* Faust prays to her in these words: "Supreme Mistress of the world! Let me behold thy secret in the outstretched azure canopy of heaven."

It was inevitable that blue should be missing for Guillaume in the tetrad of colors, because of its feminine nature. But, like woman herself, the anima means the height and depth of a man. Without the blue vertical circle the golden mandala remains bodiless and two-dimensional, a mere abstraction. It is only the intervention of time and space here and now that makes reality. Wholeness is realized for a moment only—the moment that Faust was seeking all his life.

5 Cf. my remarks on "inflation" in "The Relations between the Ego and the Unconscious," *Two Essays*, pp. 140ff., 166ff.

The poet in Guillaume must have had an inkling of the heretical truth when he gave the King a Queen sitting on a throne made of earth-brown crystal. For what is heaven without Mother Earth? And how can man reach fulfillment if the Queen does not intercede for his black soul? She understands the darkness, for she has taken her throne—the earth itself—to heaven with her, if only as the subtlest of suggestions. She adds the missing blue to the gold, red, and green, and thus completes the harmonious whole.

*

The vision of the "world clock" was neither the last nor the highest point in the development of the symbols of the objective psyche. But it brings to an end the first third of the material, consisting in all of some four hundred dreams and visions. This series is noteworthy because it gives an unusually complete description of a psychic fact that I had observed long before in many individual cases.[6] We have not only the completeness of the objective material but the care and discernment of the dreamer to thank for having placed us in a position to follow, step by step, the synthetic work of the unconscious. The troubled course of this synthesis would doubtless have been depicted in even greater completeness had I taken account of the 340 dreams interspersed among the 59 examined here. Unfortunately this was impossible, because the dreams touch to some extent on the intimacies of personal life and must therefore remain unpublished. So I had to confine myself to the impersonal material.

I hope I may have succeeded in throwing some light upon the development of the symbols of the self and in overcoming, partially at least, the serious difficulties inherent in all material drawn from actual experience. At the same time I am fully aware that the comparative material so necessary for a complete elucidation could have been greatly increased. But, so as not to burden the meaning unduly, I have exercised the greatest reserve in this respect. Consequently there is much that is only hinted at, though this should not be taken as a sign of superficiality. I believe myself to be fully in a position to offer ample evidence for my views, but I do not wish to give the impression that I imagine I have said anything final on this highly complicated subject. It is true that this is not the first time I have dealt with a series of spontaneous manifestations of the unconscious. I did

6 Cf. my commentary to *The Secret of the Golden Flower*, and "The Relations between the Ego and the Unconscious."

so once before, in my book *Symbols of Transformation*, but there it was more a problem of neurosis in puberty, whereas this is the broader problem of individuation. Moreover, there is a very considerable difference between the two personalities in question. The earlier case, which I never saw at first hand, ended in psychic catastrophe—a psychosis; but the present case shows a normal development such as I have often observed in highly intelligent persons.

What is particularly noteworthy here is the consistent development of the central symbol. We can hardly escape the feeling that the unconscious process moves spiral-wise round a center, gradually getting closer, while the characteristics of the center grow more and more distinct. Or perhaps we could put it the other way round and say that the center—itself virtually unknowable—acts like a magnet on the disparate materials and processes of the unconscious and gradually captures them as in a crystalline lattice. For this reason the center is—in other cases—often pictured as a spider in its web, especially when the conscious attitude is still dominated by fear of unconscious processes. But if the process is allowed to take its course, as it was in our case, then the central symbol, constantly renewing itself, will steadily and consistently force its way through the apparent chaos of the personal psyche and its dramatic entanglements, just as the great Bernoulli's epitaph [7] says of the spiral: *"Eadem mutata resurgo."* Accordingly we often find spiral representations of the center, as for instance the serpent coiled round the creative point, the egg.

Indeed, it seems as if all the personal entanglements and dramatic changes of fortune that make up the quintessence of life were nothing but hesitations, timid shrinkings, almost like petty complications and meticulous excuses for not facing the final reality of this strange and uncanny process of crystallization. Often one has the impression that the personal psyche is running round this central point like a shy animal, at once fascinated and frightened, always in flight, and yet steadily drawing nearer.

I trust I have given no cause for the misunderstanding that I know anything about the nature of the "center"—for it is simply unknowable and can only be expressed symbolically through its own phenomenology, as is the case, incidentally, with every object of experience. Among the various characteristics of the center the one that struck me from the beginning was

7 In the cloisters of Basel Cathedral.

the phenomenon of the quaternity. That it is not "simply" a question of, shall we say, the "four" points of the compass or something of that kind is proved by the fact that there is often a competition between four and three.[8] There is also, but more rarely, a competition between four and five, though five-rayed mandalas must be characterized as abnormal on account of their lack of symmetry.[9] It would seem, therefore, that there is normally a clear insistence on four, or as if there were a greater statistical probability of four. Now it is—as I can hardly refrain from remarking—a curious "sport of nature" that the chief chemical constituent of organic bodies is carbon, which is characterized by four valencies; also it is well known that the diamond is a carbon crystal. Carbon is black—coal, graphite—but the diamond is "purest water." To draw such an analogy would be a lamentable piece of intellectual bad taste were the phenomenon of four merely a poetic conceit on the part of the conscious mind and not a spontaneous production of the objective psyche. Even if we supposed that dreams could be influenced to any appreciable degree by autosuggestion—in which case it would naturally be more a matter of their meaning than of their form—it would still have to be proved that the conscious mind of the dreamer had made a serious effort to impress the idea of the quaternity on the unconscious. But in this as in many other cases I have observed, such a possibility is absolutely out of the question, quite apart from the numerous historical and ethnological parallels.[10] Surveying these facts as a whole we come, at least in my opinion, to the inescapable conclusion that there is some psychic element present which expresses itself through the quaternity. No daring speculation or extravagant fancy is needed for this. If I have called the center the "self" I did so after mature consideration and a careful appraisal of the empirical and historical data. A materialistic interpretation could easily maintain that the "center" is "nothing but" the point at which the psyche ceases to be knowable because it there coalesces with the body. And a spiritualistic interpretation might retort that this "self" is nothing but "spirit," which animates both soul and body and irrupts into time and space at that creative point. I purposely refrain from all such physical and meta-

8 This was observed chiefly in men, but whether this is an accident or not I am unable to say.
9 Observed mainly in women. But it occurs so rarely that it is impossible to draw any further conclusions.
10 I have mentioned only a few of these parallels here, but shall return to them in a later study.

physical speculations and content myself with establishing the empirical facts, and this seems to me to be infinitely more important for the advance of human knowledge than running after fashionable intellectual crazes or trumped-up "religious" creeds.

To the best of my experience we are here dealing with important "nuclear processes" in the objective psyche—"images of the goal," as it were, which the psychic process, being "purposive," apparently sets up of its own accord, without any external stimulus.[11] Externally, of course, there is always a certain psychic need, a sort of hunger, but it seeks for familiar and favorite dishes and never imagines as its goal some outlandish food unknown to consciousness. The goal which beckons to this psychic need, the image which promises to heal, to make whole, is at first strange beyond all measure to the conscious mind, so that it can find entry only with the very greatest difficulty. Of course it is quite different for people who live in a time and environment when such images of the goal have dogmatic validity. These images are then *ipso facto* held up to consciousness, and the unconscious is thus shown its secret reflected image in which it recognizes itself and so joins forces with the conscious mind. A prerequisite for this is that consciousness should be gripped by the images.

As to the question of the origin of the mandala motif, from a superficial point of view it looks as if it had gradually come into being in the course of the dream-series. The fact is, however, that it only *appeared* more and more distinctly and in increasingly differentiated form; in reality it was always present and even occurred in the first dream—as the nymphs say later: "We were always there, only you did not notice us." It is therefore more probable that we are dealing with an *a priori* "type," an archetype which is inherent in the collective unconscious and thus beyond individual birth and death. The archetype is, so to speak, an "eternal" presence, and the only question is whether it is perceived by consciousness or not. I think we are forming a more probable hypothesis, and one that better explains the observed facts, if we assume that the increase in the clarity and frequency of the mandala motif is due to a more accurate perception of an already

11 The image that presents itself in this material as a goal may also serve as the origin when viewed from the historical standpoint. By way of example I would cite the conception of paradise in the Old Testament, and especially the creation of Adam in the Slavonic Book of Enoch. Cf. Max Förster: "Adams Erschaffung und Namengebung: ein lateinisches Fragment des s.g. slawischen Henoch," *Archiv für Religionswissenschaft* (Leipzig), XI (1908), 478ff.

existing "type," rather than that it is generated in the course of the dream-series.[12] The latter assumption is contradicted by the fact, for instance, that such fundamental ideas as the hat which epitomizes the personality, the encircling serpent, and the *perpetuum mobile* appear right at the beginning (first series: dream 1 and vision 5; second series: dream 9).

If the motif of the mandala is an archetype it ought to be a collective phenomenon, i.e., theoretically it should appear in everyone. In practice, however, it is only to be met with in distinct form in relatively few cases, though this does not prevent it from functioning as a concealed pole round which everything ultimately revolves. In the last analysis every life is the realization of a whole, that is, of a self, for which reason this realization can also be called "individuation." All life is bound to individual carriers who realize it, and it is simply inconceivable without them. But every carrier is charged with an individual destiny and destination, and the realization of these alone makes sense of life. True, the "sense" is often something that could just as well be called "nonsense," for there is some incommensurability between the mystery of existence and human understanding. "Sense" and "nonsense" are merely man-made labels which serve to give us a reasonably valid sense of direction.

As the historical parallels show, the symbolism of the mandala is not just a unique curiosity; we can well say that it is a regular occurrence. Were it not so there would be no comparative material, and it is precisely the possibility of comparing the mental products of all times from every quarter of the globe that shows us most clearly what immense importance the *consensus gentium* has always attached to the processes of the objective psyche. This is reason enough not to make light of them, and my medical experience has only confirmed this estimate. There are people, of course, who think it unscientific to take anything seriously; they do not want their intellectual playground disturbed by graver considerations. But the doctor who fails to take account of man's feeling for values commits a serious blunder, and

12 If we divide the four hundred dreams into eight groups of fifty each, we come to the following results:

I	6 mandalas	V	11 mandalas
II	4 "	VI	11 "
III	2 "	VII	11 "
IV	9 "	VIII	17 "

So a considerable increase of the mandala motif takes place in the course of the whole series.

if he tries to correct the mysterious and well-nigh inscrutable workings of nature with his so-called scientific attitude, he is merely putting his shallow sophistry in place of nature's healing processes. Let us take the wisdom of the old alchemists to heart: *"Naturalissimum et perfectissimum opus est generare tale quale ipsum est."* [13]

13 "The most natural and perfect work is to generate what is like to itself."

M. C. Cammerloher

The Position of Art in the Psychology of Our Time

Ever since Greek philosophers, who were not artists, began to subject art to scientific investigation, there has been no end to this presumptuous mischief.

It all began with Socrates. His remarks about art are deplorable and reveal the total inadequacy of rational thought in a field essentially alien to it. Greek philosophy, which before him had been intimation and intuition of the world in its entirety, now surrendered to logic, in the belief that everything could be apprehended and explained with the help of this new instrument. Plato stated it bluntly: thought was the only form in which the truth could be known. And Socrates disparaged the artist because his work did not originate in reflection and understanding, but "only" in natural aptitude and inspiration.

Aristotle, it is true, recognized the fundamental difference between conceptual knowledge and artistic endeavor. This insight might have led to an understanding of the nature of art as the fulfillment and objectivization of the visual process beginning with optical sensation. What is more, here lay the germ of an insight into the essential diversity of the psychological functions. But the time was not yet ripe. In his *Nicomachean Ethics*, Aristotle went back to Plato's view that the only form of knowledge was the logical procedure of discursive thought; according to this view, nature is a copy of ideas and art is a copy of nature, hence a copy of a copy. Art thus encompasses less truth than thought and less reality than nature.

This view prevailed for two thousand years. Philosophers and aestheticians spoke and wrote irrelevancies, while the artists said nothing, but created painting and sculpture. When one of the rare articulate artists did speak, the "thinkers" ignored him; like children playing a game, they said, "That doesn't count."

All philosophers since Plato have been absolutely convinced that art is a copy or imitation of nature. This fallacy has been taken as an axiom, never to be re-examined or even doubted. It runs through the whole literature of art criticism even to our own day, although recent philosophy might have offered an excellent basis for reconsidering the old question and formulating a theory consonant with the facts. The only philosopher who has had anything sound to say on this subject, Konrad Fiedler, friend and patron of Hans von Marées, is totally ignored by the academic world, by philosophers as well as art historians.

And the nineteenth-century attempts to explain art on the basis of evolution were no better. Until quite recently archaeologists were still saying that the art of primitive peoples arose from their need to have images of their gods—historical hysteron proteron if ever there was one, just about as useful as saying that James Watt invented the steam engine because Englishmen were sick of the slow stagecoach and had finally made up their minds to have regular locomotives and railroads.

From the standpoint of Sukshma,[1] there would be a certain element of truth in such an assertion, provided we had in mind a "coming to pass" in the sense of the Biblical phrase "And when the time was accomplished . . ."; provided we take "time" in this sense as a substance and not as an empty abstraction of a succession of events. It has never seemed to me, however, that Sukshma was the prevailing attitude in European science.

If we are to attain deeper insight into the essence and meaning of art, we must drop all preconceived opinions, including the notion of imitation and copy.

It lies in the very nature of the German word *nachahmen* (imitate or mimic) that it can refer only to something living, involved in motion or change. One can mimic the faces, posture, and gestures of a man, the movements of an animal or of the wind (as children often do), the puffing of a locomotive. But one cannot mimic dead, motionless things, a block of stone or a suitcase.

Thus the word implies something that has nothing whatever to do with the perceptive function but pertains to intuition, one might almost say presentiment. Of course there is an imitative impulse, else we should not have the word. Children observe the facial expressions, gestures, attitudes of grownups, often imitate them purposely, and in this simple way, through

1 [*Sūkshma* (Sanskrit), "subtle"; *sūkshma-sharīra*, "subtle body": the inner world of thoughts, emotions, dreams, visions, fantasies, ideas, etc., underlying and motivating the visible "gross body" (*sthūla-sharīra*). Art, then, might be interpreted as a coming-to-manifestation of the *sūkshma-sharīra*, "subtle aspect," of existence or of things. —Ed.]

psychophysical correlation, learn the meaning of the gestures and at the same time the inner connections between their own body and mind. For every physical occurrence is also psychic, and conversely.

There are imitative arts, those generally known as "representative": the dance and, what is in essence the same thing, the drama. They do not, like the plastic arts, embody the perception of things, but represent a psychophysical relationship; they "are" not something, but "mean" something; thus they belong to the sphere of intuition.

There is, however, a sensuous element in the representative arts, since the representation appeals to the eye, and often to the ear as well. But whereas in the plastic arts the visual perception is the central experience, the beginning and end of the work, in the representative arts the eye serves only as receiver and transmitter, just as it does for the scientist and thinker. And in the representative art it is easy to tell when the visual, sensory element begins to predominate over the "meaning." Then the art is debased; the opera or drama becomes a costume piece or a review.

It might be argued that I have no need to insist on the word "imitate" but might use another word, such as "portray" or "reproduce." But I did not invent the concept; it lies at the base of scientific theories of art (a contradiction in terms), and of popular notions as well.

All of these verbal designations arise from the false assumption that nature exists as something to be copied or imitated, that it is already present and given as a model, so that the artist has no other function than to "render" it in some material or other, as Plato supposed—to what end has never been explained.

But there is no nature in this sense. For nature—from the standpoint of art, i.e., of the perceptive function—can only mean the sum of our visual sensations and images. It is only with regard to these sensations and images that we can make any statement. Concerning their causes or stimuli, which in their totality we call our world, we know nothing.

We may go further. A philosophical inquiry from the standpoint of sensation—and such an inquiry would be fully as justified and meaningful as one from the standpoint of conceptual thought—must come to the conclusion that to speak of stimuli, cause, and effect is inadmissible and must lead to insoluble contradictions. We must rather say that perceptions and thoughts are not effects of a Being situated outside us and forever unattainable, a Being accessible to us only in the form of perception or conceptual

426

thought, but are themselves forms of this Being, forms in which it experiences—i.e., perceives or thinks—itself.

And now the real question arises: If there is no nature in the sense of an object to be imitated, if nature is only the sum of our perceptions and ideas, what then is art?

I should formulate the answer as follows: From the point of view of man, its creator, art is the conscious experience of his own store of perceptions and images through formative effort; in it perception and image achieve their fulfillment, their visible and demonstrable form; seen from the vantage point of the thing, the work itself, or of the effective force (which is in this case identical), art is the autonomous self-representation of perception.

Thus nature ceases to exist as a mere object. It becomes subject and object in one. It is nature that in the consciously perceiving and creating man, the artist, who is himself nature, becomes aware of itself, experiences itself, in so far as it is perceptive. Thus the dichotomy of subject and object, of seeing and seen, is resolved: the two have become one.

As long as this formative activity of art is lacking in a people or in a man, perceptions, though present, are utterly unconscious. In reference to sense perception—in the present case, the sense of vision—the people or individual then find themselves in a state of *participation mystique* with their environment. But when at a high level of art the perceptions are *formed*, the original *participation mystique* (which also constituted an identification with the environment, though an unconscious one)— is annulled.

Just as fallacious as the popular idea that art consists in imitating or copying is the notion that a special type of talent is required for artistic creation. Of course there are different degrees of talent. But just as we expect every civilized man to have the power of communicating his thoughts in clear, intelligible form, and to understand what has been clearly and intelligibly stated, we must also expect to find in every man the ability to give a clear and graphic representation of his visual perceptions. The varying simplicity or development of the form then provides an absolutely unmistakable picture of the level his perceptions have attained. And everyone is able to furnish such a picture. We often hear people say that they cannot draw. This usually masks the unconscious meaning: My perceptions are in such a barbarous state that I am ashamed to disclose them and prefer to plead incompetence.

Conversely, the perceptions of a man who does not cultivate them by constantly enhancing his consciousness in formative activity remain at a barbarous, undeveloped, rudimentary stage, as do the ideas of a man who does not repeatedly clarify them through language. Language in its highest form, that of scientific and philosophical exposition, is the forming of ideas; art is the language, the communication of perceptions.

Actually, people "without talent" often produce perfectly passable drawings and paintings when impelled by an inner need to give form to the world of their perceptions. And the best proof of this is that their ability vanishes with the disappearance of the inner pressure. Such persons then return to the function through which they are accustomed to orient themselves in life.

The questions we have dealt with up to now belong intrinsically to the field of epistemology and are thus accessible to rational inquiry. But the theory of art in the more restricted sense presupposes artistic experience on the part of the inquirer. Here everything depends on the function of visual sensation, on perception and the actualization of perceptions. None of this is susceptible to logical analysis or rational explanation. The entire process is irrational and inaccessible to the understanding, for the act and product of sensation cannot be elucidated or demonstrated; hence the process is axiomatic—familiar and intelligible only to those who know the workings of the function. For this, one need not be an artist, but one does require a certain insight based on experience, approximating in scope the insight which, for example, enables an educated man to understand and reflect on a philosophical or scientific work. In other words, one requires a relative familiarity with drawing and painting.

The first question raised by the theory of art is, How does art come into being? What is the origin of artistic activity, what are its stages? Can we assimilate it to certain norms—comparable, let us say, to the Aristotelian categories of thought? Concerning these questions there is an immense body of little-known literature, to wit the writings of artists themselves, from Leonardo and Dürer through Hogarth and Delacroix, Marées, Hildebrand and Böcklin, and down to the moderns. Recently Britsch, who unhappily died while still a young man, ably reconsidered the theory of art in accordance with modern views of cultural development.

At the dawn of the Christian era, when the ancient civilizations had grown old and tired and man was gathering his forces for a cultural rebirth, he cast about for an image, an *eidolon* of his highest potentialities, a symbol to lead and guide him. He sought it, as always, in his antithesis, in what he had hitherto not been. Consider the Dionysian rites and the cult of Adonis; the temple prostitution, which had long ceased to be sacred; and worse, the temple beasts, of which a Greek historian wrote that it was not fitting to speak of them aloud; consider the never-ending scandals of both gods and men in the ancient world, as described by Juvenal in his *Satires;* consider all this, and you will understand why the antithesis to this mankind was the primal man dwelling in the metaphysical beyond, Adam Kadmon, the Christ who, as St. John said, was before the world was.

Since then, nearly two millennia have passed, and we have experienced Western intellectualism with its incomparable world of abstract science, acknowledging the perceptive functions of sensation and intuition only as handmaidens; we have lived amid the eminently spiritual religion of Christianity, in which all flesh was looked upon as sinful.

Thus today our opposite lies again in the antispirit, in the realm of primitive beginnings, of the savage, the animal, and the child. This accounts for Darwinism and the S.P.C.A.; today we are living in the century of the child, and our primal man is no longer called Adam Kadmon, but Homo Neanderthalensis or Heidelbergensis.

Accordingly we do not ask, Why did God give art to man? but, How did man first come to engage in art, to *form?* And how is this phylogenetic fact disclosed ontogenetically in the child of today? These questions must be answered if we wish to obtain an insight in keeping with our present-day attitudes.

If we now ask at what stage we first encounter a manifestation which might pass as a point of departure for further formative activity, which can therefore be regarded as the first step a man takes on his road to acquiring his perceptions as a conscious possession, there is a clear and unmistakable answer. Here it is:

Fig. 1

What does it mean?

In the life of the child there comes a day when he watches someone writing and suddenly declares categorically, "Me write too." And then the child does something of this sort. This is what I would call the flailing stage of formative activity. A play movement. The child's occupations during the first year of his life are eating, sleeping, and flailing. This last serves not only the purpose of strengthening the muscles, which are not yet strong enough to support the infant body, but also the far more immediate purpose of experiencing and becoming acquainted with this whole complex apparatus of limbs, bones, muscles, and nerves. The infant does not yet possess his body, for he cannot yet use it. He must acquire it by experiencing it. This flailing on the child's part is not intentional; the infant has no intentions. He does not yet grasp, because the bodily function of grasping has not yet been experienced, and far less has the idea of an aim been developed. It is the infant's free-flowing energy that creates out of itself this movement which alone of all types of movement is "timely." We are quite familiar with this free flowing of energy in other contexts. When we lie in the grass, doing nothing, wanting nothing, and, as they say, thinking nothing, we experience this free flowing of thoughts. It is perfectly effortless. Only when we wish to hold a thought fast and pursue it does the work and exertion begin.

Caruso's friends report that he sang several hours each day, but he did not sing arias, he sang tones that came of themselves. He gave free play to his voice. This, he maintained, was the best sort of practice for the singer. And Caruso was one to know. Here again we have to do with free-flowing energy, which in the last analysis is the secret of every great achievement. The creative man is often as playful as a child. The philistine calls this laziness, and he is right. Work is an entirely different matter. But the creative man knows this too; he knows it more profoundly. When work takes hold of him, he does not stop at an eight-hour day.

These periods of idleness are the really fruitful ones. Undeterred by any will, purpose, or aim, those ideas, perceptions, intuitions, images can emerge that wish to, that are ripe. The unconscious can move freely. This was known to man in the remotest past, and he made full use of it. For this is the attitude of the man who questions the oracle. First he calms himself, relaxes. Then for a time he engages in seemingly meaningless, irrelevant, playful activity—which, however, serves to banish attention. The arranging of little sticks in the *I Ching*, the tossing of ifa pits among the Yorubas, the laying down of cards, and all such activities that strike the intellectual European as absurd superstition serve the purpose of allowing the unconscious to act and raise to the light of consciousness things which are otherwise held submerged by the everyday will, but which are recognized to be more significant than anything the diurnal man can achieve with his knowledge and will.

This talent for giving oneself entirely to the free flow of one's thoughts or ideas, feelings or intuitions, this ability to play, to be lazy in the bourgeois sense, or, as Jung says, to let things happen inwardly—this action in non-action, this *wu wei*, is the secret of the creative mind.

For to play means to devote oneself so completely to the psychic process that one becomes its body: the psychic finds its fulfillment in the physical, and becomes form. To play means to let oneself be driven by vital energy, without any purpose; for purpose is an act of the will and immediately blocks the free flow of energy, which itself knows best what it wants. Only when it has found its goal are we commanded to work, and then it is up to the will to carry out the order, to obey the word of God, for it is the word of God.

All this may seem very simple and convenient, but it implies something extremely difficult to possess: courage.

It is not easy to speak quite clearly and without ambiguity in this matter. I might also have said above: Play means that the psychological process finds its expression in the physical. There would be little argument to the contrary, and yet further insight would be hopelessly frustrated by a misunderstanding. For like "imitation," "copy," etc., "expression" is one of those terms which, though not totally false in this connection, miss the mark, because they designate more the result, the manifestation and effect, than the function, the causative force that is needed to produce the result.

The moment we speak of expression we presuppose a dualism, as though we had on the one hand a psychic process as such, and on the other hand an expression for it, which might be present or not present. In the latter case we should simply have an unexpressed psychic process.

But this cannot be, for there is no psychic process that is not simultaneously a physical process, and conversely. If there were, the question would inevitably arise wherein the parallelism or relation between the two consisted, i.e., we should need some sort of *tertium comparationis* that would make their mutual dependency a mere comparison. Moreover, we should be confronted by the second question: Under what conditions does physical expression for a psychic occurrence take place? And this would lead to the odd and absurd inference that one and the same physical process could be connected with two different psychic processes.

As a rule the layman, for lack of experience of his own, finds these processes hard to understand. But I shall be easily understood if I shift to a generally known field of experience. What is laughter? Is it a mere expression of inner psychic merriment, or is it not merriment itself in its most perfect form?

Of course we are cultivated people; we have learned to control our facial expression and conceal laughter when it is out of place. But everyone knows from repeated experience how the merriment, the inner tension, which we feel quite without distinguishing between the psychic and the physical, seeks another way out, and finding none avenges itself for the frustration by shifting into its opposite, into physical pain.

It is not joy that finds its expression in a physical process; it is rather the physical process that is necessary in order for the joy to be joy, in order for the laughter to be laughter. It is the form in which the sensation manifests itself—i.e., assumes outward form, seizes hold of the whole man—and only by so doing comes into itself.

And thus art is also the form in which the sensation of the eye comes to itself, by becoming visible in the material form of the picture and thus aware of itself. It is the form in which sensation knows life, in so far as it is visual. Art is knowledge. The word itself says so.[2]

This stage of playful submission to free-flowing energy, along the line of least resistance and in a form determined by the energy itself—that is to say, through the most sensitive organ and its prenatally differentiated function—is the beginning of all things. All beginnings are easy; only completion is difficult. And the scribble in Figure 1, above, represents this beginning. Without such a beginning, Rembrandt and Michelangelo would have been impossible; and each of us not only begins in this way but in every single work repeats this same step, though in very much abbreviated form. Primitive man also passed through this stage; through various fortunate accidents such scribblings have come down to us from prehistoric times.

In this scribbling the child first of all experiences the possibility, new to

2 [A reference to the German word *Kunst*.—Tr.]

432

him, of forming the visual with his hand. Of course he is not conscious of this; he does not express himself in such terms. He is conscious of nothing at all, except for the force and pleasure of seeing and forming; he expresses nothing and does not reflect; he experiences himself, experiences himself with pleasure, and that suffices. Reflections and modes of expression become necessary only when something becomes unclear. But nothing is clearer and less ambiguous than experience and forming.

And then, just as matter coagulates into suns amid the primal mists of space, a form, a figure, a something one day emerges from this scribbling. It looks like this:

Fig. 2

And it is called Papa or Mama, Baby or Bow-wow. What has happened? In a study of the names for numbers in the languages of the South Sea Islands, Frobenius has made it appear likely that the earliest numbers refer to unclear concepts such as "many" and "few," and originally designated something quite vague; sharpness is introduced only with the number proper. But before this number could come into being, the clearly delimited individual thing had to be consciously recognized as such. The spots in Figure 2 have no sharp boundaries, but they are nevertheless distinguished from the undelimited scribble of Figure 1. They symbolize the first appearance of the self-circumscribed image that strives to differentiate and isolate itself from the rise and fall of the free-flowing images.

This, in the conscious mind, constitutes the same process as, in the unconscious, the newborn infant's first learning to see. Even we grownups occasionally experience this state, though it usually passes unnoticed. Between sleeping and waking there is sometimes a brief interval of one or two seconds, during which we blink our eyes and the usually familiar surroundings of our bed seem utterly strange. We see no object at all, but only a space full of colored spots without contour or form. This impression is so strange, in a way so terrifying, that its very strangeness immediately awakens us to full consciousness. And now to our amazement we suddenly recognize that this or that group of colored spots is the table, the chair, a glass, or the roof of the house across the street. For the space of an instant we had gone back to the vision of the first days of our infancy. This is how the infant sees at first, and it explains why he does not look at anything; he does not fixate the objects of his environment, because the image complex "object" is not yet formed.

Ultimately, all painting strives toward this primal visual experience. Hence it attains its high point and its finest perfection through the complete dissolution of form in European impressionism and in the Chinese-Japanese gouache paintings of a Meng Yu-chien or a Sesshu. It is not immediately apparent why the fourth and last epoch of every civilization, the epoch of science and rationalism, is also that of the highest development in painting. What the two have in common is the power to dissolve all the forms and figures—which the three preceding epochs have molded through the centuries—into the primal experience of undifferentiated but creation-pregnant chaos, thus opening the road to the development of new forms.

The same process takes place in the meditation of the Chakras. In the transition from one Chakra to another, every form and every content of the preceding Chakras must be fully dissolved and poured into the molds of experience provided by the new one. If an undissolved remnant is left behind, it causes an obstruction. We have the same process as in the pupation of the caterpillar; the body is not gradually transformed, but is first dissolved into a kind of homogeneous mucus, from which the butterfly is born.

This process, which is an entirely unconscious learning-to-see, is repeated in exactly the same way when the child, following the impulse of his vital energy, embarks on a conscious learning-to-see. The scribble means undifferentiated representation and experience of the organism and its function. The vaguely delimited spot means the first differentiation, a first coagulation and delimitation. Thus it is a universally valid symbol for this stage, as is also the first number, the number one. It says: "I see the difference between thing and unthing, and I can also show it, make it visible to myself and others."

The next step is the sharp boundary. The child paints a series of dumpling-like shapes.

Fig. 3

But with delimitation, the part inside the boundary takes on a new meaning in relation to the undelimited environment, the world outside. For the present, it can still refer to any object whatever; what is achieved with this step in the realization of a visual conception is the fact of sharp delimitation as such. This delimited form is the magic circle, and the force that has effected it is magic. For with the drawing of this boundary a new force is acquired and grasped, the force of creative action, which from the point of view of the doer is realization and from the point of view of the beholder is effect. Here lies the secret of the skin from which all living form arises, and this is the first step on the road to individuation, which is a rising to conscious life from the boundless flow of a collective, undifferentiated sea.

The stage in which thing is differentiated from unthing, thing from environment, the delimited from the undelimited, is followed by the inner development of things, the differentiation and delimitation of their parts. Thus, for example:

Fig. 4

Here details are differentiated within the boundary, things within the thing; and concomitantly, a new visual category is attained: direction. A beginning has been made in the ascertainment and differentiation of directions, but the parts are not yet precisely articulated.

The differentiation of directions now progresses and becomes more distinct:

Fig. 5

These drawings show how the new knowledge of difference in direction is realized clearly and sharply. The most radical differentiation of direction, that between the vertical and the horizontal, is expressed by the right angle. And this distinct realization of direction strikingly demonstrates that what is represented is not ready-made "nature," which would be utterly inaccessible to the child mind.

435

The child can now distinguish thing from environment, the delimited from the undelimited, but he cannot yet differentiate between things. This ability first develops only with the knowledge of direction and of the relations between directions. When contour can be discerned within contour, the "face" complex is distinguished from the "man" complex. And this is merely another way of saying that the object of representation develops parallel to the child's faculty of differentiation, that it is a product of artistic activity and is not already present as a presupposed something that can serve as a "model" for a "copy."

Since this is a very fundamental matter, I should like to include one more example, Britsch's classical series of heads:

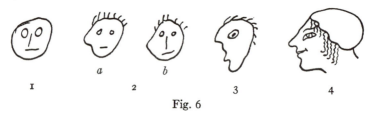

Fig. 6

In no. 1 we have a delimited spot, internally developed through partial perceptions. The boundary line itself shows no perception of direction, and approximates a perfect circle.

In no. 2(a) the artist has become aware that the boundary is not symmetrical. In some cases the directional stroke "nose" is still retained (b); this means not that the face has two noses but that an older perception is for a time retained side by side with a newer and more developed one—a phenomenon familiar to us in every sphere of life.

There is still no full perception of the connection between the parts. The protuberance on the left cannot be definitely identified as a nose; it tells us only that very general differences of direction are now recognized in the contour, the details being still uncertain. We have to do with a process of refinement progressing logically, step by step.

Thus in no. 3, although the boundary shows changes throughout its length, there is still no precise statement of detail. This last is achieved only in no. 4, a type we encounter in almost the same form and degree of refinement in Etruria, Crete, early Greece, and Egypt. At this stage the mutual relations of situation, direction, and dimension are established with great sharpness.

436

But we cannot say that no. 4 is more correct than nos. 1–3. Each statement corresponds to the degree of knowledge attained. The ability to state perceptions clearly and consciously has reached this precise level, and will in a few weeks or months attain to a higher stage.[3]

It is not my purpose here, nor is it possible, to develop a complete theory of plastic art or even to suggest the immensity of the problems involved. I should only like to hint at the fundamental difference between ancient cultures and those of the Christian era.

All the ancient cultures with the exception of the Hellenistic stopped at the stage of recognizing and depicting variability of direction. The next step, that of understanding the variable boundary, makes possible the following product:

Fig. 7

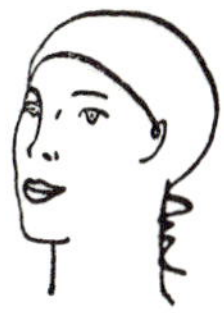

This is what we inexactly call a half or three-quarter profile, and the principle is known as foreshortening, a development fully realized only in European art, but mastered in varying degrees in the Indian and East Asian art of the two millennia of the Christian era.

For peoples who have advanced this far in perceptive knowledge of the world, things begin to lose their rigidity, their singleness of meaning and immutability. Space is no longer the void between solid objects, but acquires a meaning of its own, while things lose their former substantiality; in drawing they are transformed into lines and spots (Rembrandt); in painting, into air, tonality and light; in physics, into energy and waves. Static vision becomes dynamic; numbers, even, lose their singleness of meaning and become functions. Relativity, which despite the *panta rhei* of Heraclitus was a concept almost unintelligible to the ancient world, finally becomes the prevailing view. This is the road of development that China, India, and Europe have traveled up to now. Thus the three-quarter profile is the symbol of relativity in the realm of vision. Art is philosophy in images and symbols.

We have seen how from the simple boundary, from the distinction be-

3 The foregoing is partly quoted from Britsch. [I.e., Gustav Britsch, *Theorie der bildenden Kunst*, ed. Egon Kornmann (Munich, 1926, 1930).—ED.]

tween "thing and unthing" or "thing and environment," the object of representation comes into being step by step through the progressive differentiation of perception; we have seen not that a pre-existing object is represented, copied, imitated, but that the representation itself creates the object, just as thought does not copy or imitate nature but creates its object, the concept.

What is represented, i.e., what is made visual in a given medium, is not outward object but an inner perceptive relationship, an inner de-veloping in the fullest sense of the word, the unraveling of an image from its involvement in the involuntary perceptive process. It is an inner clarification of the image and its structure; a clarification that is not intellectual but visual. And it is made fully conscious by a process of development, of "forming" and actualization. Hence the visible forming in the medium is not something beside or apart from the image; it is the last stage in its development and fulfillment, just as thought attains its fulfillment only in the utterable and communicable proposition.

For the artist himself, moreover, it is the only possible demonstration of the stage of development attained by his images, and without this visible form no one can know how precise, how rich, or how well-ordered his images are; just as no one can be certain of his own thoughts until he has formed them in utterable and communicable words and propositions. And finally, it is the only way in which the artist can act upon the outside world, the only way in which he can give back to the collectivity the fruit of its collective soil.

Thus all such terms as "imitation," "copy," etc., prove meaningless.

In becoming conscious of his own images and their structure, in progressively transcending his visual *participation mystique*, and in transforming himself from an object of unconscious stimulation, as defined in Uexküll's theory of the "surrounding world," into a subject of conscious experience, and in placing the product of his knowledge before the world in visible works, the artist also helps others to stronger consciousness of their ideas and overcomes, though in far lesser degree than in himself, their *participation mystique*.

The artistic act is a way of redemption in the sense that every step we take away from our involvement in the world of stimuli, away from the state of being lived from outside, hence away from our *participation mystique*, brings us closer to redemption.

438

Hitherto redemption, consecration, illumination, or whatever we may call this strange process of becoming-whole, was possible only for the religious man, and the only possible guidance lay in intuition. Thereby, all those whose favored function was not intuition were excluded from redemption. But the time of mysteries in the narrower sense is past. European and Asiatic mankind, taken as a whole, has reached a stage at which every function can become the key to a mystery. The best and simplest road to consecration is one's own trade.

And here I should like to point to the difference between artistic and analytical psychology, between the psychology of creative construction and that of rational dissection, or, as we might roughly and inadequately put it, the difference between synthesis and analysis. Synthesis means a putting together, a harmonization of particulars on the basis of a pre-existing general idea—that is, the creation of a whole. Analysis means dissolution and dissection. Its purpose, to be sure, is understanding, but inevitably it has also a killing effect, whether it is applied to the anatomical study of plant, animal, or man; or to the grandiose process of undermining a culture by subjecting it to rational questioning, as happens in the fourth and last stage of every culture; or, finally, to the analytical study and understanding of a psychological whole.

As long as the stream of life flows undisturbed, i.e., as long as man can follow the twistings and turnings of his free-flowing energy, analytical inquiries are unnecessary, and simply do not occur. Only when a block arises, a damming of energy, through some obstruction that cannot be cleared away by the usual means—only when uncertainty appears, and suddenly something "becomes a problem"—does the question "Why?" emerge and rational thought enter in.

If a man's own forces and faculties suffice for the answering of the question, the solution of the problem, then the obstruction is overcome and the psychological block eliminated; his life and work return to their tranquil flow.

But perhaps—and it happens more and more frequently in our time—a man will be unable to remove a block of this sort by his own efforts, even over a period of years or decades, and it will take on dangerous forms, threatening his health and his very existence. Then the help of a brother man becomes necessary, the help of the healer, priest, father confessor, who today, since the historical failure of religion, has been replaced by the analyst.

439

And now everything turns upon this question: is the core of the neurosis an error or a truth? That is, does it originate in the realm of inhibitions, in the individual unconscious, or in the collective unconscious?

A lingering in the emotional atmosphere of childhood, misunderstood as sexuality, as well as inferiority masked as an urge for power are the proper spheres of analytical treatment. The neurotic looks backward, clinging to a life form that has ceased to be timely, resisting the new and timely form.

The problems raised by life's typical tasks—the choice of a profession, the founding of a family, the rearing of children, i.e., by the tasks of self-preservation and preservation of the species—have been solved by hundreds of generations before us; they lie within us as a heritage, and our fellow men are continually performing them before our eyes.

Failure in the performance of these tasks, because of inability to effect the transition from childhood to adulthood, may be called an individual error; accordingly, the individual can correct it, if a psychoanalyst is able to disclose the false roads his patient has traveled, if he can trace the neurosis back to the mistake from which it resulted.

The core of the neurosis may, however, be a new truth that is not yet understood. Just as the tasks of the first half of life can be construed as a preparation for life, so can those of the second half be called a preparation for death. The tasks that now arise must be regarded as a new truth because, in a way quite unlike those of the first half of life, they are always new for every individual. For while the tasks of youth are always more or less a part of a man's heritage, while they confront him again and again in his immediate and broader environment, while accordingly he cannot mistake or misunderstand them but only arrive at false solutions arising from his special, individual form of life, the tasks of his maturity do not constitute a part of his heritage, and they are not in any intelligible way solved by his environment.

Though innumerable men may already have solved these problems, it lies in the very nature of man and of the problem itself that such solutions occur at an age in which children are seldom or never begotten; and moreover, because of the specific nature and difficulty of the tasks, they have been associated, in historical cultures, primarily with the life of the ascetic, the hermit, the monk, hence with a state of removal from active life.

The man who is seized by a new inner truth of this sort stands in our world almost without outward help, while from within he is continually assailed by new and increasingly incomprehensible images which are inaccessible to analytical reflection—since they present nothing that can be split apart—but disclose themselves only to intuitive vision.

Here discursive, logical thought cannot help us. It can only lead us astray and entangle us in irrelevancies. Here only creative activity finds an issue, by raising the inner world of images to consciousness, by satisfying its urge for externalization, by objectifying it in the forms of the favored function.

It is along these lines that the various schools of modern psychology since Jung have aimed to establish contact with the emotional forces of the psyche, to encourage the patient's unconscious to "externalize" itself, whether through writing, dancing, or painting. In this way, even the noncreative man learns to communicate with his unconscious, to recognize and accept that element within himself which had formerly been alien and hostile. He learns to fulfill the process of the creators who from depths unknown to them raise thoughts, ideas, and images and project them as scientific theories, artistic works, or new life forms—that is to say, as works, for which they are prepared to fight and if necessary to die, because they feel within them a force that is stronger than themselves.

From such activity there issues a liberating and in the fullest sense of the word "redeeming" effect, because it removes a block that has come into being through failure to understand a new truth, the truth of one's own life, which analytical understanding, discursive thought, would never have found, but can only understand later on, when it has taken on life and form.

Thus the artistic-formative and the analytical-dissecting psychology are not merely in disagreement but constitute an essential antithesis, standing to each other in a kind of polar relationship, and belonging to each other as day and night, life and death. And if we represent this polarity in graphic form, we see that in synthetic activity, the activity which constitutes the whole, there lies a dark kernel emanating from the contrary pole, because at the bottom of all synthesis there lies something akin to analysis—a dissection and destruction of the unity of chaos—and because without this analytical element, selection would be impossible. For creation requires fixed form, and all form requires boundary, or skin. The chaos is split into the part within the boundary, and the part outside it. And similarly there lies at the bottom of all analysis and dissection the urge to transcend all dissection and

Fig. 8

441

dissolution and arrive at a new totality. The most magnificent example of this in our time is modern astronomy.

We seem to have gone far afield. But only seemingly. For the very fact that this digression was possible proves that art, when truly experienced and understood, implies far more than the question of oil or tempera, madonna or bunch of asparagus, and that from it—i.e., from the perceived and perceiving world—roads lead to every sphere of the outer and inner cosmos, as far as man can apprehend it.

We have recognized three stages of artistic knowledge of the world, determined by the categories of delimitation, direction, and variability of boundaries and direction.

Only now, since a theory of the categories of vision has been devised in the world of art, since it has become possible to make statements concerning the visual nature of things and having the same universal validity as the philosophical systems from Aristotle to Kant in the realm of thought; only now, since the relativity of direction and delimitation and a number of other problems not mentioned here have been recognized, has it become possible to make a "picture" of something. Only now am I able to have a point of view, because I have become aware of the possibility of changing the point of view. And only now has it become possible, for example, to devise a scientific, i.e., calculable and constructible, perspective. And only now can we assign to art the task of making a picture or representation. But this means the practical utilization of the knowledge we have attained and has as much and as little to do with art as technical exploitation with scientific thought and scientific inquiry.

And only now have we a conception of nature as the sum of all our potentialities and realizations. Only now have we a sentiment of nature; only now have we pastoral plays and English gardens, Alpinism, week-end cottages and sun bathing—a return to nature—because only now has it become possible to recognize, see, and feel nature as such.

What science is for thought, philosophy and psychology for intuition, and the whole intricate structure of human society for affectivity, the arts are for the realm of sensation. According to their kind, the arts mold the whole world into visible or audible form. With the theory of functions, the age-old theory of correspondences is resurrected.

It can be asked whether from the point of view of the beholder any investigations are necessary or profitable. I can only answer this question in the negative; they do not concern him at all. For he is a beholder only in so far as he beholds, but not in so far as he reflects. And in the good times of an artistic culture, people did not concern themselves with such questions. The sensory and perceptive functions operated of their own accord, in the creator as well as the layman. But today we live in the last, the intellectual, phase of an intellectual culture. The intellectual attitude has so far thrust back and tinged the other functions that they have virtually lost their power to stand alone, and in order to reflect upon them, one must invoke scientific method.

But it is only the product, not the essence, of a function that can be apprehended through another function. This assertion, it is true, stands in obvious contradiction to the prevailing view that conceptual thought is omnipotent and can apprehend everything. A brief discussion will show the error of this conception.

Scientific thought can subject a work of art, i.e., the product of the activity of the perceptive function, to investigation from every conceivable standpoint, historical, anthropological, technical, chemical, etc. Conversely, perception can in its own way consider a work of the rational function, i.e., of scientific activity; it can perceive and form it. Or to speak concretely, I can draw or paint a telescope, a motorcar, a torpedo boat. But anyone who maintains that the understanding, the rational function, can also understand and penetrate the essence and functioning of perception must also admit the reverse, and is then invited to speculate on the possibilities of rendering Darwin's theory of the origin of species in a sonata, or Jung's theory of functions in a tapestry.

Thus confusion was inevitable and a fundamental clarification and reordering was necessary. And that is all I am concerned with now. What I say here will give no one a better understanding of a work of art, but it may remove obstacles to understanding, and help us to a sound approach.

However, the theory of the four functions tells us one more thing. It shows us not only that man possesses these four functions as four different possibilities of reacting to his environment, but above all that they are a part of the whole man, in whom they are all present at once, though the emphasis may vary.

Consequently, specialized investigations and specialized activities—i.e., those which lift a function or one of its parts out of the general harmony and endeavor to develop it for itself—have immediate meaning and value only for those who engage in them, and not for everyone. All specialized endeavor remains intrinsically limited to a small circle of the initiate. Somehow and somewhere, however, even the most specialized of all endeavors must flow back into the Whole; the fruits of labor must be given back to the totality from whose soil they have grown, if the work of redemption is to advance.

Art as mere specialization, as *l'art pour l'art* in the most extreme sense, would mean complete renunciation of its ultimate, one might almost say transcendent, meaning. And artists have never had any such thing in mind; to be understood and accepted has always been the profoundest desire of all creative men.

And this means simply that art has two aspects, a twofold meaning, one for the artist and the other for the beholder, just as the treatment and cure of an illness has entirely different meanings for the sick man and for the physician. For the artist, as we have seen, the meaning of art lies in the apprehension of a perceptive context that is clarified and fulfilled in the work, and at the base of the whole process lies the biological purpose of attaining a higher level of consciousness, thus annulling a *participation mystique*.

The beholder remains completely unaware of this, as one can see from the popular conceptions of imitation, etc. The new doctrine, the new discovery that lies in the work, the whole labor that the artist has had to perform, comes to the beholder by way of the unconscious; he takes it in like the air he breathes.

But the beholder is acutely conscious of one thing. He knows whether the work appeals to him, whether it moves him; he consciously seeks to know what the work means. According to their temperament, artists tend to smile or grow angry at this question. It would be hard to understand why they grow angry if their anger itself did not provide a psychological indication. Anger, like hatred, is a sign of impotence, of failure to understand. It is foolish to ask an artist about the meaning of his work; as an artist, he cannot understand the question; for him all meaning lies in the interplay of light and shade, of lines and colors, of directions and movements. He apprehends the whole world as perception, as visuality; each work means only itself, because for him it is perception through and through, and as such cannot be referred to anything else, hence can have no "meaning" outside of perception; so that any further question is inquiry into something that is not art.

444

Nevertheless the question exists for the beholder; it must in some way stem from his whole approach; and this we have no right to prescribe.

To my knowledge no one has ever seriously inquired into the significance of the objective element in art; in other words, why do the painters of a given period all paint more or less the same subject matter, though with individual differences? Why was Rembrandt so passionately addicted to the painting of ugly, old people, why did Degas paint ballet dancers and race horses, Michelangelo prophets and sibyls, Segantini sheep, cows, and shepherds?

Where these questions receive any consideration at all, they receive only the vague answer that choice of subject matter is determined by the general interests of an epoch or the personal interests of the artist. But the fact of the matter is that the artist does not choose his subject matter at all; the subject matter chooses him. And the word "interest" is much too weak and colorless to designate the force with which the various themes impose themselves, unless we qualify the interest with an epithet such as "burning." It is far more than a mere interest—it is a burning interest, a fascination, a seizure. It is quite simply the archetypes at work in time that rise up in him; it is the substance of time itself which in personal form, characteristic of him alone, creates in him these images, with all their radiance, their light that is often a dark light, a glittering darkness. They seize upon him, and he seizes upon them, clutches them, bites into them, and does not let them loose because they do not let him loose—until he has wrought them, acquired them, made them his possession, and shaped them into a work. It is like Jacob's wrestling with the angel; and often the hollow of the artist's thigh is thrown out of joint.

The artist as creator is not conscious of all this. He has his idea and that is enough. The unconscious processes must have been completed before he so much as draws a line. He knows as little as other men about the emergence of archetypes and visions, and he knows even less why precisely these and not others rise up within him. He has no need to know. It is not important. Important is only that he has an idea, a projection, which takes hold of him sufficiently to call forth his creative powers.

And everything that flows in upon him from his unconscious and finally takes form in lines and colors, light and shade, is contained in his work, as form, as color, as movement, and as the interrelations of all these elements. And that is precisely what the beholder now sees in the work—sees con-

445

sciously, understands, and wants to understand. But from this it follows that the more or less conscious activity of the beholder is not sensory perception, is not seeing. The seeing is for him a means to an end. The sensory, visual knowledge, the authentic product of the artist's work, enters into him unconsciously; he receives it gratis as it were. His own activity is the intuitive apprehending of the archetypes and their meaning. He seeks and finds, whether he knows it or not, the symbolic content of the work.

Thus art becomes the symbolic forming of archetypes working in time. The picture becomes symbol and prototype. Therein lies the magic of the work, and that is why all artistically living epochs have recognized art to be magic. This is true even of the Catholic Church. For at the time when magic force was still at work within it, it forbade certain themes in art. And at an early Church council the proposition that art belongs to the artist but its themes belong to the Church was taken as a dogma. Prohibition and rejection are a sort of recognition.

The beholder remains aware of the artist's conscious effort in his work; and the artist is aware of what the beholder seeks in the work and consciously receives from it. Woe to the artist when this is not true. Then purpose, will, the "message," enter the work, and the result is trash.

What the beholder receives from the work is the artist in all his great or small humanity, along with the values of his time, values of which he himself is unconscious. Hence every complete work is greater than its creator.

We have come to the end. I have tried to suggest that art should be conceived and experienced as a spontaneous reflection of the autonomous perceptive process. In other words, I conceive of art as a biological function. It is not a gratuitous human invention, but a method, disclosed and willed by life itself, of transcending through formative creation the primal, nature-given, and naturally necessary involvement in the world of stimuli sometimes known as *participation mystique*. Sensation, spontaneously seeking fulfillment, strives to become conscious of itself. Beginning with the visual process of sensory perception, sensation attains to its ultimate physical development in the work which as formed material is again external—and as universal symbol of a given stage of knowledge is brought to life and brought to bear upon life.

I should like to conclude by saying with Konrad Fiedler that as long as men look upon art merely as a luxury article, carrying on its aloof existence apart from the serious business of human life, as the pleasure and delectation of idle moments, we shall not accord the artist his due recognition. For the artist performs a serious and necessary part of the spiritual daily work of mankind, and without it men would lose not only an exalted pleasure but a whole category of higher existence as well.

To say that art is divine is a euphemism and an evasion, meaning that its human content has not been understood.

APPENDICES

Biographical Notes

RUDOLF BERNOULLI, Ph.D. Born 1880, Basel; died 1948, near Zurich. 1924–47, curator of the graphics collection, Federal Polytechnic Institute, and lecturer in art (from 1935, professor). 1906–23, posts in various museums and libraries, Berlin. Organized many local exhibitions, which helped to systematize Swiss graphic art from a historical perspective, and exchange exhibitions, which made Swiss art known internationally. 1947, organized definitive exhibition of "Swiss Graphic Art of the Classic and Romantic Periods." Professor Bernoulli lectured at the Eranos conferences of 1934 and 1935.

MARTIN BUBER, Ph.D. (hon., Hebrew University, Jerusalem), D.H.L. (hon., Hebrew Union College, Cincinnati). Born 1878, Vienna. Since 1938, professor of social philosophy (now emeritus), Hebrew University, Jerusalem. 1901–30, editor and publisher, Austria and Germany; founded *Der Jude*, leading organ of German-speaking Jewry (1916–24, its editor), and the Jüdischer Verlag. 1923–30, professor of comparative religion, University of Frankfurt a. M., and director, College of Jewish Studies. 1938, as spiritual leader of Jews against Nazism, left Germany and settled in Palestine. 1949, founded Institute for Adult Education, to train teachers in the immigrant camps of Israel. 1954, awarded the Goethe Prize, Hamburg. Special interest: the interpretation of Judaism, particularly Hasidism. Has lectured widely in America and western Europe. Chief among his numerous works, in English translation: *I and Thou* (New York, 1937; rev. edn., 1959); *Moses* (Oxford, 1946); *Between Man and Man* (New York, 1947); *Hasidism* (New York, 1948); *For the Sake of Heaven* (2nd edn., New York, 1953); *Hasidism and the Way of Man* (New York, 1960). Professor Buber has been at work on a translation of the Bible, with Franz Rosenzweig, from Hebrew into German: to date, 15 vols., from Genesis through Proverbs. Lectured at the second Eranos meeting, in 1934.

MORIZ CARL CAMMERLOHER, Ph.D. (Vienna). Born 1882, Vienna; died there, 1945. Student of art, Oriental culture and religion, and medicine. Worked as a painter, a translator from the Sanskrit, and later in life a consultant in analytical psychology. Published papers on art and depth psychology; doctoral thesis, "Comparison between Linguistic and Pictorial Representations and Their Elements."

451

Following the death of his wife in the Auschwitz concentration camp, his health rapidly declined and he died in extremity. Dr. Cammerloher lectured at the Eranos meeting of 1934.

THEODOR-WILHELM DANZEL, Ph.D. (Leipzig). Born 1886, Hamburg; died 1954. 1928–54, professor of ethnology, University of Hamburg (1933–46, tenure interrupted by the Nazi regime). 1924–45, curator and departmental chief, Museum für Völkerkunde, Hamburg. 1928, field work in the United States and Mexico; 1931–32, in China and Japan; fellow of Academia Sinica and guest professor, Central University, Nanking. Chief interests: folk and cultural psychology, pre-Columbian ethnology and archaeology. Principal works: *Die Anfänge der Schrift* (Leipzig, 1912 and 1929); *Entwicklungspsychologie (Kultur und Gesellschaft)* (Berlin and Vienna, 1921 and 1931); *Mexiko I* and *II* (Hagen and Darmstadt, 1922: studies in religion, culture, art); *Handbuch der präkolumbischen Kulturen in Lateinamerika* (Hamburg and Berlin, 1927 and 1936). Professor Danzel lectured at the 1937 Eranos meeting.

MIRCEA ELIADE, Ph.D. Born 1907, Bucharest. Since 1956, professor of the history of religion, University of Chicago. 1928–32, predoctoral studies at the University of Calcutta, studies in the techniques of Yoga at Rishikesh. 1933–39, maître de conférences, University of Bucharest. 1945–56, lecturer in comparative religion at the École des Hautes-Études, Sorbonne. Founder and editor, *Zalmoxis: Revue des études religieuses* (Paris and Bucharest, 1938–42). Haskell Lecturer, University of Chicago, 1957. Special fields: Indian philosophy and comparative religion. Author also of several popular novels. Principal works: *Patterns in Comparative Religion* (tr., New York, 1958; original, Paris, 1949); *The Myth of the Eternal Return* (tr., New York and London, 1954; original, Paris, 1949); *Le Chamanisme* (Paris, 1951; English tr. in preparation); *Images et symboles* (Paris, 1952); *Yoga: Immortality and Freedom* (tr., New York and London, 1958; original, Paris, 1954); *Forgerons et alchimistes* (Paris, 1956). Has lectured at all Eranos meetings since 1950.

FRIEDRICH HEILER, Ph.D. (Munich), D.Theol. (hon., Kiel), D.D. (Glasgow). ˙Born 1892, Munich. Since 1920, professor of the comparative history of religion, Marburg University. In 1934, in protest against the enactment by the Nazis of the Nuremberg Laws, resigned from the theological faculty at Marburg and was invited to the philosophical faculty at Greifswald University; in 1935, joined the philosophical faculty, Marburg; in 1948, recalled to the theological faculty. Has lectured or served as guest professor at the universities of Uppsala, Lund, Chicago, Saloniki, Athens, and Ankara, and the Episcopal Seminary in Alexandria, Vir-

452

ginia. 1958–59, traveled and lectured in Japan, Java, Siam, Burma, and India. Since 1929, president of the Evangelical-Ecumenical Union; since 1953, president of the German branch of the International Union for the History of Religion. Among many published works on Eastern and Western religion may be mentioned: *Prayer, A Study in the History and Psychology of Religion* (orig. 1918; tr., London and New York, 1932); *The Spirit of Worship* (orig., 1921; tr., London, 1926); and *The Gospel of Sadhu Sundar Singh* (orig., 1923; tr., London, 1927). His writings have been translated also into French, Swedish, Italian, Dutch, and Japanese. Professor Heiler lectured at the first two Eranos meetings.

C. G. JUNG, M.D., L.L.D. (hon., Clark, Fordham, Allahabad, Calcutta), Litt.D. (hon., Benares, Geneva), Sc.D. (hon., Harvard, Oxford, Federal Polytechnic Inst., Zurich). Born 1875, Kesswil, Canton Thurgau, Switzerland. 1900–1909, psychiatric work at Burghölzli Clinic and the university, Zurich, and studies (1902) with Pierre Janet at the Salpetrière, Paris. 1907–14, associated with Freud in the psychoanalytical movement. Subsequently, medical and psychotherapeutic practice, scientific research, and writing. 1933–42, professed at the Federal Polytechnic Inst., Zurich. 1944, called to the University of Basel to occupy the chair of medical psychology, established for him, but forced to resign owing to illness after a year. His eightieth birthday, 1955, was celebrated by a convocation of friends and students from many countries, and the 1955 Eranos meeting was dedicated to him. Undertook many expeditions: to North and Central Africa, the American West, and India. In recent years, engaged in studies in symbolism, Küsnacht and Bollingen, near Zurich. The Collected Works of C. G. Jung, in 18 or more vols., are being published in both English and German; a French edition is projected. His publications otherwise number over 150. Professor Jung lectured at thirteen Eranos meetings, beginning with the first, in 1933; special volumes of the *Eranos-Jahrbuch* were published in honor of his 70th and 75th birthdays.

C. KERÉNYI, Ph.D. Born 1897, Temesvár, (then) Hungary. Formerly professor of classical studies and the history of religion, universities of Szeged and Pécs, Hungary. Resident of Switzerland since 1943. Lecturer, C. G. Jung Institute, Zurich. Founder and editor of the Albae Vigiliae series (Zurich) on mythology, art, and related subjects. Principal works: *Apollon* (2nd edn., Amsterdam, 1940); *Die antike Religion* (3rd edn., Dusseldorf, 1951); with C. G. Jung, *Essays on a Science of Mythology* (New York, 1949; London, 1950, as *Introduction to a Science of Mythology*); *Niobe* (Zurich, 1949); *The Gods of the Greeks* (New York and London, 1951); with C. G. Jung and Paul Radin, *The Trickster* (London, 1956); *The Heroes of the Greeks* (London, 1959). A series of interrelated works on Archetypal Images in Greek Religion is in course of publication, beginning with *Asklepios*

APPENDICES

(New York and London, 1959). Dr. Kerényi lectured frequently at Eranos meetings in the 1940's.

JOHN LAYARD, M.A. (Cantab. and Oxon.), D.Sc. (Oxon.). Born 1891, London. Studied anthropology under A. C. Haddon and W. H. R. Rivers. 1914–15, field work in Malekula, New Hebrides. Subsequent shift of main interest to psychotherapy; analytical work with Homer Lane, Wilhelm Stekel, H. G. Baynes, and C. G. Jung. Professional Practicing Member of The Society of Analytical Psychology, practicing in London and Oxford. Fellow, Royal Anthropological Institute and British Psychological Society. Founder, Oxford University Society for the Discussion of Psychology and Religion. Lecturer, C. G. Jung Institute, Zurich. Author of *Stone Men of Malekula* (London, 1942), *The Lady of the Hare: A Study in the Healing Power of Dreams* (London, 1944), and numerous periodical publications in anthropology and psychology. Dr. Layard lectured at the Eranos meetings of 1937, 1948, 1955, and 1959, and contributed to the 1945 Jung *Festschrift*.

FRITZ MEIER, Ph.D. Born 1912, Basel. Since 1949, professor of Oriental philology, University of Basel. Philological research in the mosque libraries of Istanbul (1936) and Iran (1937). 1946–48, maître de conférences, University of Farouk I, Alexandria. His special field is Islamic religion and mysticism. Principal publications: *Vom Wesen der islamischen Mystik* (Basel, 1943); *Die Vita des Scheich Abū Ishāq al-Kāzarūnī* (Bibliotheca Islamica, vol. 14; Leipzig, 1948); *Die 'Fawā'ih al-ğamāl wa fawātih al-ğalāl' des Nağm ad-dīn al-Kubrā* (a study of Islamic mysticism from A.D. 1200; Basel, 1953). He has lectured at the Eranos meetings of 1944, 1945, 1946, and 1954.

MAX PULVER, Ph.D. Born 1889, Bern; died 1952. Writer and poet. In his later years, an internationally known graphologist, working in Zurich. He had a special interest in Gnosticism, and lectured on this and related subjects. Principal works: *Symbolik der Handschrift* (Zurich, 1931); *Trieb und Verbrechen* (Zurich, 1934); *Person, Charakter, Schicksal* (Zurich, 1944); *Intelligenz im Schriftausdruck* (Zurich, 1949); and several volumes of belles-lettres, drama, and poetry. He lectured at Eranos meetings in 1940–45.

ERWIN ROUSSELLE, Ph.D., Jur.D. (both Heidelberg). Born 1890, Hanau a. M., Germany; died 1949, Upper Bavaria. Scholar of Semitic and Oriental philology, specializing in Chinese, Tibetan, and Sanskrit and in related studies in Buddhism. 1924–29, professor of German philosophy, Chinese National University, guest professor of comparative linguistics, Tsing Hua University, and director, Sino-Indian Institute, Yenching University. 1931, succeeded Richard Wilhelm as director, China Institute, Frankfurt a. M.; 1935, appointed extraordinary professor, University of Frankfurt. 1938–40, travels in the interior and other parts of China on research for the China Institute. Subsequently removed from both posts by the Nazi regime, on political grounds; 1943, officially silenced; 1948, restored to both directorate and professorial chair. Publications include *Mysterium der Wandlung: Der Weg zur Verwandlung in den Weltreligionen* (Darmstadt, 1923); a translation of the Tao Teh Ching into German (Frankfurt, 1950; an earlier edition was destroyed in the war); and many articles in the China Institute periodical *Sinica*. Professor Rousselle lectured at the first three Eranos meetings, 1933–35.

HEINRICH ZIMMER, Ph.D. (Berlin). Born 1890, Greifswald, Germany; died 1943, New York. 1923–38, professor of Indology, Heidelberg University; dismissed because of his anti-Nazi views. 1939–40, guest at Balliol College, Oxford. 1941–43, lecturer, Columbia University. He was son of Heinrich Zimmer, eminent scholar of Celtic philology; was student of Sanskrit, Pali, Pahlavi, Arabic, Chinese, Gaelic, Gothic, Old Norse, Greek, Latin, as well as modern European languages; married Christiane von Hofmannsthal, daughter of the Austrian poet. Influenced the work of C. G. Jung as well as that of Thomas Mann, who dedicated his novel *The Transposed Heads* to him. The first volume of Bollingen Series (1943) was dedicated to his memory; four posthumous works, completed and edited by Joseph Campbell, were subsequently published in the Series: *Myths and Symbols in Indian Art and Civilization* (1946), *The King and the Corpse* (1948), *Philosophies of India* (1951), and *The Art of Indian Asia* (2 vols., 1955). Other posthumata were *Der Weg zum Selbst*, ed. C. G. Jung (Zurich, 1944), and *Hindu Medicine*, ed. Ludwig Edelstein (Baltimore, 1948). Other principal works: *Kunstform und Yoga* (Berlin, 1926), *Spiel um den Elefanten* (Munich, 1929), *Ewiges Indien* (Zurich, 1930), *Indische Sphären* (1955), *Maya: Der Indische Mythos* (Stuttgart and Berlin, 1936; 2nd edn., Zurich, 1952), and *Weisheit Indiens* (Darmstadt, 1938). Professor Zimmer lectured at the Eranos meetings of 1933, 1934, 1938, and 1939.

The *Eranos-Jahrbücher*

The contents of the *Eranos-Jahrbücher*, consisting of twenty-eight volumes through 1959, are listed (in translation) for reference. The respective lectures were delivered in German (chiefly), French, English, and Italian. In the first eight *Jahrbücher*, all the papers were published in German; in later volumes, they were published in their original language. An index of contributors is at the end. In the following list, the titles of papers translated in the present series are indicated by superior numbers for volumes, thus: 1. *Spirit and Nature* (1954); 2. *The Mysteries* (1955); 3. *Man and Time* (1957); 4. *Spiritual Disciplines* (1960).

I: 1933: Yoga and Meditation in the East and the West

HEINRICH ZIMMER: On the Significance of the Indian Tantric Yoga [4]
Mrs. RHYS DAVIDS: Religious Exercises in India and the Religious Man
ERWIN ROUSSELLE: Spiritual Guidance in Contemporary Taoism [4]
C. G. JUNG: A Study in the Process of Individuation
G. R. HEYER: The Meaning of Eastern Wisdom for Western Spiritual Guidance
FRIEDRICH HEILER: Contemplation in Christian Mysticism [4]
ERNESTO BUONAIUTI: Meditation and Contemplation in the Roman Catholic Church

II: 1934: Symbolism and Spiritual Guidance in the East and the West

ERWIN ROUSSELLE: Dragon and Mare, Figures of Primordial Chinese Mythology
J. W. HAUER: Symbols and Experience of the Self in Indo-Aryan Mysticism
HEINRICH ZIMMER: Indian Myths as Symbols
Mrs. RHYS DAVIDS: On the History of the Symbol of the Wheel
C. G. JUNG: The Archetypes of the Collective Unconscious
G. R. HEYER: The Symbolism of Dürer's Melancholia
FRIEDRICH HEILER: The Madonna as a Religious Symbol
ERNESTO BUONAIUTI: Symbols and Rites in the Religious Life of Various Monastic Orders
MARTIN BUBER: Symbolic and Sacramental Existence in Judaism [4]
RUDOLF BERNOULLI: On the Symbolism of Geometrical Figures and of Numbers

456

VI: 1938: The Configuration and Cult of the "Great Mother"
JEAN PRZYLUSKI: I. Origins and Development of the Cult of the Mother Goddess. II. The Mother Goddess as a Link between the Local Gods and the Universal God
CHARLES PICARD: I. The Anatolian Ephesia. II. The Great Mother from Crete to Eleusis
CHARLES VIROLLEAUD: I. Ishtar, Isis, Astarte. II. Anat-Astarte
LOUIS MASSIGNON: The Gnostic Cult of Fatima in Shiite Islam
HEINRICH ZIMMER: The Indian World Mother
V. C. C. COLLUM: The Creative Mother Goddess of the Celtic-speaking Peoples, Her Instrument, the Mystical "Word," Her Cult and Cult Symbols
ERNESTO BUONAIUTI: I. Mary and the Virgin Birth. II. St. Mary Immaculata in the Christian Tradition
C. G. JUNG: Psychological Aspects of the Mother Archetype
G. R. HEYER: The Great Mother in the Psyche of Modern Man

VII: 1939: The Symbolism of Rebirth in the Religious Imagery of Various Times and Peoples
LOUIS MASSIGNON: Resurrection in the Mohammedan World
CHARLES VIROLLEAUD: The Idea of Rebirth among the Phoenicians
PAUL PELLIOT: The Chinese Conception of the Other World
WALTER F. OTTO: The Meaning of the Eleusinian Mysteries [2]
CHARLES R. C. ALLBERRY: Symbols of Death and Rebirth in Manichaeism
HANS LEISEGANG: The Mystery of the Serpent [2]
HEINRICH ZIMMER: Death and Rebirth in the Light of India
ERNESTO BUONAIUTI: Rebirth, Immortality, and Resurrection in Early Christianity
RICHARD THURNWALD: Primitive Rites of Initiation and Rebirth
C. G. JUNG: The Different Aspects of Rebirth

VIII: 1940–41: The Trinity, Christian Symbolism, and Gnosis
ANDREAS SPEISER: The Platonic Doctrine of the Unknown God and the Christian Trinity
C. G. JUNG: A Psychological Approach to the Dogma of the Trinity
C. KERÉNYI: Mythology and Gnosis
C. G. JUNG: Transformation Symbolism in the Mass [2]
ERNESTO BUONAIUTI: Christ and St. Paul
MAX PULVER: Gnostic Experience and Gnostic Life in Early Christianity (from the Sources)
ERNESTO BUONAIUTI: Christology and Ecclesiology in St. Paul

IX: 1942: The Hermetic Principle in Mythology, Gnosis, and Alchemy
C. KERÉNYI: Hermes Guide of Souls: The Mythologem of the Masculine Origin of Life

458

* Title changed in *Spirit and Nature* to "The Phenomenology of the Spirit in Fairy Tales."

461

ADOLF PORTMANN: The Problem of Archetypes from the Biological Standpoint

XIX: 1950: Man and Rite

C. KERÉNYI: Dramatic Divine Presence in Greek Religion

LOUIS BEIRNAERT: The Symbolism of Ascension in Christian Liturgy and Mysticism

ERICH NEUMANN: On the Psychological Significance of Myth

GERSHOM G. SCHOLEM: Tradition and Creation in Cabalistic Ritual

HENRY CORBIN: Sabaean Ritual and Ismailian Exegesis of the Ritual

MIRCEA ELIADE: The Psychology and History of Religions: the Symbolism of the "Center"

PAUL RADIN: The Esoteric Rituals of the North American Indians

LOUIS MASSIGNON: The Living Rite

ADOLF PORTMANN: Animal Rites

RAFFAELE PETTAZZONI: The Babylonian Rite of Akitu and the Epic of Creation

F. J. J. BUYTENDIJK: On the Phenomenology of the Encounter

XX: 1951: Man and Time

ERICH NEUMANN: Art and Time [3]

HENRI-CHARLES PUECH: Gnosis and Time [3]

GILLES QUISPEL: Time and History in Patristic Christianity [3]

LOUIS MASSIGNON: Time in Islamic Thought [3]

HENRY CORBIN: Cyclical Time in Mazdaism and Ismailism [3]

MIRCEA ELIADE: Time and Eternity in Indian Thought [3]

LANCELOT LAW WHYTE: Time and the Mind-Body Problem: A Changed Scientific Conception of Progress

C. G. JUNG: On Synchronicity [3]

ERWIN R. GOODENOUGH: The Evaluation of Symbols Recurrent in Time, as Illustrated in Judaism

HELLMUT WILHELM: The Concept of Time in the Book of Changes [3]

HELMUTH PLESSNER: On the Relation of Time to Death [3]

MAX KNOLL: The Transformations of Science in Our Age [3]

ADOLF PORTMANN: Time in the Life of the Organism [3]

XXI: 1952: Man and Energy

MIRCEA ELIADE: Power and Sacrality in the History of Religions

GERSHOM G. SCHOLEM: On the Development of the Cabalistic Conception of the Shekhinah

GILLES QUISPEL: Man and Energy in Patristic Christianity

ERICH NEUMANN: The Psyche and the Transformation of the Planes of Reality

KARL LÖWITH: The Dynamics of History, and Historicism

HERBERT READ: The Dynamics of Art

MARTIN D'ARCY: The Power of Caritas and the Holy Spirit
ADOLF PORTMANN: The Significance of Images in the Living Transformation of Energy
MAX KNOLL: Quantum Conceptions of Energy in Physics and Psychology
LANCELOT LAW WHYTE: A Scientific View of the "Creative Energy" of Man

XXII: 1953: Man and Earth

ERICH NEUMANN: The Significance of the Earth Archetype for Modern Times
MIRCEA ELIADE: Terra Mater and Cosmic Hierogamies
GILLES QUISPEL: Gnosis and Earth
HENRY CORBIN: Celestial Earth and the Body of the Resurrection according to Various Iranian Traditions: I. Mazdean Imago Terrae. II. Hurqalya's Mystical Earth (Shaikhism)
GERSHOM G. SCHOLEM: The Conception of the Golem and Its Tellurian and Magical Contexts
GIUSEPPE TUCCI: Earth as Conceived of in Indian and Tibetan Religion, with Special Regard to the Tantras
DAISETZ SUZUKI: The Role of Nature in Zen
JEAN DANIÉLOU: Earth and Paradise in Greek Mysticism and Theology
ERNST BENZ: I. The Sacred Cave in Eastern Christianity. II. The Charismatic Type of the Russian Saints
ADOLF PORTMANN: The Earth as the Home of Life

XXIII: 1954: Man and Transformation

MIRCEA ELIADE: Mysteries and Spiritual Regeneration in Non-European Religions
FRITZ MEIER: The Transformation of Man in Mystical Islam
HENRY CORBIN: Divine Epiphany and Initiatic Birth in Shiite Gnosis
ERICH NEUMANN: The Creative Principle in Psychic Transformation
PAUL TILLICH: New Being as the Central Concept of a Christian Theology
DAISETZ SUZUKI: The Awakening of a New Consciousness in Zen
LANCELOT LAW WHYTE: The Growth of Ideas, Illustrated by Man's Changing Conception of Himself
ERNST BENZ: Theogony and the Transformation of Man in Schelling
JEAN DANIÉLOU: The Transfiguration of Man in Early Byzantine Mysticism
ADOLF PORTMANN: Metamorphosis in Animals

XXIV: 1955: Man and the Sympathy of All Things

ERICH NEUMANN: The Experience of the One Reality and the Sympathy of Things
GERSHOM G. SCHOLEM: Transmigration and the Sympathy of Souls in Jewish Mysticism

LOUIS MASSIGNON: The Mohammedan Experience of Compassion, integrated with the Universal in connection with Fatima and Ḥallāj
ERNST BENZ: Man and the Sympathy of All Things at the End of the Ages
HENRY CORBIN: Sympathy and Theopathy among the "Fedeli d'Amore" in Islam
WALTER F. OTTO: The Primordial Myth in the Light of the Sympathy of Man and the World
JOHN LAYARD: Identification with the Sacrificial Animal
CHUNG-YUAN CHANG: Tao and the Sympathy of All Things
MAX KNOLL: Endogenous Rhythms and Biological Time
ADOLF PORTMANN: The Organism: A Pre-established Relationship

XXV: 1956: Man and the Creative Principle
ERICH NEUMANN: Creative Man and the "Great Experience"
HENRY CORBIN: Creative Imagination and Creative Prayer in Mystical Experience
MIRCEA ELIADE: Mythology and Creativity
GERSHOM G. SCHOLEM: Creatio ex Nihilo and God's Self-Immersion
KARL REINHARDT: Prometheus
ERNST BENZ: The Holy Ghost as Creator in Joachim de Fiore
HERBERT READ: Poetic Consciousness and the Creative Experience
HELLMUT WILHELM: The Creative Principle in the Book of Changes
CHUNG-YUAN CHANG: Creativity as Process in Taoism
LAURENS VAN DER POST: The Creative Pattern in Primitive Africa
ADOLF PORTMANN: Levels of Organic Life

XXVI: 1957: Man and Meaning
ERICH NEUMANN: The Individual and the Problem of Meaning
HENRY CORBIN: The Interiorization of Meaning in Iranian Ṣūfī Hermeneutics
MIRCEA ELIADE: Meanings of the "Inner Light"
GERSHOM G. SCHOLEM: Religious Authority and Mysticism
KARL REINHARDT: The Crisis of Meaning in Euripides
HERBERT READ: The Creative Nature of Humanism
HELLMUT WILHELM: The Meaning of Events According to the Book of Changes
WALTER CORTI: The Platonic Academy Down Through History and as a Task of Our Time
JOSEPH CAMPBELL: The Symbol without Meaning
ADOLF PORTMANN: The Interpretation of Meaning as a Biological Problem

XXVII: 1958: Man and Peace
ERICH NEUMANN: Peace as a Symbol of Life
HENRY CORBIN: Peace and Disquiet of the Soul in the Ṣūfism of Rûzbehân Baqlî of Shîrâz

Index of Contributors

References are to volumes in the foregoing list. Places of residence at the time of publication are noted in parentheses.

ABBREVIATIONS

AEO	*Archives d'études orientales.* Stockholm.
AM	*Athenische Mitteilungen (Mitteilungen des Kaiserlich Deutschen Archäologischen Instituts,* Athenische Abt.). Berlin or Athens.
ANCL	Ante-Nicene Christian Library. Edinburgh.
Baynes/Wilhelm	*The I Ching, or Book of Changes.* The Richard Wilhelm translation from German, translated into English by Cary F. Baynes. New York and London, 1950. 2 vols.
BI	Bibliotheca Islamica. Leipzig and Istanbul.
BS	Bollingen Series. New York.
CWJ	Collected Works of C. G. Jung. New York and London.
EI	*Encyclopedia of Islam.* Leiden and London, 1908–36.
EJ	*Eranos-Jahrbuch.* Zurich.
GCS	*Die griechischen christlichen Schriftsteller.* Ed. by O. Stählin. Berlin, 1905–36. 4 vols.
JAI	*Jahrbuch des [Deutschen] Archäologischen Instituts.* Berlin.
JAOS	*Journal of the American Oriental Society.* Boston.
LCL	Loeb Classical Library. Cambridge, Mass. (orig. New York) and London.
Migne, *PG* and *PL*	J. P. Migne, ed. *Patrologiae cursus completus.* *PG* = Greek Series. Paris, 1857–66. 166 vols. *PL* = Latin Series. Paris, 1844–64. 221 vols. Refs. are to columns.

PEY	Papers from the Eranos Yearbooks (the present series).
PW	*Paulys Real-Encyclopädie der classischen Alter-tumswissenschaft.* Begun by Georg Wissowa, ed. by Wilhelm Kroll. Stuttgart, 1894– . Refs. are to columns.
Roscher's *Lexikon*	W. H. Roscher, ed. *Ausführliches Lexikon der griechischen und römischen Mythologie.* Leipzig, 1884–1937. 6 vols. Refs. are to columns.
SBE	Sacred Books of the East. Ed. by F. Max Müller. London.
ZDMG	*Zeitschrift der Deutschen Morgenländischen Gesellschaft.* Leipzig.

INDEX

INDEX

A

Aaron, 170
abbots, Taoist, 61
abdomen, 74
abhayada, 30
Abraham, 169, 173, 302, 303*n;* path of, 328
abstinence, 109
Abū Bakr 'Atīq-i Sūrābādī, 277*n*
ace of clubs, 357, 396
acetum fontis, 356
Acheloos, 157, 158, 159
Actaeon, 338
action(s): effortless, 64; sacred, 62
active and contemplative life, 195, 198; *see also vita activa*
activity, actionless, 85
actor, 406
Acts of the Apostles, Book of, 195, 325*n*
Acts of St. John, 254&*n*
acupuncture, 72
Adam, 270, 278, 287, 288; creation of, 421*n;* "forgetting," 271*n;* Kadmon, 429; old, 113
Adam's Peak, 270
Ademarus, 397*n*
'Adī ibn Musāfir, 271, 283*n*
admission, certificate of, 63, 67, 87
Adonis, 429
adoration, perpetual, 219
Advent, 209
adversary, God's, 240
Aeneas, 77, 149
aenigma regis, 372, 406
aeons, 183
Aeschylus, 153*n*, 157, 169
Aesculapius, 402
'Affān, 280

Africa, 310
Agathodaemon, 415
age, and spiritual progress, 95
Agnes, St., 19
Ahmed ibn-Tulun, 375
Ahriman, 249
air, 111, 331
αἰσχρυλογία, 360
Ajax, 37
ajña, 80
a-khila, 39
Akhmim, Codex of, 349*n*
Akko, 156
alb, 215
alchemy, 71*n*, 280, 305*ff*, 350, 356&*n*, 361-2, 371-2, 388*n*, 396; approaches to, 320*f;* Arabic, 309*f;* Chinese, 357; goal of, 313, 317; medieval, 310; nature of, 313; origins of, 308; in pictures, 320*ff;* three aspects of, 319; two kinds of, 318
alcheringa, 380
Alexander (the Great), 15, 294
Alföldi, A., 156*n*
Aloysius, St., 19
A(lpha) and Ω (Omega), 317
alphabet, 317
Alphito, 156
Alphonsus Liguori, St., 201
altar, 206, 208, 217, 225
Ambrym, 117, 120, 128, 129, 131-2, 134, 135, 147, 148
America, 353, 383; civilizations of, 103
amice, 215
Amitabha, 365
amṛta, 90
amulets, 184
an, 87, 91
ἀναδρομή, 250

473

belly, 30
Benedict, St., 197, 237
Benedict XIV, Pope, 235
Benedictines, 200
Benedictus, 212
Bengalis, 10
Benndorf, O., 164*n*
Berlin, 104
Bern, 104
Bernard of Clairvaux, St., 197*ff*, 201, 203, 223*f*, 226, 230, 233*n*, 237
Bernoulli, Rudolf, 419
Béroalde de Verville, François, 349*n*
Berthelot, Marcellin, 350*n*, 376*n*
Besserer chapel, 104
Bethlehem, 48
Beya, 389*n*
Beyen, H. G., 152*n*
Bhagavad-Gita, 375
bhakti, 12, 18
bhakti-yoga, 24
bhoga, 326
bhrātri-sphota, 6*f*
Bible, 171; *see also* New Testament; Old Testament; *names of separate books*
Bidermann, Jakob, 37*n*
Bieber, M., 153*n*, 154*n*, 158*n*, 160*n*, 161*n*, 167*n*
Binde, 204
bird(s), 131, 303; black with red head, 148
blacksmith, 20
Blake, William, 203
blood, 56; sacrificial, 105; blood-letting, 110
boar(s), 118, 121, 131, 133; sacrifice of, 119*f*, 122*ff*, 128*ff*; boar's head, 47
Böcklin, A., 428
Bodhidharma, 78, 89, 100
Bodhisattva(s), 19, 25, 38, 379
body, 99, 247*f*, 332; celestial, 249; diamond, 72, 77, 89, 99*f*, 380; and the gods, 30*ff*, 52; immortal, 244; luminous, 246, 256; spiritual and fleshly, 242*f*; tomb of soul, 244; transformation, 99
Boehme, Jakob, 203, 222*f*

Boeotia, 165
Boll, Franz Johannes, 312*n*
Bonaventure, St., 198*f*
bond, sacrament and, 176*f*, 181
Bong-na-un, 128, 131, 135
book, sealed, 175
Book of Changes, 63, 81*n*, 82; *see also I Ching*
Book of the Dead, Tibetan, 32*ff*, 38, 48
Book of Rites, 92
Book of That Which Is in the Underworld, 108
Borgia Codex, 110
borrowing, cultural, 103*f*
Bosch, Hieronymus, 48
Bot-gharambi, 128
bough, golden, 149
Bousset, Wilhelm, 254*n*, 255, 257
bow(s), 69*n*
bowl, 165; silver, 162*f*
Brahma, 13, 30, 57; city of, 370
Brāhmanism, Vedāntic, 186
brain, 83, 97–8
bread, 160
breath, 26, 66, 69, 71*f*, 83, 97, 99; ocean of the, 79; sea of, 74, 87; tongues of, 105
breathing exercises/regulations/technique, 66, 80, 87, 266
Breughel, 48
breviary, 70, 88; Latin, 208
bride price, 121
bridge, 82*f*, 94, 403; rainbow, 351, 352, 373, 412
Brimo, 156
Britsch, Gustav, 428, 436, 437*n*
Bronze Age, 116
brotherhood, Taoist, 85
brothers, ten petromorphic, 118, 129
Brothers of the Common Life, 200
brother-sister rite, 6*f*
Browne, Edward G., 276*n*
Bry, Theodore de, 336
Bubastis, 360; B.-Aphrodite, 249
bucket, 324–5
Buddha(s), 19, 23, 24*f*, 33, 39, 83, 91, 112, 365, 370, 379; footprint of, 270;

D

daemons of fertility, 154
dagger, bone, 110
daimon, 27f, 247
Dale, Andrew M., 177n
dance(s): god of, 105; ritual, 380; of dead, 128, 132
dancers, masked, 159
dancing ground, 119
dangers, of contemplative life, 234
Daniel, Book of, 15ff
Dante, 37, 109, 198, 349, 399, 400n
darkness, 233, 239f, 245; in alchemy, 318
dark night of the soul, 236
Darmstädter, Ernst, 309n, 317n
David, star of, 337
David-Neel, Alexandra, 54
Davids, Mrs. C. A. F. Rhys, 112n
Dawkins, R. M., 167n
Dawlatshāh, 302n
day(s): seventh, 136, 250; of week, 209
Dāya, 288n
Deacon, A. Bernard, 118n, 137n
dead: fear of, primitive, 119; masks and the, 153; spirits of the, 118; world of, 108
Dead, Cave of the, see Cave
Dead, Home of the, 120, 134
Dead, Journey of the, 115ff, 123f, 127ff, 135ff
Dead, Land of the, 119, 121, 132, 141, 144
death, 34f, 105, 158, 244, 380; creative, 222; god of, 9; spiritual, 360; waters of, 136f
"Deathless," 7
death's-head, 360
de Boer, T., 285n
Deborah, 170
Deedes, C. N., 142
deer, 338
Degas, 445
De Groot, J. J. M., 61n, 322n, 323
deification, 196, 231f
δεικνύμενον(-α), 62, 192
deity(-ies): 265; Christian, 388; chthonic, 89; inwardness of, 13; tutelary, 36

Delacotte, Joseph, 415n
Delacroix, 428
Delatte, A., 162n, 163n
delimitation, 435
delusions, 235
Demeter, 155f; Erinys, 156; Kidaria, 155; sanctuary of, 156n
Democritus/Demokritos, 331; pseudo-, 356n
demon, 66
demonism, 5, 14, 17, 21, 39, 51, 56
Denis the Carthusian, 198
Deo concedente, 372
descent, 333, 335
desire, sexual, 275
desolation, 236
destiny, 247; see also fate
deus absconditus, 239
Deussen, Paul, 316, 369n
Deutero-Isaiah, 182
devaguna, 30
devil(s), 46ff, 55, 347; the, 278, 287, 364, 384; — as fourth person, 388
Devouring Ghost, see ghost
dew, 6f
Dhahabī, 275n
dhāranā, 87
dharma, 83; see also wheel of dharma
dharmacakra, 88
Dharmagupta, 80
dharmapāla, 96
Dhatar, 30
diamond, 397, 407, 420
diamond body, see body
Diamond Sūtra, 95
Dickins, G., 167n
diet, 366
Dieterich, Albrecht, 269n, 286n, 300n, 301n, 348n
Diez, Ernst, 298n
differentiation, 316, 436ff
Digulleville, Guillaume de, 415ff
δικήριον, 207
dimension, fourth, 23
Dionysius the Areopagite, 195f, 198f, 202, 208, 233, 260f, 264
Dionysos/Dionysus, 159f, 166f, 363; cult/rites/worship of, 154, 383, 429;

I

W